GRE
核心词汇
考法精析

陈琦 周书林 / 主编

陈 琦 周书林 杨 珺 王东东
陶 睿 马 驰 肖 雪 颜余真 编著

群言出版社
QUNYAN PRESS

图书在版编目(CIP)数据

GRE核心词汇考法精析 / 陈琦主编. —北京：群言
出版社，2011（2016.1重印）
ISBN 978-7-80256-254-7

Ⅰ. ①G… Ⅱ. ①陈… Ⅲ. ①GRE—词汇—自学参考资
料 Ⅳ. ①H313

中国版本图书馆CIP数据核字（2011）第131499号

责任编辑：张　茜
封面设计：大愚设计

出版发行：群言出版社
社　　址：北京市东城区东厂胡同北巷1号（100006）
网　　址：www.qypublish.com
自营网店：http://xdfdytushu.tmall.com（天猫旗舰店）
　　　　　http://qycbs.shop.kongfz.com（孔夫子旧书网）
　　　　　http://www.qypublish.com（群言出版社官网）
电子信箱：bj62605588@163.com　qunyancbs@126.com
联系电话：010-62418641　62605019　65267783　65263836
经　　销：全国新华书店
法律顾问：北京天驰君泰律师事务所

印　　刷：北京四季青印刷厂
版　　次：2011年9月第1版　2016年1月第16次印刷
开　　本：787mm×1092mm　1/16
印　　张：29
字　　数：888千字
书　　号：ISBN 978-7-80256-254-7
定　　价：55.00元

献给所有为 GRE 奋斗的人以及那逝去的青春。

序 一

提着昨日种种千辛万苦，向明天换一些美满和幸福。

——周华健《风雨无阻》

2004年，我第一次踏上北京新东方学校GRE类比反义课堂的讲台，这一讲就是六年。GRE的类比反义对于单词量的要求是迄今为止所有以英语为载体的能力测试中最高的。在课上，我要求学生们把俞敏洪老师的《GRE词汇精选》背诵50遍。我深知背单词是一件苦差事，要想背好海量单词，没有捷径，只能反复重复。但是既然选择去美国深造，我们终究逃不过单词这一关。

记得在大二备考GRE的那个学期，我每天背着双肩书包，手里拿着富光杯的透明水壶，耳朵上塞着耳机听俞敏洪老师的GRE词汇串讲，匆匆地走在去自习教室的路上。那段时间，我的生活重心就在自习教室。用现在流行的话来描述我的生活轨迹应该是"要么我在自习教室，要么我在去自习教室的路上"。每晚将近1点钟才能完成一天的学习任务，而11点时，北航教学区的门就被锁上了。为了能够尽早回到宿舍休息而不走远路，我需要从北航教学区大门旁3米高的铁栏杆翻出教学区。一开始翻的时候，心里会很心酸，但是日子久了，我告诉自己每翻一次就距离我的美国梦又近了一步。有一天我发现那个经常翻的栏杆断了，我意识到在学校里有很多我未曾谋面的同学，他们也为了自己的梦想，每天下自习很晚而走捷径翻这个栏杆。在那个学期，我目睹栏杆断了多次，但后来都被学校的后勤及时地焊上了。毕业的时候，我除了去学校的图书馆拍了毕业照，也去当年翻的这个栏杆拍了我大学四年里最有意义的一张照片。因为这个栏杆，我不是北航里的匆匆过客，它时常让我想起我曾经像一个骄傲的英雄一样每天执着地追逐着自己的梦想。有事做本身就是一件幸福的事，在那段准备GRE的日子里，GRE是我的第二次高考，我有幸能够在大二的时候就接触到它，因为这个考试，我拥有了新东方的工作，让我过上了自己当年想都不敢想的生活。

在新东方讲课除了可以大大改善自己的生活，还可以去影响别人的生活。我曾经将自己备考GRE的经历讲给学生听，这些可爱的学生们也会把他们的故事说给我听。北大光华管理学院的卢璐在2006年10月的GRE考试中取得了Verbal 750的高分，她的高分是每天自习到凌晨3点多，坚持两个月换来的。这个女孩和我提及这段经历的时候告诉我，"每天晚上下了自习，自习所在的北大老4教的楼门都锁了，我每晚是从一层的男厕所开着的窗户翻出来的。每当我翻的时候，我就想到当时课上老师讲的翻栏杆的故事，我觉得我也应该坚持下来。只不过我要是毕业的话，拍毕业照的地方就不是特别合适了"。当我听到卢璐的描述后，当我知道她是北京四中的理科高考状元后，当我知道她家庭背景非常好，全身都是Prada的时候，我意识到有些人的存在就是让你不舒服的。他们既聪明又有好的出身，但和别人一样甚至比别人还要勤奋。当我们面对这样的人的时候，我们没有任何懈怠的借口。每当我们看到他人成功的时候，不要只看结果，多问问他们都吃了哪些苦。因为要吃的苦很多，所以成功走下来的人并不多。

吃苦是守恒的，早吃苦总比晚受苦要好得多。在各位考生背单词受挫的时候，请学会调整自己的心态。唐僧当年也是经过九九八十一难才成功到达西天取得真经的，而背诵GRE单词也只是我们去西方发达国家取经道路中的小小一步。我们不妨将每次挫折都当成是一次锻炼自己的机会，熬过它，我们就距离我们的梦想更近一些。

成功的人经常毅然地选择去做他们不喜欢的事情。如果只愿意挑喜欢的、容易做的事情，我们就好比在跑步机上跑步，即使努力很多，在距离上还是原地踏步。如果说你现在想要开始GRE单词的征程，你一定要能够坚持。毕竟这一路走过来，你必须学会承受各种挫败与打击。背单词的过程是需要积累的，是爆发式的增长。如果你不想坚持了，请参看本段第一句话。

悉数从 2003 年 3 月份第一次参加GRE 考试，到 2009 年的 10 月，我总共参加了 11 次 GRE 考试，Verbal 部分平均分 700+。我在课上总跟学生说我的词汇量不大。除了那些基础的四、六级词汇，我能记得的 GRE 单词只是 GRE 考试里主考的那些高频词，只不过对这些高频词，我太熟悉——不是简单的只知道意思，而是对于它们的种种考法了如指掌。

和 GRE 纠结了这么多年，我决定把自己花了六年时间精心分析筛选的 GRE 高频词和大家分享一下了。于是，我和我的团队成员们共同编写了这本用心良苦的 GRE 词汇书。在这本书中，我们对 GRE 考试中最常做主考的 3000 多个单词的考法进行了全新的演绎，让那些想花最少的时间和精力在 Verbal 部分取得 600 分以上的同学，免去大量无意义单词的背诵，免去大量无用处题目的反复，免去与《韦氏大学词典》以及《美国传统词典》之间的磨磨唧唧。

感谢为本书倾注时间与精力的团队成员们（周书林、杨珺、王东东、陶睿），因为你们，那些备受 GRE 单词煎熬的同学们可以在备考时大大减负；

感谢为了本书的出版付出心血和努力的所有编辑，因为你们，这本书可以如此快地出版；

感谢为本书题词的小牛人俱乐部的 25 位同学和 5 位名校录取的学员（曹楚楠、金宇航、朱晨光、蒋喆、罗弥、武阳乐、童心、卢璐、王彦妮、底骞、温韬、刘琼、周慧杰、汪洋、刘宜君、赵禾、徐碧慧、宋歆怡、赵墨非、杨璐、吕秋莹、相舒、蔺琳、周晟茹、姚佳雄、李丹、刘栩志、陈曦、翟冰、薄瓜瓜），因为你们，阅读本书的读者可以看到他们美好的将来；

感谢新东方曾经影响过我的老师（王鹏、王海波、黄颀、戴云、张晓楠、孙继军、张旭、宋昊、郭行），你们的智慧、才华、洒脱是当年吸引我来新东方的主要动因；

感谢新东方正在影响我的同事，与你们的碰撞是我在新东方快乐工作的原因；

感谢我所有的学生，因为你们，我有了被需要的理由；

感谢我的爸爸妈妈，我永远爱你们！

最后，祝各位同学在 GRE 之旅中一切顺利。为了享受明天美好的生活，也希望你学会享受当下的艰辛与感动。

陈　琦
Jason Chen

序 二

"我不去想是否能够成功/既然选择了远方/便只顾风雨兼程"

——《热爱生命》，汪国真

2008 年的冬天，在和 Jason 的一次聊天中，谈起市面上几乎人手一本的 GRE 红宝书。这本厚厚的红宝书收录了 8000 多词条，而 GRE 考试中类比、反义、填空常考词汇只占其中的一部分。为了能让同学们节省备考时间，提高备考效率，Jason 和我决定开始合作写一本赋予全新理念的 GRE 考试词汇书。在这本词汇书中，我们只收录 GRE 考试类反、填空部分的核心词汇，并对每个词汇的词义解释和考点考法进行详尽的分析。

经济学十大原理之一就是，某种东西的成本是为了得到它所放弃的东西。于我而言，这本词汇书的成本就是在工作辛苦忙碌之余仅有的那一点休息时间。工作日每天上午 7 点起床，晚上 9 点多到家，从 10 点一直编写到 12 点然后睡觉。每个周末不睡懒觉并不是为了看心爱的 NBA，而是为了从上午 9 点一直到晚上 1 点的编写工作。就这样，在把几乎所有的闲暇时间挤出来以后，经历了 3 个多月的努力，把陈琦精心筛选出来的 3000 多个词在《韦氏大学词典》和《美国传统词典》里统统查了一遍，对照着曾经考过的题，将一个个对应的词汇意思摘录出来，终于初步完成了词义筛选工作。Jason 对初稿进行校稿，添加和删除一些内容。由于种种原因，这本词汇书曾一度搁浅。电脑里所有的初稿被我堆进一个文件夹，之后，又被我扔进了移动硬盘的某个角落。

过了许久，我和 Jason 重提这本词汇书的事。毕竟这本书对于每一位考 G 人来说是那么的重要，而且我们也花了那么多心血，不能就这么轻易放弃。这时，幸得几位同学以及 Jason 的同事也一起参与进来，形成了一个编辑团队。大家对初稿所有词条又重新校一遍，并补充了很多新的内容。2009 年夏天，Jason 忙着新东方的暑假 GRE 班，我亦被派到外地出差，这一去就是几个月，这本词汇书又被耽搁了下来。2009 年 12 月 31 日的晚上，Jason 跟我说，他教了这么多年的 GRE 类反，有必要为每一个考 GRE 的同学做一点事情了，于是我们决定将这本词汇书完成，并放到网上，让更多人能自由地获取，免费地阅读这本电子书。

在 2010 年年初的寒假班中，Jason 对同学们做出了承诺，一定会让这本书上线。这是男人的承诺。Jason 每天晚上 9 点下课后，从京郊的房山、琉璃河赶到家编写，第二天上午 6 点继续赶去上课。我将 Jason 编写的内容进行审阅并站在阅读者的角度提出修改意见，Jason 再进行二次修稿。这样来来回回地斟酌敲定，只为将这本"用心良苦"的词汇书付诸实现。Jason 是一个典型的完美主义者，我也喜欢 flawless 的东西，于是从内容到排版，从字体到颜色，Jason 和我都反复商量，终于在 2 月的最后一天，将这本词汇书的第一个 List 终稿完成并上传到网上。本书一共有 30 个 List，我戏谑地称之为"要你命三千"。搞定这些词，"你"就是 ETS；搞不定，"你"就只是你自己。

就在我们逐步将终稿完成的时候，ETS 正式宣布将于 2011 年 8 月对 GRE 考试进行改革。于是我们在保证质量的前提下加快了进度，只为能让那些在 GRE 改革前参加考试的同学们可以尽早获取到这本书。在这个艰难的时刻，我们非常感谢北京新东方大愚文化传播有限公司对出版这本"短命"的词汇书的肯定和支持，若没有他们，这本词汇书将永远停留在 0 和 1 的世界里。针对改革后的 GRE，我和 Jason 已决定将在第一时间为广大考生编写出一本应对全新 GRE 考试的全新词汇书。

最后，谨以此书献给所有看过这本书，考完 GRE，出国深造的同学，希望你们能够披荆斩棘，实现自己的梦想，和心中所爱的人一起创造人生的辉煌。同时，我也要把这本书献给那些在我遭遇挫折困苦的时候，在我人生低谷中给我鼓励和帮助的每一位朋友，以及我心中所爱的人。谢谢你们！

周书林

Franklin Chow

于杭州

迎接改变

2011年2月，万泉河教学区101的讲台上，我在新东方最后一节GRE强化班的类反课因为GRE考试改革而正式落幕。之前的"要你命3000"也被GRE改革要了命。面对新GRE的变化，我多次犹豫是否还有必要做本书的改编。倘若改编，耗时耗力。而在这一年间，"要你命3000"团队成员的生活轨迹也发生了巨大的变化。周书林去香港读书了，陶睿毕业了，杨珺去美国留学了，王东东创业了，我从新东方的北美部调岗至多语种部了。

3000团队的成员在新的环境下一定需要一段适应时间。就像对我来说，面对一个新的部门，面对多语种部六门自己一窍不通的语言，我更是诚惶诚恐，不知所措。岗位上的巨变，对于缺乏管理经验的我来说，无异于七年前，一个内向木讷的理工男双腿发抖地在四百多学生面前讲课时的巨大挑战。但是面对改变，面对新的事物，我们需要将对它本能的恐惧转化成进步的动力。在多语种部工作的这一年，自己成长了很多，认识了很多朋友，喝了很多酒。虽然每天过得很辛苦，但是刻骨铭心。因为我相信如果我们能够把每天的艰辛、痛苦、委屈当作生活的常态，我们的内心就会更加丰富。

每晚拖着疲惫的身躯回到家，想想当年讲台上的日子，百感交集。怀念讲台下那些渴望知识、渴望美好生活的学生；怀念讲台上同台搭档的好朋友。与其怀念，不如行动。最终，我还是决定做这本书的改编。因为这本书对我来说最大的意义，就是永远留在我逝去青春中的——陪我一路走过的学生和朋友。

在此，我要感谢刘宜君、路鹭，因为你们的爬虫程序，使得"新3000"的编写效率大增；感谢颜余真和肖雪，我能理解每个夜晚你们泪眼婆娑地看着屏幕仔细做修订的辛苦；感谢新浪微博GRE机器人常年"要你命3000"的单词更新，让移动背词成为可能；恭喜小牛人俱乐部今年申请的同学，你们持之以恒的努力，让读者在list题词中见证了你们申请的成功！

最后，感谢老GRE，让我的青春那么美好。

新GRE来了，让我们洒脱地迎接它！

琦叔
Jason Chen
于北京

序二(新版)

依稀记得当年上小学五年级的时候,学校第一次开了英语课。那时候有许多外资进入中国,大家觉得学好英语可以去外企,工资也会比国企高。这就是当时我对为什么要学英语的全部理解了。升入初中以后,为了应对三年后的中考,英语作为三门主课之一,贯穿了整个初中阶段。也是在那个时候,新东方英语、李阳疯狂英语等培训班声名鹊起,并逐渐走入莘莘学子的学习生活中。那时的我觉得学英语的目标就是为了应付这门课、这门考试,以期望考上一所好的高中。

后来进入高中才发现,原来高中本质上和初中没有什么两样,学习目的简单而纯粹——考出好的分数,上一所好的大学。经历了大学时代和工作的这些年,当年死记硬背下来的内容大都已经忘得一干二净,甚至于面对今年的高考卷,我都答不上来那些化学生物题,唯有语文、数学和英语如今还在使用。随着阅历的增长,我才逐渐发现了学习英语的意义。

英语作为国际社会的通用语,是解读现代文明世界的工具之一。这句话毫不夸张地道出了现实:中国总体情况的落后是大家深有体会的,而西方国家总体情况的先进也是不可否认的。每年有众多留学生选择去发达国家学习深造,以期学到那些先进的思想文化与科学技术。自然而然,英语成了每一位留学西方国家的同学的必修课。这便是学习英语的基本意义——进入和了解西方世界的通行证。

然而学习英语本身并不能创造出推动社会向上的动力。《十月围城》里,陈少白在被软禁中对他的学生阎孝国说的那句话给我留下了深刻的印象:"功课优秀,头脑愚蠢,一介莽夫,难为大才"。接受西式教育的阎孝国却有着保守固化、不愿接受变革的思想观念。社会的进步是螺旋上升的,期间必定伴随着新陈代谢——这既是自然界的生物法则也是人类社会的发展法则。中国所经历的几千年轮回般的帝制才刚刚在一百年前得以终结,可是封建时期的许多影响在当下社会却依然残留着,这不是靠改良制度就可以祛除的,也不是单靠知识分子们在高等学府里讲课就可以根治的,更不是靠一场文化革命就可以革除的。思想文化的革新是一个漫长而痛苦的过程,需要一代又一代全体中国人民的自我觉醒。学习英语的深层次意义,就是用这个工具将先进的思想解码并传之于中华大地,使全体中国人民能通过了解自身、了解周围、了解世界来建立对社会有益的人生观、价值观和世界观,获得自我觉醒。这也是每一个知识分子乃至每个中国人的使命。

我愿与大家一道,为中国的未来而努力,为建设心目中所希望的中国而奋斗!最后,写下一句屈原先生的话同大家共勉:路漫漫其修远兮,吾将上下而求索。

書林

Franklin Chow

于香港

笔者根据新 GRE 考试特点，在上一版基础上进行了较大幅度改版，推出此"再要你命3000"纸版书籍。本书共收录 GRE 考试中最常做主考的 3072 个单词，给出每个单词常考的中英文释义，配有精选例句、同义词群以及反义词群。部分单词还增加了派生词汇。

本书特色具体如下：

结构科学：本书共有 31 个 List，每个 List 包含 10 个 Unit，每个 Unit 的单词量为 10 个，考生可以循序渐进地进行学习，更加牢固地掌握每个单词。

收词精准：本书针对新 GRE 考试重新设计，删除旧版中只在类反题目中考查的单词，收录历年 GRE 考试中常考的核心词汇，同时增补了最近考试中出现的主考词，以及新 GRE 官方指南中的重点词汇。本书最后四个 list 以星号标注，全部是新增加的重点词汇。

释义权威：所有单词的解释均结合 GRE 考试的常考含义进行筛选。英文释义出自《美国传统词典》（*American Heritage Dictionary*）及 GRE 官方指定的《韦氏大学词典》（*Merriam-Webster's Collegiate Dictionary*），并辅以例句，便于考生在情景中理解词义。

结合实战：每条英文解释中均以加粗和下划线标记出单词考点所在，便于考生迅速把握单词的特征，在平时背诵的过程中逐步由中式思维转换为英式思维。另外，删除旧版中的类反题目，增加新 GRE 考试重点考查的同、反义词，参照以往 GRE 出题频率以及《韦氏同义词反义词词典》（*Merriam-Webster Thesaurus*），为每个主词条精挑细选同义词群和反义词群。

词汇延展：词条中给出派生词汇，扩大了横向词汇，达到举一反三的效果。

去年初夏第一版上架之后，很高兴收到非常多考生的来信，有认真指出纰漏的，也有希望能见到新版面市的。我们编辑团队倾听大家的意见和反馈，力争做得最好。再次感谢这些热心的考生。

关于本书的用法，我们想在这里做一个详细的说明。

首先，关于本书的定位。本书收录的是历次 GRE 考试中的超高频词汇，掌握好这些单词是考生取得理想分数的必要条件。学习这些词，考生需要在认知方面具有一定的深度。事实上，如果能够真正踏踏实实地掌握好本书中的所有内容，考生的词汇知识和能力将达到一个新的水平，可以力争在新 GRE 考试中取得优异成绩。不过，如果背诵本书单词后，在练习中依然遇到大量生词，请考生选择四六级以及托福的单词书，做好基础单词的巩固工作。

其次，关于本书该在备考的哪个阶段使用以及如何使用。本书专门针对新 GRE 考试设计，无论是前期准备、中期巩固还是后期冲刺均是必备利器。本书和市面上其他词汇书最大的不同，同时也是本书精华所在，就是用加粗带下划线的形式突出了单词的"特征点"，即"考点"，所以请务必精读本书，掌握每个单词的考点所在，力求做到"看到词就想到该词的特征"。

最后，关于本书的权威性。本书单词释义都是 GRE 考试中的常考含义，经笔者精挑细选，量身定制，帮助考生避免面对词典中的大量解释而无从下手的尴尬处境。英文释义取自以上两部美国权威词典，曾被 ETS 在出题时选用过，具有极高的准确性和参考价值，中文释义则是与英文释义相对应的正确解释。因此请考生尽可能掌握这些词义。

愿这本书能助各位考生一臂之力！

使用说明

GRE 高分、名校录取学员备考 GRE 的真挚感言

标注星号的最后四个 list 是新版中增补的重点词汇，来自最近考试中出现的主考词汇以及新 GRE 官方指南。这些单词和前面 27 个 list 的词一样重要，考生务必重点掌握。

英文释义中加粗和下划线的部分是单词的核心意思，也是单词在 GRE 考试中经常出现的考点所在，请考生务必熟记。

单词配以经典、实用的例句，便于考生在具体语境中加深对单词的理解。

List 28*

"如果出国是一种信念，那GRE便是是否能坚守的第一道考验。"

（陈曦，录取院校：University of Pennsylvania 材料科学与工程系）

Unit 1

■ ABREAST　　■ ABSENT　　■ ACCLAIM　　■ ACCOMPLISH　　■ ACCORD
■ ACKNOWLEDGE　■ ACQUIRE　　■ ACQUISITIVE　　■ ADJUDICATE　　■ ADVERSITY

abreast [əˈbrest]
【考法 1】 *adv.* 并排地：**beside one another with bodies in line**
例 a group of youths riding four abreast 四个一排骑着车的一群年轻人
近 alongside, side by side
反 aimlessly, desultorily, erratically, haphazardly, irregularly, randomly, willy-nilly 随意地
【考法 2】 *adj.* 熟知的：up to a particular standard or level especially of **knowledge of recent developments**
例 She tried to keep abreast of the latest fashion trends. 她总是尽可能地跟上时尚的潮流。
近 acquainted, conversant, informed, knowledgeable, versed, well-informed
反 ignorant, unacquainted, unfamiliar, uninformed, unknowledgeable 无知的，不熟悉的

absent [ˈæbsənt]
【考法 1】 *adj.* 未出现的，缺乏的：**not present**, attending or existing
例 The city's usual stir of activity was conspicuously absent due to the report of an escaped lion from the zoo. 一则动物园狮子逃跑的消息让这座城市缺少了往日的繁华热闹。
近 away, lacking, missing, nonexistent, wanting
反 existent, present 存在的，出现的
【考法 2】 *adj.* 不专心的，走神的：**lost in thought**
例 He seemed absent because he nodded but didn't say anything. 他只点了点头但没说话，看起来像是走神了。
近 abstracted, distracted
反 alert, vigilant, watchful, wary 警惕的；attentive, heedful, mindful, preoccupied 专注的

acclaim [əˈkleɪm]
【考法 1】 *n.* 称赞：**public acknowledgment or admiration** for an achievement
例 Many people were involved in the search, but the person who actually found the missing girl got all the acclaim. 许许多多的人都参与了搜索行动，但是只有真正找到那个迷失的小女孩的人才受到了称赞。
近 accolade, applause, credit, distinction, homage, honor, kudos, laud, laurels
【考法 2】 *vt.* 赞扬，赞颂：to declare enthusiastic **approval** of
例 He was acclaimed as the country's greatest modern painter. 他被盛赞为国内最优秀的现代画家。
近 accredit, applaud, cheer, commend, endorse, exalt, hail, praise, salute, tout
反 castigate, excoriate, lambaste, pan, slam 猛烈抨击

accomplish [əˈkɑːmplɪʃ]
【考法】 *vt.* 完成，实现：to carry through (as a process) to **completion**
例 I don't think we can accomplish our goal unless we cooperate. 我认为只有合作才能实现我们的目标。
近 achieve, commit, execute, fulfill, make, perpetrate, prosecute, carry out
反 fail 失败
派 accomplishment *n.* 成就；accomplished *adj.* 有造诣的

accord [əˈkɔːrd]
【考法 1】 *n.* 一致：a state of **consistency**
例 This map doesn't seem to be in accord with the current layout of the streets. 这幅地图似乎与当前的街道情况不一致。
近 accordance, agreement, conformity, congruence, congruity, consonance, harmony, tune
反 conflict, disagreement, incongruence, incongruity, incongruousness 不一致

单词释义均结合考试的常考含义给出，参考《美国传统词典》(American Heritage Dictionary) 及 GRE 官方指定的《韦氏大学词典》(Merriam-Webster's Collegiate Dictionary)，帮助考生精确了解词义，培养英语思维。

同义词群和反义词群是新 GRE 考试着重考查的词汇题目，参照以往 GRE 出题频率以及《韦氏同义词反义词词典》(Merriam-Webster Thesaurus) 给出。

词条中给出派生词汇，扩大了横向词汇，达到举一反三的效果。

目 录

List 1

"考好 GRE 的唯一捷径就是重复，重复，再重复。"
（曹楚楠，2008 年 10 月，Verbal 750，Quantitative 800，AW 5.5，
录取学校：Princeton, MIT, M. Fin）

Unit 1

■ ABANDON	■ ABASE	◉ ABASH	■ ABATE	■ ABBREVIATE
■ ABDICATE	■ ABERRANT	■ ABET	■ ABEYANCE	■ ABHOR

abandon [əˈbændən]

【考法 1】 *n.* 放纵：carefree, freedom from **constraint**
- 例 add spices to the stew with complete abandon 肆无忌惮地向炖菜里面加调料
- 近 unconstraint, uninhibitedness, unrestraint

【考法 2】 *v.* 放纵：to give (oneself) over **unrestrainedly**
- 例 abandon oneself to emotion 感情用事 ‖ abandon herself to a life of complete idleness 她放纵自己过着闲散的生活
- 近 indulge, surrender

【考法 3】 *v.* 放弃：to **withdraw** from often in the face of danger or encroachment
- 例 abandon the ship/homes 弃船；离家
- 反 salvage 救援

【考法 4】 *v.* 停止做某事：to **put an end to** (something planned or previously agreed to)
- 例 The bad weather forced NASA to abandon the launch. 坏天气迫使 NASA 停止了发射。
- 近 abort, drop, repeal, rescind, revoke, call off, give up
- 反 keep, continue, maintain, carry on 继续

abase [əˈbeɪs]

【考法】 *v.* 降低(地位、职位、威望或尊严)：to **lower** in rank, office, prestige, or esteem
- 例 He was unwilling to abase himself by pleading guilty to a crime that he did not commit. 他不愿意屈就自己去承认一个莫须有的罪名。
- 近 debauch, degrade, profane, vitiate, discredit, foul, smirch, take down
- 反 elevate, ennoble, uplift, aggrandize, canonize, deify, exalt 使高贵，使有声望

abash [əˈbæʃ]

【考法】 *vt.* 使尴尬，使羞愧：to destroy the self-possession or **self-confidence** of, disconcert, **embarrass**
- 例 Nothing could abash him. 没有什么可以使他感到难堪。
- 近 discomfit, disconcert, discountenance, faze, fluster, nonplus, mortify
- 反 embolden 使大胆

abate [əˈbeɪt]

【考法 1】 *v.* 减轻(程度或者强度)：to **reduce** in **degree** or **intensity**
- 例 abate his rage/pain 平息他的愤怒 / 减轻他的痛苦
- 近 moderate, recede, subside, remit, wane, die (away or down or out), let up, phase down, taper off
- 反 intensify 加强，加剧

【考法 2】 *v.* 减少(数量)，降低(价值)：to **reduce** in **amount or value**
- 例 abate a tax 降低税收
- 近 de-escalate, deplete, downscale, dwindle, ratchet (down)
- 反 augment, promote 增加

【考法 3】 *v.* 停止，撤销：to put an **end** to
- 例 abate a nuisance 停止伤害
- 近 abrogate, annul, invalidate, nullify, rescind, vacate

abbreviate [əˈbriːvieɪt]

【考法】 *v.* 缩写，缩短：to make **briefer**
- 例 abbreviate the word "building" as "bldg." 将"building"缩写作"bldg."
- 近 abridge, curtail, cut back, syncopate, truncate
- 反 extend, protract, elongate, lengthen, prolong 延长

abdicate	[ˈæbdɪkeɪt]
【考法】	*v.* 正式放弃（权力、责任）: to renounce a **throne**, to relinquish (power or responsibility) formally
例	abdicate the throne/crown 退位
近	cede, relinquish, renounce, resign, step down (from)
反	constitute, assume, usurp 任命；承担；篡位

aberrant	[æˈberənt]
【考法】	*adj.* 异常的，非常规的: **deviating** from the usual or natural type
例	This behavior might be aberrant enough to draw attention. 这样的行为已经异常得足以引起人们的注意。
近	abnormal, anomalous, peculiar, singular, unwonted, uncustomary
反	normal, natural, regular, standard, typical 正常的，标准的，典型的

abet	[əˈbet]
【考法1】	*v.* 帮助，怂恿: to **assist or support** in the achievement of a purpose
例	aid and abet <法律>协助教唆
近	ferment, foment, provoke, instigate, stir (up), whip (up)
【考法2】	*v.* 鼓励: to actively **encourage** (as an activity or plan)
近	aid, assist, back, support, prop (up)
反	stymie, frustrate, obstruct, thwart, impede, forestall, hinder 阻挠

abeyance	[əˈbeɪəns]
【考法】	*n.* 中止，搁置: temporary **inactivity**
例	hold the plan in abeyance 使计划暂停
近	doldrums, quiescence, moratorium, latency, dormancy, suspension, cold storage, deep freeze
反	continuance, fulfillment 继续；履行

abhor	[əbˈhɔːr]
【考法】	*vt.* 深恶痛绝，极度厌恶: to regard with **extreme repugnance**
例	He abhors the way people leave their trash at the picnic sites in the park. 他很厌恶人们把垃圾留在公园的野餐点。
近	abominate, despise, detest, execrate, loathe
反	greatly admire 非常崇拜

Unit 2

◧ABIDING	◧ABJECT	◧ABJURE	◧ABNEGATE	◧ABOMINATE
◧ABOVEBOARD	◧ABRADE	◧ABRIDGE	◧ABROGATE	◧ABSCOND

abiding	[əˈbaɪdɪŋ]
【考法】	*adj.* 永久的: lasting for a long time; **enduring**
例	an abiding love of Espanol 对西班牙语持久的热爱
近	ageless, enduring, eternal, everlasting, perennial, perpetual, timeless
反	evanescent, ephemeral 短暂的

abject	[ˈæbdʒekt]
【考法1】	*adj.* 无精打采的: cast down in spirit, **spiritless**
例	a man made abject by suffering 被苦难折磨得无精打采的人
近	spiritless
反	spirited, excited, exultant 狂喜的，令人兴奋的
【考法2】	*adj.* (地位、身份)悲惨、凄凉的: sunk to or existing in a **low state** or condition
例	abject poverty 让人绝望的贫穷
【考法3】	*adj.* 卑微的，讨好的: expressing or offered in a **humble** and often ingratiating spirit
例	abject flattery 卑躬屈膝般的恭维 ‖ an abject apology 讨好般的道歉
近	base, humble, menial, servile, slavish

abjure	[əbˈdʒʊr]
【考法1】	*v.* 发誓放弃: a firm and final **rejecting** or **abandoning** often made under oath
例	abjure one's belief 发誓放弃信仰
近	recant, renege, renounce, abnegate, forswear, repudiate
反	affirm, espouse, embrace 接受，拥护
【考法2】	*v.* 抵制，避免: to **resist** the temptation of
例	abjure extravagance 抵制铺张浪费
近	keep (from), refrain (from), withhold (from)
反	bow to, give in to, submit to, succumb to, surrender to, yield to 屈从于

abnegate [ˈæbnɪɡeɪt]

【考法 1】 *v.* 否认 : **deny**, **renounce**

例 abnegate the idea of freedom 放弃自由的观念

近 recant, renege, repudiate, unsay, forswear, take back

反 reaffirm 再肯定，重申

【考法 2】 *v.* 投降，放弃，交出（权力等）: **surrender**, **relinquish**

例 abnegate her powers 交出她拥有的权力

近 cede, resign, step aside (from), step down (from)

反 adhere to 依附；坚持

abominate [əˈbɑːmɪneɪt]

【考法】 *v.* 憎恶 : to hate or loathe intensely, **abhor**

例 We abominate jokes that make fun of people who have physical disabilities. 我们鄙视拿有生理缺陷的人开玩笑。

近 despise, detest, execrate, loathe

反 esteem, love, adore 尊敬，爱

aboveboard [əˈbʌvbɔːrd]

【考法】 *adj.* 无欺诈的，光明正大的 : **free from** all traces of **deceit or duplicity**

例 This transaction was totally aboveboard, so there was no reason to question it. 这项交易完全公开公正，没有必要质疑。

反 surreptitious, underhanded 偷偷摸摸的

abrade [əˈbreɪd]

【考法】 *v.* 磨损，精神上折磨 : to rub or **wear away** especially **by friction**; wear down spiritually

例 My skin was abraded. 我的皮肤被磨损了。

近 chafe, excoriate, rasp, graze, scuff

反 augment 增加

abridge [əˈbrɪdʒ]

【考法 1】 *v.* 缩短，缩小 : to **shorten** in duration or extent

例 The modern transportation abridges distance. 现代运输方式缩短了路途。

近 curtail, truncate, cut back

反 extend in length, protract, amplify 延长，放大

【考法 2】 *v.* 在不改变本意的条件下删减词语，缩写 : to **shorten** by omission of words without sacrifice of sense

例 an abridged edition 精简版

近 abbreviate, curtail, condense, syncopate

abrogate [ˈæbrəɡeɪt]

【考法 1】 *v.* 官方的正式废除 : to abolish by authoritative action, **annul**

例 abrogate the law/treaty 废除法律、条约

近 disannul, invalidate, nullify, quash, rescind, roll back, strike down

反 embrace, uphold, institute 采纳；支持；建立

【考法 2】 *v.* 无视（某事的）存在 : to treat as **nonexistent**

例 abrogate their responsibilities 抛开、不顾他们的责任

abscond [əbˈskɑːnd]

【考法】 *v.* 偷偷离开 : to **depart secretly** and hide oneself

例 abscond from the prison 越狱

近 flee, lam, run off, break out (of), clear out

Unit 3

| ABSOLUTE | ABSOLVE | ABSTAIN | ABSTEMIOUS | ABSTRACT |
| ABSTRUSE | ABSURD | ABUNDANT | ABUSE | ABUT |

absolute [ˈæbsəluːt]

【考法 1】 *adj.* 专制的 : **unconstrained** by constitutional or other provisions

例 absolute ruler 专制的统治者

近 arbitrary, autocratic, despotic, dictatorial, monocratic, tyrannical

【考法 2】 *adj.* 无限的 : **unqualified** in extent or degree; total

例 absolute silence 鸦雀无声

近 complete, utter, deadly, downright, out-and-out

反 qualified 有限的，有保留的

【考法3】	*adj.* 完美的，纯净不掺杂的：**free from imperfection**; free or relatively free from **mixture**
例	absolute alcohol 无水酒精（纯酒精）
近	plain, refined, unadulterated, unalloyed, undiluted, unmixed
反	adulterated, alloyed, diluted, impure, mixed 掺杂的，不纯的
【考法4】	*adj.* 不容置疑的，确凿的：positive, **unquestionable**
例	absolute proof 确凿的证据
近	clear, deciding, decisive, definitive
反	inconclusive, indecisive, unclear 不明确的

absolve [əbˈzɑːlv]

【考法】	*v.* 使无罪，解除责任：to set **free from** an obligation or the consequences of **guilt**, **exculpate**
例	absolve somebody from blame 使某人免受责备
近	acquit, exonerate, vindicate
反	blame, criminate, incriminate 定罪

abstain [əbˈsteɪn]

【考法】	*v.* 自我克制，主动戒绝：to **refrain** from something **by one's own choice**
例	abstain from smoking/voting 戒烟；弃权
近	forgo, keep from, refrain from, withhold (from)
反	bow to, give in to, submit to, succumb to, surrender to, yield to 屈服于

abstemious [əbˈstiːmiəs]

【考法】	*adj.* （吃喝等）有节制的，节俭的：marked by **restraint** especially in the consumption of **food or alcohol**, **sparing**
例	an abstemious diet 有节制的饮食 ‖ abstemious meals 节俭的饭餐
近	continent, temperate, self-abnegating, self-denying
反	indulgent 放纵的

abstract [æbˈstrækt]

【考法1】	*vt.* 做总结，概括：to make an **abstract** of, **summarize**
例	abstract the 135-page report in three short paragraphs 将一份 135 页的报告概括为三段话
近	digest, recapitulate, synopsize, sum up, boil down
反	elaborate 详细描述
【考法2】	*vt.* 使分心：to draw **away** the **attention** of
例	Personal problems abstracted him. 私人问题让他分心。
近	detract, divert, call off, throw off
派	abstraction *n.* 心不在焉
反	attention 关注

abstruse [əbˈstruːs]

【考法】	*adj.* 难以理解的：difficult to comprehend: **recondite**
例	the abstruse calculations 复杂深奥的计算
近	arcane, esoteric, hermetic (*also* hermetical), recondite
反	accessible, patent, shallow, superficial 可了解的，肤浅的

absurd [əbˈsɜːrd]

【考法】	*adj.* 不合理的：ridiculously **unreasonable**, unsound, or incongruous
例	an absurd argument 无稽之谈
近	wild, bizarre, ludicrous, insane, nonsensical, preposterous, half-baked
反	rational, sensible, realistic, reasonable 理性的，合理的

abundant [əˈbʌndənt]

【考法】	*adj.* 大量的：marked by **great plenty** (as of resources)
例	an abundant land 一片富饶的土地
近	ample, cornucopian, teeming, replete, abounding
反	infrequent, rare, uncommon, inadequate, scanty, scarce 稀少的，罕见的

abuse [əˈbjuːz]

【考法1】	*v.* 辱骂，抨击：to **condemn or vilify** usually unjustly, intemperately, and angrily
例	He alleged that he was verbally abused by his colleagues. 他声称受到了同事的言语攻击。
近	assail, bash, castigate, excoriate, lambaste
派	abusive *adj.* 辱骂的
【考法2】	*v.* 不正当或不合理使用：to put to a **wrong or improper use**；过分过量使用：to **use excessively**
例	abuse a privilege 滥用特权 ‖ abuse alcohol 酗酒
近	misemploy, misuse

abut [əˈbʌt]
【考法】 *v.* 邻接，毗邻：to touch at one end or side; lie **adjacent**
例 Our land abuts a wildlife preserve. 我们的土地靠近一片野生动物保护区。
近 skirt, verge on, border on, butt on, march with

Unit 4

■ ABYSMAL ■ ACCEDE ■ ACCELERATE ■ ACCESSIBLE ■ ACCESSORY
■ ACCIDENTAL ■ ACCLIMATE ■ ACCOLADE ■ ACCOMMODATE ■ ACCOST

abysmal [əˈbɪzməl]
【考法 1】 *adj.* 极低的，极可怜的：**immeasurably low** or wretched
例 abysmal living conditions 极可怜的生活条件
近 bottomless
【考法 2】 *adj.* (程度) 很深的；极端的：**immeasurably great**
例 abysmal ignorance 极端的无知 ‖ an abysmal cliff 深不见底的悬崖
近 profound
反 shallow, shoal, skin-deep, superficial 浅的；肤浅的

accede [əkˈsiːd]
【考法 1】 *v.* 赞成：to express **approval** or give **consent**
例 accede to their pleas 同意他们的请愿
近 acquiesce, assent, consent, subscribe, come round
反 demur, dissent 反对
【考法 2】 *v.* 就任，就职：to arrive at or **come into an office** or dignity
例 accede to the throne 就任国王

accelerate [əkˈseləreɪt]
【考法 1】 *v.* 加速：to cause to move **faster**
例 accelerate his steps 他加快脚步
近 balloon, escalate, snowball, mushroom, proliferate, burgeon, build up
反 retard 减速
【考法 2】 *v.* 使提前发生：to bring about at an **earlier** time
例 accelerate their departure 提前离开
【考法 3】 *v.* 变大，变多：to become **greater** in size, extent, volume, amount, or number
例 Toy purchases accelerate dramatically during the Christmas season. 玩具销售量在圣诞期间暴涨。
近 accumulate, balloon, enlarge, escalate, mushroom, proliferate, snowball, roll up
反 contract, decrease, diminish, dwindle, lessen, recede, wane 减小，减少

accessible [əkˈsesəbl]
【考法 1】 *adj.* 可以到达的：situated **within easy reach**
例 the town accessible by rail 有铁路通达的城镇
近 handy, reachable
反 inconvenient, unhandy, unreachable, untouchable 无法到达的，不方便的
【考法 2】 *adj.* 可理解的：capable of being **understood** or appreciated
例 The information ought to be made more accessible. 信息应该更清晰易懂。
近 apprehensible, fathomable, legible, scrutable
反 abstruse, incoherent, incomprehensible, inscrutable, insensible 深奥的；难以理解的
【考法 3】 *adj.* 能够获得的：possible to **get**
例 The data is not currently accessible. 该数据目前还不可用。
近 available, attainable, obtainable, procurable
反 unattainable, unavailable, unobtainable 无法获得的

accessory [əkˈsesəri]
【考法 1】 *adj.* 辅助的，附属的：having a **secondary**, **supplementary**, or **subordinate** function
例 accessory features such as call-waiting 类似呼叫等待的附属功能
近 peripheral, supplementary
反 of primarily importance, chief, main, principal 主要的
【考法 2】 *n.* 帮凶：**one** associated with another in **wrongdoing**
例 Two accessories, the driver of the getaway car and the dishonest bank teller, were charged in the robbery case. 两个帮凶，逃逸车辆的司机和不诚信的银行出纳，在抢劫案中被控告。
近 abettor, confederate

accidental [ˌæksɪˈdentl]

【考法 1】 *adj.* 意外发生的，偶然的：occurring **unexpectedly** or by chance

例 The discovery of gold was entirely accidental. 黄金的发现纯属偶然。

近 incidental, fortuitous, unintended, unintentional, unpremeditated, unwitting

反 calculated, deliberate, intended, planned, premeditated 预先计划好的

【考法 2】 *adj.* 附带的，不重要的：**not being a vital part** of or belonging to something

例 Its commercial value was accidental. 它的商业价值微乎其微。

近 alien, extraneous, external, adventitious

反 inherent, innate, intrinsic 内在的，固有的

acclimate [ˈækləmeɪt]

【考法】 *vt.* 使适应：**to change** (something) **so as to make it suitable** for a new use or situation

例 acclimate oneself to a nine-to-five office job 适应朝九晚五的坐班生活

近 adjust, accommodate, shape, suit, tailor

反 make unfamiliar with 使不熟悉

accolade [ˈækəleɪd]

【考法 1】 *n.* 同意，赞赏：an expression of **approval**

例 The director won virtually every accolade that the film world offered. 这位导演赢得了电影界几乎一致的赞赏。

近 applause, credit, distinction

反 disapprobation 不赞成

【考法 2】 *v.* 赞扬：to **praise** or honor

反 excoriate, criticise, reprobate, castigate, derogate, reproof, denigrate, denunciate 批评，谴责

accommodate [əˈkɑːmədeɪt]

【考法 1】 *v.* 提供所需（例如服务、借贷、寄宿）：to **provide** with something desired, needed, or suited (as a helpful service, a loan, or lodgings)

例 This cruise ship was big enough to accommodate over 600 people. 该游轮可以为 600 多人提供食宿。

近 fit, hold, take

【考法 2】 *v.* 改变以适应新情况、新场景：to change (something) so as to **make** it **suitable** for a new use or situation

例 accommodate the lectern to the height of the guest speaker 将讲台的高度调节得适合客座讲演者

近 acclimate, adjust, condition, conform, doctor, edit, shape, suit, tailor

【考法 3】 *vt.* 使和谐：to bring to a state **free of conflicts**, inconsistencies, or differences

例 The idea that the United States could harmoniously accommodate all was a fiction. 认为美国能够和谐一切的想法只是幻想。

近 attune, conciliate, conform, coordinate, reconcile

反 disharmonize 使不和谐

accost [əˈkɔːst]

【考法】 *vt.* 以挑衅的形式搭讪：to approach and speak to often in a **challenging or aggressive way**

例 accosted by three gang members 被三个混混搭讪

Unit 5

■ ACCRETE	■ ACCUMULATE	■ ACERBIC	■ ACME	■ ACQUIESCE
■ ACRID	■ ACRIMONIOUS	■ ACUMEN	■ ACUTE	■ ADAMANT

accrete [æˈkriːt]

【考法】 *v.* 逐渐增长：to **grow** or increase **gradually**, as by addition

例 silt accreting at the mouth of the river 泥沙在河口淤积

近 accumulate, build up, pile (up), stack (up)

反 wear away 衰退

派 accretion *n.* 慢慢增加

accumulate [əˈkjuːmjəleɪt]

【考点】 *vi.* 逐渐增长：to **increase gradually** in quantity or number

例 accumulate a fortune 积攒了一笔财富

近 mount, swell, garner, snowball, build up, bulk (up)

反 dissipate, diminish, dwindle, recede, wane 消散，减少

acerbic [əˈsɜːrbɪk]

【考法】 *adj.* （心情、心境或者语调）尖酸的：marked by the use of **wit** that is intended to **cause hurt feelings**

例 acerbic commentary 尖酸的评论

近 pungent, sardonic, satiric, scalding, scathing

反 sweet, saccharine 甜的

派 acerbity *n.* 尖酸，刻薄

acme [ˈækmi]

【考法1】 *n.* 顶点，极点：the **highest** point or stage, as of achievement or development

例 the acme of his career 他事业的巅峰

近 culmination, pinnacle, tip-top, high-water mark

反 bottom, nadir, rock bottom 最低点

【考法2】 *n.* 最佳典范：the **most perfect type** or example

例 The movie has come to be regarded as the acme of the Hollywood musical. 这部影片被认为是好莱坞音乐剧的典范。

近 apotheosis, epitome, exemplar

acquiesce [ˌækwiˈes]

【考法】 *v.* 勉强同意；默许：to **accept**, comply, or submit **tacitly or passively**

例 acquiesce to my own fleecing 默许我的敲竹杠行为

近 assent, consent, subscribe, come round

反 resist, defy, dissent 抵制，不同意

acrid [ˈækrɪd]

【考法1】 *adj.* 辛辣的，刺鼻的：sharp and **harsh** or unpleasantly pungent in **taste** or **odor**: irritating

例 acrid smell of tobacco 烟草刺鼻的味道

【考点2】 *adj.* 刻薄的：marked by the use of **wit** that is intended to **cause hurt feelings**

例 acrid temper 刻薄的性情

反 gentle 温和的

acrimonious [ˌækrɪˈmoʊniəs]

【考法】 *adj.* 刻薄的，充满仇恨的：having or showing **deep-seated resentment**

例 the acrimonious debate between the two candidates 两位候选人之间言辞激烈的辩论

近 embittered, hard, rancorous, resentful, sore

○ acumen [ˈækjəmən]

【考法】 *n.* 不同寻常的洞察力和鉴别力：**exceptional discernment and judgment** especially in practical matters

例 the business acumen 商业方面的洞察力

近 keenness, shrewdness, canniness, clear-sightedness, hardheadedness

反 unable to discern 不能辨别的

acute [əˈkjuːt]

【考法1】 *adj.* 敏锐的：marked by **keen discernment** or intellectual perception especially of subtle distinctions, penetrating

例 an acute thinker 思维敏锐的思想者

近 delicate, fine, keen, perceptive, sensitive

【考法2】 *adj.* 严重的，急性的：needing **immediate attention**

例 acute appendicitis 急性阑尾炎

近 exigent, imperative, compelling, urgent

反 mild, noncritical, nonurgent 轻微的，不严重的

【考法3】 *adj.* （程度、影响）极强的：**extreme** in degree, or effect

例 She was experiencing acute distress over the misunderstanding with her best friend. 她因与死党之间发生误会而陷入了深深的痛苦中。

近 dreadful, excruciating, profound

反 light, moderate, soft 温和的

adamant [ˈædəmənt]

【考法】 *adj.* 固执的，不可动摇的：**unshakable** or insistent especially in maintaining a position or opinion, **unyielding**; **inflexible**

例 adamant about staying here 执意留下来

近 hardheaded, headstrong, intransigent, pertinacious, obdurate, uncompromising

反 vacillatory, incline to yield, amenable, compliant, relenting, yielding 动摇的，易屈从的

Unit 6

adapt [ə'dæpt]
【考法】 *v.* 修改，使(适应)：to **modify** according with the changing circumstances
例 adapt to the change 适应变化 ‖ adapt the novel for the screen 改编小说为影视作品
近 adjust, conform, edit, accommodate, shape, suit, tailor

addict
【考法 1】 [ə'dɪkt] *v.* 沉溺，上瘾：to devote or **surrender** (oneself) to something habitually or **obsessively**
例 be addicted to drug/alcohol 沉溺于毒品、酒
【考法 2】 ['ædɪkt] *n.* 对某事上瘾的人：a person with a strong and **habitual liking** for something
例 science-fiction addicts who eagerly await each new installment in the series 科幻小说爱好者，等待着系列的每一次更新
近 devotee, enthusiast, fanatic, maniac
反 nonfan 非粉丝

adhere [əd'hɪr]
【考法 1】 *v.* 依附，粘着：to cause to **stick** fast
例 adhere to the surface 附着在表面
近 cleave, cling, hew
反 detach 分离
【考法 2】 *v.* 服从，遵守：to act **according to the commands** of
例 adhere to the rules 遵守规定
近 cling to, hew to, stand by, stick to, comply with
反 defy, disobey, rebel against 不服从，反抗
【考法 3】 *v.* 坚定地支持：to give **steadfast support** to
例 Our coach adheres to the belief that we can win this game if we just have a positive attitude. 我们的教练坚定地相信，只要我们有积极的态度，就能拿下比赛。
近 keep to, stand by, stick to or with
反 defect from 叛变
派 adherent *n.* 追随者：a follower of a leader, party, or profession
反 forerunner 先行者

adjourn [ə'dʒɜːrn]
【考法】 *vi.* 延期，休会：to **suspend** a session indefinitely or to another time or place
例 The meeting adjourned for a week. 会议延期一周。
近 prorogate, prorogue, recess, suspend
反 convoke 召集，召开会议

adjunct ['ædʒʌŋkt]
【考法】 *n.* 附属物，非必须部分：something joined or added to another thing but **not essentially a part** of it
例 Massage therapy can be used as an adjunct along with the medication. 按摩治疗可以作为药物治疗的补充疗法。
近 appendage, appliance, attachment, add-on
反 essential element 重要部分

ad-lib [ˌæd'lɪb]
【考法】 *adj.* 即兴的：made or done **without previous thought or preparation**
例 not bad for an ad-lib comedy routine 对即兴喜剧表演来说已经不错了
近 extempory, impromptu, improvisational, offhanded
反 considered, planned, premeditated, rehearsed 预先计划的

admonish [əd'mɑːnɪʃ]
【考法 1】 *v.* 建议：to **give advice** to
例 admonish the patient to eat more healthy foods 建议患者多吃健康食品
近 counsel
【考法 2】 *v.* 责备：to **reprove gently** but earnestly
例 admonish her for littering 责备她乱扔垃圾
近 chide, reprimand, reproach, reprove, tick off
派 admonishment *n.* 责备

adore [əˈdɔːr]
【考法 1】 *vt.* 喜爱，因…感到愉悦: to take **pleasure** in
例 I adore those earrings. 我相中那对耳环了。
近 fancy, relish, savor, delight in, rejoice in
【考法 2】 *vt.* 宠爱: to feel passion, devotion, or **tenderness** for
例 adore his wife 宠爱他的妻子
近 cherish
反 abhor, abominate, despise, detest, execrate, loathe 讨厌，嫌弃

adulate [ˈædʒəleɪt]
【考法】 *v.* 极度谄媚: to **praise too much**
例 incompetent assistants who spend all their time adulating her 成天恭维她的不称职的下属
近 overpraise, belaud, soft-soap, butter up
反 scorn, disdain, vituperate, disparage 鄙视

adulterate [əˈdʌltəreɪt]
【考法】 *vt.* 掺杂，加入低等成分: to corrupt, debase, or make **impure** by the **addition** of a foreign or inferior substance or element
例 adulterate its products with cheap additives 在产品中掺杂廉价的添加剂
近 alloy, contaminate, pollute, taint, water down
反 enrich, fortify, strengthen 加入(养分)使增强

Unit 7

| ■ ADUMBRATE | ■ ADVENTITIOUS | ■ ADVERSARY | ■ ADVERT | ■ ADVOCATE |
| ■ AFFABLE | ■ AFFINITY | ■ AFFLUENT | ■ AGGRANDIZE | ■ AGGRAVATE |

adumbrate [ˈædəmbreɪt]
【考法 1】 *vt.* 部分地或有保留地揭露: to **disclose** partially or guardedly
例 adumbrate a plan 透露计划
反 revelation 完全显示
【考法 2】 *vt.* 预示着: to **give a slight indication** of beforehand
例 The strife in Bloody Kansas adumbrated the civil war that would follow. 发生在堪萨斯州的流血冲突预示了之后的南北内战的爆发。
近 forerun, harbinger, herald, prefigure

adventitious [ˌædvenˈtɪʃəs]
【考法】 *adj.* 外来的，后天的，非内在的: coming from another source and **not inherent or innate**
例 Moral considerations are adventitious to the study of art. 道德的考量对于艺术研究来说是不必要的。
近 alien, extraneous, external, foreign, supervenient
反 constitutional, essential, intrinsic, inborn, inbred, innate, inherent 天生的，内在的

adversary [ˈædvərseri]
【考法】 *n.* 敌手，对手: one that contends with, opposes, or **resists**: **enemy**
例 political adversary 政敌
近 antagonist, foe, opponent
反 ally, amigo, friend 联盟；朋友

advert [ədˈvɜːrt]
【考法】 *vi.* 引起注意；提到: to call attention; **refer**
例 He adverted to the problem in the opening paragraph. 他开门见山地提出了问题。
派 advertent *adj.* 留意的
反 inattentive, remiss, heedless, negligent 疏忽的

advocate [ˈædvəkeɪt]
【考法】 *vt.* 支持，提倡: to speak, plead, or argue in favor of; **support**
例 advocate traditional teaching methods 提倡传统教学方法
近 back, champion, endorse, patronize
反 impugn 提出异议

affable [ˈæfəbl]
【考法】 *adj.* 和蔼的，温和的: characterized by **ease** and **friendliness**
例 an affable manner 随和的举止
近 cordial, genial, hospitable, sociable, good-natured, good-tempered, well-disposed
反 irascible, testy, ill-tempered, unamiable, ungenial 易怒的，不随和的

affinity [ə'fɪnəti]

【考法1】 *n.* 喜欢，倾向：a habitual **attraction** to some activity or thing

例 She always had an affinity for nurturing living things. 她总是喜欢养一些活物。

近 bent, penchant, predilection, predisposition, proclivity, propensity

反 aversion, repugnance, antipathy 厌恶

【考法2】 *n.* 相似：the fact or state of having something **in common**

例 a study showing an affinity between obesity and socioeconomic status 一项显示了肥胖程度和社会经济水平之间相似性的研究

近 association, kinship

affluent ['æfluənt]

【考法】 *adj.* 富裕的：having a generously **sufficient** and typically increasing supply of material possessions

例 affluent society 富裕的社会

近 opulent, loaded, deep-pocketed, silk-stocking, well-endowed, well-off, well-to-do

反 needy, impecunious, impoverished, indigent, penurious 贫困的

aggrandize [ə'ɡrændaɪz]

【考法】 *vt.* 增加、提高（力量、财富、地位、声誉）等：to **enhance** the power, wealth, position, or reputation of

例 exploit the situation to aggrandize himself 借势而上使得自己地位提升、财富增长

近 augment, boost, expand, magnify, add (to), pump up

反 relegate, disparage, efface, abase, demean 降级；贬低

aggravate ['æɡrəveɪt]

【考法1】 *vt.* 加重，恶化：to make **worse**, more **serious**, or more **severe**

例 Stress and lack of sleep could aggravate the situation. 压力和睡眠不足使情况恶化。

近 complicate, worsen

反 alleviate, succor, console, assuage, mitigate, relieve 减轻，抚慰

【考法2】 *vt.* 使恼火：to **disturb** the peace of mind of (someone) especially by repeated disagreeable acts

例 It really aggravates me; when I arrived 10 minutes before the stated closing time, the store had closed already. 我在规定的打烊时间前10分钟到达，但发现商店已经关门了，这让我很恼火。

近 annoy, bother, nettle, vex

Unit 8

■ AGGREGATE	■ AGGRESSIVE	■ AGGRIEVE	■ AGITATE	■ AGOG
■ AGONIZE	■ AIRTIGHT	■ ALACRITY	■ ALIBI	■ ALIENATE

aggregate

【考法1】 ['æɡrɪɡət] *n.* 集合体：a mass or body of **units or parts** somewhat loosely **associated** with one another

例 An empire is the aggregate of many states under one common head. 帝国是由一个共同领袖领导的若干国家的集合体。

近 sum, summation, totality

反 isolated units 隔离的单位

【考法2】 ['æɡrɪɡeɪt] *v.* 集合，聚集：to **collect or gather** into a mass or whole

例 aggregate content from many other sites 搜罗集合许多其他网站的内容

近 coalesce, join together

反 disperse 分散

派 disaggregate *v.* 分解

aggressive [ə'ɡresɪv]

【考法1】 *adj.* 好斗的：having a quality of anger and determination that makes it ready to **attack** others

例 aggressive behavior 具有攻击性的行为

近 fierce, assaultive, combative, militant, confrontational, go-getting, self-assertive, truculent, pugnacious

反 even-tempered, nonbelligerent, pacific, uncombative, uncontentious 心平气和的，不好斗的

【考法2】 *adj.* 强有力的，强烈的：marked by or uttered with **forcefulness**

例 an aggressive campaign to win the African-American vote 一次能够获得非裔美国人选票的强有力的竞选

近 dynamic, energetic, full-blooded, vigorous

aggrieve [əˈgriːv]
【考法】 *vt.* 使苦恼，使悲痛：to give **pain** or **trouble** to, **distress**
反 gratify 使高兴，满足
派 aggrieved *adj.* 苦恼的，怨念的
例 a line of aggrieved ticket-holders, demanding a refund for the cancelled play 一队心怀怨念的购票者，为取消的话剧要求退款
近 discontent, disgruntled, displeased, dissatisfied, malcontent

agitate [ˈædʒɪteɪt]
【考法 1】 *v.* 煽动，激起：to attempt to **arouse** public feeling
例 agitate for better conditions 为得到更好的条件而煽动
近 debate, dispute, bat (around or back and forth), hash (over or out), talk over
【考法 2】 *vt.* 使不安：to excite and often **trouble the mind** or feelings of: **disturb**
例 There's no need to agitate the patient about little things. 没必要因为鸡毛蒜皮的事让患者烦躁。
近 bother, discomfort, discompose, perturb
反 calm, compose, soothe, tranquilize 平息，抚慰

agog [əˈgɑːg]
【考法】 *adj.* 极度感兴趣的：showing **urgent desire or interest**
例 Children were agog over new toys. 孩子们见到了新玩具极其兴奋。
近 avid, ardent, enthusiastic, solicitous, voracious
反 apathetic, indifferent, uneager, unenthusiastic 漠不关心的，冷淡的

agonize [ˈægənaɪz]
【考法】 *v.* (使)非常痛苦：to (cause to) feel **deep sadness** or mental pain
例 agonizes over every decision 做每一个决定都非常痛苦
近 anguish, suffer

airtight [ˈeɪrtaɪt]
【考法 1】 *adj.* 无瑕疵的：having **no** noticeable weakness, **flaw**, or loophole
例 an airtight argument 滴水不漏、无懈可击的论断
【考法 2】 *adj.* 密封的，不透气的：**impermeable to air** or nearly so
例 an airtight seal 不透气的封口

alacrity [əˈlækrəti]
【考法】 *n.* 反应迅速，乐意，欣然：promptness in response: cheerful readiness
例 accept the invitation with alacrity 欣然接受邀请
近 amenability, gameness, obligingness, willingness
反 dilatoriness, hesitance and reluctance 拖延、犹豫和不情愿

alibi [ˈæləbaɪ]
【考法】 *n.* 不在场的证明；托辞，借口：an **excuse** usually intended to avert blame or punishment(as for failure or negligence)
例 He always has a very creative alibi for undone homework. 他对于不完成作业总是有各种新奇的借口。
近 defense, justification, plea, reason

alienate [ˈeɪliəneɪt]
【考法 1】 *v.* 疏远，离间：to **make unfriendly**, or indifferent especially where attachment formerly existed
例 He has alienated most of his colleagues with his bad temper. 因为他的坏脾气，很多同事都和他疏远了。
近 disaffect, disgruntle, sour
反 unite, reunite, reconcile 联合，重新联合，和好
【考法 2】 *v.* 转移、变卖（财产或权利）：to **convey or transfer**(as property or a right) usually by a specific act rather than the due course of law
例 A landowner has a right to alienate his right of ownership. 地主有权利变卖自己的地产。
近 assign, cede, deed, make over

Unit 9

| ■ ALIGN | ■ ALLAY | ■ ALLEGIANCE | ■ ALLEVIATE | ■ ALLUDE |
| ■ ALLURE | ■ ALLY | ■ ALOFT | ■ ALOOF | ■ ALTRUISM |

align [əˈlaɪn]
【考法 1】 *vt.* 使排成一行：to bring into **line** or alignment
例 align the cars with the curb 使车与路缘对齐
派 alighed *adj.* 排成一行的
反 askew, awry, warped 歪斜的

【考法 2】 *vt.* 调准，校准：to **adjust** to produce a proper relationship or orientation
例 align the wheels of the truck 调整卡车的轮子
派 aligned *adj.* 对准的，均衡的
反 improperly adjusted, irregular 调整不当的，不规则的

allay [ə'leɪ]
【考法】 *vt.* 减轻：to **subdue** or **reduce** in **intensity or severity**, alleviate
例 allay one's fears or doubts 减轻某人的恐惧或怀疑
近 assuage, ease, mitigate, mollify, palliate, relieve, soothe, alleviate
反 excite, aggravate, foment, increase the intensity of, exacerbate 激起，使加重

allegiance [ə'liːdʒəns]
【考法】 *n.* 忠诚：**devotion or loyalty** to a person, group, or cause
例 They swore their allegiance to the USA. 他们宣誓效忠美国。
近 commitment, dedication, piety, faithfulness, steadfastness
反 inconstancy, infidelity, perfidiousness, treachery 不忠实，背叛

alleviate [ə'liːvieɪt]
【考法】 *v.* 缓和，减轻：**relieve, lessen**
例 alleviate pain/suffering 减轻痛苦
近 ease, assuage, mitigate, mollify, palliate, soothe, allay, relieve
反 excite, aggravate, foment, increase the intensity of, exacerbate 激起，使加重

allude [ə'luːd]
【考法】 *vi.* 间接提到：to convey an idea **indirectly**
例 He also alluded to his rival's past marital troubles. 他还间接提到了对手过去的婚姻问题。
近 imply, indicate, infer, insinuate, intimate, suggest

allure [ə'lʊr]
【考法 1】 *vt.* 吸引：to **attract or delight** as if by magic
近 entice, seduce, solicit, tempt, captivate, enchant, lead on
派 alluring *adj.* 诱惑的，有吸引力的
例 an alluring smile 迷人的微笑
反 unattractive 无吸引力的
【考法 2】 *v.* 诱惑做（某事）：to **lead** away from a usual or proper course by offering some **pleasure or advantage**
例 Allured by the promise of big bucks, he decided to have a go at a job on the trading floor of the stock market. 被赚大钱的许诺所引诱，他决定投身股票市场工作。
近 bait, beguile, decoy, entice, seduce, lead on, tempt, solicit

ally
【考法 1】 ['ælaɪ] *n.* 盟友，支持者：one in helpful **association** with another
例 enter the war as an ally of America 以美国的同盟者身份加入战争
近 supporter, confederate, sympathizer
反 adversary, rival 对手
【考法 2】 [ə'laɪ] *v.* 加入联盟：to **enter** into an alliance
例 several tribes allied to fend off the invaders 几个部落联合起来抵抗侵略者
反 disband 解散

aloft [ə'lɔːft]
【考法】 *adv.* 在空中：in the air especially: **in flight** (as in an airplane)
例 The balloon stayed aloft for days. 气球在空中停留了很多天。
近 overhead
反 grounded 着陆地

aloof [ə'luːf]
【考法】 *adj.* 孤高的，不合群的：removed or **distant** either physically or emotionally
例 an aloof church 一座孤零零的教堂 ‖ stood apart with aloof dignity 带着超然的尊严站在一旁
近 detached, offish, unsociable, withdrawn, standoffish
反 sociable 好社交的

altruism ['æltruɪzəm]
【考法】 *n.* 利他主义：**unselfish** regard for or devotion to the welfare of others
例 ambition that is masked as altruism 利他主义掩盖下的野心
反 egoism 利己主义
派 altruistic *adj.* 利他的
反 egotistic, self-centered, self-concerned, selfish 自私的

Unit 10

amalgamate ［ə'mælgəmeɪt］
【考法】 *v.* 合并，混合：to **combine** into a **unified** or integrated whole; **unite**
例 amalgamate with an American company 与一家美国公司合并
近 mix, fuse, intermix, compound, meld, mingle, integrate, intermingle
反 separate, isolate 分开，隔离

ambiguous ［æm'bɪgjuəs］
【考法】 *adj.* 有多种理解方式的；不确定的：open to **more than one** interpretation; **doubtful** or **uncertain**
例 Students have ambiguous feelings about their role in the world. 学生们为他们在世界中的角色感到迷茫。
frustrated by ambiguous instructions 因为不明确的指示而受挫
近 doubtful, equivocal, unclear, uncertain
反 distinct, pellucid, patent, blatant, explicit, lucid, perspicuous 清楚的，明显的

amble ［'æmbl］
【考法】 *vi./n.* 漫步，闲逛：to **walk slowly** or **leisurely**; **stroll**
例 Every evening, they ambled along the bank. 他们每晚沿河边散步。
近 ramble, saunter, stroll, wander, dally, dawdle
反 step quickly 快走

ambrosial ［æm'brəʊzɪəl］
【考法】 *adj.* (食物)特别美味的；香的：something **extremely pleasing** to taste or smell
例 The ambrosial aroma of the roast stimulated our appetites. 烤肉的香气刺激了我们的食欲。
近 savory, aromatic, perfumed, redolent, odorous
反 fetid, noisome, stenchy, malodorous, rancid 恶臭的

ameliorate ［ə'miːlɪəreɪt］
【考法】 *vt.* 改善，改进：to make or **become better**; **improve**
例 ameliorate the suffering of people who have lost their jobs 缓解失业人员的痛苦
近 improve, recuperate
反 aggravate, worsen, deteriorate (使)恶化
派 ameliorator *n.* 改良物
反 damper 抑制因素

amenable ［ə'miːnəbl］
【考法】 *adj.* 顺从的，服从的：readily brought to **yield**, **submit**, or cooperate
例 The high-spirited and rebellious girl is not at all amenable to persuasion. 这个泼辣而反叛的女孩根本不听从劝告。
近 compliant, docile, submissive, tractable, obedient
反 intransigent, contumacious 不妥协的；intractable, recalcitrant, refractory 倔强的；uncontrollable, ungovernable, unruly 难管束的

amenity ［ə'menəti］
【考法 1】 *n.* (环境、设备等的)舒适，人性化：something that conduces to **comfort**, convenience, or enjoyment
例 the amenity of the new surroundings 新环境的舒适宜人
近 comfort, convenience, affability
【考法 2】 *n.* 融洽，和谐：the quality of being **pleasant** or **agreeable**
例 a discussion conducted in perfect amenity 在和谐融洽的气氛中进行的讨论
近 agreeability, harmony, accord, concord, consonance
反 discordance, inharmony 不和谐

amiable ［'eɪmɪəbl］
【考法】 *adj.* 好脾气的，友好易相处的：being **friendly**, sociable, and congenial
例 an amiable teacher not easily annoyed 一个不易惹恼、易相处的老师
近 friendly, affable, amicable, genial, easy to get along with
反 disagreeable, ill-natured, ill-tempered, unamiable, ungenial, ungracious, unpleasant 坏脾气的，令人不愉快的

amicable	[ˈæmɪkəbl]

【考法】 *adj.* 友善的：characterized by **friendly** goodwill; **amiable**

例 maintain amicable relations 保持友好关系 ‖ an amicable divorce 和平离婚

近 friendly, affable, amiable, genial, easy to get along with

反 antagonistic, hostile, unfriendly 有敌意的

amity	[ˈæməti]

【考法】 *n.* 友好关系，亲善和睦：**friendship**; especially: **friendly** relations between nations

例 live in amity with his neighbors 与邻居和睦相处 ‖ They parted in amity. 他们友好地分别了。

近 friendship

反 enmity, hostility 敌意

Man errs so long as he strives.

人只要奋斗就会犯错误。

——德国诗人、剧作家 歌德
（Johann Wolfgang Goethe, German poet and dramatist）

List 2

Unit 1

■ AMORPHOUS	■ ANALGESIC	■ ANARCHIST	■ ANATHEMA	■ ANCILLARY
■ ANECDOTE	■ ANEMIC	■ ANESTHETIC	■ ANIMATE	■ ANIMUS

amorphous [əˈmɔːrfəs]
【考法1】 *adj.* 无固定形状的：having no **definite** form: **shapeless**
例 an amorphous cloud mass 一团无定形的云
近 shapeless, unformed, unshaped
【考法2】 *adj.* 不可归类的：being without definite character or nature: **unclassifiable**
例 an amorphous segment of society 不可归类的社会阶段
近 unclassifiable

analgesic [ˌænəlˈdʒiːzɪk]
【考法】 *n.* 镇痛剂：a **medication** that **reduces** or **eliminates pain**
例 Aspirin is a kind of analgesic. 阿司匹林是一种止痛剂。
近 anesthetic, anodyne

○ **anarchist** [ˈænərkɪst]
【考法】 *n.* 反抗权威的人：a person who **rebels against any authority**, established order, or ruling power
同 rebel, insurgent
派 anarchy *n.* 混乱：a state of lawlessness or political disorder due to the absence of governmental authority
近 chaos, disarray, topsy-turviness, commotion, turmoil
反 order 有序

anathema [əˈnæθəmə]
【考法】 *n.* 诅咒：a ban or **curse** solemnly pronounced by ecclesiastical authority and accompanied by excommunication
近 curse, execration, imprecation, malediction
反 benediction, benison, blessing 祝福

○ **ancillary** [ˈænsəleri]
【考法1】 *adj.* 次要的：of **secondary importance**
例 The company hopes to boost its sales through ancillary products. 公司想通过辅助产品来增加销量。
近 subordinate, subsidiary
反 main, paramount 主要的
【考法2】 *adj.* 辅助的，补充的：**auxiliary, supplementary**
例 the need for ancillary evidence 对补充证据的需要 ‖ Some practice in the deft use of words may well be ancillary to the study of natural science. 某些熟练使用文字的练习对于自然科学的研究也是有辅助作用的。
近 auxiliary, supplementary

○ **anecdote** [ˈænɪkdoʊt]
【考法】 *n.* 短小有趣的故事：a usually **short narrative** of an **interesting, amusing**, or biographical incident
例 He told us all sorts of humorous anecdotes about his childhood. 他告诉了我们所有关于他童年的奇闻趣事。
He is a master raconteur with endless anecdotes. 他是讲故事的超级高手，总有讲不完的奇闻趣事。

○ **anemic** [əˈniːmɪk]
【考法】 *adj.* 缺乏力量、活力、精神的：**lacking force**, vitality, or spirit
例 an anemic economic recovery 毫无活力的经济复苏 ‖ Investors are worried about the stock's anemic performance. 投资者担心股市低迷的表现。
近 sapless, infirm, feeble, decrepit, wan, pale, pallid, effete, lethargic
反 vigorous, spirited 精力充沛的；forceful 有力量的

anesthetic [ˌænəs'θetɪk]

【考法 1】 *n.* 止痛剂: something (as a drug) that **relieves pain**
例 The dentist waited until the anesthetic took effect. 牙医一直等到止痛药生效。
近 analgesic, anodyne

【考法 2】 *adj.* 无感觉的，麻木的: **lacking awareness or sensitivity**
例 be anesthetic to their feelings 对他们的感受麻木不仁
反 sensate 有感觉的

animate

【考法 1】 ['ænɪmət] *adj.* 活的: having or showing **life**
例 The lecture was about ancient worship of animate and inanimate objects. 演讲是关于对生命体和非生命体的古代崇拜。
近 breathing, live, living
反 dead, expired, deceased, lifeless, nonliving 无生命的

【考法 2】 *adj.* 有活力的: having much **high-spirited energy** and movement
例 Animate dance will get the blood pumping. 有活力的舞蹈会让人热血沸腾。
近 bouncing, brisk, energetic, sprightly, vivacious
反 inactive, lackadaisical, languid, listless, leaden 没有活力的，无精打采的

【考法 3】 ['ænɪmeɪt] *vt.* 使有活力，支持: to give **spirit** and **support** to
例 The writer's humor animates the novel. 作者的幽默使小说富有生命力。
近 brace, energize, enliven, invigorate, ginger (up), pep up, vitalize 使有活力
反 damp, dampen, deaden 使没活力，使沮丧
派 animation *n.* 生命力，活力: the quality or condition of being alive, active, spirited, or vigorous
反 lassitude, lethargy 疲倦，疲乏

【考法 4】 *vt.* 使行动，驱使: to move to **action**
例 a criminal animated by greed 一个受贪婪驱使的罪犯
近 goad, prod, spur, galvanize, stimulate

【考法 5】 *vt.* 使活灵活现，使栩栩如生: to make or design in such a way as to create apparently spontaneous **lifelike movement**
例 *Kongfu Panda*'s very realistic panda was animated by CG. 《功夫熊猫》这部电影通过 CG 技术使熊猫变得活灵活现。

animus ['ænɪməs]

【考法】 *n.* 敌意: a usually prejudiced and often **spiteful** or **malevolent** ill will, **enmity**
例 She felt no animus toward those who had wronged her. 她对那些冤枉了她的人没有敌意。
近 animosity, antagonism, antipathy, hostility, rancor
反 friendliness, amity, amenity 友好

Unit 2

■ ANNOY	■ ANNUL	■ ANOMALOUS	■ ANONYMOUS	■ ANTAGONIZE
■ ANTEDILUVIAN	■ ANTERIOR	■ ANTIC	■ APATHY	■ APHORISM

annoy [ə'nɔɪ]

【考法】 *vt.* 不断烦扰: to **disturb** or irritate especially by **repeated** acts
例 Mosquitoes annoy us in the summer. 夏天蚊子总是不断烦扰我们。 ‖ The sound of footsteps on the bare floor annoyed the downstairs neighbors. 楼上地板的脚步声吵得楼下住户心烦。
近 aggravate, bother, chafe, gall, grate, irk, nettle, peeve, pique, rile, ruffle, spite, vex
反 soothe, defuse, allay, conciliate, propitiate, mitigate, assuage, appease, pacify, placate, calm, settle, subdue, solace, mollify 平息，抚慰

annul [ə'nʌl]

【考法 1】 *vt.* 宣告无效，取消: to declare or make **legally invalid** or void
例 The marriage was annulled last month. 婚约上个月取消了。
近 disannul, cancel, invalidate, abrogate, nullify, repeal, rescind
反 make legal 使合法；enact 制定

【考法 2】 *vt.* 抵消: to **balance** with an equal force so as to make **ineffective**
例 Unfortunately, his arrogant attitude annuls the many generous favors he does for people. 不幸的是，他傲慢的态度抵消了他之前对人们的慷慨恩惠。
近 counterbalance, neutralize

anomalous [əˈnɑːmələs]

【考法 1】 *adj.* 不普通的，不平常的：being **out** of the **ordinary**

例 He is in an anomalous position as the only part-time teacher in XDF. 他和别人不一样的是，他是 XDF 唯一的兼职老师。

近 aberrant, abnormal, atypical, phenomenal, singular, uncustomary, unwonted

反 unexceptional, unextraordinary 普通的，平常的

派 anomaly *n.* 反常：deviation or departure from the normal or common order, form, or rule

【考法 2】 *adj.* 反常的，不正常的：**departing** from some accepted **standard** of what is **normal**

例 an anomalous burst of anger from this usually easygoing person 这个随和的人的一反常态的暴怒

反 natural 自然的；standard 标准的

anonymous [əˈnɑːnɪməs]

【考法 1】 *adj.* 匿名的：**not named** or **identified**

例 He made an anonymous phone call to the police. 他给警察打了一个匿名电话。 ‖ The donor wishes to remain anonymous. 捐赠者希望保持匿名身份。

近 incognito, innominate, unnamed, unidentified, untitled

反 dubbed, named, termed 有名字的

【考法 2】 *adj.* 无特色的：**lacking individuality**, distinction, or recognizability

例 the anonymous faces in the crowd 大众脸

antagonize [ænˈtæɡənaɪz]

【考法 1】 *vt.* 与…敌对，反对：to act in **opposition** to：**counteract**

例 He did not mean to antagonize you. 他并没有要反对你。 ‖ antagonize a bill 反对一项议案

近 counteract, disagree

反 agree, concede, grant，win over（使）同意

【考法 2】 *vt.* 激怒：to **incur** or **provoke** the **hostility** of

例 His remark antagonized his friends. 他的评述激怒了他的朋友。

近 aggravate, exasperate, gall, inflame, nettle, provoke, peeve, pique, irritate, rile, roil, chafe, grate, ruffle, vex

反 soothe, defuse, allay, conciliate, propitiate, mitigate, assuage, appease, pacify, placate, calm, settle, subdue, solace, mollify 平息，抚慰

antediluvian [ˌæntɪdɪˈluːviən]

【考法 1】 *adj.* 非常古老的；过时的：**extremely old** and **antiquated**

例 He has antediluvian notions about the role of women in the workplace. 他对职场女性抱有老掉牙的看法。
an antediluvian automobile 古董级的汽车

近 aged, age-old, prehistoric, antique, immemorial

反 modern, new, recent 新的

【考法 2】 *n.* 保守的人：a person with **old-fashioned** ideas

例 an antediluvian who thought a woman without talent is virtuous 一个认为"女子无才便是德"的保守的人

近 reactionary

反 modern, trendy 潮人

anterior [ænˈtɪriər]

【考法】 *adj.* 前面的：coming **before** in time or development

例 finish the work anterior to the schedule 提早完成任务 ‖ tests anterior to the college entrance examination 高考前的考试

近 antecedent, foregoing, former, forward, precedent, preceding, prior

反 after, ensuing, following, posterior, subsequent, succeeding 后面的，后来的

antic [ˈæntɪk]

【考法】 *adj.* 滑稽可笑的：characterized by **clownish** extravagance or absurdity

例 The clown came on with many antic gestures. 那个小丑上场表演了许多滑稽动作。

近 chucklesome, comedic, comic, droll, farcical, laughable, ludicrous, hilarious

反 humorless, unamusing, uncomic, unfunny, unhumorous 不好笑的；grave, serious, solemn, somber 严肃的，庄重的

apathy [ˈæpəθi]

【考法 1】 *n.* 冷漠，缺乏情感：**lack** of **feeling** or **emotion**

例 People have shown surprising apathy toward these important social problems. 人们对于这些重要的社会问题显示出了令人惊讶的冷漠。

近 affectlessness, emotionlessness, impassiveness, impassivity, insensibility, numbness, phlegm

反 emotion, feeling, sensibility 有感情

【考法 2】 *n.* 缺乏兴趣，不关心：**lack** of **interest** or **concern**
例 She heard the story with apathy. 她毫无兴趣地听完了这个故事。 ‖ Her poor grades are proof enough of her apathy concerning all matters academic. 她可怜的分数足以证明她对所有的学术问题都没兴趣。
近 disinterestedness, disregard, incuriosity, insouciance, nonchalance, unconcern
反 concern, interest, regard 关心，有兴趣，在意

aphorism [ˈæfərɪzəm]
【考法】 *n.* 格言，警句：a **short witty** sentence which expresses a general truth or comment
例 When decorating, remember the familiar aphorism, "less is more." 装修时需要记住一句格言"少即是多"。
近 adage, epigram, maxim, proverb

Unit 3

■ APOCALYPTIC	■ APOCRYPHAL	■ APOPLECTIC	■ APOSTASY	■ APPALL
■ APPEAL	■ APPEALING	■ APPLAUSE	■ APPOSITE	■ APPRECIABLE

apocalyptic [əˌpɑːkəˈlɪptɪk]
【考法 1】 *adj.* 预言的，启示的：of a revelatory or **prophetic** nature
例 No one listened to her apocalyptic predictions. 没有人听她的预言。
近 prophetic, predictive, prognostic, farsighted
【考法 2】 *adj.* 重要的，转折点的：of, relating to, or being a **major turning** point
例 The apocalyptic Battle of Stalingrad led to the ultimate defeat of Nazi Germany. 具有转折点意义的斯大林格勒战役导致了最后纳粹德国的战败。
反 trivial, petty, minor, immaterial, inconsequential, insignificant 不重要的
【考法 3】 *adj.* 夸大的：wildly **unrestrained**：**grandiose**
例 apocalyptic tone 夸大的语气

apocryphal [əˈpɑːkrɪfl]
【考法】 *adj.* 假的：of **doubtful authenticity**：**spurious**
例 an apocryphal story about the president's childhood 一个关于总统童年的假的故事
近 spurious, unauthentic, ungenuine
反 factual, true, truthful, authentic 真的

apoplectic [ˌæpəˈplektɪk]
【考法】 *adj.* 极度愤怒的：**extremely angry**; **furious**
例 He became apoplectic about wasteful government spending. 他对政府的浪费开销感到怒不可遏。 The coach was so apoplectic when the player missed the free throw that he threw his clipboard onto the court. 教练对球员罚篮不进非常恼怒，把战术板扔到了球场上。
近 choleric, enraged, furious, incensed, indignant, infuriated, irate, ireful, outraged
反 angerless, delighted, pleased 不生气的，高兴的

apostasy [əˈpɑːstəsi]
【考法 1】 *n.* 放弃宗教信仰：**renunciation** of a religious **faith**
例 Some people completely abandon the faith after apostasy. 有些人在放弃自己的宗教信仰后就再也不信仰任何其他宗教了。
【考法 2】 *n.* 变节，背叛：**abandonment** of a **previous loyalty**：defection
例 He was looked down upon for apostasy. 他因为背叛而受到鄙视。
近 defection, perfidy, treacherousness, recreancy
反 fidelity, allegiance, loyalty, piety 忠诚，虔诚

appall [əˈpɔːl]
【考法】 *vt.* 使惊恐：to overcome with **consternation**, shock, or dismay
例 He felt appalled by the whole idea of marriage so we broke up. 结婚使他恐惧，因此我们分手了。
近 dismay, terrify, intimidate, frighten, horrify, daunt, deter
反 embolden, encourage, nerve 使大胆，鼓起勇气

appeal [əˈpiːl]
【考法 1】 *n.* 申请：an **application** (as to a recognized authority) for corroboration, vindication, or decision
例 a piteous appeal for help 哀怜地请求帮助 ‖ make an appeal to the public to donate needed blood 向公众提出献血请求
近 adjuration, conjuration, entreaty, petition, pleading, supplication

【考法2】 *n.* 起诉：to **charge** with a **crime**: **accuse**
例 My lawyer said the court's decision wasn't correct and that we should file for an appeal. 我的律师说，法庭的判决不对，我们应该起诉。
近 charge, accuse, incriminate, inculpate, indict
反 absolve 赦免；exonerate, exculpate 开脱罪责；vindicate 辩护

appealing [ə'piːlɪŋ]
【考法】 *adj.* 吸引人的：**attractive**, **inviting**
例 The large salary made Goldman Sachs's offer more appealing to him. 高薪使高盛的工作对他更有吸引力。
近 alluring, captivating, charismatic, charming, enchanting, engaging, entrancing, luring, seductive
反 repellent, repelling, repugnant, repulsive, unalluring 令人厌恶的，不吸引人的

applause [ə'plɔːz]
【考法】 *n.* 鼓掌；认可：**approval** publicly expressed (as by clapping the hands)
例 Her appearance was greeted with applause. 她的出现被报以热烈的掌声。
近 acclamation, cheer, cheering, ovation, plaudit, rave
反 hissing, booing 发出嘘声

apposite ['æpəzɪt]
【考法】 *adj.* 相关的，合适的：highly **pertinent** or **appropriate**: apt
例 enrich his essay with some very apposite quotations from famous people 用名人名言来丰富他的文章
近 applicable, apropos, germane, pointed, relative, relevant
反 extraneous, irrelevant, impertinent, irrelative, pointless 无关的

appreciable [ə'priːʃəbl]
【考法】 *adj.* 可感知的，明显的：capable of being perceived or measured; **perceptible**
例 the appreciable changes in temperature 气温明显的变化 ‖ There doesn't seem to be any appreciable difference between this piece and that one. 这个和那个看上去没什么差别。
近 apprehensible, perceptible, detectable, discernible, palpable, distinguishable, sensible
反 impalpable, imperceptible, inappreciable, indistinguishable, insensible, undetectable 不能感知的

Unit 4

■ APPREHENSION   ■ APPRISE   ■ APPROBATION   ■ APPROPRIATE   ■ APROPOS
■ APT   ■ ARCHAIC   ■ ARCHETYPE   ■ ARDOR   ■ ARDUOUS

apprehension [ˌæprɪ'henʃn]
【考法1】 *n.* 忧虑，恐惧：**suspicion** or **fear** especially of future evil
例 She had a strong apprehension about her sister's health. 她非常担心她姐姐的健康。
近 dread, foreboding, misgiving, anxiousness, unease, uneasiness, worry
反 composure, equanimity 镇定；unconcern 冷漠
【考法2】 *n.* 逮捕：seizure by legal process: **arrestment**
例 apprehension of the thief 逮捕小偷
近 arrest
反 discharge 释放
【考法3】 *n.* 理解：the knowledge gained from the process of coming to know or **understand** something
例 a good apprehension of how computer systems work 对计算机是如何工作的有很好的理解
近 understanding, comprehension
反 incomprehension

apprise [ə'praɪz]
【考法】 *v.* 通知，告知：to give notice to; **inform**
例 apprise him of the danger that may be involved 告知他可能涉及的危险
近 inform, acquaint, make known to
反 withhold information 隐瞒信息

approbation [ˌæprə'beɪʃn]
【考法】 *n.* 同意：an expression of warm **approval**
例 The proposal met his approbation. 这项建议得到了他的同意。
近 approval, favor
反 disapproval, disapprobation, disfavor 不同意

appropriate

【考法 1】 [əˈprouprieɪt] *v.* 私自挪用：to **take possession** of or make use of exclusively for oneself, often **without permission**

例 appropriate private property 盗用私人财产 ‖ The economy has been weakened by corrupt officials who have appropriated the country's resources for their own use. 经济因为腐败的官员们私自挪用国家资源而被削弱了。

近 purloin, pirate, embezzle, peculate, usurp

【考法 2】 [əˈproupriət] *adj.* 适当的：especially **suitable** or compatible: **fitting**

例 Red wine is a more appropriate choice with the meal. 红酒更适合这顿饭。 ‖ I don't think jeans and a T-shirt are appropriate attire for a wedding. 我觉得穿牛仔裤和 T 恤衫去参加婚礼不太得体。

近 apt, becoming, felicitous, fitting, proper, meet, suitable, apposite, apropos

反 improper, inapposite, inappropriate, inapt, unmeet, unseemly, unsuitable 不合适的

apropos [ˌæprəˈpou]

【考法 1】 *adj.* 相关的：being both **relevant** and opportune

例 The actor announced to reporters that he would only answer to apropos questions about the movie. 演员向记者表示，他只回答和电影有关的问题。

近 applicable, apposite, germane, pointed, relative, relevant

反 extraneous, irrelevant, impertinent, irrelative, pointless 无关的

【考法 2】 *prep.* 关于，有关：**having to do with**

例 make a number of telling observations apropos the current political situation 做了很多关于当前政治形势有力的观察

近 apropos, apropos of, as far as, as for, as regards (*also* as respects), as to, concerning, regarding, respecting, touching, toward (*or* towards)

apt [æpt]

【考法 1】 *adj.* 恰当的，合适的：exactly **suitable**; **appropriate**

例 apt remark/choice/description 恰当的评述/选择/描述

近 apropos, germane, relative, relevant, appropriate

反 extraneous, irrelevant, impertinent, irrelative 无关的；inappropriate, improper, unseemly 不恰当的，不合时宜的

【考法 2】 *adj.* 有…倾向的，可能的：having a **tendency**: **likely**

例 He is apt to fly out in rage. 他容易发脾气。

近 likely, inclined, tending, given

反 unlikely 不可能的；disinclined 没有…倾向的

【考法 3】 *adj.* 聪明的：keenly **intelligent** and **responsive**

例 an apt pupil 一个聪明的小学生 ‖ He is apt at mathematics. 他擅长数学。

近 brilliant, clever, quick-witted, ready-witted, smart

反 foolish, dull, dumb, stupid, unintelligent 傻的，愚蠢的

archaic [ɑːrˈkeɪɪk]

【考法】 *adj.* 过时的，久远的：**no** longer **current** or applicable; **antiquated**

例 archaic laws 过时的法律

近 antiquated, outdated, outmoded, prehistoric, superannuated

反 fashionable 流行的；up-to-date, fresh, modern, new, novel 新的

派 archaism *n.* 古语：the use of archaic diction or style

反 modern diction 新语

archetype [ˈɑːkitaɪp]

【考法 1】 *n.* 典范，榜样：an **ideal** example of a type

例 an archetype of the successful entrepreneur 成功企业家的典范

近 ideal, a perfect example, quintessence

【考法 2】 *n.* 先驱，鼻祖：something belonging to an **earlier** time from which something else was later developed

例 The abacus is sometimes cited as the archetype of the modern digital calculator. 算盘是现代计算器的鼻祖。

近 antecedent, foregoer, forerunner, precursor, predecessor

【考法 3】 *n.* 原型：something from which **copies** are made

例 "'Frankenstein' . . . 'Dracula' . . . 'Dr. Jekyll and Mr. Hyde' . . . the archetypes that have influenced all subsequent horror stories" (*New York Times*)   "'弗兰肯斯坦'…'德拉库拉'…'杰基尔博士和海德先生'是影响了所有继之而来的恐怖故事的原型"（《纽约时报》）

近 prototype

ardor [ˈɑːrdər]

【考法】 *n.* 狂热：**strong enthusiasm** or **devotion**; **zeal**

例 His ardor was damped. 他的热情被泼了冷水。

近 avidity, zeal, fervor, fervency, fervidness, passion, passionateness, vehemence

反 apathy, torpor, impassivity, insensitivity 冷漠，麻木

arduous [ˈɑːrdʒuəs]

【考法】 *adj.* 难以做到的，费劲的：hard to accomplish or achieve: **difficult**

例 a long and arduous undertaking 一项长期艰苦的任务 ‖ an arduous journey across miles of desert 艰苦的沙漠之旅

近 grueling, laborious, taxing, onerous, burdensome

反 easy, simple, unchallenging, undemanding, facile, effortless 不费劲的

Unit 5

| ■ ARGOT | ■ ARREST | ■ ARRESTING | ■ ARRHYTHMIC | ■ ARROGANCE |
| ■ ARTICULATE | ■ ASCENDANT | ■ ASCETIC | ■ ASEPTIC | ■ ASKEW |

argot [ˈɑːrɡət]

【考法】 *n.* 隐语，黑话，行话：a **specialized** vocabulary or set of idioms used by a **particular** group

例 groups communicating in their own secret argots 用秘密的行话交流的团体

近 cant, jargon, shoptalk

反 standard language 标准的语言；common verbalism 大众的言语

arrest [əˈrest]

【考法1】 *vt.* 使不活跃：to make **inactive**

例 arrest the growth of the tumor 抑制肿瘤生长

近 check, rein, curb, contain, hamper, thwart, bring to a halt

反 vitalize, activate, animate, invigorate 使有生气；prod, goad, spur, galvanize, provoke, stimulate 刺激

【考法2】 *n./v.* 停止：the **stopping** of a process or activity; to bring to a **standstill**

例 Science cannot yet arrest the process of aging. 科学不能阻止衰老。

近 cease, cessation, closure, conclusion, discontinuance, discontinuation, ending, halt, stop, termination; check, stop, cease, close, conclude, discontinue, end, halt, terminate

反 continuance, continuation 继续

【考法3】 *v.* 逮捕：to take or **keep** under one's control by authority of law

例 She was charged with resisting arrest. 她因为拒捕受到起诉。

近 apprehend

反 discharge 释放

【考法4】 *v.* 吸引(某人)注意力：to **hold** the **attention** of as if by a spell

例 The behavior of the daredevil arrested pedestrians. 冒失鬼的行为吸引了行人们的注意力。

近 enchant, fascinate, bedazzle, grip, hypnotize, mesmerize

arresting [əˈrestɪŋ]

【考法】 *adj.* 吸引人的：**attracting** and holding the attention; **striking**

例 an arresting spectacle 吸引人的奇观

近 absorbing, engaging, engrossing, enthralling, fascinating, gripping, immersing, intriguing, riveting

反 boring, drab, tedious, monotonous, uninteresting 乏味的，单调的

arrhythmic [əˈrɪðmɪk]

【考法】 *adj.* 不规律的：**lacking** rhythm or **regularity**

例 arrhythmic pulse 不规律的脉搏

近 irregular, disorderly

反 regular, orderly 规律的

arrogance [ˈærəɡəns]

【考法】 *n.* 傲慢，自大：**overbearing pride**

例 Her arrogance has earned her a lot of enemies. 她的傲慢给她带来了很多敌人。

近 assumption, bumptiousness, haughtiness, hauteur, imperiousness, loftiness, peremptoriness, pomposity, pompousness, presumptuousness, superciliousness

反 humility, modesty, humbleness, unassumingness 谦虚，谦逊

articulate

【考法 1】 [ɑːrˈtɪkjuleɪt] *v.* 清晰地表达：to utter **clearly** and **distinctly**

例   He cannot articulate his thoughts. 他不能清楚地表达他的想法。 ‖ a theory first articulated by ancient philosophers 被古时哲学家阐明的理论

近   enunciate

反   murmur, mumble, mutter, slur 含糊地说

【考法 2】 [ɑːrˈtɪkjələt] *adj.* 表达清晰的：**able** to **express** oneself **clearly** and well

例   The television crew covering the science fair were looking for photogenic and articulate students to explain their projects on the air. 负责报道科学展览的电视工作人员正在寻找上镜的、表达清晰的学生，请他们在节目中解释其(科学)项目。

近   eloquent, fluent, silver-tongued, well-spoken

反   inarticulate, ineloquent, unvocal 表达不清楚的

ascendant   [əˈsendənt]

【考法 1】 *adj.* 有影响力的，主宰的：**dominant** in position or **influence**; **superior**

例   This idea was in the ascendant. 这种思想处于主导地位。

近   superior, dominant, sovereign

反   having no influence/power 没有影响力的

【考法 2】 *adj.* 上升的：moving **upward**: **rising**

例   The teacher told the students to write even numbers in ascendant order. 老师让学生们按升序写出偶数。

反   declining 下降的

ascetic   [əˈsetɪk]

【考法 1】 *adj.* 苦行的，克己的；禁欲的：practicing strict **self-denial** as a measure of personal and especially spiritual discipline

例   This is an ascetic diet of rice and beans. 这是一顿苦行餐，只有米饭和豌豆。

近   abstemious, abstinent, self-denying

反   sumptuous, luxurious 奢侈的；licentious, sybaritic, voluptuous 放荡的，沉溺于酒色的

【考法 2】 *n.* 禁欲者：a **person** who renounces material comforts and leads a life of austere **self-discipline**, especially as an act of religious devotion

例   We normally see an ascetic meditating in a Yogic pose. 我们通常会看见一个苦行者以瑜伽的姿势来冥想。

近   stoic, spartan

反   sybarite, hedonist, voluptuary 奢侈逸乐的人，享乐主义者，酒色之徒

aseptic   [ˌeɪˈseptɪk]

【考法 1】 *adj.* 消毒的，无菌的：**preventing infection**

例   Surgery must be in aseptic environments. 手术必须在无菌环境下进行。

近   sterile, germfree

反   germy, unsterile 有细菌的；contaminated, tainted 被污染的

【考法 2】 *adj.* 缺乏活力的：**lacking vitality**

近   inactive, lackadaisical, languid, listless, spiritless

反   active, animated, energetic, vivacious 有活力的

【考法 3】 *adj.* 冷漠的：**lacking emotion**, or warmth

例   aseptic essays 没有感情的文章 ‖ an aseptic smile 漠然的微笑

近   affectless, emotionless, impassive, insensible, numb, phlegm

反   emotional, feeling, sensible 有感情的

askew   [əˈskjuː]

【考法】 *adj./adv.* 不成直线的(地)，歪的(地)：out of line, **awry**

例   The picture hung askew. 画挂歪了。 ‖ His tie was askew. 他的领带歪了。

近   crooked, cockeyed, oblique, lopsided, skewed, aslant, slanted, slanting, listing, tilted, awry

反   aligned 列成一行的；straight, erect 直的

Unit 6

■ ASPECT	■ ASPERITY	■ ASPERSION	■ ASPIRANT	■ ASSENT
■ ASSERT	■ ASSERTIVE	■ ASSESS	■ ASSIDUOUS	■ ASSUAGE

aspect   [ˈæspekt]

【考法】 *n.* 外表，容貌：**appearance** to the eye or mind

例   His face had a frightening aspect. 他的脸很吓人。

近   appearance, look, figure, presence, mien

asperity [æˈsperəti]

【考法 1】 *n.* (举止、性情)粗暴: **roughness** of manner or of temper

例 She responded with such asperity that we knew she was offended by the question. 她如此粗鲁地回答问题，我们知道这个问题冒犯了她。

近 roughness, crudity, rudeness, poignancy, harshness

反 softness, mildness 脾气好

【考法 2】 *n.* (环境)艰苦: **rigor**, **severity**

例 He has encountered more than his share of asperities on the road to success. 在成功的道路上，他已经遇到过比他应该承受的更多的艰辛。

近 severity, hardness, hardship, rigor

aspersion [əˈspɜːrʒn]

【考法】 *n.* 诽谤，中伤: a false or misleading charge meant to **harm** someone's **reputation**

例 cast aspersions on my loyalty 诽谤我的忠诚

近 defamation, besmirchment, calumny, calumniation, maligning, obloquy, vilification

反 glowing tribute, eulogy, extolling, laudation, praise, commendation, compliment 热情赞赏，表扬; flattery, adulation 拍马屁

aspirant [əˈspaɪərənt]

【考法 1】 *n.* 有抱负者，有野心者: one who **aspires**, as to advancement, honors, or a high position

例 a bevy of ever-smiling aspirants for the Miss America title 一群想当美国小姐的少女 ‖ Envy can make oneself backward; self-confidence can tell oneself to be an aspirant. 妒忌能使自己落后，自信能使自己上进。

近 seeker

反 noncandidate 非候选人

【考法 2】 *adj.* 想成为…的: **seeking** to attain a desired position or status

例 The pilot was an aspirant astronaut. 这个飞行员想成为航天员。

assent [əˈsent]

【考法】 *vi.* 同意: to **agree** to something especially after thoughtful consideration

例 The general proposed a detailed plan and the president assented. 将军提出了一个细节化的计划，总统同意了该计划。

近 accede, agree, consent, subscribe, come round

反 dissent, disagree 不同意

assert [əˈsɜːrt]

【考法】 *vt.* 断言，肯定地说出: to state or **declare** positively and often **forcefully** or **aggressively**

例 assert one's innocence 坚称自己无罪 ‖ He asserted that there were corrupt officials in the government. 他断言政府里面一定存在腐败的官员。

近 aver, allege, avow, avouch, insist

反 deny, gainsay 否认

assertive [əˈsɜːrtɪv]

【考法】 *adj.* 自信的: inclined to **bold** or confident **assertion**; aggressively **self-assured**

例 You will have to make many personal judgments when being assertive. 如果你要表现得坚定自信(坚持自己的立场和主张)，就必须做出很多个人判断。

近 assertory, self-assured, self-assertive, peremptory

反 diffident 不自信的

assess [əˈses]

【考法 1】 *v.* 评估(重要性、尺寸、价值等): to **determine** the importance, size, or **value** of

例 We need to assess whether or not the system is working. 我们需要评估这个系统是否有效。 ‖ Damage to the boat was assessed at $5,000. 对这艘船的损失的评估是 5,000 美元。

近 evaluate, appraise, guesstimate

【考法 2】 *v.* 征收费用(如罚款): to establish or apply as a **charge** or **penalty**

例 The utility company will assess a fee if your payment is late. 如果你付款晚了，公共事业公司会罚款。

近 assess, charge, exact, fine, lay, levy, put

反 remit 免除(债务)

assiduous [əˈsɪdʒuəs]

【考法】 *adj.* 勤勉的，专心仔细的: marked by **careful** unremitting attention or persistent application; busy

例 He always tended his garden with assiduous attention. 他总是专心仔细地照看他的花园。 ‖ The project required some assiduous planning. 该项目需要细心的规划。

近 diligent, industrious, sedulous

反 idle, inactive, unbusy, unemployed, unoccupied 空闲的

派 assiduity *n.* 勤勉: persistent application or diligence; unflagging effort

assuage [əˈsweɪdʒ]

【考法 1】 *vt.* 缓和，减轻：to **lessen** the **intensity** of
- 例 He couldn't assuage his guilt over the divorce. 他无法减轻自己在离婚中的内疚。
- 反 aggravate, exacerbate 加强，使恶化

【考法 2】 *vt.* 平息，抚慰：to **pacify** or **calm**
- 例 Life contains sorrows that cannot be assuaged, and it is important to be honest in acknowledging this. 生活中存在着无法平息的悲伤，诚实地承认这个事实是重要的。
- 近 compose, soothe, calm, pacify, placate, appease, lighten, relieve, alleviate, assuage, allay, mitigate, moderate, conciliate, propitiate
- 反 aggravate, annoy, enrage, exasperate, incense, infuriate, ire, irk, irritate, madden, nettle, peeve, provoke, rile, roil, vex 煽动，激怒

【考法 3】 *vt.* 使满足：to put an end to by **satisfying**
- 例 assuage his thirst 解渴 ‖ That meal certainly assuaged my hunger. 那顿大餐满足了我的口腹之欲。
- 近 satisfy, sate, satiate, quench

Unit 7

| ■ ASTOUNDING | ■ ASTUTE | ■ ASUNDER | ■ ASYLUM | ■ ASYMMETRICAL |
| ■ ATONE | ■ ATROCIOUS | ■ ATTENUATE | ■ AUDACIOUS | ■ AUGUR |

astounding [əˈstaʊndɪŋ]

【考法】 *adj.* 令人吃惊的，出乎意料的：causing **astonishment** or **amazement**
- 例 The richness and variety of the undersea environment are astounding. 丰富多样的海底环境是令人惊奇的。
- 近 amazing, astonishing, blindsiding, dumbfounding, shocking, startling, stunning, stupefying
- 反 unsurprising 平常的

astute [əˈstuːt]

【考法】 *adj.* 机敏的，有洞察力的：having or showing **shrewdness** and **perspicacity**
- 例 Astute salesmen know how to invest emotionally. 精明的推销员知道如何进行感情投资。
- 近 canny, smart, shrewd, perspicacious, clear-eyed, clear-sighted, savvy, hardheaded
- 反 unknowing 无知的

asunder [əˈsʌndər]

【考法 1】 *adv.* 分离成多部分或多片地：into **separate parts** or **pieces**
- 例 broken asunder 打碎 ‖ Buildings were burst asunder. 建筑物已经被炸成碎片了。
- 近 piecemeal
- 反 in a piece 完整一片；together 在一起

【考法 2】 *adv.* 分离地：**apart** from each other in position
- 例 A quiet conscience sleeps in thunder, but rest and guilt live far asunder. 平静的良心能在雷声中入睡，而安宁和负罪则无法毗邻。 ‖ Our opinions are wide as the poles asunder. 我们的意见完全相反。
- 近 apart
- 反 together 在一起

asylum [əˈsaɪləm]

【考法】 *n.* 收容所，保护所：an inviolable place of **refuge** and protection giving shelter to criminals and debtors/something (as a building) that offers cover from the weather or **protection** from danger
- 例 an insane asylum 疯人院 ‖ The embassy serves as an asylum for that country's nationals in need of help. 大使馆作为那国需要帮助的公民的保护所。
- 近 harbor, haven, refuge, sanctuary, sanctum

asymmetrical [ˌeɪsɪˈmetrɪkl]

【考法】 *adj.* 不平衡的，不对称的：having **no balance** or **symmetry**
- 例 the asymmetrical construction 非对称的建筑
- 近 asymmetric, nonsymmetrical, unsymmetrical, unbalanced
- 反 symmetrical 对称的；balanced 平衡的

atone [əˈtoʊn]

【考法】 *v.* 赎罪，弥补：to make **amends**, as for a sin or fault
- 例 Blood must atone for blood. 以命抵命。 ‖ Even death cannot atone for the offence. 罪不容诛。
- 近 redeem

atrocious [əˈtroʊʃəs]

【考法 1】 *adj.* 极坏的，极其残忍的：**extremely wicked**, brutal, or cruel
例 Murder is an atrocious crime. 犯罪是一种极其恶劣的犯罪活动。
近 heinous
反 benign, kind, kindhearted, benignant, good-hearted, humane, sympathetic, tenderhearted 善良的，好的
【考法 2】 *adj.* 让人极为不满意的：**extremely unsatisfactory**
例 The service on plane was atrocious. 飞机上的服务让人极为不满意。
反 satisfactory 令人满意的；wonderful 精彩的，极好的

attenuate [əˈtenjueɪt]

【考法】 *v.* 降低(数量、力量、价值)：to **lessen** the amount, force, magnitude, or value of
例 an investment attenuated by inflation 一项因通货膨胀而贬值的投资
近 cheapen, devalue, downgrade, reduce, write down
反 appreciate, enhance, upgrade, mark up 升值，提升
派 attenuation *n.* 减弱，贬值

audacious [ɔːˈdeɪʃəs]

【考法 1】 *adj.* 大胆的，(但往往)愚勇的：**fearlessly**, often **recklessly** daring; bold
例 an audacious plan 一个冒进的计划
近 bold, adventurous, brash, brassy, brazen, rash, reckless
反 cautious, circumspect, guarded, wary 小心谨慎的
【考法 2】 *adj.* 蔑视(法律、礼节)的，无礼的：**contemptuous of law**, religion, or decorum
近 impertinent, impudent, insolent
反 timid, meek 温顺的
派 audacity *n.* 大胆，不敬
【考法 3】 *adj.* 乐于冒险的：inclined or willing to **take risks**
例 audacious adventurers risking everything they had for a shot at glory 为了荣誉而孤注一掷的冒险家们
近 daring, emboldened, enterprising, nervy, venturesome
【考法 4】 *adj.* 大胆创新的：marked by originality and **verve**
例 an audacious interpretation of two dramas 对两部戏剧的创造性阐述

augur [ˈɔːgər]

【考法 1】 *n.* 预言家：one who **predicts** future events or developments
例 The ancient Roman augurs predicted the future by reading the flight of birds. 古罗马的预言家们通过鸟类的航线来预测未来。
近 forecaster, foreseer, diviner, foreteller, prophesier, visionary
【考法 2】 *vi.* 出现好兆头：to show **signs of** a favorable or **successful outcome**
例 This augurs well for us. 这是一个好兆头。
近 promise
【考法 3】 *vt.* 预言：to **tell** of or describe **beforehand**
例 The fortune-teller augured nothing but a series of calamities for me. 占卜人预言在我身上将会有一系列大灾难发生。
近 forecast, predict, presage, prognosticate, prophesy, forebode

Unit 8

■ AUTHENTIC	■ AUTHORITY	■ AUTOCRACY	■ AUTONOMY	■ AVARICE
■ AVER	■ AVERSION	■ AVID	■ AWASH	■ AWE

authentic [ɔːˈθentɪk]

【考法 1】 *adj.* 真实的，非仿造的：being **exactly** as appears or as claimed
例 found an authentic Native American arrowhead 发现了一支美洲土著的箭头
近 bona fide, certified, genuine
反 bogus, counterfeit, fake, mock, phony, spurious 伪造的
派 authenticity *n.* 真实，真实性
【考法 2】 *adj.* 准确的，相符合的：following an **original** exactly
例 an authentic reconstruction of the Parthenon 帕台农神殿的准确复制
近 accurate, exact, precise, right, veracious
反 corrupt, false 错误的

authority [əˈθɔːrəti]
【考法 1】 *n.* (某领域的)权威人士：a person with **a high level of knowledge** or skill in a field
- 例 a leading authority on neural anatomy 一名神经解剖学领域的权威人士
- 近 expert, connoisseur, maestro, master, virtuoso
- 反 amateur 业余爱好者; inexpert 非专家

【考法 2】 *n.* 管辖权，控制：**lawful control** over the affairs of a political unit (as a nation)
- 例 The sheriff had authority over the whole county. 郡守对于整个郡都有管辖权。
- 近 administration, governance, regime, regimen

【考法 3】 *n.* 影响力：the **power to direct** the thinking or behavior of others usually indirectly
- 例 He speaks with a persuasive authority on matters of public health. 他就公共健康事务发表了具有影响力的、令人信服的评论。
- 近 clout, credit, leverage, weight

【考法 4】 *n.* (管束他人的)权力：the **right** or means to command or **control others**
- 例 By the authority vested in me, I now pronounce you married. 依我所拥有的权力，我宣布你们成为夫妻。
- 近 arm, command, control, dominion, reign
- 反 impotence, powerlessness 无权力

【考法 5】 *n.* 根据，理由：a **warrant** for action
- 例 On what authority do you make such a claim? 你的指控有何理由?
- 近 grounds, justification

autocracy [ɔːˈtɑːkrəsi]
【考法】 *n.* 独裁政府：**government** in which a person possesses **unlimited power**
- 例 It signified the British rejection of autocracy by constituting the first formal restraining of the power of the monarch. 英国对于独裁体制的反抗表现在它对君王权力进行的正式约束。
- 近 absolutism, dictatorship, totalitarianism, tyranny
- 反 democracy 民主，民主制度
- 派 autocratic *adj.* 独裁的

autonomy [ɔːˈtɑːnəmi]
【考法 1】 *n.* 政治上的独立：the quality or state of being **self-governing**
- 例 The province has been granted autonomy. 这个省份被授予了自治权。
- 近 self-governance, sovereignty
- 反 dependence, subjection 附属，依赖

【考法 2】 *n.* 自我主导的自由，(尤其是)精神独立：self-directing freedom and especially moral **independence**
- 例 a teacher who encourages individual autonomy 一个鼓励精神独立的老师
- 近 independence, liberty, free will
- 反 constraint, duress 限制
- 派 autonomous *adj.* 自治的

avarice [ˈævərɪs]
【考法】 *n.* 贪财，贪婪：excessive or **insatiable** desire for wealth or gain
- 例 The bank official's embezzlement was motivated by pure avarice. 银行官员盗用公款纯粹是出于贪婪。
- 近 acquisitiveness, avidity, covetousness, cupidity, greediness, rapacity
- 反 generosity, magnanimity 慷慨
- 派 avaricious *adj.* 贪婪的

aver [əˈvɜːr]
【考法 1】 *v.* 声称为真：to **state** as a fact usually **forcefully**
- 例 was tearfully averring his innocence 涕泪俱下地声明他的清白
- 近 allege, assert, avouch, avow, declare, purport, warrant
- 反 deny, gainsay 否认

【考法 2】 *v.* (态度强硬而明确地)声明：to **state clearly** and strongly
- 例 She averred that she didn't need any help choosing her own clothes. 她态度强硬地声明：在买衣服的问题上不需要别人指手画脚。
- 近 affirm, insist, maintain, profess

aversion [əˈvɜːrʒn]
【考法 1】 *n.* 非常讨厌，极厌恶：a **dislike** so strong as to cause stomach upset or queasiness
- 例 a natural aversion toward insects 天生对昆虫的反感
- 近 distaste, horror, loathing, nausea, repugnance, repulsion, revulsion

【考法 2】 *n.* 令人厌恶的事物：something or **someone that is hated**
- 例 Clichés should be the aversion of every good writer. 陈词滥调应该是让每个优秀的作家都感到厌恶的。
- 近 abhorrence, abomination, antipathy, detestation, execration
- 反 love 令人喜爱的事物

avid ['ævid]

【考法 1】 *adj.* 急切渴望的：marked by keen interest and **enthusiasm**

例 avid movie fans 急切的影迷

近 agog, ardent, eager, keen, impatient, thirsty

反 apathetic, indifferent 不在乎的

【考法 2】 *adj.* 贪婪（钱财）的：having or marked by an **eager** and often selfish desire especially **for material possessions**

例 She stared at the jewels with an avid glint in her eye. 她带着贪婪的目光注视着那些珠宝。

近 acquisitive, avaricious, covetous, greedy, rapacious

派 avidity *n.* 贪婪

---

awash [ə'wɔːʃ]

【考法 1】 *adj.* 被淹没的：containing, covered with, or thoroughly penetrated **by water**

例 The streets were awash from the heavy rains. 街道因为大雨被水淹没了。

近 doused, drenched, saturated, sodden, soggy, soaked

反 dry, arid, dehydrated, drained 干燥的

【考法 2】 *adj.* （如洪水般）泛滥的：**filled**, **covered**, or completely **overrun** as if by a flood

例 The program is currently awash in submissions and will not be accepting any more until next term. 该项目的申请人数过多，因此下一轮之前不会再接受任何申请。

近 abounding, abundant, flush, fraught, replete, swarming, teeming, thronging

反 dearth, insufficient, scant 匮乏的

---

awe [ɔː]

【考法】 *n./v.* 敬畏：an emotion variously combining **dread**, **veneration**, and **wonder** that is inspired by authority or by the sacred or sublime

例 She gazed in awe at the great stone. 她敬畏地凝视着那块巨石。

近 admiration, reverence, respect, veneration; admire, revere, respect, venerate

反 irreverence, insolence, scorn, superciliousness 蔑视，不敬

派 awesome *adj.* 令人敬畏的

Unit 9

■ AWKWARD	■ AWNING	■ AWRY	■ AXIOMATIC	■ BABBLE
■ BACKHANDED	■ BADGER	■ BADINAGE	■ BAIT	■ BALE

---

awkward ['ɔːkwərd]

【考法 1】 *adj.* 缺乏灵活性和技巧的：**lacking dexterity** or skill

例 awkward with a needle and thread 缺乏灵巧的针线活技术

近 handless, maladroit

反 adroit, deft, dexterous, proficient, skilled 灵巧的

【考法 2】 *adj.* （处理问题）缺乏手段和智谋的：showing or marked by **a lack of skill and tact** (as in dealing with a situation)

例 Her awkward handling of the seating arrangements resulted in many hurt feelings. 她那缺乏智谋的座次安排伤害了许多人的感情。

近 botched, bungling, fumbled, inept, inexpert, maladroit

【考法 3】 *adj.* 臃肿笨拙的，不优雅的：**lacking ease** or grace (as of movement or expression)

例 an awkward design 一份粗劣的设计

近 clumsy, gauche, graceless, gawkish

反 elegant, graceful, polished, lithe, coordinated 优雅的

【考法 4】 *adj.* 令人尴尬的：causing **embarrassment**

例 the awkward situation of having to listen as your host and hostess quarrel loudly in the next room 不得不听着你的主人和他太太在隔壁大声争吵的尴尬境地

近 discomfiting, disturbing, disconcerting, embarrassing, flustering

【考法 5】 *adj.* （因过大过重或设计问题）难以操作的：**difficult to use** or operate especially because of size, weight, or design

例 The manual can opener is too awkward to hold. 那个手动启瓶器太难握了。

近 ponderous, ungainly, unhandy, unwieldy, bunglesome, cranky

反 handy 容易操纵的

awning ['ɔːnɪŋ]
【考法】 n. 雨篷，遮阳篷：a piece of material attached to a caravan or building which provides **shelter** from the rain or sun
例 stay under the awning outside the Starbucks during the rainstorm 在星巴克外面的遮阳棚下避雨
近 ceiling, cover, roof, tent

awry [ə'raɪ]
【考法1】 adj. 弯曲的，扭曲的：in a **turned** or **twisted** position or direction
例 Her sunglass is awry. 她的墨镜戴歪了。
近 askew, aslant, lopsided, slanted
反 aligned, direct, even, straight 成行的，笔直的
【考法2】 adj./adv. 走样的(地)，出差错的(地)：**off** the correct or expected **course**
例 Operation Redwing was initially launched by US special-operation troops in hopes of capturing or killing a Taliban leader but went awry. 由美军特种部队发起、代号为"红翼"的军事行动的最初目的是捕获或击杀一名塔利班头目，然而行动在执行过程中出现了差错。
近 amiss, aside, astray, erroneous
反 right, well 无差错的

axiomatic [ˌæksɪə'mætɪk]
【考法1】 adj. 公理的：based on or involving an **axiom** or system of axioms
例 Euclidean geometry is based on five axiomatic principles. 欧几里得几何学是在五条公理的基础上建立的。
近 fundamental
派 axiom n. 公理
【考法2】 adj. 不言自明的：taken for granted, **self-evident**
例 an axiomatic truth 一个不言而明的真理
近 self-evident, prima facie
反 controversial 有争议的

babble ['bæbl]
【考法1】 v. 发出含糊无意义的嘟囔声，胡乱说：to **utter** a **meaningless** confusion of words or sounds
例 Babies babble before they can talk. 婴儿在会说话以前含糊不清地发音。
近 drivel, gabble, gibber, jabber, prattle
反 articulate 清晰地说出
【考法2】 v. 闲聊：to engage in casual or **rambling conversation**
例 The little girls babbled contentedly for the whole ride home. 小姑娘们在回家的路上高兴地闲聊。
近 chatter, prate

backhanded [ˌbæk'hændɪd]
【考法】 adj. 间接的，含沙射影的，虚情假意的：**indirect**, devious, especially sarcastic
例 a backhanded compliment 虚情假意的恭维话
近 feigned, roundabout, sarcastic, hypocritical, two-faced, double-faced, left-handed
反 forthright 直截了当的；artless, candid, genuine, honest, sincere 真挚的，真诚的

badger ['bædʒər]
【考法】 vt. 不断纠缠或骚扰：to **harass** or annoy **persistently**
例 badger him into purchasing 不断地骚扰劝说他购买
近 bait, plague

badinage [ˌbædən'ɑːʒ]
【考法】 n. 打趣，善意的玩笑：playful repartee, **banter**
例 the sophisticated badinage of the characters in plays by Oscar Wilde 奥斯卡·王尔德作品中意味深长的玩笑话
近 banter, persiflage, repartee

bait [beɪt]
【考法1】 vt. 逗弄，激怒：to **persecute** or **exasperate** with unjust, malicious, or persistent attacks
例 bait him with gibes about his humble origin 取笑他的平凡出身以激怒他
近 badger, annoy, harass, heckle
反 appease, pacify, mollify, disarm 平息，使缓和
【考法2】 vt. 引诱：to **lead away** from a usual or proper course by offering some pleasure or advantage
例 The investment scheme baits the greedy and the unscrupulous. 这份投资计划吸引贪婪者和轻信者上钩。
近 allure, decoy, entice, seduce
【考法3】 n. 诱饵：**something** (as food) used in **luring** especially to a hook or trap
例 The squad leader has finally realized that his team was a bait. 队长终于意识到他的队伍是一个诱饵。
近 allurement, snare, trap, temptation

bale [beɪl]

【考法】 *n.* 痛苦，悲哀：woe, **sorrow**

例 relieve spirit from the bale 从悲痛中解脱

近 misery, suffering, anguish, grief

反 joy 快乐

Unit 10

■ BALEFUL	■ BALK	■ BALKY	■ BALLAD	■ BALLOON
■ BALM	■ BANAL	■ BANE	■ BANISH	■ BANTER

baleful [ˈbeɪlfl]

【考法 1】 *adj.* 有害的：**harmful** or malignant in intent or effect

例 a policy with baleful effects 一个带来不良后果的政策

近 harmful, pernicious, detrimental

反 beneficent 有益的

【考法 2】 *adj.* 凶兆的；凶恶的：foreboding or threatening **evil**

例 a baleful look 面露凶色

近 direful, doomy, ominous, ill-boding, minatory, portentous, sinister

反 unthreatening 不构成威胁的

【考法 3】 *adj.* 致命的：likely to cause or capable of **causing death**

例 a medicine that is beneficial in small doses but baleful in large 是药三分毒

近 deadly, fatal, lethal

反 healthy, wholesome 有益健康的

balk [bɔːk]

【考法 1】 *vt.* 阻碍：to **check** or stop by or as if by an **obstacle**

近 circumvent, frustrate, foil, thwart

反 advance, forward, foster, nurture, promote 推进

【考法 2】 *v.* 不愿接受，拒绝：to show **unwillingness** to accept, do, engage in, or agree to

例 She balked at the very idea of compromise. 她固执地拒绝了妥协的想法。

近 decline, refuse, spurn, repudiate, turn down

反 accept, approve 同意

派 balky *adj.* 倔强的

balky [ˈbɔːlki]

【考法】 *adj.* 不服管束的，倔强的：**refusing** or likely to refuse to proceed, act, or function as directed or expected

例 a balky mule 犟骡子

近 contumacious, defiant, perverse, intractable, obstreperous, refractory, unruly, wayward, willful

反 compliant, docile, subdued, submissive, tractable 顺从的

ballad [ˈbæləd]

【考法】 *n.* （由简单诗节和叠句组成的）民歌：a narrative **poem**, often of folk origin and intended to be sung, consisting of simple stanzas and usually having a refrain

例 a haunting ballad about loneliness 一段有关寂寞的萦绕于心的民谣

近 ditty, jingle, lyric, vocal

balloon [bəˈluːn]

【考法】 *v.* 迅速增加：to **increase** rapidly

例 The use of computers has ballooned. 电脑的使用量迅速增长。

近 inflate, escalate, expand, burgeon, mushroom, snowball

反 decrease, taper, dwindle, diminish, recede, wane 减少

balm [bɑːm]

【考法 1】 *n.* 香油，止痛膏；安慰物：a **sweet-smelling oil** that heals wounds or reduce pain; things that **soothe** the mind

例 Friendship is the finest balm in need. 危难关头，友情是最好的安慰。

反 irritant 刺激物

派 balmy *adj.* 止痛的

【考法2】 *n.* 香气： a sweet or **pleasant smell**
例 The balm of the restaurant's backyard garden enhances the aura of romance. 餐馆后院传来的阵阵芳香增加了浪漫的情调。
近 aroma, fragrance, incense, perfume, redolence
反 fetor, malodor, stench, stink 恶臭

banal [bə'nɑːl]
【考法】 *adj.* 非原创的，陈腐的： lacking originality, freshness, or novelty; **trite**
例 The slogan is too banal. 这口号已是陈词滥调了。
近 cliché, hackneyed, stereotyped, threadbare, trite, timeworn, shopworn, stale, moth-eaten
反 novel, innovative, arresting 新颖的
派 banality *n.* 陈腐

bane [beɪn]
【考法1】 *n.* 祸根： a source of harm or **ruin**
例 Drinking was the bane of his life. 饮酒是他一生的祸根。
近 affliction, curse, nemesis, scourge
反 blessing, boon, felicity, windfall 福根
【考法2】 *n.* 有害的物质： a substance that by chemical action can **kill or injure a living thing**
例 a plant that is believed to be the bane of the wolf 一种被认为对狼有毒害作用的植物
近 toxic, toxin, venom
派 baneful *adj.* 有害的

banish ['bænɪʃ]
【考法1】 *vt.* 驱逐出境： to require by authority to **leave** a **country**
例 Since the diplomatic relation between the two nations has been broken, diplomats were all banished. 随着两国外交关系的破裂，所有的外交人员都被驱逐出境。
近 deport, exile, expatriate, expel
反 repatriate 遣返
【考法2】 *vt.* 赶出： to drive or **force out**
例 The troublemakers were permanently banished from the youth recreational center. 肇事者被永久地剥夺了进入青年娱乐中心的权力。
派 banishment *n.* 驱逐

banter ['bæntər]
【考法】 *n./v.* 幽默、打趣的(地)谈话： good-**humored**, playful conversation
例 banter with someone 和某人调侃
近 badinage, persiflage, repartee

Today is the first day of the rest of my life, I wake as a child to see the world begin. On monarch wings and birthday wonderings, want to put on faces, walk in the wet and cold. And look forward to my growing old, to grow is to change, to change is to be new, to be new is to be young again, I barely remember when.

——美国乡村歌手约翰·丹佛(John Denver)

List 3

Unit 1

■ BARB	■ BARBAROUS	■ BAREFACED	■ BARGAIN	■ BAROQUE
■ BARRAGE	■ BARREN	■ BARRICADE	■ BARTER	■ BATCH

barb ［bɑːrb］
【考法】 *n.* 尖锐而严厉的批评：a biting or pointedly **critical** remark or comment
例 He delivered one last barb to his ex-girlfriend as he stalked away. 在他转身离去之前，给他前女友留下了最后一句尖锐的批评。
近 affront, criticism, offense, outrage, sarcasm
反 praise, applause, compliment 称赞

barbarous ［ˈbɑːrbərəs］
【考法 1】 *adj.* 野蛮的，凶残的：**mercilessly** harsh or cruel
例 insulted by barbarous language 被粗暴的言语侵犯
近 brutal, atrocious, fiendish, heartless, savage, truculent, vicious
反 merciful, benevolent , humane, sympathetic 仁慈的
【考法 2】 *adj.* 未开化的：**uncivilized**
例 some barbarous behaviors such as eating with your fingers 一些没有教养的举止，比如直接用手拿东西吃
近 wild, uncultivated
反 civilized, decent, decorous 举止得体的

barefaced ［ˈberfeɪst］
【考法】 *adj.* 公然的，厚颜无耻的：undisguisedly bold; **brazen**
例 a barefaced lie 一个公然的谎言
近 apparent, plain, bald, evident, manifest, obvious, perspicuous
反 secret, furtive, clandestine, surreptitious 秘密的

bargain ［ˈbɑːrgən］
【考法 1】 *n.* 协议：an **agreement** between parties settling what each gives or receives in a transaction
例 They made a bargain that one would help the other next week. 他们达成了一项协议：下周其中一人将帮助另外一人。
近 accord, compact, contract, covenant, deal, pact, settlement
【考法 2】 *vi.* 讨价还价：to **negotiate** over the terms of a purchase
例 bargain over the price 讨价还价
近 haggle, negotiate

baroque ［bəˈroʊk］
【考法 1】 *adj.* 装饰华丽的，过分雕琢的，复杂的：characterized by **extravagance**, **complexity**, or **flamboyance**
例 a baroque prose 一篇辞藻华丽的散文
近 byzantine, complicated, convoluted, elaborate, fancy, intricate, knotty, labyrinthine, lavish, tangled
反 austere, plain, simple 朴实无华的
【考法 2】 *adj.* （程度上）过分的：going **beyond** a normal or acceptable **limit** in degree or amount
例 Eventually even the movie seems bored by its baroque violence. 到最后，这电影也因为其中过度的暴力元素而显得让人厌烦。
近 exorbitant, extravagant, lavish, overdue
反 moderate, modest, temperate 适度的

barrage ［bəˈrɑːʒ］
【考法 1】 *n.* 弹幕：a heavy **curtain** of artillery fire directed in front of friendly troops to protect them
例 Troops are advancing under the shield of barrage. 部队在弹幕的掩护下前进。
近 bombardment, fusillade

【考法 2】 *n.* 有压倒之势的、集中的倾泻(如言语)：an **overwhelming**, concentrated **outpouring**, as of words

例 The announcement was met with a barrage of criticism and protests. 此公告一出，批评和抗议的声音四起。

近 salvo, hail, cannonade, shower, storm, volley

【考法 3】 *v.* (同时)袭来：to **attack with** a rapid or **overwhelming outpouring** of many things at once

例 The athlete was barraged with requests for an autograph. 请求这位运动员签名的呼声如排山倒海般袭来。

近 bomb

---

barren 〔ˈbærən〕

【考法 1】 *adj.* 不育的：**incapable** of **producing** offspring

例 a poor, barren woman 一名可怜的不孕女子

近 fruitless, impotent, infertile, effete

反 prolific, fecund 多产的

【考法 2】 *adj.* 不产生结果的，无效的：producing **no results**; unproductive

例 That line of investigation proved barren, so the police tried other avenues. 那个方向的调查已经被证明是没有结果的了，所以警察开始尝试其他的途径。

近 bootless, ineffective, inefficacious, unavailing, vain

反 effective, successful, productive, virtuous 有效的，成功的

【考法 3】 *adj.* 贫瘠的：**deficient** in production of vegetation and especially crops

例 barren deserts and wastelands 贫瘠的沙漠和荒野

近 desolate, impoverished, waste

反 arable, fruitful, luxuriant, verdant 富饶的，繁茂的

【考法 4】 *adj.* 极度匮乏的：utterly **lacking** in something needed, wanted, or expected

例 Their proposal for revitalizing the downtown business district is utterly barren of practical methods. 他们意图重振中心商业区的计划缺乏能够起效的方法。

近 bare, bereft, destitute, void

反 filled, flush, fraught, full, replete, rife 充沛的

---

barricade 〔ˌbæriˈkeɪd〕

【考法 1】 *n.* 障碍物：an **obstruction** or **rampart** thrown up across a way or passage

例 The police put up barricades to block off the parade route. 警察设立了路障来阻挡游行的队伍。

近 fence, hedge, wall, barrier, obstacle, blockade, obstruction

【考法 2】 *vt.* 用障碍物阻止通过：to **prevent access** to by means of a barricade

例 Streets have been barricaded by authorities. 街道被当局封锁了。

近 bar, check, hinder, impede, obstruct, wall off

反 permit 允许

---

barter 〔ˈbɑːrtər〕

【考法】 *v.* 以物换物：to **trade** (goods or services) **without** the exchange of **money**

例 barter wheat for cotton 以小麦换棉花

近 swap, trade

---

batch 〔bætʃ〕

【考法 1】 *n.* 一批次的量：a number of things considered as a **unit**

例 a batch of cookies 一批次烘烤的饼干

近 array, collection, package, parcel, group

【考法 2】 *n.* 一小群人：a usually **small number of persons** considered as a unit

例 Show the next batch of applicants in, please. 请带下一批申请人进来。

近 band, body, cluster, party

Unit 2

■ BATHETIC ■ BAWDY ■ BEDECK ■ BELABOR ■ BELEAGUER
■ BELIE ■ BELLWETHER ■ BENEFICENT ■ BENIGN ■ BERATE

---

bathetic 〔bəˈθetɪk〕

【考法】 *adj.* 平凡的，陈腐的：characterized by exceptional **commonplaceness**

例 a bathetic funeral scene 平凡的葬礼场面

近 trite, cliché, commonplace, hackneyed, stale, stereotyped

反 offbeat 离奇的；exceptional 不平常的，非凡的

派 bathos *n.* 平凡的事物

bawdy [ˈbɔːdi]

【考法】 *adj.* 下流的，猥亵的：boisterously or humorously **indecent**

例 a bawdy joke 黄色笑话 ‖ a bawdy house 妓院

近 obscene, lewd, ribald, vulgar

反 decent, decorous 得体的；chaste, noble 贞洁的，高贵的

bedeck [bɪˈdek]

【考法】 *vt.* 装饰，点缀：to **make more attractive** by adding something that is beautiful or becoming

例 flag bedecking the balcony 用以装饰阳台的旗子 ‖ bedeck with jewels 用珠宝装饰

近 adorn, beautify, decorate, dress, embellish, emblaze

反 strip 剥去；blemish, deface, mar, spoil 损害，破坏

belabor [bɪˈleɪbər]

【考法1】 *vt.* (当众)严厉批评：to **criticize** harshly and usually publicly

例 It's not wise to belabor other people's flaws when you're hardly perfect yourself. 如果你自己还做不到完美，去指责他人是不明智的。

近 beat, baste, batter, excoriate, lambaste, abuse, assail, vituperate, scathe

反 applaud, extol, eulogize, endorse, acclaim 赞扬

【考法2】 *vt.* 就…作过度的说明，喋喋不休：to **explain** or insist on **excessively**

例 belabor the obvious 就显而易见的问题喋喋不休

近 dwell on, harp on

反 disregard, omit, ignore, neglect, slight, slur over 忽略

beleaguer [bɪˈliːgər]

【考法1】 *vt.* 包围，围攻：**to surround** (as a fortified place) with armed forces for the purpose of capturing or preventing commerce and communication

例 beleaguered the castle for months 围攻堡垒长达数月

近 siege, besiege, invest, blockade

反 retreat, withdraw 撤退

【考法2】 *vt.* 使困扰，使烦恼，使消沉：**trouble**, harass, beset

例 We are still beleaguered by the very problem. 我们仍然为这一个问题感到困扰。

近 annoy, harass, pester, plague, tease

反 delight 使愉悦

派 beleaguering *adj.* 扰人的

belie [bɪˈlaɪ]

【考法1】 *vt.* 错误地描述；误述：to **picture falsely**; misrepresent

例 The report belied the real severity of the aftermath. 这个报道错误地评价了后果的严重性。

近 misrepresent, falsify

反 betray, reveal 表明，暴露，揭露(伪装)

【考法2】 *vt.* 证明…为假：to show (something) to be **false** or **wrong**

例 Practical experience belies this theory. 实践证明这个理论是错误的。

近 debunk, discredit, refute, shoot down

反 attest, confirm, validate, verify 证实

【考法3】 *vt.* 掩饰：to keep secret or **shut off from view**

例 Security Council issued false assurances that belied the true gravity of the situation. 安理会发布了不真实的承诺，掩盖了局势的严重性。

近 conceal, curtain, disguise, mask

反 disclose, expose 揭露

【考法4】 *vt.* 与…相对立；与…相矛盾：to be **counter** to; contradict

例 At first glance, life at the boarding school seemed to belie all the bad things I had heard about it. 乍看之下，寄宿学校的生活似乎不同于我所听说的有关它的糟糕情形。

近 contradict, contravene

反 agree 与…相一致

bellwether [ˈbelweðə]

【考法】 *n.* 领导者，带头人：one that takes the **lead** or initiative

例 Paris is a bellwether of the fashion industry. 巴黎是一座引领时尚潮流的都市。

近 leader, pacemaker, pilot, trendsetter

反 follower, disciple, imitator 跟随者，弟子，模仿者

beneficent [bɪˈnefɪsnt]

【考法 1】 *adj.* 仁慈的，好慈善的：characterized by or performing acts of kindness or **charity**

例 a beneficent couple who are regular volunteers at an orphan 一对常在孤儿院做义工的慈善的夫妇

近 kind, altruistic, benevolent, philanthropic, benign, compassionate, sympathetic

反 atrocious, barbarous, truculent, vicious 残忍的

派 beneficently *adv.* 仁慈地

【考法 2】 *adj.* (对个人或社会)有益的：promoting or **contributing** to personal or social well-being

例 the beneficent effect of sunshine 日光浴的益处

近 helpful, advantageous, favorable, kindly, profitable, salutary

反 detrimental, harmful, noxious, toxic 有害的

benign [bɪˈnaɪn]

【考法 1】 *adj.* 好心的，仁慈的：showing **kindness** and **gentleness**

例 a benign coach 一名仁慈的教练

近 beneficent, gentle, kind

反 abrasive, caustic, coarse, hard, harsh, rough, scathing, stern 粗暴的，严厉的

【考法 2】 *adj.* 无害的：**not causing** or being capable of causing injury or **hurt**

例 Don't worry; his eccentricities are entirely benign. 别担心，他那些古怪行为不会给人带来伤害。

近 harmless, innocent, innocuous, inoffensive

反 baleful, deleterious, detrimental, harmful, injurious, pernicious 有害的

berate [bɪˈreɪt]

【考法】 *vt.* (长时间)严厉指责：to **scold** or condemn **vehemently** and **at length**

例 He berated them in public. 他公开谴责他们。

近 castigate, flay, lambaste, scold, rail, upbraid, reproach, reprimand

反 commend, compliment, praise 表扬，赞颂

Unit 3

| ■ BESEECH | ■ BESMIRCH | ■ BIFURCATE | ■ BIGOT | ■ BLAND |
| ■ BLANDISHMENT | ■ BLASÉ | ■ BLAST | ■ BLATANT | ■ BLAZON |

beseech [bɪˈsiːtʃ]

【考法】 *vt.* (急切地)恳求：to **beg** for urgently or anxiously

例 They besought the military to act immediately. 他们恳求军方立即采取行动。

近 appeal, conjure, entreat, implore, petition, plead, supplicate

反 demand (依据权力等)要求

besmirch [bɪˈsmɜːtʃ]

【考法 1】 *vt.* 弄脏，弄污：to **make dirty**; soil

例 They besmirched the white bed sheets with their dirty hands. 他们的脏手把白床单弄脏了。

近 foul, smirch, smudge, taint

反 clean, cleanse 清洁

【考法 2】 *vt.* 诽谤，玷污：to **detract from the honor** or luster of

例 besmirch your reputation by fabricating scandals 通过捏造丑闻来玷污你的名声

近 defile, smear, soil, stain, smirch

反 honor 授予荣誉

bifurcate [ˈbaɪfərkeɪt]

【考法】 *v.* (使)分成两支：(to cause) to divide into **two branches** or parts

例 Their visions of the company's future slowly began to bifurcate. 我们关于公司未来的构想慢慢出现分歧。

近 divide, diverge, fork

反 coalesce 联合；converge 汇合

bigot [ˈbɪgət]

【考法】 *n.* 固执己见者，有偏见的人：a person **obstinately devoted** to his own opinions and prejudices

例 He is a bigot, or "a slave of dogma". 他是一个固执己见的人，换言之，就是教条主义的奴隶。

近 dogmatist, partisan

反 depreciator, disparager 贬低他人的人

派 bigoted *adj.* 固执己见的

bland	[blænd]
【考法1】	*adj.* 味道平淡的，不刺激的：not irritating or stimulating; **soothing**
例	stick to bland diet to lose weight 坚持清淡的饮食以减肥 ‖ bland food that was good for babies and invalids 对婴儿和病患有益的温和的食物
近	mild, light, soft, soothing, tender
反	pungent, tangy, zesty 味道刺激的
【考法2】	*adj.* 无趣的：**dull**, insipid
例	a bland story with naïve plot 一个情节幼稚的无聊故事
近	banal, sapless, insipid
反	riveting, enchanting 诱人的
【考法3】	*adj.* 温和的，和蔼的：**not harsh** or stern especially in nature or effect
例	his face expanding in a bland smile 他的脸上绽开了温和的笑容
近	balmy, benign, delicate, mellow, nonabrasive
反	abrasive, caustic, coarse, hard, harsh, rough, scathing, stern 刺激性的；尖刻的，严厉的

blandishment	[ˈblændɪʃmənt]
【考法】	*n.* 甜言蜜语，讨好某人的话：something that tends to **coax** or **cajole**
例	Our blandishment left her unmoved. 纵使甜言蜜语她也无动于衷。
近	flattery, adulation

blasé	[blɑːˈzeɪ]
【考法】	*adj.* (过度放纵之后)厌倦享乐的，腻烦的：**apathetic** to pleasure or excitement as a result of excessive indulgence or enjoyment
例	Years of extravagance has made him totally blasé. 长期的奢华生活已使他彻底麻木。
近	indifferent, jaded, unconcerned, world-weary
反	zealous, fanatic 狂热的；curious 好奇的

blast	[blæst]
【考法1】	*n.* 爆炸：an **explosion** or violent detonation
例	blast wave of a nuclear bomb 原子弹的冲击波
近	burst, detonation, eruption, outburst
反	implosion 向内爆裂
【考法2】	*n.* 一阵猛烈的强风：a violent **gust** of wind
例	blasts of bleak air 阵阵阴风
近	blow, flurry
【考法3】	*n.* 巨响：a **loud** explosive **sound**
例	A sharp blast of the horn startled the other driver. 一声尖锐刺耳的喇叭声惊吓到了另一名司机。
近	bang, boom, thunderclap
反	murmur, whisper 轻言轻语
【考法4】	*vt.* 炸裂，爆破：to **cause to break open** or into pieces by or as if by an explosive
例	The highway engineers will have to blast that hill in order to put a road through here. 为了建设一条通过这里的公路，道路工程师们必须对那座山施行爆破。
近	demolish, explode, smash, blow up
【考法5】	*vt.* 斥责，抨击：to **criticize harshly** and usually publicly
例	blast the new governor for every little misstep 就每一个小的失误抨击新的执政官
近	abuse, assail, belabor, castigate, lambaste, scathe, vituperate

blatant	[ˈbleɪtnt]
【考法1】	*adj.* 大声喧哗的：**noisy**, especially in a vulgar or offensive manner
例	blatant radios 喧闹恼人的电台
近	boisterous, clamant, clamorous, vociferous
反	quiet, reticent, taciturn 安静的，沉默少语的
【考法2】	*adj.* (让人生厌地)惹人注目的：very **noticeable** especially for being incorrect or bad
例	a blatant lie 明目张胆的谎言 ‖ a blatant error in simple addition 简单加法运算中的一个明显错误
近	conspicuous, flagrant, glaring, patent, striking, pronounced
反	subtle, unimpressive 细微的

blazon	[ˈbleɪzn]
【考法1】	*vt.* 使知名：to **make known openly** or publicly
例	Their very public canoodling has pretty much blazoned the fact that they are having an affair. 他们彼此间公开的亲昵举动让他们之间的恋情大白于天下。
近	annunciate, broadcast, declare, publicize, proclaim
反	withhold 保留，不透露

【考法 2】 *v.* 修饰，装扮：to **make more attractive** by adding something that is beautiful or becoming
例 The university's dormitory has been blazoned with banners celebrating graduation. 大学宿舍被那些庆祝毕业的横幅装饰一新。
近 adorn, bedeck, embellish, garnish
反 blemish, deface, mar, spoil 损害，破坏

Unit 4

blemish [ˈblemɪʃ]
【考法 1】 *n.* 缺点，污点：a noticeable **imperfection**
例 The first LCD had several blemishes on its surface, so we took it back to the store. 第一块液晶显示屏有许多坏点，所以我们拿回商场去退货了。
近 blotch, defect, fault, flaw, mar, spot, scar
【考法 2】 *vt.* 损害，玷污：to **reduce** the soundness, effectiveness, or perfection of
例 A scratch blemished the finish on the car. 一道刮痕破坏了车子表面的涂层。
近 break, disfigure, harm, hurt, impair, injure, spoil, vitiate
反 fix, renovate, repair, revamp 翻新，维修
派 unblemished *adj.* 纯洁的，无瑕疵的

blight [blaɪt]
【考法 1】 *v.* (使)枯萎：to **affect** (as a plant) with blight
近 wither, shrivel
反 flourish 生长繁茂
【考法 2】 *v.* 损害：to **impair** the quality or effect of
例 Illness blighted his career. 伤病毁了他的职业生涯。
近 damage, deteriorate, harm, impair, mar, ruin
派 blighted *adj.* 枯萎的；毁坏的

bliss [blɪs]
【考法 1】 *n.* 极度快乐：extreme happiness; **ecstasy**
例 Ignorance is bliss ——The Matrix. 无知者，幸也。（电影《黑客帝国》）
近 beatitude, joy, ecstasy, elation
反 grief, misery 悲痛
【考法 2】 *n.* 极乐世界：a dwelling **place of perfect happiness** for the soul after death
例 the road to eternal bliss 通往永恒乐土的道路
近 heaven, paradise
反 hell 地狱
派 blissful *adj.* 带来幸运的

blithe [blaɪð]
【考法 1】 *adj.* 愉快高兴的：of a **happy lighthearted** character or disposition
例 Everyone loved her for her blithe spirit. 所有人都喜欢她开朗的性格。
近 bright, buoyant, gay, jocular, jocund, jovial
反 dour, gloomy, morose, saturnine, sulky, sullen 忧郁的
【考法 2】 *adj.* 无忧无虑的；漫不经心的：having or showing **freedom from worries** or troubles
例 He has a blithe attitude about ever having to earn a living because he knows there's a trust fund in his future. 他对生活无忧无虑，因为他知道他的未来有信托基金可以倚靠。
近 debonair, insouciant, lighthearted
反 careworn 焦虑的

blueprint [ˈbluːprɪnt]
【考法 1】 *n.* 蓝图，详细计划：a photographic print used especially for **architects' plans**
例 a blueprint for the new library 新图书馆的建造蓝图
近 arrangement, design, plan, scheme
【考法 2】 *vt.* 事先计划：to **work out** the details of (something) **in advance**
例 blueprint the schedule of events for the festival right down to the last detail 把节日活动的每一个细节都事先安排好
近 arrange, budget, calculate, organize, frame, lay out

blunder [ˈblʌndər]

【考法 1】 *n.* 过失：a gross **error** or **mistake** resulting usually from stupidity, ignorance, or carelessness

例 That's your second blunder today. 这是你今天犯的第二个低级错误了。

近 mistake, gaffe, lapse, error

【考法 2】 *v.* 在…方面犯了很愚蠢且通常很严重的错误；糟蹋：to **make a stupid**, usually serious **error** in; botch

近 screw up, mess up

【考法 3】 *v.* 蹒跚：to move **unsteadily** or confusedly

例 Without my glasses I blundered into the wrong room. 因为没戴眼镜，所以我蹒跚地走入了错误的房间。

近 stumble, falter, limp, plod

派 blundering *adj.* 蹒跚行走的

blunt [blʌnt]

【考法 1】 *vt.* 使变钝：to make **less sharp** or definite

近 dull, deaden, hebetate, benumb, enfeeble

反 whet, sharpen 磨尖

【考法 2】 *vt.* 减弱（力度等）：to reduce or **weaken in strength or feeling**

例 The abrupt music blunted the effect of the movie's final tragic scene. 突兀的音乐让电影结束时悲剧场景的氛围大打折扣。

近 dampen, deaden, attenuate

【考法 3】 *adj.* 直率的：being or characterized by **direct**, **brief**, and potentially rude speech or manner

例 He values honesty and is quite blunt about telling people what he doesn't like about them. 他重视诚实，经常直率地告诉别人他们何处使他不满。

近 abrupt, bluff, brusque, curt, gruff

反 circuitous, mealy-mouthed 拐弯抹角的

blur [blɜːr]

【考法 1】 *v.* （使）变得朦胧，（使）变得不清楚：to (cause sth. to) become **vague** or indistinct

例 Sorrowful tears blurred her eyes. 悲伤的眼泪模糊了她的双眼。

近 shroud, becloud, befog, obscure

反 clear 使清晰

派 blurring *adj.* 朦胧的

【考法 2】 *vt.* 使不易理解：to make (something) **unclear to the understanding**

例 An article for the layman that blurs the distinction between the two kinds of cholesterol. 一篇针对普通读者的文章对两种胆固醇的区别表述得糊不清。

近 obfuscate

反 clarify, illuminate 阐明，说清楚

blurt [blɜːt]

【考法】 *vt.* 突然说出，冲动地说：to utter **abruptly** and impulsively

例 blurt out the secret 脱口说出了秘密

近 burst, bolt, ejaculate, cry out

反 muffle, mute 使缄默

bluster [ˈblʌstər]

【考法 1】 *v.* 狂妄自大地大声说：to speak in a **loudly arrogant** or bullying manner

例 He was blustering alone in the meeting, which triggered wide dissatisfaction. 他一人在会议上夸夸其谈，引得众人不满。

近 roar, clamor, rattle

反 whisper 小声嘀咕

【考法 2】 *n.* 大声吹嘘；恐吓：**loudly** boastful or threatening speech

近 grandiloquence, braggadocio

【考法 3】 *n.* 喧闹的状态：a state of **noisy**, confused activity

例 a mayor who got things done without a lot of bluster 一个能把事情低调解决的市长

近 disturbance, pandemonium, tumult, turmoil

派 blustering *adj.* 大吵大闹的

Unit 5

boggle ['bɑːgl]

【考法 1】 *v.* (因为怀疑、恐惧)犹豫: to **hesitate** because of doubt, fear, or scruples

例 boggle at the dilemma 身处困境而犹豫不决

近 hesitate, falter, waver

【考法 2】 *v.* 笨拙地做: to make or do (something) in a clumsy or **unskillful way**

例 She boggled her first effort to make Christmas cookies. 她第一次笨手笨脚尝试做圣诞蛋糕。

近 botch, bungle

boisterous ['bɔɪstərəs]

【考法】 *adj.* 喧嚷的，吵闹的: **noisily** turbulent

例 a boisterous queue in front of the pavilion 场馆前喧闹的队伍 ‖ boisterous mirth 喧闹的欢笑

近 rowdy, vociferous, blatant, clamorous, raucous, rambunctious

反 quiet, sedate 安静的

派 boisterousness *n.* 喧闹

bolster ['boʊlstər]

【考法 1】 *n./v.* 支撑(物): a structural part designed to eliminate friction or **provide support** or bearing

例 pillars that bolster the building 支撑房屋的柱子

近 brace, buttress, bear, sustain, undergird, underpin, uphold, prop up

【考法 2】 *vt.* 鼓励，使有精力: to give a **boost** to

例 news that bolsters the morale of the troops 鼓舞军队士气的消息

近 buoy, reinforce

反 dampen 泼冷水

bombast ['bɑːmbæst]

【考法】 *n.* 夸大的言辞: grandiloquent, **pompous** speech or writing

例 "Their eloquence is all bombast", said Charles Kingsley. "他们的雄辩是虚张声势"，查尔斯·金斯利如此说道。

近 braggadocio, grandiloquence, exaggeration

反 understatement 保守的观点

派 bombastic *adj.* 夸大的

bonhomie [ˌbɑːnə'miː]

【考法】 *n.* 温和，和蔼: a pleasant and affable disposition; **geniality**

近 affability, amiability, geniality

派 bonhomous *adj.* 和蔼的

boo ['buː]

【考法】 *n./v.* 嘘(以表示不满或嘲笑): a sound uttered to show **contempt**, **scorn**, or **disapproval**

例 boo the actor off the stage 把演员嘘下舞台

近 jeer, scorn

反 applaud 鼓掌

boon [buːn]

【考法 1】 *n.* 恩惠，福利: **benefit**, favor

例 The new solar battery booster is a boon for photographers. 这个光伏充电器是摄影师们的福音。

近 gift, benevolence, present, windfall

反 misfortune, scourge 灾祸

【考法 2】 *adj.* 喜欢集体行动的: likely to seek or **enjoy the company of others**

近 convivial, extroverted, gregarious, social, outgoing

反 reclusive 隐居

boor [bʊr]

【考法】 *n.* 粗鲁的人，不敏感的人: a **rude** or insensitive person

例 acting like a boor 表现得很粗鲁

近 peasant, barbarian, buffoon

反 sentimentalist 多愁善感的人

bootless [ˈbuːtləs]
【考法】 *adj.* 无用的：**useless**, unprofitable, futile

例 The meeting turns out to be a bootless attempt. 这个会议被证明是一次徒劳的尝试。

近 barren, ineffective, futile, abortive, fruitless, vain

反 worthy 有价值的

bound [baʊnd]
【考法 1】 *n.* 界限：a real or imaginary point **beyond which a person or thing cannot go**

例 The language in the novel really is beyond the bounds of decency. 这本小说的语言实在太不得体了。

近 environs, limit, confines, perimeter

反 unrestrainedness 无边无际

【考法 2】 *vt.* 给…设置限制：to **set limits** or bounds to

例 The country is bounded by river. 这个国家的领土以河水为界。

近 limit, demarcate, delimit

反 enfranchise, free, liberate 释放

【考法 3】 *adj.* 投入的，坚定的：**fully committed** to achieving a goal

例 I am bound and determined to write a novel before I turn 30. 我下定决心在 30 岁之前要写本小说。

近 resolute, determined, single-minded, bent on

反 faltering, hesitant, vacillating, wavering, weak-kneed 动摇的

派 boundless *adj.* 无边无际的，无约束的

Unit 6

■ BOYCOTT	■ BRACING	■ BRAKE	■ BRASH	■ BRASSY
■ BRAVADO	■ BRAVURA	■ BRAZEN	■ BREACH	■ BREVITY

boycott [ˈbɔɪkɑːt]
【考法】 *vt.* 联合抵制，拒绝参与：to engage in a **concerted refusal** to have dealings with（as a person, store, or organization）usually to express disapproval or to force acceptance of certain conditions

例 This brand is being boycotted for damaging environment. 因为破坏环境，这个品牌正在被抵制。

近 refuse

反 patronize 经常光顾

bracing [ˈbreɪsɪŋ]
【考法】 *adj.* 令人振奋的，给人带来活力的：**giving strength**, vigor, or freshness

例 a bracing news from the frontline 来自前线的振奋人心的消息

近 invigorating, rejuvenating, reviving, stimulating

反 vapid 乏味的

派 brace *v.* 支持，使充满活力

brake [breɪk]
【考法】 *v.* 刹车：to cause to move or proceed at a **less rapid** pace

例 A seagull swooped down in front of her car, causing her to slam on the brakes. 一只海鸥忽然俯冲到车窗前，她猛踩刹车。

近 decelerate, retard, slacken

反 accelerate, hasten, rush, speed up 加速

brash [bræʃ]
【考法 1】 *adj.* 愚勇的，鲁莽的：**foolishly adventurous** or bold

例 that brash motorcyclist likes to show off by riding on only one wheel 那个鲁莽的摩托车手喜欢炫耀单轮骑车

近 audacious, brassy, daredevil, madcap, reckless, temerarious

反 circumspect, guarded, heedful, prudent, wary 谨慎的

【考法 2】 *adj.* 缺乏判断力的，不明智的：showing **poor judgment** especially in personal relationships or social situations

例 He was reprimanded for his brash comments to the media about the team's coaching staff. 他因对媒体说了一些有关教练组的不明智的评论而遭到指责。

近 imprudent, injudicious, tactless, undiplomatic

反 advisable, discreet, tactful 明智的

brassy ['bræsɪ]

【考法 1】 *adj.* 厚脸皮的，不知羞耻的：displaying or marked by **rude boldness**

例 brassy reporters 厚颜无耻的记者

近 audacious, bold-faced, brazen, impertinent, impudent, insolent

反 diffident, unassertive, retiring, timid 羞怯的，谦逊的

【考法 2】 *adj.* 华而不实地炫耀的：cheap and **showy**; flashy

反 furtive 隐秘的

bravado [brə'vɑːdəʊ]

【考法 1】 *n.* 假装勇敢：a **pretense** of bravery

例 I remembered his youthful bravado. 我还记得他的年少鲁莽。

【考法 2】 *n.* 虚张声势：blustering **swaggering** conduct

例 strive to prevent our courage from turning into bravado 努力阻止我们的勇气变成虚张声势

bravura [brə'vʊərə]

【考法】 *adj./n.* 优秀演技(的)：**brilliant** technique or style in performance

例 a truly bravura performance of the ballet 一场极其精彩的芭蕾舞演出

近 adroit, artful, dexterous, masterful

反 amateur, artless, unprofessional, unskillful 业余的，拙劣的

brazen ['breɪzn]

【考法 1】 *adj.* 蛮横大胆的，厚颜无耻的：marked by **contemptuous boldness**

例 a brazen disregard for the rules 蛮横大胆地漠视规则

近 bold-faced, impertinent, impudent, insolent

反 modest, self-effacing, diffident, retiring, timid 谦虚的，胆小的

【考法 2】 *v.* 大胆自信地去面对或从事：to face or undergo with **bold self-assurance**

例 brazen out the crisis 沉着面对危机 ‖ Some people prefer to brazen a thing out rather than admit defeat. 有的人不愿承认失败，而是宁肯厚着脸皮干下去。

近 confront, outface, defy

反 dodge, duck, shirk, sidestep 躲开，避谈

breach [briːtʃ]

【考法 1】 *n.* (对伦理、法律准则的)破坏：a **breaking** of a **moral or legal code**

例 cheating on the exam was a serious breach of the military academy's honor code 考试作弊是对军校的荣誉准则的严重破坏

近 malefaction, transgression, trespass, violation, wrongdoing

【考法 2】 *v.* 违背：to **fail to keep**

例 a builder being sued by a homeowner for breaching a contract 建筑商因违约被房主起诉

近 contravene, fracture, infringe, transgress

反 obey, observe, comply with, conform to 遵守

brevity ['brevəti]

【考法 1】 *n.* 简短，简洁：**shortness** of duration

例 The best quality a graduation speech can have is brevity. 好的毕业演讲必须简洁。

近 briefness, conciseness, shortness

反 lengthiness 冗长

【考法 2】 *n.* 精炼：the quality or state of being marked by or using only **few words** to convey much meaning

例 If brevity is the soul of wit, then that speech wasn't at all witty. 如果说精炼是智慧的灵魂，那么那个演讲毫无智慧可言。

近 conciseness, pithiness, sententiousness, terseness

反 diffuseness, long-windedness, prolixity, verbosity, wordiness 冗长，啰嗦

Unit 7

| ■ BRIBE | ■ BRIDLE | ■ BRISK | ■ BRISTLE | ■ BRITTLE |
| ■ BROACH | ■ BROMIDE | ■ BROOK | ■ BROWBEAT | ■ BRUIT |

bribe [braɪb]

【考法】 *v.* 贿赂，收买：to **give** something, such as **money** or a favor, to a person in a position of trust to influence that person's views or conduct

例 They bribed him to keep quiet about the incident. 他们收买他，希望其保持缄默。

近 corrupt, pay off, square

bridle	[ˈbraɪdl]
【考法】	v. 限制: to keep from exceeding a desirable degree or level (as of expression)
例	Try to bridle your criticism next time so that it is helpful and not hurtful. 下回尽量控制好批评的语气，让其既顺耳又有益。
近	check, contain, curb, constrain, inhibit, regulate, restrain, tame, rein in

brisk	[brɪsk]
【考法 1】	adj. 充满生机的，有活力的: marked by much life, movement, or **activity**
例	brisk and concise response 轻快而简洁的回答
近	animated, bouncing, bustling, frisky, kinetic, sprightly, vibrant
反	lackadaisical, languid, leaden, dead, inactive, lifeless 没有生机的
【考法 2】	adj. (言辞或方式)尖刻辛辣的，刻薄的: **keen or sharp** in speech or manner
例	a brisk greeting 尖刻的祝贺

bristle	[ˈbrɪsl]
【考法 1】	v. 怒不可遏，咆哮: to express one's **anger** usually violently
例	bristle at the suggestion of gay marriage 对基情怒不可遏
近	bluster, fulminate, rampage, fume, storm
反	cower 畏缩
【考法 2】	v. 供应充足，充满: to be **copiously** supplied
例	starting a new life in New York city bristling with possibilities 在有着无限机会的纽约开始新生活
近	brim, overflow, swarm, teem

brittle	[ˈbrɪtl]
【考法 1】	adj. 易碎的，脆弱的，易坏的: easily **broken**, cracked, or snapped
例	as brittle as glass 像玻璃一样脆弱
近	crispy, crumbly, flaky, friable
【考法 2】	adj. 不热心的，不真心的: **lacking in friendliness** or warmth of feeling
例	a brittle apology that was anything but heartfelt 一个毫不真诚的道歉
近	chilly, frigid, frosty, glacial, unfriendly, unsympathetic
反	cordial, genial, warmhearted 热心的

broach	[broʊtʃ]
【考法 1】	vt. 开启，启封: to **open** for the first time
例	broach a keg of beer 开一小桶酒
近	break
反	close off 关闭
【考法 2】	vt. 提出讨论: to **present** or bring forward for discussion
例	broach the topic of plans for next year's parade 将明年的游行活动计划提上讨论日程
近	moot, place, raise, bring up

bromide	[ˈbroʊmaɪd]
【考法】	n. 陈词滥调: a commonplace or **hackneyed** statement or notion
例	A newspaper editorial offered the timeworn bromide that people should settle their differences peacefully. 报纸编辑又拿出那一套呼吁和平解决纷争的陈词滥调。
近	banality, cliché, platitude, homily, truism, chestnut, shibboleth

brook	[brʊk]
【考法 1】	vt. 忍受，容许: to stand for, **tolerate**
例	brook no interference with his plans 不能容忍别人对他的计划进行干涉
近	abide, countenance, endure, stomach
【考法 2】	n. 小溪流: a natural stream of water normally smaller than and often tributary to a river: **creek**
例	There are tiny fish and frogs in that brook. 那条小溪里有小鱼和青蛙。
近	creek, rivulet

browbeat	[ˈbraʊbiːt]
【考法】	vt. 恐吓: to **intimidate** by a stern manner or arrogant speech: bully
例	They would often browbeat the younger child until he cried. 他们总是把小朋友欺负到哭为止。
近	blackjack, bulldoze, bully, cow, hector, intimidate

bruit	[ˈbruːt]
【考法】	vt. (未经证实地)散播(消息): to **make** (as a piece of information) **the subject of common talk** without any authority or confirmation of accuracy
例	It's been bruited that... 到处传播…
近	circulate, whisper, noise about
反	keep secret 保持秘密

Unit 8

buck [bʌk]

【考法 1】 *v.* 阻止，反对：to **refuse assent**, to refuse to give in to
例 buck the system 不遵守制度
近 defy, fight, oppose, repel, withstand
反 assent to, bow to, submit to, succumb to, surrender to, yield to 赞成，服从

【考法 2】 *v.* 转移，交接：to **shift possession** of (something) from one person to another
例 buck each box to the next person in line 将每一个盒子传给队伍中的后一人
近 transfer, hand over

budge [bʌdʒ]

【考法 1】 *v.* (使)改变立场或态度：to **alter a position** or attitude
例 Nothing would budge him. 没有什么可以让他改变主意。

【考法 2】 *v.* 停止抵抗，屈服：to **cease resistance** (as to another's arguments, demands, or control)
例 Despite hours of intense pressure, she refused to budge from her position. 尽管被连续施压几小时，她仍旧不肯让步。
近 concede, relent, submit, succumb, surrender
反 resist 拒绝，抵抗

bulge [bʌldʒ]

【考法 1】 *n.* 凸起：a **protuberant** or swollen part or place
例 a bulge in his jacket 他衣服上鼓起来的一块
近 convexity, projection, protrusion, protuberance, swell
反 depressed region, cavity, dent, indent, recess, pit 凹陷，坑
派 bulging *adj.* 凸起的
例 bulging eyes 暴鱼眼

【考法 2】 *n.* 比赛中的优势地位：the **more favorable condition** or position in a competition
例 Somehow she got the bulge on him in the race for the statehouse. 她在州议员竞选中领先了他。
近 high ground, inside track, upper hand, whip hand
反 disadvantage, drawback, handicap, liability 劣势

【考法 3】 *n.* 暴涨，突增，在数目或数量上突然而且是临时性的增加：a **sudden, usually temporary increase** in number or quantity
例 The baby boom created a bulge in school enrollment. 生育高峰造成学校入学人数的暴涨。

【考法 4】 *vi.* 充满：to be **copiously supplied**
例 This guidebook to San Francisco positively bulges with useful information. 这本关于旧金山的指南包含了很多有用信息。
近 brim, bristle, overflow, swarm, teem

bully [ˈbʊli]

【考法 1】 *n.* 欺凌弱小者：a person who habitually treats others in an overbearing or **intimidating manner**
例 They had to deal with the local bullies. 他们要对付当地恶霸。
近 bullyboy, hector, intimidator
反 underdog 被欺负的人

【考法 2】 *adj.* 最好的，最棒的：of the very **best** kind
例 That's a bully idea for reviving the town's retail center. 真是个重整镇上零售中心的好主意。
近 awesome, fabulous, fantastic, superb, marvelous, unsurpassed, excellent

bumptious [ˈbʌmpʃəs]

【考法】 *adj.* 专横傲慢的，自以为是的：having a feeling of **superiority** that shows itself in an overbearing attitude
例 a bumptious young man whose family wealth gave him a sense of entitlement 一个傲慢的富二代 ‖ be bumptious over one's inferiors 对下级态度傲慢
近 assumptive, supercilious, imperious, overweening, peremptory, pompous, presuming, presumptuous, self-assertive, haughty
反 humble, modest, unarrogant, unpretentious 谦虚的，低调的

bungle ['bʌŋgl]
- 【考法】 *vt.* 办糟，失败：to act or **work clumsily** and awkwardly
- 例 bungle a job 搞砸了一项工作
- 近 boggle, bumble, fumble, mess up, screw up
- 反 bring off 成功

buoy [bɔɪ]
- 【考法】 *vt.* 使充满勇气和力量，使振作：to fill with **courage or strength** of purpose
- 例 The sudden improvement in his health buoyed him up. 身体的突然好转让他很振奋。
- 近 embolden, hearten, inspire, bear up, buck up
- 反 daunt, discourage, dishearten, dispirit 使沮丧，泼冷水

buoyant ['buːjənt]
- 【考法 1】 *adj.* 有浮力的：capable of **floating**
- 例 a buoyant balloon 一个能浮起来的气球
- 反 leaden 沉重的
- 【考法 2】 *adj.* 心情好的：having or showing a **good mood or disposition**
- 例 in a buoyant mood 轻松快乐的心情
- 近 blithe, chipper, eupeptic, lightsome, upbeat, winsome, effervescent
- 反 dour, gloomy, morose, saturnine, sullen 沮丧的

burgeon ['bɜːrdʒən]
- 【考法】 *vi.* 迅速成长扩大，蓬勃发展：to **grow** and expand **rapidly**; **flourish**
- 例 My confidence began to burgeon. 我的信心开始迅速增强。
- 近 accelerate, accumulate, balloon, boom, build up, escalate, mount, multiply, mushroom, proliferate, roll up, snowball, wax, flourish, prosper
- 反 wane, wither, waste away, subside, subdue 衰退

burlesque [bɜːr'lesk]
- 【考法】 *n./v.* 夸张滑稽地模仿以嘲弄他人的文学艺术作品，恶搞：to copy or exaggerate （someone or something） in order to **make fun of**
- 例 Burlesquing the teacher's nervous tic isn't very nice. 恶搞老师紧张的痉挛不是好的行为。
- 近 caricature, imitate, mock, parody, spoof, travesty

Unit 9

| ■ BURNISH | ■ BUTTRESS | ■ BYZANTINE | ■ CACHE | ■ CACHET |
| ■ CACOPHONY | ■ CADGE | ■ CAJOLE | ■ CALCIFY | ■ CALIBRATE |

burnish ['bɜːrnɪʃ]
- 【考法】 *v.* 擦亮，磨光：to **make smooth or glossy** usually by repeatedly applying surface pressure
- 例 burnish the knife 磨光刀
- 近 buff, polish, furbish, grind, smoothen

buttress ['bʌtrɪs]
- 【考法 1】 *n.* 扶墙：a projecting structure for **supporting** or giving stability to a **wall** or **building**
- 近 anchor, mainstay, pillar, reliance, standby
- 【考法 2】 *vt.* 为…提供支撑的证据或者信息：to **provide evidence or information for** (as a claim or idea)
- 例 A mass of circumstantial evidence buttresses the prosecutor's case. 大量证据都支持起诉人的案件。
- 近 back, bolster, corroborate, reinforce, substantiate, shore up
- 反 contravene, challenge 反对，质疑

byzantine ['bɪzəntiːn]
- 【考法】 *adj.* 错综复杂的：**complicated** or **secretive**, having many parts or aspects that are usually **interrelated**
- 例 a bill to simplify the byzantine tax structure 一项试图简化繁琐税收制度的提案
- 近 convoluted, intricate, involved, labyrinthine, sophisticated, tangled
- 反 straightforward, plain, simple, uncomplicated 直截了当的，不复杂的

cache [kæʃ]
- 【考法 1】 *n.* 囤货，藏货：a **supply** stored up and often hidden away
- 例 maintain a cache of food in case of emergencies 保存食物，以防万一
- 近 stash, stockpile, store, deposit, hoard, reserve

【考法2】 *v.* 隐藏：to put into a **hiding** place

例 The fugitive slaves were cached in their cellar until they could make their way to Canada. 奴隶们被藏匿在房间的地下室直到他们能够顺利逃去加拿大。

近 conceal, ensconce, secrete, squirrel away

反 display, exhibit 展示

cachet [kæˈʃeɪ]

【考法1】 *n.* 同意：an indication of **approval** carrying great prestige

近 approval, authorization, concurrence, endorsement, license, permission, sanction, warrant

反 interdiction, prohibition, proscription 禁止

【考法2】 *n.* 声望：**prestige**

例 being rich...doesn't have the cachet it used to 富甲一方，再也不像过去拥有那么高的声望了

cacophony [kəˈkɑːfənɪ]

【考法】 *n.* 刺耳的声音：loud, confused, and usually **inharmonious sound**

例 the cacophony of a pet store full of animals 宠物商店里各种动物叽叽呱呱的声音

近 blare, bluster, clamor, din, discordance, racket

反 quiet, silence, still, stillness 安静

cadge [kædʒ]

【考法】 *v.* 乞讨，乞求：**beg**, sponge

例 cadge a free cup of coffee 讨到一杯免费的咖啡

反 earn 赚钱

cajole [kəˈdʒoʊl]

【考法】 *v.* 哄骗：to urge with gentle and repeated appeals, teasing, or flattery; **wheedle**

例 He cajoled her into doing his laundry for him. 他哄骗她帮他洗衣服。

近 blandish, blarney, palaver, wheedle, soft-soap, sweet-talk

calcify [ˈkælsɪfaɪ]

【考法】 *vt.* 使僵化：to make **inflexible** or **unchangeable**

例 a leg that calcified 一条麻木僵直的腿

近 harden, ossify

反 make malleable, make pliant, make more flexible 使灵活

calibrate [ˈkælɪbreɪt]

【考法1】 *vt.* 调整，使标准化：to **standardize**（as a measuring instrument）by determining the deviation from a standard so as to ascertain the proper correction factors

例 calibrate the polling procedures to ensure objectivity 为保证客观性而使投票过程标准化

反 unstandardize 使不标准

【考法2】 *vt.*（根据标准）精确测量：to **measure precisely** especially: to measure against a standard

Unit 10

■ CALLIGRAPHY	■ CALLOUS	■ CALLOW	■ CALUMNIATE	■ CAMARADERIE
■ CAMEO	■ CAMOUFLAGE	■ CANARD	■ CANDOR	■ CANON

calligraphy [kəˈlɪɡrəfi]

【考法】 *n.*（优美的）书法：artistic, stylized, or **elegant handwriting** or lettering

例 She specializes in scrollwork with beautiful calligraphy. 她很擅长花体字。

近 longhand, manuscript, penmanship, script

callous [ˈkæləs]

【考法】 *adj.* 无同情心的, 冷漠的：emotionally hardened; **unfeeling**

例 a callous indifference to the suffering of others 对他人痛苦的漠不关心

近 affectless, uncharitable, unsparing, remorseless, indurate, ruthless

反 sympathetic, compassionate, merciful, tender, warmhearted 有同情心的

callow [ˈkæloʊ]

【考法】 *adj.* 不老练的, 不成熟的：**lacking** in adult **experience** or maturity

例 callow young man 未经世事的年轻人

近 green, immature, inexperienced, juvenile, unfledged, unripened, puerile

反 adult, experienced, grown-up, mature, ripe 成熟的

calumniate	[kə'lʌmnɪeɪt]

【考法】 *v.* 诽谤，造谣，中伤：to utter maliciously **false statements**, charges, or imputations about

近 asperse, blacken, defame, libel, malign, smear, traduce, vilify

反 vindicate 辩护

派 calumnious *adj.* 造谣的

反 flattering 谄媚的

派 calumny *n.* 诽谤，中伤：a false statement maliciously made to injure another's reputation

反 approbation 嘉许

camaraderie	[ˌkɑːməˈrɑːdəri]

【考法】 *n.* 友情：a spirit of **friendly** good-fellowship

例 There is great camaraderie among the teammates. 组员之间有着深厚的情谊。

近 brotherhood, comradeship, fellowship

反 enmity 敌意

cameo	[ˈkæmioʊ]

【考法1】 *n.* 栩栩如生的描绘，简洁生动的描述或刻画：a **brief**, **vivid portrayal** or depiction

例 a literary cameo 文学描写

【考法2】 *v.* 客串：to make a **brief but dramatic appearance**, as in a film

例 She cameoed as Anne Boleyn in *A Man for All Seasons*. 在《四季之人》中她客串安妮·博林。

camouflage	[ˈkæməflɑːʒ]

【考法】 *v./n.* 伪装；伪装手段：behavior or artifice designed to **deceive** or **hide**

例 The soldiers must wear protective jungle camouflage while on patrol. 士兵们在巡逻的时候必须穿上迷彩服来保护自身安全。

近 costume, guise, cloak, dress up

反 unmask 揭露

canard	[kə'nɑːrd]

【考法】 *n.* 谣传，误传：an unfounded or false, deliberately **misleading** story.

例 It's a popular canard that the actress died under scandalous circumstances. 有一种广泛的说法声称，女演员死于绯闻的压力。

近 story, whisper

candor	[ˈkændər]

【考法】 *n.* 坦白，直率，诚挚：unreserved, **honest**, or **sincere** expression

例 The members of the rock band speak with candor about their recent squabbling. 摇滚乐队成员对于他们最近的内讧直言不讳。

近 bluntness, forthrightness, frankness, unreservedness, straightforwardness

反 artifice, mendacity, dissembling, dissimulation, indirection 谎言，不直接

canon	[ˈkænən]

【考法1】 *n.* 准则，标准：a basis for judgment; a **standard** or **criterion**

例 the canons of polite society 文明社会的法规

近 dogma

【考法2】 *n.* 真经，正典：the **authentic** works of a writer

反 apocrypha 伪经

派 canonical *adj.* 正统的，标准的：conforming to a general rule or acceptable procedure : orthodox

反 heterodox, nontraditional 非正统的

派 canonize *v.* 作为神圣的来对待，使神圣化：to treat as sacred; glorify

近 adore, adulate, idolize, deify, worship

反 abase, degrade, demean, humiliate 贬低

List 4

Unit 1

| ■ CANVASS | ■ CAPITULATE | ■ CAPRICE | ■ CAPTIVATE | ■ CAREWORN |
| ■ CARDINAL | ■ CARICATURE | ■ CARNAL | ■ CAROUSE | ■ CARP |

canvass ['kænvəs]

【考法 1】 *v.* 仔细检查，详尽讨论：to **examine carefully or discuss thoroughly**; scrutinize

例 The evidence had been repeatedly canvassed in American courts. 该项证据已在美国的法庭中反复被审查过。

【考法 2】 *v.* 游说，去（一个地区）的各处或找到（个人）来拉选票或订单：to go through (a region) or go to (persons) to **solicit votes or orders**

例 canvass voters 拉选票

近 interview, poll, solicit, survey

capitulate [kə'pɪtʃuleɪt]

【考法】 *v.* 投降，默许：to **give up all resistance**; acquiesce; yield

例 One side finally capitulated when it became clear that they couldn't win the argument. 意识到他们不能拿下这场辩论后，该方投降了。

近 budge, concede, relent, submit, succumb, surrender, knuckle under

反 resist, oppose 抵抗

caprice [kə'priːs]

【考法 1】 *n.* 一时冲动的决定：an **impulsive change** of mind

例 An out-of-character caprice led him to take the day off from work and go to the beach. 一时冲动让他决定休假一天，去海滩度假。

近 crank, fancy, vagary, vagrancy, whimsy

【考法 2】 *n.* 反复无常，善变：an inclination to **change** one's mind **impulsively**

例 His knack for picking racetrack winners appears to owe as much to caprice as it does to a canny assessment of horseflesh. 他赌马屡赌屡赢，似乎要归功于自己的反复无常而不是对于赛马本身独到精明的评估。

近 freakishness, impulsiveness, whimsicalness

反 confirmation 确认

派 capricious *adj.* 反复无常的，善变的

反 steadfast, resolute, constant, pertinacious 坚定不变的

captivate ['kæpɪveɪt]

【考法】 *vt.* 吸引：to **attract** and hold by charm, beauty, or excellence

例 I was captivated by her brilliant mind. 我被她的才华横溢所吸引。

近 allure, beguile, bewitch, enchant, fascinate, magnetize

反 repulse 使反感

careworn ['kerwɔːrn]

【考法】 *adj.* 忧心忡忡的，焦虑的：showing the effect of **grief** or **anxiety**

例 a careworn face 忧心忡忡的脸

反 lighthearted 心情愉快的

cardinal ['kɑːrdinl]

【考法】 *adj.* 主要的，非常重要的：of **foremost importance**; paramount

例 the cardinal rule of medicine: do no harm 药物的首要标准就是无害

近 dominant, overbearing, overriding, paramount, preeminent, primal, supreme

反 minor 次要的

caricature [ˈkærɪkətʃər]

【考法1】 *n.* 用讽刺歪曲等手法的夸张，漫画，讽刺画：**exaggeration** by means of often ludicrous distortion of parts or characteristics

派 caricaturist *n.* 漫画家

【考法2】 *v.* 嘲笑性模仿或夸张：to **copy** or **exaggerate**（someone or something）in order to make fun of

例 caricature the supervisor's distinctive walk 模仿督导员独特的走路方式

近 burlesque, imitate, mock, parody, spoof, travesty

carnal [ˈkɑːrnl]

【考法1】 *adj.* 肉体的，物质的：relating to the **physical**

例 seen with carnal eyes 用肉眼看 ‖ carnal remains 遗体

近 corporal, corporeal, fleshly, material, somatic

反 spiritual 精神的

【考法2】 *adj.* 世俗的：**worldly**

例 a carnal mind 凡心

近 earthborn, mundane, temporal, terrestrial, worldly

carouse [kəˈraʊz]

【考法】 *vi.* 畅饮，狂饮作乐：to **drink** liquor **freely** or excessively

例 stay at home instead of going out and carousing with friends 呆在家里而不是出去和朋友们狂饮作乐

近 binge, revel, roister, wassail

carp [kɑːrp]

【考法】 *vi.* 对小事吹毛求疵，挑剔，表现不满：to make often **peevish criticisms** or **objections** about matters that are minor, unimportant, or irrelevant; to **express dissatisfaction**, pain, or resentment usually **tiresomely**

例 carp about the order of names on the wedding invitations 对于婚礼请柬上的名单顺序吹毛求疵

近 cavil, fuss, niggle, nitpick, gripe, grizzle, grouch, grouse, grumble, wail

Unit 2

◼ CARVE	◼ CAST	◼ CASTIGATE	◼ CATALYZE	◼ CATASTROPHE
◼ CATEGORICAL	◼ CATHOLIC	◼ CAUSTIC	◼ CAVEAT	◼ CAVIL

carve [kɑːrv]

【考法1】 *v.* 雕刻：to create a **three-dimensional representation** of（something）using solid material

例 carve a statue out of rare marble 用纯的大理石雕刻一尊雕像

近 sculpture

【考法2】 *v.*（通过长期不懈努力）开创，开拓：to **produce or bring about** especially by long or repeated effort

例 He finally carved out a niche for the sport in the school's athletic program. 他终于在学校运动计划中寻找到了自己的定位。‖ carve out a way through the enemy 从敌营中杀出一条血路

近 forge, grind out, thrash out, work out, work up

cast [kæst]

【考法1】 *n.* 演员，演员阵容：**a set of characters** or persons

【考法2】 *vt.* 选派（演员）：to **assign**（as an **actor**）to a role or part

近 He was cast in the leading role. 他被选为男一号。

【考法3】 *vt.* 提出：to put forth, **give off**, to place as if by throwing

例 cast doubt on their reliability 对它们的可靠性提出质疑

近 discharge, emanate, irradiate, issue, shoot, throw out, give out

【考法4】 *v.* 抛弃：to **get rid of** as useless or unwanted

例 Once she became rich and didn't need them anymore, she cast off all her old friends like so much junk. 当她有钱了不再需要朋友了，她把老友像糟粕一样抛弃了。

近 ditch, dump, jettison, toss

castigate [ˈkæstɪgeɪt]

【考法1】 *vt.* 强烈（公开）指责：to **criticize** harshly and usually publicly

例 The author castigated the prime minister as an ineffective leader. 该作者谴责首相行政无作为。

近 berate, chastise, lambaste, reprimand, reproach, rebuke, vituperate, excoriate, rail（at or against）

反 approbate, accolade, extol 认可，赞美

【考法 2】 *vt.* 惩罚: to inflict a **penalty** on for a fault or crime

例 a judge who believes in castigating criminals to the full extent of the law 认为应该最大程度地惩罚罪犯的法官

近 chasten, chastise, correct, discipline, penalize

反 excuse, pardon, spare 宽恕

catalyze [ˈkætəlaɪz]

【考法】 *vt.* 成为…的导火索，导致: to **be the cause of** (a situation, action, or state of mind)

例 A reinstitution of the draft would catalyze protests around the country. 草案的提出会激发全国范围的抗议。

近 breed, beget, effectuate, engender, generate, prompt, spawn, yield, result in , bring (about)

反 retard, prevent, inhibit 阻挠，抑制

派 catalyst *n.* 催化剂: an agent that provokes or speeds significant change or action

例 a catalyst for change of lifestyle 生活方式变化的催化剂

反 inhibitor 抑制剂

catastrophe [kəˈtæstrəfi]

【考法 1】 *n.* 大灾难: the final event of the dramatic action especially of a **tragedy**

近 apocalypse, calamity, cataclysm, debacle, tragedy

【考法 2】 *n.* 彻底的失败: **utter failure**: fiasco

例 The party was a catastrophe. 该派对就是一个杯具。

近 bummer, debacle, disaster, fiasco, fizzle, washout

反 blockbuster, hit, smash, success, winner 大胜

categorical [ˌkætəˈɡɔːrɪkl]

【考法】 *adj.* 没有例外的，无条件限制的；绝对的: being **without** exception or **qualification**; **absolute**

例 a categorical denial 完全的否认

近 definite, downright, fair, utter, thorough, unalloyed, unconditional, unqualified

反 conditional, qualified 有条件的

catholic [ˈkæθlɪk]

【考法】 *adj.* 普遍的，包容的: **not limited or specialized** in application or purpose

例 a catholic taste in music 对于音乐的兼容并包的品味

近 unlimited, unqualified, unrestricted, unspecialized, all-around (also all-round)

反 narrow, limited, restricted, specialized 狭隘的

caustic [ˈkɔːstɪk]

【考法 1】 *adj.* 腐蚀性的: capable of **destroying** or **eating away** by chemical action: corrosive

例 The chemical was so caustic that it ate through the pipes. 化学性质具有如此强的腐蚀性，把管道都腐蚀了。

反 palliating 减缓的

【考法 2】 *adj.* 挖苦讽刺的，刻薄的: marked by **incisive sarcasm**

例 caustic movie reviews 尖酸刻薄的影评

近 acerbic, acrid, barbed, mordant, pungent, sardonic, satiric, scathing, sharp

反 genial, smooth, kind, innocuous 和蔼的，（言论行为等）无害的

caveat [ˈkæviæt]

【考法】 *n.* 警告，告诫: a **warning of a specific limitation** of something such as information or an agreement

例 a final caveat 最终的告诫

近 warning, admonish

cavil [ˈkævl]

【考法】 *v.* 挑剔，吹毛求疵: to find fault unnecessarily; raise trivial objections: **quibble**

例 Let us not cavil too much. 我们别太挑剔。 ‖ cavil about the price of a cup of coffee 对一杯咖啡的价钱挑剔

近 carp, fuss, niggle, nitpick, quibble

Unit 3

| ■ CAVORT | ■ CEDE | ■ CEMENT | ■ CENSOR | ■ CENSORIOUS |
| ■ CENSURE | ■ CENSUS | ■ CESSATION | ■ CHAFF | ■ CHAGRIN |

cavort [kəˈvɔːrt]

【考法】 *vi.* 欢快地蹦跳或行走，雀跃: to bound or prance about in a **sprightly** manner; caper

例 Children are cavorting in the sand. 孩子们在沙子中嬉戏。

近 caper, disport, frisk, gambol, rollick, romp

反 trudge 蹒跚地走

	cede	[siːd]
	【考法】	*vt.* (根据条约)放弃，割让：to **surrender possession of**, especially by treaty
例		cede the island to America 把岛屿割让给了美国
近		relinquish, render, yield, renounce, resign, turn in, turn over, step aside (from), give up, hand over, lay down
反		possess 拥有

	cement	[sɪˈment]
	【考法】	*n./v.* 粘合，粘合剂：a **uniting** or **binding** force or influence
例		Justice is the cement that holds a political community together. 正义是让政治个体团结的粘合剂。
近		cord, knot, link, tie

	censor	[ˈsensər]
	【考法】	*vt.* 审查并删除不良的东西：to **examine** in order to suppress or **delete** anything considered objectionable
例		censor the news 审查新闻
近		bowdlerize, expurgate, red-pencil, clean up
派		censorship *n.* 审查制度

	censorious	[senˈsɔːriəs]
	【考法】	*adj.* 挑剔指责的：highly **critical**
例		censorious comment 尖刻的评论
反		eulogistic 赞美的

	censure	[ˈsenʃər]
	【考法】	*v.* 公开表示反对，谴责：to express **public** or **formal disapproval** of
例		He was censured by the committee for his failure to report the problem. 他因为未上报事故受到了委员会的指责。
近		condemn, denounce, objurgate, rebuke, reprimand, reproach, reprehend, pan
反		commend, extol, laud, endorse 支持，赞同

	census	[ˈsensəs]
	【考法】	*n.* 人口普查：an official **survey** of the **population** of a country that is carried out in order to find out how many people live there and to obtain details of such things as people's ages and jobs
近		tale, tally

	cessation	[seˈseɪʃn]
	【考法】	*n.* 终止，暂停：the **stopping of a process** or activity
例		The cessation of the storm was a relief. 暴风雪终于停了，真是让人欣慰。
近		check, cutoff, closure, discontinuance, expiration, halt, shutdown, termination
反		commencement, start, continuation 开始，继续

	chaff	[tʃæf]
	【考法】	*v.* 开玩笑：to **make jokes**
例		A coworker likes to chaff at others' expense, and this often results in hurt feelings. 同事喜欢开别人玩笑，往往会伤害他人感情。
近		banter, jape, jest, quip

	chagrin	[ʃəˈɡrɪn]
	【考法】	*n.* （因为失败、出糗而导致的）不安，焦虑：disquietude or **distress of mind** caused by humiliation, disappointment, or failure
例		Edgar's chagrin at having bungled the simple assignment was clear from his trembling lips and averted eyes. 从埃德加颤抖的嘴唇和躲闪的目光中可以看出他搞砸简单任务之后的不安。
近		anxiety, concern, disquiet, inquietude, restiveness, solicitude, unease, unrest, worry
反		aplomb, composure, countenance, equanimity, sangfroid 镇定自若，淡定

Unit 4

■ CHAMELEON	■ CHAMPION	■ CHAOS	■ CHARADE	■ CHARLATAN
■ CHARY	■ CHASE	■ CHASM	■ CHAUVINISTIC	■ CHECK

	chameleon	[kəˈmiːliən]
	【考法】	*n.* 变色龙，善变的人：a person who dexterously and expediently **changes or adopts opinions**
例		At the summer resort he acquired a reputation as a social chameleon—someone who could be whatever his hosts wanted him to be. 在度假胜地，他被称为"社交多面手"——可以变成主人想要的任何角色。
近		chancer, opportunist, temporizer, timeserver, trimmer, weathercock

champion ['tʃæmpiən]

【考法】 *vt.* 支持: to fight for, defend, or **support** as a champion

例 champion the cause of civil rights 支持民权事业

近 advocate, back, endorse, patronize, plump for

反 disparage, impugn, oppose 贬低，反对

chaos ['keiɑːs]

【考法】 *n.* 混乱: a condition or place of great **disorder** or **confusion**

例 The boy's room is in such chaos that it looks as though a tornado had struck. 小男孩的房间如此混乱，看起来像台风来袭。

近 disarrangement, dishevelment, disorder, disarray, havoc, mess, muddle, jumble, welter

反 order 有秩序

派 chaotic *adj.* 混乱的，无序的: happening in a state of complete disorder and confusion

反 strictly structured 构造严谨的

charade [ʃəˈreɪd]

【考法 1】 *n.* 装模作样: a display of emotion or behavior that is insincere or **intended to deceive**

例 His concern was a charade. 他的关心只是装模作样。

近 disguise, façade, playacting, pretense, put-on, semblance

【考法 2】 *n.* 动作字谜: a game in which **words** or phrases are **represented in pantomime**

charlatan [ˈʃɑːrlətən]

【考法】 *n.* 骗子，装懂的人: a person who makes elaborate, **fraudulent**, and often voluble claims to skill or knowledge; a quack or fraud

例 The famed broker turned out to be a charlatan. 一位有声望的经纪人结果是个骗子。

近 fake, fraud, hoaxer, mountebank, phony, pretender, quack, imposter

chary [ˈtʃeri]

【考法】 *adj.* 非常谨慎的: very **cautious**

例 chary investors who weren't burned by the dot-com bust 那些没有受到互联网萧条影响的谨慎投资者们

近 alert, cautious, circumspect, conservative, gingerly, guarded, heedful, wary

反 rash, bold 鲁莽的

chase [tʃeɪs]

【考法 1】 *v.* 镂雕(金属)以装饰: to **decorate** (metal) by engraving or embossing

【考法 2】 *v.* 驱赶: to drive or **force out**

例 chase the cat out of the garden 把猫赶出园子

近 banish, dismiss, expel, extrude, kick out, cast out

chasm [ˈkæzəm]

【考法】 *n.* 分歧, (意见、利益或忠诚上的)明显差异: a **pronounced difference** of opinion, interests, or loyalty

近 contradiction, dissent, disjunction, discord, conflict, rift, rivalry, dichotomy

chauvinistic [ˌʃoʊvɪˈnɪstɪk]

【考法】 *adj.* 盲目爱国的: having or showing **excessive favoritism** towards one's own country

例 At times I have also been aggressive, chauvinistic and hot-tempered. 我曾经非常好斗，热烈爱国，还脾气暴躁。

近 jingoist, jingoistic, nationalistic, superpatriotic

check [tʃek]

【考法 1】 *vt.* 使突然停止，阻止: to **arrest** the motion **abruptly**

例 A tree finally checked the skidding car. 一辆滑行的车终于被大树停住了。

近 arrest, stall, bridle, contain, curb, tame, bring up, draw up, hold up, pull up

反 propagate, goad, hasten 扩增，驱使，促进

【考法 2】 *v.* 同意，一致: to be **in agreement** on every point

例 Their story of what happened checks with the report of the eyewitness. 他们的说法和目击者的供词一致。

近 accord, cohere, conform, correspond, dovetail, fit, harmonize, jibe, tally

反 differ, disagree with 反对

Unit 5

cherubic [tʃəˈruːbik]

【考法】 *adj.* 天使般可爱的 : innocent-looking usually chubby and **rosy**

例 A representation of Cupid as a naked, cherubic boy usually is used as a symbol of love. 丘比特作为小天使般的少年裸体画像被用作爱的象征。

反 fiendish, devilish 恶魔般的

chicanery [ʃɪˈkeɪnəri]

【考法】 *n.* 诡计多端，欺骗 : **deception** by artful subterfuge or sophistry

例 Well-doer never does chicanery and person who is good at chicanery does not belong well-doer. 善者不辩，辩者不善。‖ He wasn't above using chicanery to win votes. 他不是用欺骗来赢得选票的。

近 deception, artifice, legerdemain, wile, subterfuge

反 aboveboard action 光明正大的行为; honest dealing 诚实的行为; forthrightness 坦白

chide [tʃaɪd]

【考法】 *v.* 责备 : to **scold mildly** so as to correct or improve

例 My wife chided me for forgetting to offer our guests some refreshments. 我妻子责备我忘记给客人们上点心。

近 reprove, reprimand, reproach, tick off

反 praise, commend 称赞

choleric [ˈkɑːlərɪk]

【考法 1】 *adj.* 易怒的，暴躁的 : easily **angered**; bad-tempered

例 choleric disposition 易怒的性情 ‖ Men of the choleric type take to kicking and smashing. 易怒的人喜欢踢和打碎东西。

近 crabby, cranky, irascible, peevish, petulant, bad-tempered, hot-tempered, short-tempered, testy

反 difficult to provoke, pacific, placid, calm, serene, tranquil, composed, nonchalant 难以被激怒的，平静的

派 choler *n.* 易怒 : ready disposition to irritation: irascibility also: anger

【考法 2】 *adj.* 生气的 : feeling or showing **anger**: angry, **irate**

例 I absolutely get choleric when a salesman calls during the dinner hour. 当一个推销员午休时间打来电话的时候，我彻底愤怒了。

近 angered, apoplectic, ballistic, enraged, furious, incensed, inflamed, enflamed, infuriated, irate, ireful, outraged, rankled, riled, wrathful

反 angerless, delighted, pleased 不生气的; 高兴的

chord [kɔːrd]

【考法】 *vi.* 与…和谐一致; 符合 : to be in **accord**; **agree**

例 The revised system chords perfectly with the original goals. 新版的系统非常符合最初的目标。

近 accord, agree, conform, consist, correspond, dovetail, fit, harmonize, jibe, rhyme, square, tally

反 differ from, disagree with 与……不同，有分歧

chromatic [krəˈmætɪk]

【考法】 *adj.* 彩色的 : relating to **colors** or color

例 the chromatic paintings of Matisse and the other Fauvists 马蒂斯和其他野兽派画家的彩色画

近 colored, colorful, motley, multicolored, multihued, varicolored, variegated, kaleidoscopic

反 colorless, pallid, blanched 无色的; monochromatic, monochromic, monotone, self-colored 单色的

chronic [ˈkrɑːnɪk]

【考法 1】 *adj.* 经常发生的，复发的 : marked by long duration or **frequent recurrence**

例 chronic disease 慢性病

近 frequent, usual, routine

反 sporadic 偶然发生的; infrequent 不经常的

【考法 2】 *adj.* 习惯性的，不可能改变的 : being such by habit and **not likely** to **change**

例 a chronic smoker who has quit many times 一个戒了很多次烟的老烟民

近 inveterate

churl [tʃɜːrl]

【考法 1】 *n.* 粗野的人：a **rude**, **boorish** person

例 By the 19th century, "churl" had a new and pejorative meaning, "one inclined to uncivil or loutish behavior". 19 世纪的时候，churl 有了一个新的带有贬义的意思，即"一个粗鲁没有教养的人"。

近 boor, lout

派 churlish *adj.* 粗野的，暴躁的：of, like, or befitting a churl; boorish or vulgar

近 crude, coarse, boorish, loutish, uncultured, unpolished

反 genteel, complaisant, courtly, polished 文雅的，彬彬有礼的；sophisticated 机智圆滑的

【考法 2】 *n.* 吝啬鬼：a **mean** grasping person who is usually **stingy** with money

例 Don't bother asking a churl for donations. 别自找麻烦向一个吝啬鬼要捐款。

近 miser, niggard, skinflint, penny-pincher

反 generous/liberal/munificent person 慷慨的人；waster, wastrel, spendthrift, prodigal, profligate, dissipater 败家子

cipher ['saɪfər]

【考法 1】 *n.* 无影响或无价值的人：a person of **no importance** or **influence**

例 The intern is a mere cipher in the company. 这个实习生在公司里是个无足轻重的小人物。

近 dwarf, half-pint, insect, insignificancy, lightweight, morsel, nonentity, nothing, nullity, snippersnapper, whippersnapper, zero

反 big shot, big wheel, bigwig, eminence, figure, personage 要人，名人

【考法 2】 *v.* 计算（价值）：to **determine** (a value) by doing the necessary **mathematical operations**

例 We were surprised by how much we had spent on the cruise after we had ciphered out the grand total. 当我们算出我们沉船游览的总花费时，我们都惊呆了。

近 compute, work out

【考法 3】 *n.* 密码：a method of transforming a text in order to **conceal** its meaning

例 convert their messages into cipher 把他们的信息转换成密码

近 code, secret message

circuitous [sərˈkjuːɪtəs]

【考法 1】 *adj.* 迂回的，不直接的：**not** being **forthright** or **direct** in language or action

例 We took a circuitous route to the airport so as to avoid the massive traffic jam. 我们走了一条迂回的路线去机场来躲避堵车。

近 indirect, circular, roundabout

反 direct, straight, straightforward 直接的

派 circuity *n.* 不直接：lack of straightforwardness

反 straightforwardness, direction 直接

【考法 2】 *adj.* 冗长的：using or containing **more** words than **necessary** to express an idea

例 a circuitous explanation for what seems like a fairly basic concept 对一个非常基本的概念的冗长解释

近 circumlocutory, diffuse, long-winded, prolix, rambling, verbose, windy

反 compact, concise, pithy, succinct, terse 简洁的

Unit 6

> ■ CIRCUMLOCUTION　　■ CIRCUMSCRIBE　　■ CIRCUMSPECT　　■ CIRCUMVENT　　■ CIVILITY
> ■ CLAIM　　　　　　　■ CLANDESTINE　　　■ CLARION　　　　■ CLARITY　　　　■ CLASP

circumlocution [ˌsɜːrkəmləˈkjuːʃn]

【考法 1】 *n.* 绕圈子的说话：the use of **unnecessarily** wordy and **indirect** language, **evasion** in speech

例 The other son of your parents' is a circumlocution for your brother. 你父母的"另一个儿子"是你"兄弟"的绕圈子的说法。

近 equivocation, shuffle, tergiversation

反 pithy utterance, straightforward utterance, succinct expression 简洁的表达；direct encounter 直接面对

派 circumlocutory *adj.* 绕圈子的

反 direct 直接的

【考法 2】 *n.* 冗长：the use of **too many** words to express an idea

例 Your papers have to be five pages long, but that's five pages of substance, not circumlocution. 你的论文要求 5 页，但是那 5 页都是实质内容，不是废话。

近 diffuseness, diffusion, long-windedness, prolixity, redundancy, verbalism, verboseness, verbosity, windiness, wordage, wordiness

反 conciseness, concision, pithiness, succinctness, terseness 简洁

circumscribe [ˈsɜːkəmskraɪb]

【考法 1】 *vt.* 限制：to **limit** narrowly; restrict
例 Teammates circumscribed his enthusiasm so as not to make the losing side feel worse. 队员们抑制了他们的热情，为了不让失败者更难过。
近 cap, limit, confine, delimit, restrict
反 exceed 超过，超越

【考法 2】 *vt.* 包围，围绕：to **surround** by or as if by a boundary
例 fields circumscribed by tall trees 被高树包围的地方 ‖ Circumscribe a circle around a square. 画正方形的外接圆。
近 surround, encompass

circumspect [ˈsɜːrkəmspekt]

【考法】 *adj.* 谨慎的，小心的：**careful** to consider all circumstances and possible consequences: prudent
例 The banks should have been more circumspect in their dealings. 银行本应该在它们的交易当中更加谨慎。
近 alert, careful, gingerly, guarded, heedful, prudent, cautious, chary, wary
反 careless, incautious, unmindful, unwary 不小心的，不谨慎的；audacious, reckless 大胆的，鲁莽的

circumvent [ˌsɜːrkəmˈvent]

【考法】 *vt.* 躲避，不遵从：to **avoid** having to **comply** with (something) especially through cleverness
例 circumvent all the red tape 绕过所有官方程序繁文缛节 ‖ He found a way to circumvent the law. 他发现了一个逃避法律的方法。
近 avoid, bypass, dodge, sidestep, skirt, get around
反 comply with, follow, obey, observe 遵从；confront, directly encounter 直接面对

civility [səˈvɪləti]

【考法】 *n.* 彬彬有礼：**courteous** behavior; **politeness**
例 They greeted us with civility. 他们有礼貌地招呼我们。
近 politeness, courtesy, politeness, genteelness, gentility, graciousness
反 discourteousness, discourtesy, impoliteness, incivility, rudeness, surliness, ungraciousness 无礼，粗鲁

claim [kleɪm]

【考法 1】 *n./v.* 要求（权利）：to **ask for** especially as a **right**
例 a fragile claim to fame 对名誉不切实际的要求 ‖ After many years had passed, he suddenly appeared to claim his inheritance. 很多年已经过去，他突然出现并要求继承遗产。
近 call for, command, quest
反 renounce 放弃

【考法 2】 *vt.* 断言：to **state as a fact** usually forcefully
例 People claim that they have been kidnapped by aliens. 人们断言，他们被外星人绑架了。
近 allege, assert
反 deny, gainsay 否认

【考法 3】 *vt.* 剥夺生命：to **deprive** of **life**
例 Cancer claims hundreds of thousands of Americans each year. 癌症每年要剥夺成千上万美国人的生命。
反 animate 使有生命

【考法 4】 *n.* 权利：a legal **right** to participation in the advantages, profits, and responsibility of something
例 A shareholder has a claim in the business. 股东在企业中有权利(收益权、选举权等)。

clandestine [klænˈdestɪn]

【考法】 *adj.* 隐藏的，秘密的：kept or done in **secret**, often in order to conceal an **illicit** or **improper** purpose
例 their clandestine love affair 他们的秘密恋情
近 secret, covert, furtive, surreptitious, sneaky, stealthy, undercover, underground, underhand, underhanded
反 open, overt, public 公开的；aboveboard 光明正大的

clarion [ˈklæriən]

【考法】 *adj.* 清楚响亮的：**loud** and **clear**
例 clarion call for democracy 对民主的高声呼吁 ‖ *The internationale* is a clarion call to the labouring people of the world. 《国际歌》是唤起全世界劳动人民的响亮号角。
反 soft and indistinct 柔和模糊的

clarity [ˈklærəti]

【考法 1】 *n.* 清晰，清楚：the quality or state of being **clear**: **lucidity**
例 Clarity of diction is vital for a XDF teacher. 发音清楚对新东方老师来说是至关重要的。
近 clarity, explicitness, lucidity, lucidness, perspicuity, perspicuousness
反 obscureness, obscurity, unclarity 模糊，不清晰
派 clarify *v.* 澄清，使清晰：to free of confusion
例 clarify his mind 理清思路；clarify a subject 澄清某一问题
近 purify, clear, elucidate, explain, illuminate, illustrate
反 obfuscate, obscure 使模糊

【考法 2】 *n.* 清澈透明: the state or quality of being **easily seen through**

例 mountain streams with water of incredible clarity 难以置信的清澈透明的山涧

近 clearness, limpidity, limpidness, translucence, translucency, transparency

反 cloudiness, opacity, opaqueness, turbidity, turbidness 浑浊, 不透明

clasp [klæsp]

【考法】 *n./v.* 紧握: the act or manner of **holding**

例 Be careful that your clasp on the cat isn't too tight, or she could get hurt. 注意别抓那只猫太紧, 否则她会受伤的。

近 clench, grapple, grasp, grip, handgrip, handhold

Unit 7

■ CLEMENT	■ CLICHÉ	■ CLOG	■ CLOT	■ CLOUDBURST
■ CLOUT	■ CLOYING	■ CLUMSY	■ COAGULATE	■ COALESCE

clement ['klemənt]

【考法 1】 *adj.* 宽容的, 善良的: **tolerant** and **kind** in the judgment of and expectations for others

例 Clement judge reduced the sentence. 仁慈的法官减轻了刑罚。

近 charitable, lenient, merciful

反 harsh, severe, stern, strict 严厉的, 严格的

派 clemency *n.* 仁慈

【考法 2】 *adj.* 气候温和的: marked by temperatures that are **neither** too **high** nor too **low**

例 Hawaii is known for its delightfully clement climate. 夏威夷以它宜人的温和气候著称。

近 mild, genial, gentle, balmy, equable

反 harsh, inclement, severe 严酷的

cliché [kliːˈʃeɪ]

【考法】 *n./adj.* 陈词滥调(的): a **hackneyed** theme, characterization, or situation

例 Cliché is a feature of bad news. 拙劣新闻的特征是使用陈词滥调。

近 banality, bromide, platitude; trite, bathetic, hackneyed, stereotypical

反 fresh, new, original, creative 新的, 创造性的

clog [klɑːɡ]

【考法 1】 *n.* 阻碍物: **something** that makes **movement** or **progress difficult**

例 impede with a clog 用障碍物阻止

近 balk, bar, block, deterrent, drag, fetter, holdback, hurdle, impediment, inhibition, interference, obstacle, obstruction, shackles, stop, stumbling block, trammel

【考法 2】 *v.* 阻碍: to create **difficulty** for the work or activity of

例 They always clog the courts. 他们一直阻挠法庭工作。

近 encumber, fetter, hinder, hold back, hold up, impede, inhibit, interfere with, obstruct, shackle, stymie, tie up, trammel

反 aid, assist, help 帮助; facilitate 促进

【考法 3】 *v.* 堵塞: to **prevent** passage **through** by filling with something

例 Within a few years the pipe began to clog up. 没有几年, 管子就开始堵塞了。

近 block, choke, clot, gum up, jam, obstruct, occlude, stop up, stuff

反 clear, free, open up, unblock, unclog, unstop 清除, 排除障碍

clot [klɑːt]

【考法 1】 *n.* 密集的一群: **a number of things** considered as **a unit**

例 A clot of daisies occupied one corner of the flower bed. 一簇雏菊占据了花床的一角。

近 array, assemblage, band, block, bunch, cluster, clutch, collection, constellation, grouping, huddle, knot, lot, muster, package

【考法 2】 *v.* 堵塞: to **prevent** passage **through** by **filling with something**

近 block, choke, clog, gum up, jam, obstruct, occlude, stop up, stuff

反 clear, free, open up, unblock, unclog, unstop 清除, 排除障碍

【考法 3】 *v.* 凝结: to turn from a liquid into a substance resembling **jelly**

例 Scabs form over cuts when your blood starts to clot. 当血液开始凝结的时候, 伤口处会形成血痂。

近 congeal, jell, jelly

cloudburst	[ˈklaʊdbɜːrst]
【考法】	n. 突然一场暴雨 : a sudden copious **rainfall**
例	The weatherman warned of possible cloudbursts in the afternoon. 天气预报员警告下午可能有暴雨。
近	downfall, downpour

◯ clout	[klaʊt]
【考法】	n. 权力，影响力 : **influence**; pull
例	The queen may have privilege but she has no real political clout. 女王有特权，但无真正的政治影响力。
近	power, influence, capacity, heft, leverage
反	impuissance, impotence 无力

◯ cloying	[ˈklɔɪɪŋ]
【考法】	adj. 甜得发腻的；感情用事的 : excessively **sweet**; **sentimental**
例	the cloying sentiments of so many Mother's Day cards 这么多母亲节贺卡(所蕴含)的甜蜜感情
近	lovey-dovey, maudlin, mawkish, saccharine, sentimental
反	unsentimental 不动感情的

clumsy	[ˈklʌmzi]
【考法 1】	adj. 笨拙的 : **lacking** or showing a lack of **nimbleness** in using one's hands; a **lack** of **skill** and tact
例	turn out to be a clumsy sleight of hand 弄巧成拙
近	awkward, ham-handed, heavy-handed, maladroit, unhandy, bungling, inept
反	adroit, deft, dexterous, handy 熟练的，灵巧的
【考法 2】	adj. 不文雅的 : **lacking** social **grace** and assurance; showing an **inability** to move in a **graceful** manner
例	be clumsy on the dance floor 在舞池里表现不优雅的
近	awkward, graceless, ungainly, gauche, inelegant, rustic, ungraceful
反	graceful, urbane, refined 优雅的
【考法 3】	adj. 不精致的 : hastily or **roughly** constructed
例	a clumsy mock-up of the real thing 一个粗糙的实物模型
近	rough, unrefined
反	refined 精致的

coagulate	[koʊˈægjuleɪt]
【考法】	v. (使)凝结，(使)变稠 : to (cause to) become viscous or thickened into a **coherent** mass: curdle, **clot**
例	The blood coagulates to stop wounds bleeding. 血液会凝结以防止伤口流血。
近	clot, congeal, jelly
反	melt, liquefy, fluidify, dissolve 融化，溶解；thin 使变稀薄
派	coagulant n. 凝结剂 : an agent that causes a liquid to coagulate

coalesce	[ˌkoʊəˈles]
【考法】	v. 合并，融合 : to unite into a **whole**: **fuse**
例	Different units coalesced into one army. 不同的党派融合成了一支部队。
近	associate, combine, conjoin, connect, couple, fuse, interfuse, join, link (up), unify, unite
反	break up, dissever, section, separate, sever, split, sunder, unlink, disband 分开，解散

Unit 8

■ COAX	■ CODA	■ COERCE	■ COEVAL	■ COGENT
■ COGNIZANT	■ COLLAPSE	■ COLLUDE	■ COLOSSAL	■ COLTISH

coax	[koʊks]
【考法】	v. 哄骗 : to persuade or try to persuade by **pleading** or **flattery**; **cajole**
例	coax a child to take his medicine 哄小孩吃药
近	blandish, cajole, wheedle, palaver

◯ coda	[ˈkoʊdə]
【考法】	n. 终曲 : the **concluding passage** of a movement or composition
例	A song includes prelude, loud song and coda. 一首歌包括前奏、高潮和尾声。
近	finale, epilogue
反	overture, prelude 前奏

coerce [koʊˈɜːrs]

【考法】 *vt.* (以武力)强制：to achieve by **force** or **threat**

例 be coerced into agreeing 被迫同意 ‖ A confession was coerced from the suspect by police. 嫌犯被警察逼供。

近 force, threaten, compel

派 coercion *n.* 强力压迫：the act of persuading someone forcefully to do something that they do not want to do

反 voluntary behavior 自愿的行为

coeval [koʊˈiːvl]

【考法】 *adj.* 同时代的，同龄的：of the same or **equal age**, antiquity, or duration

例 Two stars thought to be coeval because they have nearly the same mass and brightness. 两个星星被认为是同龄，因为他们的质量和亮度几乎相同。

近 coetaneous, coexisting, concurrent, contemporaneous, simultaneous, synchronic, synchronous

反 asynchronous, noncontemporary, nonsimultaneous 不同时的

cogent [ˈkoʊdʒənt]

【考法 1】 *adj.* 令人信服的：appealing forcibly to the mind or reason: **convincing**

例 Six Sigma is one of the most cogent methods for modern enterprises to control quality and optimizing process. "六西格玛"方法是现代企业进行质量控制和工艺优化最令人信服的方法之一。

近 convincing, compelling, conclusive, telling, persuasive, satisfying

反 unconvincing, unpersuasive 不令人信服的

【考法 2】 *adj.* 相关的：**pertinent**, relevant

例 a cogent analysis 一项相关的研究

近 apropos, germane, relative, relevant

反 extraneous, irrelevant, impertinent, irrelative 无关的

cognizant [ˈkɑːɡnɪzənt]

【考法】 *adj.* 知道的，意识到的：fully informed; conscious; **aware**

例 We are cognizant of the problem. 我们已经意识到了这个问题。

近 aware, conscious, witting, apprehensive, sensible

反 oblivious, unconscious, unaware, unmindful 没意识到的

派 incognizance *n.* 不认识；没知觉

collapse [kəˈlæps]

【考法 1】 *vi./n.* 突然倒塌或收缩：to **fall** or **shrink** together abruptly and completely

例 President Bush is vowing to rebuild the bridge which collapsed last year. 布什总统发誓要重建这座去年坍塌的桥梁。‖ One ant-hole may cause the collapse of a thousand-li dyke. 千里之堤，毁于蚁穴。

近 compact, condense, constrict, constringe, contract, implode, squeeze

反 decompress, expand, open, outspread, outstretch 展开，扩张

【考法 2】 *n.* 完全耗尽体力：a complete **depletion** of **energy** or **strength**

例 He suffered a mental collapse under the strain of studying for his bar exam. 他在紧张的律师考试的复习下脑力消耗殆尽。

近 exhaustion, tiredness, lassitude, weariness

反 refreshment, rejuvenation, revitalization 重新充满活力

【考法 3】 *v./n.* 失败：to be **unsuccessful**; a falling short of one's goals

例 The legal case collapsed in the face of the opposition's evidence. 面对反方的证据，这个法律案件败诉了。

近 defeat, nonachievement, nonsuccess

反 accomplishment, achievement, success 成功，成就

collude [kəˈljuːd]

【考法】 *v.* 串通，共谋（做坏事）：to act **together secretly** to achieve a **fraudulent**, illegal, or **deceitful** purpose; **conspire**

例 collude with competitors to control the price 与竞争者合谋以控制价格

近 connive, conspire, contrive, intrigue, machinate, put up

反 act independently 单独行动

colossal [kəˈlɑːsl]

【考法】 *adj.* 巨大的：of a **size**, **extent**, or **degree** that elicits awe or taxes belief; **immense**

例 a colossal waste of public money 对公共财产的巨大浪费

近 huge, giant, titanic, gargantuan, mammoth, tremendous, elephantine, prodigious

反 tiny, micro, minute, miniature, minuscule, wee, infinitesimal 微小的

| | coltish | ['koʊltɪʃ] |

【考法 1】 *adj.* 不守纪律的：**not subjected** to **discipline**

反 disciplined 遵守纪律的

【考法 2】 *adj.* 爱开玩笑的：given to good-natured **joking** or **teasing**

例 Off camera the actor is high-spiritedly coltish, but turns serious once the camera starts rolling. 镜头下这个演员很喜欢开玩笑，但是当镜头开启，他就马上变得严肃起来。

近 antic, frisky, frolicsome, larky, sportful

反 earnest, serious-minded, sober 严肃的

Unit 9

■ COMA	■ COMBUSTIBLE	■ COMELY	■ COMITY	■ COMMENCEMENT
■ COMMEND	■ COMMENSURATE	■ COMMINGLE	■ COMMITMENT	■ COMMITTED

coma ['koʊmə]

【考法 1】 *n.* 昏迷，深度无知觉：a state of **profound unconsciousness** caused by disease, injury, or poison

例 The girl lay in a coma for three days after the accident. 那个女孩在事故之后昏迷了三天。

近 insensibility, blackout, knockout

反 consciousness, awareness 有知觉

【考法 2】 *n.* 迟钝，冷漠：a state of mental or physical **sluggishness**: torpor

近 sluggish, torpor

反 activity, animation 有活力；alacrity 敏捷

combustible [kəm'bʌstəbl]

【考法 1】 *adj.* 可燃的：capable of **igniting** and burning

例 release a combustible gas 释放出可燃性气体

近 burnable, combustive, flammable, ignitable, inflammable

反 incombustible, nonburnable, noncombustible, nonflammable, noninflammable, unburnable 不可燃的；fire-proof 防火的

【考法 2】 *adj.* 容易激动的：**easily excited**

例 a high-strung combustible temper 一碰就火的性格

近 excitable, agitable, touchy

comely ['kʌmli]

【考法】 *adj.* 漂亮的，吸引人的：**pleasing** and **wholesome** in appearance; **attractive**

例 a comely young woman 年轻美丽的女人

近 attractive, cute, fair, good-looking, gorgeous, handsome, lovely, pretty, ravishing, well-favored, seemly, stunning

反 homely, ill-favored, ugly, unattractive, unbeautiful, uncomely, uncute, unhandsome, unlovely, unpleasing, unpretty 不好看的

comity ['kɑːmɪti]

【考法】 *n.* 友好，社会和谐：**friendly** social atmosphere: social **harmony**

例 group activities promoting comity 促进和谐氛围的团队活动 ‖ comity of nations 国际礼节

近 compatibility, concord, peace

反 conflict, discord, dissension 冲突，不和

commencement [kə'mensmənt]

【考法 1】 *n.* 开始：a **beginning**; a start

例 There was a large turnout at the commencement of the conference, but the numbers dwindled as it progressed. 在会议开始的时候，有很多人出席。但是随着会议的进行，人慢慢变少了。

近 birth, onset, outset, start, genesis, inception, nascence, threshold

反 close, conclusion, end, ending 结束

【考法 2】 *n.* 毕业典礼：the ceremonies or the day for **conferring** degrees or diplomas

例 The purpose of a commencement speaker is to dispense wisdom. 毕业典礼上演讲者的目的是传播智慧。

反 matriculation 录取入学

commend [kə'mend]

【考法 1】 *vt.* 赞扬：to mention with **approbation**: **praise**

例 Jason commended his students' studious attitude. Jason 表扬了他的学生用功的态度。

近 approbate, praise, acclaim, applaud, compliment, eulogize, extol

反 blame, criticize, reprehend, reprobate, chide, rebuke, reprimand, reproach, reprove, censure, admonish berate, deplore, execrate 责备，批评，谴责，憎恶，痛骂

【考法2】 *vt.* 委托保管: to **entrust** for care or preservation
例 I commend my fate into your hands. 我的命运就拜托给你了。
近 commit, delegate, deliver, entrust, confide, consign, hand over
反 hold, keep, retain 保留
【考法3】 *vt.* 推荐: to **recommend** as worthy of confidence or notice
例 I commend this book to anyone interested in learning more about American history. 我把这本书推荐给所有对美国历史感兴趣的人。

commensurate [kə'menʃərət]
【考法1】 *adj.* 同样大小的: **equal** in measure or extent
例 Five yards is commensurate with fifteen feet. 5 码等于 15 英尺。
近 equal, tantamount
反 unequal, disparate, preponderant 不相同的, (重量, 重要性, 数量上) 超过的
【考法2】 *adj.* 相称的, 相当的: corresponding in size or degree; **proportionate**
例 a job commensurate with her abilities 一份与她能力相称的工作
近 commensurable, proportionate
反 disproportionate 不相称的

commingle [kə'mɪŋgl]
【考法】 *v.* 充分混合: to **blend** thoroughly into a harmonious whole
例 Ground waters originating in different beds commingle. 来源于不同层位的地下水相互混合。‖ Fact and fiction commingle in the story. 事实和虚构混合成了故事。
近 amalgamate, fuse, mix, immix, commix, compound, mingle, immingle, intermingle, intermix, merge
反 break down, break up, separate, unmix 分开

commitment [kə'mɪtmənt]
【考法1】 *n.* 致力, 投入: the state or an instance of being **obligated** or emotionally **impelled**
例 a commitment to a cause 投身于某项事业
近 dedication, devotedness, fealty, piety, steadfastness
【考法2】 *n.* 确信: a strong **belief** in something
近 conviction, belief, faith
【考法3】 *n.* 承诺, 表态: the act of **revealing one's view** of
例 He made a commitment to pay the rent on time. 他承诺按时交房租。
反 ambivalence, equivocation 矛盾, 含糊其辞

committed [kə'mɪtɪd]
【考法】 *adj.* 忠诚的, 忠实的: **loyal** to a belief, organization, or group, and willing to work hard for it
例 remain committed to one's youthful ideal 坚持不懈地追求自己年轻时的理想
近 loyal, faithful, allegiant
反 disloyal 不忠诚的
派 noncommittal *adj.* 不明确的: giving no clear indication of attitude or feeling
例 a noncommittal reply 一个不明确的回答
反 confirmable 确定的

Unit 10

■ COMMODIOUS ■ COMMONSENSICAL ■ COMMOTION ■ COMPENDIUM ■ COMPLACENCY
■ COMPLAISANCE ■ COMPLIANT ■ COMPLIMENT ■ COMPLY ■ COMPOSE

commodious [kə'moʊdiəs]
【考法】 *adj.* 宽敞舒适的: comfortably or conveniently **spacious**: roomy
例 a commodious closet 宽敞的衣橱
近 spacious, roomy
反 constricted, cramped, snug, constringed 狭窄的

commonsensical [ˌkɑːmən'sensɪkl]
【考法】 *adj.* 符合常识的, 有依据的: displaying **common sense**, based on **sound** reasoning or information
例 The only commonsensical solution would be to divide the children into groups according to age. 唯一合理的解决办法就是按照年龄把孩子分成组。
近 justified, logical, rational, reasonable, reasoned, valid, well-founded, levelheaded
反 groundless, illogical, invalid, irrational, nonrational, nonsensical, nonvalid, unfounded, uninformed, unjustified, unreasonable, unreasoned, unsound 无逻辑的, 不合理的; preposterous 荒谬的

commotion [kəˈmoʊʃn]

【考法】 *n.*骚乱：an agitated **disturbance**

例 The commotion was created when the nation's top rock band arrived in town. 当全国顶级摇滚乐队来到小镇时，人们骚乱了。

近 tumult, turmoil, pandemonium, hurry-scurry

反 tranquility, calmness, quiet, serenity 安静；order 有序

compendium [kəmˈpendiəm]

【考法1】 *n.*摘要：a brief **summary** of a larger work or of a field of knowledge: **abstract**

例 a compendium of information 资料概要

近 abstract, brief, overview

派 compendious *adj.*简洁而全面的：concise and comprehensive

例 his compendious knowledge of this subject 他关于这一学科的全面知识

近 concise, brief, laconic, compendiary, succinct

【考法2】 目录：各种项目的列表或集合：a **list** or **collection** of various items

例 Compendium of Materia Medica《本草纲目》

近 compilation, miscellany

complacency [kəmˈpleɪsnsi]

【考法】 *n.*自满，无忧患意识：a feeling of **self-satisfaction**, coupled with an **unawareness of trouble**

例 Complacency is the enemy of study. 自满乃学习之敌。‖ A momentary complacency was quickly dispelled by the shock of cold reality. 短暂的自满很快就被残酷的现实赶跑了。

近 conceit, pomposity, pompousness, pride, self-admiration, self-assumption, smugness, vanity

反 anxiety 忧虑；humbleness, humility, modesty 谦虚

complaisance [kəmˈpleɪzəns]

【考法】 *n.*愿意顺从，讨好，彬彬有礼：disposition to please or **comply**: **affability**

例 She speaks with complaisance. 她说话彬彬有礼。‖ The complaisance of his girlfriend is such that she meekly goes along with everything he says. 他的女朋友讨好他，对他言听计从。

近 affability, amenability, amiability, good-naturedness

反 obstinacy 固执；churlishness 粗野

compliant [kəmˈplaɪənt]

【考法】 *adj.*顺从的：ready or disposed to comply: **submissive**

例 a corrupt regime aided by a compliant television station 一个在顺从的电视台帮助下的腐败政府

近 amenable, conformable, docile, submissive, tractable

反 balky, contumacious, disobedient, incompliant, insubordinate, intractable, noncompliant, obstreperous, rebel, rebellious, recalcitrant, refractory, unamenable, ungovernable, unruly, willful, wayward 顽固的，难驾驭的

compliment *n.* [ˈkɑːmplɪmənt] *v.* [ˈkɑːmplɪment]

【考法1】 *n./vt.*称赞，恭维：an expression of **praise**, admiration, or congratulation

例 a man meriting the compliments and homage of his fellows 一个值得他的伙伴们尊敬和称赞的人

近 praise, commend, eulogize, extol, laud

反 vituperate 责骂

派 complimentary *adj.*称赞的：expressing or containing a compliment

反 vituperative 责骂的

【考法2】 *n.*敬意，免费赠送的礼物：formal and **respectful** recognition: honor

例 How about a delicious dessert then, with our compliment? 给您上点甜点怎么样，算是我们小小的敬意。

comply [kəmˈplaɪ]

【考法】 *vi.*遵从：to **conform**, **submit**, or adapt （as to a regulation or to another's wishes）as required or requested

例 The devices comply with industry standards. 该设备符合工业标准。‖ There will be penalties against individuals who fail to comply. 谁不遵从谁就会受到惩罚。

近 conform, submit, observe

反 defy, disobey, rebel against, violate, breach, transgress 违背

compose [kəmˈpoʊz]

【考法1】 *vt.*使镇定：to free from agitation: **calm**

例 She took a deep breath and composed herself. 她做了一个深呼吸，使自己安定下来。

近 contain, settle

反 agitate, discompose, disquiet, disturb, perturb, upset, vex 使激动，使不安

派 composed *adj.*镇静的，安定的：free from agitation: calm

反 distraught, restless 发狂的，不平静的

派 composure *n.*镇定：a calmness or repose especially of mind, bearing, or appearance

例 composed of many ingredients 由很多配料组成
近 constitute, comprise, make up

Ordinary people merely think how they shall spend their time; a man of talent tries to use it. 普通人只想到如何度过时间，有才能的人设法利用时间。

——德国哲学家 叔本华（Arthur Schopenhauer, German philosopher）

List 5

"最初的梦想要靠坚持才能到达，一路上的无限风景见证着我的勇敢与执着。"
（罗弥，2007 年 10 月，Verbal 730，Quantitative 800，AW 6.0）

Unit 1

■ COMPOUND	■ COMPRESS	■ COMPROMISE	■ COMPUNCTION	■ CONCATENATE
■ CONCAVE	■ CONCEAL	■ CONCEDE	■ CONCENTRATE	■ CONCERTED

compound
- 【考法 1】 [ˈkɑːmpaʊnd] *n.* 混和物：**something composed** of or resulting from union of separate elements, ingredients, or parts
  - 例 mixed the chemicals together to form a new compound 将化学试剂混合形成新的化合物
  - 近 admixture, alloy, amalgam, amalgamation, cocktail, combination, composite, fusion, intermixture, meld, mix, conflation, synthesis
- 【考法 2】 [ˈkɑːmpaʊnd] *adj.* 混合的：**consisting** of two or more substances, ingredients, elements, or parts
  - 例 a compound word 复合词 ‖ "Steamboat" is a compound noun. "汽船"是一个复合名词。
  - 近 amalgamated
  - 反 noncompound 非混合的
- 【考法 3】 [kəmˈpaʊnd] *vt.* 混合：to put or bring **together** so as to form a new and longer whole
  - 例 the German language's propensity for compounding words 德语喜欢复合单词
  - 近 chain, conjugate, couple, hook, interconnect, interlink, join, link, yoke
  - 反 disconnect, disjoin, disjoint, dissever, disunite, separate, unchain, uncouple, unhitch, unyoke 分开
- 【考法 4】 *v.* 扩大，增多：to make **greater** in size, amount, or number
  - 例 We compounded our error by waiting too long to call for help. 我们等着不寻求帮助增大了我们的错误。
  - 近 aggrandize, amplify, augment, boost, enlarge, escalate, expand, extend, raise, swell
  - 反 abate, decrease, diminish, dwindle, lessen, lower, minify, reduce 缩小，减少
- 【考法 5】 *v.* 和解：to **agree** for a consideration not to prosecute (an offense)
  - 例 compound a felony 私了案件

compress [kəmˈpres]
- 【考法】 *vt.* 压缩(体积)：to **reduce** in **size** or **volume** as if by squeezing
  - 例 compress a computer file 压缩电脑文档 ‖ The science textbook compresses a lot of information about human reproduction into a few short chapters. 科学教科书将人类的繁育知识压缩成了几个短章节。
  - 近 capsule, collapse, compact, condense, constrict, constringe, contract, shrink, telescope
  - 反 increase in volume, decompress, expand, balloon 体积增大；outspread, outstretch 伸展，扩张

compromise [ˈkɑːmprəmaɪz]
- 【考法 1】 *v.* 妥协：to adjust or settle by mutual **concessions**
  - 例 Eventually we reached a compromise on the number of hours per week that would be devoted to piano practice. 最后我们在每周练琴的时间上妥协了。
  - 近 accommodation, negotiation
- 【考法 2】 *vt.* 使危险：to place in **danger**
  - 例 Officials were concerned that his statements would compromise national security. 官员们认为他的言论会危害国家安全。
  - 近 hazard, imperil, jeopardize, menace, peril, venture

compunction [kəmˈpʌŋkʃn]
- 【考法】 *n.* 焦虑，内疚，良心不安：**anxiety** arising from awareness of **guilt**
  - 例 compunction of conscience 良心不安 ‖ a brutal murderer who killed without compunction 一个野蛮没有良心的杀人犯

近 anxiety, misgiving, scruple

反 absence of misgiving 不担忧

concatenate [kənˈkætɪneɪt]

【考法】 *v.* 连结，混合：to put or **bring together** so as to form a new and longer whole

例 The movie actually concatenates several episodes from various books into one extended narrative. 这部电影把很多书中的片段混合成了一个故事。

近 catenate, chain, couple, hook, interconnect, interlink, join, link, yoke

反 disconnect, disjoin, disjoint, dissever, disunite, separate, unchain, uncouple, unhitch, unyoke 分开

concave [kɑːnˈkeɪv]

【考法】 *adj.* 凹的：**curved** like the inner surface of a sphere

例 a concave lens 凹透镜

近 dented, depressed, dished, indented, recessed

反 bulging, convex, protuberant 凸的

conceal [kənˈsiːl]

【考法】 *v.* 隐藏，隐瞒：to **prevent disclosure** or recognition of

例 Drunkenness reveal what soberness conceal. 酒后吐真言。

近 cache, secrete, disguise, mask, occult, ensconce

反 display, exhibit 展示；bare, disclose, expose, reveal, uncover, unmask 揭露

concede [kənˈsiːd]

【考法 1】 *vt.* 承认：to **grant** as a right or privilege

例 She grudgingly conceded his point. 她不情愿地承认了他的观点。

近 acknowledge, grant, confess

反 refuse to grant, deny 拒绝承认，否认

派 concession *n.* 让步：the act of yielding

反 aggression 侵犯

【考法 2】 *v.* 停止抵抗：to **cease resistance** (as to another's arguments, demands, or control)

例 He conceded as soon as it became clear that he could not win. 当他明显赢不了的时候他就停止了抵抗。

近 capitulate, give in, quit, submit, succumb, surrender

反 resist 抵抗

concentrate [ˈkɑːnsntreɪt]

【考法 1】 *v.* 集中：to bring or direct toward a common center or objective：**focus**

例 concentrate one's efforts 集中精力

近 center, focus, rivet

反 deploy, dispel, disperse, dissipate 散开，驱散

【考法 2】 *vt.* 浓缩：to make **less dilute**

例 Prolonged boiling is required to concentrate the sap when making maple syrup. 制作枫糖浆时，要进行长时间的煮，使汁液充分浓缩。

近 condense

反 dilute, water down 稀释

【考法 3】 *v.* 聚集：to come **together** in one body or place

例 Recent immigrants tend to concentrate in port cities. 近来的移民倾向于聚集在海港城市。

近 accumulate, amass, assemble, collect, congregate, garner

反 dispel, disperse, dissipate, scatter, break up, disband 驱散，解散

concerted [kənˈsɜːrtɪd]

【考法】 *adj.* 共同完成的：planned or **accomplished together**

例 The ITER project, commendable though it is, should be merely a component of a concerted effort. "国际热核聚变实验堆"计划虽然是值得称赞的，但是它仅仅是（人类）齐心协力的一部分。‖ A victory results from the concerted effort of the entire team. 一项成功来自整个团队的齐心协力。

近 collaborative, combined, cooperative, united

反 separate 分开的；individual, single, sole, solitary 单独的

Unit 2

conciliate ［kənˈsɪlieɪt］

【考法 1】 *v.* 平息，抚慰：to **lessen the anger** or agitation of

例 A principal tried to conciliate the parents who did not receive their tickets to the graduation ceremonies. 校长试着平息没有收到他们学校毕业晚会门票的家长的气愤情绪。

近 appease, pacify, assuage, mollify, placate, propitiate, calm (down), ease, soothe, palliate, disarm

反 annoy, enrage, vex, nettle, rile, incense, inflame, exasperate, infuriate, discompose, disturb, perturb, upset 烦扰，激怒，打扰

【考法 2】 *vt.* 调解：to make **compatible**: **reconcile**

例 It will be hard to conciliate the views of labor and management regarding health benefits. 调解劳资双方对于健康保险金的观点很难。

近 attune, reconcile, coordinate, accommodate

反 discontent 不满；disharmonize 使不和谐

派 conciliatory *adj.* 调和的，安抚的

反 contentious 好争吵的；belligerent 好战的

concise ［kənˈsaɪs］

【考法】 *adj.* 简洁的：marked by **brevity** of expression or statement

例 a clear and concise account of the accident 一份清楚简洁的事故描述 ‖ Concise Design of Spacecraft Automatic System 航天器自动控制系统简要设计

近 aphoristic, compendious, curt, laconic, pithy, succinct, terse, elliptical

反 circuitous, circumlocutory, diffuse, long-winded, prolix, verbose, windy, wordy 冗长的

concord ［ˈkɑːŋkɔːrd］

【考法】 *n.* 一致，和睦：**harmony** or **agreement** of interests or feelings; accord

例 No discord, no concord. 不打不成交。

近 comity, compatibility, peace

反 conflict, discord, dissension, variance 冲突，不和

concur ［kənˈkɜːr］

【考法 1】 *vi.* 同意：to express **agreement**

例 concur with an excellent opinion 同意一个好的想法

近 agree, coincide

反 differ, disagree 不同意

【考法 2】 *vi.* 同一时间发生、存在：to occur or exist at the **same time**

例 The race to the moon, the Vietnam War, and the civil rights movement all concurred in the 1960s. 登月、越战和人权运动都发生在二十世纪六十年代。

近 coexist, synchronize, co-occur

【考法 3】 *vi.* 团结合作：to participate or assist in a **joint** effort to accomplish an end

例 All people concurred to pass the reform legislation. 所有人都联合起来使改革法案通过。

近 band together, collaborate, concert, conjoin, league, team up, unite

condescending ［ˌkɑːndɪˈsendɪŋ］

【考法】 *adj.* 摆出高人一等的姿态的：displaying a **patronizingly superior** attitude

例 treat sb in a condescending manner 以屈尊俯就的态度对待某人

近 patronizing

派 condescension *n.* 屈尊俯就：patronizing attitude or behavior

condign ［kənˈdaɪn］

【考法】 *adj.* 应得的，恰当的：**deserved**, appropriate

例 condign punishment 应得的惩罚 ‖ A suspension without pay is condign punishment for breaking the company's code of business ethics. 停职是违反公司商业道德准则应得的惩罚。

近 due, deserved, merited, justified, warranted

反 undeserved, undue, unmerited 不应得的

condole ［kənˈdoʊl］

【考法】 *vi.* 表达同情：to express **sympathetic** sorrow

例 We condole with him on the death of his father. 我们对他父亲的死深表同情。

近 compassionate, sympathize with, yearn over

派 condolence *n.* 同情：sympathy with another in sorrow

condone [kənˈdoʊn]

【考法】 *vt.* 宽恕；忽视：to overlook, **forgive**, or disregard（an offense）without protest or censure

例 By his silence, he seemed to condone their behavior. 他的沉默流露出了他对他们行为的宽恕。|| He is too quick to condone his friend's faults. 他太快了，忽视了他朋友的过错。

近 disregard, ignore, overlook, remit, shrug off, gloss over

反 denounce 谴责；exact 强求

conducive [kənˈduːsɪv]

【考法】 *adj.* 有益的，有促进作用的：tending to **promote** or assist

例 be conducive to education 于教育有利的 || The state's long-standing low tax is conducive to entrepreneurship. 政府长期的低税率有利于创业者。

近 facilitative, useful

反 unhelpful, useless 无用的

confident [ˈkɑːnfɪdənt]

【考法】 *adj.* 有信心的，自信的：having or showing **assurance** and **self-reliance**

例 Thicker and fuller hair would make a man more confident at work. 越来越浓密的头发让男人在工作中更加自信。

近 assured, self-assured, self-confident

反 diffident 不自信的

Unit 3

■ CONFINE	■ CONFLUENCE	■ CONFRONT	■ CONFOUND	■ CONGEAL
■ CONGENIAL	■ CONGRUENT	■ CONJECTURE	■ CONNIVE	■ CONNOISSEUR

confine [kənˈfaɪn]

【考法 1】 *vt.* 禁闭，监禁：to shut or keep in, especially to **imprison**

例 The thief was confined in a prison. 小偷被关在监狱里。

近 imprison, commit, confine, immure, incarcerate, jail

反 discharge, free, liberate, release 释放

【考法 2】 *vt.* 限制：to keep within **limits**

例 Please confine yourself to the subject. 请不要离题。

近 limit, circumscribe, restrict

反 exceed 超越，超过

confluence [ˈkɑːnfluəns]

【考法】 *n.* 汇合，混合：the coming **together** of two or more things to the **same** point

例 a happy confluence of beautiful weather and spectacular scenery during our vacation 旅途中美好的天气和壮丽的景色——令人欣喜的汇合

近 conjunction

反 divergence 分叉

confront [kənˈfrʌnt]

【考法】 *vt.* 直接对抗，直面：to come **face to face** with, especially with defiance or hostility

例 You must confront your fear in order to conquer it. 要战胜你的恐惧，就必须首先敢于面对。

近 affront, brazen, encounter, face, meet

反 dodge, duck, parry, shirk, sidestep 躲避

派 confrontation *n.* 对抗，冲突

confound [kənˈfaʊnd]

【考法 1】 *vt.* 使困惑：to throw into a state of mental **uncertainty**

例 We are all confounded by his self-contradictory claims. 我们都对他自相矛盾的言论感到困惑。

近 baffle, bewilder, confuse, muddle, perplex, puzzle

反 clarify 使清醒

【考法 2】 *vt.* 无法区分，混淆：to **fail to differentiate**（a thing）from something similar or related

例 I think you must have confounded astrology with astronomy. 我想你一定是把占星术和天文学搞混了。

近 misidentify, mistake, mix up

反 discriminate, distinguish 区分

【考法3】 *vt.* 证明为假，证伪：to prove to be **false**
例 new discoveries that confounded much of what archaeologists thought they have known about the ancient Mayan civilization 一些新的发现颠覆了考古学家们长期以来对于古代玛雅文明的认识
近 belie, debunk, falsify, disprove, rebut, refute
反 confirm, validate, verify 证实，证明为真
派 confounding *adj.* 使人困惑的

▷ **congeal** [kən'dʒiːl]
【考法】 *v.* 凝固，固化：to change from a fluid to a **solid state** by or as if by cold
例 The blood had started to congeal. 血液开始凝结了。
近 coagulate, solidify, indurate, clot
反 melt, liquefy 熔化，液化
派 congealment *n.* 凝固

congenial [kən'dʒiːniəl]
【考法1】 *adj.* 和善的，友好的：having or marked by **agreement** in feeling or action
例 a congenial host who invited us for a feast 一位邀请我们美餐一顿的友好主人
近 agreeable, amicable, compatible, unanimous
反 discordant, incompatible 不和睦的，不和谐的
派 congeniality *n.* 友善
【考法2】 *adj.* 令人愉悦的：**giving pleasure** or contentment to the mind or senses
例 a couple relaxing in the congenial atmosphere of a luxury health SPA 一对沉浸在奢华水疗寓所中令人愉快气氛里的夫妻
近 delightful, dulcet, felicitous, palatable
反 unpleasant 令人不悦的

◯ **congruent** ['kɑːŋgruənt]
【考法1】 *adj.* 和谐一致的：being **in agreement**, harmony, or correspondence; congruous
例 a theory congruent with the known facts 一个与已知事实相一致的理论
近 consonant, compatible, consistent, harmonious, accordant
反 disagreeable 不一致的；conflicting, incompatible 冲突的，不可协调的
派 congruity *n.* 和谐一致
【考法2】 *adj.* 全等的：**coinciding** exactly when superimposed
例 These two triangles are congruent. 这两个三角形是全等的。
近 identical, exact
反 disparate 迥异的

conjecture [kən'dʒektʃər]
【考法1】 *n.* 推测，猜测：a **conclusion** deduced **by surmise** or guesswork
例 That was only a conjecture, not a fact. 那只是猜测而非事实。
近 speculation, supposition, surmise, theory
反 fact 事实；axiom 公理
【考法2】 *v.* 猜测，估计（大小、数量等）：to **decide** the size, amount, number, or distance of（something）**without actual measurement**
近 calculate, estimate, guess, gauge
反 prove 证明
【考法3】 *v.* （没有依据地）认为：to **form an opinion** from little or no evidence
例 conjecture that this disease is caused by a defective gene 揣测这种疾病是由基因缺陷导致的
近 assume, imagine, presume, speculate, suppose

◯ **connive** [kə'naɪv]
【考法1】 *vi.* 暗中合作，共谋：to **cooperate secretly** or have a secret understanding; collude
例 They connived to take over the throne. 他们密谋篡位。
近 conspire, intrigue, plot, collude, machinate, put up
派 conniver *n.* 共谋者
【考法2】 *vi.* 纵容：假装忽视或并未采取措施阻止错误：to **pretend ignorance** of or fail to take action against something one **ought to oppose**
例 The guards were suspected of conniving at the prisoner's escape. 警卫人员有纵容犯人越狱的嫌疑。
近 blink, disregard, overlook, wink
反 disapprove 反对

connoisseur [ˌkɑːnə'sɜːr]
　　【考法1】 *n.* 鉴赏家（尤指艺术领域）：a person who enjoys **with discrimination** and **appreciation** of subtleties and details especially in matters of culture or art
　　　例　a connoisseur of wine and cigarette 烟酒鉴赏的行家
　　　近　aesthete, cognoscente
　　【考法2】 *n.* 专家：a person with a **high level of knowledge** or skill in a field
　　　例　works that are highly prized by connoisseurs of art glass 被玻璃艺术制品专家高度赞誉的作品
　　　近　adept, artist, authority, maestro, master, maven, proficient, virtuoso
　　　反　amateur, inexpert, nonexpert 业余者，非专业者；tyro, neophyte 新手

Unit 4

| ■ CONSCIENTIOUS | ■ CONSENSUS | ■ CONSEQUENCE | ■ CONSERVATIVE | ■ CONSERVATORY |
| ■ CONSERVE | ■ CONSIDERABLE | ■ CONSOLE | ■ CONSOLIDATE | ■ CONSONANT |

conscientious [ˌkɑːnʃi'enʃəs]
　　【考法1】 *adj.* 仔细的，一丝不苟的：taking, showing, or **involving great care** and effort
　　　例　a conscientious researcher 一丝不苟的研究者
　　　近　careful, exact, heedful, meticulous, painstaking, scrupulous
　　　反　careless, remiss 粗心大意的
　　【考法2】 *adj.* 有良心的，正直的：**governed by** or conforming to the dictates of **conscience**
　　　例　a conscientious police officer 一名有良心的警察
　　　近　conscionable, ethical, honest, moral, upright, principled, scrupulous
　　　反　unscrupulous 不正直的
　　　派　conscience *n.* 良心

consensus [kən'sensəs]
　　【考法】 *n.* 一致同意：**general agreement**; unanimity
　　　例　The board has finally reached a consensus. 董事会最终达成了一致。
　　　近　accord, assent, agreement, harmony, unanimity, unison
　　　反　disagreement 不同意见

consequence ['kɑːnsəkwens]
　　【考法1】 *n.* 结果：something **produced by** a **cause** or necessarily following from a set of conditions
　　　例　negative consequences of the war 战争带来的负面后果
　　　近　aftermath, effect, outcome, result
　　　反　source, origin, cause, antecedent 根源，原因
　　【考法2】 *n.* 重要性，价值：significance; **importance**
　　　例　a mistake of no consequence 不重要的错误
　　　近　moment, magnitude, weight
　　　反　triviality 琐碎的事
　　　派　consequential *adj.* 重要的

conservative [kən'sɜːrvətɪv]
　　【考法1】 *adj.* 守旧的，不愿改变的：favoring traditional views and values; tending to **oppose change**
　　　例　a conservative political stance 一个守旧的政治立场
　　　近　hidebound, reactionary, die-hard
　　　反　radical, aggressive 激进的
　　【考法2】 *adj.* 不招摇的，低调的：**not** excessively **showy**
　　　例　dressing in conservative outfits so as to make a good impression at job interviews 身着低调得体的套装以期待在面试时留下一个好印象
　　　近　muted, repressed, low-key, understated, unpretentious
　　　反　flamboyant, ostentatious, splashy 浮夸的，张扬的
　　【考法3】 *adj.* 谨慎小心的：having or showing a **close attentiveness** to avoid danger or trouble
　　　例　He made conservative investments, and so he wasn't ruined when the market went into a free fall. 他只进行谨慎保守的投资，因此市场崩盘时他并没有受到严重损失。
　　　近　alert, heedful, cautious, circumspect, gingerly, guarded, wary, vigilant
　　　反　heedless 不谨慎的，莽撞的

conservatory [kən'sɜːrvətɔːri]
　　【考法1】 *n.* 温室：a **greenhouse** for growing or displaying plants
　　　例　The college's conservatory is entirely devoted to cultivating and displaying orchids. 学校的温室几乎全部用于兰花的种植和观赏了。
　　　近　greenhouse, hothouse

【考法 2】 *n.* 艺术学院：a **school** specializing in one of the fine **arts**

例 an opera conservatory 歌剧学院

conserve [kənˈsɜːrv]

【考法】 *vt.* 保存，避免浪费：to **keep** in a safe or sound state, especially to **avoid wasteful** or destructive use

例 conserve natural resources 保护自然资源

近 husband, preserve, save

反 dissipate, lavish, waste, squander 浪费

派 conservation *n.* 保护

considerable [kənˈsɪdərəbl]

【考法 1】 *adj.* (数量上)可观(而值得注意)的：sufficiently **large** in size, amount, or number to merit attention

例 a considerable amount of fortune 一笔可观的财富

近 extensive, substantial, large-scale

【考法 2】 *adj.* 值得考虑的，重要的：worth consideration; **significant**

例 a considerable artist 一位举足轻重的艺术家

近 important, significant, consequential, momentous, weighty

反 trivial 不值一提的；insubstantial, negligible, nominal, trifling 不重要的，可忽视的

console [kənˈsoʊl]

【考法】 *vt.* 安慰，藉慰：to **alleviate** the grief, sense of loss, or trouble of; **comfort**

例 Only her children could console her when her husband died. 当她丈夫去世时，只有她的孩子们才能抚慰她的悲痛。

近 comfort, solace, soothe, calm

反 distress, torment, torture 使痛苦

派 consolation *n.* 安慰

consolidate [kənˈsɑːlɪdeɪt]

【考法 1】 *vt.* 使联合，统一：to **join together** into one whole; unite

例 consolidate several small school districts 合并了几个小的校区

近 unify, combine, amalgamate

反 dissolve, sunder, fragment 解散

【考法 2】 *vt.* 加固，使安全：to **make firm** or secure; strengthen

例 consolidate the defense line 加固防线

近 enhance, strengthen, fortify, reinforce

反 abate, attenuate, undermine, weaken 削弱

派 consolidation *n.* 合并；加固

consonant [ˈkɑːnsənənt]

【考法】 *adj.* 和谐一致的：being **in agreement** or harmony; free from elements making for discord

例 His performance was rarely consonant with his reputation. 他的表现与名气大不相符。

近 harmonious, compatible, congenial, consistent, congruous, correspondent

反 conflicting, dissonant, discrepant, inconsistent 不和谐的，不一致的

派 consonance *n.* 和谐，一致

Unit 5

■ CONSPICUOUS	■ CONSPIRE	■ CONSTITUTE	■ CONSTRAIN	■ CONSTRINGE
■ CONSTRUCT	■ CONSUMMATE	■ CONTAGIOUS	■ CONTAMINATE	■ CONTENT

conspicuous [kənˈspɪkjuəs]

【考法】 *adj.* 显而易见的；吸引人的：**obvious** to the eye or mind; attracting attention

例 a conspicuous change in her appearance 她外貌的明显改变

近 apparent, clear, distinct, evident, manifest, plain, patent, noticeable

反 hidden, concealed 隐藏的

派 conspicuousness *n.* 显然，明显性

conspire [kənˈspaɪər]

【考法】 *v.* 合谋，秘谋：to **plan** together **secretly** to commit an illegal or wrongful act or accomplish a legal purpose through illegal action

例 A group of POWs conspired to abscond. 一批战俘密谋潜逃。

近 plot, contrive, connive, cogitate, intrigue, put up

派 conspiracy *n.* 密谋

constitute [ˈkɑːnstətuːt]

【考法 1】 *vt.* 指派，任命：to **appoint** to an office, function, or dignity

例 He was constituted manager. 他被任命为经理。

近 nominate, designate, authorize

反 discharge, dismiss 撤除职务；abdicate, resign 退位，辞职

【考法 2】 *vt.* 构成：**make up**, form, compose

例 Water constitutes the greater part of the human body. 人体中包含着大量的水分。

近 compose, comprise, form

派 constitution *n.* 构成；宪法；体格

constrain [kənˈstreɪn]

【考法 1】 *vt.* 限制：to force by imposed stricture, **restriction**, or limitation

例 Low temperature constrains the chemical reactivity. 低温降低了化学反应活性

近 bridle, check, confine, imprison, restrain, trammel

反 release 释放

派 constrained *adj.* 受限的

【考法 2】 *vt.* 使人屈服于（压力、感情等）：to cause (a person) to **give in to pressure**

例 constrained by his conscience to tell the truth 受良心的驱使，他说了实话

近 coerce, compel, oblige, sandbag

constringe [kənˈstrɪndʒ]

【考法】 *vt.* 使紧缩：to make narrow or **draw together**

例 A styptic pencil stopped the bleeding by constringing the small blood vessels at the site of cut. 止血笔通过挤压伤口处的血管阻止了出血。

近 capsule, constrict, narrow, compress, squeeze, telescope

反 broaden, expand, outstretch 扩展，扩宽

construct [kənˈstrʌkt]

【考法 1】 *vt.* 建造，建立：to **form** by assembling or combining parts

例 construct a new library 建一座新图书馆

近 assemble, build, fabricate, make, produce, rear, set up

反 demolish, destroy, raze 摧毁

派 construction *n.* 建设，建造

【考法 2】 *vt.* 创造，想出：to **create** or think of by clever use of the **imagination**

例 He managed to construct a theory that fits all the facts. 他成功提出了一个与所有事实相吻合的理论。

近 contrive, devise, excogitate, fabricate, vamp up

consummate [ˈkɑːnsəmət]

【考法 1】 *adj.* 专业的，有造诣的：**extremely skilled** and accomplished

例 a consummate liar 一个老练的骗子

近 accomplished, finished, virtuosic, versed, veteran

反 amateur 业余的

【考法 2】 *adj.* 无纰漏的，完美的：complete in every detail; **perfect**

例 The difficult aria displayed her consummate skill. 高难度的咏叹调展示了她完美的技巧。

近 flawless, impeccable, perfect

反 defective 有漏洞的

【考法 3】 *adj.* 最高档次的，最大规模的：of the greatest or **highest degree** or quantity

近 maximum, paramount, supreme, top, utmost

反 minimal 最少量的

contagious [kənˈteɪdʒəs]

【考法 1】 *adj.* 传染的：**communicable** by contact; catching

例 contagious diseases 传染病

近 infectious, pestilent, transmissible, epidemic

反 incommunicable 不传染的

派 contagiousness *n.* 可传染性

【考法 2】 *adj.* （情绪等）唤起共鸣的：**exciting a similar feeling** or reaction in others

例 The enthusiasm of the new club members was contagious. 新成员的热情具有很强的感染力。

近 catching, spreading

contaminate [kənˈtæmɪneɪt]

【考法】 *vt.* 污染，感染：to soil, **stain**, corrupt, or infect by contact or association

例 Bacteria contaminated the wound. 细菌感染了伤口。

近 pollute, defile, taint, infect

反 purify, sanitize 净化

派 contamination *n.* 污染；contaminant *n.* 污染物

content

【考法1】 [kənˈtent] *vt.* 使满足：to **appease** the desires of

例 One glass of beer every day could content him. 每天一杯啤酒就能满足他。

近 satisfy, gratify, rejoice

反 discontent 不满足

派 contented *adj.* 满足的

【考法2】 [ˈkɑːntent] *n.* 主题：a **major object of interest** or concern (as in a discussion or artistic composition)

例 Although I appreciate the poem's lyrical qualities, I don't understand its content. 虽然我很欣赏这首诗歌的节奏美，但我无法理解其主题。

近 motive, subject, theme, topic

【考法3】 *n.* 内容，内涵：the **idea that is conveyed** or intended to be conveyed to the mind by language, symbol, or action

例 The speech was filled with fancy words but devoid of any real content. 这篇演讲辞藻华丽，但是没什么实质性内容。

近 intention, purport, sense, significance

Unit 6

■ CONTENTIOUS　　■ CONTIGUOUS　　■ CONTORT　　■ CONTRACT　　■ CONTRAVENE
■ CONTRITE　　■ CONTUMACIOUS　　■ CONUNDRUM　　■ CONVALESCE　　■ CONVENIENCE

---

contentious [kənˈtenʃəs]

【考法1】 *adj.* 引起争论的：likely to cause contention; **argumentative**

例 contentious contents in a movie 电影中引发争论的内容

近 controversial, disputatious, polemical

【考法2】 *adj.* 好争论的，好战的：exhibiting an perverse and wearisome **tendency** to **quarrels** and disputes

例 The Tartars were a contentious people who terrorized much of Asia and eastern Europe during the Middle Ages. 鞑靼是一个好斗的民族，他们在中世纪时期统治了亚洲和东欧的大片土地。

近 belligerent, bellicose, combative, truculent, litigious, pugnacious, scrappy

反 dovish, peace-loving 爱好和平的

contiguous [kənˈtɪɡjuəs]

【考法】 *adj.* 接壤的，相邻的：**sharing an edge** or boundary; touching

例 contiguous nations at war 交战中的邻国

近 adjacent, abutting, neighboring, juxtaposed, verging

反 apart, separate 分开的

派 contiguity *n.* 接壤

contort [kənˈtɔːrt]

【考法】 *vt.* 扭曲：to **twist**, wrench, or bend severely out of shape

例 a contorted version of the truth 被歪曲的真相

近 deform, distort, warp, misshape

派 contortion *n.* 扭曲

contract

【考法1】 [ˈkɑːntrækt] *n.* 契约，合同：a **binding agreement** between two or more persons or parties, especially one that is written and enforceable by law

例 a billion-dollar contract from Department of Defense 来自国防部的巨额合同

近 agreement, compact, convention, treaty

【考法2】 [kənˈtrækt] *v.* 收缩：to **reduce** in **size** by drawing together; shrink

例 contract muscle 收缩肌肉

近 compress, condense, concentrate

反 expand 扩展；inflate 膨胀

【考法3】 *v.* 感染疾病：to **become affected** by a disease or disorder
- 例 He contracted a severe cold that later turned into pneumonia. 他染上了重感冒，最终发展成为肺炎。
- 近 catch, get, sicken
- 反 heal 痊愈

contravene [ˌkɑːntrəˈviːn]
【考法】 *vt.* 违反，反对：to **violate**, to **oppose** in argument: contradict
- 例 contravene the proposal with no reservation 毫无保留地反对这一提案
- 近 breach, infringe, transgress, fracture, deny, contradict, gainsay, reject
- 反 uphold, support, buttress 支持；comply, conform, observe 顺从
- 派 contravention *n.* 反对；违反，触犯

contrite [kənˈtraɪt]
【考法】 *adj.* （因为有罪孽或过错而感到）后悔悲痛的：feeling or **showing** sorrow and **remorse** for a sin or shortcoming
- 例 too late to feel contrite 现在后悔为时已晚
- 近 compunctious, regrettable, remorseful, apologetic, penitent, repentant, rueful
- 反 impenitent, unrepentant 不知悔改的

contumacious [ˌkɑːntuˈmeɪʃəs]
【考法】 *adj.* 不服从的，倔强的：stubbornly **disobedient**; rebellious
- 例 Contumacious insurgents refuse to talk. 不愿服从命令的叛军拒绝对话。
- 近 balky, contumacious, defiant, insubordinate, intractable, obstreperous, rebellious, recalcitrant, refractory, restive, ungovernable, unruly, untoward, wayward, willful
- 反 obedient, docile, ruly 顺从的
- 派 contumacy *n.* 不服从，反抗

conundrum [kəˈnʌndrəm]
【考法】 *n.* 无法解决的问题，迷：a paradoxical, **insoluble**, or difficult problem; a **dilemma**
- 例 a difficult conundrum even for the experts 一道即便是专家也束手无策的难题
- 近 enigma, mystery, puzzlement, riddle, secret

convalesce [ˌkɑːnvəˈles]
【考法】 *vi.* 渐渐康复，渐愈：to **recover** health and strength **gradually** after sickness or weakness
- 例 the time needed to convalesce after an operation 手术后需要用来康复的时间
- 近 heal, recover, recuperate, recoup, snap back
- 反 aggravate, deteriorate, intensify 恶化，加剧

convenience [kənˈviːniəns]
【考法】 *n.* 便利，方便：**fitness** or **suitability** for performing an action or fulfilling a requirement
- 例 the convenience of living in megacity 住在大城市的便利
- 近 accommodation, amenity, ease, facility
- 反 burden, millstone 负担
- 派 convenient *adj.* 方便的，便捷的

Unit 7

■ CONVENTION	■ CONVERGE	■ CONVERSANT	■ CONVERT	■ CONVEX
■ CONVEY	■ CONVICTION	■ CONVOKE	■ CONVOLUTED	■ CONVULSION

convention [kənˈvenʃn]
【考法1】 *n.* 常规，习俗：general **agreement** on or **acceptance** of certain practices or attitudes
- 例 By convention, north is at the top of most maps. 按照常规，北方在大多数地图的上部。
- 近 custom, ritual, manner
- 反 deviation 背离（习俗）
- 派 conventional *adj.* 传统习俗上的

【考法2】 *n.* 公约，协议：a general **agreement** about basic principles or procedures
- 例 Under this circumstance Geneva convention does not comply. 此情形下《日内瓦公约》无效。
- 近 treaty, agreement, compact, contract

【考法3】 *n.* 大会，集会：a **coming together** of a number of persons for a specified purpose
- 例 attend a convention of mathematicians in California 参加加州的一次数学家集会
- 近 assembly, congress, council, gathering

converge [kən'vɜːrdʒ]

【考法】 *v.* 汇集，交汇于一点：tending to **move toward one** point or one another
例 The main streets converge on a central square. 众主干道在中央广场交汇。
近 meet, focus, concentrate
反 diverge, deviate, digress 分离，分岔
派 convergent *adj.* 汇集的；convergence *n.* 汇集

conversant [kən'vɜːrsnt]

【考法】 *adj.* 熟悉的：having frequent or **familiar** association
例 conversant with the accounting system 熟知会计系统
近 acquaint, aware, familiar, informed, versed
反 ignorant, unfamiliar 无知的，不熟悉的
派 conversance *n.* 熟知，造诣

convert

【考法1】 ['kɑːnvɜːrt] *n.* 被改变宗教信仰的人：one that is **converted**
近 proselyte
【考法2】 [kən'vɜːrt] *vt.* 使改变信仰：to **bring over from** one belief, view, or party to another
例 European missionaries converted thousands to Christianity. 欧洲传教士使成千上万的人改信了基督教。
近 persuade, proselytize, bring, lead
【考法3】 *vt.* 改变，转化：to **alter** the physical or chemical nature or properties of especially in manufacturing
例 convert water into ice 将水转化成冰
近 alter, change, transform, transfigure
派 converter *n.* 转换器；convertible *adj.* 可转变的 *n.* 敞篷跑车

convex ['kɑːnveks]

【考法】 *adj.* 凸起的：having a surface or boundary that **curves** or bulges **outward**, as the exterior of a sphere
例 A convex function has the property that a line joining any two points on its graph lies on or above the graph. 凸函数具有如下的性质：其图像上任何两点之间的连线都在这两点间函数曲线的上方。
近 bulging
反 dent, concave 凹陷的

convey [kən'veɪ]

【考法1】 *vt.* 运输：to take or carry from one place to another; **transport**
例 goods conveyed by sea 海路运输的货物
近 carry, transfer, ferry, transmit
【考法2】 *vt.* 传递，交流：to impart or **communicate** by statement, suggestion, gesture, or appearance
例 He was struggling to convey his feelings. 他正在挣扎着表达他的情感。
近 conduct, communicate, impart, pass on
反 withhold 隐瞒

conviction [kən'vɪkʃn]

【考法1】 *n.* 深信，确信：the state of **being convinced**
例 a warrior of strong conviction 一名信念坚定的战士
近 assurance, certainty, certitude
反 dubiety, incredulity 怀疑；uncertainty, incertitude 不确定性
【考法2】 *n.* 证明有罪：state of being found or **proved guilty**
例 evidence that led to the suspect's conviction 证明嫌疑犯有罪的证据
近 sentence
反 acquittal 宣告无罪
派 convict *v.* 宣判有罪

convoke [kən'voʊk]

【考法】 *v.* 召集开会：to **bring together** by or as if by summons
例 convoke Parliament 召开国会
近 assemble, convene, summon, muster
反 adjourn 休会

convoluted ['kɑːnvəluːtɪd]

【考法】 *adj.* 复杂的，费解的：**complicated**; intricate
例 a convoluted way of describing a simple mechanism 用令人费解的方法解释一个简单的原理
近 complex, knotty, involved, sophisticated, twisted, tangled, labyrinthine
反 straightforward 直截了当的

convulsion [kənˈvʌlʃn]

【考法 1】 *n.* 痉挛（强烈的、无法控制的肌肉收缩）：an abnormal violent and **involuntary contraction** of the muscles

例 Convulsions are usually accompanied by loss of consciousness. 痉挛常常伴随着失去意识。

【考法 2】 *n.* 骚乱：a violent **disturbance**

例 a regime in convulsion 动荡中的政权

近 commotion, ferment, tumult, upheaval, clamor, tempest, uproar

反 serenity, tranquility 宁静

派 convulse *v.* 剧烈震动；痉挛

Unit 8

| ■ COOP | ■ COPIOUS | ■ COQUETTE | ■ CORDON | ■ CORNUCOPIA |
| ■ CORONATION | ■ CORPOREAL | ■ CORROBORATE | ■ CORROSIVE | ■ CORRUGATED |

coop [kuːp]

【考法】 *vt.* 监禁，困于…之中：to **confine** in a restricted and often crowded area

例 Those restless kids were cooped up in the house on a rainy. 雨天那些好动的孩子们被困在房子里。

近 box, cage, corral, encage, enclose, envelop, fence, hedge, immure, include, pen, wall

反 free, liberate, release 释放

copious [ˈkoʊpiəs]

【考法】 *adj.* 丰富的，大量的：large in quantity; **abundant**

例 a copious harvest 大丰收

近 plentiful, abundant, ample, gushing

反 sparse, dearth, scant 稀少的，缺乏的

coquette [koʊˈket]

【考法 1】 *n.* 调情的女子：a woman who makes teasing sexual or romantic overtures; a **flirt**

例 A coquette though she might appear to be at first, Violetta from Verdi's *La Traviata* is actually yearning for true love. 乍看之下，威尔第歌剧《茶花女》中的维奥莱塔是一个轻浮的女子，但实际上她渴望真爱。

近 vamp, flirt

【考法 2】 *v.* 调情；不认真对待：to flirt; to deal with something **playfully** rather than seriously

例 He is interested only in coquetting with her, not marrying her. 他只想与她保持暧昧关系，而不结婚。

近 trifle, dally, flirt, mess around

派 coquet *v.* 不认真对待，调情；coquettish *adj.* 调情的

cordon [ˈkɔːrdn]

【考法 1】 *n.* 警戒线：a **line** or ring of police, soldiers, or vehicles **preventing** people from entering an area

例 a cordon of police 警察围成的警戒线

近 perimeter

【考法 2】 *v.* 围成一道防线：to **form** a protective or restrictive **cordon** around

例 cordon off the area around the explosion scene 在爆炸现场周边设置警戒线

近 close, obstruct, block

cornucopia [ˌkɔːrnjuˈkoʊpiə]

【考法】 *n.* 大量：an **overflowing** store; an abundance

例 a cornucopia of employment opportunities 大量的就业机会

近 plentitude, plethora, wealth, profusion, affluence

反 lack, pittance, deficiency 缺乏，少量

coronation [ˌkɔːrəˈneɪʃn]

【考法】 *n.* 加冕，加冕礼：the act or ceremony of **crowning** a sovereign or the sovereign's consort

例 Two different musical pieces by Mozart (a piano concerto and a mass) are both titled "Coronation". 莫扎特两部不同的音乐作品（一部钢琴协奏曲和一部弥撒）都被称作"加冕"。

近 enthronement, crowning

反 abdication 退位

派 coronate *v.* 加冕

corporeal [kɔːrˈpɔːriəl]

【考法 1】 *adj.* 肉体的：**not spiritual**

例 corporeal suffering 肉体上的折磨

近 bodily, carnal, corporal, somatic, physical, fleshly

反 spiritual 精神上的

【考法2】 *adj.* 有形的，实体的：**not immaterial** or intangible
近 material, physical, substantial, sensible, tangible
反 intangible, disembodied, immaterial 无形的，无实体的

corroborate [kəˈrɑːbəreɪt]
【考法1】 *vt.* 用证据或权威证实：to **support with evidence** or authority; make more certain
例 new evidence to corroborate the defendant's story 能证实被告的故事的新证据
近 confirm, authenticate, justify, substantiate, validate, verify
反 controvert, contradict, deny 反驳，否认
【考法2】 *vt.* 为…提供证据，支持：to **provide evidence** or information for（as a claim or idea）
例 My personal experience does not corroborate your faith in the essential goodness of people. 我的经历可不赞同你关于"人性本善"的信念。
近 back, bolster, buttress, reinforce, support
派 corroboration *n.* 证实

corrosive [kəˈroʊsɪv]
【考法1】 *adj.* 腐蚀性的：tending to **destroy slowly** by chemical action
例 Concentrated sulfur acid is highly corrosive. 浓硫酸有极强的腐蚀性。
近 erosive, caustic
反 noncorrosive 无腐蚀性的
派 corrosion *n.* 侵蚀
【考法2】 *adj.* 讽刺性的：bitingly **sarcastic**
例 corrosive satire 讽刺性的作品
近 sarcastic, barbed, acerbic, satiric, acrid, mordant, tart

corrugated [ˈkɔːrəgeɪtɪd]
【考法】 *adj.* 褶皱的：shaped into a series of regular **folds** that look like waves
例 corrugated paper 褶皱的纸
近 wrinkled, creased, folded
反 smooth 光滑的
派 corrugation *n.* 褶皱，折痕

Unit 9

| ■ COSMOPOLITAN | ■ COSSET | ■ COUNTENANCE | ■ COUNTERFEIT | ■ COUNTERMAND |
| ■ COURT | ■ COVERT | ■ COVETOUS | ■ COW | ■ COWARDICE |

cosmopolitan [ˌkɑːzməˈpɑːlɪtən]
【考法】 *adj.* 有世界性眼光的，包容的：having **worldwide** rather than limited or provincial scope or bearing
例 a cosmopolitan traveler 云游四海的旅行者
近 universal, catholic, global, worldwide
反 insular, provincial 狭隘的
派 cosmopolitism *n.* 世界主义，天下主义

cosset [ˈkɑːsɪt]
【考法】 *vt.* 宠爱：to treat as a pet; **pamper**
近 caress, cuddle, dote, pet, mollycoddle
反 slight 怠慢；abuse 虐待
派 cosseted *adj.* 被宠坏的

countenance [ˈkaʊntənəns]
【考法1】 *vt.* 容忍：to **put up with**（something painful or difficult）
例 The college administration will not countenance cheating. 该大学管理部门决不容忍作弊的存在。
近 abide, endure, stand, stomach, wear
【考法2】 *vt.* 赞成，推崇：to have a **favorable opinion** of
例 I don't countenance such behavior in children of any age. 对于任何年龄的孩子，我都不推崇那种行为。
近 accept, favor, subscribe
反 disapprove, frown 反对

【考法 3】 *n.* 沉着，冷静：**evenness** of emotions or temper

例 The doctor's purposeful countenance was in stark contrast to everyone else's hysteria. 医生带有目的性的沉着与其他人的歇斯底里形成了巨大的反差。

近 aplomb, calmness, composure, sangfroid, serenity

反 agitation, discomposure, perturbation 急躁，焦虑

counterfeit [ˈkaʊntərfɪt]

【考法 1】 *adj.* 仿制的，假冒的：made in **imitation** of something else with intent to deceive

例 counterfeit money 假币

近 forged, bogus, spurious, pseudo, feigned, artificial, phony

反 authentic, genuine 真实的

【考法 2】 *vt.* 仿制：to make a **fraudulent replica** of

例 counterfeit the signature 仿造签名

近 copy, forge, imitate, simulate, mimic

【考法 3】 *vt.* 伪装成：to present a **false appearance** of

例 counterfeit a happy expression while visiting a sick friend 在看望患病的朋友时装出一副高兴的样子

近 affect, assume, fake, pretend

countermand [ˈkaʊntərmænd]

【考法】 *vt.* 取消，撤销：to **revoke**（a command）by a contrary order

例 countermand an order 撤销命令

近 annul, repeal, rescind, revoke, cancel

反 approve, permit, sanction 批准

court [kɔːrt]

【考法】 *vt./n.* 追求，献殷勤：to **seek** the **affections** of

例 court the young lady by bring her flowers every day 通过每天送花追求那个年轻女孩

近 woo, pursue, invite

反 spurn, snub 摒弃，怠慢

派 courteous *adj.* 殷勤的；彬彬有礼的

covert [ˈkoʊvɜːrt]

【考法 1】 *adj.* 隐蔽的，秘密的：**not** openly **shown**, engaged in, or avowed

例 covert alliance 秘密联盟

近 cloistered, hidden, secret, sheltered

反 open, overt, aboveboard 公开的

【考法 2】 *n.* 隐秘掩护所：a place where a person goes to hide or to **avoid others**

例 set up a covert from which to watch wildlife without being detected 设立了一个隐蔽的野生动物观测点

近 concealment, hermitage, hideaway, nest, lair

covetous [ˈkʌvətəs]

【考法】 *adj.* 贪婪的，渴求财富的：marked by **inordinate desire** for wealth or possessions or for another's possessions

例 cast covetous eyes on their neighbors' fields 对他邻居的土地垂涎

近 acquisitive, avaricious, avid, rapacious, grasping

反 easily-satiated 容易满足的；unenvious 不艳羡的

派 covet *v.* 觊觎，贪婪

cow [kaʊ]

【考法】 *vt.* 恐吓，威胁：to **frighten** with threats or a show of force

例 cow sb. into doing sth 威胁某人做某事

近 intimidate, browbeat, bully, hector, awe

反 embolden, encourage, inspirit 鼓励

派 cowed *adj.* 被吓倒的

cowardice [ˈkaʊərdɪs]

【考法】 *n.* 懦弱，不坚定：**lack** of **courage** or resolution

例 cowardice in the face of danger 面对危险时的懦弱

近 cravenness, dastardliness, gutlessness, poltroonery, pusillanimity, spinelessness

反 courage, guts, pluck, intrepidness, nerve, stoutness, valiance, valor 勇气

派 coward *n.* 懦夫

Unit 10

cower [ˈkauʊr]

【考法】 *vi.* 畏缩：to **cringe** in fear

例 The dog cowered under the table. 狗吓得蜷缩在桌子下面。

近 fawn, flinch, grovel, quail, recoil, wince

cozen [ˈkʌzn]

【考法】 *v.* 诱骗：to **mislead** by means of a petty trick or fraud; deceive

例 The salesman cozened the old lady into buying his goods. 推销员诱使老太太买下了他的东西。

近 bamboozle, dupe, cheat, deceive, beguile, delude, take in

cramped [kræmpt]

【考法】 *adj.* 狭小的，狭窄的：uncomfortably **small** or restricted

例 a cramped cubbyhole in an office 办公室里狭小的隔间

近 confined, limited, restrained

反 commodious, spacious 宽敞的

派 cramp *n.* 狭窄

crass [kræs]

【考法】 *adj.* 粗俗的，愚钝的：so crude and **unrefined** as to be in discrimination and sensibility

例 crass receptionist 粗俗的招待员

近 coarse, crude, rude, incult, uncouth, vulgar

反 civilized, polished, refined, urbane, genteel 有教养的

crave [kreɪv]

【考法】 *vt.* 热望：to have an **intense desire** for

例 crave alcohols and cigarettes 渴望烟酒

近 need, yearn, desire, pine, thirst, itch, long, yen

反 spurn 摒弃

派 craving *n.* 迫切的渴望

craven [ˈkreɪvn]

【考法】 *adj.* 非常懦弱的，因胆小而遭人鄙视的：**lacking** the least bit of **courage**; contemptibly fainthearted

例 a craven deserter 一个懦弱的逃兵

近 cowardly, gutless, pusillanimous, spineless

反 dauntless, fearless, gallant, gutsy, intrepid, stalwart, stout, stouthearted, valiant, valorous 勇敢的

crease [kriːs]

【考法】 *n.* 折痕：a line made by pressing, **folding**, or wrinkling

例 flatten the creases of the map 抚平地图上的折痕

近 wrinkle, corrugation, fold, furrow

派 creased *adj.* 有折痕的

credence [ˈkriːdns]

【考法】 *n.* 坚信：**firm belief** in the integrity, ability, effectiveness, or genuineness of someone or something

例 give credence to gossip 相信绯闻

近 belief, credit, faith, trust, reliance

反 doubt, skepticism 怀疑

credulous [ˈkredʒələs]

【考法】 *adj.* 轻信的，易受骗的：disposed to believe too readily; **gullible**

例 accused of swindling credulous investors 被控欺骗轻信的投资者

近 believing, unwary, gullible, naïve, unsuspecting

反 disbelieving, skeptical 怀疑的

派 credulity *n.* 轻信

creek [kriːk]

【考法】 *n.* 小溪，小河：a natural stream of water normally **smaller** than and often tributary to a **river**

例 go wading in the creek 在小溪中涉水而行

近 stream, branch, brook, rivulet

Every day I remind myself that my inner and outer life are based on the labors of other men, living and dead, and that I must exert myself in order to give in the same measure as I have received and am still receiving.

每天我都提醒着自己：我的精神生活和物质生活都是以别人的劳动为基础的，我必须尽力以同样的分量来报偿我所获得的和至今仍在接受着的东西。

————美国科学家 爱因斯坦（Albert Einstein, American scientist）

List 6

（武阳乐，2007 年 10 月，Verbal 700，Quantitative 800，AW 5.0，
录取院校：Princeton 物理系）

Unit 1

■ CREEP	■ CRESCENDO	■ CREST	■ CRESTFALLEN	■ CRONYISM
■ CROOK	■ CROON	■ CROUCH	■ CRUCIAL	■ CRUMPLE

creep ［kriːp］
【考法 1】 *vi./n.* 缓慢地行进：to go very **slowly**
例 creep through the crowd 在人潮中缓慢前行
近 drag, loiter, tarry
反 scurry, run 快步走，跑
【考法 2】 *vi.* 匍匐前进：to move slowly with the **body close to the ground**
例 The kitten crept silently across the floor before suddenly pouncing on the mouse. 小猫静静地匍匐穿过地板，然后突然向老鼠发起猛扑。
近 crawl, grovel, slide, slither
反 swagger 昂首阔步

crescendo ［krəˈʃendoʊ］
【考法 1】 *n./v.*（声音）渐强：a **gradual increase** in volume of a musical passage
例 The movement begins with a crescendo of a clarinet. 乐章伴随着渐强的单簧管奏响。
反 decrescendo（声音）渐弱
【考法 2】 *n.*（渐强之后到达的）顶峰：the **peak** of a gradual increase
例 Complaints about stifling smog conditions reach a crescendo. 对让人窒息的烟雾的抱怨到达了顶峰。
近 apex, acme, apogee, climax, crest, peak, pinnacle, summit, zenith
反 nadir 最低点

crest ［krest］
【考法】 *n.* 顶部，浪尖，山顶：the top, as of a hill or wave
例 on the crest of a wave 如日中天，非常成功
近 apex, acme, apogee, climax, crescendo, peak, pinnacle, summit, zenith
反 bottom 底部

crestfallen ［ˈkrestfɔːlən］
【考法】 *adj.* 垂头丧气的，沮丧的：dispirited and **depressed**; dejected
例 be crestfallen at the failure 因失败而垂头丧气
近 downcast, dispirited, low, gloomy, melancholic, sorrowful, woeful
反 elated, buoyant, excited, exhilarated, exultant 激动的，欢悦的

cronyism ［ˈkroʊniɪzəm］
【考法】 *n.* 任人唯亲，对好朋友的偏袒：**favoritism** shown to old **friends** without regard for their qualifications
例 officials practicing cronyism 任人唯亲的官员
近 favoritism

crook ［krʊk］
【考法】 *vt.* 使弯曲：to cause to turn **away from a straight line**
例 Crook your finger to pull the trigger. 弯曲你的手指来扣动扳机。
近 arch, bow, curve, hook, swerve
反 straighten, unbend, uncurl 拉直，伸直

croon ［kruːn］
【考法】 *v.* 低声歌唱或说话：to sing or speak in a gentle **murmuring** manner
例 croon mellow tunes 低声唱柔和的调子
近 whisper, grumble, mumble, murmur
反 shout, yell 大声喊叫

crouch [kraʊtʃ]

【考法】 *v.* 蹲伏：to **lower** the body **stance** especially by bending the legs

例 He crouched behind a rock and watched vigilantly. 他蹲伏在石头后面，警惕地观察着。

近 huddle, squat

反 arise, stand 站立

crucial [ˈkruːʃl]

【考法】 *adj.* 非常重要的，决定性的：**extremely significant** or important

例 a crucial step in his professional career 他职业生涯中具有决定性的一步

近 critical, decisive, key, pivotal, vital

反 inconsequential, insignificant, trivial 不重要的

crumple [ˈkrʌmpl]

【考法 1】 *v.* 弄皱：to press, **bend**, or crush out of shape

例 crumple a piece of paper 弄皱一张纸

近 rumple, crimple, crease, fold, wrinkle

反 smooth 使平滑

【考法 2】 *v.* (因外力挤压而) 垮塌：to **fall down** or in as a result of physical pressure

例 The box crumpled when I accidentally dropped a brick on it. 我不小心扔了块石头在箱子上，它就倒塌了

近 collapse, founder, implode, tumble, yield

Unit 2

■ CRUTCH	■ CRUX	■ CRYPTIC	■ CULPABLE	■ CULTIVATE
■ CUMBERSOME	■ CUNNING	■ CURMUDGEON	■ CURSORY	■ CURT

crutch [krʌtʃ]

【考法】 *n./v.* 支撑，支柱：something that **supports** or sustains

例 a crutch for local economy 当地的经济支柱

近 brace, buttress, column, stay, support, underpinning, underpropping

crux [krʌks]

【考法】 *n.* 中心，关键点：the basic, central, or **critical point** or feature

例 the crux of the problem 问题的核心所在

近 core, substance, kernel, gist, pivot

反 trifle, triviality 无价值之物

cryptic [ˈkrɪptɪk]

【考法 1】 *adj.* 秘密的：**secret** or occult

例 cryptic message 秘密的信息

近 covert, furtive, secret, stealthy

反 public, open 公开的

【考法 2】 *adj.* 含义模糊的：having or seeming to have a hidden or **ambiguous meaning**

例 The senator made some cryptic explanations about the military operations. 参议员就军事行动给出了含糊其辞的解释。

近 ambiguous, equivocal, nebulous, obscure, unclear, vague

反 clear, explicit, obvious, plain 清晰的

【考法 3】 *adj.* 超出理解能力的：being **beyond one's powers to know**, understand, or explain

例 They were puzzled by the cryptic e-mail message left on his computer. 他们被他电脑里让人费解的电子邮件所迷惑。

近 arcane, enigmatic, impenetrable, inscrutable, mystic, occult, uncanny

反 comprehensible, understandable 可以理解的

culpable [ˈkʌlpəbl]

【考法】 *adj.* 该受谴责的，有罪的：**deserving** of **blame** or censure as being wrong, evil, improper, or injurious

例 culpable behaviors 该受谴责的行为

近 blameworthy, censurable, guilty, reprehensible, sinful, reproachable

反 inculpable, innocent 无罪的

派 culpability *n.* 有罪

cultivate [ˈkʌltɪveɪt]

【考法 1】 *vt.* 提升，加强：to **improve** by labor, care, or study

例 cultivate the mind 开化心智

近 educate, instruct, illuminate, nurse

反 degrade, deteriorate, impair 损坏，降低品质

【考法 2】 *vt.* 种植，培养：to **promote** the **growth** of（a biological culture）

例 cultivate vegetables 种植蔬菜

近 grow, breed, produce, raise, develop, nurture

反 balk, frustrate, thwart 阻碍

派 cultivation *n.* 栽培

cumbersome ['kʌmbərsəm]

【考法】 *adj.* 笨重的，难处理的：**difficult to handle** because of weight or bulk

例 a cumbersome piece of machinery 一件笨重的机器

近 unhandy, ponderous, heavy, unwieldy, onerous, thorny

反 light, weightless 轻的；handy 容易处理的

cunning ['kʌnɪŋ]

【考法 1】 *adj.* 狡猾的：marked by or given to **artful** subtlety and **deceptiveness**

例 cunning tactics 狡猾的战术

近 artful, crafty, devious, foxy, sly, tricky, wily

反 artless, naïve, unsophisticated 天真无邪的

【考法 2】 *adj.*（手工）灵巧的：**skillful** with the hands

例 Only the most cunning cabinetmaker could have crafted such a beautifully proportioned chest of drawers. 只有手工超凡的家具工才能打造出如此精致协调的衣柜。

近 clever, deft, handy

反 heavy-handed, ham-handed 笨拙的

【考法 3】 *n.* 欺诈，欺骗：the inclination or **practice of misleading** others through lies or trickery

例 She used cunning and subterfuge to work her way up the corporate ladder. 她通过欺骗在公司中步步攀升。

近 artifice, deception, fraud

反 ingenuousness, sincerity 真诚

curmudgeon [kɜːr'mʌdʒən]

【考法】 *n.* 脾气坏的、爱抱怨的人：an **irritable and complaining** person

例 a terrible old curmudgeon 一个坏脾气老头

近 crosspatch, fusser, griper, grouser, growler, grumbler, whiner

反 agreeable person 令人愉快的人

cursory ['kɜːrsəri]

【考法】 *adj.* 匆忙的，不注意细节的：acting or done with **excessive or careless speed**

例 a cursory glance at the headline 匆匆地瞥了一眼标题

近 headlong, overhasty, pell-mell, precipitate, precipitous, rash

反 fastidious, thorough, deliberate, unhurried, unrushed 极关注细节的，考虑周到的，不匆忙的

curt [kɜːrt]

【考法 1】 *adj.* 言词简略的，直接（以至显得粗鲁）的：being or characterized by **direct, brief, and potentially rude** speech or manner

例 his curt reply 他简略而略显粗鲁的回答

近 abrupt, bluff, brusque, downright, unceremonious

反 circuitous, mealymouthed 迂回的

【考法 2】 *adj.* 言简意赅的：marked by the use of few words to **convey much information** or meaning

例 On a daily basis she e-mailed to her commanders curt reports on the situation. 她每天向长官做简短汇报。

近 aphoristic, compendious, elliptical, laconic, pithy, sententious, succinct, terse

反 diffuse, long-winded, prolix, verbose 冗长啰嗦的

Unit 3

☑ CURTAIL	■ CYNIC	■ DABBLE	■ DAFT	■ DAIS
■ DALLY	■ DAMPER	■ DANDY	■ DANK	■ DAPPER

curtail [kɜːr'teɪl]

【考法】 *vt.* 缩短，削减：to make **less in extent or duration**

例 curtail your holiday 缩短你的假期

近 abbreviate, abridge, syncopate, truncate, cut back

反 elongate, protract, prolong, extend, lengthen 延长

cynic [ˈsɪnɪk]

【考法】 *n.* 愤世嫉俗者：a person who believes all people are motivated by **selfishness**

例 A cynic might think that the governor visited the hospital just to gain votes. 一个愤世嫉俗者认为州长去医院探视仅仅是为了拉票。

近 misanthrope, naysayer, pessimist

dabble [ˈdæbl]

【考法】 *vi.* 涉猎，对…浅尝辄止：to work or involve oneself **superficially** or intermittently especially in a secondary interest

例 dabble in arts 对艺术稍有涉猎

反 dedicate, specialize 投入，专门研究

派 dabbler *n.* 涉猎者，浅尝辄止者：one not deeply engaged in or concerned with something

例 He's not a dedicated musician, just a dabbler. 他并不是专门的音乐家，只不过是个业余爱好者

反 specialist 专家

daft [dæft]

【考法1】 *adj.* 神经错乱的：having or showing a very **abnormal** or **sick state of mind**

例 The king was clearly daft, talking to trees and rocks. 国王俨然已经疯了，对着树和石头说话。

近 demented, deranged, lunatic, psychotic, unbalanced, unsound

反 balanced, sane 头脑正常的

【考法2】 *adj.* 不明智的：showing or marked by a **lack of good sense or judgment**

例 This is a daft plan, doomed to wretched failure and merciless ridicule. 这是一个不明智的决定，最终难逃悲催的结局和被无情嘲讽的下场。

近 fatuous, featherheaded, nonsensical, preposterous, senseless

反 judicious, prudent, sagacious, sapient, wise 明智的

dais [ˈdeɪɪs]

【考法】 *n.* 主席台，嘉宾席：a **raised platform**, as in a lecture hall, for speakers or **honored** guests

例 The speaker took his place at the front of the dais. 演讲者在主席台就坐。

近 podium, rostrum, tribune

dally [ˈdæli]

【考法1】 *vi.* 虚度时光：to spend time **doing nothing**

例 I kept dallying at my desk until I couldn't put off doing my work any longer. 我一直浪费时间直到作业不能再拖了。

近 dawdle, loll, lounge, hang around

【考法2】 *vi.* 玩乐：to engage in activity for **amusement**

例 He spent his college years dallying, seemingly determined to acquire as little knowledge as possible. 他在大学里面尽情玩乐，不学习。

近 disport, frolic, recreate, rollick, sport

【考法3】 *vi.* 慢吞吞，磨磨蹭蹭：to move or act **slowly**

例 Don't dally on the way to the interview. 别在去面试的路上磨磨蹭蹭。

近 crawl, creep, dillydally, drag, lag, linger, loiter, tarry

反 dash, hasten, scoot, scurry 匆忙

damper [ˈdæmpər]

【考法】 *n.* 抑制因素：one that deadens, **restrains**, or **depresses**

例 Rain put a damper on our picnic plans. 下雨打破了我们的野餐计划。

反 ameliorator 促进物

dandy [ˈdændi]

【考法1】 *n.* 纨绔子弟，爱打扮的人：a man who gives exaggerated attention to personal **appearance**

例 That dandy was willing to spend thousands of dollars just to get the Hermes Birkin for his girlfriend. 那个纨绔子弟愿意花数千美元，只为他的女朋友买 Hermes Birkin 的包包。

近 fop, gallant

【考法2】 *adj.* 最佳的，最好的：of the **very best kind**

例 That's a dandy new racing bike. 真是辆最好的比赛用自行车。

近 awesome, fabulous, superb, sensational, splendid, unsurpassed

反 atrocious, awful, execrable, lousy, pathetic, wretched 糟糕的，差劲的

dank [dæŋk]

【考法】 *adj.* 阴湿的：slightly or moderately **wet**

例 Vegetables tended to go bad quickly in the dank cellar. 蔬菜在潮湿的地下室很容易变坏。

近 damp, wettish

dapper [ˈdæpər]

【考法】 *adj.* 衣冠整洁的：being **strikingly neat and trim** in style or appearance

例 The students all looked very dapper in their uniforms. 学生们穿着校服显得非常整洁。

近 natty, sharp, snappy, spruce

反 frowsy, unkempt, slovenly 不整洁的

Unit 4

■ DAPPLED	■ DAREDEVIL	■ DART	■ DAUNT	■ DAWDLE
■ DEADPAN	■ DEARTH	■ DEBACLE	■ DEBARK	■ DEBASE

dappled [ˈdæpld]

【考法 1】 *adj.* 有斑点的，花的：**marked with small spots** or contrasting with the background; **mottled, spotted**

例 a dappled fawn 一只小花鹿

近 blotchy, mottled, specked, piebald, splotched, stippled, spotted

反 unspotted 没有斑点的

【考法 2】 *adj.* 色彩斑斓的：having blotches of **two or more colors**

例 a forest that was vibrant with the dappled foliage of autumn 充满秋天的生机、色彩斑斓的森林

近 marbled, mottled, piebald, pinto, splotched

daredevil [ˈderdevl]

【考法 1】 *adj./n.* 大胆鲁莽的(人)：**foolishly** adventurous or bold

例 His daredevil stunts are sure to end in disaster someday. 玩火者必自焚。

近 audacious, brash, madcap, overbold, reckless, temerarious

反 circumspect, guarded, heedful, prudent, wary 小心谨慎的

【考法 2】 *adj.* 不考虑后果的：having or showing **a lack of concern for the consequences** of one's actions

例 a daredevil driver who thinks that racing on city streets is a harmless game 不计后果的司机认为在大街上飙车对人无害

近 foolhardy, irresponsible, harum-scarum

反 responsible 负责任的

dart [dɑːrt]

【考法 1】 *vi.* 突然移动，猛冲，狂奔：to move **suddenly** and rapidly

例 The dog darted across the street. 狗飞奔过马路。

近 flitter, flutter

【考法 2】 *n.* 公开侮辱：an act or expression showing scorn and usually **intended to hurt another's feelings**

例 The darts flew fast and furiously when the two former lovers bumped into each other at the party. 旧情人在 party 上偶遇，立马开始激烈的人身攻击。

近 affront, barb, offense, sarcasm, slight, slur

daunt [dɔːnt]

【考法】 *vt.* 使胆怯，吓倒：**to lessen the courage** or confidence of

例 She was not at all daunted by the size of the problem. 她根本没有被问题的大小给吓倒。

近 demoralize, dishearten, dismay, dispirit, frustrate, unnerve

反 embolden, make resolute, hearten 使大胆，鼓舞

派 dauntless, undaunted *adj.* 无畏的，大胆的

反 pusillanimous, trepid, craven, easily discouraged, meek, timorous 胆怯的

dawdle [ˈdɔːdl]

【考法 1】 *v.* 闲荡，虚度光阴：to **spend time idly**

例 dawdle the day away 闲荡一天

近 bum, dally, loll, loaf, lounge, hang about, kick around

反 hie 匆忙，抓紧

【考法 2】 *v.* 拖拖拉拉：to move or act **slowly**

例 If you continue to dawdle, we'll be late for sure. 你要是再拖拉，我们铁定要迟到了。

近 crawl, creep, dally, dillydally, lag, linger, loiter, tarry

反 bolt, hasten, course, dash, speed, scurry 匆忙，疾行

deadpan [ˈdedpæn]

【考法】 *n.* 无趣的，无生气的，不活泼的：marked by **impassively** matter-of-fact, as in style, behavior, or expression

例 a deadpan comedy 一个没有笑点的喜剧

近 expressionless, impassive, inexpressive, stolid, vacant

反 demonstrative, expressive 有表现力的

dearth [dɜːrθ]

【考法】 *n.* 供应不足：an **inadequate** supply

例 a dearth of evidence 证据不足

近 want, deficit, insufficiency, paucity, pinch, scantiness, scarcity, undersupply

反 plethora, spate, copiousness, abundance, adequacy, amplitude, opulence 过剩，丰富

debacle [deɪˈbɑːkl]

【考法】 *n.* 溃败：a **complete failure**; fiasco

例 the debacle of the war 战争的彻底失败

近 bummer, calamity, catastrophe, cataclysm, fiasco, fizzle, flop, washout

反 complete success, éclat, blockbuster 大成功

debark [diˈbɑːrk]

【考法】 *v.* (使)下船(飞机、车等)；卸(客、货)：to **unload**, as **from a ship or an airplane**; disembark

例 The seasick passengers debarked as soon as the ship dropped anchor. 晕船的乘客等到轮船一靠岸抛锚就立即下船。

近 land

反 embark 上船，装货

debase [diˈbeɪs]

【考法】 *v.* 贬低，贬损：to reduce to a **lower standing** in one's own eyes or in others' eyes

例 Our failure to win a single game completely debased our image. 我们一场未胜的战绩彻底让我们的形象一落千丈。

近 abase, debauch, degrade, demean, demoralize, deprave, deteriorate, profane, subvert, vitiate

反 aggrandize, canonize, deify, elevate, exalt, ennoble 使神圣

Unit 5

| ■ DEBILITATE | ■ DEBRIS | ■ DEBUNK | ■ DEBUT | DECADENCE |
| ■ DECANT | ■ DECIPHER | ■ DECODE | ■ DECORUM | DECREPIT |

debilitate [diˈbɪliteɪt]

【考法】 *vt.* 使衰弱：to impair the **strength** of; enfeeble

例 The virus debilitates the body's immune system. 病毒削弱了免疫系统。

近 devitalize, enervate, enfeeble, prostrate, sap

反 invigorate, fortify, strengthen, beef up 使有活力，加强

debris [dəˈbriː]

【考法】 *n.* 废墟：**discarded** or **useless material**

例 the unsightly debris left after mining operations had ceased 采煤工程中止后留下来的难看的废墟

近 dross, dust, litter, offal, refuse, effluvium, junk

debunk [ˌdiːˈbʌŋk]

【考法 1】 *vt.* 揭穿⋯的真面目：to reveal the **true nature** of

例 debunk a supposed miracle drug 揭穿所谓的灵丹妙药的真面目

近 uncloak, uncover, undress, unmask, show up

反 camouflage, cloak, disguise, mask 继续伪装，掩盖

【考法 2】 *vt.* 证明⋯为假：to prove to be **false**

例 a Web site that assiduously debunks urban legends 一个不遗余力证明假传闻的网站

近 belie, confound, confute, discredit, falsify, rebut, refute

反 confirm, establish, validate, verify 证明⋯为真

debut [deɪˈbjuː]

【考法】 *n.* 初次登台，出道：a **first** public **appearance**

例 made her single debut 完成了她的处女秀

反 farewell performance 告别演出

	decadence	['dekədəns]
	【考法】	*n.* 衰落，颓废：a process, condition, or period of **deterioration** or **decline**; a change to a lower state or level
	例	The book condemns the decadence of modern society. 该书批判了现代社会的堕落。
	近	degeneracy, degeneration, degradation, deterioration, downfall, eclipse
	反	ascent, rise, upswing 提高，提升

	decant	[dɪ'kænt]
	【考法】	*vt.* 轻轻倒出：to pour off (wine, for example) **without disturbing** the sediment
	例	The bottles were uncorked and the wine was decanted an hour before the meal. 瓶塞被打开，美酒在正餐前一小时倒出。

	decipher	[dɪ'saɪfər]
	【考法1】	*vt.* 破译：to read or **interpret** (ambiguous, obscure, or illegible matter)
	例	We deciphered the hidden message to find out when we were supposed to meet. 通过破解暗语，我们得知何时要碰头。
	近	break, crack, decrypt, decode
	反	cipher, encipher, encode, encrypt 加密
	【考法2】	*vt.* 对…有清晰想法，理解，解读：to have a **clear idea** of
	例	a convoluted thriller, the plot of which I was never able to actually decipher 一部错综复杂的恐怖电影，情节我一直没有理解
	近	apprehend, perceive, recognize, seize, sense, make out

	decode	[ˌdiː'koʊd]
	【考法1】	*vt.* 解码：to **change** (as a secret message) from code **into ordinary language**
	例	The agents worked into the night to decode the intercepted message from the enemy spy. 情报人员夜以继日地破解从敌方间谍拦截的信息。
	近	break, crack, decipher, decrypt
	【考法2】	*vt.* 对…有清晰想法，理解，解读：to have a **clear idea** of
	例	a complex literary text difficult for many people to decode 一个深奥的文学文本，许多人都无法理解
	近	apprehend, perceive, recognize, seize, sense, make out

	decorum	[dɪ'kɔːrəm]
	【考法】	*n.* 礼仪，得体：**appropriateness** of behavior or conduct; **propriety**
	例	High standards of decorum are usually required when attending the opera. 去听歌剧的时候需要遵守高标准的礼节。
	近	form, propriety
	反	impropriety, indecency 不得体
	派	decorous *adj.* 有礼貌的：marked by propriety and good taste
	例	decorous behavior 得体的举止
	反	mangy, unseemly 低贱的，不得体的
	派	indecorous *adj.* 不合礼节的
	反	proper 适当的

	decrepit	[dɪ'krepɪt]
	【考法】	*adj.* 虚弱的，衰老的，破旧的：**weakened**, worn out, impaired, or broken down by old age, illness
	例	a decrepit old man 一个虚弱的老年人
	反	vigorous, sturdy, sound, robust, hale 健壮的

Unit 6

■ DEFAULT	■ DEFER	■ DEFERENCE	■ DEFICIENCY	■ DEFILE
■ DEFT	■ DEFUSE	■ DEFY	■ DEHYDRATE	■ DEIFY

	default	[dɪ'fɔːlt]
	【考法】	*n.* 不履行义务，玩忽职守：the **nonperformance** of an assigned or expected action
	例	default on a loan 拖欠贷款
	近	delinquency, dereliction, misprision, nonfeasance, oversight

	defer	[dɪ'fɜːr]
	【考法1】	*v.* 推迟，延期：to put off; **postpone**; defer
	例	We agreed to defer a discussion of the issue. 我们决定推迟问题的讨论。
	近	delay, remit, shelve, hold off, hold over, lay over, put off

【考法2】 *vi.* 遵从：to submit to another's wishes, opinion, or governance usually through deference or **respect**
例 defer to her father's wishes 遵从她父亲的意愿

deference [ˈdefərəns]
【考法】 *n.* 尊崇，顺从：a readiness or willingness to **yield to** the wishes of others
例 He is shown much deference by his colleagues. 他的同事很尊敬他。
近 acquiescence, compliancy, docility, obedience, submissiveness
反 contempt, defiance, disobedience, intractability, recalcitrance 轻视，不服从
派 deferential *adj.* 表示尊重的，恭敬的：showing or expressing deference
反 imperious, impudent 专横无礼的

deficiency [dɪˈfɪʃnsi]
【考法】 *n.* 缺乏，不足：the quality or state of being deficient: **inadequate**
例 There is a deficiency of fresh food in the diet of many of the working poor. 很多劳工阶层的饮食都缺乏新鲜食物。
近 want, dearth, deficit, famine, paucity, scantiness, scarcity
反 surfeit, abundance, adequacy, amplitude, opulence, sufficiency 过度，充足

defile [dɪˈfaɪl]
【考法1】 *n.* (山间)小道：**a narrow passage** or gorge
例 They climbed up the mountain through a defile. 他们通过一条小路爬到山上。
【考法2】 *vt.* 亵渎：to **treat** (a sacred place or object) shamefully or **with great disrespect**
例 Art conservators were careful not to do anything that might defile the holy relic. 公物管理员要防止任何玷污圣迹的行为。
近 profane, violate
【考法3】 *vt.* 使腐坏，污损：to **make unfit for use** by the addition of something harmful or undesirable
例 supplies of meat that had been defiled by maggots 肉已经生蛆了，不能再食用了
近 befoul, foul, pollute, taint
反 decontaminate, purify 使纯净

deft [deft]
【考法】 *adj.* 灵巧的，熟练的：characterized by facility and **skill**
例 He finished off the painting with a few deft strokes of the brush. 他简单熟练地用几笔便完成了画作。
近 cunning, adroit, dexterous, expert, masterful, virtuoso
反 awkward, maladroit, ham-handed, amateur, artless, unprofessional, unskillful 笨拙的，不精通的

defuse [ˌdiːˈfjuːz]
【考法】 *vt.* 抚慰，减轻：to **make less** dangerous, **tense**, or hostile
例 defuse the crisis 平息危机
反 foment 煽动

defy [dɪˈfaɪ]
【考法】 *vt.* 反抗，违抗：to **go against** the commands, prohibitions, or rules of
例 defy the court 蔑视法庭
近 mock, rebel, oppose, confront
反 acquiesce, obey, comply with, conform to 默默接受，遵守；capitulate to, submit to, succumb to, surrender to, yield to 屈服

dehydrate [diːˈhaɪdreɪt]
【考法1】 *vt.* 去除水分，使干燥：to **remove water** from; make anhydrous
例 She bought a dehumidifier in order to dehydrate the damp basement. 她买了一个除湿器来给地下室除湿。
近 dampen, desiccate, parch, scorch, sear
反 hydrate, saturate with water, reconstitute 用水浸润
【考法2】 *v.* 使失去活力：to **deprive of vitality** or savor
例 Years of being trapped in a loveless marriage had dehydrated his spirit. 多年不幸的婚姻消磨了他的活力。
近 deaden, devitalize, enervate, petrify, sap
反 brace, energize, enliven, invigorate, vitalize, vivify 使生机勃勃

deify [ˈdeɪɪfaɪ]
【考法1】 *vt.* 把…当作神来崇拜：to **offer honor or respect to** (someone) as a divine power
例 Some ancient pagans deified such objects of nature as trees and rivers. 很多古代的异教徒将一些自然事物比如树木、河流当作崇拜对象。
近 glorify, revere, venerate

【考法 2】 *vt.* 过分喜爱：to **love or admire** too much

例 materialistic people who deify money 那些眼里只有钱的物质之人

近 adore, adulate, canonize, dote

【考法 3】 *vt.* 尊敬，尊崇：to assign a **high status or value to**

例 Valentino was virtually deified by legions of female fans. 瓦伦蒂诺被大批女粉丝崇拜。

近 aggrandize, canonize, dignify, ennoble, glorify, magnify

反 abase, degrade, demean, humble, humiliate 贬低，羞辱

派 deification *n.* 崇拜

反 debasement 贬低

Unit 7

■ DEJECT	■ DELETERIOUS	■ DELIBERATE	■ DELICACY	■ DELIRIUM
■ DELUSION	■ DELUGE	■ DELVE	■ DEMAGOGUE	■ DEMANDING

deject ［dɪ'dʒekt］

【考法】 *vt.* 使沮丧：to **lower the spirits** of; **dishearten**

例 Nothing dejects a TV pundit than the reality check that nobody cares what he thinks. 没有什么比大家都漠不关心更让电视节目专家沮丧了。

近 oppress, sadden, weigh down, bum out

反 brighten, buoy, lighten, rejoice, cheer up 使高兴

deleterious ［ˌdelə'tɪriəs］

【考法】 *adj.* 有害的：**harmful** often in a subtle or unexpected way

例 deleterious to health 对健康有害的

近 adverse, baleful, baneful, detrimental, mischievous, nocuous, noxious, pernicious

反 beneficial, salutary, salubrious, wholesome, benign, harmless, innocuous 有益的，安全无害的

deliberate ［dɪ'lɪbərət］

【考法】 *adj.* 深思熟虑的：characterized by or resulting from **careful** and thorough consideration

例 a deliberate decision 一个慎重的决定

近 calculated, considered, reasoned, thoughtful

反 impetuous, casual, unadvised, uncalculated, unconsidered, unstudied 随意的，未经过深思的

delicacy ［'delɪkəsi］

【考法】 *n.* (外貌、结构等)精致：**fineness** of appearance, construction, or execution; elegance

例 lace of great delicacy 精致的蕾丝

近 daintiness

反 crudity, coarseness, roughness 粗糙

delirium ［dɪ'lɪriəm］

【考法】 *n.* 精神错乱；极度兴奋，发狂：an acute **mental disturbance** characterized by **confused** thinking and disrupted attention usually accompanied by disordered speech and hallucinations; frenzied exitement

例 Shoppers were running around in a delirium the day before Christmas. 购物者在圣诞节前夕疯狂扫货。

近 agitation, distraction, hysteria, rage, rampage, uproar

delusion ［dɪ'luːʒn］

【考法】 *n.* 错觉，妄想：a **false** idea

例 This was not optimism, it was delusion. 那不是乐观主义，那是妄想。

近 hallucination, illusion, unreality, falsehood, misconception

反 truth, verity 真实

派 delusive *adj.* 欺骗的：false, deceptive

反 transparent 坦诚的

deluge ［'deljuːdʒ］

【考法 1】 *n.* 大暴雨：a **drenching rain**

反 drizzle 毛毛雨

【考法 2】 *n.* 大量：a **great flow** of water or of something that overwhelms

例 receive a deluge of offers 收到一大堆 offer

近 inundation, overflow, spate, torrent

delve [delv]

【考法】 *v.* 探究，钻研：to make a careful or **detailed search for information**

例 The book delves into the latest research. 这本书深入探究了最近的研究。

近 probe, investigate, inquire into, look into, dig into

demagogue ['deməgɑːg]

【考法】 *n.* 蛊惑民心的政客：a **leader** who makes use of popular prejudices and **false claims** and promises in order to gain power

例 That politician is just a demagogue who preys upon people's fears and prejudices. 那就是一个蛊惑民心的政客，利用民众的害怕和偏见来欺骗他们。

近 firebrand, fomenter, incendiary, instigator, kindler, provocateur

demanding [dɪ'mændɪŋ]

【考法 1】 *adj.* 难取悦的，难满足的：not easily **satisfied** or pleased

例 His mother could be demanding at times. 他母亲有时候很难取悦。

近 exacting, fastidious, finical, finicking, fussy, picky

【考法 2】 *adj.* 费时间花心思的：**requiring** much time, effort, or **careful attention**

例 The demanding assignment kept them working all night long. 那项劳神的任务使得他们熬夜。

近 arduous, burdensome, challenging, exacting, grueling, killing, laborious, onerous, persnickety, taxing, toilsome

反 light, unchallenging, undemanding 不费劲的，轻而易举的

Unit 8

■ DEMOLITION　　■ DEMONSTRATE　　■ DEMORALIZE　　■ DEMOTIC　　■ DEMUR
■ DENIGRATE　　■ DENOUEMENT　　■ DENOUNCE　　■ DENT　　■ DENUDE

demolition [ˌdeməˈlɪʃn]

【考法】 *n.* 破坏，毁坏：the act or process of wrecking or **destroying**, especially destruction by explosives

例 the demolition of dangerous buildings 危楼的拆毁

近 annihilation, decimation, devastation, havoc, wreckage

反 building, construction, erection, raising 建造

demonstrate ['demənstreɪt]

【考法 1】 *vt.* (通过证据)证明，表明：to show or **make clear** by **using examples**

例 The paleontologist hopes to demonstrate that dinosaurs once existed in central Peru by unearthing the fossil evidence. 通过发掘化石，古生物学家试图证明恐龙曾经在秘鲁中部生活过。

近 exemplify, instance

反 unable to prove 不能证明

【考法 2】 *vt.* 使明白易懂：to **make plain or understandable**

例 A few striking facts should demonstrate the complex nature of our topic. 一些显著的事实可以使我们的复杂话题变得好懂。

近 clarify, construe, demystify, elucidate, explicate, illuminate

反 obscure 使模糊

【考法 3】 *vt.* 表现，表露：to **make known** (something abstract) through outward signs

例 The babysitter's actions during the emergency demonstrate beyond doubt her general dependability. 保姆在紧急情况下的表现毋庸置疑地展示了她一贯的可靠性。

近 bespeak, betray, display, evince, manifest, reveal

demoralize [dɪ'mɔːrəlaɪz]

【考法 1】 *vt.* 使士气低落：to undermine the confidence or morale of; **dishearten**

例 demoralize the staff 使员工士气低落

近 daunt, dishearten, dismay, dispirit, unnerve

反 invigorate, cheer 鼓舞

【考法 2】 *vt.* 贬低，使堕落：to **lower in character**, dignity, or quality

例 We refused to be demoralized by our humiliating defeat. 我们拒绝由于这场屈辱的战败而被贬低。

近 abase, corrupt, debauch, degrade, demean

反 elevate, ennoble, uplift 使崇高，提升

| demotic | [dɪˈmɑːtɪk] |

【考法】 *adj.* 通俗的，大众化的：popular, **common**
例　demotic entertainments 大众化的娱乐
反　profound 深奥的

| demur | [dɪˈmɜːr] |

【考法 1】 *n./vi.* 表示异议，反对：to voice **opposition**; **object**
例　demur at the suggestion 反对提议
近　challenge, exception, expostulation, fuss, kick, protest, remonstrance, stink
反　accept, accede 接受

【考法 2】 *n.* 犹豫：hesitation（as in doing or accepting）usually based on **doubt** of the **acceptability** of something offered or proposed; **qualm**
例　We accepted his offer to pay for our dinners without demur. 我们毫不犹豫地同意了他买单。

| denigrate | [ˈdenɪɡreɪt] |

【考法】 *vt.* 诋毁，污蔑：to express **scornfully** one's low opinion of
例　denigrate one's opponents 诋毁某人的对手
近　belittle, depreciate, derogate, dismiss, disparage
反　honor, acclaim, applaud, exalt, extol, glorify, magnify 给以…荣誉，赞扬

| denouement | [ˌdeɪnuːˈmɑː] |

【考法】 *n.*（小说的）结局：the **final resolution** or clarification of a dramatic or narrative plot
例　a surprising/unexpected denouement 令人惊奇的、出人意料的结局

| denounce | [dɪˈnaʊns] |

【考法 1】 *vt.* 公开指责：to express **public or formal disapproval** of
例　The governor has denounced the court's decision and vows to press for a constitutional amendment. 州长公开指责法庭判决不公，准备投票进行修宪。
近　condemn, objurgate, rebuke, reprimand, reproach, reprove
反　cite, commend, endorse 支持，称赞
派　denunciation n. 谴责：an act of denouncing especially: a public condemnation
反　panegyric, accolade, eulogy 赞颂，颂词

【考法 2】 *vt.* 宣称…道德上错误、可耻：to declare to be **morally wrong** or evil
例　The church council denounced the bishop's teachings, officially declaring them to be heresy. 该教理事会指责主教的布道可耻，声称它们是异端学说。
近　anathematize, censure, execrate, reprehend, reprobate

| dent | [dent] |

【考法 1】 *n.* 凹陷，凹痕：a **depression** in a surface made by pressure or a blow
例　a dent in the side of a car 汽车侧面一处凹陷
近　cavity, depression, hollow, indenture, recess
反　bulge, convexity, projection, protrusion, protuberance 凸起

【考法 2】 *vt.*（数量、程度上）削弱：to make smaller in amount, volume, or extent
例　Hopefully this vacation won't dent our bank account too much. 但愿这次旅行不会让我们银行存款缩水太多。
近　abate, downscale, downsize, dwindle
反　aggrandize, amplify, augment, boost, enlarge, escalate 增大，增强

| denude | [dɪˈnuːd] |

【考法】 *vt.* 脱去，使赤裸：to divest of covering; make **bare**
例　Drought has completely denuded the hills of grass. 干旱"脱去"了山上的草使山变得光秃秃的。
反　cover 遮盖

Unit 9

| ■ DEPLETE | ■ DEPLORE | ■ DEPLOY | ■ DEPORTATION | ■ DEPOSE |
| ■ DEPOSIT | ■ DEPRAVITY | ■ DEPRECATE | ■ DEPRECIATE | ■ DEPRESSED |

| deplete | [dɪˈpliːt] |

【考法】 *vt.* 耗尽，使衰竭：to decrease the fullness of; to **make complete use** of
例　Miners depleted the vein of copper ore after only a few months. 矿工们在短短几个月内就把一整片铜矿开采完了。
近　consume, devour, drain, exhaust, draw down, play out, use up
反　enrich, renew, replace 使富有，更新

deplore [dɪˈplɔːr]
【考法】 *vt.* 哀悼：to feel or express **sorrow** for
例 a statement from the bishops deploring the loss of life in the war overseas 一份来自主教们的声明，对海外战争中遇难的生命表示沉痛哀悼
近 mourn, bewail, grieve for, wail for
反 delight, exult in, glory in, rejoice in 高兴

deploy [dɪˈplɔɪ]
【考法】 *v.* (有目的地)展开；调度，部署：to **spread out**, utilize, or arrange for a deliberate purpose
例 deploy a sales force 展开部署销售力量
反 concentrate 集中

deportation [ˌdiːpɔːrˈteɪʃn]
【考法】 *n.* 放逐：the **removal from a country** of an alien whose presence is unlawful or prejudicial
例 the deportation of all illegal immigrants 驱逐所有非法移民
近 banishment, displacement, expatriation, expulsion, relegation

depose [dɪˈpoʊz]
【考法 1】 *vi.* 宣誓作证：to **testify** to under oath or by affidavit
例 He was nervous when the time to depose before the jury finally arrived. 他很紧张，在陪审团面前作证的时刻终于到来了。
近 attest, swear
反 perjure 作伪证
【考法 2】 *vt.* 废黜，罢免：to **remove from a throne** or other high position
例 a military junta deposed the dictator after he had bankrupted the country 军阀罢黜了使国家陷入赤贫的独裁者
近 defrock, deprive, oust, uncrown
反 crown, enthrone 授予王权
【考法 3】 *vt.* 摆放：to **arrange** something in a certain spot or position
例 She deposed her fan and gloves on the dressing table. 她把扇子和手套放在梳妆台上。
近 deposit, dispose, emplace, situate

deposit [dɪˈpɑːzɪt]
【考法 1】 *n.* 自然积累，沉积，矿藏：a natural **accumulation** (as of iron ore, coal, or gas)
例 rich deposits of oil and natural gas 丰富的石油和天然气矿藏
近 dregs, precipitate, sediment, settlings, hoard, reserve
反 process of eroding 腐蚀过程
【考法 2】 *vt.* 存钱：to **put in** an **account**
例 We quickly deposited the check in a bank account. 我们火速把支票存入银行账户。
反 withdraw 取款

depravity [dɪˈprævəti]
【考法】 *n.* 道德败坏：**immoral** conduct or practices **harmful or offensive** to society
例 He was sinking into a life of utter depravity. 他自甘堕落。
近 debauchery, iniquitousness, licentiousness, perversion, turpitude, dissoluteness
反 morality, virtue 美德

deprecate [ˈdeprəkeɪt]
【考法 1】 *vt.* 不喜欢：to hold an **unfavorable opinion** of
例 They deprecates TV sitcoms as childish and simpleminded. 他们批评电视情景喜剧既幼稚又脑残。
近 deprecate, discountenance, disesteem, disfavor, frown (on or upon)
反 approve, favor 喜欢
【考法 2】 *vt.* 贬低，轻视：to **express scornfully** one's low opinion of
例 They boys deprecate the comedy as the stupidest movie of the year. 男孩们认为这部喜剧是年度最傻逼电影。
近 belittle, denigrate, dismiss, disparage, cry down
反 acclaim, applaud, exalt, extol, glorify 赞扬
【考法 3】 *vt.* 降低…的重要性，使低调：**play down**, to make little of
例 She deprecated her facility for languages. 她不炫耀自己对于语言的天赋。
反 vaunt 夸张，吹嘘

depreciate [dɪˈpriːʃieɪt]
【考法 1】 *vt.* 贬低…的价值：to **lower** the price or estimated **value** of
例 New cars start to depreciate as soon as they are on the road. 新车一上路便开始贬值。
近 cheapen, depress, devalue, downgrade, mark down
反 appreciate, enhance, upgrade, mark up 提价，升值

【考法2】 *vt.* 轻视：to **lower** in **estimation** or **esteem**

例　He dared to depreciate Shakespeare, saying his works have no relevance for modern audiences. 他胆敢贬低莎大人，说他的作品对于现代观众来说没有意义。

近　denigrate, disparage, play down, talk down

反　acclaim, exalt, extol, glorify, magnify 赞扬

---

depressed ［dɪˈprest］

【考法1】 *adj.* 不开心的，情绪不高的，消沉的：feeling **unhappiness**

例　I was depressed and didn't feel much like going to the party. 我感到很沮丧，不想去参加聚会。

近　crestfallen, dejected, despondent, gloomy, low-spirited, wretched

反　blissful, buoyant, gleeful, joyous, jubilant 情绪高的

【考法2】 *adj.* 生活境况悲催的：kept from having the necessities of life or a **healthful environment**

例　a depressed class of people whose living conditions are abominable even by third world standards 境况悲惨的一群人，即使用第三世界标准来看他们的生存条件也是很糟的

近　disadvantaged, underprivileged

反　advantaged, privileged 具有优势的、特权的

Unit 10

| ■ DEPRIVATION | ■ DERACINATE | ■ DERELICT | ■ DERIDE | ■ DERIVATIVE |
| ■ DESCEND | ■ DESCENDANT | ■ DESECRATE | ■ DESICCATE | ■ DESIGNATE |

deprivation ［ˌdeprɪˈveɪʃn］

【考法】 *n.* 匮乏：the condition of being deprived; **privation**

例　serious sleep deprivation caused by long work hours 由长时间工作导致的严重睡眠不足

反　fecundity 丰饶

---

deracinate ［ˌdiːˈræsɪneɪt］

【考法】 *vt.* 根除：to **pull out** by the roots; uproot

反　plant 种植

---

derelict ［ˈderəlɪkt］

【考法1】 *adj.* 玩忽职守的，不认真的：**lacking** a sense of **duty**; marked by a **carelessly** easy manner

例　The guards were judged derelict in their duty. 守卫们被判玩忽职守罪。

近　disregardful, lax, neglectful, neglecting, remiss, slack

反　extremely careful, attentive, conscientious, nonnegligent 特别仔细的

【考法2】 *n.* 被社会遗弃的人：a destitute homeless **social misfit**

例　a section of the city that seemed to be frequented mostly by derelicts 这座城市里流浪汉的集中区

近　deserted, desolate, disused, forgotten, forsaken, rejected

反　pillar of society 社会的栋梁

---

deride ［dɪˈraɪd］

【考法】 *vt.* 嘲弄，嘲笑：to speak of or treat with **contemptuous mirth**

例　My brothers derided our efforts, but were forced to eat their words when we won first place. 我的兄弟嘲笑我们的努力，但是当我们得了第一名以后他们不得不收回那些话。

近　gibe, jeer, mock, scout, shoot down, laugh at

反　praise 赞美

派　derision *n.* 嘲弄：contemptuous or jeering laughter; ridicule

反　veneration 尊敬

---

derivative ［dɪˈrɪvətɪv］

【考法】 *adj.* 非原创的：lacking **originality**: banal

例　their dull, derivative debut album 他们毫无新意的首张专辑

近　secondhand

反　original, innovative, precursory 原创的，先驱的

---

descend ［dɪˈsend］

【考法1】 *v.* 下降：to lead or extend **downward**

例　The pathway descends to the river bank. 通道一直向下延伸到河岸。

近　dip, fall, plunge, sink

反　arise, ascend, climb, mount, upsweep, upturn 上升，登上

【考法2】 *v.* 世代相传：to originate or come from an ancestral stock or source, to **pass by inheritance**

例　The house has descended through four generations. 这座房子已经传了四代。‖ a tradition descending from colonial days 殖民时期传递下来的一项传统

descendant [dɪˈsendənt]

【考法】 *n.* 后代：one **deriving directly from** a precursor or prototype

例　They are descendants of the original English and Scottish settlers. 他们是最早一批英格兰和苏格兰定居者的后裔。

反　forbears 祖先

desecrate [ˈdesɪkreɪt]

【考法】 *vt.* 亵渎，玷污：to **treat** (a sacred place or object) **shamefully** or with great disrespect

例　desecrate the shrine 亵渎圣地

近　defile, profane, violate

反　sanctify, revere, hallow 尊敬，将…视为神圣

desiccate [ˈdesɪkeɪt]

【考法1】 *vt.* 使(食物)脱水以保存，使干燥：to preserve (a food) by **drying**

例　add a cup of desiccated coconut to the mix 加一杯椰蓉进行搅拌

近　dehydrate, parch, scorch, sear

反　add water to, hydrate, drench 加水，浸透

派　desiccant *n.* 干燥剂：a drying agent (as calcium chloride)

【考法2】 *vt.* 使缺乏活力：to **deprive** of emotional or intellectual **vitality**

例　That historian's dryasdust prose desiccates what is actually an exciting period in European history. 那位历史学家枯燥无味的散文让欧洲一段扣人心弦的历史变得乏味单调。

近　castrate, dampen, deaden, devitalize, enervate

反　brace, energize, enliven, invigorate, stimulate, vitalize 使生机勃勃

designate [ˈdezɪgneɪt]

【考法1】 *vt.* 任命：to **pick** (someone) by one's authority **for a specific position or duty**

例　He has yet to designate his successor as head of the firm. 他还没有给公司选定接班人。

近　assign, commission, constitute, nominate, place

反　discharge, dismiss, expel, fire 解雇，开除

【考法2】 *vt.* 命名：to **give a name to**

例　He was designated Air Jordan by his fans. 他被粉丝们称为"飞人乔丹"。

近　denominate, dub, entitle, label, style, term, title

A man is not old as long as he is seeking something. A man is not old until regrets take the place of dreams.

只要一个人还有所追求，他就没有老。直到后悔取代了梦想，一个人才算老。

——美国演员 巴里穆尔(J. Barrymore, American actor)

List 7

"刷词，刷题，刷《再要你命 3000》，为你刷出新世界"

（童心，2007 年 10 月，Verbal 700，Quantitative 800，AW4.0
录取院校：Princeton University 运筹与金融工程）

Unit 1

■ DESPICABLE	■ DESPISE	■ DESPOTIC	■ DESULTORY	■ DETACH
■ DETAIN	■ DETER	■ DETERIORATION	■ DETOUR	■ DETRACT

despicable [dɪˈspɪkəbl]

【考法 1】 *adj.* 令人鄙视的：arousing or deserving of one's **loathing and disgust**

例 Even within the prison population, pedophiles are regarded as particularly despicable. 即使在囚犯内部，恋童癖者也是极其让人鄙视的。

近 contemptible, detestable, dishonorable

反 admirable, commendable, creditable, meritorious, praiseworthy 值得赞扬的

【考法 2】 *adj.* 不荣耀的，不得体的：**not** following or in accordance with standards of **honor** and decency

例 the cad's despicable behavior toward women 公车售票员对女性不得体的举动

近 currish, dirty, execrable, ignominious, sordid, wretched

反 honorable, lofty, noble, upright, venerable, virtuous 崇高的

despise [dɪˈspaɪz]

【考法】 *vt.* 极其不喜欢：to **dislike strongly**

例 I despise anchovies on pizza, and I refuse to eat them. 我鄙视披萨上的凤尾鱼，所以从来不吃。

近 abhor, abominate, detest, execrate, loathe, disregard, flout

反 love 喜欢

despotic [dɪˈspɑːtɪk]

【考法】 *adj.* 专制的，暴虐的：arbitrary, autocratic, monocratic, **tyrannical**

例 a despotic tyrant 专制的暴君

近 authoritative, dictatorial, imperious, overbearing, peremptory, tyrannous

desultory [ˈdesəltɔːri]

【考法 1】 *adj.* 无计划的，无目的的：**lacking** a definite **plan**, purpose, or pattern

例 a desultory search for something of interest on TV 漫无目的地换台

近 digressive, excursive, meandering, rambling, wandering

反 carefully planned, strictly methodical, assiduous 精心计划的，有条理的，专心致志的

【考法 2】 *adj.* 令人失望的：**disappointing** in progress, performance, or quality

例 a desultory fifth place finish 让人失望的第五名

detach [dɪˈtætʃ]

【考法】 *vt.* 使分离：to **separate** or unfasten; disconnect

例 Detach the white part of the application form and keep it. 撕下申请表的白色部分并予以保留。

反 tether 束缚

detain [dɪˈteɪn]

【考法】 *vt.* 拘留，扣留：to **hold** or **keep** in or as if in custody

例 detained by the police for questioning 被警察扣留下问讯

反 manumit 释放

deter [dɪˈtɜːr]

【考法】 *vt.* 吓住，威慑：to **prevent** or **discourage** from acting, as by means of fear or doubt

例 We wouldn't be deterred by threats. 我们不会被威胁吓住。

近 dissuade, inhibit

反 spur, encourage, persuade 激励

派 deterrent *adj./n.* 威慑的；威慑力量

例 deterrent weapons 威慑性武器 || a deterrent to theft 对偷窃的威慑

反 inducement, incentive 引诱，刺激

deterioration [dɪ͵tɪrɪə'reɪʃn]

【考法】 *n.* 恶化；堕落：a gradual **sinking** and wasting away of mind or body

例 a continuing deterioration in relations between the two countries 两国关系的持续恶化

近 decadence, degeneration, deterioration, devolution, downfall, downgrade

反 improvement, recovery, recuperation, rehabilitation, revitalization 改进，改善

detour ['diːtʊr]

【考法 1】 *n.* 偏离正常标准：a turning **away from** a course or **standard**

例 We'll regard this relapse as just a brief detour on your road to recovery from substance abuse. 我们把这次旧病复发看成你戒瘾道路上的一个小偏离。

近 deflection, departure, deviation, divergency

【考法 2】 *v.* 改变方向或者路线，绕道：to **change** one's course or **direction**

例 We had to detour for a few miles around the section of highway under construction. 为了避开正在维修的高速公路路段，我们不得不绕远儿公里。

近 deviate, diverge, sheer, swerve, veer

detract [dɪ'trækt]

【考法 1】 *vt.* 贬低，降低价值：to **diminish** the importance, value, or effectiveness of something

例 It is wrong to detract from the achievements of other people in the same field. 贬低同行是不对的。

近 belittle, depreciate, derogate, disparage, dispraise, write off

反 extol, praise, eulogize, laud, panegyrize 赞美

【考法 2】 *vt.* 使分心：to **draw** the **attention** or mind to something else

例 Numerous typos in the text detract the reader's attention from the novel's intricate plot. 许多打印错误让读者分心，不关注复杂的情节了。

近 divert, call off

Unit 2

| ■ DETRITUS | ■ DEVOTED | ■ DEVOUT | ■ DEXTEROUS | ■ DIABOLIC |
| ■ DIAPHANOUS | ■ DIATRIBE | ■ DIDACTIC | ■ DIEHARD | ■ DIFFIDENT |

detritus [dɪ'traɪtəs]

【考法】 *n.* 废品，碎屑，遗骸：a **product** of **disintegration**, **destruction**, or wearing away: **debris**

例 the detritus of war 战争的残迹

近 debris, residue, wreck

反 valuable product 有用的物品

devoted [dɪ'voʊtɪd]

【考法 1】 *adj.* 投入的；忠诚的：characterized by **loyalty** and **devotion**

例 Good teachers are devoted to learning. 好老师会专心学习。

近 constant, loyal, allegiant, dedicated, devout, loyal, pious, staunch, steadfast

反 disloyal, faithless, perfidious, unfaithful 不忠诚的；recreant, traitorous, treacherous 背叛的

【考法 2】 *adj.* 示爱的，恩爱的：feeling or showing **love**

例 A devoted couple will enjoy sharing their lives with one another. 一对恩爱的情侣喜欢和对方一起度过自己的人生。

近 adoring, affectionate, fond, tender, tenderhearted

反 unloving 无爱心的，冷漠的

devout [dɪ'vaʊt]

【考法 1】 *adj.* （对于宗教）虔诚的：**devoted to religion** or to religious duties or exercises

例 a devout Buddhist 虔诚的佛教徒

近 pious, religious, sainted

反 antireligious, impious 不虔诚的

【考法 2】 *adj.* 忠诚的：firm in one's **allegiance** to someone or something

例 Devout Mavericks fans never lost faith in Nowitzki. 忠诚的小牛队球迷从来没有对诺维斯基失去信心。

近 constant, loyal, allegiant, dedicated, pious, staunch, steadfast

反 disloyal, faithless, perfidious, unfaithful 不忠诚的；recreant, traitorous, treacherous 背叛的

dexterous ['dekstrəs]

【考法 1】 *adj.* 动作灵活的：**ready** and **skilled** in physical movements

例 a dexterous surgeon 技术娴熟的外科医生 ‖ The dexterous watchmaker was able to repair the antique watch's delicate gears and parts. 手巧的手表匠能够修理古董手表精密的齿轮和部件。

近 deft, handy

反 ham-fisted, ham-handed, handless, heavy-handed, unhandy 手笨的

【考法2】 *adj.* 头脑灵活的：**mentally adroit** and **skillful**: clever

近 adroit, clever, cunning

反 dull, foolish, silly, fatuous, unwise 傻的

diabolic [ˌdaɪəˈbɑːlɪk]

【考法】 *adj.* 恶魔一般的：of, relating to, or characteristic of the **devil**

例 The police quickly mobilized to track down the diabolic serial killer. 警察迅速行动起来追查这个恶魔般的连环杀人狂。

近 demoniac, demonian, demonic, devilish, satanic

反 angelic, seraphic 天使般的

diaphanous [daɪˈæfənəs]

【考法1】 *adj.* 模糊的；非实在的：**vague** or **insubstantial**

例 only a diaphanous hope of success 只有一丝成功的希望

近 vague, obscure, unexplicit, insubstantial, immaterial

反 substantial 实在的；clear, distinct 清晰的

【考法2】 *adj.* (质地精致得)几乎透明的：of such fine texture as to be **transparent** or **translucent**

例 The bride wore a diaphanous veil. 新娘戴着透明的面纱。

近 transparent, translucent, transpicuous, gossamer

反 opaque, impermeable of light 不透明的，不透光的

diatribe [ˈdaɪətraɪb]

【考法1】 *n.* 长篇抨击性演讲：a **long** angry speech or **scolding**

例 He was forced to sit through a long diatribe. 他被迫耐着性子听完一个长篇抨击性演讲。

近 tirade, harangue, jeremiad, philippic, rant

【考法2】 *n.* 挖苦，讽刺的指责：**ironic** or **satirical** criticism

例 The movie reviewer wrote a diatribe of the movie describing it as having excessive sex and violence. 那个影评人指责这个电影含有过多的色情和暴力。

近 irony, satire

反 encomium, eulogy, panegyric, tribute, laudatory piece of writing 颂词，赞赏作品

didactic [daɪˈdæktɪk]

【考法】 *adj.* 喜欢说教的：designed or intended to **teach**

例 Parents' speech to their kids often seems to be painfully didactic. 父母对他们孩子说的话似乎都是让人痛苦的说教。

近 homiletic, preachy, moralistic, sententious

反 undidactic 不喜欢说教的

diehard [ˈdaɪhɑːrd]

【考法】 *adj.* 顽固的，保守的 *n.* 顽固的人，保守的人：strongly or fanatically **determined** or **devoted** / someone who **opposes change** and **refuses** to accept **new ideas**

例 Some diehard smokers belied the doctors' suggestion. 一些顽固的烟民违背了医生们的建议。

近 conservative, hidebound, old-fashioned, reactionary, ultraconservative

反 liberal, nonconservative, open-minded, liberal 自由的，开放的

diffident [ˈdɪfɪdənt]

【考法1】 *adj.* 不自信的：hesitant in acting or speaking through **lack** of **self-confidence**

例 He is diffident to express his opinions in public. 他在公共场合表达自己的观点时有点害羞。

近 unassured, bashful, retiring, self-effacing, withdrawn

反 confident, assured, self-assured, self-confident 自信的

【考法2】 *adj.* 内向的：**reserved** in manner; unassertive

例 She was diffident about stating her opinion. 她很内向，表达自己观点的时候有点害羞。

近 introverted

反 extroverted, outgoing 外向的

Unit 3

■ DIFFUSE	■ DIGRESS	■ DILAPIDATE	■ DILATE	■ DILATORY
■ DILETTANTE	■ DILIGENT	■ DILUTE	■ DIMINISH	■ DIN

diffuse
【考法 1】 ［dɪˈfjuːs］ *adj.*啰嗦的：being at once **verbose** and ill-organized
例 a diffuse report 冗长的报告
近 circuitous, circumlocutory, long-winded, prolix, verbose, windy, rambling
反 concise, pithy, succinct, terse, laconic 简洁的
【考法 2】 *adj.*不集中的，扩散的：**not concentrated** or localized
例 diffuse lighting 散射光
反 concentrated 集中的
【考法 3】 ［dɪˈfjuːz］ *v.*扩展，散开：to **extend**, **scatter**
例 The photographer uses a screen to diffuse the light. 摄影师用一个屏幕来分散光线。
近 spread, extend, disperse, disseminate, scatter
反 concentrate, center, centralize, focus 集中

digress ［daɪˈgres］
【考法】 *v.*脱离主题：to **turn aside** especially from the **main subject** of attention or course of argument
例 digress from her prepared subject 脱离她准备好的主题 ‖ He digressed so often that it was hard to follow what he was saying. 他经常跑题，我们很难跟上他说的内容。
近 excurse, ramble, diverge, get off the subject
派 digressive *adj.* 偏离的
近 discursive
派 digression *n.* 题外话，跑题：the act or an instance of digressing in a discourse
近 aside

dilapidate ［dɪˈlæpɪdeɪt］
【考法】 *v.*（使）荒废：to bring into a condition of decay or partial **ruin**
例 The house has been dilapidated by neglect. 由于没人照看，这所房子已经要荒废了。
近 ruin, wreck
反 be in use 还在使用；restore 恢复使用；mend, repair 修理；rejuvenate, renew, renovate 翻新

dilate ［daɪˈleɪt］
【考法 1】 *v.*（使）膨胀，扩大：to **enlarge** or **expand** in bulk or extent; to become **wide**
例 The cat dilated its eyes in the darkness. 猫在黑暗中睁大眼睛。‖ The drug dilates the blood vessels. 药使血管膨胀。
近 expand, amplify, enlarge
反 contract 收缩；narrow 使变窄
【考法 2】 *v.*详细表达：to express **more fully** and in **greater detail**
例 He refused to dilate upon his plan for improving the economy in the event that he won the election. 他拒绝在他赢得选举的情况下透露更多关于振兴经济计划的细节。
近 amplify, develop, elaborate on, flesh out, enlarge on
反 abbreviate, abridge, condense, shorten 删减，缩短

dilatory ［ˈdɪlətɔːri］
【考法】 *adj.*拖延的，磨蹭的：tending or intended to **cause delay**, characterized by **procrastination**
例 dilatory tactics 拖延战术 ‖ The homeowner is claiming that local firefighters were dilatory in responding to the call. 业主声称本地的消防队员对（火警）电话有拖延。
近 delaying, procrastinating, dragging, lagging, tardy
反 rapid, fast, fleet, precipitate, rocketing, swift, hasty, hurrying, scurrying 快速的

dilettante ［ˌdɪləˈtænti］
【考法】 *n./adj.*业余爱好者（对艺术或知识领域涉猎浅薄者）/缺乏专业技术的：a person having a **superficial interest** in an art / **lacking** or showing a lack of **expert skill**
例 Dilettante watch the scene of bustle, adept guard the entrance. 外行看热闹，内行看门道。‖ Many dilettante efforts could be seen at the sidewalk art show. 街边艺术展上可以看到很多技术业余的作品。
近 dabbler, amateur, nonexpert, cognoscente; nonprofessional, amateur
反 authority, expert, pro, professional, specialist 专家

diligent [ˈdɪlɪdʒnət]

【考法】 *adj.* 勤勉的，辛勤的：characterized by **steady**, **earnest**, and **energetic** effort: painstaking

例 A new bride is diligent for three days. 新娶媳妇三日勤。‖ a student who has been unceasingly diligent in pursuit of a degree in mathematics 一个不断勤奋追求数学学位的学生

近 assiduous, industrious, sedulous, engaged, hopping, tied-up

反 idle, inactive, unbusy, unemployed, unoccupied 空闲的

dilute [daɪˈluːt]

【考法 1】 *vt.* 稀释 / *adj.* 经稀释的：to make thinner or less **concentrated** by adding a liquid such as water/of relatively **low strength** or **concentration**

例 dilute a color 稀释色彩 ‖ a dilute acid that's safe to handle in the classroom 稀释了的可以安全在教室处理的酸

近 thin

反 condense, densify, concentrate, thicken 使浓缩

【考法 2】 *vt.* 削弱：to **diminish** the **strength**, **flavor**, or **brilliance** of by admixture

例 The hiring of the new CEO diluted the power of the company's president. 新的 CEO 削弱了公司董事长的权力。

近 weaken

反 fortify, strengthen 增强

diminish [dɪˈmɪnɪʃ]

【考法 1】 *v.* (使)变小，(使)减少：to (cause to) become **smaller** or **less**

例 diminish an army's strength 削弱军队力量 ‖ The sound of the train diminished as our distance from it increased. 当我们距离火车越远时，火车的声音就越小。

近 abate, dwindle, lessen, lower, reduce, decline

反 aggrandize, amplify, augment, boost, enlarge, escalate, expand, increase, raise, balloon 增加，增大

【考法 2】 *v.* 轻视，贬低：to **lessen** the authority, dignity, or reputation of: **belittle**

例 diminish a rival's accomplishments 贬低对手的成就

近 belittle, deprecate, depreciate, disparage

反 acclaim, applaud, exalt, extol, glorify, laud, praise 赞美

din [dɪn]

【考法 1】 *n.* 喧闹声，嘈杂声：a **loud** continued **noise**

例 The din of the engines was deafening. 引擎的嘈杂声震耳欲聋。‖ There's always a great din from the cafeteria during lunch. 午餐时间经常从餐厅里传来很大的喧闹声。

近 blare, bluster, cacophony, chatter, clamor, discordance, racket, rattle, roar

反 quiet, silence, still 安静

【考法 2】 *v.* 重复，使人厌烦地反复灌输：to say or state **again**

例 Safety lessons dinned into us over and over. 我们一遍又一遍地进行安全教育。

近 iterate, rehearse, reiterate

Unit 4

| ■ DINGY | ■ DIOCESAN | ■ DIPLOMATIC | ■ DIRE | ■ DIRGE |
| ■ DISABUSE | ■ DISAFFECTED | ■ DISARM | ■ DISARRAY | ■ DISAVOW |

dingy [ˈdɪndʒi]

【考法】 *adj.* 昏暗的；肮脏的：**darkened** with smoke and grime; **dirty** or discolored

例 A dingy room is always Dickensian image of the poor. 一个肮脏而昏暗的房间经常作为狄更斯时代的穷人形象。‖ The bed sheets were pretty dingy so we threw them in the laundry pile. 床单太脏了，我们把它扔进了脏衣服堆。

近 darkened, dirty, bedraggled, bemired, besmirched, dusty, mucky, muddy, nasty, smudged, soiled, sordid, stained, sullied

反 clean, cleanly, immaculate, spotless, stainless, unsoiled, unstained, unsullied 干净的

diocesan [daɪˈɑːsɪsn]

【考法】 *adj.* 主教管辖区的：of or relating to a **diocese**

例 national or diocesan authority 国家或教区权利

反 ecumenical 世界范围的

diplomatic	[ˌdɪpləˈmætɪk]

【考法】 *adj.* 使用策略的，机智的：employing **tact** and conciliation especially in situations of stress
例 be very diplomatic with awkward clients 总是有办法对付难缠的顾客
近 politic
反 gauche, impolitic, tactless, undiplomatic, untactful 笨拙的，不机智的

dire	[ˈdaɪər]

【考法 1】 *adj.* 不吉利的，不祥的：being or showing a sign of **evil** or **calamity** to come
例 a dire forecast of a plunge in stock prices 股市大跌不祥的预测
近 baleful, direful, foreboding, ill-boding, inauspicious, menacing, minatory, portentous, sinister, threatening
反 propitious, unthreatening 吉利的，吉祥的

【考法 2】 *adj.* 可怕的，恐怖的：causing **fear**
例 a series of dire tremors that hinted at a volcanic eruption 一系列暗示火山爆发的恐怖的震动
近 alarming, direful, dread, dreadful, fearsome, forbidding, formidable, frightening, frightful, ghastly, hair-raising, horrendous, horrible, horrifying, intimidating, redoubtable, scary, shocking, terrible, terrifying

【考法 3】 *adj.* 迫切的：needing **immediate** attention; **urgent**
例 There is a dire need for food and medicine in the famine-stricken country. 在闹饥荒的国家迫切需要食物和药品。
近 immediate, burning, compelling, critical, crying, emergent, exigent, imperative, imperious, importunate, instant, necessitous, pressing, urgent
反 nonurgent, noncritical 不迫切的

【考法 4】 *adj.* 悲惨的：causing or marked by an atmosphere **lacking** in **cheer**
例 With stock prices steadily falling, these are dire days on the trading floor. 股价不断走低，交易大厅一片悲惨的景象。
近 cheerless, chill, depressing, depressive, desolate, disconsolate, dismal, drear, dreary, funereal, glum, lugubrious, miserable, morose, saturnine, somber, sullen, sunless, wretched
反 bright, cheerful, cheering, cheery, festive, gay, sunshiny 愉快的

dirge	[dɜːrdʒ]

【考法】 *n.* 挽歌：a slow, **solemn**, and **mournful** piece of **music**
例 This funeral dirge is for the dead friend. 这首葬礼挽歌是写给故去的朋友的。
近 elegy, requiem

disabuse	[ˌdɪsəˈbjuːz]

【考法】 *vt.* 打消错误念头，纠正：to **free from error**, **fallacy**, or **misconception**
例 disabuse sb of the notion that... 打消某人的…观点 ‖ I must disabuse you of your feelings of grandeur. 我必须消除你的傲气。
近 disenchant, undeceive
反 lead into error 导致错误；mislead 误导

disaffected	[ˌdɪsəˈfektɪd]

【考法】 *adj.* 不满的，叛逆的：**discontented** and resentful especially against authority; **rebellious**
例 gangs of disaffected teenagers 一群叛逆的年轻人 ‖ The soldiers were disaffected toward the government. 那些士兵对政府不满.
近 discontented, dissatisfied, malcontent, rebellious, insubordinate, contumacious
反 satisfied, contented 满足的
派 disaffect *vt.* 使不安，使不满：to fill with discontent and unrest; disaffection *n.* 不满，疏远：estrangement
近 dissatisfy, agitate, upset
反 mollify 平息，抚慰

disarm	[dɪsˈɑːrm]

【考法 1】 *v.* 解除武装：to give up or **reduce armed forces**
例 disarm the captured soldiers 解除被捕士兵的武装 ‖ The defeated nation was disarmed so that it would never again be a threat to international order. 战败国被解除武装，这样一来它就不会再对国际秩序造成威胁。
近 demilitarize
反 arm, militarize, put on guard 装备武器

【考法 2】 *vt.* 使息怒，平息，抚慰：to **lessen** the anger or agitation of
例 Her future father-in-law was totally disarmed by her words. 她未来的继父听了她的话彻底没脾气了。
近 appease, assuage, conciliate, gentle, mollify, placate, propitiate
反 anger, enrage, incense, inflame, enflame, infuriate, ire, madden, outrage 煽动，激起

【考法 3】 *vt.* 使无害：to make **harmless**
例 disarm a bomb 拆除炸弹

disarray [ˌdɪsəˈreɪ]

【考法1】 *n.* 混乱，无秩序：a **lack** of **order** or sequence

例 The room was in disarray. 房间一片混乱。

近 confusion, disarrangement, disorder, disorderliness, disorganization, havoc, mess, messiness, misorder, muddle, muss, shambles, jumble, welter

反 order, orderliness 有序

【考法2】 *vt.* 使混乱：to **undo** the proper **order** or **arrangement** of

例 Changing offices disarrayed my papers completely. 办公室搬迁使我的文件全部乱套了.

近 confuse, disarrange, discompose, dishevel, dislocate, disorganize, disrupt, disturb, hash, jumble, muddle, muss, rumple, scramble, upset, mess up, mix up

反 arrange, array, dispose, order, organize, range, regulate, straighten up 使有序

disavow [ˌdɪsəˈvaʊ]

【考法】 *vt.* 拒绝承认，否认：to **disclaim** knowledge of, responsibility for, or association with; to declare **not** to be **true**

例 disavow the rumor 否认谣言 ‖ She disavowed the testimony that she had given earlier in the trial. 她在审判中否认了自己之前的证词。

近 deny, repudiate, disaffirm, disclaim, disconfirm, gainsay, negate

反 acknowledge, avow, concede 承认

Unit 5

■ DISCERN	■ DISCHARGE	■ DISCIPLE	■ DISCOMBOBULATE	■ DISCOMFIT
■ DISCOMMODE	■ DISCOMPOSE	■ DISCONCERT	■ DISCORD	■ DISCREDIT

discern [dɪˈsɜːrn]

【考法】 *v.* 识别，辨别差异：to **perceive** with the eyes or intellect; **detect**

例 discern the motives 辨识出动机 ‖ too young to discern between right and wrong 太年轻而辨别不了是非

近 behold, descry, distinguish, espy, perceive, regard, differentiate, discriminate

反 confuse, mix up 混淆

派 discerning *adj.* 有洞察力的，洞悉的：showing insight and understanding

例 a very discerning art critic 眼光敏锐有洞察力的艺术评论家 ‖ She has a discerning palate. 她的味觉很敏锐。

近 insightful, incisive

反 myopic, shortsighted 目光短浅的；undiscerning 无辨别能力的

派 discernible/discernable *adj.* 可辨识的，可辨别的：perceptible

例 a discernible mark 可辨别的痕迹

近 perceptible, detectable, distinguishable

反 indiscernible, imperceptible 不可辨识的

discharge

【考法1】 [dɪsˈtʃɑːrdʒ] *vt.* 解雇：to **dismiss** from employment

例 discharge a worker/soldier 开除员工/军籍

近 fire, dismiss

反 employ, engage, hire, take on, sign up or on 雇佣

【考法2】 *vt.* 释放：to set **free** (as from slavery or confinement)

例 discharge the prisoners upon the signing of the peace treaty 根据和平条约释放罪犯

近 disenthrall, emancipate, enfranchise, liberate, loose, manumit, release, spring, unbind, uncage, unchain, unfetter

反 bind, confine, enchain, fetter 监禁，束缚

【考法3】 [ˈdɪstʃɑːrdʒ] *n.* 不承担责任：a **freeing** from an **obligation** or **responsibility**

例 a full discharge from responsibility for the accident 对事故完全不负有责任

近 delivery, quietus, quittance

disciple [dɪˈsaɪpl]

【考法】 *n.* 信徒，追随者：one who accepts and assists in spreading the doctrines of another, **follower**

例 A circle of dedicated disciples who conscientiously wrote down everything the prophet said. 一圈忠实的信徒认真地记下了先知所说的话。

近 acolyte, adherent, convert, epigone, partisan, votary

反 leader, coryphaeus 领导者

discombobulate [ˌdɪskəmˈbɑːbjuleɪt]

【考法】 *vt.* 使不安，使混乱：**upset, confuse**

例 invent cool new ways to discombobulate the old order 发明新的好方法打乱了旧秩序

近 upset, addle, baffle, bamboozle, befog, befuddle, confound, fuddle, gravel, muddle, muddy, mystify, perplex, puzzle, vex

反 compose, soothe, calm, pacify 使安定

discomfit [dɪsˈkʌmfɪt]

【考法 1】 *vt.* 使尴尬：to put into a state of perplexity and **embarrassment**

例 He was discomfited by the awkward situation of having his ex-girlfriend meet his current one. 他的前女友看到他现任女友的情况让他很尴尬。

近 embarrass, abash, faze, fluster, mortify, nonplus, rattle

【考法 2】 *vt.* 阻碍：to **prevent** from achieving a goal

例 Constant interruptions discomfited her in her attempt to finish the speech. 经常打断她讲话导致她无法完成演讲。

近 balk, foil, thwart, baffle, checkmate

反 advance, forward, foster, further, promote 推进，促进；encourage 鼓励

discommode [dɪskəˈmoʊd]

【考法】 *vt.* 打扰，使不便：to cause inconvenience to: **trouble**

例 The breakdown of her car didn't discommode her seriously. 车的故障没有给她带来很大麻烦。

近 disturb, trouble, incommode, put out

反 accommodate, assist, oblige, favor 帮忙

discompose [ˌdɪskəmˈpoʊz]

【考法 1】 *vt.* 使不安：to **disturb** the **composure** or calm of; **perturb**

例 GRE does not seem to discompose Jason; on the contrary, he looks rather relaxed. GRE 没有使 Jason 感到慌乱，正相反，他看上去很轻松。

近 agitate, bother, discomfort, disquiet, distemper, disconcert, disturb, perturb, upset, weird out

反 calm, compose, quiet, settle, soothe, tranquilize 平息，抚慰

【考法 2】 *vt.* 使混乱：to **undo** the proper **order** or **arrangement** of

例 The wind ruffled her hair and discomposed her carefully arranged papers. 风凌乱了她的头发，吹乱了她细心整理的纸张。

近 disarrange, disarray, disorganize

反 arrange, array, order, organize, range 使有序

disconcert [ˌdɪskənˈsɜːrt]

【考法】 *vt.* 使不安：to **disturb** the composure of

例 We were disconcerted by the unexpected changes to the program. 我们对项目未预料到的变化感到不安。

近 abash, discomfit, discountenance, mortify, rattle

反 calm, compose, quiet, settle, soothe, tranquilize 平息，抚慰

discord [ˈdɪskɔːrd]

【考法】 *n.* 意见不一致，不和谐：**lack** of **agreement** or **harmony**（as between persons, things, or ideas）

例 No discord, no concord. 不打不成交。

近 conflict, disaccord, discordance, disharmony, dissension, dissidence, dissonance, disunion, disunity, division, friction, inharmony, schism, strife, row, divergence

反 accord, agreement, concord, concordance, harmony, consensus, unanimity 和谐，一致

派 discordant *adj.* 不和谐的，刺耳的：disagreeable in sound; harsh or dissonant

近 dissonant, cacophonous, disharmonic, disharmonious

反 concordant, harmonious 和谐的

discredit [dɪsˈkredɪt]

【考法 1】 *vt.* 羞辱，使丧失名誉：to **damage** in **reputation**; **disgrace**

例 discredit his opponents 羞辱他的对手

近 abase, debase, degrade, demean, disgrace, dishonor, humiliate, shame, sink, smirch, take down

反 aggrandize 提高名誉；canonize, deify 神化；elevate 提升；exalt 赞扬

【考法 2】 *vt.* 怀疑，不相信：to think **not** to be **true** or **real**

例 I discredit the story that the old house is haunted. 我怀疑那个房子闹鬼不是真的。

近 negate, doubt, distrust

反 accept, believe, credit 接受，相信；confirm, prove, validate, verify 证实

Unit 6

discrepancy [dɪsˈkrepənsi]

【考法】 *n.* (在事实和宣称之间的)差异或矛盾：**divergence** or **disagreement**, as between facts or claims

例 a large discrepancy between the ideal image and the reality 理想与现实之间的巨大差距

近 contrast, disagreement, disparity, dissimilarity, distance, distinction, diversity

反 convergence, concord, consonance 一致，和谐；analogousness, community, resemblance, similarity 相似

discrete [dɪˈskriːt]

【考法】 *adj.* 离散的，不连续的：constituting a **separate** entity

例 a discrete variable 离散变量

近 detached, disconnected, unattached, unconnected, separate

反 continuous 连续的；attached, connected, joined, linked 连接的

discretion [dɪˈskreʃn]

【考法 1】 *n.* 谨慎：the quality of being **discreet**; **circumspection**

例 You must show discretion in choosing your teammates. 你选择队友时必须慎重。

近 discreetness, prudence

反 imprudence, indiscretion 轻率

派 indiscretion *n.* 不谨慎，不符合社会道德规范：an act at variance with the accepted morality of a society

例 resign because of financial indiscretions 因为财政方面的不检点而辞职

【考法 2】 *n.* 自制，节制：the **checking** of one's true feelings and impulses when dealing with others

例 In that job you'll be expected to show discretion and act like a professional at all times. 那项工作要求你时刻保持自制，表现得像一个专业人士。

近 continence, discipline, inhibition, refrainment, restraint, self-control, self-restraint

反 disinhibition, incontinence, unconstraint 不自制，不节制

discretionary [dɪˈskreʃəneri]

【考法】 *adj.* 自主决定的：left to discretion: exercised at **one's own discretion**

例 In many restaurants, discretionary tipping is being replaced by a standard service charge. 在很多饭店，标准的服务价格取代了随意支付的小费。

近 elective, voluntary

反 compulsory, mandatory, nonelective, nonvoluntary, obligatory, required 强制性的，非自愿的

discriminate [dɪˈskrɪmɪneɪt]

【考法 1】 *vt.* 区分：to **perceive** the **distinguishing** features of; **recognize** as distinct

例 discriminate different kinds of animals 区分不同的动物

近 differentiate, discern, distinguish

反 confuse, mistake, mix up 混淆

【考法 2】 *vi.* 歧视：to make a **difference** in treatment or favor on a basis other than individual merit

例 The new law discriminated against lower-paid workers. 这条新法律歧视低工资的工人。

派 discriminatory *adj.* 差别对待的：marked by or showing prejudice; biased

近 prejudiced, biased

反 equitable, impartial, unbiased, impersonal, unprejudiced 公平的

discursive [dɪsˈkɜːrsɪv]

【考法】 *adj.* (谈话内容)杂乱的：moving from topic to topic **without order**

例 a long, discursive article 冗长杂乱的文章 ‖ The speaker's discursive style made it difficult to understand his point. 演讲者讲话杂乱，很难让人理解他的观点。

近 desultory, digressional, excursive, meandering, rambling, wandering

反 keen on title, concentrated 关注主题的，集中的

disdain [dɪsˈdeɪn]

【考法】 *vt.* 轻视，鄙视：to look on with **scorn**

例 disdain that man for snobbishness 鄙视那个势利小人

近 contemn, disrespect, slight, sniff, snub, look down

反 honor, respect 尊敬；treat favorably 亲切地对待

disengage [ˌdɪsɪnˈɡeɪdʒ]

【考法】 *vt.* 分开，使脱离：to **set free** from **entanglement** or difficulty

例 Disengage the gears when you park the car. 当你停车的时候要把（传动）齿轮分开。‖ seek to disengage myself from the embarrassing situation 试图把我自己从尴尬的气氛中解救出来

近 disengage, disentangle, untangle

反 embroil, entangle 卷入；mesh 啮合

disgorge [dɪsˈɡɔːrdʒ]

【考法 1】 *v.* 呕吐出：to **discharge** by the throat and mouth; **vomit**

例 He cannot disgorge a fish bone without the doctor's assistant. 没有医生的帮助他吐不出鱼刺来。‖ The volcano disgorged lava. 火山喷出岩浆。

近 belch, disgorge, eject, eruct, expel, jet, spew, spout

反 swallow, ingest 吞下，咽下

【考法 2】 *v.* 被迫放弃：to **give up** on request or under pressure

例 The corrupt officials refused to disgorge his ill-gotten gains. 贪官们拒绝放弃赃款。

disgruntle [dɪsˈɡrʌntl]

【考法 1】 *vt.* 使发怒，使不满意：to make ill-humored or **discontented**

例 be disgruntled with sb 对某人不满

近 disaffect, displease, dissatisfy

反 content, gratify, please, satisfy 使满意

【考法 2】 *vt.* 使疏远，使不友好：to cause to change from friendly or loving to **unfriendly** or uncaring

近 alien, alienate

反 reconcile 调解，使和谐

Unit 7

■ DISGUISE   ■ DISINCLINATION   ■ DISINFECT   ■ DISJOINTED   ■ DISINTER
■ DISINTERESTED   ■ DISJUNCTIVE   ■ DISMANTLE   ■ DISMAY   ■ DISPARAGE

disguise [dɪsˈɡaɪz]

【考法 1】 *vt.* 伪装（防止被认出）：to modify the manner or appearance of in order to **prevent recognition**

例 The raiders disguised themselves as security guards. 袭击者装扮成了保安人员。

近 camouflage, costume, mask

反 unmask 使露出真相

【考法 2】 *vt.* 隐藏，掩饰：to keep **secret** or **shut off** from view

例 That investigative reporter usually does a good job of disguising her true motives for interviewing a person. 采访时，那个调查记者通常会很好地隐藏自己的真实目的。‖ He always disguises his true feelings. 他经常掩饰自己的真实感受。

近 belie, blanket, conceal, cover, curtain, occult, veil

反 bare, disclose, display, divulge, expose, reveal, show, uncover, unmask, unveil 暴露，展现

disinclination [ˌdɪsɪnklɪˈneɪʃn]

【考法】 *n.* 不喜欢，厌恶，不情愿：a **lack** of **willingness** or **desire** to do or accept something

例 show a marked disinclination 表现出明显的不情愿

近 aversion, disfavor, disliking, disrelish, mislike, unwillingness

反 appetite, favor, fondness, liking, partiality, preference, relish, inclination 喜欢；willingness 情愿

disinfect [ˌdɪsɪnˈfekt]

【考法】 *vt.* 消毒，使无菌：to **free from infection** especially by destroying harmful microorganisms

例 disinfect with bleaching powder 用漂白粉消毒

近 sterilize

反 infect, pollute, contaminate, taint 感染，污染

disjointed [dɪsˈdʒɔɪntɪd]

【考法 1】 *adj.* 机能失调的：being thrown **out** of **orderly function**

例 a disjointed society 混乱的社会

近 chaotic, disorderly

反 orderly, regular, systematic 有序的，规律的，系统的

【考法 2】 *adj.* 不连贯的：**not** clearly or logically **connected**

例 a disjointed speech about a hodgepodge of things 关于一大堆杂事的不连贯的演讲

近 disconnected, unconnected

反 coherent, connected 连贯的

---

disinter [ˌdɪsɪnˈtɜːr]

【考法】 *vt.* (从墓地里)掘出：to **take out** of the grave or tomb

例 The Egyptian mummy was carefully disinterred in hopes that it would yield secrets about the Old Kingdom. 那个埃及木乃伊被小心地挖掘出来，人们希望它可以告诉我们关于这个古老王国的一些秘密。

近 unbury, unearth

反 bury, inter, tomb, inhume 埋葬

---

disinterested [dɪsˈɪntrəstɪd]

【考法 1】 *adj.* 公正的，无偏见的：**free from selfish** motive or interest: **unbiased**

例 a disinterested decision 公正的决定

近 equal, evenhanded, impartial, just, nonpartisan, dispassionate, objective, square, unbiased, unprejudiced

反 biased, inequitable, nonobjective, one-sided, partial, partisan, prejudiced, unjust 不公正的，有偏见的

【考法 2】 *adj.* 没有兴趣的：having or showing a **lack** of **interest** or **concern**

例 The city's philistines, naturally disinterested in art, voted to cut the museum's budget. 城市里对艺术本来就不感兴趣的俗人们，投票表决要缩减博物馆的预算。

近 apathetic, incurious, insouciant, nonchalant, perfunctory, unconcerned

反 concerned, interested 关心的，感兴趣的

---

disjunctive [dɪsˈdʒʌŋktɪv]

【考法】 *adj.* 分离的：marked by **breaks** or **disunity**

例 a disjunctive narrative sequence 分散的叙述顺序

近 discrete, separate, disconnected, disunited

反 combined, connected, jointed, mixed, united 连接的，混合的

---

dismantle [dɪsˈmæntl]

【考法】 *vt.* 分解，分拆：to take to **pieces** also: to **destroy** the **integrity** or functioning of

例 dismantle a machine 分拆机器

近 break down, knock down

反 assemble, construct 组装

---

dismay [dɪsˈmeɪ]

【考法 1】 *vt.* 使失去勇气：to cause to **lose courage** or resolution

例 The excessive homework dismayed ourselves. 过量的作业让我们失去了信心。

近 chill, daunt, dishearten, dispirit, frustrate, unnerve

反 embolden, encourage, hearten, nerve 鼓励，使勇敢

【考法 2】 *vt.* 使不安，使焦虑：to **trouble** the mind of; to make **uneasy**

例 Parents became increasingly dismayed by their son's GPA. 父母对他们儿子的平均成绩非常焦虑。

近 agitate, bother, discomfort, discompose, disquiet, distemper, distress, perturb, unsettle, upset

反 calm, compose, quiet, soothe, tranquilize 平息，抚慰

---

disparage [dɪˈspærɪdʒ]

【考法】 *vt.* 贬低；轻蔑地说：to **lower** in rank or reputation; to speak of in a slighting or **disrespectful** way; belittle

例 use the past to disparage the present 借古讽今 ‖ Voters don't like political advertisements in which opponents disparage one another. 选民不喜欢看到竞争对手互相贬低的政治广告。

近 belittle, denigrate, deprecate, depreciate, derogate, degrade

反 acclaim, applaud, exalt, extol, glorify, laud 赞扬

Unit 8

■ DISPARATE	■ DISPASSIONATE	■ DISPATCH	■ DISPOSE	■ DISREGARD
■ DISSECT	■ DISSEMBLE	■ DISSEMINATE	■ DISSENSION	■ DISSENT

---

disparate [ˈdɪspərət]

【考法】 *adj.* 迥然不同的：fundamentally **distinct** or **different** in kind; entirely **dissimilar**

例 This couple of seemingly disparate topics have something in common. 这两个看似无关的主题其实有些相同之处。

近 dissimilar, distinct, distinguishable, diverse, nonidentical, unalike

反 alike, identical, indistinguishable, kindred, like, parallel, same, similar 相似的，相同的

dispassionate [dɪsˈpæʃənət]

【考法】 *adj.* 客观公正的，不易被情绪或偏见影响的：devoid of or **unaffected** by passion, emotion, or **bias**

例 Journalists should aim to be dispassionate observers. 记者们应该朝着成为一个公正的观察者努力。

近 disinterested, equal, equitable, evenhanded, impartial, just, nonpartisan, objective, unbiased, unprejudiced

反 biased, inequitable, nonobjective, one-sided, partial, partisan, prejudiced, unjust 有偏见的，不公正的

dispatch [dɪˈspætʃ]

【考法 1】 *n.* 迅速：**promptness** and efficiency in performance or transmission

例 do sth with dispatch 迅速地做某事

近 alacrity, haste, swiftness, expedition, promptitude

反 leisureliness, delay, procrastination 悠然；拖延

【考法 2】 *vt.* 发送，派遣：to cause to go or be taken from **one place to another**

例 to dispatch a messenger with urgent news 发送一个紧急消息

近 transfer, transmit, transport, pack off

反 accept, receive 接收

【考法 3】 *vt.* 使死亡：to **deprive** of **life**

例 dispatch a criminal 处决罪犯 ‖ The man dispatched the termites with professional efficiency. 那个男人技术纯熟地杀死了白蚁。

反 animate 使有生命

【考法 4】 *vt.* 获胜，胜过…：to achieve a **victory** over

例 They dispatched the other team with breaking a sweat. 他们险胜其他的队。

近 conquer, defeat, subdue, triumph over, prevail over

反 lose to 输给…

dispose [dɪˈspoʊz]

【考法 1】 *vt.* 使倾向于：to give a **tendency** to: **incline**

例 faulty diet disposes one to sickness 营养不全面导致疾病

派 disposed *adj.* 喜欢的：willing or likely, inclined

例 not feel disposed to argue with her 不喜欢与她争执

近 willing, inclined, predisposed, prone

反 disinclined, indisposed 不喜欢的

【考法 2】 *vi.* 处理掉（与 of 连用，dispose of）：to **get rid of**; **throw out**

派 disposal *n.* 处理，不再利用：the act of getting rid of something that is no longer wanted or needed

例 the permanent disposal of radioactive wastes 对放射性废物的永久处理

【考法 3】 *vt.* 有序地布置：to place, distribute, or arrange especially in an **orderly** way

例 Dispose the surgical instruments in the exact order in which they would be needed. 把手术仪器按他们被需要的顺序放置。

近 array, arrange

反 disarrange, disarray, disorder, upset, mess up, muss up 使混乱

disregard [ˌdɪsrɪˈɡɑːrd]

【考法 1】 *vt.* 漠视，不关注：to pay **no attention** to

例 disregard the advice of his executives 漠视管理者的建议

近 ignore, overlook, slight

反 heed, mind, regard, attend to 关注

【考法 2】 *n.* 缺乏兴趣，缺乏关心：lack of **interest** or **concern**

例 Revelers fired guns in the air with complete disregard for the possible consequences. 饮酒狂欢者朝空中乱开枪，一点也不关心可能产生的后果。

近 apathy, disinterestedness, incuriosity, nonchalance, torpor, unconcern

反 concern, interest, regard 关心，感兴趣

dissect [dɪˈsekt]

【考法 1】 *vt.* 仔细分析：to **examine**, **analyze**, or criticize in **minute** detail

例 dissect some basic problems in mathematics analysis 仔细研究数学分析中的一些基本问题 ‖ Let's dissect the plot of this thriller to see what makes it thrilling. 让我们来仔细分析一下这个恐怖电影为什么恐怖。

近 analyze

【考法 2】 *vt.* 切成片（尤其是为了解剖研究）：to **cut apart** or **separate** (tissue), especially for anatomical study

例 dissect the brain of Einstein 解剖爱因斯坦的大脑

近 anatomize, assay, break down

dissemble [dɪˈsembl]
【考法】 v. 用假象隐藏真相，掩饰: to put on a **false** appearance
例 dissemble fear with a smile 用微笑来掩饰恐惧 ‖ He dissembled happiness at the news that his ex-girlfriend was getting married to someone else. 他听到前女友结婚的消息后假装高兴。
近 dissimulate, affect, assume, bluff, counterfeit, fake, sham
反 behave honestly 表现诚恳

disseminate [dɪˈsemɪneɪt]
【考法】 vt. 散播，传播: to **spread** abroad; **promulgate**
例 disseminate Marxism-Leninism 传播马列主义 ‖ The Internet allows us to disseminate information faster. 互联网让我们更快地传播信息。
近 broadcast, circulate, propagate
反 gather, amass, garner 收集

dissension [dɪˈsenʃn]
【考法】 n. 意见不合: **difference** of opinion; **disagreement**
例 Although we have dissension, we are friend all the same. 虽然我们意见不合，但我们还是朋友。‖ There is a continued dissension among historians on the exact spot of Columbus's first landing. 对于哥伦布第一次的准确登陆地点这个问题，历史学家们总是存在分歧。
近 conflict, disaccord, discordance, discordancy, disharmony, dissent, dissidence, dissonance, disunion, disunity, division, friction, inharmony, schism, strife, row, divergence
反 accord, agreement, concord, concordance, harmony, consensus, unanimity 和谐，一致

dissent [dɪˈsent]
【考法1】 vi. 持异议，不同意: to **differ** in opinion
例 I dissent from what you said. 我不同意你说的话。‖ Anyone who dissented was encouraged to speak out while they had the chance. 如果谁有异议，有机会都可以发言。
近 differ, disagree, nonconcur
反 agree, assent, concur 同意
【考法2】 n. 反对正统: **departure** from a generally **accepted** theory, opinion, or practice
例 The church reacted to any form of dissent by promptly excommunicating its proponents. 教堂会立即开除任何反对正统教义的人。
近 heterodoxy, nonconformity
反 conformity 遵从; orthodoxy 正统
【考法3】 n. 意见不一致，不和谐: a **lack** of agreement or **harmony**
近 conflict, disaccord, discordance, discordancy, disharmony, dissesion, dissidence, dissonance, disunion, disunity, division, friction, inharmony, schism, strife, row, divergence
反 accord, agreement, concord, concordance, harmony, consensus, unanimity 和谐，一致

Unit 9

| ■ DISSIPATE | ■ DISSOLUTE | ■ DISSOLVE | ■ DISSONANCE | ■ DISSUADE |
| ■ DISTAIN | ■ DISTAL | ■ DISTEND | ■ DISTILL | ■ DISTORT |

dissipate [ˈdɪsɪpeɪt]
【考法1】 vt. 驱散: to **drive away**; **disperse**
例 The wind finally dissipated the smoke. 风终于吹散了雾气。
近 disband, dispel, disperse, scatter
反 accumulate, gather, amass, cluster, assemble, concentrate, congregate 积聚
【考法2】 vt. 浪费: to spend or expend intemperately or **wastefully**: **squander**
例 dissipate too much time and effort 挥霍了太多的时间与精力
近 waste, squander, lavish
反 conserve 节省
【考法3】 vi. 放纵: to **indulge** in the **intemperate** pursuit of pleasure, especially: to drink to excess
近 indulge

dissolute [ˈdɪsəluːt]
【考法】 adj. 放荡的，无节制的: lacking moral **restraint**; **indulging** in sensual pleasures or vices
例 lead a dissolute life 过着放荡无节制的生活
近 dissipated, libertine, rakish, reprobate
反 abstinent, abstemious, temperate, ascetic, stoic, spartan, self-denying 自我节制的; pure, uncorrupt, uncorrupted 纯洁的，未堕落的

dissolve [dɪˈzɑːlv]

【考法 1】 *v.* 溶解，融化：to cause to pass into **solution**; to reduce (solid matter) to liquid form; **melt**
- 例 Sugar dissolves in the water. 糖在水中溶解。
- 近 liquefy, melt
- 反 coagulate, solidify, freeze 凝结，凝固，结冰

【考法 2】 *v.* 解散：to **break into** component **parts**; **disintegrate**
- 近 disintegrate, disband, break up
- 反 consolidate, unify 使联合

【考法 3】 *v.* 驱散；(使)消失：to (cause to) **cease** to be **visible**; to (cause to) **cease** to **exist**
- 例 The mist dissolved in the morning sun. 雾消失在朝阳中。
- 近 dematerialize, vanish
- 反 appear 出现；materialize 使实物化

【考法 4】 *v.* 废除，撤销：to put an **end** to by formal action
- 例 The king dissolved parliament. 国王废除了议会。
- 近 terminate, abrogate, annul, cancel, disannul, invalidate, negate, null, nullify, repeal, rescind

dissonance [ˈdɪsənəns]

【考法】 *n.* (音调)不和谐，刺耳；不一致，分歧：a harsh, **disagreeable** combination of sounds; **discord**; lack of agreement, consistency, or harmony; conflict
- 例 cognitive dissonance 认识上的分歧 ‖ Dissonance among the three partners doomed the project. 三个股东间的不调和注定了那计划的失败。
- 近 conflict, disaccord, discordance, discordancy, disharmony, dissent, dissidence, disunion, disunity, division, friction, inharmony, schism, strife
- 反 accord, agreement, concord, concordance, harmony, consensus, unanimity 和谐，一致

dissuade [dɪˈsweɪd]

【考法】 *vt.* 劝阻，反对：to **deter** (a person) from a course of action or a purpose by **persuasion** or **exhortation**
- 例 dissuade sb from (doing) sth 劝阻/反对某人做某事 ‖ Her parents tried to dissuade her from her intention to drop out of college. 她的父母劝她不要退学。
- 近 deter, inhibit
- 反 encourage 鼓励；persuade 说服

distain [dɪsˈteɪn]

【考法 1】 *vt.* 贬损，伤害(某人的)名誉：to cause to **lose honor**, **respect**, or **reputation**
- 近 dishonor, belittle, denigrate, deprecate, depreciate, degrade
- 反 praise, acclaim, applaud, exalt, extol, glorify, laud 赞扬

【考法 2】 *vt.* 弄脏：to make **dirty**
- 例 hands distained with blood 被血弄脏的手
- 近 bemire, besmirch, daub, muddy, smirch, smudge, soil, stain, sully
- 反 clean 使干净

distal [ˈdɪstl]

【考法】 *adj.* 远离中心的，(神经)末梢的：**situated away** from the point of attachment or origin or a **central** point
- 例 the distal end of nerve 神经末梢
- 反 proximal 接近中心的

distend [dɪˈstend]

【考法】 *v.* (使)膨胀：to (cause to) swell out or **expand** from or as if from internal pressure
- 例 The stomachs of starving people often distend. 饥民的肚子经常涨起来。
- 近 expand, dilate, inflate, swell
- 反 constrict, compress 收缩，压缩

distill [dɪˈstɪl]

【考法 1】 *vt.* 对…用蒸馏法提高纯度：to **increase** the concentration of, separate, or **purify** by or as if by distillation
- 例 Distill the water before pouring it in the steam iron. 在把水倒到熨斗里前蒸馏一下
- 近 purify, filter, refine, fine
- 派 distillate *n.* 蒸馏物，纯化物，精华：a purified form; an essence

【考法 2】 *v.* (使)渗出；(使)滴下：to **fall** or let fall in or as if in **drops**
- 例 The basement walls distill water every time it rains heavily. 每次下大雨时，地下室的墙壁都会渗出水来。
- 近 dribble, drop, trickle

distort [dɪˈstɔːrt]

【考法】 *vt.* 扭曲，歪曲：to **twist** out of the true meaning or proportion

例 A painter may exaggerate or distort shapes and forms. 画家可能会夸张或扭曲形状。‖ The coach's message was so distorted after passing through so many people that it was unintelligible. 教练的信息在经过许多人传递后已经被歪曲得很难看懂了。

近 deform, misshape, torture, falsify, misinterpret, misrepresent, pervert, twist

Unit 10

■ DISTRACT	■ DISTRAUGHT	■ DIURNAL	■ DIVERGE	■ DIVERSITY
■ DIVERT	■ DIVESTITURE	■ DIVULGE	■ DODDER	■ DODGE

distract [dɪˈstrækt]

【考法1】 *vt.* 转移（注意力），使分心：to **draw** or **direct**（as one's attention）to a **different** object

例 be distracted by a sudden noise 被突然的噪音分心

近 abstract, divert, detract, call off

派 distracted *adj.* 精力分散的

反 rapt 全心投入的

【考法2】 *vt.* 使焦虑，使不安：to **trouble** the mind of; to make **uneasy**

例 The students are easily distracted before the exam. 学生们在考试前很容易焦虑不安。

近 agitate, bother, discomfort, discompose, dismay, disquiet, distress, perturb, upset

反 calm, compose, quiet, soothe, tranquilize 平息，抚慰

【考法3】 *adj.* 疯狂的：**insane**, **mad**

近 insane, delirious, hysterical

distraught [dɪˈstrɔːt]

【考法】 *adj.* 精神狂乱的，极疯狂的：deeply **agitated**, as from emotional conflict; **insane**

例 Her distraught mother had spent all night waiting by the phone. 她母亲忧心如焚，在电话旁守了一个晚上。

近 agitated, delirious, distracted, frenzied, hysterical

反 collected, composed, recollected, self-collected, self-composed, self-possessed 镇静的，平静的

diurnal [daɪˈɜːrnl]

【考法1】 *adj.* 白天发生或行动的：occurring or active during the **daytime** rather than at night

例 diurnal animals 昼行性动物

反 nocturnal 夜晚的

【考法2】 *adj.* 每天的：occurring, done, produced, or appearing **every day**

例 a love as constant and certain as the diurnal tides 像每天潮汐一样始终如一的爱情

近 daily, day-to-day

【考法3】 *adj.* 期刊：a **publication** that appears **at regular intervals**

例 A microfilm contains a collection of diurnals. 一个微缩胶片里包含很多期刊的合集。

近 bulletin, magazine, periodical, review, serial, journal

diverge [daɪˈvɜːrdʒ]

【考法1】 *vt.* 改变方向：to **change** one's course or direction

例 The deer abruptly diverged from its intended path the moment it spied the waiting lion. 当那只鹿发现潜伏的狮子的时候就突然改变了自己原来的路线。

近 detour, deviate, sheer, swerve, turn off

【考法2】 *vt.*（使）分叉，散开：to (cause to) go or move in **different directions** from a **central** point

例 At that point the road and the railroad tracks diverge. 公路和铁路在那个点分叉了。

近 branch out, divide, spread

反 converge, join 会合

【考法3】 *vi.* 分歧：to become or be **different** in character or form: **differ** in opinion

近 differ, disagree

反 conform 遵从

派 divergence *n.* 分歧，不同意：disagreement

【考法4】 *vi.* 离题：to **depart from** a set course or norm; deviate

近 excurse, ramble, get off the subject

diversity [daɪˈvɜːrsəti]

【考法1】 *n.* 多样性：**variety** or **multiformity**

例 the diversity of species 物种的多样性

近 diverseness, multifariousness, multiplicity, variousness, miscellaneousness

【考法2】 *n.* 分歧，不同点：the quality or state of being **different**

例 There is no fundamental diversity between the two ideologies. 这两种思想意识之间并没有根本的分歧。

近 contrast, disagreement, discrepancy, disparateness, disparity, dissimilarity, dissimilitude, distinction, otherness, unlikeness

反 alikeness, analogy, likeness, resemblance, sameness, similarity 相同，相似

divert [daɪˈvɜːrt]

【考法1】 *vt.* 使转向：to **turn** from one course or use to another: **deflect**

例 divert traffic to a side street 使交通转至辅路

近 deflect, redirect, swing, veer, wheel

反 fix, set, settle 固定

【考法2】 *vt.* 使消遣：to cause (someone) to pass the time **agreeably** occupied

例 A light comedy divert the tired business executive. 一个轻松的喜剧让疲惫的企业主管人员得到了放松。

近 disport, entertain, regale, solace

【考法3】 *vt.* 使分心：to **draw** the attention or mind to **something else**

例 divert one's attention 转移某人注意力 || The parents tried to divert the child with a toy while the doctor was giving her a shot. 当医生要给那个孩子打针的时候，她的父母试图用玩具转移其注意力。

近 abstract, detract, call off

divestiture [daɪˈvestɪtʃər]

【考法】 *n.* 剥夺：the act of **taking away** from a person

例 Melodramas were popular because they offered the audience a divestiture of neutrality. 情节剧之所以受到欢迎是因为他们给观众一个缺乏中立的(世界)。

近 deprivation, dispossession

反 acquisition 获得；endowment 捐赠

divulge [daɪˈvʌldʒ]

【考法】 *vt.* 泄漏(秘密)：to make **known** (as a **confidence** or **secret**)

例 refuse to divulge details of the negotiations 拒绝透露谈判的细节内容 || We tried to make him divulge the name of the winner, but he wouldn't budge. 我们试图让他透露胜利者的名字，但是他没有那样做。

近 bare, disclose, discover, expose, uncover, unmask, unveil

反 conceal, cover up, hide, mask, shroud, veil 保密，隐藏

dodder [ˈdɑːdər]

【考法】 *vi.* 蹒跚，颤巍巍地行进：to **progress** feebly and **unsteadily**

例 He could only dodder along after the operation. 他手术后只能步履蹒跚地走。

近 careen, lurch, teeter, totter, waddle

dodge [dɑːdʒ]

【考法】 *v.* 躲避：to **avoid** (a blow, for example) by moving or shifting quickly aside

例 dodge a storm of bullets 躲避枪林弹雨 || He dodged the first punch but was hit by the second. 他躲过了第一次打击，但是没有躲过第二次。

近 avoid, escape, shirk, malinger, goldbrick, evade, parry, sidestep, circumvent, fence, hedge, avert, elude, shun, skirt, bilk, eschew, weasel

List 8

Unit 1

■ DOFF	■ DOGGED	■ DOGMA	■ DOLDRUMS	■ DOLOROUS
■ DOLT	■ DOMICILE	■ DOMINANT	■ DON	■ DONOR

doff [dɑːf]

【考法】 *vt.* 脱下：to **take off**; **remove**

例 The blazing sun soon had the men doffing their jackets. 炙热的太阳很快就让男人们脱掉了夹克。

近 put off, take off

反 don, put on 穿上

dogged [ˈdɔːɡɪd]

【考法 1】 *adj.* 坚持的，坚决的：**continuing** despite difficulties, opposition, or discouragement; showing no signs of **slackening** or **yielding** in one's purpose

例 gain respect through sheer dogged determination 凭借单纯的坚决赢得了尊重 ‖ a madman who spent his life in dogged pursuit of power 一个一生都坚持追求权力的疯子

近 insistent, persevering, pertinacious, tenacious, determined

反 easily discouraged 容易气馁的；yielded 屈服的

【考法 2】 *adj.* 固执的，任性的：**sticking to** an opinion, purpose, or course of action in spite of reason, arguments, or persuasion

例 Your dogged adherence to a really lame argument is embarrassing. 你固执地坚持一个站不住脚的观点令人很尴尬。

近 adamant, hardheaded, headstrong, inflexible, intransigent, mulish, obdurate opinionated, ossified, pertinacious, self-opinionated, self-willed, stubborn, unbending, uncompromising, unrelenting, unyielding, willful

反 acquiescent, amenable, compliant, complying, flexible, pliable, pliant, relenting, yielding 顺从的

dogma [ˈdɔːɡmə]

【考法】 *n.* 教条，信条：a **doctrine** or body of doctrines concerning faith or morals formally **stated** and **authoritatively** proclaimed by a church

例 People are beginning to question the old dogmas. 人们开始质疑旧的信条。‖ The newspaper seeks to be independent of political dogma. 这份报纸力求不受政治信条影响。

近 credo, doctrine, gospel

反 heresy, heterodoxy 异端邪说

派 dogmatic *adj.* 独断的，武断的：characterized by an authoritative, arrogant assertion of unproved principles

例 a dogmatic critic 独断的评论家

近 dictatorial, dictative, authoritarian, authoritative, magisterial

doldrums [ˈdouldrəmz]

【考法 1】 *n.* 低迷，中断：a state or period of **inactivity**, stagnation, or slump

例 August is a time of doldrums for many enterprises. 对于许多企业来说八月是一个低迷期。‖ The economy is in the doldrums. 经济低迷。

近 abeyance, dormancy, latency, quiescence, moratorium

反 continuation 持续

【考法 2】 *n.* 情绪不佳：a state or spell of **low spirits**

例 The team had been in the doldrums ever since losing the championship. 整个队伍自从输了锦标赛以来一直情绪不佳。

近 dejection, depression, desolation, despondence, dolefulness, gloom, melancholy, unhappiness

反 bliss, ecstasy, elation, exhilaration, exuberance, exultation, jubilation, rapture, felicity 极度欢喜

dolorous [ˈdoʊlərəs]

【考法】 *adj.*忧伤的：causing, marked by, or expressing **misery** or **grief**
例 He lifted a pair of sapphire, dolorous eyes. 他抬起了一双忧郁的、蓝宝石般的眼睛。
近 agonized, bemoaning, bewailing, deplorable, grievous, miserable, plaintive, rueful, sorrowful, woeful
反 happy, joyful, jovial, jubilant 高兴的

dolt [doʊlt]

【考法】 *n.*笨蛋：a **stupid** person
例 What a dolt I have been! 我是多么的愚蠢啊!
近 idiot, fool, moron, simpleton, dullard
反 illuminati, intellectual 智者；genius 天才
派 doltish *adj.* 愚笨的

domicile [ˈdɑːmɪsaɪl]

【考法 1】 *n.*住所，住宅：a **residence**; a home
例 an alternate domicile in emergency 紧急情况下的住所
近 home, dwelling, habitation, abode, house, lodging
【考法 2】 *vt.*为…提供住处：to establish in or **provide** with a **domicile**
例 The university domiciles students in a variety of buildings in and around its urban campus. 大学在城区校园周围为学生提供了多样化的宿舍。
近 accommodate, bestow, lodge, harbor, put up
反 banish, expel 驱逐

dominant [ˈdɑːmɪnənt]

【考法 1】 *adj.*处于支配地位的：commanding, **controlling**, or prevailing over all **others**
例 the dominant culture 主流文化
近 ascendant, leading, outweighing, paramount, prevalent, principal, supreme
反 subordinate (等级上)低的
派 dominate *v.* 占主导地位，统治；dominance *n.* 主导，主流
【考法 2】 *adj.*(基因)显性的：of, relating to, or exerting ecological or **genetic dominance**
反 recessive 隐性的
派 dominance *n.* (基因的)显性

don [dɑːn]

【考法】 *vt.*穿上：to **put on** (an article of clothing)
例 He donned a raincoat for his trip. 他为出行穿上雨衣。
近 assume, wear, put on
反 doff 脱下

donor [ˈdoʊnər]

【考法】 *n.*捐赠人，给体：one that gives, **donates**, or presents something
例 donors of funds to research foundations 研究基金的捐赠人
近 donator, presenter, contributor, subscriber, patron, sugar daddy
反 acceptor 受体

Unit 2

| ■ DOODLE | ■ DORMANT | ■ DOUR | ■ DOUSE | ■ DOWNPLAY |
| ■ DOWNPOUR | ■ DOYEN | ■ DOZE | ■ DRACONIAN | ■ DRAWL |

doodle [ˈduːdl]

【考法 1】 *vi.*(无目的地)乱涂乱画：to scribble **aimlessly**, especially when preoccupied
例 I often doodle when I'm on the phone. 打电话时我经常乱写乱画。
近 mess around
【考法 2】 *vi.*漫无目的地打发时光：to spend time in **aimless activity**
例 I plan to spend the entire vacation just doodling. 我打算整个假期就随便做点事打发时间。
近 dawdle, trifle

dormant [ˈdɔːrmənt]

【考法 1】 *adj.*静止的，不活跃的：in a state of rest or **inactivity; inoperative; in abeyance**
例 volcanoes which have been dormant for thousand years 休眠了上千年的火山
近 dead, latent, lurking, abeyant, quiescent, inert
反 active, busy, operating 活跃的

【考法 2】 *adj.* (动物)冬眠的：having biological activity **suspended**

例 The bears lay dormant in their den during the winter. 在冬季，熊在他们的穴里冬眠。

近 asleep, resting, napping, slumbering

反 awake 清醒的

派 dormancy *n.* 不活跃；冬眠

dour [ˈdaʊər]

【考法 1】 *adj.* 闷闷不乐的，死气沉沉的：sullen, **gloomy**

例 The captain's dour look depressed us all. 船长闷闷不乐的脸色使我们所有人倍感低落。

近 morose, sulky, surly, moody

反 gay 欢快的

【考法 2】 *adj.* 严厉的：**harsh** and threatening in manner or appearance

例 His dour criticism made us regret having undertaken the job. 他严厉的批评让我们后悔接下这活儿了。

近 strict, sharp, austere, exacting, fierce, gruff, intimidating, rough, stark, stern

反 benign, gentle, mild, tender 温和的

douse [daʊs]

【考法 1】 *vt.* 熄灭：to **put out** (a light or fire)

例 douse a fire with water 用水熄灭火焰

近 quench, extinguish, put out

反 kindle, ignite, inflame 点燃

【考法 2】 *vt.* 弄湿：to make **wet**

例 The heavy rains thoroughly doused the tourists. 大雨把游客淋得透湿。

近 deluge, bathe, drench, soak, sodden, sop, wet

反 dehydrate, desiccate, dry 脱水，干燥；parch, scorch, sear 烧焦，烤焦

downplay [ˌdaʊnˈpleɪ]

【考法】 *vt.* 轻描淡写，不予重视：to **minimize** the **significance** of, play down

例 downplay the bad news 对坏消息轻描淡写

近 de-emphasize, disregard, ignore, overlook, neglect, understate, play down

反 address, emphasize, underscore 强调

downpour [ˈdaʊnpɔːr]

【考法】 *n.* 倾盆大雨：a **heavy** fall of **rain**

例 power failure due to the downpour 暴雨导致的电力中断

近 deluge, downfall, cloudburst, rainstorm

反 drizzle, sprinkle 细雨

doyen [ˈdɔɪen]

【考法 1】 *n.* 有经验的人，资深人士：a person considered to be **knowledgeable** or uniquely skilled as a result of long **experience** in some field of endeavor

例 a doyen in the industry 业界的元老

近 authority, expert, master, maven, veteran, virtuoso

反 amateur, layman 业余爱好者，门外汉；tyro, novice, neophyte, rookie, fledgling 新手

【考法 2】 *n.* (加入时间较长的)高级会员：the **senior member** of a group

例 He's the doyen of the admission committee, and his opinion has considerable weight. 他是招生委员会里的老人了，所以他的话格外有分量。

近 elder, senior

反 junior 新人

doze [doʊz]

【考法】 *vi./n.* 小憩：to sleep **lightly** or briefly

例 He dozed off during the lecture. 他在讲座上睡着了。

近 drowse, nap, wink, slumber

反 wake 醒来

draconian [drəˈkoʊniən]

【考法】 *adj.* 极其残酷的；十分严厉的：exceedingly **harsh**; very severe

例 abolish a draconian legal code 废除一部严酷的法典

近 rigid, ironhanded, strict, stringent

反 mild, genial, lenient 温和的

○ **drawl** [drɔːl]

【考法】 *v.* 慢吞吞地说：to **speak slowly** with vowels greatly prolonged

例 The old woman was drawling on and on. 老太太慢吞吞地说个没完。

近 extend, lengthen, prolong, protract, draw out

反 drivel, gibber 快速(而模糊)地说

Unit 3

■ DREARY	■ DRENCH	■ DRIVEL	■ DRIZZLE	■ DROLL
■ DRONE	■ DRUDGERY	■ DUBIOUS	■ DUCTILE	■ DULCET

○ **dreary** [ˈdrɪri]

【考法 1】 *adj.* 单调乏味的：having **nothing** likely to provide **cheer**, comfort, or interest

例 The day is cold, rainy, and dreary. 天气寒冷，阴暗而沉闷。

近 desolate, gloomy, sullen, dull, monotone, pedestrian, somber

反 jocund 令人欢乐的

【考法 2】 *adj.* 令人不悦的：**causing unhappiness**

例 The couple decided to see a professional counselor in order to save their dreary marriage. 这对夫妇决定咨询专业人士以拯救他们悲剧式的婚姻。

近 depressing, dismal, heartbreaking, mournful, pathetic, melancholy

反 cheering 令人高兴的

派 drearily *adv.* 令人厌烦地

○ **drench** [drentʃ]

【考法】 *vt.* 使湿透，浸透：to **wet thoroughly**

例 The thunderstorm drenched us to the skin. 雷雨把我们浇了个透。

近 bathe, deluge, douse, soak, saturate, sodden, sop, wet

反 dehydrate, desiccate, dry 脱水，干燥；parch, scorch, sear 烧焦，烤焦

○ **drivel** [ˈdrɪvl]

【考法 1】 *n.* 胡言乱语：unintelligible or **meaningless** talk

例 My roommate talks in her sleep, but it's just drivel. 我的室友会说梦话，但都是些没有意义的呓语。

近 abracadabra, nonsense, prattle, gabble

【考法 2】 *v.* 胡言乱语，说傻话：to **talk stupidly** and carelessly

例 He always drivel on about his "distinguished" family. 他总是痴痴地说着他所谓的"名门"出身。

近 babble, gabble, gibber, jabber

○ **drizzle** [ˈdrɪzl]

【考法】 *vi./n.* (下)细小、轻柔、似雾的雨，毛毛雨：a fine **misty rain**

例 The intermittent drizzle was just heavy enough to spoil all of our outdoor activities. 断断续续的小雨恰好大到让我们所有的户外活动都泡汤。

近 mist, sprinkle

反 deluge, downpour 倾盆大雨

派 drizzling *adj.* (雨)细小的

○ **droll** [droʊl]

【考法】 *adj.* 古怪有趣的，离奇可笑的：**amusingly odd** or whimsically comical

例 a droll man with a strong dialect 一个带着浓郁口音的有意思的人

近 antic, comic, farcical, funny, hilarious, laughable, humorous, ridiculous, ludicrous, uproarious, whimsical

反 lame, unamusing, uncomic, unfunny, unhumorous, unhysterical 不幽默的，无趣的

派 drollness *n.* 古怪

○ **drone** [droʊn]

【考法 1】 *v.* 低沉单调地说；嗡嗡地叫：to **talk** in a persistently dull or **monotonous** tone

例 droning bees 嗡嗡作响的蜜蜂

近 hum, buzz, bumble

【考法 2】 *n.* (昆虫振翅般)单调嗡嗡的声音：a **monotonous sound** like that of an insect in motion

例 hear the drone of an helicopter overhead 听到头顶直升机嗡嗡的声音

近 burr, whir

【考法3】 *vi.* 混日子: to spend time **doing nothing**
例 Instead of getting a job, he preferred to drone and live off his parents. 相对于找个工作来说，他更喜欢什么也不做，依靠他的父母过日子
近 dally, dawdle, hang, laze, loll, lounge

drudgery [ˈdrʌdʒəri]
【考法】 *n.* 苦工；单调、卑贱或无趣的工作: **tedious**, menial, or unpleasant **work**
例 get away from the drudgery of their everyday lives 摆脱每日单调无聊的工作
近 labor, slavery, toil, travail, grind
反 sinecure 闲职，美差；fun, play 玩耍，娱乐

dubious [ˈduːbiəs]
【考法1】 *adj.* 充满不定性的，值得怀疑的: giving rise to **uncertainty**; **questionable** or suspect as to true nature or quality
例 a dubious assertion 一个值得怀疑的论调
近 debatable, doubtful, disputable, equivocal, problematic, questionable, shaky
反 certain, incontestable, undeniable 确定的，毋庸置疑的；reliable 可靠的
【考法2】 *adj.* (对事实等)持怀疑态度的: **not feeling sure** about the truth, wisdom, or trustworthiness of someone or something
例 dubious about a diet that claims I can eat all I want and still lose weight 对于一份声称可以一边随心所欲地吃而一边减肥的节食方案表示怀疑
近 distrustful, skeptical, suspicious, unsure
反 convinced, positive, sure 持肯定态度的，确信的
派 dubiety *n.* 可疑，怀疑
【考法3】 *adj.* 迟疑不决的，不愿行动的: **slow to begin** or proceed with a course of action **because of doubts** or uncertainty
例 I'm dubious about our plan to go hang gliding without having had any training. 我对于不做任何训练就去玩滑翔感到很迟疑
近 undecided, disinclined, loath, reluctant, reticent
反 disposed, inclined 倾向于…的

ductile [ˈdʌktaɪl]
【考法1】 *adj.* 可塑的，有延展性的: easily molded or shaped, **malleable**
例 Gold is a kind of ductile metal. 金是一种有延展性的金属。
近 malleable, moldable
反 inflexible 僵硬的
【考法2】 *adj.* 易受影响的: **easily led** or influenced
例 a ductile personality 易受他人影响的性格
近 pliant, yielding, supple
反 adamant, intractable, refractory, obdurate 倔强的，不易改变立场的

dulcet [ˈdʌlsɪt]
【考法】 *adj.* 悦耳的，令人愉悦的: pleasing to the ear; **melodious**; generally pleasing or agreeable
例 dulcet tones from harps and flutes 竖琴和长笛发出的悦耳音调
近 sweet, agreeable, delightful, euphonic, mellifluous, tuneful, winsome
反 cacophonous, grating 刺耳的

Unit 4

| ■ DULLARD | ■ DUPE | ■ DUPLICITY | ■ DWINDLE | ■ DYSPEPTIC |
| ■ EARNEST | ■ EARSHOT | ■ EARSPLITTING | ■ EAVESDROP | ■ EBULLIENT |

dullard [ˈdʌlɑːrd]
【考法】 *n.* 笨蛋: a **stupid** or unimaginative person
近 moron, simpleton, idiot, fool
反 wit 机智的人；genius 天才
派 dull *adj.* 愚笨的

dupe [duːp]
【考法1】 *n.* 复制品，复制: something that is made to look **exactly like something else**
例 He built a dupe of the original model which is locked in a vault. 他仿造保险柜里的模型做了一个复制品。
近 clone, duplicate, facsimile, imitation, mock, replica
反 archetype, original, prototype 原型

【考法2】 *n.* 易受骗的人：one that is **easily deceived** or cheated

例　The swindler was able to escape with all of the dupe's money. 骗子带着受骗人的财产成功逃跑了。

近　fool, victim, gull

反　connoisseur 行家，鉴赏家

【考法3】 *vt.* 欺骗：to **deceive**（an unwary person）

例　The public is easily duped by extravagant claims in advertising. 大众极易被广告中夸大的介绍误导。

近　bamboozle, beguile, cheat, cozen, delude, gull, hoax, hoodwink

派　dupable *adj.* 易受骗的

duplicity [duːˈplɪsəti]

【考法】 *n.* 欺骗，口是心非：deliberate **deceptiveness** in behavior or speech

例　accidentally reveal their duplicity 不经意间暴露了他们的口是心非

近　artifice, deceit, craft, cunning, fraudulence, guile

反　honesty, artlessness, forthrightness, guilelessness, ingenuousness, sincerity 诚实，坦诚

dwindle [ˈdwɪndl]

【考法】 *vi.* 逐渐减少：to become **gradually less** until little remains

例　His vast fortune is dwindling away. 他的巨额财富正在慢慢缩水。

近　abate, decrease, drop, diminish, reduce, shrink, taper, wane, knock down

反　aggrandize, balloon, burgeon, increase 增加；accumulate 累积

派　dwindling *adj.* 减少的

dyspeptic [dɪsˈpeptɪk]

【考法1】 *adj.* 脾气坏的：**bad-tempered**

例　The sultry day makes us dyspeptic. 闷热潮湿的天气让我们变得脾气暴躁。

近　cantankerous, disagreeable, irritable, fretful, irascible, peevish, splenetic, surly

反　amiable, easygoing, genial, good-humored, good-natured, good-tempered 随和的，和蔼的

【考法2】 *adj.* 消化不良的：pertaining to, subject to, or suffering from **dyspepsia**

派　dyspepsia *n.* 消化不良

earnest [ˈɜːrnɪst]

【考法】 *adj.* 严肃认真的：characterized by or proceeding from an intense and **serious** state of mind, **grave**

例　an earnest machine operator 一丝不苟的机器操作员

近　grave, serious, solemn, staid, sober

反　facetious, frivolous, flip, flippant, playful 轻浮的

earshot [ˈɪrʃɑːt]

【考法】 *n.* 听力所及的范围：the **range** within which one may **hear** a person's unaided voice

例　wait until he was out of earshot 等到他听不见的时候

近　hail, hearing, sound

earsplitting [ɪrˈsplɪtɪŋ]

【考法】 *adj.* 震耳欲聋的：**distressingly loud** or shrill

例　earsplitting noise of airplane engines 飞机引擎的巨大噪音

近　blaring, blasting, deafening, loud, piercing, plangent, resounding, roaring, stentorian, thunderous

反　gentle, soft（音乐）轻柔的

eavesdrop [ˈiːvzdrɑːp]

【考法】 *vi.* 偷听：to **listen secretly** to the private conversation of others

例　eavesdrop on the conversation 偷听谈话

近　overhear, wiretap

ebullient [ɪˈbʌliənt]

【考法】 *adj.* 热情奔放的：**zestfully** enthusiastic

例　The ebullient dancers left an enduring impression on us. 热情洋溢的舞者给我们留下了难以磨灭的印象。

近　boiling, exuberant, effervescent, vivacious

反　tepid, torpid 无精打采的

派　ebullience *n.* 热情洋溢

Unit 5

eccentric [ɪk'sentrɪk]
【考法】 *adj.* 行为出格的，不循规蹈矩的：**deviating** from **conventional** or accepted usage or conduct
例 an eccentric millionaire 行为怪异的百万富翁
近 strange, bizarre, erratic, idiosyncratic, odd, offbeat, outlandish, quaint, weird
反 ordinary, regular 常规的
派 eccentricity *n.* 古怪

éclat [eɪ'klæ]
【考法】 *n.* 辉煌成就：brilliant or conspicuous **success**
例 The premier of Mozart's *Le Nozze di Figaro* enjoyed a great éclat in 1786. 莫扎特歌剧《费加罗的婚礼》于1786 年的首演获得了极大的成功。
近 fame, renown, brilliance, triumph
反 debacle, fiasco 惨败

eclipse [ɪ'klɪps]
【考法 1】 *n.* 下降，衰退：a change to a **lower state** or level
例 the eclipse of the town from a grand seaside resort to a tacky tourist trap 该城镇从壮丽辉煌的海边旅游圣地退化成了俗气的坑人景点
近 decadence, degeneration, degradation, deterioration, ebb, fall
反 ascent, rise, upswing 上升，崛起
【考法 2】 *vt.* 使声望下降，使黯然失色：to obscure or **diminish** in **importance**, fame, or reputation
例 Her score eclipsed the old record. 她的分数使旧的纪录黯然失色。
近 adumbrate, obscure, overshadow
【考法 3】 *vt.* （在数量、品质上）超越：to **be greater**, better, or stronger than
例 The brilliant young pianist now eclipsed even his own mentor in musical artistry. 这位极富天赋的小钢琴家如今甚至已超越了他的音乐导师。
近 beat, exceed, excel, outshine, outstrip, surpass, transcend
反 fall behind 落后

ecstasy ['ekstəsi]
【考法 1】 *n.* 无法自控的情绪：a state of being **beyond** reason and **self-control**
例 an ecstasy of rage 无法自控的愤怒
近 mania, rhapsody
反 self-control 自控，自制；composure, sangfroid 镇定
【考法 2】 *n.* 狂喜：**intense joy** or delight
例 be in ecstasy over the offer from Harvard University 因被哈佛录取而欣喜若狂
近 delight, elation, euphoria, exhilaration, rapture, transport
反 depression, melancholy 沮丧

ecumenical [ˌiːkjuː'menɪkl]
【考法 1】 *adj.* 全球基督教会的：of, relating to, or representing the **whole** of a body of **churches**
近 catholic
反 diocesan 主教管辖特定小教区的
【考法 2】 *adj.* 世界范围的，普遍性的：**worldwide** or general in extent, influence, or application
例 an ecumenical scope 国际视野
近 universal, cosmopolitan, global, planetary, worldwide
反 provincial, insular 狭隘的

edible ['edəbl]
【考法】 *adj.* 可食用的：fit to be **eaten**
例 No chemicals in the laboratory is edible. 实验室中的任何化学试剂都不能食用。
近 eatable, comestible, consumable, digestible, esculent
反 inedible 不可食用的
派 edibility *n.* 可食用

edifice [ˈedɪfɪs]

【考法 1】 *n.* 大厦；大建筑物: a large or **massive structure**

例 The Capitol is one of the most impressive edifices in the United States. 国会山是美国最令人印象深刻的建筑之一。

近 building, erection, palace

反 cottage 小棚舍

【考法 2】 *n.* 基础，基本构架: the arrangement of parts that gives something its **basic form**

例 The edifice of the argument is quite simple, once you get past the fancy language. 只要你看透了表面花哨的语言，你会发现这段论证的基本构架是非常简单的。

近 architecture, configuration, framework, skeleton, structure

efface [ɪˈfeɪs]

【考法】 *vt.* 擦掉，抹去；使不明显: to eliminate or **make indistinct** by or as if by wearing away a surface

例 efface those unpleasant memories 抹去那些不快的记忆

近 eradicate, erase, expunge, exterminate, extirpate, liquidate, eclipse, obliterate, wipe, root out

反 blazon, decorate 装饰；emboss 使凸起，使显现

派 self-effacing *adj.* 谦卑的，低调的

effervesce [ˌefərˈves]

【考法 1】 *vi.* 冒泡: to **bubble**, hiss, and foam as gas escapes

例 effervesce with bubbles 冒气泡

近 bubble, foam, froth

【考法 2】 *vi.* 兴奋，热情洋溢: to show **high spirits** or animation

例 effervesce over the news of victory 因胜利的消息而兴奋

近 rejoice, exult, jubilate, triumph

反 grieve 感到极度悲伤

派 effervescent *adj.* 热情洋溢的；effervescence *n.* 热情洋溢

effete [ɪˈfiːt]

【考法 1】 *adj.* 衰弱的，衰落的: **depleted** of vitality, force, or effectiveness

例 an effete monarchy 奄奄一息的君主制

近 consumed, debilitated, decadent, degenerate, depleted, drained, exhausted, feeble

反 hale, sound, robust 强健的，充满活力的

派 effetely *adv.* 衰弱地

【考法 2】 *adj.* 缺乏信念的，懦弱的: **lacking strength of will** or character

例 The government is too effete to take out the powerful special interests that really ruin this state. 该国政府过于懦弱，不敢去摧毁那些祸害国家的特殊利益集团。

近 frail, invertebrate, nerveless, spineless

反 backboned, firm, hard, strong, tough 刚毅的

Unit 6

| ■ EFFLUVIUM | ■ EFFRONTERY | ■ EFFULGENT | ■ EFFUSIVE | ■ EGALITARIAN |
| ■ EGOISTIC | ■ ELABORATE | ■ ELASTIC | ■ ELATE | ■ ELEEMOSYNARY |

effluvium [ɪˈfluːviəm]

【考法 1】 *n.* 难闻的气味: an **offensive** exhalation or **smell**

例 Repulsive effluvia made us vomit. 这恶臭让我们作呕。

近 malodor, stink, stench

反 fragrance, aroma 芳香

派 effluvial *adj.* 恶臭的

【考法 2】 *n.* 没用的副产品，废品: a **by-product** especially in the form of **waste**

例 With nothing but effluvia obtained, researchers decided to abandon this method. 由于得不到目标产物，研究者们决定放弃这种方法。

近 dross, refuse, rubbish, trash, waste

effrontery [ɪˈfrʌntəri]

【考法】 *n.* 厚颜无耻，放肆大胆: flagrant **disregard** of **courtesy** or propriety and an arrogant assumption of privilege

例 The man had the effrontery to insult her father. 这个男人胆敢辱骂她的父亲。

近 audacity, brashness, brazenness, insolence, nerve, presumption, temerity

反 decorum, propriety, courtesy, grace 得体；timidity 胆小

○ **effulgent** [ɪˈfʌldʒənt]
　　【考法】 *adj.* 光辉灿烂的: shining brilliantly; **resplendent**
　　例 an effulgent sunset on the Atlantic 大西洋上壮丽辉煌的日落
　　近 bright, beaming, glorious, luminous, radiant, splendid
　　反 dim, murky, dull 模糊的，黯淡的
　　派 effulgence *n.* 光辉

○ **effusive** [ɪˈfjuːsɪv]
　　【考法】 *adj.* 感情泛滥的/溢于言表的；感情表达不节制的/过度的；过分多情的: **unrestrained** or excessive **in emotional expression**
　　例 The principal delivered an effusive address at the commencement ceremony. 校长在毕业典礼上做了充满感情的演讲。
　　近 emotional, expansive, demonstrative, gushy, passionate
　　反 inhibited, reserved, restrained 节制的；undemonstrative, unemotional 不易动情的；numb, torpid 麻木不仁的
　　派 effusion *n.* 流出，溢出

egalitarian [iˌɡælɪˈteriən]
　　【考法】 *adj.* 平等主义的: affirming, **promoting**, or characterized by belief in **equal** political, economic, social, and civil **rights** for all people
　　例 the egalitarian principle guiding his endeavor 引导他奋斗的平等主义原则
　　近 disinterested, impartial, unprejudiced, unbiased, objective
　　反 inequitable, discriminating, unfair 有偏见的，不公平的
　　派 egalitarianism *n.* 平等主义

egoistic [ˌeɡoʊˈɪstɪk]
　　【考法】 *adj.* 利己的，以自我为中心的: being **centered in** or preoccupied with **oneself** and the gratification of one's own desires
　　例 egoistic behaviors others detest 令他人厌恶的利己行为
　　近 egocentric, self-centered, individualistic, navel-gazing
　　反 altruistic, selfless 利他的，无私的
　　派 ego *n.* 自大，自我；egoism *n.* 利己主义；egoist *n.* 以自我为中心的人

○ **elaborate**
　　【考法 1】 [ɪˈlæbərət] *adj.* 详细的，复杂的: marked by **complexity**, fullness of detail, or ornament
　　例 an elaborate manual 内容详尽的使用手册
　　近 circumstantial, complex, complicated, intricate, knotty, minute, particular, particularized, sophisticated
　　反 sketchy, brief, compendious, summary 概要性的
　　【考法 2】 [ɪˈlæbəreɪt] *vt.* 详细阐述: to expand something **in detail**
　　例 The defense committee asked the PhD candidate to elaborate one critical assumption in his thesis. 答辩委员会要求答辩的博士进一步说明他毕业论文中的一个关键假设。
　　近 develop, expand, amplify, explain
　　反 abstract, abbreviate, condense, simplify 简化；downplay, ignore, neglect, overlook 忽视，忽略

elastic [ɪˈlæstɪk]
　　【考法 1】 *adj.* 有弹性的: easily **resuming** original **shape** after being stretched or expanded
　　例 elastic rubber band 弹性橡胶圈
　　近 bouncy, flexible, malleable, resilient, stretchable, supple
　　反 rigid, stiff 僵化的
　　派 inelastic *adj.* 无弹性的，非弹性的
　　【考法 2】 *adj.* 能（迅速从伤痛中）恢复的: capable of **recovering** quickly especially **from depression** or disappointment
　　例 owe her success to an elastic optimistic nature 将她的成功归因于能迅速走出悲伤的乐观品质
　　近 adaptable, adjustable, buoyant, pliable, volatile
　　反 established, fixed, immutable 不变的

○ **elate** [iˈleɪt]
　　【考法】 *vt.* 使开心，使自豪: to fill with joy or pride
　　例 The phenomenal sales record elated him. 卓越的业绩让他高兴不已。
　　近 cheer, excite, exhilarate, inspire, stimulate
　　反 depress, dishearten, sadden 使沮丧
　　派 elated *adj.* 高兴的；elation *n.* 高兴

eleemosynary [ˌeliːˈmɑːsɪˌneri]

【考法】 *adj.* 慈善的：of, relating to, or supported by **charity**

例 an eleemosynary foundation funded by the Bill Gates 由比尔·盖茨夫妇资助的慈善基金

近 benevolent, charitable, humane, humanitarian, philanthropic

反 parsimonious 吝啬的

Unit 7

■ ELEGY	■ ELEPHANTINE	■ ELEVATE	■ ELICIT	■ ELLIPTICAL
■ ELUCIDATE	■ EMACIATE	■ EMANCIPATE	■ EMBARGO	■ EMBARK

elegy [ˈelədʒi]

【考法】 *n.* 哀歌(诗)，挽歌(诗)：a song or poem **expressing sorrow** or lamentation

例 a moving elegy played at the funeral 葬礼上演奏的催人泪下的挽歌

近 dirge, lamentation, requiem

反 ode 颂歌，颂词

elephantine [ˌeliˈfæntiːn]

【考法 1】 *adj.* 巨大的：having **enormous size** or strength

例 an elephantine meteor crate 巨大的陨石坑

近 huge, colossal, enormous, gargantuan, gigantic, massive, prodigious, tremendous

反 microscopic, minute, tiny, infinitesimal 细微的，微小的

【考法 2】 *adj.* 笨拙的：**clumsy**, ponderous

例 elephantine movements 笨拙的行动

近 awkward, graceless, maladroit

反 graceful 优雅的

elevate [ˈelɪveɪt]

【考法 1】 *vt.* (在道德、智力、文化水平上)提升：to **improve** morally, intellectually, or culturally

例 a novel that both entertains and elevates readers 一本寓教于乐的小说

近 advance, boost, enhance, ennoble, raise, upgrade

反 abase, debase, demote, degrade 贬低

派 elevation *n.* 提升

【考法 2】 *vt.* 使兴奋：to **raise** the **spirits** of

例 one of the most elevating moments in their lives 生命中最让人兴奋的时刻之一

近 elate, enrapture, exhilarate, intoxicate, transport

反 depress 使沮丧

elicit [iˈlɪsɪt]

【考法】 *vt.* 激起，唤起：to draw forth or **bring out**

例 The king's speech elicited lasting cheer and applause. 国王的演讲激起了持续的欢呼和掌声。

近 arouse, evoke, excite, inspire, provoke, raise

反 appease, placate, mollify, pacify 平息

elliptical [ɪˈlɪptɪkl]

【考法 1】 *adj.* 含糊不清的：of or relating to deliberate **obscurity** (as of literary or conversational style)

例 give an elliptical response to the inquiry 就问题给出一个含糊其辞的回答

近 ambiguous, arcane, cryptic, enigmatic, equivocal, inscrutable, murky, nebulous, occult, opaque, vague

反 clear, explicit, unambiguous, unequivocal 清晰明确的

【考法 2】 *adj.* 椭圆的：of, relating to, or shaped like an **ellipse**

近 oval, ovate

反 circular, round 圆形的

派 ellipse *n.* 椭圆

elucidate [iˈluːsɪdeɪt]

【考法】 *v.* 阐明：to **make lucid** especially by explanation or analysis

例 elucidate an abstruse equation in quantum mechanics 阐明一个深奥难懂的量子力学方程

近 clarify, clear, construe, explain, explicate, expound, illustrate

反 confuse, obfuscate, obscure 使困惑；garble 曲解

派 elucidation *n.* 阐释，阐明

emaciate [ɪˈmeɪʃieɪt]

【考法1】 *vt.* 使消瘦，使衰弱：to cause to lose flesh so as to **become** very **thin**
例 become emaciated by long illness 因长年累月的病痛而消瘦
反 fatten 变胖；invigorate 使充满活力
派 emaciation *n.* 虚弱

【考法2】 *vt.* 削弱：to make **feeble**
例 His hesitation emaciated the force of his argument. 他的迟疑削弱了他论证的力度。
近 droop, flag, sag, decay, enfeeble, enervate, languish, wane, wither

emancipate [ɪˈmænsɪpeɪt]

【考法】 *vt.* 解放，解除束缚：to **free** from bondage, oppression, or restraint
例 emancipate students from excessive assignments 将学生从题海中解放出来
近 discharge, enfranchise, free, liberate, loose, manumit, release
反 bind, shackle 束缚；enslave, enthrall 奴役
派 emancipation *n.* 解放，获得自由

embargo [ɪmˈbɑːrɡoʊ]

【考法】 *n.* 贸易禁止令：a legal **prohibition on commerce**
例 a trade embargo on luxuries 对奢侈品的禁运令
近 ban, interdiction, proscription, sanction, veto
反 approval, license, permission, prescription 许可

embark [ɪmˈbɑːrk]

【考法1】 *vi.* 上船：to **go aboard** a vessel or aircraft, as at the start of a journey
例 With all cargos embarked, the ship weighed the anchor. 所有货物都上船了，货船拔锚起航。
近 board
反 disembark 下车，下船

【考法2】 *vi.* 开始从事：to make a **start**
例 embark on a world tour 开始了环游世界的旅程
近 begin, commence, launch, initiate, start
反 conclude, end, finish, terminate 结束

Unit 8

| ■ EMBARRASS | ■ EMBED | ■ EMBEZZLE | ■ EMBOLDEN | ■ EMBOSS |
| ■ EMBRACE | ■ EMBROIDER | ■ EMIGRATE | ■ EMINENT | ■ EMOLLIENT |

embarrass [ɪmˈbærəs]

【考法1】 *vt.* 使尴尬：to cause to **experience** a state of self-conscious **distress**
例 bawdy jokes that embarrassed her 让她尴尬的荤段子
近 abash, discomfit, disconcert, faze, fluster, mortify, nonplus
派 embarrassing *adj.* 令人窘迫的；embarrassment *n.* 尴尬

【考法2】 *vt.* 阻挠，制造障碍：to **create difficulty** for the work or activity of
例 A lot of this paperwork is unnecessary and just embarrasses the organization. 这些文案工作很多都是多余的，只会妨碍组织的工作。
近 encumber, handicap, hinder, impede, inhibit, obstruct, shackle, stymie, trammel
反 aid, facilitate 促进

embed [ɪmˈbed]

【考法】 *vt.* 嵌入：to **enclose** closely in or as if in a matrix
例 The thorn was embedded in her thumb. 刺扎入了她的拇指。
近 entrench, fix, ingrain, root
反 extract, dislodge, uproot 取出，移出
派 embedded *adj.* 嵌入（式）的

embezzle [ɪmˈbezl]

【考法】 *vt.* 盗用：to **appropriate** (as property entrusted to one's care) fraudulently to one's own use
例 limitations on the right of the state to embezzle private property 限制政府挪用私人财产的权利
近 appropriate, peculate
反 confiscate 没收充公
派 embezzlement *n.* 挪用，盗用

embolden [ɪmˈbəʊldən]

【考法】 *vt.* 鼓励，使大胆：to **instill** with boldness or **courage**

例 be emboldened by the wine 借酒壮胆

近 encourage, animate, cheer, hearten, strengthen

反 daunt, discourage, dishearten, dispirit 使沮丧，使丧失信心

emboss [ɪmˈbɔːs]

【考法】 *vt.* 以浮雕效果妆点，装饰：to raise the surface of into bosses; especially to **ornament with raised work**

例 embossed with a design of Shanghai skyline 用刻有上海城市轮廓的浮雕图案进行装饰

近 adorn, beautify, bedeck, blazon, ornament, garnish

反 flatten, efface 抹平，抹去

embrace [ɪmˈbreɪs]

【考法 1】 *vt.* 乐于接受：to take up **willingly** or **eagerly**

例 embrace the opportunity to study further 乐于接受继续深造的机会

近 accept, adopt, espouse, welcome

反 abjure, abrogate, renounce, spurn 废除，摒弃，放弃

【考法 2】 *vt.* 包围：to **surround** or cover closely

例 The stone walls that embrace the monastery serve to symbolize its function as a retreat from an unquiet world. 包围着修道院的石墙是它远离喧嚣尘世的象征。

近 circle, encompass, envelop, wrap

embroider [ɪmˈbrɔɪdə(r)]

【考法】 *v.* （时常伴有夸张和想象内容地）详细说明：to **give** an **elaborate account** of, often with florid language and fictitious details

例 embroider the story of his adventures in the army 细说他服役时惊险的经历

近 elaborate, embellish, exaggerate, magnify, overstate, hyperbolize

反 downplay, de-emphasize 轻描淡写

emigrate [ˈemɪɡreɪt]

【考法】 *vi.* 移民，移居海外：to **leave** one's place of residence or country to live elsewhere

例 have to emigrate to the United States due to political persecution 因政治迫害而不得不移民美国

近 migrate

反 immigrate 移入，入境；repatriate 遣返

派 emigrant *n.* （向外的）移民；emigration *n.* （向外）移居，迁徙

eminent [ˈemɪnənt]

【考法】 *adj.* 杰出的：exhibiting eminence especially in standing **above others** in some quality or position

例 an eminent young scientist 一名杰出的青年科学家

近 famous, celebrated, distinguished, famed, notable, prominent, renowned

反 mediocre, undistinguished 中庸的，平凡的

派 eminence *n.* 杰出，显赫

emollient [iˈmɑːliənt]

【考法】 *adj.* 起缓和作用的：making **less intense** or harsh

例 soothe us in our grieves with emollient words 用安慰的话语抚平我们的悲伤

近 appeasing, assuaging, mollifying, mitigating, relieving

反 aggravating, intensifying 使（局势、情况）加剧恶化的

Unit 9

■ EMULATE	■ ENACT	■ ENAMEL	■ ENCOMIUM	■ ENCOMPASS
■ ENCUMBER	■ ENDEMIC	■ ENDORSE	■ ENERVATE	■ ENFRANCHISE

emulate [ˈemjuleɪt]

【考法】 *vt.* 效仿并努力超越：to strive to equal or **excel**, especially **through imitation**

例 a role model worthy emulating 值得效仿的榜样

近 copy, imitate, mimic, mime

派 emulation *n.* 模仿

enact [ɪ'nækt]
【考法】 *vt.* 制定或颁布(法律): to **establish** by legal and authoritative act
例 Congress enacted the tax reform bill. 国会颁布了税法改革案。
近 constitute, establish, legislate, pass, ratify, ordain, lay down
反 abolish, repeal, rescind, revoke 废除
派 enactment *n.* 颁布

enamel [ɪ'næml]
【考法1】 *vt.* 涂亮漆; 使具有光滑或亮泽的表面: to **give a glossy** or brilliant **surface** to
近 glaze, varnish
反 efface 抹去
【考法2】 *vt.* 用亮丽的表面装饰: to **adorn** with a brightly colored surface
近 adorn, beautify, bedeck, decorate, embellish, garnish, ornament
反 disfigure 破坏…的外形

encomium [en'koʊmiəm]
【考法】 *n.* 赞颂之词: glowing and warmly enthusiastic **praise**
例 receive encomiums from literary critics 受到文学评论家的好评
近 accolade, applause, compliment, eulogy, laud, panegyric, salutation, tribute
反 criticism 批评; abuse, invective, vituperation 辱骂

encompass [ɪn'kʌmpəs]
【考法1】 *vt.* 组成, 包含: to constitute or **include**
例 a plan that encompasses multiple aims 一项包含了多个目标的计划
近 contain, comprehend, embody, entail, involve, subsume
反 exclude 排除
【考法2】 *vt.* 包围: **envelop**
例 Berlin had already been encompassed by the Red Army and all Soviet soldiers were patiently waiting for the order to put a final nail in Nazi Germany's coffin. 柏林已被红军包围, 苏联士兵们静静地等待着最后的命令, 彻底消灭纳粹德国。
近 circle, embrace, enclose, environ, surround

encumber [ɪn'kʌmbər]
【考法1】 *vt.* 阻碍; 妨碍: to **impede** or hamper the function or activity of
例 Negotiation between the two parties were encumbered by a lack of trust. 两党之间的谈判因缺乏信任而受到阻碍。
近 hamper, hinder, impede, obstruct, retard, stymie
反 promote, further 推动; aid, assist, facilitate, help 帮助
【考法2】 *vt.* 给…增添负担: to **place** a weight or **burden** on
例 Don't encumber your pack animal so much that it can hardly move. 别让你的牲畜驮这么多东西, 它都走不动了。
近 burden, lade, lumber, saddle
反 unload 卸下

endemic [en'demɪk]
【考法】 *adj.* 地方性的: prevalent in or peculiar **to a particular** locality, **region**, or people
例 an endemic disease 地方性疾病
近 aboriginal, indigenous, native, domestic
反 exotic, foreign, nonindigenous, nonnative 国外的, 外来的

endorse [ɪn'dɔːrs]
【考法】 *vt.* 公开支持, 推崇: to **express** support or **approval** of publicly and definitely
例 endorse a presidential candidate 公开支持一名总统候选人
近 advocate, back, approve, certify, champion, sanction, support, uphold
反 deprecate, impugn, oppose 反对
派 endorsement *n.* 支持, 赞同

enervate ['enərveɪt]
【考法1】 *vt.* 使衰弱: to **weaken** or destroy the strength or vitality of
例 His constitution was enervated by lustful lifestyle. 他荒淫无度的生活习惯已使他身体虚弱。
近 debilitate, disable, enfeeble, fatigue, sap
反 fortify, strengthen 强化; energize, invigorate, vitalize 给…注入活力
派 enervation *n.* 虚弱

【考法2】 *vt.* 使麻木: to **deprive of emotional** or intellectual **vitality**
例 A lifetime of working in dreary jobs had enervated his very soul. 一生忙于无聊的工作让他变得无比麻木。
近 dampen, deaden, petrify
反 brace, energize, enliven, invigorate, vitalize, vivify 使充满活力

○ **enfranchise** [ɪnˈfræntʃaɪz]
【考法1】 *vt.* 给予…权利（例如选举权）: to **endow** with the **rights** of citizenship, especially the right to vote
例 Slaves in US were emancipated in 1863 but were not enfranchised until the Fifteenth Amendment went into effect in 1870. 尽管在美国奴隶于 1863 年就获得了解放，但他们直到 1870 年《第五修正案》正式生效才获得选举权。
反 disenfranchise, disempower 剥夺权利
【考法2】 *vt.* 解放: to **set free** (as from slavery)
例 In a way, modern labor-saving appliances enfranchised people, giving them much more leisure time. 从某种意义上来说，那些节省劳动力的现代设备将人们解放出来，给予人们更多的休闲时间。
近 discharge, emancipate, free, liberate, manumit, rescue, unfetter
反 bind, confine, enfetter 束缚; subjugate, subdue; enthrall 使臣服; 使成为奴隶

Unit 10

| ■ ENGENDER | ■ ENGROSS | ■ ENIGMA | ■ ENLIGHTEN | ■ ENMITY |
| ■ ENNOBLE | ■ ENNUI | ■ ENSEMBLE | ■ ENSCONCE | ■ ENSUE |

○ **engender** [ɪnˈdʒendər]
【考法1】 *vt.* 引起，使发展: to **cause** to exist or to develop
例 Her latest book has engendered a lot of controversy. 她的新书引发了很多争议。
近 beget, cause, catalyze, generate, induce, invoke, produce, spawn
【考法2】 *vi.* 产生，出现: to **come into existence**
例 Feelings of confidence and independence were only just beginning to engender within her. 她的自信和独立的感觉才刚刚产生
近 actualize, appear, arise, form, materialize, spring
反 cease 停止; disappear, perish 消逝，死亡; eradicate 根除; quash 平息; terminate 终止

○ **engross** [ɪnˈɡroʊs]
【考法】 *vt.* 使全神贯注: to **occupy exclusively**
例 He was completely engrossed in his work. 他全神贯注于他的工作之中。
近 absorb, engage, enthrall, fascinate, grip, immerse
派 engrossed *adj.* 全神贯注的

enigma [ɪˈnɪɡmə]
【考法】 *n.* 难以理解或解释的事物，谜: something **hard to understand** or explain
例 The smile on Da Vinci's masterpiece *Mona Lisa* has been an enigma for hundred years. 数百年来，达·芬奇名作《蒙娜丽莎》上的微笑一直是个不解之谜。
近 mystery, conundrum, puzzle, riddle
派 enigmatic *adj.* 谜一般的

enlighten [ɪnˈlaɪtn]
【考法1】 *vt.* 使知道，启发: to give information to; **inform** or **instruct**
例 enlighten us about the thorny problem 启发我们思考这个棘手的问题
近 apprise, instruct
反 bewilder, confuse, confound, perplex 使疑惑
【考法2】 *vt.* （在道德或精神上）进行教育: to **provide** (someone) with **moral** or spiritual **understanding**
例 Many people around the world have been enlightened by the teachings of Gautama Buddha. 释迦摩尼的说教启迪了世界上许许多多的人的灵魂。
近 edify, educate, illuminate, nurture
派 enlightening *adj.* 具有启发性的

enmity [ˈenməti]
【考法】 *n.* 敌意: positive, active, and typically **mutual hatred** or ill will
例 an unspoken enmity between two factions 两个派系间心照不宣的仇恨
近 animosity, animus, antagonism, antipathy, feud, gall, hostility, rancor
反 amity, comity 友好; concord 和睦

ennoble [ɪˈnoʊbl]

【考法】 *vt.* 使尊贵: to make **noble**

例 Her skill and talent ennoble her profession. 技能和天赋使她成为业界领军人物。

近 aggrandize, canonize, deify, dignify, glorify, magnify

反 debase, abase, degrade, demean, humble, humiliate 贬低

ennui [ɑːnˈwiː]

【考法】 *n.* 倦怠；缺乏兴趣: **listlessness** and dissatisfaction resulting from **lack of interest**

例 The kind of ennui comes from having too much time on one's hands and too little will to find something productive to do. 倦怠来自手上有大把时间却没有有益的事可做。

近 doldrums, listlessness, tedium, weariness

反 keen interest, energy, enthusiasm, exuberance 强烈的兴趣，生气盎然

ensemble [ɑːnˈsɑːmbl]

【考法】 *n.* 合唱，合奏曲: a work for **two or more vocalists** or instrumentalists

例 The actor performed an ensemble piece. 该演员参与了合唱。

反 solo 独唱

ensconce [ɪnˈskɑːns]

【考法1】 *vt.* 安置: to **settle**（oneself）**securely** or comfortably

例 ensconce oneself in a new job 在一个新职位安定下来

近 install, lodge, nestle, perch, roost, settle

反 unsettle, dislodge, displace 使从安置好的地方移开，驱逐

【考法2】 *vt.* 隐藏: to put in a **hiding** place

例 ensconce the spare house key in a place where no thief would think to look 把备用钥匙藏在小偷根本不会注意的地方

近 bury, cache, conceal, secrete

反 display, exhibit 展示

ensue [ɪnˈsuː]

【考法】 *vi.* 紧随其后: take place **afterward** or as a result

例 A brief but embarrassing silence ensued. 一阵短暂且令人尴尬的沉默随之而来。

近 follow

You have to believe in yourself. That's the secret of success.

人必须相信自己，这是成功的秘诀。

——美国演员 卓别林（Charles Chaplin, American actor）

List 9

Unit 1

■ ENTANGLE	■ ENTHUSIASM	■ ENTICE	■ ENTRANCE	■ ENTRAP
■ ENTREAT	■ ENUNCIATE	■ EPHEMERAL	■ EPIC	■ EPICURE

entangle ［ɪnˈtæŋgl］
【考法 1】 vt. 使卷入，使纠缠: to **twist** together into a usually **confused mass**
例 We managed to entangle the string of lights into a hopeless mess of wires. 我们将小灯泡的线纠缠成了一堆。
近 interlace, intertwist, knot, snarl, tangle
【考法 2】 vt. 使变复杂或困难: to make **complex or difficult**
例 The history of Alexander the Great is entangled by variant accounts of his exploits. 亚历山大大帝的生平历史被不同版本的记录搞得很纠结。
近 complexify, perplex, sophisticate
反 simplify, streamline 简化

enthusiasm ［ɪnˈθuːziæzəm］
【考法】 n. 热情，兴趣: urgent **desire or interest**
例 In my enthusiasm to get going, I forgot to pack any foul-weather clothing. 在强烈的出游热情下，我忘记带上防备坏天气的衣服了。
近 ardor, avidity, desirousness, impatience, keenness, lust, thirst
反 apathy, indifference 无动于衷，漠不关心
派 enthusiastic adj. 热情的
反 halfhearted 心不在焉的

entice ［ɪnˈtaɪs］
【考法】 vt. 诱使: to attract artfully or adroitly or by arousing hope or desire: **tempt**; **lure**
例 entice sb into doing sth 诱使某人做某事
近 allure, bait, beguile, decoy, seduce, solicit, tempt, lead on
派 enticing adj. 诱人的
反 formidable 可怕的

entrance
【考法 1】 ［ˈentrəns］ n. 进入权，进入许可: the **means** or right **of entering or participating in**
例 Entrance to the club is by invitation only. 该俱乐部只接受受邀入会。
近 access, admission, admittance, gateway, ingress, passport, ticket
【考法 2】 ［ɪnˈtræns］ vt. 使入迷: to fill with delight, **wonder**, or **enchantment**
例 be entranced by the view 陶醉于景色
近 enrapture, enthrall, ravish, transport, carry away
反 bore, disappoint, disgust, repel, repulse 使厌烦
派 entrancing adj. 使人欣喜的
反 unprepossessing 不讨人喜欢的

entrap ［ɪnˈtræp］
【考法】 vt. 诱骗: to **lure** into a compromising statement or act
例 A string of inconsistent statements finally entrapped the witness. 一系列不一致的陈述最终蒙骗了目击者。
近 ensnare, ensnarl, entoil, mesh, net, snare, catch up
反 disentangle, untangle 使解脱

entreat ［ɪnˈtriːt］
【考法】 vt. 恳求: to **plead** with especially in order to **persuade**, **ask urgently**
例 He entreated his boss for another chance. 他恳求老板再给他一次机会。
近 beseech, besiege, conjure, implore, importune, solicit, supplicate, plead to, appeal to

enunciate [ɪˈnʌnsieɪt]

【考法 1】 *v.* 清晰地说：to utter **articulate** sounds

例 Enunciate your words, and then you won't have to repeat them so often. 把话说清楚，你就不用经常重复了。

近 articulate

【考法 2】 *vt.* 公开宣布，宣称：to make known **openly or publicly**

例 Today the President enunciated a new foreign policy. 总统在今天宣布了一项新的对外政策。

近 annunciate, broadcast, declare, herald, proclaim, promulgate, publicize, release, give out

ephemeral [ɪˈfemərəl]

【考法】 *adj.* 短暂的：lasting a **very short time**

例 ephemeral pressures 暂时的压力

近 evanescent, fleeting, impermanent, temporary, transient, transitory, fugacious, fugitive

反 eternal, permanent, perpetual, enduring, everlasting, ceaseless, immortal, undying 永久的

epic [ˈepɪk]

【考法】 *adj.* 宏大的，超凡脱俗的：**surpassing the usual** or ordinary, particularly in scope or size

例 His genius was epic. 他聪明过人。

近 august, grandiose, imposing, magnificent, majestic, monumental

反 humble, unheroic, unimpressive, modest 适度的，印象不深的

epicure [ˈepɪkjʊr]

【考法】 *n.* 美食家：one with sensitive and **discriminating tastes** especially in food or wine

例 Thomas Jefferson was one of America's first great epicures. 托马斯·杰斐逊算得上是美国早期美食家一枚。

近 bon vivant, gastronomist, gourmand, gourmet

Unit 2

■ EPIGRAM	■ EPILOGUE	■ EPITHET	■ EPITOMIZE	■ EQUABLE
■ EQUITY	■ EQUIVALENT	■ EQUIVOCATE	■ ERODE	■ ERRANT

epigram [ˈepɪɡræm]

【考法】 *n.* 机智的短诗，警句：a **short**, **witty** poem expressing a single thought or observation

例 Benjamin Franklin's most famous epigram, "Remember that time is money." 本杰明·富兰克林最著名的警句就是，时间就是金钱。

近 adage, aphorism, apothegm, byword, maxim, proverb

epilogue [ˈepɪlɔːɡ]

【考法 1】 *n.* 文学作品的结局：a **concluding section** that rounds out the design of a **literary** work

反 preface 序文

【考法 2】 *n.* 戏剧的收场白：the **final scene of a play** that comments on or summarizes the main action

近 coda

epithet [ˈepɪθet]

【考法】 *n.* 外号，绰号：a **descriptive** or familiar **name** given instead of or in addition to the one belonging to an individual; a disparaging or abusive word or phrase

例 King Richard I of England was given the very laudatory epithet "the Lion-Hearted". 英王理查一世因英勇大胆被赞誉为"狮心理查"。

近 alias, cognomen, sobriquet

epitomize [ɪˈpɪtəmaɪz]

【考法 1】 *vt.* 摘要，概括：to make into a **short statement** of the **main points** (as of a report)

例 His personal code of behavior on the playing field is epitomized by his favorite saying, Nice guys finish last. 他在赛场上的座右铭是：好男坚持到底。

近 abstract, digest, encapsulate, outline, recapitulate, synopsize, sum up

【考法 2】 *vt.* 代表，体现，是…的典型范例：to **represent** in visible form; to be a **typical example of**

例 The Parthenon in Athens epitomizes the ancient Greek ideal of architectural beauty. 雅典的巴特农神庙体现了古希腊对于建筑美感的理念。 || behavior that epitomizes selfishness 典型的自私行为

近 body, express, externalize, incarnate, incorporate, instantiate, manifest, materialize, substantiate

equable [ˈekwəbl]

【考法】 *adj.* (脾气、性情)温和的：not easily disturbed; **serene**

例 equable temperament 温和的性情

近 balmy, genial, gentle, moderate, temperate

反 harsh, inclement, intemperate, severe 严厉的

派 equanimity *n.* 温和

反 agitation, excitability 激动

equity [ˈekwəti]

【考法】 *n.* 不偏不倚，公平：**lack of favoritism** toward one side or another

例 The lower wages paid to women for equal work violated the notion of equity. 同等工作付给女性更低的报酬违背了公平的理念。

近 disinterestedness, evenhandedness, fairness, impartiality, neutrality, nonpartisanship

反 bias, favoritism, nonobjectivity, one-sidedness, partiality, partisanship, prejudice 歧视，偏见；偏爱

派 equitable *adj.* 公平的

反 biased, discriminatory 偏袒的，差别对待的

equivalent [ɪˈkwɪvələnt]

【考法】 *adj./n.* 等价的，相等的：**equal** in force, amount, or value

例 That huge mansion is the equivalent of five ordinary houses. 那栋巨大的公馆有五套一般户型的房子那么大。

近 coequal, coordinate, counterpart, peer, rival, parallel

equivocate [ɪˈkwɪvəkeɪt]

【考法】 *vi.* (带有欺骗目的地)模棱两可地说，说谎话：to use **equivocal** language especially with intent to deceive

例 When asked about his tax plan, the candidate didn't equivocate. 当被问到税收方案时，候选人直言不讳。

近 fudge, hedge, weasel, prevaricate, palter

反 communicate straightforwardly 直率地说

派 equivocal *adj.* 模棱两可的：open to two or more interpretations and often intended to mislead; ambiguous; equivocation *n.* 模棱两可的话

反 clarity 清楚

erode [ɪˈroʊd]

【考法】 *v.* 侵蚀，慢慢减少：to **consume** or wear away **gradually**

例 Flooding eroded the hillside. 洪水冲刷着山坡。‖ inflation eroding buying power 通货膨胀导致购买力下降

近 corrode, fret, gnaw, nibble, bite at

errant [ˈerənt]

【考法1】 *adj.* 居无定所的：traveling **from place to place**

例 the errant gunslinger as a standard character in western novels 在西部题材小说中，居无定所的持枪歹徒是经典形象

近 ambulant, fugitive, nomadic, perambulatory, roaming, roving, vagabond, vagrant, wandering

【考法2】 *adj.* 误入歧途的，犯错误的：**straying** from the **proper course or standards**

例 errant youngsters 误入歧途的青少年

近 misbehaving, mischievous

反 behaved, behaving, nice, orderly 行为规矩的

Unit 3

| ■ ERRATIC | ■ ERUDITE | ■ ESCALATE | ■ ESCHEW | ■ ESOTERIC |
| ■ ESPOUSE | ■ ESTEEM | ■ ESTIMABLE | ■ ESTRANGE | ■ ETCH |

erratic [ɪˈrætɪk]

【考法1】 *adj.* 善变的：**not** staying **constant**

例 Business at the fast-food restaurant has been so erratic lately that the manager never knows how much staff to have on hand. 快餐店的生意最近非常起伏以至于经理也不清楚需要多少人手。

近 changing, fluctuating, irregular, unequal, unstable, unsteady, varying

反 changeless, constant, stable, steady, unchanging, unvarying 不变的

【考法2】 *adj.* 异常的，不同寻常的：**different from the ordinary** in a way that causes curiosity or suspicion

例 The key to the code was the erratic punctuation the killer used. 解开密码的关键是杀手使用的不同寻常的标点符号。

近 bizarre, eccentric, offbeat, outlandish, out-of-the-way, peculiar, quaint, queer, remarkable, screwy, spaced-out, way-out, weird

erudite	[ˈerudaɪt]	

erudite [ˈerudaɪt]
【考法】 *adj.* 博学的：characterized by erudition; **learned**
例 an erudite scholar 渊博的学者
近 knowledgeable, learned, lettered, literate, scholarly, well-read
反 ignorant, unlettered, benighted, illiterate, uneducated, unscholarly 无知的

escalate [ˈeskəleɪt]
【考法】 *v.* (使)(战争等)升级，扩大：to **increase** in extent, volume, number, amount, intensity, or scope
例 We don't want to escalate the war. 我们不想使战争扩大。
近 aggrandize, amplify, augment, boost, expand, pump up, build up
反 wane, diminish 减弱

eschew [ɪsˈtʃuː]
【考法】 *vt.* 刻意避开；戒绝：to **avoid** habitually especially on moral or practical grounds
例 The minister eschews involvement in local politics, since he doesn't want to diminish his moral authority in the community. 首相回避参与当地政治，因为他不想降低其道德权威。
近 dodge, elude, evade, shirk, shun, weasel out of
反 embrace, greet, welcome, habitually indulge in, seek 乐于接受，寻觅

esoteric [ˌesəˈterɪk]
【考法 1】 *adj.* 深奥难懂的：**difficult** for one of ordinary knowledge or intelligence **to understand**
例 esoteric terminology 深奥难懂的专业术语
近 abstruse, arcane, hermetic, recondite
反 shallow, superficial 肤浅的
【考法 2】 *adj.* 少数人知道的：**not known** or meant to be known **by the general** populace
例 The actor must have had some esoteric motive for leaving stage. 该演员淡出舞台肯定有不为人知的原因。
近 confidential, inside, intimate, nonpublic, privy, secret
反 commonly accepted, generally known, open, public 公开的，普遍接受的

espouse [ɪˈspaʊz]
【考法 1】 *vt.* 支持；拥护：to take up and **support** as a cause
例 espouse the revolutionary cause 支持革命事业
近 embrace, take on, take up
反 abjure, repudiate 誓绝
【考法 2】 *vt.* 与…结婚：to take in **marriage**; **marry**

esteem [ɪˈstiːm]
【考法】 *n./v.* 尊重：to regard with **respect**; **prize**
例 be held in high esteem 被高度敬仰
近 appreciation, estimation, favor, regard, respect
反 disfavor, odium 不喜欢，憎恶

estimable [ˈestɪməbl]
【考法】 *adj.* 值得尊敬的：deserving of esteem; **admirable**
例 an estimable adversary 一位值得尊敬的对手
近 prestigious, reputable, applaudable, commendable, creditable, meritorious, praiseworthy
反 contemptible, infamous, censurable, discreditable, illaudable, reprehensible 令人鄙视的

estrange [ɪˈstreɪndʒ]
【考法】 *vt.* 使疏远，离间，使感情失和：to arouse especially mutual **enmity** or **indifference** in where there had formerly been love, affection, or **friendliness**
例 He estranged several of his coworkers. 他和好多同事疏远了。
近 alienate, disaffect, disgruntle, sour
反 reconcile 使和好

etch [etʃ]
【考法 1】 *v.* 蚀刻：to produce （as a pattern or design）on a hard material by eating into the material's surface （as by acid or laser beam）
例 The artist etched his landscape on a copper plate. 艺术家将风景画刻在铜盘上。
近 grave, incise, inscribe
【考法 2】 *v.* 留下深刻印象，铭记：to **produce a vivid impression** of
例 In just a few pages the writer etched an unforgettable portrait of one of the more remarkable First Ladies. 仅用数页，作者刻画出了一位杰出的第一夫人令人难忘的形象。
近 impress, imprint, infix, ingrain

Unit 4

■ ETERNAL　　　■ ETHEREAL　　　■ ETHICS　　　■ EULOGIZE　　　■ EUPHEMISM
■ EUPHONIOUS　　■ EUPHORIA　　　■ EVACUATE　　■ EVANESCENT　　■ EVASIVE

eternal [ɪˈtɜːrnl]
【考法】 *adj.* 永恒的：having **infinite duration**; **everlasting**; **perpetual**
例　eternal love 永恒的爱
近　ageless, everlasting, immortal, imperishable, perennial, perpetual, undying
反　ephemeral 短暂的

ethereal [iˈθɪriəl]
【考法 1】 *adj.* 轻巧精致的：resembling air in **lightness**, **highly refined**; **delicate**
例　The bakery's scrumptious pastries have a wonderfully ethereal consistency. 面包师可口的糕点有着一种奇妙的蓬松轻巧的质感。
近　fluffy, gossamer, light
反　heavy, leaden, ponderous 沉重的
【考法 2】 *adj.* 天国的：of, relating to, or suggesting **heaven**
例　a land of ethereal beauty and tranquility 具有缥缈的美感和宁静的一片土地
近　elysian, empyreal, heavenly, supernal
反　chthonic, hellish, infernal, Tartarean 地狱的
【考法 3】 *adj.* 非物质的，精神（上）的：not of this world; **spiritual**; **not composed of matter**
例　that ethereal attribute that every performer should have—charisma 每位演奏者都应该具有一种精神上的特质——个人魅力
近　bodiless, formless, incorporeal, insubstantial, nonmaterial, nonphysical, spiritual
反　bodily, corporeal, material, physical, substantial 物质的，有实体的

ethics [ˈeθɪks]
【考法】 *n.* 道德规范：rules or standards **governing** the **conduct** of a person or the members of a profession
例　an old-fashioned work ethics 传统的工作行为规范
近　ethos, morality, morals, norms, principles, standards

eulogize [ˈjuːlədʒaɪz]
【考法】 *vt.* 称赞；颂扬：to **speak** or write **in high praise of**
例　He was eulogized at his funeral as a caring husband and a good father. 他在悼词中被称赞为一个好丈夫、一个好爸爸。
反　defame, pan 诬蔑，指责

euphemism [ˈjuːfəmɪzəm]
【考法】 *n.* 婉言，委婉的说法：the substitution of an agreeable or **inoffensive expression** for one that may offend or suggest something unpleasant
例　using "eliminate" as a euphemism for "kill" "杀死"的委婉说法是"灭掉"

euphonious [juːˈfoʊniəs]
【考法】 *adj.* 悦耳的：**pleasing** or agreeable to the ear
近　mellifluous, melodious, canorous, harmonizing, symphonious, tuneful
反　cacophonous, discordant, disharmonious, dissonant, tuneless, unmelodious 刺耳的

euphoria [juːˈfɔːriə]
【考法】 *n.* 感觉极其愉快：a state of **overwhelming usually pleasurable** emotion
例　The initial euphoria following her victory in the election has now subsided. 选举成功最初带给她的欢愉感现在已经消失。
近　elation, exhilaration, intoxication, transport, rapture, rhapsody
反　depression 沮丧

evacuate [ɪˈvækjueɪt]
【考法 1】 *vt.* 撤空：to **empty or remove** the contents of
例　They were ordered to evacuate the building. 他们被命令搬出大楼。
近　clear, vacate, void
反　fill up, occupy, load 填满
【考法 2】 *vt.* 撤退：to **remove** especially from a military zone or dangerous area
例　During World War II, children were evacuated from London to the country. 二战期间，伦敦市的儿童被撤离到郊区。
反　conquer 占领

evanescent [ˌevəˈnesnt]

【考法】 *adj.* 逐渐消失的，短暂的：tending to **vanish** like vapor

例 Beauty is as evanescent as a rainbow. 容颜易老，年华易逝。

近 ephemeral, fleeting, impermanent, temporary, transient, transitory

反 ceaseless, endless, enduring, eternal, everlasting, immortal, permanent, perpetual, timeless, undying, unending, abiding, lasting 持久的

evasive [ɪˈveɪsɪv]

【考法】 *adj.* 难以发现、捕捉、分离的；含糊其辞的：hard to find, capture, or isolate; **equivocal**

例 an evasive statement 模棱两可的陈述

近 fugitive, slippery

反 unequivocal 明确的

Unit 5

■ EVERLASTING	■ EVICT	■ EVINCE	■ EVOKE	■ EXACERBATE
■ EXACTING	■ EXALT	■ EXASPERATE	■ EXCAVATE	■ EXCEPTIONAL

everlasting [ˌevərˈlæstɪŋ]

【考法】 *adj.* 永恒的，持久的：lasting **forever**; eternal

例 To his everlasting credit, he never once gave in to temptation. 他人品非常好，从来没有屈服于诱惑。

近 ageless, enduring, eternal, immortal, imperishable, perennial, perpetual, undying

反 impermanent, mortal, temporary, transient, ephemeral 短暂的

evict [ɪˈvɪkt]

【考法】 *vt.* 赶出，逐出：to put out (a tenant, for example) by legal process; **expel**

例 Her landlord has threatened to evict her if she doesn't pay the rent soon. 她的房东威胁说如果再不交房租就要把她赶出去。

反 harbor 收容

evince [ɪˈvɪns]

【考法】 *vt.* 表明：to **make known** (something abstract) through outward signs

例 evince a strong desire 明显地表现出强烈的欲望

近 bespeak, betray, declare, demonstrate, expose, manifest, reveal, give away

反 conceal, keep hidden 隐藏

evoke [ɪˈvoʊk]

【考法】 *vt.* 唤起，引发：to **call** forth or **up**

例 evoke memories 唤起回忆

近 elicit, inspire, raise

exacerbate [ɪgˈzæsərbeɪt]

【考法】 *vt.* 使加剧，使恶化：to make more violent, bitter, or **severe**

例 a heavy rainfall that exacerbated the flood problems 大雨恶化了洪水问题

近 aggravate, complicate, worsen

反 allay, alleviate, assuage, mitigate, relieve, palliate 缓和

exacting [ɪgˈzæktɪŋ]

【考法 1】 *adj.* 严格的，苛求的：making severe demands; **rigorous**

例 an exacting instructor 一位严苛的导师

近 choosy, demanding, fastidious, finical, fussy, pernickety, persnickety, picky

派 exact *vt.* 强求，索取：to force the payment or yielding of

例 exact tribute from a conquered people 从征服的人民手中强取贡品

反 condone, forgive 赦免，免除(债务)

【考法 2】 *adj.* 费时间花心思的：**requiring** much **time**, **effort**, or careful **attention**

例 Editing and proofreading will always be an exacting task. 编辑和校对是花时间花心思的工作。

近 arduous, burdensome, challenging, grueling, killing, laborious, onerous, taxing, toilsome

反 light, unchallenging, undemanding 要求不高的

exalt [ɪɡˈzɔːlt]

【考法 1】 *vt.* 提升，提拔：to **raise** in rank, character, or status; elevate

例 Popular support and media hype have exalted Super Bowl Sunday to the level of a national holiday. 大众广泛的支持和媒体的大肆宣传已然将"超级碗美式足球冠军赛"变成了一个全民狂欢的大节日。

近 aggrandize, canonize, deify, dignify, elevate, ennoble, magnify

反 abase, degrade, demean, humble, lower in status 贬抑，降低身份

【考法 2】 *vt.* 赞扬：to glorify, **praise**, or honor

近 emblazon, extol, glorify, laud, magnify

反 condemn 谴责

exasperate [ɪɡˈzæspəreɪt]

【考法】 *vt.* 激怒：to **excite** the anger of

例 I was exasperated by the flight delays. 我被飞机延误激怒了。

近 aggravate, gall, nettle, peeve, rile, ruffle, vex, burn up

反 mitigate, mollify 平息

excavate [ˈekskəveɪt]

【考法】 *v.* 挖掘，挖空：to **dig out** and remove

例 excavate soil from one area 从某处挖土出来

反 fill in 填满

exceptional [ɪkˈsepʃənl]

【考法】 *adj.* 例外的，特别的，非凡的：being an exception; **uncommon**; **extraordinary**

例 exceptional bravery 非凡的勇敢

近 aberrant, abnormal, anomalous, exceeding, extraordinary, peculiar, unwonted

反 commonplace, prosaic, customary, normal, ordinary, typical, unextraordinary, usual 平凡常见的

Unit 6

■ EXCORIATE	■ EXCRETE	■ EXCRUCIATE	■ EXCULPATE	■ EXCURSIVE
■ EXECRATE	■ EXEMPLARY	■ EXEMPT	■ EXHAUST	■ EXHILARATE

excoriate [ˌeksˈkɔːrieɪt]

【考法】 *vt.* 严厉批评：to **criticize harshly** and usually **publicly**

例 She was excoriated as a racist. 她被指责是一个种族歧视者。

近 abuse, assail, belabor, castigate, lambaste, vituperate

反 accolade, extol, flatter, praise lavishly 赞扬

excrete [ɪkˈskriːt]

【考法】 *vt.* 排泄：to separate and **discharge**（waste matter）from the blood, tissues, or organs

例 excrete sweat 排汗

反 absorb, ingest 吸收

excruciate [ɪkˈskruːʃieɪt]

【考法】 *vt.* 折磨，使痛苦：to inflict severe **pain** on; torture

例 She has long been excruciated by a persistent pain in her back. 她长久以来被背痛折磨。

近 agonize, anguish, plague, rack, torment, torture, harrow

反 exult 使欢跃

exculpate [ˈekskʌlpeɪt]

【考法】 *vt.* 声明无罪；开脱，使无罪：to **clear** from alleged **fault** or **guilt**

例 I have gathered evidence that will exculpate my client. 我已经搜集到能够证明委托人无罪的证据了。

近 absolve, acquit, clear, exonerate, vindicate

反 attribute guilt, inculpate, indict, criminate, incriminate 归罪，控告

excursive [ɪkˈskɜːrsɪv]

【考法】 *adj.* 离题的；散漫的：**passing** from one topic to another

例 an excursive story line that some readers of Melville's novel find very rewarding 梅尔维尔小说的一些读者非常喜欢松散的故事主线

近 desultory, digressive, meandering, rambling, wandering

execrate [ˈeksɪkreɪt]

【考法 1】 v. 谴责: to declare to be **morally wrong or evil**

例 Leaders from all over the world execrated the terrorists responsible for the bomb blast. 世界各国首脑强烈谴责对爆炸袭击负责的恐怖分子。

近 anathematize, censure, decry, denounce, reprehend, reprobate

反 bless 保佑

【考法 2】 v. 痛恨: to **dislike strongly**

例 execrate anyone who would physically abuse children or animals 痛恨那些虐待儿童或动物的人

近 abhor, abominate, despise, detest, loathe

反 love 爱

exemplary [ɪgˈzempləri]

【考法 1】 adj. 榜样的, 值得效仿的: constituting, serving as, or worthy of **being a pattern** to be **imitated**

例 As a hospital volunteer he has given exemplary service to his community. 他作为医疗志愿者为社区起到了模范的作用。

近 archetypal, imitable, paradigmatic, quintessential

派 exemplify vt. (通过榜样)示范, 显示: to show or illustrate by example

【考法 2】 adj. 作为警告的: serving as or offering a **warning**

例 Armies have traditionally used public execution as an exemplary punishment for the crime of desertion. 军队通常将公开处决作为玩忽职守罪的惩罚, 以儆效尤。

近 admonishing, admonitory, monitory, premonitory, warning

exempt [ɪgˈzempt]

【考法】 vt. 使免除: to **release** or deliver from some **liability** or requirement to which others are subject

例 a man exempted from military service 免服军役的人

exhaust [ɪgˈzɔːst]

【考法 1】 vt. 耗尽: to **consume entirely**: to make **complete use of**

例 We exhausted our funds in a week. 我们在一周内就耗尽了经费。

近 consume, devour, drain, expend, spend, use up

派 exhaustive adj. 彻底的, 完整的, 详尽的: testing all possibilities; thorough; complete

例 conduct an exhaustive investigation 做详尽的调查

反 incomplete, partial 不完全的

【考法 2】 vt. 使筋疲力尽: to **wear out** completely

例 exhausted by overwork 加班使得筋疲力尽

近 fatigue, frazzle, harass, wear out, weary, knock out

exhilarate [ɪgˈzɪləreɪt]

【考法】 vt. 使高兴; 使兴奋: to make **cheerful** and **excited**

例 be exhilarated by her success 为她的成功感到兴奋

近 electrify, galvanize, intoxicate, pump up, turn on

反 sadden, depress 使悲哀, 使沮丧

派 exhilarating adj. 令人兴奋的

反 soporific 昏昏欲睡的

Unit 7

exhort [ɪgˈzɔːrt]

【考法】 vt. 敦促, 力劝: to **urge** by **strong**, often stirring argument, admonition, advice, or appeal

例 The speaker exhorted the graduating students to go forth and try to make a difference in the world. 演讲者鼓励毕业生们向广阔天地前进, 有所作为。

近 encourage, goad, nudge, prod, prompt, egg on

exigent [ˈeksɪdʒənt]

【考法】 adj. 紧急的: requiring **immediate** aid or action

例 exigent circumstances 紧急情况

近 compelling, dire, emergent, imperative, importunate, necessitous, pressing, urgent

反 deferrable, noncritical, nonurgent 可拖延的, 不紧急的

exodus ['eksədəs]
【考法】 *n.* 大批离去：a mass **departure**
例 the mass exodus from the cities for the beaches on most summer weekends 在多数夏季的周末，大批都市人奔向海滩
近 gush, outpour, outpouring
反 influx, flux, inflow, inrush 涌入

exonerate [ɪgˈzɑːnəreɪt]
【考法】 *vt.* 免除责备：to **free from blame**
例 An investigation exonerated the school from any blame. 一项调查使该学校免受责备。
近 absolve, acquit, clear, vindicate
反 censure, incriminate, inculpate, prove guilty 责难，证明有罪

exorbitant [ɪgˈzɔːrbɪtənt]
【考法】 *adj.* 过度的：**exceeding the customary or appropriate limits** in intensity, quality, amount, or size
例 exorbitant prices 过高的价格
近 extravagant, intolerable, lavish, overdue, overweening, unconscionable
反 middling, moderate, modest, reasonable, temperate 适度的，合适的

exotic [ɪgˈzɑːtɪk]
【考法】 *adj.* 外来的，不同寻常的：excitingly or mysteriously **unusual**
例 She's famous for her exotic tastes. 她以有异域风情著称。
近 outlandish, strange
反 indigenous, familiar, nonglamorous, plain-Jane, unexotic 本地的；平常的

expansive [ɪkˈspænsɪv]
【考法 1】 *adj.* 广阔的：having a **great expanse** or extent
例 expansive beach 广阔的沙滩
近 broad, extended, far-reaching, rangy
反 limited, narrow 有限的
【考法 2】 *adj.* 话多的，健谈的：characterized by high spirits, generosity, or **readiness to talk**
例 The first Moon explorers were rarely expansive in describing their surroundings; on the contrary, their reports tended to be laconic. 初期的探月者们很少对所处的周遭环境进行大量描述；相反，他们的报告显得格外简洁。
近 communicative, eloquent, garrulous, glib, loquacious, talkative, vocative, voluble
反 laconic, reserved, reticent, taciturn 话少的，沉默寡言的

expedite ['ekspədaɪt]
【考法】 *vt.* 加快进程：to **speed up the progress** of; accelerate
例 expedite your plans 加快你的计划
反 retard 减速，阻碍

expedition [ˌekspəˈdɪʃn]
【考法】 *n.* 动作迅速：**speed** in performance; promptness
例 deal with the order with the greatest possible expedition 以可能的最快的速度处理订单
近 haste, celerity, dispatch
反 foot-dragging 拖拉

expiate ['ekspieɪt]
【考法】 *vt.* 赎罪，纠正：to **extinguish the guilt** incurred by
例 expiate one's sin 赎罪
近 mend, redeem, atone for

Unit 8

| ■ EXPIRE | ■ EXPLICIT | ■ EXPLOIT | ■ EXPONENT | ■ EXPURGATE |
| ■ EXQUISITE | ■ EXTANT | ■ EXTEMPORIZE | ■ EXTENUATE | ■ EXTINCT |

expire [ɪkˈspaɪər]
【考法 1】 *v.* 断气，死亡：to breathe one's last breath; **die**
例 The patient expired early this morning. 病人今早逝世了。
近 conclude, elapse, terminate, decease, leave off, let up
反 come to life 出生
【考法 2】 *v.* 到期：to **come to an end**
例 My membership in the club has expired. 我的会员资格到期了。
近 discontinue, elapse, end, finish, terminate, wind up, wink out
反 continue, persist, hang on 持续，续期

explicit [ɪk'splɪsɪt]

【考法 1】 *adj.* 表达清晰的: **fully revealed or expressed** without vagueness, implication, or ambiguity

例 explicit instructions 表达清晰的指示说明

近 clear-cut, definite, specific, unambiguous, unequivocal, univocal

反 obscure, implicit, implied, inferred, ambiguous, circuitous, equivocal, indefinite, unspecific, vague 模糊的

【考法 2】 *adj.* 成熟的, 完全形成的: **fully developed** or formulated

例 an explicit plan 成熟的计划

反 inchoate 未完成的, 未形成的

exploit

【考法 1】 ['eksplɔɪt] *n.* 英雄行为: a **notable** or heroic **act**

例 his wartime exploits 他在战争期间的英勇行为

【考法 2】 [ɪk'splɔɪt] *vt.* 最大程度地利用: to **employ** to the greatest possible advantage

例 exploit your opponent's weakness 利用你对手的弱点

近 abuse, leverage, play on, capitalize on, impose on

exponent [ɪk'spoʊnənt]

【考法 1】 *n.* 倡导者, 支持者: one that speaks for, represents, or **advocates**

例 Exponents of space exploration earnestly called for more missions to the outer reaches of the solar system. 太空探险的支持者强烈要求对太阳系的外边缘进行探索。

近 advocator, backer, booster, champion, espouser, friend, promoter, proponent

反 adversary, antagonist, opponent 反对者

【考法 2】 *n.* 实践者, 典型代表: one who brings an art or science to **full realization**

例 She has long reigned as the nation's leading exponent of modern dance. 她长期以来被认为是该国现代舞的集大成者。

近 expounder, guru, interpreter, practitioner, high priest

expurgate ['ekspərgeɪt]

【考法】 *vt.* 净化 (书等), 删去 (不当处): to **remove** erroneous, vulgar, obscene, or otherwise objectionable material from (a book, for example) before publication

例 an expurgated edition of the letters 信件的删减版

近 bowdlerize, obliterate, launder, red-pencil, clean up

exquisite [ɪk'skwɪzɪt]

【考法 1】 *adj.* 程度强烈的: **extreme** in degree, power, or effect

例 suffer exquisite pain 遭受强烈的痛感

近 acute, dreadful, excruciating, explosive, ferocious, fierce, furious, intensive, keen, profound, terrible, vehement, vicious

反 light, moderate, soft 适当的

【考法 2】 *adj.* 精致精巧的: having qualities that appeal to a **refined taste**

例 exquisite pen-and-ink drawings of city scenes 精巧的城市钢笔画

近 dainty, delicate, elegant, recherché, select

extant [ek'stænt]

【考法】 *adj.* 现存的: still in existence; **not destroyed**, **lost**, or **extinct**

例 the most charming writer extant 目前活着的作家中最有魅力的一位 ‖ extant manuscripts 未毁坏的手稿

近 current, immediate, ongoing, present-day, existent

反 destroyed, extinct, lost, missing, dead, nonextant 丢失的, 不存在的

extemporize [ɪk'stempəraɪz]

【考法】 *v.* 即兴表现: to do or perform (something) **without prior preparation** or practice

例 A good talk show host has to be able to extemporize the interviews when things don't go as planned. 一个好的脱口秀主持人要能够在计划之外即兴表现。

反 follow a script 参考草稿

派 extemporaneous *adj.* 即席的

反 planned 有计划的

extenuate [ɪk'stenjueɪt]

【考法】 *vt.* 减轻罪过: to lessen or to try to **lessen the seriousness** or extent of by making partial excuses

例 Try to extenuate their vandalism with the old refrain of "Boys will be boys." 企图用"江山易改本性难移"的俗语为他们的暴行开脱。

近 deodorize, excuse, explain away, gloss over, gloze over

extinct [ɪkˈstɪŋkt]

【考法】 *adj.* 灭绝的：**no longer existing** or living

例 extinct species 灭绝的物种

近 bygone, bypast, defunct, expired, nonextant, vanished

反 alive, extant, existing, living, resuscitated 现存的

派 extinction *n.* 灭绝

反 perpetuation 永存

Unit 9

■ EXTINGUISH	■ EXTOL	■ EXTORT	■ EXTRACT	■ EXTRACTION
■ EXTRANEOUS	■ EXTRAVAGANT	■ EXTRICATE	■ EXUBERANT	■ EXUDE

extinguish [ɪkˈstɪŋgwɪʃ]

【考法 1】 *vt.* 熄灭：to **put out** (a fire, for example); quench

例 The fire in the skillet was quickly extinguished by slamming the lid on. 盖上锅盖后，平底锅的火苗很快熄灭了。

近 blanket, douse, quench, put out, snuff out

反 ignite, rekindle 点燃

【考法 2】 *vt.* 终止：to **bring to a complete end** the physical soundness, existence, or usefulness of

例 a fatal blunder that extinguished all hope that the team would actually win the play-offs 一个致命的失误使得队伍赢得季后赛的希望完全破灭

近 annihilate, decimate, demolish, desolate, devastate, pulverize, ruin, shatter, smash, tear down, pull down, rub out

反 build, construct, erect, raise, rear, set up, put up 建立

extol [ɪkˈstoʊl]

【考法】 *vt.* 赞美；吹捧：to **praise** highly; glorify

例 extol the virtues of... 赞美……的优点

近 carol, exalt, glorify, laud, magnify, resound

反 censure, impugn, malign, deprecate, detract, rail, vilify, excoriate 批评

extort [ɪkˈstɔːrt]

【考法】 *vt.* 勒索：to obtain from a person by **force**, **intimidation**, or undue or illegal power

例 The criminals extorted large sums of money from their victims. 绑匪向受害者勒索大笔钱财。

近 wrest, wring

extract [ɪkˈstrækt]

【考法】 *vt.* 用力拔出：to pull or **take out** forcibly

例 extract a wisdom tooth 拔出一颗智齿

近 pull, uproot, wrest, wring, yank, root out, tear out

反 embed 嵌入

extraction [ɪkˈstrækʃn]

【考法】 *n.* 血统：**origin**; lineage; **ancestry**

例 a family of French extraction 有法国血统的家族

近 bloodline, breeding, descent, genealogy, lineage, origin, family tree

extraneous [ɪkˈstreɪniəs]

【考法 1】 *adj.* 无关的：having **no relevance**

例 an extraneous digression 无关的跑题

近 impertinent, inapplicable, irrelative, accidental, adventitious, external

反 applicable, apposite, apropos, germane, pertinent, relative, relevant 相关的

【考法 2】 *adj.* 非主要因素的：**not** forming an **essential** or vital part

例 The architect's streamlined modern style shuns any sort of extraneous ornamentation. 建筑师流线型的现代设计避免了一切多余的装饰。

近 accidental, adventitious, alien, external, foreign

反 essential, inherent, innate, intrinsic 本质的，核心的

extravagant [ɪkˈstrævəgənt]

【考法 1】 *adj.* 挥霍的：given to **spending money freely** or foolishly

例 She has always been extravagant with her money. 她总是挥金如土。

近 profligate, spendthrift, squandering, thriftless, unthrifty, wasteful

反 frugal, conserving, economical, penny-pinching, scrimping, skimping, thrifty 节省的

【考法2】 *adj.* 过度的，不必要的：going **beyond** a **normal** or **acceptable limit** in degree or amount

例 The book doesn't quite merit the extravagant praise that it has received. 这本书被盛赞过度。

近 baroque, exorbitant, immoderate, inordinate, lavish, overdue, overmuch, overweening, plethoric, unconscionable, unmerciful

反 middling, moderate, modest, reasonable, temperate 适当的，适度的

extricate [ˈekstrɪkeɪt]

【考法】 *vt.* 使解脱，救出：to **free** or remove from an **entanglement** or difficulty

例 extricate himself from financial difficulties 使他摆脱财政困境

近 disengage, disentangle, free, liberate, release, untangle

反 enmesh, entangle, embroil 使卷入

exuberant [ɪɡˈzuːbərənt]

【考法1】 *adj.* 非常高兴的，热情洋溢的：**joyously unrestrained** and enthusiastic

例 Exuberant crowds rushed to greet the returning national champions. 激动的人群争先恐后地向凯旋的全国冠军表示问候。

近 ebullient, effervescent, frolic, buoyant, bouncy, vivacious

反 austere 克制的；sullen 闷闷不乐的

【考法2】 *adj.* 大量的，充分的：produced in extreme **abundance**

例 an exuberant imagination 丰富的想象力

近 ample, lavish, lush, luxuriant, opulent, plentiful, prodigal, profuse, riotous

反 meager, scant, sparse 匮乏的

exude [ɪɡˈzuːd]

【考法】 *v.* 分泌，流出：to **flow forth** slowly through small openings

例 a sticky resin exuded from the bark 从树皮中分泌出来的黏稠的树脂

近 bleed, ooze, seep

反 absorb 吸收

Unit 10

■ EXULT	■ FABLE	■ FABRICATE	■ FACETIOUS	■ FACILE
■ FACILITATE	■ FACTION	■ FALLACIOUS	■ FALLOW	■ FAIL-SAFE

exult [ɪɡˈzʌlt]

【考法】 *vi.* 感到欢喜：to **rejoice** especially with feelings or display of triumph or self-satisfaction

例 exult in a triumph 沉浸在胜利的欢喜当中

近 delight, glory, jubilate, joy, rejoice, triumph

反 lament, mourn 哀悼；bemoan 叹息，悲伤

派 exultant *adj.* 狂喜的

fable [ˈfeɪbl]

【考法1】 *n.* 寓言故事：a **story** intended to **teach a basic truth** or moral about life

例 This classic Christmas film is essentially a fable showing how every person's life has meaning. 这部经典的基督教电影本质上来说是一个寓言，它告诉我们每个人的生命都是有意义的。

近 apologue, parable

派 fabulous *adj.* 寓言般的，难以置信的

【考法2】 *n.* 神话，传说：a legendary **story of supernatural happenings**

例 According to an ancient fable, the waters of the mountain spring are the tears of a woman weeping for her lost children. 根据一个古老的传说，山中的这眼泉水是一名失去孩子的母亲所流下的眼泪。

近 legend, mythos, tale

【考法3】 *n.* 谎言，虚构：a **statement** known by its maker to be untrue and made **in order to deceive**

例 The stories of lost cities of gold may have been fables deliberately concocted by Native Americans to dupe the Spanish. 所谓的"失落的黄金之都"的故事也许只是美洲土著们杜撰出来忽悠西班牙人的。

近 fabrication, falsehood, lie, mendacity, prevarication, story

反 fact 事实；truth 真相

fabricate [ˈfæbrɪkeɪt]

【考法1】 *vt.* 捏造：to **make up** for the purpose of deception

例 be accused of fabricating evidence 被指控有捏造证据的行为

近 concoct, coin, devise, forge, fake, feign, invent

【考法2】 *vt.* 搭建，组建；打造：to **bring into being by combining**, shaping, or transforming materials

例 The house was essentially fabricated at the factory and then shipped to the site for assembly. 这间房屋的核心主体在工厂内建好之后，它被运往目的地直接进行组装。|| All the key parts are fabricated from high quality titanium alloy. 所有的关键零件都是由上好的钛合金打造的。

近 assemble, construct, erect, frame, fashion, manufacture, produce, rear, set up

反 demount, disassemble, dismantle, dismember 拆解，拆毁

派 fabrication *n.* 组建；虚构的事物

facetious [fə'si:ʃəs]

【考法】 *adj.* 喜欢开玩笑的，轻浮的：**joking** or jesting often inappropriately

例 Stop being facetious! This is the life-and-death moment. 别开玩笑了！这可是生死攸关的时刻。

近 humorous, jocose, jocular, waggish, witty

反 earnest, sincere 真挚的，真诚的；lugubrious 哀怨的

facile ['fæsl]

【考法1】 *adj.* 表面的，浅尝辄止的：having or showing a **lack of depth** of understanding or character

例 a facile slogan devised by politicians 政客们肤浅的宣传口号

近 cursory, shallow, simplistic, superficial

反 deep, profound 深刻的；comprehensive, exhaustive 全面的，详尽的

【考法2】 *adj.* 容易的，唾手可得的：**easily accomplished** or attained

例 a facile victory 一场轻松易得的胜利 || propose a facile solution to a complex problem 给一个复杂的问题提议一个容易的解决方案

近 cheap, easy, effortless, painless

反 arduous, demanding, difficult, formidable, hard, laborious, toilsome, tough 费力的，困难的

facilitate [fə'sɪlɪteɪt]

【考法】 *vt.* 使变容易，促进：to **make easy** or easier

例 The new airport will facilitate the development of tourism. 新建机场将促进旅游业的发展。

近 ease, expedite, forward, further, help

反 check, hamper, handicap, hinder, impede, obstruct, thwart, retard 阻碍，阻止；complicate 使复杂化

派 facility *n.* 设施；容易，方便

faction ['fækʃn]

【考法】 *n.* 派系：**a party** or group (as within a government) **that is often contentious** or self-seeking

例 affiliated with one faction 附属于某个党派 || North-Ocean Faction 北洋派

近 bloc, body, clique, coalition, sect, wing

派 factional *adj.* 派系的，派别的

fallacious [fə'leɪʃəs]

【考法1】 *adj.* 谬误的，不合逻辑的：**containing** or based on a **fallacy**

例 The once-common fallacious claim that girls just weren't any good at math. 曾经广为流传的一个谬论：女孩子无论如何就是学不好数学。

近 illogical, invalid, irrational, mad, reasonless, sophistic, unreasonable

反 sound 论证有力的；valid 合乎逻辑的

派 fallacy *n.* 逻辑谬误

【考法2】 *adj.* 欺骗性的：**tending to deceive** or mislead

例 fallacious testimony 不真实的证词

近 beguiling, deceiving, deceptive, deluding, delusive, delusory, false, fraudulent, misleading

反 authentic, veritable 真实的

fallow ['fælou]

【考法1】 *adj.* 休耕的：left **untilled** or unsown after plowing

例 The field was lying fallow. 那田地正在休耕中。

近 untilled, uncultivated

【考法2】 *adj.* 闲置的：**not being in a state of use**, activity, or employment

例 The coal mine has been lying fallow since the drop in prices made it unprofitable. 自从煤价下跌造成亏损，这个煤矿就一直处于停工状态。

近 dead, dormant, inert, inoperative, latent, unused, vacant

反 functioning, occupied, operative, running, working 使用中的；active 活跃的

fail-safe [feɪl-seɪf]

【考法1】 *n.* 保险措施：a measure taken **to preclude loss or injury**

例 There are so many fail-safes built into the system that a highly unlikely series of mistakes would have to be made before failure could occur. 系统中嵌入了大量的保险措施，因此在系统崩溃之前，必须要发生一系列几乎不可能出现的错误。

近 caution, palladium, preventive, safeguard

【考法2】 *adj.* 万无一失的：having **no chance of failure**

例 a fail-safe device 自动防故障装置 ‖ Men have traditionally regarded flowers as the fail-safe gift for Valentine's Day. 男士们长期以来认为鲜花是情人节永远不会错的礼物。

近 certain, foolproof, sure, unfailing

反 fallible 容易犯错的

Trouble is only opportunity in work clothes.

困难只是穿上工作服的机遇。

——美国实业家 凯泽（H.J. Kaiser, American businessman）

List 10

"背 GRE 单词的过程，让我们铭记的不仅仅是单词，更是周围人的关爱。
我们刷的不是单词，而是关爱。"　　　　　　（底骞，2009 年 10 月，Verbal 730，Quantitative 800，
录取院校：The Pennsylvania of State University, Department of Geography）

Unit 1

■ FALSEHOOD	■ FALTER	■ FANATIC	■ FANTASY	■ FARCE
■ FASCINATE	■ FAST	■ FASTIDIOUS	■ FATEFUL	■ FATHOM

falsehood [ˈfɔːlshʊd]
【考法】 *n.* 谎言：a statement known by its maker to be **untrue** and **made in order to deceive**
例 Truth always rise above falsehood, as oil rise above water. 油脂水面浮，真理胜谎言。
近 deception, fable, lie, mendacity, prevarication, untruth
反 truth, verity 真相，实话

falter [ˈfɔːltər]
【考法 1】 *vi.* 蹒跚：to **walk unsteadily**
近 lurch, stagger, stumble, teeter, totter, wobble
【考法 2】 *vi.* 犹豫，踌躇：to be **unsteady in purpose or action**, as from loss of courage or confidence
例 Mr. Garrison never once faltered in his demand that slavery be unconditionally abolished. 盖瑞森先生从不对他废除奴隶的要求存有任何的犹豫。
近 balance, halt, hesitate, vacillate, waver
派 faltering *adj.* 犹豫的

fanatic [fəˈnætɪk]
【考法 1】 *n.* 狂热者：a person marked or motivated by an extreme, **unreasoning enthusiasm**, as for a cause
例 a soccer fanatic 一个足球迷
近 bigot, devotee, enthusiast, fiend, freak, maniac, partisan, zealot
反 nonfan 非爱好者
【考法 2】 *adj.* 狂热的；盲信的：marked by excessive enthusiasm and often **intense uncritical devotion**
例 They are fanatic about sadomasochism. 他们对 SM 十分狂热。
近 extreme, rabid, radical, revolutionary, ultra
反 conservative 保守的；rational 理性的
派 fanatical *adj.* 狂热的；盲信的

fantasy [ˈfæntəsi]
【考法 1】 *n.* 幻想：**imaginative fiction** featuring especially strange settings and grotesque characters
例 indulge in a fantasy 沉迷于幻想
近 chimera, conceit, daydream, delusion, dream, hallucination, illusion, vision
反 actuality, fact, reality, truth 事实，现实
【考法 2】 *vt.* 产生幻想：to **form a mental picture** of
例 He regularly fantasies romantic encounters that he knows will never happen. 他会定期意淫一些永远不可能发生的浪漫邂逅。
近 dream, envisage, envision, fantasize, imagine, picture
派 fantastic *adj.* 梦幻般的，极好的

farce [fɑːrs]
【考法 1】 *n.* (带有嘲讽元素的)滑稽戏：a light dramatic composition marked by **broadly satirical comedy** and improbable plot
近 burlesque, caricature, parody, sham, travesty
反 serious play 正剧
【考法 2】 *n.* 闹剧：**ridiculous** or empty show
例 The enforcement of this law became a farce. 这条法律的执行过程成了一场闹剧。
近 joke, mockery, nonsense
派 farcical *adj.* 荒谬的

fascinate [ˈfæsɪneɪt]

【考法】 *vt.* 强烈吸引，使入迷：to **hold an intense interest** or attraction for

例 toys that fascinate infants 吸引婴儿们的玩具

近 allure, arrest, attract, bewitch, captivate, charm, enchant, enthrall, grip

反 disgust, repel 使厌恶，使反感

派 fascinating *adj.* 引人入胜的

fast [fæst]

【考法1】 *n.* 绝食；斋戒：an act of **abstaining from food**

例 fast to death 绝食而死

近 hunger strike

【考法2】 *adj.* 快速的：characterized by **quick** motion, operation, or effect

例 The fast pace of construction resulted in our new house being done ahead of schedule. 极快的施工使得我们的新房提前竣工。

近 brisk, expeditious, fleeting, hasty, quick, rapid, speedy, swift

反 slow 慢的

【考法3】 *adj.* 忠诚的：**firm in one's allegiance** to someone or something

例 The two girls soon became fast and inseparable friends. 这两个女孩子很快成为了忠于彼此的形影不离的好伙伴。

近 constant, dedicated, devoted, devout, loyal, pious

反 disloyal, perfidious 不忠诚的；treacherous 背叛的

【考法4】 *adj.* 稳固的，难以拆卸的：**firmly positioned** in place and difficult to dislodge

例 The rusty, old screws are so fast in the fitting that there's no hope of getting them out. 这颗生锈的老铁钉已经钉得太死了，根本不可能将其取出。

近 firm, frozen, lodged, secure, stable, staunch, strong, stuck

反 loose, shaky 松动的；insecure 不稳定的

派 fasten *v.* 系紧

fastidious [fæˈstɪdiəs]

【考法】 *adj.* 挑剔的，极仔细的，追求完美的：possessing or displaying careful, **meticulous attention to detail**

例 be fastidious about personal hygiene and appearance 极其注意个人卫生和外表

近 demanding, exacting, fussy, hypercritical, squeamish

反 undemanding 不挑剔的；cursory 粗略的，敷衍的；indiscriminate, uncritical 不加区分的

fateful [ˈfeɪtfl]

【考法1】 *adj.* 意义重大的：involving **momentous** consequences

例 make a fateful decision to declare war 做出了宣战的重大决定

近 critical, crucial, important, momentous, significant

反 inconsequential, insignificant, petty, paltry, trivial, unimportant 不重要的

【考法2】 *adj.* 带来灾难的，毁灭性的：**bringing death** or disaster

例 a fateful journey 一趟致命的旅行

近 calamitous, cataclysmic, catastrophic, deadly, destructive, disastrous, fatal, ruinous

fathom [ˈfæðəm]

【考法1】 *vt.* 测量（深度）：to **measure the depth** of (as a body of water) typically with a weighted line

例 The pilot had to continually fathom the river, which drought conditions had lowered to unprecedented levels. 舵手不得不时刻注意河水深度，因为干旱已经使水深下降到了前所未有的程度。

近 plumb

【考法2】 *vt.* 彻底理解，弄懂：to penetrate and **come to understand**

例 unable to fathom what he was talking about 无法弄懂他在说什么

近 apprehend, cognize, comprehend, grasp, know, understand

反 misunderstand 误解

派 fathomable *adj.* 可测量的；可知晓的

Unit 2

fatigue [fəˈtiːg]

【考法 1】 *n.* 疲惫: **weariness or exhaustion** from labor, exertion, or stress

例 The day-long battle against the blaze left firefighters in a state of utter fatigue. 与大火一整天的斗争使得消防员们处于极度疲惫的状态。

近 collapse, exhaustion, lassitude, tiredness, weariness

反 refreshment, rejuvenation, revitalization 恢复活力

【考法 2】 *n.* (让人厌倦的)苦差事: something, such as tiring effort or activity, that **causes weariness**

例 Although he had joined the army for action and adventure, much of his day seemed to be devoted to mindless fatigues. 尽管当初参军是为了上战场冒险的，但他生活的大部分时间似乎都耗费在了没意思的苦差上。

近 drudge, drudgery, grind, labor, sweat, toil, travail

反 fun, play 玩耍；sinecure 美差，闲职

fatuous [ˈfætʃuəs]

【考法】 *adj.* 愚笨的，昏庸的: complacently or inanely **foolish**

例 Emperor Yang in the Sui Dynasty is not only a rare fatuous tyrant but also an outstanding poet. 隋炀帝虽是少有的昏暴之君，但在文学上却是一位杰出的诗人。

近 asinine, brainless, foolish, obtuse, silly, simple, stupid, unwitty, witless

反 sagacious, sapient 聪明的，睿智的；judicious, prudent, sensible, wise 谨慎的，明智的

faultfinder [fɔːlt ˈfaɪndər]

【考法】 *n.* 吹毛求疵的人: one who is given to **petty criticism** and constant complaint

例 No sooner had we finished decorating the church than the parish faultfinder decided that she didn't like it. 我们一完成教堂的装修工作，教区里挑剔的人就说她不喜欢。

近 carper, castigator, caviler, censurer, critic, disparager, hypercritic, nitpicker

favorable [ˈfeɪvərəbl]

【考法 1】 *adj.* 赞许的: **expressing approval**

例 Favorable reviews for the movie were few. 关于这部电影的正面评价极少。

近 admiring, applauding, commendatory, complimentary, positive

反 adverse, disapproving, negative 否定的

【考法 2】 *adj.* 有利的: tending to **promote** or facilitate

例 mild climate favorable to his health 有利于他健康的温和气候

近 advantageous, benefic, beneficial, favoring, good, helpful, salutary

反 unfavorable, disadvantageous, untoward, unpropitious 不利的

fawn [fɔːn]

【考法】 *vi.* 阿谀奉承: to **seek favor** or attention **by flattery** and obsequious behavior

例 fawn on one's superior 向上司谄媚

近 cower, cringe, flatter, grovel, toady, truckle

反 domineer 统治；专横跋扈

派 fawning *adj.* 阿谀奉承的，讨好的

faze [feɪz]

【考法】 *vt.* 打扰，使尴尬: to **disturb the composure** of: disconcert, dismay

例 Nothing can faze her. 没有什么可以使她气馁。

近 abash, annoy, bother, disconcert, dismay, disturb, discomfit, embarrass, fluster, rattle

反 calm, lull 使平静，使镇定

feckless [ˈfekləs]

【考法 1】 *adj.* 无成果的，没有价值的: **having no** real **worth** or purpose

例 years of feckless negotiations 长达数年的毫无成果的谈判

近 bootless, fruitless, futile, meaningless, purposeless, useless, worthless

反 effective, effectual, efficacious 有成效的

【考法 2】 *adj.* 粗心不负责任的: **careless** and irresponsible

例 The young man was feckless and irresponsible. 这个年轻人既粗心又没有责任感。

近 careless, heedless, inadvertent, irresponsible, slipshod, sloppy

反 careful, cautious, circumspect, discreet, wary 谨慎小心的

fecund [ˈfiːkənd]

【考法】 *adj.* 多产的，肥沃的：**fruitful** in offspring or vegetation

例 fecund black soil 肥沃的黑土地

近 cornucopian, fertile, fruitful, lush, luxuriant, productive, prolific, rich

反 barren, infertile, sterile 贫瘠的

派 fecundity *n.* 多产，丰饶

feeble [ˈfiːbl]

【考法】 *adj.* 衰弱的：markedly **lacking in strength**

例 The heartbeat was feeble and irregular. 心跳虚弱且不规则。

近 debilitated, effete, enervated, faint, fragile, frail, infirm, languid, sapped

反 mighty, powerful, robust, stalwart, stout, strong 强壮的，强健的

派 enfeeble *vt.* 使衰弱

feign [feɪn]

【考法】 *vt.* 制造假象，装出…的样子：to **give a false appearance** of

例 I would never feign illness just to postpone a test. 我绝不会为了缓考而装病。

近 affect, assume, counterfeit, dissemble, pretend, profess, sham, simulate

派 unfeigned *adj.* 没有伪装的，真诚的

Unit 3

| ■ FENDER | ■ FERAL | ■ FERTILIZE | ■ FERVID | ■ FERVOR |
| ■ FESTER | ■ FETID | ■ FETTER | ■ FIASCO | ■ FICKLE |

fender [ˈfendər]

【考法】 *n.* 缓冲装置：a **cushioning device**, such as a bundle of rope or a piece of timber, used on the side of a vessel or dock to absorb impact or friction

例 a fender on the SUV 运动越野车的一个防护板

近 buffer, bumper, cocoon, cushioning, pad

feral [ˈferəl]

【考法 1】 *adj.* 野生的：**not domesticated** or cultivated

例 Animal experts discourage homeowners from trying to adopt feral animals as pets. 动物专家们不建议户主们将野生动物收养为宠物。

近 undomesticated, untamed, wild

反 cultivated 人工培养的；domestic, tame 家养的，被驯化的

【考法 2】 *adj.* 动物性的：having or showing the **nature** and appetites **of a lower animal**

例 The movie reveals just how thin the veneer of civilization is and how feral we are at bottom. 这部电影展示了所谓文明只不过是薄薄的一层纱，而内心深处我们仍然是野兽。

近 animalistic, beastly, brutal

反 rational 理性的

fertilize [ˈfɜːrtəlaɪz]

【考法】 *vt.* 使肥沃，使多产：to **make fertile**

例 Reading will fertilize vocabulary. 阅读丰富词汇。

近 enrich, manure

反 deplete, drain, exhaust 消耗，耗尽

派 fertilizer *n.* 化肥

fervid [ˈfɜːrvɪd]

【考法 1】 *adj.* 酷热的：having a notably **high temperature**

例 Set out when the fervid heat subsides. 当酷热消散之后出发。

近 boiling, hot, scorching, searing, sultry, sweltering, torrid

反 arctic, chilling, cold, freezing, frigid, frozen, glacial, icy 冰冷的，寒冷的

【考法 2】 *adj.* 热情的：marked by **great passion** or zeal

例 a fervid patriot 热情洋溢的爱国者

近 ardent, fervent, impassioned, passionate, perfervid

反 cold, cool, dispassionate, emotionless, impassive, unemotional 淡定的，不为所动的

fervor	[ˈfɜːrvər]

【考法】 *n.* 热情，狂热：**great warmth** and intensity of emotion
例 A blind patriotic fervor is called chauvinism. 盲目的爱国热情就被称为沙文主义。
近 ardor, enthusiasm, passion, zeal, zealotry
反 apathy, indifference, impassiveness, unconcern 冷漠

fester	[ˈfestər]

【考法】 *v.* 感染，溃烂，腐烂：to infect, inflame, or **corrupt**
例 A dirty wound will probably fester. 伤口弄脏了有可能会感染化脓。
近 corrupt, decompose, putrefy, rot, spoil
反 heal, cure 愈合
派 festering *adj.* 更加恶化的
例 festering dispute over sth 关于某事的争论更加恶化

fetid	[ˈfetɪd]

【考法】 *adj.* 恶臭的：having a heavy **offensive smell**
例 Ammonia has a fetid odor that sickened the people. 氨气有着令人作呕的气味。
近 foul, fusty, malodorous, noisome, reeking, smelly, stinky
反 ambrosial, aromatic, balmy, fragrant, redolent, scented 芳香的

fetter	[ˈfetər]

【考法 1】 *n.* 枷锁，限制：something that **limits one's freedom** of action or choice
例 a fetter that prevents us from trying something new 阻碍我们尝试新事物的枷锁
近 circumscription, constraint, curb, limitation, restraint, stricture
【考法 2】 *vt.* 束缚：to **restrain from motion**, action, or progress
例 be fettered by family responsibilities 被家庭责任所束缚
近 chain, clog, enfetter, hamper, manacle, restrain, shackle, trammel
反 enfranchise, free, liberate, unbind, unfetter, unshackle 解放；facilitate 促进
派 enfetter *vt.* 束缚

fiasco	[fiˈæskoʊ]

【考法】 *n.* 大失败：a **complete failure**
例 The Hitler's plot ended in a fiasco. 希特勒的阴谋最终以彻底失败告终。
近 catastrophe, debacle, disaster, failure
反 blockbuster, éclat, success 成功

fickle	[ˈfɪkl]

【考法 1】 *adj.* 易变的：**likely to change** frequently, suddenly, or unexpectedly
例 a fickle lover 感情善变的情人
近 capricious, fluid, mercurial, mutable, temperamental, volatile
反 constant, immutable, invariable, stable, steady 稳定的，不变的
【考法 2】 *adj.* 不忠诚的：**not true in one's allegiance** to someone or something
例 When the family's fortune disappeared, so did their fickle friends. 当这个家庭的财富消逝殆尽时，他们的那些虚伪的朋友也无影无踪了。
近 disloyal, perfidious, recreant, traitorous, treacherous, unfaithful
反 faithful, loyal 忠诚的

Unit 4

■ FICTITIOUS	■ FIDELITY	■ FIGURATIVE	■ FIGURINE	■ FILIBUSTER
■ FILTER	■ FINALE	■ FINESSE	■ FINICKY	■ FLACCID

fictitious	[fɪkˈtɪʃəs]

【考法】 *adj.* 虚构的：**not real** and existing only in the imagination
例 His wartime exploits turned out to be entirely fictitious, as he had never even been in the military. 他(吹嘘的)战时英勇行为是彻底虚构的，因为他根本就没有参过军。
近 chimerical, fabricated, fabulous, fictional, imagined, invented
反 actual, existing, real 事实的

fidelity	[fɪˈdeləti]

【考法】 *n.* 忠诚：the quality or state of **being faithful**
例 They have never wavered in their fidelity to the cause of liberation. 他们从不动摇对于解放事业的忠诚。
近 adherence, allegiance, commitment, devotion, faith, loyalty, piety
反 disloyalty, infidelity, perfidy 不忠；treachery 背叛
派 infidel *n.* 异教徒

figurative [ˈfɪɡərətɪv]

【考法】 *adj.* 比喻的：expressing one thing in terms normally **denoting another** with which it may be regarded as analogous

例 The word here is used in its figurative sense. 这个词在这里取它的比喻义。

近 extended, metaphorical

反 literal 字面上的，逐字逐句的

figurine [ˌfɪɡjəˈriːn]

【考法】 *n.* 小雕塑：a **small statue**

例 His collection of figurines includes toy soldiers from every war that America has fought. 他收藏的小雕塑包括了美国参与过的所有战争中的士兵模型。

近 figure, statuette

反 colossus 巨像

filibuster [ˈfɪlɪbʌstər]

【考法】 *n./v.* 拖延议事：the use of obstructionist tactics, especially prolonged speechmaking, **for the purpose of delaying legislative action**

例 The Senator used a filibuster to stop the bill. 参议员拖延了草案的实施。

近 delay, hindrance, impediment, obstruction, postponement, procrastination

filter [ˈfɪltər]

【考法1】 *v.* 过滤：to **pass through a filter**

例 Steep the tea and then filter it to get rid of the leaves. 浸泡茶叶，再将其过滤以去除废渣。

近 screen

【考法2】 *v.* 去除杂质：to **remove** (usually visible) **impurities** from

例 After frying the chicken, we filtered the oil and kept it in the refrigerator to use again. 在炸完鸡肉之后，我们将滤去了杂质的油保存起来以供日后使用。

近 clear, distill, purify

反 adulterate 掺杂；contaminate 污染

finale [fɪˈnæli]

【考法】 *n.* 终场，结局：the **closing part**, scene, or number in a public performance

例 Didier Drogba pulled one back for Chelsea in a finale. 德罗巴在终场结束时为切尔西扳回一球。

近 close, coda, conclusion, end

反 prologue 开场白；overture 序曲

finesse [fɪˈnes]

【考法1】 *n.* 娴熟技巧：mental **skill** or quickness

例 The musician shows wonderful finesse. 那位音乐家展现出了非凡的技艺。

近 adeptness, adroitness, cleverness, dexterity, proficiency

反 awkwardness, ineptitude, gaucherie, ungainliness 笨拙

【考法2】 *v.* 精心策划：to **plan out** usually **with subtle skill** or care

例 finesse the schedule 精心安排日程

近 contrive, frame, machinate, maneuver, manipulate

【考法3】 *v.* (巧妙地) 躲避：to get or **keep away from** (as a responsibility) through cleverness or trickery

例 He tried to finesse the blame for the foreign policy fiasco, even though he was Secretary of State at the time. 他竭尽所能躲避因失败的对外政策而可能遭到的指责，尽管他时任国务卿。

近 avoid, dodge, eschew, evade, shun

反 confront 直面

finicky [ˈfɪnɪki]

【考法】 *adj.* 过分讲究的，挑剔的：**extremely** or excessively particular, exacting, or **meticulous** in taste or standards

例 have a reputation for being finicky eater 有着挑食的名声

近 demanding, exacting, fastidious, fussy, nice, particular

反 undemanding, unfussy 不挑剔的

flaccid [ˈflæsɪd]

【考法】 *adj.* 不结实的，松弛的：not firm or stiff; **lacking** normal or youthful **firmness**

例 flaccid muscles 松弛的肌肉

近 droopy, floppy, lank, loose, slack, yielding

反 stiff, sturdy 结实的，坚硬的；resilient 有弹性的

Unit 5

flag [flæg]

【考法 1】 *n.* 旗帜，象征：a piece of fabric that is used as a **symbol** (as of a nation) or as a signaling device
例 We respect the flag of our fathers. 我们尊敬父辈们的旗帜。
近 banner, ensign, pendant, pennant

【考法 2】 *vi.* 变得衰弱：to **become** unsteady, **feeble**, or spiritless
例 We flagged as we neared the end of the long mountain trail. 当我们终于快到达漫长山路的终点时，已经筋疲力尽了。
近 decay, decline, deteriorate, emaciate, fade, fail, languish, sag, waste, wilt, wither
反 thrive 繁荣；revitalize, revive 恢复活力
派 unflagging *adj.* 坚持不懈的

flamboyant [flæm'bɔɪənt]

【考法】 *adj.* 艳丽夺目的，炫耀的，充满装饰的：marked by or given to **strikingly elaborate** or colorful display or behavior; ornate
例 Las Vegas showgirls wearing flamboyant headdresses 打扮花哨的拉斯维加斯舞女
近 flaring, florid, garish, ornate, ostentatious, showy
反 natural 自然的；conservative, quiet, understated 低调的
派 flamboyance *n.* 炫目，炫耀

flatter ['flætər]

【考法 1】 *vt.* 拍马屁，奉承，讨好：to **praise excessively** especially from motives of self-interest
例 Friends who flatter you to your face are not true friends. 当面拍你马屁的朋友都不是真正的朋友。
近 adulate, blandish, compliment, court, massage, overpraise, stroke, wheedle
反 abuse 辱骂；censure, criticize 批评

【考法 2】 *vt.* 自我感觉良好：to **think highly of** (oneself)
例 Don't flatter yourself that no one has ever thought of that idea before. 不要自欺欺人地认为别人没有想到过那个想法。
近 pique, plume

【考法 3】 *vt.* 使显得更漂亮：to **show** off becomingly or **advantageously**
例 Orange flatters those with golden skin tones. 橙色让黄肤色的人显得更漂亮。
近 become, enhance, suit
反 mar, spoil 破坏
派 flattering *adj.* 令人满足的，令人迷恋的

flaw [flɔː]

【考法 1】 *n.* 瑕疵，缺点：an **imperfection**, often concealed, that impairs soundness
例 The absence of flaw in beauty is itself a flaw. 完美无瑕本身就是瑕疵。
近 blight, blotch, defect, fault, imperfection, mar, scar, spot

【考法 2】 *v.* 降低，破坏，使不完美：to **reduce** the soundness, effectiveness, or **perfection** of
例 That crack has flawed the vase to the extent that its value in the antiques market is greatly reduced. 那道裂缝让这个花瓶在古董市场上大大地掉价。
近 blemish, break, compromise, cripple, harm, hurt, impair, injure, spoil, vitiate
反 fix, mend, repair, revamp 修复，改造
派 flawed *adj.* 有瑕疵的；flawless *adj.* 完美无瑕的；flawlessness *n.* 完美

fledgling ['fledʒlɪŋ]

【考法】 *n.* 新手：a person who is just **starting out in a field** of activity
例 At hockey he's still a fledgling and needs to work on his basic skating skills. 在冰球场上他还是一个菜鸟，还需要在基本的滑冰技术上加强练习。
近 apprentice, beginner, freshman, neophyte, novice, tyro, recruit, rookie
反 veteran 老兵，身经百战的人
派 fledge *v.* (鸟类)长羽毛

fleet [fliːt]

【考法 1】 *n.* 舰队，车队：a **group of vehicles** traveling together or under one management
例 fleet of the Royal Navy 皇家海军的舰队
近 armada, caravan, cavalcade, motorcade

【考法2】 *adj.* 迅速的：moving, proceeding, or acting **with great speed**
- 例 He was fleet as a deer. 他如小鹿般敏捷。
- 近 brisk, expeditious, fast, hasty, nimble, quick, rapid, rattling, speedy, swift
- 反 slow 缓慢的

【考法3】 *vi.* 快速通过：to move or **pass swiftly**
- 近 dart, flit, hurry, hustle
- 反 plod 沉重而缓慢地走
- 派 fleeting *adj.* 稍纵即逝的

flexible [ˈfleksəbl]

【考法1】 *adj.* 灵活的，可变的：capable of being **readily changed**
- 例 Our schedules are highly flexible. 我们的计划是非常灵活的。
- 近 adaptable, adjustable, alterable, changeable, elastic, fluid, malleable, modifiable, pliable, variable
- 反 fixed, immutable, inflexible, invariable 确定的，不可变的；stiff, rigid 僵化的
- 派 flexibility *n.* 灵活性

【考法2】 *adj.* 易受影响的：**susceptible to influence** or persuasion
- 例 Their boss was flexible and lenient. 他们的老板既好说话，又很仁慈。
- 近 docile, manageable, tractable
- 反 adamant, headstrong, intractable, mulish, recalcitrant, refractory, stubborn, obstinate 倔强的

flinch [flɪntʃ]

【考法】 *vi.* 畏缩；退缩：to **draw back** in fear, pain, or disgust
- 例 He met my gaze without flinching. 他毫不畏缩地与我对视。
- 近 cringe, quail, recoil, shrink, wince
- 反 face, meet 面对；confront 直面

flippancy [ˈflɪpənsi]

【考法】 *n.* 轻率，无礼：**unbecoming levity** or pertness especially in respect to grave or sacred matters
- 例 The flippancy of your answer annoyed me. 你轻率的回答让我很恼火。
- 近 facetiousness, flightiness, frivolousness, frothiness, levity, silliness
- 反 earnestness, gravity, seriousness, soberness, solemnity, solemnness 严肃，认真

flirt [flɜːrt]

【考法1】 *vi.* 调情：to **behave amorously** without serious intent
- 例 The waitress at that restaurant flirts with all single male customers. 这家餐厅的女服务员对所有的男性单身顾客都暗送秋波。
- 近 coquet, dally, frivol, toy, trifle

【考法2】 *vi.* 无规则地快速运动：to **make** an **irregular** series of quick, sudden **movements**
- 例 The beautiful lady lazily watched the butterflies flirting among the wildflowers. 这名美丽的女子慵懒地看着蝴蝶在野花丛中乱舞。
- 近 dance, dart, fleet, flick, flit, flutter, hurry, rush, zip

Unit 6

■ FLIT	■ FLOCK	■ FLORID	■ FLOUNDER	■ FLOURISH
■ FLOUT	■ FLUCTUATE	■ FLUENT	■ FLUKY	■ FLUSH

flit [flɪt]

【考法】 *vi.* 快速或突然地经过：to **pass quickly** or abruptly from one place or condition to another
- 例 Memories of the evening flitted through her mind. 关于那一晚的记忆在她脑海中一掠而过。
- 近 dance, dart, fleet, flick, flirt, flutter, hurry, rush, zip
- 反 plod 沉重缓慢地走

flock [flɑːk]

【考法1】 *n.* 人群，兽群：a great number of persons or **creatures massed together**
- 例 a flock of ill-disposed reporters at the press conference 新闻发布会上一群不怀好意的记者
- 近 army, drove, herd, legion

【考法2】 *vi.* 聚集，集体行动：to congregate or **travel in a flock** or crowd
- 例 Vacationers flocked to the towns along the shore in order to escape the August heat. 度假的人们一起涌向海岸，以躲避八月里的热浪。
- 近 mob, swarm, throng

florid [ˈflɔːrɪd]
【考法 1】 *adj.* 辞藻华丽的，花哨的：**full of** fine words and **fancy expressions**
例 gave a florid speech to attract attention 做了个辞藻华丽的演说以吸引眼球
近 bombastic, flowery, grandiloquent, magniloquent, rhetorical
【考法 2】 *adj.* 装饰华丽的：**elaborately** and often excessively **decorated**
例 a florid architectural style 华丽的建筑风格
近 baroque, bedizened, flamboyant, fussy, luscious, ornate
反 austere, plain, severe, stark, unadorned 朴素的，简单的

flounder [ˈflaʊndər]
【考法】 *vi.* 笨拙地行动，挣扎：to proceed or **act clumsily** or ineffectually
例 flounder through the desert 步履蹒跚地穿越沙漠
近 blunder, fumble, lumber, plod, struggle, trudge
反 glide, slide 滑行；breeze, waltz 轻松地行动

flourish [ˈflɜːrɪʃ]
【考法 1】 *vi.* 茂盛；繁荣：to grow luxuriantly; to **achieve success**
例 The program will flourish once it receives adequate funding. 这个项目只要有足够的资金就能大获成功。
近 bloom, burgeon, prosper, thrive
反 languish, wane 变得衰弱，衰败；fail 失败
【考法 2】 *n.* 装饰：an embellishment or **ornamentation**
例 a bedroom with cute little flourishes 一间带有可爱小装饰的卧室 || Her writing style is simple and clear, without unnecessary flourishes. 她的文风很简单清新，没有那些不必要的修饰。
近 adornment, decoration, embellishment, ornamentation

flout [flaʊt]
【考法】 *n./v.* 嘲弄性不理会，蔑视：to **treat with** contemptuous **disregard**
例 flout the academic norm by plagiarizing 通过抄袭来蔑视学术规范
近 despise, disregard, gibe, sneer, taunt
反 respect, revere, venerate 尊敬

fluctuate [ˈflʌktʃueɪt]
【考法】 *vi.* 波动，无规则地变动：to **shift back and forth** uncertainly
例 Stock prices fluctuate wildly. 股票价格大幅波动。 || Samples of ice cores collected from Antarctica suggested that the atmospheric concentration of carbon dioxide has been fluctuating periodically. 南极冰芯样本表明，大气中的二氧化碳浓度存在周期性的涨落。
近 mutate, shift, swing, oscillate, vacillate, vary, waver
反 stabilize 保持稳定；plateau 到达稳定状态
派 fluctuation *n.* 涨落，波动

fluent [ˈfluːənt]
【考法 1】 *adj.* 表达流利的：**able to express** oneself clearly and **well**
例 a very fluent speaker who always communicates his points well 一个总能明确指出要点的流利演说家
近 eloquent, silver-tongued, well-spoken
反 inarticulate, ineloquent, unvocal 说话不清楚的
派 fluency *n.* 流畅，流利
【考法 2】 *adj.* 不费力的：involving **minimal difficulty** or effort
例 a fluent performance of one of the oldest magic tricks in the book 一场毫不费力的魔术，表演的是书本上最老的魔术之一
近 effortless, facile, fluid, painless, ready, simple, smooth
反 arduous, demanding, exacting, formidable, grueling, hard, laborious, murderous, rough, toilsome, tough 费劲的，艰苦的

fluky [ˈfluːki]
【考法 1】 *adj.* 侥幸的：coming or **happening by good luck** especially unexpectedly
例 a fluky coincidence that kept me safely at home when the blizzard hit 一个侥幸的巧合让我在暴风雪来袭时安全地待在家里
近 fortuitous, lucky, providential
反 hapless, unfortunate, unlucky, ill-fated 不幸的
【考法 2】 *adj.* 偶然的：happening **by** or depending on **chance**
近 casual, chance, inadvertent, incidental, unintended, unintentional
反 calculated, deliberate, intended, intentional, planned, premeditated 蓄意的，有预谋的
派 fluke *n.* 侥幸；偶然

flush [flʌʃ]

【考法 1】 *adj.* (肤色）健康红润的：having a **healthy reddish** skin tone

近 blooming, florid, glowing, red, rosy, rubicund, sanguine

反 ashen, doughy, livid, pale, pallid, wan 苍白的，病态的

【考法 2】 *adj.* 富有的：having goods, property, or **money in abundance**

例 She's very flush now that she has her inheritance. 自从继承了那份遗产，她变得十分富有。

近 affluent, loaded, opulent, wealthy

反 destitute, impoverished, indigent, needy, impecunious 贫穷的

【考法 3】 *adj.* 大量的：marked by **abundance**

例 a field flush with flowers 长满了鲜花的原野

近 abounding, abundant, awash, fraught, lousy, replete, swarming, teeming, thronging

反 inadequate, insufficient, scant, scarce, short 匮乏的，不足的

【考法 4】 *vi.* 冲洗：to **pour liquid** over or through in order to cleanse

例 flush a wound with iodine 用碘酒冲洗伤口

近 irrigate, rinse, sluice, wash

Unit 7

■ FLUSTER	■ FOIBLE	■ FOIL	■ FOMENT	■ FOOLPROOF
■ FOOTLOOSE	■ FORBEARANCE	■ FOREBEAR	■ FORESTALL	■ FOREWORD

fluster [ˈflʌstər]

【考法】 *vt.* 使慌乱：to **put into** a state of **agitated confusion**

例 A GPA of 1.0 flusters him. 1.0 的绩点让他很慌乱。

近 abash, confound, confuse, discomfit, disconcert, discountenance, faze, mortify, nonplus, rattle

反 calm, quiet, settle, soothe, tranquilize 安抚，使情绪稳定

foible [ˈfɔɪbl]

【考法】 *n.* 小缺点：a **minor flaw** or shortcoming in character or behavior

例 They admired their teacher despite his foibles. 尽管他们的老师有些小缺点，但他们还是很敬佩他。

近 demerit, dereliction, failing, fault, frailty, shortcoming, sin, vice, want, weakness

反 merit, virtue 优点，美德

foil [fɔɪl]

【考法】 *vt.* 挫败：to **prevent from being successful**; defeat

例 foil her enemy by pulling some strings 通过一些关系和手段挫败了她的对手

近 baffle, balk, beat, checkmate, discomfit, frustrate, thwart

反 forward, foster, further, promote 帮助，促进

foment [foʊˈment]

【考法】 *vt.* 助长，煽动：to **promote the growth** or development of

例 He was accused of fomenting violence. 他被指控煽动暴力行为。

近 abet, brew, ferment, incite, instigate, provoke, raise, stir

反 quash, quell, quench, squash 平息，镇压

foolproof [ˈfuːlpruːf]

【考法】 *adj.* 十分简单以至于不会失败的：so simple, plain, or reliable as to **leave no opportunity for error, misuse, or failure**

例 Anything foolproof is impossible and what truly counts is probability. 没有万无一失的事情，真正的问题在于概率。

近 guaranteed, infallible, safe, unfailing, fail-safe

反 fallible 容易出错的

footloose [ˈfʊtluːs]

【考法】 *adj.* 无拘无束的，自由的：**having no attachments** or ties; free to do as one pleases

例 After having been chained for so long, the suddenly footloose dog ran about the yard tirelessly. 这只长期被锁链束缚的小狗因为突然之间获得了自由，在院子里不知疲倦地奔跑。

近 loose, unbound, unconfined, unfettered, unrestrained, untrammeled

反 bound, confined, restrained, tied 有束缚的

forbearance [fɔːr'berəns]
【考法1】 *n.* 克制；忍耐：**tolerance and restraint** in the face of provocation; patience
例 reach the end of my forbearance 到了让我忍无可忍的地步
近 patience, temperance, tolerance, toleration
反 impatience 不耐烦
【考法2】 *n.* 友好仁慈的态度：**kind, gentle, or compassionate treatment** especially towards someone who is undeserving of it
例 The judge showed forbearance, and gave the teenaged first offender a suspended sentence. 法官网开一面，给了初犯的少年犯一个缓刑。
近 charity, clemency, leniency, mercifulness, quarter
反 vindictiveness 恶意

forebear ['fɔːrber]
【考法】 *n.* 祖先：a person from whom one is descended; **an ancestor**
例 The son of Abraham was traditionally considered to be the forebear of the Arabs. 亚伯拉罕之子传统上被认为是阿拉伯人的祖先。
近 ancestor, antecedent, ascendant, father, grandfather, primogenitor, progenitor
反 descendant, offspring 后代

forestall [fɔːr'stɔːl]
【考法】 *vt.* 预先阻止：to delay, hinder, or **prevent** by taking precautionary measures **beforehand**
例 You can often forestall skidding on the ice simply by driving more slowly. 通常你只需慢点开车就可以防止车辆在冰面上失控打滑。
近 avert, deter, obviate, preclude, prevent
反 abet, assist, facilitate, further, precipitate, promote 帮助，促进

foreword ['fɔːrwɜːrd]
【考法】 *n.* 前言：a **preface** or an introductory note, as for a book, especially by a person other than the author
例 The foreword of this book is co-written by Jason and Franklin. 这本书的序由 Jason 和 Franklin 共同写成。
近 beginning, introduction, overture, preamble, preface, prelude, prologue
反 epilogue, coda 尾声；finale 终场

Unit 8

| ■ FORGE | ■ FORMIDABLE | ■ FORTHRIGHT | ■ FORTIFY | ■ FOSTER |
| ■ FOUNDER | ■ FRACAS | ■ FRACTURE | ■ FRAGILE | ■ FRAIL |

forge [fɔːrdʒ]
【考法1】 *v.* 伪造：to make or **imitate falsely** especially with intent to defraud
例 The boy forged his father's signature on his transcript. 小男孩在他的成绩单上伪造了父亲的签名。
近 coin, counterfeit, fabricate, fake
【考法2】 *v.* 锻造，铸就：to **form** (as metal) by or as if by heating and hammering
例 a real man forged by adversity 一个经磨难考验而成的纯爷们 || They agreed to forge closer economic and political ties. 他们就打造双边的紧密政治经济联系达成了共识。
近 build, construct, form, make, manufacture, mold, shape
派 forger *n.* 打铁匠

formidable ['fɔːrmɪdəbl]
【考法1】 *adj.* 令人害怕的：**causing fear**, dread, or apprehension
例 a nation that possesses formidable nuclear deterrence 一个拥有可怕核威慑力量的国家
近 direful, dreadful, fearsome, forbidding, ghastly, horrible, intimidating, redoubtable, terrifying
反 comforting 给人安慰的
【考法2】 *adj.* 艰难的：**requiring** considerable physical or mental **effort**
例 Running a marathon is a formidable undertaking. 跑马拉松是个困难的任务。 || They have recently made a formidable decision. 他们最近做出了一个艰难的决定。
近 arduous, challenging, demanding, exacting, grueling, heavy, laborious, sweaty, toilsome, tough, strenuous
反 easy, effortless, facile, mindless, simple 轻松的，简单的

forthright ['fɔːrθraɪt]
【考法1】 *adj.* 直率的，说话率真的：**free in expressing** one's true feelings and **opinions**
例 her forthright way of dealing with people 她率真的为人处事方式
近 candid, forthcoming, frank, honest, open, outspoken, straightforward
反 dissembling 虚伪的

【考法 2】 *adj.* 直接的，不绕弯子的：free from ambiguity or evasiveness: **going straight to the point**
例 He was forthright in appraising the problem. 他直截了当地评价这个问题。
近 direct, plain, straight
反 circuitous, indirect, roundabout 不直接的，绕弯子的

fortify [ˈfɔːrtɪfaɪ]
【考法 1】 *vt.* 加固，鼓励：to **give physical strength**, courage, or endurance to
例 This country will fortify the coastal areas. 这个国家将加强沿海地区的防御。
近 energize, harden, invigorate, reinforce, strengthen, toughen
反 debilitate, enervate, enfeeble, vitiate, weaken 使衰弱，削弱
【考法 2】 *vt.* 做好心理准备：to **prepare** (oneself) **mentally** or emotionally
例 She fortified herself for the incoming tennis tournament with a series of confidence-boosting exercises. 她通过一系列练习赛来建立自信，为即将到来的网球锦标赛做好心理准备。
近 brace, forearm, gird, nerve, poise, ready, steel

foster [ˈfɔːstər]
【考法 1】 *vt.* 促进，鼓励，培养：to **help the growth** or development of
例 detect and foster artistic talent 发现并培养艺术天分
近 advance, encourage, forward, further, incubate, promote
反 discourage, frustrate, inhibit 阻碍，妨碍
【考法 2】 *vt.* 养育：to **bring to maturity** through care and education
例 a greathearted couple fostering two adopted children as well as their own 对两个抱养的孩子像自己亲生的孩子一样培养的好心夫妇
近 breed, cultivate, nourish, nurse, nurture, raise, rear

founder [ˈfaʊndər]
【考法 1】 *n.* 建立者：**one** that founds or **establishes**
例 founders of the nation 国父们
近 architect, author, creator, father, generator, initiator, originator, sire
反 terminator 终结者
【考法 2】 *vi.* 完败：to **fail utterly**
例 The theater company foundered after its corporate funding dried up. 在其基金告罄之后，这个戏剧公司彻底失败了。
近 collapse, flunk, miss, strike out, wash out
反 succeed, work out 成功
【考法 3】 *vi.* 沉没：to **become submerged**
例 The ship struck a reef and foundered. 船因触礁而沉没。
近 sink, submerge, submerse, go down
反 float 漂浮

fracas [ˈfreɪkəs]
【考法】 *n.* 争吵，吵闹：a **physical dispute** between opposing individuals or groups; a rough and often **noisy fight** usually involving several people
例 The police were called in to break up the fracas. 警察奉命去制止骚乱。
近 battle, clash, combat, conflict, contest, hassle, skirmish, struggle, tussle

fracture [ˈfræktʃər]
【考法 1】 *n.* 破裂：the act or process of **breaking**
例 a sudden fracture of the established order 已建立起的秩序被突然打破
近 breach, break, rupture, schism, split
反 unity 统一
【考法 2】 *vt.* 打碎，破坏：to cause to **separate into pieces** usually suddenly or forcibly
例 Their happiness was fractured by an unforeseen tragedy. 他们的幸福生活被突如其来的悲剧打破了。
近 disrupt, fragment, rive
反 cement 接合

fragile [ˈfrædʒl]
【考法 1】 *adj.* 易碎的：easily **broken** or destroyed
例 a fragile piece of glass 一块易碎的玻璃
近 breakable, feeble, frail, friable, frangible, infirm, unsound, weak
反 tough, durable 抗打击的

【考法2】 *adj.* 易受伤的，脆弱的：**easily injured** without careful handling

例 Babies are extremely fragile, so remember to care for them gently. 小孩子特别容易受伤，所以要记得温柔地对待他们。

近 delicate, sensitive

派 fragility *n.* 脆弱

frail [freɪl]

【考法1】 *adj.* 虚弱的：physically **weak**

例 Working for three days without any sleep made him extremely frail. 连续三天的彻夜工作使他极为虚弱。

近 weak, effete, enervated, feeble, fragile, infirm, languid, unsubstantial

反 robust 充满活力的；hale, sturdy 健壮的

【考法2】 *adj.* (意志)薄弱的：easily led astray; morally **weak**

例 frail and pathetic humanity 容易误入歧途的可悲人性

近 characterless, invertebrate, nerveless, spineless

反 faithful, resolute 意志坚定的，有坚定信念的

派 frailty *n.* 虚弱；(意志)脆弱

【考法3】 *adj.* (希望)渺茫的：**slight**, unsubstantial

例 a frail hope of success 成功的机会渺茫

近 negligible, slight, small

反 good 很有希望的

Unit 9

| ■ FRAUDULENT | ■ FRAUGHT | ■ FRENZY | ■ FREQUENT | ■ FRETFUL |
| ■ FRIABLE | ■ FRICTION | ■ FRIGID | ■ FRINGE | ■ FRIVOLOUS |

fraudulent ['frɔːdʒələnt]

【考法】 *adj.* 欺诈的：characterized by, based on, or done by **fraud**

例 a fraudulent interpretation of experimental data 对实验数据的欺骗性解释

近 deceitful, deceptive, dishonest, duplicitous, guileful, underhanded

反 reliable, trustworthy 可信的；authentic 真实的；honest, straight 诚实的

派 fraudulence *n.* 欺骗

fraught [frɔːt]

【考法1】 *adj.* 充满的：**full** of or accompanied by something

例 an experience fraught with peril 充满危险的经历

近 abounding, abundant, awash, flush, replete, thronging

反 scarce 稀缺的

【考法2】 *adj.* 令人忧虑的：causing or characterized by **emotional distress** or tension

例 a fraught relationship between the two neighboring countries 两个邻国间令人担忧的关系

近 uneasy, agitating, anxious, distressful, disturbing, restless, tense, unsettling, nail-biting

反 calming, relaxing 使人镇静的，使人放松的

frenzy ['frenzi]

【考法】 *n.* 疯狂，狂怒：a violent **mental** or emotional **agitation**

例 She is subject to these frenzies several times a year. 她每年都要暴怒几次。

近 delirium, fever, furor, fury, hysteria, insanity, rage, rampage, uproar

反 sanity 理智

派 frenetic *adj.* 疯狂的

frequent ['friːkwənt]

【考法1】 *vt.* 时常拜访：to pay frequent visits to; be in or at **often**

例 frequent opera houses 时常造访歌剧院

近 haunt, resort, visit

反 avoid, shun 躲避

【考法2】 *adj.* 时常发生的，重复再现的：happening at **short intervals**; often repeated or occurring

例 He used to make frequent trips to Los Angeles. 他从前经常前往洛杉矶旅行。

近 common, constant, everyday, habitual, periodical, repeated

反 rare 稀有的，少见的

派 frequency *n.* 频率；频繁

fretful [ˈfretfl]

【考法】 *adj.* 易怒的，烦躁的：inclined to be **vexed** or troubled

例 Adolescence is the most fretful stages of human development. 青春期是人类发展过程中最焦躁的阶段。

近 irritable, fractious, peevish, pettish, petulant

反 easygoing 随和的

派 fret *v.* (使)烦躁

friable [ˈfraɪəbl]

【考法】 *adj.* 易碎的：**easily crumbled** or pulverized

例 friable mineral rock 易碎的矿石

近 crumbly, delicate, feeble, fragile, frail, infirm, weak

反 sturdy, substantial 坚固的

friction [ˈfrɪkʃn]

【考法1】 *n.* 摩擦：the **rubbing** of one object or surface against another

例 lubricant that significantly reduces friction 能显著减少摩擦的润滑剂

近 abrasion

【考法2】 *n.* 冲突，不和：the **clashing** between two persons or parties of opposed views

例 There is a friction between the professor and students. 教授和学生之间存在不和。

近 disagreement, conflict, contention, dissidence, schism, war

反 accord, harmony, peace, concord 和谐

派 frictional *adj.* 产生摩擦的

frigid [ˈfrɪdʒɪd]

【考法1】 *adj.* 严寒的：extremely **cold**

例 an unusually frigid winter of Wuhan 武汉一个反常的寒冬

近 cold, arctic, chilling, freezing, frosty, glacial

反 roasting, scalding, scorching, searing, seething, sizzling, sultry, sweltering, torrid 炎热的

【考法2】 *adj.* 冷漠的：**lacking warmth** or ardor

例 a formal but frigid welcome 一个正式但冷漠的招呼

近 indifferent, cold, emotionless, passionless, unresponsive

反 ardent, amorous, cordial 饱含感情的

派 frigidity *n.* 严寒；冷漠

fringe [frɪndʒ]

【考法1】 *n.* 边缘：something that resembles such a **border** or edging

例 "Don't act on the fringes of the law," warns the customs officer. 海关人员警告说："不要打法律的擦边球"。

近 border, boundary, circumference, edge, margin, perimeter, periphery, skirt

反 center, core 中心，核心

【考法2】 *vt.* 与…接壤，位于…的边缘：to **be adjacent** to

近 abut, border, neighbor, skirt, verge

frivolous [ˈfrɪvələs]

【考法1】 *adj.* 轻浮的：marked by **unbecoming levity**

例 a frivolous young woman 一个举止轻浮的年轻女子

近 giddy, shallow, superficial

反 earnest, sober, serious 严肃的

派 frivolity *n.* 轻浮，轻佻

【考法2】 *adj.* 不重要的：of **little** weight or **importance**

例 The frivolous comment was soon forgotten. 那个不值一提的评论很快就被遗忘了。

近 trivial, flimsy, light, petty, trifling

反 consequential, eventful, meaningful, momentous, weighty 重要的

Unit 10

■ FROTHY	■ FROWSY	■ FRUGAL	■ FRUSTRATE	■ FULL-BODIED
■ FULMINATE	■ FUMBLE	■ FUROR	■ FURTIVE	■ FURY

frothy [ˈfrɔːθi]

【考法1】 *adj.* 用轻薄材料制作的：made of **light** thin material

例 a frothy laptop made of carbon fiber and alloys 碳纤维以及合金制造的轻薄型笔记本电脑

近 delicate, gossamer, light

反 weighty 重的；sturdy 结实的

【考法 2】 *adj.* (内容等)欢乐轻佻、不严肃的：**gaily frivolous** or light in content or treatment
例 a frothy movie 一部有喜感的电影
近 flighty, frivolous, puerile
反 earnest, serious, sober 严肃的

frowsy [ˈfraʊzi]
【考法 1】 *adj.* 邋遢的：having a **slovenly** or uncared-for appearance
例 frowsy hair 邋遢的头发
近 slovenly, unkempt, untidy
反 dapper, neat, tidy, spruce 整洁的
【考法 2】 *adj.* 味道难闻的：having an **unpleasant smell**
例 The abandoned house was dank and frowsy and barely fit for human habitation. 这座废房子光线又暗，气味又难闻，几乎无法供人居住。
近 fetid, noisome, smelly, stinky
反 ambrosial, aromatic, fragrant, redolent 芳香的

frugal [ˈfruːɡl]
【考法】 *adj.* 节约的：characterized by or reflecting **economy** in the use of resources
例 be frugal in her expenditures 节约她的开销
近 sparing, economical, provident, stingy
反 extravagant, prodigal, sumptuous 奢侈浪费的
派 frugality *n.* 节俭

frustrate [ˈfrʌstreɪt]
【考法 1】 *vt.* 挫败，阻挠：to **prevent** from accomplishing a purpose or fulfilling a desire
例 He frustrated their scheme in time. 他及时挫败了他们的阴谋。
近 ruin, baffle, balk, circumvent, foil, thwart
反 abet 帮助，鼓舞，教唆；accomplish, fulfill 实现
【考法 2】 *vt.* 使沮丧：to **lessen the courage** or confidence of
例 frustrated by his failure 为他的失败感到沮丧
近 chill, daunt, dishearten, dismay, dispirit
反 embolden, encourage, nerve, steel 鼓舞
派 frustration *n.* 沮丧；阻挠；frustrated *adj.* 沮丧的

full-bodied [fʊl ˈbɑːdid]
【考法 1】 *adj.* 重要的：having **importance**, significance, or meaningfulness
例 a full-bodied study of genetic engineering 一项基因工程的重要研究
近 important, consequential, momentous, significant, weighty
反 trivial 不重要的
【考法 2】 *adj.* 味道浓烈的：having **richness** and intensity of **flavor** or aroma
例 full-bodied perfume in the cabin 车厢内浓郁的香水味
近 strong, concentrated
反 insipid 平淡无奇的

fulminate [ˈfʊlmɪneɪt]
【考法】 *v.* 大声斥责：to issue a **thunderous** verbal attack or **denunciation**
例 fulminate the so-called curricular reform 痛斥所谓的课程改革
近 criticize, blame, censure, condemn, denounce, denunciate, lambaste, reprehend, reprobate
反 applaud, compliment, praise 赞美
派 fulmination *n.* 训斥

fumble [ˈfʌmbl]
【考法 1】 *v.* 笨拙地做：to make **awkward attempts** to do or find something
例 fumbled in his pocket for a coin 从口袋里笨拙地摸出一枚硬币
近 botch, flounder, mess, stumble
【考法 2】 *n.* (无意识的)失误：an unintentional **departure from truth** or accuracy
例 She played the entire piano piece without a single fumble. 她完美地演绎了整首钢琴曲。
近 blunder, fault, gaffe, lapse, misstep, mistake

furor [ˈfjʊrɔːr]
【考法】 *n.* 喧闹，狂怒；激动，狂热：a general commotion; public disorder or uproar; a state of **intense excitement** or ecstasy
例 The decision to raise tax has caused a great furor among the working class. 提高税收的决定引起了工人阶级的强烈骚动。
近 delirium, frenzy, fever, fury, hysteria, outrage, rage, uproar, wrath
反 serenity, tranquility 平静，宁静；delight, pleasure 愉悦

furtive ['fɜːrtɪv]

【考法】 *adj.* 鬼鬼祟祟的；秘密的：done by **stealth**

例 a furtive glance at her 朝她投去的隐秘一瞥

近 secret, clandestine, covert, stealthy, surreptitious

反 aboveboard 光明正大的；candid, forthright 坦率的

派 furtively *adv.* 秘密地

fury ['fjʊri]

【考法】 *n.* 暴怒：intense, disordered, and often destructive **rage**

例 The gods unleashed their fury on the offending mortal. 诸神将怒火降在了那些对神明不敬的凡人身上。

近 anger, indignation, ire, mad, rage, wrath

反 forbearance 容忍；delight, pleasure 快乐，愉悦

派 furious *adj.* 狂暴的，暴怒的

If you would go up high, then use your own legs! Do not let yourselves carried aloft; do not seat yourselves on other people's backs and heads.

如果你想要走到高处，就要使用自己的两条腿！不要让别人把你抬到高处；不要坐在别人的背上和头上。

——德国哲学家 尼采（F. W. Nietzsche, German philosopher）

List 11

Unit 1

| ■ FUSSY | ■ FUSTY | ■ FUTILE | ■ GADFLY | ■ GAFFE |
| ■ GAINSAY | ■ GALL | ■ GALLANT | ■ GALVANIZE | ■ GAMBLE |

fussy ['fʌsi]

【考法 1】 *adj.* 谨慎的：taking, showing, or **involving great care** and effort
例 a fussy actuarial problem 需要谨慎处理的保险计算问题
近 careful, exact, meticulous, punctilious
反 careless 粗心大意的

【考法 2】 *adj.* 过分雕琢的：elaborately and often **excessively decorated**
例 The room, with its rococo furniture and its overabundance of knickknacks, is just too fussy for my taste. 这房间里洛可可式的家具和过量的小饰品，让我觉得装修得有点过分以至于无法接受。
近 bedizened, florid
反 austere, plain, stark 朴素的，朴实无华的

【考法 3】 *adj.* 挑剔的：**hard to please**
例 It is widely known that cats are fussy eaters. 众所周知猫对食物很挑剔。
近 choosy, delicate, demanding, exacting, fastidious, nice, particular, persnickety, picky
反 undemanding, unfussy 不挑剔的

fusty ['fʌsti]

【考法 1】 *adj.* 过时的：rigidly **old-fashioned** or reactionary
例 fusty old carpets 过时的旧地毯
近 antiquated, archaic, bygone, moldy, outdated

【考法 2】 *adj.* 腐臭的：saturated with dust and **stale odors**
例 the fusty odor of a damp cellar 潮湿的地下室里的腐臭味道
近 malodorous, fetid, musty, noisome, smelly, stale
反 ambrosial, aromatic, fragrant, perfumed, redolent, savory, scented, sweet 有香味的，芳香的

futile ['fjuːtl]

【考法 1】 *adj.* 无效的，无用的：serving no useful purpose; completely **ineffective**
例 It would be an undoubtedly futile effort to persuade him. 想说服他毫无疑问是徒劳的。
近 abortive, bootless, fruitless, ineffective, useless, vain
反 effectual, efficacious 有效的
派 futility *n.* 徒劳，无益

【考法 2】 *adj.* 不严肃的：**lacking in seriousness** or maturity
例 the futile chatter of gossip columnists about the comings and goings of Hollywood celebrities 八卦的专栏作家们对于好莱坞名人来来往往的随意闲谈
近 flighty, frivolous, frothy
反 earnest, serious 严肃认真的

gadfly ['gædflaɪ]

【考法 1】 *n.* 刺激物：one that acts as a **provocative stimulus**
近 goad, impetus, impulse, incentive, irritant, spur, stimulus
反 balm 安抚，慰藉

【考法 2】 *n.* 令人反感的人：a person who stimulates or **annoys** especially by persistent criticism
例 a tactless gadfly during post-game interviews with the losing team 在赛后采访败北方时一个令人讨厌的不懂人情世故的人
近 annoyer, bother, persecutor, teaser, pest

gaffe [gæf]

【考法1】 *n.* (社交上)失礼，失态：a **social** or diplomatic **blunder**

例 A gaffe is when a politician tells the truth. —— Michael Kinsley 所谓出丑，就是政治家说真话的时候。(迈克·金斯利)

近 impropriety, indecorum, indiscretion

反 decency, decorum, propriety 举止得体

【考法2】 *n.* 明显的错误，错误判断：a **blatant mistake** or misjudgment

例 so-called debates, which were mainly about seeing which candidate made the most gaffes 所谓的辩论，其实主要就是看哪个选手犯了最多的错误

近 blunder, lapse, misstep, oversight

gainsay [ˌɡeɪnˈseɪ]

【考法1】 *vt.* 否认：to **declare false**

近 deny, contradict, contravene, naysay

反 acknowledge, admit, avow, concede 承认；affirm 证实

【考法2】 *vt.* 反对：to **oppose**, especially by contradiction

例 No one dare to gainsay him. 没人敢反驳他。

近 disagree, refute, reject, repudiate

反 concur 同意

gall [ɡɔːl]

【考法1】 *vt.* (使)焦躁，激怒：**irritate**, vex

例 The sarcastic applause from the audience galled her. 观众反讽的掌声激怒了她。

近 aggravate, exasperate, grate, inflame, provoke, pique, roil

反 appease, assuage, calm, lull, pacify, placate 使平静，使平息

【考法2】 *n.* 深深的敌意：a deep-seated **ill will**

例 Her kindly feelings turned to gall when she found out her nephew only wanted her money. 当她发现她的侄子只想要钱时，她之前友好的感情变成了憎恨与厌恶。

近 animosity, animus, antagonism, antipathy, hostility, rancor

反 amity 友好

【考法3】 *n.* 大胆，无耻：shameless **boldness**

例 I can't believe he had the gall to ask me how much I weigh. 我不敢相信他居然胆敢问我有多重。

近 audacity, brass, nerve, presumptuousness, temerity

gallant [ˈɡælənt]

【考法1】 *adj.* 英勇的：**brave**, spirited; nobly **chivalrous** and often self-sacrificing

例 Gallant paratroopers jumped out of the plane without hesitation. 英勇的伞兵们毫不犹豫地跳出了飞机。

近 bold, courageous, dauntless, heroic, stouthearted, valorous

反 craven, pusillanimous 胆小的

派 gallantly *adv.* 英勇地

【考法2】 *adj.* 高贵的，慷慨的：having, characterized by, or arising from a **dignified and generous** nature

例 The members of that service club are known for their gallant service to the community. 那个服务社的成员因为他们对社区的慷慨贡献而为人所知。

近 chivalrous, elevated, loft, magnanimous, sublime

反 base, debased, degenerate, ignoble 卑鄙的，堕落的

galvanize [ˈɡælvənaɪz]

【考法】 *vt.* (好似用电击)刺激：to **stimulate** or **excite** as if by an electric shock

例 an issue that would galvanize public opinion 激起大众评论的问题

近 provoke, agitate, excite, intoxicate, motivate, stimulate, pump up

反 allay, lull, pacify 使平静

派 galvanizing *adj.* 刺激的

gamble [ˈɡæmbl]

【考法1】 *v.* 赌博，孤注一掷：to **bet** on an uncertain outcome, as of a contest

例 gamble on the train being late 赌火车晚点

近 bet, adventure, chance, risk, stake, venture

派 gambling *n.* 赌博

【考法2】 *vi.* (使)受到威胁，冒险：to place **in danger**

例 You don't want to gamble with your life, so buckle up. 你不会想拿命来开玩笑的，所以系好安全带。

近 compromise, hazard, imperil, jeopardize, threaten

Unit 2

gambol ['gæmbl]
【考法】 *vi.* 欢跳，雀跃：to leap about **playfully**
例 young lambs gamboling in the meadow 小羊羔在原野里欢快地跳跃
近 frolic, caper, cavort
反 plod, trudge 沉重缓慢地走

gangly ['gæŋgli]
【考法】 *adj.* 身材瘦长的：awkwardly **tall** or long-limbed
例 The suspect is a gangly high school boy. 嫌犯是一个瘦高的中学生。
近 gangling, lanky, rangy, spindling, spindly
反 stalwart 壮实的

garble ['gɑːrbl]
【考法1】 *vt.* 曲解，篡改，混淆（以至使无法理解）：to mix up or **distort** to such an extent as to make **misleading** or incomprehensible
例 The summary totally garbles the results of the investigation. 这份摘要完全曲解了调查结果。
近 misrepresent, belie, color, distort, falsify, twist, warp
反 clarify, elucidate 阐明
【考法2】 *vt.* 筛选，除杂：to **remove** usually visible impurities from
例 Garbled spices are less likely to contaminate a recipe. 经过筛选的香料应该就不会影响食谱了。
近 clear, distill, filter, purify
反 adulterate, contaminate 掺杂；污染

gargantuan [gɑːrˈgæntʃuən]
【考法】 *adj.* 巨大的：**tremendous** in size, volume, or degree
例 a gargantuan waterfall in the rainforest 热带雨林中的巨大瀑布
近 huge, astronomical, colossal, elephantine, enormous, gigantic, immense, mammoth, monstrous, titanic
反 infinitesimal, minuscule 微小的

garish ['gerɪʃ]
【考法】 *adj.* 过于鲜艳的，过于张扬的：marked by **strident color** or excessive ornamentation
例 With garish makeup on, she looks exceedingly frivolous. 浓妆艳抹之下的她显得格外轻佻。
近 gaudy, blatant, brazen, flamboyant, glaring, ostentatious
反 dim, gloomy, murky, somber 黯淡的；conservative, quiet 不张扬的

garment ['gɑːrmənt]
【考法】 *n.* 衣服：an article of **clothing**
例 pack all garments 给所有衣服打包
近 apparel, attire, costume, dress, suit

garrulous ['gærələs]
【考法】 *adj.* 啰嗦的，话多得令人厌烦的：given to excessive and often trivial or rambling talk; **tiresomely talkative**
例 garrulous traveling companions 多话的旅伴
近 talkative, chatty, loquacious, verbose, voluble
反 laconic, reserved, reticent, taciturn 缄默的
派 garrulity *n.* 啰嗦

gash [gæʃ]
【考法1】 *n.* 深长的伤口或切口：a long **deep cut**
例 He got a gash in his knee that required for stitches. 他的膝盖伤得很深，需要缝针。
近 incision, laceration, rent, rip, tear
【考法2】 *vt.* 砍伤，划开：to **make** a **gash** in
例 Her face had been gashed by the rocks as she tumbled down the embankment. 当她从堤岸上摔下来时脸上被刮了一道口。
近 cut, incise, pierce, slash, slice, slit
反 sew 缝合

gasification [ˌɡæsɪfɪˈkeɪʃn]

【考法】 *n.* 气化：conversion into **gas**

例 gasification of coals 煤的气化

近 evaporation, sublimation

反 solidification 固化；liquefaction 液化

派 gasify *v.* (使)气化

gauche [ɡoʊʃ]

【考法】 *adj.* 笨拙的，缺乏社交经验的：**lacking** social experience or **grace**

例 It would be gauche to mention the subject. 提这个话题是很无礼的。

近 awkward, clumsy, crude, inept, maladroit, rustic, tactless

反 graceful 优雅的；polished, refined, urbane 有教养的

派 gaucheness *n.* 笨拙

Unit 3

■ GAUDY	■ GAUGE	■ GEAR	■ GENIAL	■ GENTEEL
■ GERMANE	■ GIBE	■ GIDDY	■ GILD	■ GIST

gaudy [ˈɡɔːdi]

【考法】 *adj.* 俗丽的：ostentatiously or tastelessly ornamented, **excessively showy**

例 gaudy movie posters 俗丽的电影海报

近 blatant, brazen, flashy, garish, glaring, meretricious, tawdry, flamboyant

反 austere, homely, plain 朴素的；conservative, understated, unflamboyant, unflashy 不张扬的

gauge [ɡeɪdʒ]

【考法1】 *n.* 测量标准：a **measurement** (as of linear dimension) according to some **standard** or system

例 polls as a gauge of voter satisfaction 用以衡量选民满意度的投票选举

近 standard, benchmark, criterion, measure, touchstone, yardstick

【考法2】 *vt.* 判定：to **determine** the capacity or contents of

例 It is hard to gauge his mood. 要判断他的情绪很困难。

近 assess, determine, evaluate, figure, measure, scale

gear [ɡɪr]

【考法】 *v.* 调整(以配合)：to **adjust** or adapt so as to make suitable

例 gear the speech towards a conservative audience 调整演讲以适应保守的观众

近 adapt, adjust, fit, suit, tailor

genial [ˈdʒiːniəl]

【考法1】 *adj.* 和蔼亲切的：having an **easygoing** and pleasing manner especially in social situations

例 a genial host who makes a point of speaking personally to each and every guest 一个重视与每个客人私下交流的亲切的主人

近 affable, agreeable, gracious, mellow, nice, pleasant, sweet

反 caustic, mordant 尖酸刻薄的；truculent 凶残的

派 geniality *n.* 和蔼

【考法2】 *adj.* 友好的，热心的：having or showing **kindly feeling** and sincere interest

近 amicable, companionable, cordial, warmhearted

反 antagonistic, hostile 有敌意的

【考法3】 *adj.* 温暖的：marked by temperatures that are **neither too high nor too low**

例 genial sunshine in winter 冬日的暖阳

近 balmy, equable, gentle, mild, moderate, soft, temperate

反 harsh, inclement, intemperate, severe 严寒的

genteel [dʒenˈtiːl]

【考法】 *adj.* 有教养的，不粗俗的：**free from vulgarity** or rudeness

例 Her genteel behaviors at the ball make others conjecture that she must come from a distinguished noble family. 舞会上她极有教养的举止让他人纷纷猜测她一定来自名门望族。

近 courteous, decent, decorous, mannerly, polite, polished, respectable, urbane, couth, cultured, refined

反 churlish 粗暴的；loutish 蠢笨的

germane	[dʒɜːrˈmeɪn]
【考法】	*adj.* 有关的，适当的：being at once **relevant** and appropriate
例	details not germane to the discussion 与讨论无关的细节
近	applicable, apropos, apposite, pertinent, relevant
反	extraneous, irrelevant 无关的；inappropriate 不适当的

gibe	[dʒaɪb]
【考法】	*v.* 嘲弄：to deride or tease with **taunting words**
例	gibe at the umpire 嘲弄裁判员
近	deride, jeer, ridicule, mock, scoff, sneer, taunt
反	respect, revere, venerate 尊敬

giddy	[ˈgɪdi]
【考法 1】	*adj.* 轻率不严肃的：**lacking in seriousness** or maturity
例	teach a bunch of giddy Girl Scouts how to make a fire 教一群漫不经心的女童子军如何生火
近	flighty, frivolous, frothy
反	grave, serious 严肃的；earnest 认真的
【考法 2】	*adj.* 喜悦的：joyfully **elated**
例	He's clearly giddy at the news that his ailing grandfather will be fine. 听到他祖父的病将无大碍，他的喜悦之情溢于言表。
近	elated, elevated, euphoric, exhilarated, exultant, intoxicated, rapturous
反	depressed, melancholy 忧郁的

gild	[gɪld]
【考法】	*vt.* (带欺骗性地)修改，润色：to give an often **deceptively attractive** or improved appearance to
例	Any further retouch would be gilding the lily. 任何形式的润色都会是画蛇添足。
近	polish, refine, smooth

gist	[dʒɪst]
【考法】	*n.* 要点：the **main point** or part
例	the gist of the argument 论证的要点
近	core, essence, kernel, pivot, quintessence, substance
反	divergence 偏离(主旨)

Unit 4

■ GLADIATOR	■ GLAZE	■ GLIB	■ GLISTEN	■ GLITCH
■ GLOAT	■ GLOOMY	■ GLOSS	■ GLOSSY	■ GLUT

gladiator	[ˈglædieɪtər]
【考法 1】	*n.* 角斗士：a person **engaged** in a **fight** to the **death** as public entertainment for ancient Romans
例	He comes to Rome as a gladiator to seek revenge. 他化成角斗士来到罗马寻求复仇。
【考法 2】	*n.* 参与打斗或辩论的人：a person **engaging in** a public fight or **controversy**
近	boxer, fighter, belligerent, combatant

glaze	[gleɪz]
【考法 1】	*vt.* 给…上釉，妆点：to **coat** with or as if with a **glaze**
例	The storm glazed trees with ice. 暴风雪给树木镀上了一层冰装。
近	adorn, bedeck, decorate, embellish, garnish
反	strip, uncover 剥去
【考法 2】	*vt.* 使平滑：to give a smooth **glossy surface** to
近	polish, burnish, furbish, shine
反	rumple 弄皱

glib	[glɪb]
【考法 1】	*adj.* 流利圆滑的（常含有不真诚或欺诈的成分），油腔滑调的：marked by ease and **fluency** in speaking or writing often to the point of being **insincere** or **deceitful**
例	a glib politician 油嘴滑舌的政客
近	nonchalant, oily
反	taciturn 沉默寡言的；awkward 笨拙的

【考法2】 *adj.* 缺乏深度的，肤浅的：**lacking depth** and substance
例 glib solutions to the knotty problem 对复杂难解问题的肤浅的解决方案
近 cursory, shallow, superficial
反 abstruse, deep, profound 深奥的，深刻的

glisten ['glɪsn]
【考法】 *vi.* 闪光：to **shine** by reflection with a **sparkling** luster
例 The calm sea glistened in the sunlight. 日光下平静的海面波光粼粼。
近 flash, scintillate, sparkle, twinkle, winkle
反 dim 变得黯淡

glitch [glɪtʃ]
【考法】 *n.* 小故障：a **minor malfunction**, mishap, or technical problem
例 postponement due to a glitch in a spacecraft's fuel cell 宇宙飞船燃料电池故障引起的推迟发射
近 bug, defect, fault, lapse, imperfection, peccadillo
反 fatal error 致命错误

gloat [gloʊt]
【考法】 *vi.* 幸灾乐祸，自鸣得意：a feeling of great, often malicious, pleasure or **self-satisfaction**
例 gloat over his enemy's misfortune 为敌人的不幸而幸灾乐祸
近 crow, relish, triumph
反 mourn 哀悼

gloomy ['gluːmi]
【考法1】 *adj.* 黯淡无光的：being **without light** or without much light
近 black, dark, dim, dimmed, murky, obscure, stygian, pitch-dark
反 bright, luminous, lucent, lucid 明亮的
【考法2】 *adj.* 忧郁的：**low** in **spirits**
例 feel gloomy about future career 对未来的职业生涯倍感忧心
近 sullen, dejected, dour, melancholy, morose, saturnine, surly
反 frothy 欢乐轻挑的；buoyant, cheerful, jubilant 高兴的

gloss [glɑːs]
【考法1】 *n.* 简短解释：a **brief explanation** of a difficult or **obscure** word or expression
近 abstract, annotation, brief, epitome, synopsis
反 amplification 详解
派 glossary *n.* 术语表
【考法2】 *n.* (欺骗性的)光鲜外表：a deceptively **attractive** external **appearance**
例 She used a computer to give her astrological predictions the gloss of real science. 她用计算机来给她的占星预测结果套上科学的外衣。
近 façade, mask, veneer
【考法3】 *v.* 敷衍潦草做事(甚至忽略)：to deal with (a subject or problem) **too lightly** or not at all
例 gloss over the problems 不怎么理会这些问题
近 disregard, ignore, neglect, overlook
反 scrutinize 仔细研究
【考法4】 *v.* 开脱(罪名)：to make (something) seem **less bad** by offering excuses
例 I don't want to gloss over her misbehavior, but keep in mind that she's been under a lot of stress lately. 我不想为她的行为辩护，但是别忘了她最近压力很大。
近 excuse, extenuate

glossy ['glɑːsi]
【考法】 *adj.* 平滑的，有光泽的：having a **smooth**, shiny, lustrous **surface**
例 glossy surface of the floor 平整光亮的地板
近 lustrous, burnished, glistening, polished, shining
反 coarse 粗糙的；dull, dim 无光泽的

glut [glʌt]
【考法】 *vt.* 使过量，使充满：to fill **beyond capacity**, especially with food
例 glut himself with Sushi 吃寿司吃撑了
近 cloy, cram, fill, satiate, surfeit, oversupply, sate
反 lack 缺乏
派 glutted *adj.* 饱和的

Unit 5

glutinous [ˈgluːtənəs]

【考法】 *adj.* 胶状的，粘的：of the nature of or resembling **glue**

例 glutinous liquid 胶状液体

近 adherent, adhesive, cloggy, gluey, sticky, tenacious, viscid

反 fluid 流体的

glutton [ˈglʌtn]

【考法】 *n.* 贪吃者：a person who eats or consumes **immoderate** amounts of **food** and drink

例 a glutton for work 工作狂

近 gorger, gourmand

派 gluttony *n.* 暴饮暴食

goad [goʊd]

【考法】 *vt.* 刺激，驱使，激发：to **incite** or **rouse** as if with a goad

例 goad someone to do something 激励某人做某事

近 urge, abet, exhort, instigate, prod, prompt, propel, spur, stimulate

反 check, curb 阻止；lull 使安静

gobble [ˈgɑːbl]

【考法】 *vt.* 狼吞虎咽：to swallow or **eat greedily**

例 Lions gobble their prey. 狮子狼吞虎咽地啃食它们的猎物。

近 devour, gorge, guzzle, quaff, raven, swill

反 nibble 小口咬

goggle [ˈgɑːgl]

【考法】 *vi.* 凝视：to **look** long and hard in wonder or surprise

例 goggle at the characters on the stele 凝视石碑上的文字

近 blink, gawk, gaze, peer, stare

反 glance, glimpse 瞥视

goldbrick [ˈgoʊldbrɪk]

【考法】 *v.* 逃避工作和责任：to **shirk** one's assigned duties or **responsibilities**

例 goldbrick his duty as a citizen 逃避他作为公民的义务

近 idle, parry, shirk, sidestep

反 dedicate, devote 致力于

gorge [gɔːrdʒ]

【考法 1】 *n.* 峡谷：a narrow steep-walled **canyon** or part of a canyon

例 Wenchuan earthquake is said to have no detrimental effect on Three-Gorge dam. 汶川地震据称对三峡大坝没有破坏性影响。

近 gap, gulch, notch, ravine

【考法 2】 *v.* 狼吞虎咽：to **eat greedily** or to repletion

例 He gorged himself at the party. 他在聚会上狼吞虎咽。

近 cram, devour, gobble, guzzle, quaff, sate, swill

反 nibble 小口咬

gossamer [ˈgɑːsəmər]

【考法 1】 *n.* 虚无缥缈的东西：something light, delicate, or **insubstantial**

例 the gossamer of youth's dreams 年少时缥缈的梦想

近 ether, delicacy

反 substance, entity 实体

【考法 2】 *adj.* 轻薄的；薄弱的：extremely **light**, delicate, or tenuous

例 a gossamer explanation 站不住脚的解释

近 diaphanous, ethereal, filmy, light, insubstantial, tenuous

反 heavy, leaden, ponderous 沉重的

gourmand [ˈgʊrmɑːnd]

【考法】 *n.* 嗜食者，大胃王：one who is **excessively fond of eating** and drinking

例 the kind of gourmand who swallows food without even pausing to taste it 不尝味道就下咽的那种嗜食者

近 gorger, glutton

gourmet [ˈgʊrmeɪ]

【考法】 *n.* 美食家：a **connoisseur** of **food** and drink

例 a gourmet of Chinese food 中餐美食家

近 bon vivant, connoisseur, epicure

反 layman 门外汉

Unit 6

■ GRANDEUR	■ GRANDILOQUENT	■ GRANDIOSE	■ GRANDSTAND	■ GRATE
■ GRATIFY	■ GRATUITOUS	■ GREEN	■ GREGARIOUS	■ GRIEVE

grandeur [ˈɡrændʒər]

【考法】 *n.* 宏伟，壮丽：the quality or condition of being **grand**; magnificence

例 the glory that was Greece and the grandeur that was Rome 希腊的荣耀和罗马的辉煌

近 magnificence, augustness, brilliance, glory, majesty, nobility, resplendence, splendor

反 frivolousness 无关紧要

派 grand *adj.* 宏伟壮观的

grandiloquent [ɡrænˈdɪləkwənt]

【考法】 *adj.* （语言等）浮夸的：a lofty, **extravagantly** colorful, pompous, or **bombastic** style, manner, or quality especially in language

例 feel disgusted with his grandiloquent speech 对他浮夸的演讲表示厌恶

近 rhetorical, bombastic, inflated, magniloquent, pretentious

反 secretive 低调的，隐秘的；simple 简单的

派 grandiloquence *n.* 夸张的话语

grandiose [ˈɡrændioʊs]

【考法1】 *adj.* 自命不凡的，浮夸的：characterized by feigned or affected **grandeur**

例 grandiose words 自命不凡的话语

近 extravagant, flamboyant, pompous, pretentious

反 humble 谦逊的

【考法2】 *adj.* 宏大的：characterized by **greatness** of scope or intent

例 a grandiose hydroelectric project 宏伟的水电工程

近 august, glorious, grand, imposing, magnificent, monumental, splendid

反 trivial 微不足道的；humble, unimposing, unimpressive 平凡的

派 grandiosity *n.* 雄伟，壮观

grandstand [ˈɡrænstænd]

【考法】 *vi.* 为了给人留下印象而表演，哗众取宠：to play or act so as to **impress** onlookers

例 grandstand on the stage 在舞台上哗众取宠

近 act, perform, pretend

grate [ɡreɪt]

【考法1】 *v.* 刮擦（以发出刺耳的声音）：to make a **rasping** sound

例 The sled grated along the bare pavement. 雪橇与裸露的路面刮擦发出刺耳声。

近 abrade, rasp, scratch, scrape

派 grating *adj.* 刺耳的

【考法2】 *v.* 骚扰，惹恼：to **irritate** or annoy persistently

例 a noise that grates on one's nerves 使人烦躁的噪音

近 irritate, aggravate, gall, nettle, peeve, plague, provoke, vex

反 soothe 使平静，安抚

gratify [ˈɡrætɪfaɪ]

【考法】 *vt.* 使满足：to give what is **desired** to, to **please** or satisfy

例 gratify her curiosity 满足她的好奇心 || Her praise will gratify all who worked so hard to earn it. 她的表扬会使所有辛勤工作的人们高兴。

近 appease, cater, content, satisfy

反 displease 使不满；grieve 使悲痛

派 gratification *n.* 满意

gratuitous [grəˈtuːɪtəs]

【考法 1】 *adj.* 无根据的，无理由的：unnecessary or **unwarranted**

例 a dubious request based on a gratuitous assumption 基于无根据假设的可疑要求

近 unfounded, unjustified, unreasonable, baseless, groundless

反 justified, warranted 有理有据的

【考法 2】 *adj.* 无报酬的，免费的：given or granted **without return** or recompense

例 a gratuitous ticket 免费的门票

近 free, complimentary, unearned, voluntary

反 merited 应得的

派 gratuity *n.* 报酬，小费

【考法 3】 *adj.* 多余的：**not needed** by the circumstances or to accomplish an end

近 dispensable, inessential, needless, redundant, superfluous, surplus

反 critical, essential, pivotal, vital 关键的

green [griːn]

【考法】 *adj.* 无经验的：**deficient** in training, knowledge, or **experience**

例 lead a squad of green recruits 带领一队没有经验的新兵

近 inexperienced, callow, fresh, raw, unfledged, young

反 experienced, versed 经验丰富的

gregarious [grɪˈgeriəs]

【考法 1】 *adj.* 爱社交的：likely to seek or **enjoy the company** of others

近 convivial, extroverted, genial, outgoing, sociable, outgoing

反 aloof 疏远的；antisocial 不合群的；introverted, reclusive 内向的

【考法 2】 *adj.* 群居的：tending to **group with others** of the same kind

例 ecologically define human as gregarious carnivore 从生态学上将人类定义为群居类肉食动物

近 social

反 solitary 独自的

grieve [griːv]

【考法】 *vt.* (使)感到悲伤：to (cause to) feel **deep sadness** or mental pain

例 We all grieved over the lost cat. 我们都为那只丢失的猫感到伤心。

近 agonize, anguish, suffer, bemoan, bewail, deplore

反 delight, exult in, glory in, joy, rejoice in 感到高兴

Unit 7

■ GRIMACE	■ GRIN	■ GRIPE	■ GRISLY	■ GROOVE
■ GROTESQUE	■ GROVEL	■ GRUELING	■ GUILE	■ GUILT

grimace [grɪˈmeɪs]

【考法】 *v./n.* 因痛苦而面部扭曲，(作)怪相，(作)鬼脸：a sharp **contortion** of the face expressive of **pain, disgust or disapproval**

例 She made a grimace when she tasted the medicine. 她尝了一口药，然后做了一个鬼脸。

近 frown, moue, pout, scowl

grin [grɪn]

【考法】 *v.* 咧嘴笑，咧嘴笑着表示：to **express an emotion** (as amusement) by curving the lips upward

例 The boss grinned his approval. 老板咧嘴一笑表示赞许。

近 beam

反 pout 噘嘴生气

gripe [graɪp]

【考法 1】 *vi.* 抱怨：to express **dissatisfaction**, pain, or resentment usually tiresomely

例 All workers were griping about the new regulations. 所有的工人都在抱怨新规章。

近 carp, fuss, grouch, grouse, grumble, wail

反 crow, delight, rejoice 欢快，喜悦

【考法 2】 *vt.* (通过连续让人讨厌的举动)激怒，惹怒：to **disturb** the peace of mind of (someone) especially by repeated disagreeable acts

例 Constant complaints from the customers griped her to the point where she started snapping back. 顾客持续的抱怨激怒了她，让她也到了爆点，想要反驳回去。

近 aggravate, annoy, bother, chafe, exasperate, nettle, peeve, pique, rile, ruffle, vex

grisly ['grɪzli]

【考法】 *adj.* 令人反感的，令人恐惧的：inspiring **repugnance**; gruesome

例 a series grisly murders 一系列令人恐惧的谋杀

近 appalling, dreadful, ghastly, gruesome, hideous, horrifying, macabre

groove [gruːv]

【考法】 *v.* 享受，极其满意，过得快活：to **take pleasure in**

例 Thrill-seekers who groove on skiing will love snowboarding. 那些乐在滑雪中的追求刺激的人们也会喜欢滑雪板的。Il just sitting around, grooving on the music 随便坐坐，在音乐中享受一下

近 adore, fancy, savor, relish, get off on, rejoice in, revel in, delight in

grotesque [groʊ'tesk]

【考法】 *adj.* 难看的：**unpleasant** to look at

例 That bloody Halloween mask is grotesque. 那个血腥的万圣节面具丑死了。

近 hideous, homely, ill-favored, monstrous, unappealing, unattractive, uncomely, unsightly

反 aesthetic, attractive, beautiful, bonny, comely, fetching, gorgeous, knockout, ravishing, seemly, sightly, stunning, taking, well-favored 悦目的，吸引人的

grovel ['grɑːvl]

【考法】 *vi.* 卑躬屈膝：to **draw back** or crouch down in **fearful submission**

例 He made a groveling apology to the girl. 他放下身段，给那姑娘道歉。

近 cringe, creep, slither, wriggle

派 groveler *n.* 卑躬屈膝者：the one who lies with the body prostrate in token of subservience or abasement

grueling ['gruːəlɪŋ]

【考法】 *adj.* 费时间花心思的：**requiring** much time, effort, or careful attention

例 Cutting diamonds can be grueling work. 切割钻石是项劳神的活儿。

近 arduous, burdensome, laborious, onerous, taxing, toilsome

反 undemanding, facile 不费力气的

guile [gaɪl]

【考法】 *n.* 狡猾，狡诈：the inclination or practice of **misleading** others through lies or trickery

例 A person so full of guile he can't even be trusted to give you the correct time of day. 他这个人狡诈成性，说的话都不足为信。

近 artfulness, canniness, craft, cunningness, deviousness, slyness, subtleness, wiliness

反 artlessness, forthrightness, ingenuousness, sincerity 朴实

派 guileless *adj.* 朴实的：free of guile; artless

反 manipulative 操纵的

guilt [gɪlt]

【考法】 *n.* 自责，悔恨：a feeling of responsibility for **wrongdoing**

例 He was wracked with guilt after he accidentally broke his younger sister's antique grandfather clock. 在不小心弄坏他妹妹的古董老爷钟后，他备受自责的折磨。

近 contrition, penitence, remorse, repentance, self-reproach, shame

反 impenitence, remorselessness 无悔意

Unit 8

■ GULL	■ GULLIBLE	■ GUSH	■ GUST	■ GUZZLE
■ HACK	■ HACKNEYED	■ HALCYON	■ HALE	■ HALF-BAKED

gull [gʌl]

【考法】 *vt.* 欺骗：to cause to believe what is **untrue**

例 We were gulled into believing that if we answered the e-mail, we'd somehow become millionaires, but instead we just got put on a list for junk mail. 我们误以为只要回复了那封邮件，就能变身百万富翁，后来发现我们只不过是群发的垃圾邮件名单上的一员而已。

近 bamboozle, beguile, cozen, delude, dupe, fake out, gaff, hoax, hoodwink, snooker, string along, take in

反 undeceive 使醒悟

gullible ['gʌləbl]

【考法】 *adj.* 易受骗的，易被利用的：easily duped or **cheated**, readily taken advantage of

例 They sell overpriced souvenirs to gullible tourists. 他们卖高价纪念品给易上当的旅客们。

近 dewy-eyed, exploitable, naive, susceptible, unwary, wide-eyed

gush [gʌʃ]

【考法 1】 *v.* (使)大量涌出：to (cause to) flow forth suddenly in **great volume**

例 water gushing from the hydrant 水从消防栓中喷出

近 exodus, outpour, outpouring, spout

反 dribble, drip, drop, trickle 涓涓细流，滴

【考法 2】 *v.* (使)感情强烈外溢：to make an **exaggerated display** of affection or enthusiasm

例 an aunt gushing over the baby 对着婴儿母爱泛滥的姑姑

近 drool, effuse, enthuse, fuss, rave, slobber

gust [gʌst]

【考法】 *n.* 情感爆发：a **sudden intense expression** of strong feeling

例 The stressed-out coworker cried out with a gust of emotion. 压力巨大的同事开始嚎啕大哭。

近 burst, ebullition, eruption, explosion, flush, gush

guzzle [ˈgʌzl]

【考法】 *v.* 狂饮：to **drink** especially liquor **greedily**, continually, or habitually

例 guzzle beer 狂饮啤酒

近 gulp, quaff, swig, booze, soak, tipple

hack [hæk]

【考法 1】 *n.* 雇佣文人：a **writer** who aims solely for **commercial** success

【考法 2】 *v.* 乱砍；开辟：to cut or chop with repeated and **irregular blows**

例 hacking out new election districts 开辟新的选区

【考法 3】 *vt.* 成功完成：to deal with (something) usually **skillfully or efficiently**

例 just couldn't hack the new job 无法搞定新工作

近 address, contend with, cope with, manage, maneuver, manipulate

【考法 4】 *v.* 忍受：to **put up with** (something painful or difficult)

例 She's not sure she can hack that miserable job much longer. 她不知道还能忍受那项苦逼的工作多久。

近 abide, bide, brook, endure, handle, stand, stomach, sustain, tolerate

hackneyed [ˈhæknid]

【考法】 *adj.* 陈腐的，缺乏创新的：**lacking** in **freshness** or **originality**

例 hackneyed slogans 老掉牙的口号

近 banal, cliché, commonplace, hack, threadbare, trite, well-worn, stereotyped

反 fresh, offbeat, original, novel 新鲜的

halcyon [ˈhælsiən]

【考法 1】 *adj.* 宁静的，平静的：**free from** storms or physical disturbance

近 hushed, peaceful, placid, serene, tranquil, untroubled

反 tempestuous, stormy, agitated, inclement, restless, rough, turbulent, unquiet, unsettled 暴风雨的；暴躁的

【考法 2】 *adj.* 繁荣的，丰富的：prosperous, **affluent**, vigorous growth and well-being especially economically

例 halcyon years 丰年

近 booming, flourishing, lush, palmy, prospering, roaring, thriving

反 miserable, depressed, unprosperous 萧条的

hale [heɪl]

【考法 1】 *adj.* 强壮的，健壮的：**free from infirmity or illness**; sound

例 a hale and hearty old lady 硬朗矍铄的老奶奶

近 bouncing, fit, robust, sound, well-conditioned, wholesome

反 effete, infirm, anemic, wan, decrepit, blighted 衰弱的，衰老的

【考法 2】 *vt.* 拖，拉：to **cause to follow** by applying steady force on

例 The fishermen haled the huge net onto the deck of the ship. 渔民们将巨大的渔网拖到渔船甲板上。

近 drag, draw, haul, lug, tow, tug

反 drive, propel, push 推

half-baked [ˌhæf ˈbeɪkt]

【考法】 *adj.* 不明智的：showing or marked by a **lack of good sense or judgment**

例 a half-baked scheme 不明智的计划

近 daffy, daft, dippy, harebrained, half-witted, preposterous

反 judicious, prudent, sagacious, sapient, sensible, sound, wise 明智的

Unit 9

hallmark ［ˈhɔːlmɑːrk］
【考法】 *n.* 典型的特征：a **conspicuous feature** or characteristic
例 The sense of guilt is the hallmark of civilized humanity. 内疚是人类文明的特征。
近 ensign, impresa, logo, symbol, totem, trademark
反 uncharacteristic feature 不典型的特征

hallow ［ˈhælou］
【考法】 *vt.* 尊敬，把⋯视为神圣：to **respect** or honor greatly; revere
近 consecrate, sacralize, sanctify
反 desecrate, deconsecrate, desacralize, desanctify 亵渎

hallucination ［həˌluːsɪˈneɪʃn］
【考法】 *n.* 错觉：a **false idea** or belief
例 Some people have the common hallucination that gluttony during the holiday season doesn't have consequences. 一些人有种错觉，认为假期里暴饮暴食不会有什么结果。
近 chimera, daydream, delusion, fancy, figment, illusion
反 truth, verity

ham-handed ［ˈhæmhændɪd］
【考法】 *adj.* 笨手笨脚的：**lacking dexterity** or grace
例 too ham-handed to use one of those tiny cell phones 手指太不灵活了，用不了那种迷你型手机
近 awkward, handless, heavy-handed, maladroit, unhandy
反 deft, dexterous, handy, sure-handed, adroit 敏捷的

hammer ［ˈhæmər］
【考法】 *v.* 屡次重申：to make **repeated** efforts especially: to reiterate an opinion or attitude
例 The lectures all hammered away at the same points. 整场讲座都是在阐述相同的论点。 ‖ hammer the information into the students' heads 反复向学生们强调这条信息

hamper ［ˈhæmpər］
【考法】 *vt.* 阻碍：to **restrict the movement** of by bonds or obstacles: **impede**
例 Construction is hampering traffic on the highway. 高速路上的建设阻碍了正常交通。
近 cramp, encumber, fetter, handicap, hinder, impede, stymie, trammel
反 facilitate, aid, assist, help 促进

hamstring ［ˈhæmstrɪŋ］
【考法】 *vt.* 使无效，使无力：to make **ineffective** or powerless
例 The downtown development committee claims that it's hamstrung by city ordinances. 市中心发展委员会声称它受到了城市法令的阻碍。
近 cripple, immobilize, incapacitate, prostrate

hangdog ［ˈhæŋdɔːg］
【考法】 *adj.* 伤心的，沮丧的：**sad, dejected**
例 She came home with a hangdog expression on her face. 她一脸沮丧地回到了家。
近 crestfallen, dejected, despondent, disconsolate, doleful, melancholy, sorrowful
反 buoyant, elated, sprightly, blissful, delighted, joyous, jubilant, upbeat 热情高涨的

hanker ［ˈhæŋkər］
【考法】 *v./n.* 向往，渴望：to have a strong or persistent **desire**: **yearn**
例 hanker for adventure 渴望冒险
近 appetite, craving, hunger, itch, longing, lust, passion, thirst, yearning
反 odium, lack of desire 讨厌

haphazard ［hæpˈhæzərd］
【考法】 *adj.* 无秩序的，无目标的：marked by **lack of plan, order, or direction**
例 We were given a haphazard tour of the city. 我们进行了一次城市漫游。
近 aimless, arbitrary, desultory, erratic, scattered, stray
反 methodical, systematic, nonrandom, orderly, organized, regular 系统的，有序的

Unit 10

harangue [həˈræŋ]

【考法】 *v./n.* （发表）长篇大论：a **long pompous** speech, especially one delivered before a gathering

例 She harangued us for hours about the evils of popular culture. 她向我们絮叨了好几小时，批判流行文化的堕落。

近 diatribe, jeremiad, philippic, rant

反 speak temperately 有节制地说话

harass [ˈhærəs]

【考法1】 *vt.* 烦扰：to **irritate** or torment **persistently**

例 The troops harassed the defeated army throughout its retreat. 战胜的队伍在撤退过程中还不忘突袭一下败北的队伍。

【考法2】 *vt.* 耗尽…的体力：to **use up** all the physical energy of

例 The president had been visibly harassed by the demands of the presidency. 总统被事务缠身，筋疲力尽。

近 drain, fag, fatigue, outwear, tire, tucker out, wear out, knock out, burn out

harbinger [ˈhɑːrbɪndʒər]

【考法】 *n.* 预言者：one that **presages** or foreshadows what is to come

例 The October air stung my cheeks, a harbinger of winter. 十月的寒风凛冽地吹在脸上，这是冬天的预兆。

近 foregoer, herald, outrider, precursor

harbor [ˈhɑːrbər]

【考法1】 *vt.* 提供住处，隐匿：to **provide** a place, home, or **habitat** for

例 harbor a fugitive 隐匿逃亡者

近 accommodate, bestow, board, camp, chamber, domicile, lodge, quarter, take in, put up

反 evict 赶出

【考法2】 *vt.* 心怀，牢记：to **keep in one's mind** or heart

例 He had long harbored a grudge against his old employer, who had fired him without cause. 他对前老板一直耿耿于怀，因为他无缘无故炒了他。

近 bear, cherish, entertain, hold, nurse

hard-bitten [hɑːrd ˈbɪtn]

【考法】 *adj.* 顽强的，经受得住困境、压力的：able to **withstand** hardship, strain, or exposure

例 Hard-bitten Chinese people could endure both the scorching heat and the freezing cold. 坚强勇敢的中国人民既能受得住酷暑，又能受得住严寒。

近 hardened, sturdy, tough, cast-iron, inured, rugged, stout, vigorous, hardy

反 delicate, nonhardy, soft, tender, weak 柔弱的

hardy [ˈhɑːrdi]

【考法1】 *adj.* 顽强的：**able to withstand** hardship, strain, or exposure

例 Chrysanthemums are hardy enough to survive a light frost. 菊花能够经受霜打。

近 hardened, sturdy, tough, cast-iron, inured, rugged, stout, vigorous, hard-bitten

反 delicate, nonhardy, soft, tender, weak 柔弱的

【考法2】 *adj.* 愿意冒风险的：inclined or **willing to take risks**

例 hardy souls who pioneered new paths into outer space 那些愿意冒险探索外太空的先驱们

近 adventurous, audacious, daring, dashing, emboldened, enterprising, gutsy, venturous

反 unadventurous, unenterprising 没有冒险精神的

harmonious [hɑːrˈmoʊniəs]

【考法】 *adj.* 和谐一致的：having the parts **agreeably related**

例 a harmonious arrangement of archways and doorways in the palace courtyard 宫殿的庭院、拱门和门廊排列有序协调

近 balanced, congruous, consonant, eurythmic, harmonic, accordant, coherent, compatible, concordant, conformable, congruent, consonant, correspondent, nonconflicting

反 disharmonic, disharmonious, incongruous, unbalanced 不协调的；conflicting, incompatible, incongruous, inconsistent 冲突的

harness ['hɑːrnɪs]

【考法】 *vt.* 利用：**utilize**

例 harness the sun's rays as a source of energy 利用阳光作为一种能源

近 apply, employ, exercise, exploit, operate, utilize

反 fail to utilize 没能够利用

harrow ['hæroʊ]

【考法】 *vt.* 折磨，使苦恼：to inflict great **distress** or **torment** on

例 The villagers were gaunt and sickly, harrowed by years of disease and starvation. 村民们枯瘦如柴，体弱多病，都是被多年的疾病和饥饿折磨的。

近 agonize, beset, besiege, torment, torture, excruciate, plague

反 assuage 减轻（苦恼）

harry ['hæri]

【考法】 *vt.* 不断烦扰，骚扰：to disturb or **distress** by or as if by repeated attacks; **harass**

反 comfort, mollify 安慰

Every man's work, whether it be literature of music of pictures or architecture of anything else, is always a portrait of himself.

每个人的工作，不管是文学、音乐、美术、建筑还是其他工作，都是自己的一幅画像。

——美国教育家 勃特勒（Samuel Brtler, American educator）

List 12

Unit 1

■ HARSH	■ HASTEN	■ HASTY	■ HAUNT	■ HAUTEUR
■ HAVEN	■ HAVOC	■ HEADLONG	■ HEARKEN	■ HEARTEN

harsh [hɑːrʃ]
【考法 1】 *adj.* 粗糙的，不具有美感的：unpleasantly **coarse** and **rough** to the touch, **disagreeable** to one's aesthetic or artistic **sense**
例 The harsh lighting in the cafeteria makes the food look slightly off-color. 咖啡厅劣质刺眼的灯光让食物看起来卖相不佳。
近 grating, grotesque, jarring, unaesthetic
反 soft, aesthetic 柔和的，有美感的
【考法 2】 *adj.* 严厉的：unduly **exacting**, given to exacting standards of discipline and self-restraint
例 a harsh judge when it comes to drug users and especially drug dealers 对瘾君子特别是毒贩处罚格外严厉的法官
近 afflicting, agonizing, cruel, excruciating, galling, grievous, harrowing
反 clement, forbearing, gentle, indulgent, lax, lenient, tolerant 温和的，宽松的

hasten [ˈheɪsn]
【考法】 *vt.* 促进：to **speed up**; **accelerate**
例 The man's death was hastened by alcohol abuse. 酗酒加速了这个人的死亡。
近 accelerate, bundle, fast-track, rush, speed up
反 slow the progress of, check, retard, brake, decelerate, retard, slow down 阻碍，放慢

hasty [ˈheɪsti]
【考法】 *adj.* 轻率的：fast and typically **superficial**; acting or done with **excessive or careless speed**
例 a hasty decision 轻率的决定
近 cursory, headlong, precipitate, rash, rushed, pell-mell
反 deliberate, well-considered, unhurried, unrushed 深思熟虑的，不慌不忙的

haunt [hɔːnt]
【考法 1】 *vt.* 常去拜访：to visit often; **frequent**
例 haunt the movie theater 常去影院
近 affect, habituate, visit, hang at, resort to
反 avoid, shun 避开
【考法 2】 *vt.* 不断地想起，萦绕心头：to come to mind continually; **obsess**
例 a riddle that haunted me all morning 整个早上萦绕在我心头的谜

hauteur [hɔːˈtɜːr]
【考法】 *n.* 傲慢，自大：haughtiness in bearing and attitude; **arrogance**
例 He looked at her with the hauteur of someone who is accustomed to being instantly obeyed. 他看着她，带着向来被顺从惯了的傲慢。
近 bumptiousness, imperiousness, peremptoriness, pomposity, presumptuousness, pretentiousness, superciliousness, superiority
反 humility, humbleness, modesty, unassumingness, unpretentiousness 谦虚

haven [ˈheɪvn]
【考法】 *n.* 安全的地方：a **place of safety**
例 a haven for artists 艺术家们的圣地
近 asylum, harbor, refuge, retreat, sanctuary
反 unsafe place, dangerous place 不安全的地方

havoc [ˈhævək]

【考法 1】 *n.* 大混乱：a state in which everything is **out of order**

例 The blackout caused havoc in the city. 断电造成了城市一片混乱。

近 disarrangement, disarray, dishevelment, muddle, muss, tumble, welter

反 order, orderliness 有序

【考法 2】 *n.* 大范围破坏：the state or fact of being rendered **nonexistent**, physically **unsound, or useless**

例 The powerful hurricane wreaked havoc all along the coast. 威力巨大的飓风摧毁着沿岸的一切。

近 annihilation, decimation, demolishment, desolation, devastation, extermination, extinction, obliteration, ruin, wreckage

反 building, construction, erection, raising 建设

headlong [ˈhedlɔːŋ]

【考法】 *adj.* 鲁莽的：**without deliberation**

例 terrified forest creatures in a headlong retreat from the rapidly spreading fire 受惊的动物们惊慌失措地从不断蔓延的森林大火中逃离出来

近 cursory, overhasty, precipitate, precipitous, rash, pell-mell, helter-skelter

反 deliberate, unhurried, unrushed 深思熟虑的

hearken [ˈhɑːrkən]

【考法】 *vi.* 倾听，关注：to give respectful **attention**

近 attend, harken, heed, mind

反 ignore 不理睬

hearten [ˈhɑːrtn]

【考法】 *vt.* 给予鼓励，鼓舞：to give strength, **courage**, or hope to; **encourage**

例 Thinking we were hopelessly lost, we were heartened by the sight of a familiar farmhouse. 悲催地以为我们完全迷路了时，前方一座熟悉的农场给了我们新的希望。

近 embolden, inspire, inspirit, buck up, buoy up, cheer up

反 daunt, dismay, discourage, dishearten, dispirit 使胆怯

Unit 2

■ HEARTRENDING	■ HEDONISM	■ HEGEMONY	■ HEINOUS	■ HEW
■ HERALD	■ HERESY	■ HERETICAL	■ HERMETIC	■ HESITANCE

heartrending [ˈhɑːrtˌrendɪŋ]

【考法】 *adj.* 令人心碎的：causing intense **sorrow** or **distress**

例 a heartrending choice between saving his mother or his wife 先救老妈还是先救老婆的纠结选择

hedonism [ˈhiːdənɪzəm]

【考法】 *n.* 享乐主义：the **doctrine** that **pleasure** or happiness is the sole or chief good in life

例 Their spring break trip to Mexico became an exercise in heedless hedonism. 他们春季的墨西哥之行变成了一次未加注意的享乐之旅。

近 carnality, debauchery, sybaritism, voluptuousness

反 abstinence, asceticism, sobriety, temperance 禁欲，节制

hegemony [hɪˈdʒemoʊni]

【考法】 *n.* 霸权，统治权：**preponderant** influence or **authority** over others

例 battle for hegemony in Asia 争夺在亚洲地区的霸权地位

近 ascendancy, dominance, dominion, predominance, preeminence

反 lack of authority 缺少权利

heinous [ˈheɪnəs]

【考法】 *adj.* 可憎的，十恶不赦的：**hatefully** or shockingly evil, abominable

例 a heinous crime 十恶不赦的罪行

反 commendable 值得赞美的

hew [hjuː]

【考法 1】 *vi.* 遵守：**confirm**, adhere, to **hold to something firmly** as if by adhesion

例 hew to tradition 遵守传统

近 adhere, cling, conform

【考法 2】 *v.* 支持：to give **steadfast support** to

例 He was no longer able to hew to the party line, so he switched political parties. 不再赞同该党的纲领，他投奔了另一个党。

近 cling to, keep to, stand by, stick to

反 defect from 脱离，叛变

herald [ˈherəld]

【考法 1】 *vt.* 告知，宣布：to **make known** openly or publicly

例 herald the great tidings to all the world 将重大消息告知全世界

近 annunciate, broadcast, declare, enunciate, proclaim, promulgate

【考法 2】 *vt.* 预示，预兆：to give a slight **indication of beforehand**

例 The reshuffle of the company's management heralded the sweeping changes to come. 公司管理层的重新洗牌预示着即将到来的巨大变革。

近 adumbrate, forerun, harbinger, prefigure

heresy [ˈherəsi]

【考法】 *n.* 异教，和普遍观点相悖的说法：a **controversial or unorthodox opinion** or doctrine, departure from a generally accepted theory, opinion, or practice

例 the heresy of asserting that Shakespeare was not a great writer 声称莎士比亚不是伟大作家的非主流观点

近 dissent, dissidence, heterodoxy, nonconformity

反 dogma, conformity, orthodoxy 正教，正统

heretical [həˈretɪkl]

【考法】 *adj.* 异教的，异端邪说的：**departure** from established beliefs or **standards**

例 The belief that women should be allowed to have careers outside the home was once considered heretical. 女人应该拥有自己的事业这一观点一度被认为是异端邪说。

近 heterodox, nonconformist, unconventional, unorthodox

反 conforming, conformist, conventional, orthodox 正统的

hermetic [hɜːrˈmetɪk]

【考法】 *adj.* 深奥的：relating to or characterized by occultism or **abstruseness**

例 wrote hermetic poetry 写晦涩难懂的诗歌

近 abstruse, arcane, esoteric, recondite

反 easily comprehended, shallow, superficial 容易理解的，肤浅的

hesitance [ˈhezɪtəns]

【考法】 *n.* 犹豫，不情愿：the quality or state of being **hesitant**, **reluctance**

例 Sales figures for the month were up, as consumers began to overcome their hesitance about purchasing big-ticket items. 月销售额有所上涨，因为消费者对于大件商品的购买由观望转向消费。

近 faltering, indecision, irresolution, vacillation, wavering, wobbling

反 alacrity, impetuosity, inclination, willingness 冲动，乐意

Unit 3

■ HETERODOX	■ HIDEBOUND	■ HIDEOUS	■ HIE	■ HIKE
■ HILARIOUS	■ HISTRIONIC	■ HIVE	■ HOARD	■ HOARY

heterodox [ˈhetərədɑːks]

【考法】 *adj.* 非正统的，异端的：holding **unorthodox opinions** or doctrines, not rigidly following established form, custom, or rules

例 Her heterodox approach to teaching science initially met with some resistance from her peers. 她对于教学的一些非正统方法最开始受到了同辈的抵触。

近 dissenting, out-there, unconventional, unorthodox

反 conforming, conventional, orthodox, regular, routine 正常的，正统的

hidebound [ˈhaɪdbaʊnd]

【考法】 *adj.* 死板的，极度保守的：**tending to favor** established ideas, conditions, or institutions

例 The hidebound innkeeper refused to see the need for a Web site. 死板的旅店老板坚决不肯装宽带。

近 archconservative, brassbound, die-hard, old-fashioned, standpat, ultraconservative

反 broad-minded, large-minded, liberal, nonconservative, nonconventional, nonorthodox, nontraditional, open-minded, progressive 进步的，开放包容的

hideous [ˈhɪdɪəs]

【考法】 *adj.* 非常丑陋的：exceedingly **ugly**

例 The old man wore a hideous Halloween mask that made the kids all jump with fright. 老头戴着一个丑陋的万圣节面具，把小孩子全都吓跑了。

近 homely, ill-favored, monstrous, uncomely, unsightly

反 pulchritudinous, aesthetic, attractive, comely, gorgeous, handsome, knockout, ravishing, seemly, stunning, taking, well-favored 美丽的，有吸引力的

派 hideousness *n.* 丑陋

反 affinity 吸引力

hie [haɪ]

【考法】 *vi.* 匆匆忙忙：to go quickly, **hasten**

例 We had best hie home before the rain gets worse. 我们最好在雨下大之前赶快回家。

近 bustle, dash, hustle, scoot, scurry, scuttle, shoot, trot

反 dawdle, crawl, creep, poke 闲荡，爬行

hike [haɪk]

【考法】 *v.* (使)上涨：to (cause to) **rise up**, to move from a lower **to a higher place or position**

例 hike rents 涨租金

近 boost, elevate, heighten, hoist, upraise

反 backset, drop, lower 使倒退，下降

hilarious [hɪˈleriəs]

【考法】 *adj.* 非常好笑的：marked by or causing hilarity: **extremely funny**

例 hilarious cartoons that the whole family can enjoy 适合全家观看的搞笑动画片

近 hysterical, ludicrous, ridiculous, screaming, sidesplitting, uproarious

反 humorless, lame, unamusing, uncomic, unfunny 不好笑的

histrionic [ˌhɪstriˈɑːnɪk]

【考法】 *adj.* 戏剧的；演员的：of or **relating to actors**, acting, or the theater

例 a penchant for dish throwing, door slamming, and other histrionic displays of temper 有倾向做出一些砸盘子、摔门和其他一些电视剧里的经典生气动作

近 melodramatic, operatic, stagy, theatrical

反 undramatic 平淡无奇的

hive [haɪv]

【考法 1】 *n.* 忙碌之地：a place swarming with **activity**

例 The house was a hive of activity as we prepared for the party. 我们筹备派对时，房子里很是熙熙攘攘。

【考法 2】 *v.* 储备，积累：to **store up**; accumulate

hoard [hɔːrd]

【考法】 *v.* 贮藏，秘藏：to **keep hidden** or private

例 He's been hoarding empty yogurt containers all winter. 他整个冬天都在攒空酸奶瓶。

近 cache, stash, stockpile, store, squirrel, stockpile

反 lavish 挥霍

hoary [ˈhɔːri]

【考法】 *adj.* 极老的：**extremely old**

例 hoary legends 上古的传说故事

近 aged, antique, dateless, immemorial, antediluvian

反 modern, new, recent 新的

Unit 4

■ HOAX	■ HODGEPODGE	■ HOMAGE	■ HOMELY	■ HOMILY
■ HOMOGENIZE	■ HONE	■ HOODWINK	■ HORTATIVE	■ HOVEL

hoax [hoʊks]

【考法】 *n./vt.* 欺骗：to **cause to believe** what is **untrue**

例 a skilled forger who hoaxed the art world into believing that the paintings were long-lost Ve:meers 一个老道的骗子成功让艺术界相信那些画作是遗失多年的维米尔的真迹

近 bamboozle, beguile, bluff, con, cozen, delude, dupe, fake out, gull, hoodwink, take in

hodgepodge	[ˈhɑːdʒpɑːdʒ]

【考法】 *n.* 大杂烩：a **mixture** of **dissimilar** ingredients; a jumble

例 a hodgepodge of styles 混搭风格 ‖ The exhibit was a hodgepodge of mediocre art, bad art, and really bad art. 整场展览就是中庸、烂和非常烂的艺术作品的大杂烩。

近 agglomeration, assortment, collage, medley, mishmash, pastiche, potpourri

homage	[ˈhɑːmɪdʒ]

【考法】 *n.* 尊敬，敬意：expression of high regard: **respect**

例 Homage to Catalonia 向加泰罗尼亚致敬

近 commendation, eulogy, hymn, paean, panegyric, salutation, tribute, dithyramb

反 disrespect 不尊敬

homely	[ˈhoʊmli]

【考法】 *adj.* 其貌不扬的，朴素简单的：**not attractive** or good-looking

例 homely truth 朴素的真理

近 hideous, unappealing, unattractive, uncomely, unsightly

反 pulchritudinous, aesthetic, attractive, beautiful, comely, gorgeous, handsome, knockout, lovely, pretty, ravishing, seemly, sightly, stunning, taking, well-favored 美丽的

homily	[ˈhɑːməli]

【考法】 *n.* 冗长乏味的道德讲演或训诫：a tedious moralizing lecture or **admonition**

例 a TV movie filled with the usual hokey homilies about people triumphing over life's adversities 一档说教性质的、充满了介绍逆境中的人们如何成就自我的电视节目

近 banality, bromide, chestnut, cliché, groaner, platitude, shibboleth

homogenize	[həˈmɑːdʒənaɪz]

【考法】 *vt.* 使统一化：to **make agree** with a **single established standard** or model

例 plans to homogenize the science curriculum in public high schools throughout the state 计划将全州的公立高中的课程安排统一化

近 formalize, normalize, regularize

hone	[hoʊn]

【考法】 *vt.* 磨快：to **sharpen** or smooth with a whetstone

例 hone the knife's blade to razor-like sharpness 把小刀磨得像剃刀一样锋利 ‖ He honed his crossword-puzzle skills by reading the dictionary. 他通过背字典把填词游戏的水平练得炉火纯青。

近 edge, grind, strop, whet

反 blunt, dull 弄钝

hoodwink	[ˈhʊdwɪŋk]

【考法】 *vt.* 欺骗：to take in by **deceptive** means; deceive

例 Don't let yourself be hoodwinked into buying things you don't need. 别被忽悠着去买用不着的东西。

近 beguile, con, delude, dupe, fool, hoax, humbug

反 disabuse 消除…的错误念头

hortative	[ˈhɔːrtətɪv]

【考法】 *adj.* 鼓励的：giving **exhortation**

hovel	[ˈhʌvl]

【考法】 *n.* 茅屋：a **small**, **wretched**, and often **dirty** house

近 cabin, camp, hooch, hut, hutch, hutment, shanty

Unit 5

■ HUBRIS	■ HUMBLE	■ HUMILITY	■ HUMOR	■ HURRICANE
■ HUSBAND	■ HUSK	■ HUSKY	■ HYBRID	■ HYMN

hubris	[ˈhjuːbrɪs]

【考法】 *n.* 狂妄自大：**exaggerated pride** or **self-confidence**

例 His failure was brought on by his hubris. 就是他的狂妄自大才导致了失败。

反 humility 谦逊

humble ['hʌmbl]

【考法 1】 *adj.* 谦逊的：marked by **meekness** or **modesty** in behavior, attitude, or spirit; not arrogant or prideful

例 a medical scientist who remained remarkably humble even after winning the Nobel Prize 获得诺贝尔奖之后仍然保持谦逊的医学家

近 modest, unassuming, unpretentious, demure, down-to-earth

反 arrogant, bumptious, conceited, egotistic, haughty, high-and-mighty, imperious, lordly, overweening, peremptory, pompous, presuming, presumptuous, pretentious, self-assertive, supercilious, superior, toplofty, uppish, uppity 傲慢的

【考法 2】 *adj.* 顺从的，谦卑的：showing, expressing, or offered in a spirit of **humility or unseemly submissiveness**

例 Please accept my humble thanks. 请接受我的卑微的感谢。

近 base, humble, menial, servile, slavish

humility [hju:'mɪləti]

【考法】 *n.* 谦卑，谦逊：the **absence of any feelings** of being **better** than others

例 Haughtiness invites disaster; humility receives benefit. 满招损，谦受益。

近 demureness, humbleness, lowliness, meekness, modesty

反 arrogance, assumption, bumptiousness, hauteur, pomposity, presumption, superciliousness 傲慢，自大

humor ['hju:mə]

【考法 1】 *n.* 幽默，令人发笑的事物：something that is or is designed to be **comical or amusing**

例 The speech is full of wit and humor. 演讲妙趣横生。

近 comedy, comic, drollery, drollness, funniness, hilariousness

反 pathos 令人伤感的事物

【考法 2】 *vt.* 迎合，迁就：to **comply with** the wishes or ideas of

例 Parents need to know how to humor kids when they are upset. 父母需要知道当孩子烦躁的时候怎么哄孩子。

近 cater, gratify, indulge

hurricane ['hɜːrəkən]

【考法 1】 *n.* 飓风：a **violent rotating storm** or system of winds

例 The hurricane struck the coast early today. 飓风今晨袭击了海岸。

近 storm, typhoon

反 calm 风平浪静

【考法 2】 *n.* 飓风般的事物，引起动荡的事物：something **resembling a hurricane** especially in its turmoil

例 economic news that unleashed a hurricane on the trading floor 在交易大厅掀起轩然大波的经济新闻

近 disturbance, furor, pandemonium, tumult, turmoil, uproar

husband ['hʌzbənd]

【考法】 *vt.* 节俭，勤俭持家：to **use** sparingly or **economically**

例 Husbanding precious resources was part of rural life. 节俭使用珍贵的资源是农村生活的一部分。

近 budget, conserve, economize

反 dissipate, lavish, prodigalize, squander, waste 挥霍，浪费

派 husbandly *adj.* 节俭的；husbandry *n.* 节俭

husk [hʌsk]

【考法 1】 *n.* (果类或谷物的)外壳：a usually dry or membranous **outer covering** (as a pod or one composed of bracts) of various seeds and fruits (as barley and corn)

例 a grey squirrel nibbling on a peanut husk 一个啃着花生壳的灰松鼠

近 bark, chaff, hull, shell

反 core, kernel 核

【考法 2】 *vt.* 剥去：to **remove** the natural covering of

例 the tedious task of husking coconuts 无聊的任务——剥椰子

近 bark, flay, hull, shell, shuck, skin

husky ['hʌski]

【考法 1】 *adj.* (尤指声音)沙哑的，粗糙的：hoarse or **rough** in quality

例 a voice husky with emotion 富有感情的沙哑声音

近 coarse, grating, gravelly, harsh, rasping, rusty, scratchy, throaty

反 mellifluous (声音)甜蜜的，甜美的

【考法 2】 *adj.* 高大威猛的：big and **muscular**

例 a very husky young man, built like a football player 一个体格像橄榄球运动员一样的高大的男孩

近 beefy, burly, hefty, muscular, powerful, strapping, rugged

反 dwarf 矮小的

hybrid [ˈhaɪbrɪd]

【考法 1】 n. 杂交品种，混合品种：something of **mixed origin** or composition

例 a hybrid of medieval and Renaissance styles 中世纪和文艺复兴的混搭风

近 amalgam, bastard, compound, mixture, mule

【考法 2】 adj. 杂交的：being offspring produced by **parents of different races**, breeds, species, or genera

例 a hybrid rose called "American Beauty" 一种被称为"美国丽人"的杂交玫瑰

近 crossbred, mongrel

反 purebred 纯种的

hymn [hɪm]

【考法 1】 n. 赞歌，赞美诗：a **song of praise** or joy

例 They sang a hymn of praise to God. 他们唱赞歌赞美上帝。

近 eulogy, homage, hymn, ode, paean, panegyric, psalm, salutation, tribute

反 dirge, elegy 哀诗，挽歌

【考法 2】 v. 赞美：to **proclaim the glory** of

例 During the honeymoon following the inauguration, newspaper articles seemed to hymn the president's every move. 在上任后的"蜜月期"之中，报纸新闻似乎在赞美总统的每一项措施。

近 bless, carol, celebrate, emblazon, exalt, extol, glorify, laud, magnify, resound

反 blame, censure, reprehend, reprobate 责难，斥责

Unit 6

| ■ HYPERBOLE | ■ HYPNOTIC | ■ HYPOCRITICAL | ■ ICONOCLAST | ■ IDOLATRIZE |
| ■ IDYLL | ■ IGNITE | ■ IGNOMINY | ■ ILLITERACY | ■ ILLUMINATI |

hyperbole [haɪˈpɜːrbəli]

【考法】 n. 夸张：a figure of speech in which **exaggeration** is **used for emphasis** or effect

例 The debate was carried on with increasing rhetorical hyperbole. 随着辩论的进行，双方修辞当中的夸张越来越多。

近 coloring, embellishment, embroidering, exaggeration, magnification, overstatement

反 understatement 有节制的陈述

hypnotic [hɪpˈnɑːtɪk]

【考法】 adj. 催眠的：tending to **cause sleep**

例 Her eyes soon grew heavy from the hypnotic rhythm of the train's wheels. 伴随着催眠的铁轨声，她很快就有了睡意。

近 drowsy, narcotic, opiate, sleepy, slumberous, soporific

反 stimulating 刺激性的；refreshing 使人精神焕发的

hypocritical [ˌhɪpəˈkrɪtɪkl]

【考法】 adj. 虚伪的：**not being** or expressing **what one appears to be** or express

例 It's hypocritical to say mean things behind someone's back, and then to act nice when you want something from her. 这种在背后说别人坏话、而有求于人时又装出另一副样子的人就是虚伪。

近 artificial, backhanded, feigned, mealy-mouthed, phony, pretended, unctuous

反 artless, candid, genuine, honest, sincere, undesigning, unfeigned 真诚的，诚实的

派 hypocrite n. 虚伪的人，伪君子

iconoclast [aɪˈkɑːnəklæst]

【考法】 n. 特立独行的人：a person who does **not conform** to generally **accepted standards** or customs

例 He was an iconoclast who refused to be bound by tradition. 他是个不愿被传统所束缚的叛逆者。

近 bohemian, deviant, heretic, maverick, non-conformer

反 conformer, conformist 循规蹈矩的人

派 iconoclastic adj. 特立独行的

idolatrize [aɪˈdɑːlətraɪz]

【考法】 vt. (通常盲目)崇拜：**admires intensely** and often blindly

例 Some teenagers idolatrized Hitler more than their own parents. 曾经有一些青少年崇拜希特勒超过自己的父母。

近 adore, adulate, canonize, deify, dote, worship

反 abhor, abominate, detest, dislike, hate, loathe 痛恨，憎恶

派 idolatry n. 崇拜

idyll ['aɪdl]

【考法】 *n.* 无忧无虑的生活：a **carefree episode** or experience

例 a summer idyll on the coast of the Mediterranean 地中海岸的悠闲夏日

近 frisk, frolic, gambol, revel, lark

ignite [ɪg'naɪt]

【考法1】 *vt.* 点燃：to cause to burn; to **set fire to**

例 The bombs ignited a fire which destroyed some 60 houses. 炸弹引发的大火摧毁了大约 60 间房屋。

近 enkindle, fire, inflame, kindle, light, torch

反 douse, extinguish, quench, put out 熄灭

【考法2】 *vt.* 激起，唤起（感情等）：to **arouse the passions** of

例 The insults ignited my anger. 那些侮辱让我倍感愤怒。

近 arouse, incite, instigate, pique, spark, stimulate, stir

反 appease, assuage, calm, conciliate, mollify, pacify, placate, propitiate, soothe 平息怒火，安抚

ignominy ['ɪgnəmɪni]

【考法】 *n.* 耻辱：the state of having **lost the esteem** of others

例 He spent the remainder of his life in ignominy after being involved in a bribery scandal. 因为卷入了受贿丑闻当中，他在耻辱中度过余生。

近 discredit, disesteem, dishonor, disrepute, infamy, obloquy, odium, opprobrium, reproach, shame

反 glory, honor 荣耀；esteem, respect 敬意

派 ignominious *adj.* 可鄙的

illiteracy [ɪ'lɪtərəsi]

【考法】 *n.* 文盲：the condition of being **unable to read and write**

例 a nationwide campaign against illiteracy 全国扫盲运动

近 ignorance

反 learning, literacy 受过教育

派 illiterate *adj.* 不识字的

illuminati [ɪ,luːmiː'nɑːtiː]

【考法1】 *n.* 智者：persons who claim to be unusually **enlightened**

近 clerisy, intellectual, intelligentsia, literati

反 fool, dolt, dullard, idiot, simpleton 傻子

【考法2】 *n.* 精英：individuals carefully selected as being the **best of a class**

例 a book launching party to which only New York's cultural illuminati were invited 一个只邀请了纽约上层文化精英的新书发布会

近 aristocracy, elite, upper crust

Unit 7

| ■ ILLUMINATE | ■ ILLUSORY | ■ IMBIBE | ■ IMBROGLIO | ■ IMITATION |
| ■ IMMACULATE | ■ IMMANENT | ■ IMMATERIAL | ■ IMMATURE | ■ IMMEMORIAL |

illuminate [ɪ'luːmɪneɪt]

【考法1】 *vt.* 照明：to **make** luminous or **shining**

例 illuminate with a spotlight 用聚光灯照亮

近 bathe, beacon, emblaze, illume, illumine, irradiate, lighten

反 blacken, darken, obfuscate 使黯淡，使昏暗

【考法2】 *vt.* 阐明：to **make plain** or understandable

例 Roosevelt's New Deal illuminates what the role of government is in Keynesian Economics. 罗斯福新政阐明了政府在凯恩斯主义中的作用。

近 clarify, clear, construe, demonstrate, demystify, elucidate, explicate, expound, illustrate, interpret

反 obscure 使费解

【考法3】 *vt.* 启迪，启发：to provide（someone）with moral or **spiritual understanding**

例 how man is illuminated by a higher spirit 人们是如何被更高境界的思想开化的

近 edify, educate, enlighten, inspire, nurture

反 confuse, perplex, puzzle 使困惑

派 illumination *n.* 照明；启迪

illusory [ɪˈluːsəri]

【考法】 *adj.* 幻觉的，虚幻的：produced by, based on, or having the nature of an **illusion**

例 the illusory definition of nationhood 国家的虚幻定义

近 chimerical, fanciful, fantastic, fictional, fictitious, imaginary, suppositious, unreal

反 factual 事实的

派 illusion *n.* 幻觉

imbibe [ɪmˈbaɪb]

【考法】 *v.* 喝水，摄取水分：to **take in** (something **liquid**) through small openings

例 Plants can imbibe water through their roots. 植物可以通过它们的根摄取水分。

近 drink, guzzle, hoist, quaff, sip, sponge

反 urinate 排尿

imbroglio [ɪmˈbroʊlioʊ]

【考法 1】 *n.* 困境，复杂的局面：an intricate or **complicated situation**

例 What investor would willingly become involved in this imbroglio? 怎样的投资者才会像这样明知山有虎，偏向虎山行呢？

近 complexity, complication, embarrassment, entanglement, involvement, misunderstanding, quandary

【考法 2】 *n.* 纷争：an often noisy or **angry expression of differing opinions**

例 an imbroglio involving some big names in the entertainment industry 一场涉及娱乐圈数位明星的纷争

近 altercation, controversy, disagreement, dispute, fight, quarrel, squabble, wrangle

反 harmony 和谐

imitation [ˌɪmɪˈteɪʃn]

【考法】 *n.* 仿制品：something that is made to look exactly **like something else**

例 She usually wore imitations of her costly jewels. 她通常只戴她那些贵重珠宝的仿制品。

近 clone, copy, dupe, duplication, facsimile, mock, reduplication, replica, replication, reproduction

反 archetype, original, prototype 原型

派 imitating *adj.* 仿制的

immaculate [ɪˈmækjələt]

【考法 1】 *adj.* 干净的，纯净的：**free from dirt** or stain; free from any trace of the coarse or indecent

例 an immaculate soul 一个纯净的灵魂

近 antiseptic, chaste, clean, decent, modest, pristine, pure, spotless, stainless, virgin

反 coarse, indecent, obscene, vulgar 粗俗的，下流的；besmirched, dirty, filthy, foul, spotted, stained, sullied 有污点的，不干净的

【考法 2】 *adj.* 完美的，没有任何错误的：being entirely **without fault** or flaw

例 an immaculate rendering of the Queen of the Night 's aria《魔笛之夜后》咏叹调的完美演绎

近 absolute, faultless, flawless, impeccable, indefectible, irreproachable, perfect, seamless, unblemished

反 amiss, defective, faulty, flawed, imperfect 有错误的，有误差的

immanent [ˈɪmənənt]

【考法】 *adj.* 内在的：being a part of the **innermost** nature of a person or thing

例 Beauty is not something imposed but something immanent. 美丽是内在的品格而非外加的东西。

近 constitutional, essential, inborn, inbred, indigenous, ingrained, innate, integral, intrinsic, natural

反 adventitious, extrinsic, extraneous 外在的，非本源的

immaterial [ˌɪməˈtɪriəl]

【考法 1】 *adj.* 非实体的：**not composed of matter**

例 It is only possible to study immaterial forces like gravity by observing their effects on the physical world. 要研究那些非实体的作用力，例如万有引力，只能观察它们对于现实世界的影响。

近 ethereal, formless, incorporeal, insubstantial, nonmaterial, spiritual

反 bodily, corporeal, material, physical, substantial 实体的

【考法 2】 *adj.* 无关的，不重要的：of **no** importance or **relevance**

例 While undoubtedly upsetting, that story is immaterial to the question of why you are late. 尽管那个故事的确很让人遗憾，但是和你为什么迟到没有半点关系。

近 extraneous, impertinent, inapplicable, inapposite, irrelevant

反 applicable, apposite, apropos, germane, pertinent, relevant 相关的；crucial, important, significant 重要的

immature [ˌɪməˈtʃʊr]

【考法 1】 *adj.* 未完全发展的，未发育成熟的：**lacking complete growth**, differentiation, or development

例 Immature frogs are called "tadpoles". 未发育成熟的青蛙被称为"蝌蚪"。

近 adolescent, juvenile, youngish, youthful

【考法2】 *adj.* (思维、举止)不够成熟的：**lacking** in adult experience or **maturity**

例 Many high school students are still too immature to foresee the consequences of their actions. 很多高中生还是不够成熟，不能意识到他们的行为所带来的后果。

近 green, inexperienced, puerile, raw, unfledged, unripe

反 adult, experienced, mature, ripe 成年的，成熟的

immemorial [ˌɪməˈmɔːriəl]

【考法】 *adj.* 古老的：dating or surviving **from the distant past**

例 a modern version of an immemorial myth 一个远古传说的现代版本

近 aged, age-old, antediluvian, antique, dateless, hoary, old, venerable

反 contemporary, modern 当代的，现代的；recent 近来的

Unit 8

■ IMMUNE	■ IMMURE	■ IMMUTABLE	■ IMPASSIVE	■ IMPECCABLE
■ IMPECUNIOUS	■ IMPEDE	■ IMPENDING	■ IMPENETRABLE	■ IMPENITENT

immune [ɪˈmjuːn]

【考法1】 *adj.* 不易被感染的，有免疫力的：of, relating to, or **having resistance to infection**

例 The blood test will tell whether you are immune to the disease. 验血可以判断你是否对这种疾病免疫。

近 resistant

反 susceptible, vulnerable 易感染的，易受攻击的

派 immunity *n.* 免疫性

【考法2】 *adj.* 不受影响的：**not affected by** a given **influence**

例 immune to persuasion 不听劝

近 insusceptible, unaffected, unresponsive

反 ductile, pliable, pliant, yielding 易受影响的

【考法3】 *adj.* 不受约束的，免除的：**not subject to an obligation** imposed on others

例 immune from taxation 免税

近 exempt, free

反 liable, responsible 负有责任的

immure [ɪˈmjʊr]

【考法】 *vt.* 监禁，禁闭；使闭门不出：to **confine** within or as if within walls

例 immure oneself for GRE 闭门苦读 GRE

近 confine, constrain, incarcerate, intern, jail, imprison

反 discharge, release 释放；enfranchise, free, liberate 解放

immutable [ɪˈmjuːtəbl]

【考法】 *adj.* 不可变的：**not capable of changing** or being changed

例 One of the immutable laws of television is that low ratings inevitably lead to cancellation. 电视行业中一个不变的原则就是：低收视率的节目必然会被撤掉。

近 constant, fixed, inalterable, inflexible, invariable, unalterable, unchangeable

反 alterable, changeable, elastic, flexible, mutable, variable 可变的

派 immutability *n.* 不变性

impassive [ɪmˈpæsɪv]

【考法】 *adj.* 冷漠的，无感情的：giving **no sign of feeling** or emotion

例 She remained impassive as the officers informed her of her son's death. 她面不改色地听着警官宣读她儿子的死讯。

近 affectless, apathetic, cold-blooded, deadpan, emotionless, numb, phlegmatic, stoic, undemonstrative

反 demonstrative, emotional, fervent, fervid, impassioned, passionate, vehement 充满感情的

impeccable [ɪmˈpekəbl]

【考法1】 *adj.* 无罪的：**free from sin**, guilt or blame

例 the belief that there can be no such thing as an impeccable soul 不相信存在无罪的灵魂

近 blameless, clear, guiltless, inculpable, pure, sinless

反 guilty, sinful 有罪的

【考法2】 *adj.* 无瑕的，无可挑剔的：**free from fault** or blame

例 She had impeccable taste in clothes. 她有着无可挑剔的穿衣品味。

近 absolute, faultless, flawless, immaculate, indefectible, irreproachable, perfect, seamless, unblemished

反 amiss, defective, faulty, flawed, imperfect 有错误的，有误差的

impecunious [ˌɪmpɪˈkjuːniəs]

【考法】 *adj.* 贫穷的：having very little or **no money**

例 They were so impecunious that they couldn't afford to give one another even token Christmas gifts. 他们穷到了连象征性的圣诞礼物都互送不起的地步。

近 beggared, destitute, impoverished, indigent, necessitous, needy, penniless, penurious, threadbare

反 affluent, flush, opulent, rich, wealthy 富有的

impede [ɪmˈpiːd]

【考法】 *vt.* 妨碍，阻碍：to interfere with or **slow the progress of**

例 Storms at sea impeded our expedition. 海上的风暴阻碍了我们的远征。

近 clog, embarrass, encumber, fetter, hinder, inhibit, obstruct, retard, shackle, stymie, trammel

反 aid, assist, facilitate, help 促进，帮助

派 impediment *n.* 障碍，阻碍

impending [ɪmˈpendɪŋ]

【考法】 *adj.* 即将发生的：being **soon to** appear or **take place**

例 an impending celebration of the 100th anniversary of the college's founding 即将来临的百年校庆

近 approaching, coming, imminent, nearing, pending, proximate, upcoming, around the corner

反 late, recent 最近发生的；distant, remote 遥远的

impenetrable [ɪmˈpenɪtrəbl]

【考法 1】 *adj.* 不可渗透的，不可穿透的：**impossible to get through** or into

例 The ancient temple was surrounded by vast stretches of impenetrable jungle. 包围着古老的神庙的是密不可穿的灌木丛。

近 impassable, impermeable, impervious, impregnable

反 passable, penetrable, permeable, pervious 可通过的

【考法 2】 *adj.* 难以理解的：**incapable of being comprehended**

例 The textbook's language is completely impenetrable, at least to me. 至少在我看来，这个教材就是天书。

近 arcane, cryptic, enigmatic, incomprehensible, inscrutable, unfathomable, ungraspable, unintelligible

反 fathomable, intelligible, understandable 可以理解的

impenitent [ɪmˈpenɪtənt]

【考法】 *adj.* 不悔悟的：**not** feeling or expressing humble or **regretful** pain or sorrow for sins or offenses

例 remain impenitent about her criminal past 对她过去所犯罪行执迷不悟

近 remorseless, regretless, shameless, unashamed, unrepentant

反 contrite, regretful, remorseful, rueful, penitent 感到悔恨的

Unit 9

■ IMPERATIVE　　■ IMPERIAL　　■ IMPERIOUS　　■ IMPERTINENT　　■ IMPERTURBABLE
■ IMPERVIOUS　　■ IMPETUOUS　　■ IMPIOUS　　■ IMPLACABLE　　■ IMPLEMENT

imperative [ɪmˈperətɪv]

【考法 1】 *n.* 命令：a statement of what to do that **must be obeyed** by those concerned

例 a secretary of defense who was fond of issuing harshly worded imperatives 一个很喜欢发布措辞严厉的命令的国防部长

近 command, decree, dictate, direction, directive, instruction, order, word

【考法 2】 *adj.* 命令的，强制性的：**forcing one's compliance** or participation by or as if by law

例 requests that grew more and more imperative 命令性越来越强的请求

近 compulsory, forced, involuntary, obligatory, peremptory, required

反 optional 可选择的；voluntary 志愿性的

【考法 3】 *adj.* 迫切的：**needing immediate attention**

例 an imperative need for medical supplies in the earthquake-ravaged country 地震灾区国家对于医疗物资的迫切需求

近 clamant, compelling, critical, crying, emergent, exigent, imperious, importunate, pressing, urgent

反 noncritical, unimportant 不重要的

【考法 4】 *adj.* 必要的：**impossible to do without**

例 Proper equipment is imperative for the success of this chemical experiment. 合适的仪器是这个化学实验成功必不可少的条件。

近 indispensable, necessary, necessitous, requisite, vital

反 dispensable, inessential, needless, unnecessary 非必须的

imperial [ɪmˈpɪriəl]

【考法 1】 *adj.* 帝国的，帝王的：of, relating to, or suggestive of an **empire** or a sovereign, especially an emperor or empress

例 Imperial College London 帝国理工学院

近 kingly, queenly, regal, royal

【考法 2】 *adj.* 巨大的，令人惊叹的：large and **impressive in size**, grandeur, extent, or conception

例 People envisioned an imperial city that would rival the capitals of Europe for beauty and magnificence. 人们幻想着一个比欧洲各国首都更为动人和壮丽的巨大城市。

近 august, epic, glorious, grand, imposing, magnificent, monumental, noble, splendid

反 common, humble, inferior, low 低下的，平凡的

imperious [ɪmˈpɪriəs]

【考法 1】 *adj.* 爱发号施令的：fond of **ordering people** around

例 an imperious little boy who liked to tell the other scouts what to do 一个爱发号施令的小男孩，总是喜欢指挥别的童子军做事

近 authoritarian, autocratic, despotic, dictatorial, domineering, masterful, tyrannical

【考法 2】 *adj.* 傲慢的，专横的：**arrogantly domineering** or overbearing

例 an imperious movie star who thinks she's some sort of goddess 一个把自己当成某种女神的傲慢的影星

近 arrogant, bumptious, haughty, lofty, lordly, peremptory, pompous, presumptuous, supercilious, superior

反 humble, lowly, modest 谦逊的

【考法 3】 *adj.* 迫切的：intensely **compelling**

例 As war casualties mounted, the need for trained nurses became imperious. 随着战争伤亡人数的攀升，对于受训护士的需求变得愈发迫切。

近 clamant, compelling, critical, crying, dire, emergent, exigent, imperative, importunate, pressing, urgent

反 noncritical, unimportant 不重要的

impertinent [ɪmˈpɜːrtnənt]

【考法 1】 *adj.* 无关紧要的：**not having** a clear decisive **relevance** to the matter in hand

例 Your résumé needlessly lists extracurricular experiences that are impertinent to the PhD program for which you are applying. 你的简历里列出的一些课外活动和你申请的博士项目是毫不相关的。

近 extraneous, immaterial, inapplicable, inapposite, irrelevant

反 germane, pertinent, relevant 相关的；crucial, important, significant 重要的

【考法 2】 *adj.* 粗鲁无礼的，大胆的：given to or characterized by **insolent rudeness**

例 I don't like strangers who ask impertinent questions. 我很讨厌那些问无礼问题的陌生人。

近 audacious, bold, brash, brassbound, brassy, brazen, impudent, insolent

反 meek, mousy, retiring, shy, timid 内敛的，胆小的

【考法 3】 *adj.* 不守礼节的，不为他人着想的：showing a **lack of manners** or consideration for others

例 impertinent salesmen who telephone people during the dinner hour 在就餐时间打电话骚扰别人的无礼销售员

近 discourteous, disrespectful, inconsiderate, rude, thoughtless

反 civil, courteous, genteel, gracious, mannerly, polite 有礼貌的；considerate 为他人着想的

imperturbable [ˌɪmpərˈtɜːrbəbl]

【考法】 *adj.* 沉着冷静的，淡定的：marked by **extreme calm**, impassivity, and steadiness

例 The chef was absolutely imperturbable—even when the kitchen caught on fire. 这个厨师可谓淡定到了极致——他连厨房着火的时候都依然沉着。

近 collected, composed, cool, disimpassioned, nonchalant, unflappable, unruffled

反 choleric, touchy 暴躁的，易怒的

impervious [ɪmˈpɜːrviəs]

【考法 1】 *adj.* 不可渗透的，不可穿透的：**not allowing entrance** or passage

例 The material for this coat is supposed to be impervious to rain. 这件大衣的材料应该是能防雨的。

近 impassable, impenetrable, impermeable, impregnable

反 passable, penetrable, permeable, pervious 可渗透的

【考法 2】 *adj.* 不能被破坏的：**not capable of being damaged** or harmed

例 a carpet impervious to rough treatment 耐用的地毯

近 bulletproof, imperishable, indestructible, inextinguishable, invulnerable

反 delicate, sensitive, vulnerable 脆弱的，敏感的

【考法 3】 *adj.* 不为所动的：**not capable of being affected** or disturbed

例 These sailors are impervious to fear. 这些水手无所畏惧。

近 immune, insusceptible, unaffected, unresponsive

反 ductile, pliable, pliant, yielding 易受影响的

177

impetuous [ɪmˈpetʃuəs]

【考法 1】 *adj.* 冲动的，性急的，轻率的：marked by **impulsive vehemence** or passion

例 He is young and impetuous. 他年轻冲动。

近 ardent, hasty, headlong, impassioned, impulsive, passionate, rash, vehement

反 cautious, circumspect, wary 谨慎的，小心的

【考法 2】 *adj.* 剧烈的，猛烈的：marked by force and **violence of movement** or action

例 an impetuous wind 猛烈的风

近 abrupt, hasty, hurried, precipitate, precipitous, rushing, sudden, violent

反 calm, halcyon, placid, quiet 风平浪静的

派 impetus *n.* 推动力

impious [ˈɪmpiəs]

【考法】 *adj.* 不敬神的：**lacking reverence** for holy or sacred matters

例 make impious remarks about the church 对教会做出不敬的评论

近 blasphemous, irreverent, profane, sacrilegious

反 pious 虔诚的；reverent 敬神的

派 impiety *n.* (对神的)不敬

implacable [ɪmˈplækəbl]

【考法 1】 *adj.* 固执的：**sticking to an opinion**, purpose, or course of action in spite of reason, arguments, or persuasion

近 adamant, dogged, headstrong, intransigent, mulish, obdurate, pertinacious, stubborn, unyielding

反 acquiescent 默认的；compliant, flexible, pliable, pliant, yielding 易受影响的

【考法 2】 *adj.* 无法平息的：**not capable of being appeased**, significantly changed, or mitigated

例 an implacable enemy 无法与之和解的敌人

近 determined, grim, relentless, unappeasable

反 placable 可平息的，可缓和的

implement [ˈɪmplɪmənt]

【考法 1】 *n.* 工具：a **device** used in the performance of a task

例 gardening implements such as hoes, spades, and pruners 诸如锄头、铲子和修枝剪一类的园艺工具

近 apparatus, device, instrument, tool, utensil

【考法 2】 *vt.* 执行，实施：to put into practical effect; **carry out**

例 implement the new online application procedures 实行新的网申程序

近 administer, apply, effect, enforce, execute, invoke, perform

反 cancel, repeal, rescind, revoke 撤销

派 implementation *n.* 执行，履行

Unit 10

■ IMPLODE	■ IMPORTUNE	■ IMPOSING	■ IMPOSTOR	■ IMPOTENT
■ IMPRECISE	■ IMPROMPTU	■ IMPROVISE	■ IMPRUDENT	■ IMPUDENT

implode [ɪmˈpləʊd]

【考法】 *v.* (使)剧烈收缩，(使)坍缩，(使)内爆：to (cause to) **collapse inward** violently

例 The flask imploded during the vacuum distilling. 做低压蒸馏的时候烧瓶发生了内爆。

近 buckle, founder, tumble, yield

反 explode 外爆，爆炸

importune [ˌɪmpɔːrˈtuːn]

【考法】 *vt.* 恳求，迫切请求：to make a request to (someone) in an earnest or **urgent manner**

例 beggars importuning passers-by 在恳求着过路人的乞丐

近 appeal, beseech, besiege, conjure, entreat, impetrate, implore, petition, plead, pray, solicit, supplicate

反 demand 要求，强求

imposing [ɪmˈpəʊzɪŋ]

【考法】 *adj.* 宏伟壮丽的：**impressive** in size, bearing, dignity, or grandeur

例 The corporation's imposing headquarters were designed by one of the nation's cutting-edge architects. 这家公司宏伟壮丽的总部是由该国最优秀的建筑师之一设计的。

近 august, epic, glorious, grand, imperial, magnificent, monumental, noble, splendid

反 common, humble, inferior, low 低下的，平凡的

impostor	[ɪmˈpɑːstər]
【考法】	*n.* 冒充者：one that **assumes false identity** or title for the purpose of deception
例	The man who claimed to be a prince turned out to be an impostor. 那个自称是王子的人原来是冒充的。
近	charlatan, fake, fraud, hoaxer, mountebank, phony, pretender, quack, sham

impotent	[ˈɪmpətənt]
【考法1】	*adj.* 无生育能力的：**unable to produce fruit** or offspring
例	Most mules are impotent. 绝大多数的骡子都无法生育。
近	barren, fruitless, infertile, unfruitful
反	fecund, fertile, fruitful, productive 高产的，硕果累累的
【考法2】	*adj.* 无力的，无能的：**lacking in power**, strength, or vigor
例	an impotent ruler who was just a figurehead 一个无能的傀儡统治者
近	hamstrung, handcuffed, helpless, impuissant, paralyzed, weak
反	mighty, potent, powerful, puissant, strong 强大的，有能力的

imprecise	[ˌɪmprɪˈsaɪs]
【考法】	*adj.* 不精确的：**not precise**
例	incomplete and imprecise satellite data 既不完整又不精确的卫星数据
近	approximate, inaccurate, loose, squishy
反	accurate, exact, precise, veracious 精确的，准确的
派	imprecision *n.* 不准确，不精确

impromptu	[ɪmˈprɑːmptuː]
【考法1】	*n.* 即席的表演：something, such as a speech, that is made or **done extemporaneously**
近	improvisation, extemporization
【考法2】	*adj.* 即席的，即兴的：composed **without previous preparation**
例	Our dinner guest thanked us with an impromptu song. 客人们即兴高歌一首以表达谢意。
近	ad-lib, extempory, improvised, offhand, unplanned, unpremeditated, unprepared, unrehearsed
反	considered, planned, premeditated, prepared, rehearsed 事先有所准备的

improvise	[ˈɪmprəvaɪz]
【考法】	*v.* 即兴而作：to invent, compose, or **perform with little or no preparation**
例	Since the award was a complete surprise, I improvised an acceptance speech. 因为那个奖项完全是个惊喜，所以我即兴发表了一个获奖演说。
近	ad-lib, extemporize
反	plan, premeditate 计划，预先考虑

imprudent	[ɪmˈpruːdnt]
【考法】	*adj.* 不明智的：**lacking** discretion, wisdom, or **good judgment**
例	an imprudent investment he made many years ago 他许多年前做的一笔不明智的投资
近	impolitic, inadvisable, indelicate, injudicious, tactless, undiplomatic, unwise
反	advisable, politic, prudent, tactical, wise 明智的

impudent	[ˈɪmpjədənt]
【考法】	*adj.* 放肆大胆的，无礼的：marked by contemptuous or cocky **boldness or disregard** of others
例	Some children were well behaved, while others were impudent. 一些孩子表现得很得体，另一些则很无礼。
近	audacious, barefaced, bold, brash, brazen, impertinent, insolent, shameless
反	courteous, genteel, mannerly, polite, proper 举止得体的
派	impudence *n.* 放肆无礼

List 13

"无论多久后的将来，无论当我遇到什么困难险阻，每当我回想起当年奋战GRE的日子，我的血液中仍然迸发着那种不安分的激情和冲劲，让我继续舔着伤口，在荆棘丛中勇往直前。"

（周慧杰，2006年10月，Verbal 720，Quantitative 800，AW 5.5，现就职于凯雷投资集团，中国香港）

Unit 1

■ IMPUGN	■ IMPUISSANCE	■ INADVERTENT	■ INALIENABLE	■ INANE
■ INANIMATE	■ INAUGURATE	■ INCANDESCENT	■ INCANTATION	■ INCARNATE

impugn ［ɪmˈpjuːn］
【考法】 *vt.* 责难，攻击，抨击：to **attack as false** or questionable; challenge in argument
例 impugn a political opponent's character 就政治对手的人品发难
近 attack, assail, contradict, contravene, cross, disaffirm, deny, gainsay, negate, negative, traverse
反 advocate, back, support, uphold 支持；authenticate 证实，证明

impuissance ［ɪmˈpjuːɪsns］
【考法】 *n.* 无权，虚弱：**lack of power** or effectiveness
例 In spite of their impuissance the group remains highly active. 尽管手中无权，但这个组织仍然十分活跃。
近 impotence, powerlessness, weakness
反 clout, potency, power, puissance 权势
派 impuissant *adj.* 无权无势的，无能的

inadvertent ［ˌɪnədˈvɜːrtənt］
【考法 1】 *adj.* 偶然发生的：happening **by chance**
例 an inadvertent encounter with a rattlesnake 偶遇响尾蛇
近 casual, fluky, incidental, unintentional, unplanned, unpremeditated, unwitting
反 calculated, deliberate, intended, intentional, planned, premeditated 有计划的，有预谋的
【考法 2】 *adj.* 疏忽的，不留意的：marked by **unintentional lack of care**
例 The military has said it was an inadvertent error. 军方表示这是个疏忽大意的错误。
近 careless, feckless, heedless, irreflective, thoughtless, uncaring
反 advertent, careful, heedful, mindful 留意的，小心的

inalienable ［ɪnˈeɪliənəbl］
【考法】 *adj.* 不可剥夺的，不能让与的：**cannot be transferred** to another or others
例 inalienable rights of the citizen 公民不可予夺的权利
近 untransferable
反 alienable 可让与的

inane ［ɪˈneɪn］
【考法】 *adj.* 空洞的：**lacking significance**, meaning, or point
例 inane comments 空洞的评论
近 empty, insubstantial, pointless, senseless
反 meaningful, significant 有意义的；deep, profound 深刻的

inanimate ［ɪnˈænɪmət］
【考法】 *adj.* 无生命的：**not** having the qualities associated with active, **living** organisms
例 He thinks that inanimate objects have a life of their own. 他认为无生命的事物其实也是有生命的。
近 dead, lifeless, insensible, insentient, senseless, unfeeling
反 animate, living 有生命的

inaugurate ［ɪˈnɔːɡjəreɪt］
【考法 1】 *vt.* 使就职：to **induct into an office** by a formal ceremony
例 A new leader will be inaugurated soon. 新的领导即将就职。
近 induct, initiate, install, instate, invest, seat
反 abdicate, resign 辞职，退位

【考法2】 *vt.* 开始：to cause to **begin**, especially officially or formally

例 inaugurate a new immigration policy 实施新的移民政策

近 begin, commence, establish, institute, introduce, launch, open, plant, start

反 cease, close, end, terminate 结束

派 inauguration *n.* 就职；开始

incandescent [ˌɪnkænˈdesnt]

【考法1】 *adj.* 明亮灿烂的：strikingly **bright**, radiant, or clear

例 incandescent light bulbs 明亮的灯泡

近 beaming, brilliant, dazzling, effulgent, glowing, lucent, luminous, lustrous, radiant, refulgent, shining

反 dim, dull, lackluster 黯淡的

【考法2】 *adj.* 热情饱满的，感情强烈的：characterized by glowing **zeal**

例 It makes me incandescent with fury. 它让我愤怒不已。

近 ardent, demonstrative, emotional, fervid, impassioned, passionate, torrid, vehement

反 cold, cool, dispassionate, emotionless, impassive, unemotional 无感情的，漠然的

incantation [ˌɪnkænˈteɪʃn]

【考法】 *n.* 咒语：a spoken word or set of words believed to have **magic power**

例 Hovering over the sick child, the witch doctor muttered mysterious incantations. 巫医在生病的小孩子身边走来走去，嘴里念着神秘的咒语。

近 abracadabra, bewitchment, charm, conjuration, enchantment, glamour, hex, invocation

incarnate

【考法1】 [ɪnˈkɑːrnət] *adj.* 化身的，人形化的：invested with **bodily nature and form**

例 He referred to her as devil incarnate. 他把她视作恶魔的化身。

近 embodied, materialized, personified, typified

【考法2】 [ɪnˈkɑːrneɪt] *vt.* 使（思想、理论）具化，体现：to **constitute an embodiment** or type of

例 the general view that Hitler incarnated extreme egotism 通常认为希特勒代表了极端的以自我为中心

近 epitomize, incorporate, manifest, materialize, personalize, personify, substantiate, symbolize

反 disembody 使（灵魂等）脱离躯体

派 incarnation *n.* 化身

Unit 2

■ INCENDIARY	■ INCENSE	■ INCEPTION	■ INCESSANT	■ INCH
■ INCHOATE	■ INCINERATE	■ INCIPIENT	■ INCITE	■ INCLEMENT

incendiary [ɪnˈsendieri]

【考法1】 *n.* 煽动者：a **person who stirs up** public feelings especially of discontent

例 behind-the-scenes incendiaries who were intending to overthrow the government 企图推翻政府的幕后煽动者

近 demagogue, exciter, firebrand, fomenter, inciter, instigator, kindler, provocateur

【考法2】 *adj.* 煽动性的：**tending to inflame**

例 an incendiary speech 煽动性的演说

近 agitational, instigative, provocative, seditious

反 conciliatory, pacific 安抚性的

incense

【考法1】 [ˈɪnsens] *n.* 芳香：a sweet or **pleasant smell**

例 the heavenly incense of spring flowers 春天花朵发出的美妙芳香

近 aroma, balm, bouquet, fragrancy, perfume, redolence, scent, spice

反 fetor, malodor, reek, stench, stink 恶臭

【考法2】 [ɪnˈsens] *vt.* 激怒：to cause to be **extremely angry**

例 This proposal will certainly incense female activists. 这个提案肯定会激怒女权主义者。

近 aggravate, enrage, exasperate, inflame, infuriate, madden, outrage, rankle, rile, roil

反 delight, gratify, please 取悦；appease, conciliate, mollify, pacify, placate, propitiate, soothe 缓和

inception [ɪnˈsepʃn]

【考法】 *n.* 开端，开始：an act, process, or instance of **beginning**

例 This seemed like a good program at its inception, but it isn't working out as planned. 一开始这像是个不错的项目，但是它没有按照我们的预期发展。

近 beginning, birth, commencement, dawn, genesis, kickoff, launch, nascence, onset, outset, start, threshold

反 close, conclusion, end, termination,omega 结束，终止

派 inceptive *adj.* 开端的，初生的

incessant [ɪnˈsesnt]

【考法】 *adj.* 无间断的：continuing or following **without interruption**

例 The incessant noise from an outside repair crew was a real distraction during the test. 考试时，窗外维修工发出的持续不断的噪音着实让人分心。

近 ceaseless，continual，nonstop，perpetual，running，unbroken，unceasing，uninterrupted，unremitting

反 interrupted 中断的；discontinuous, intermittent 有间断的

inch [ɪntʃ]

【考法 1】 *n.* 少量，很短的距离：a very **small** distance or **degree**

例 Give them an inch, and they'll take a mile 得寸进尺。 ‖ Inch by inch, we're making progress toward our fund-raising goal. 我们在慢慢地接近筹款目标。

近 ace, hairbreadth, skip, neck, step

【考法 2】 *v.* (使)慢慢移动：to move or cause to **move slowly** or by small degrees

例 The car inched carefully across the snow-covered bridge. 汽车慢慢地通过被大雪覆盖的桥梁。

近 crawl, creak, creep, limp, plod, slouch, snail

反 dart, fleet, flit, scurry 飞奔，疾行

inchoate [ɪnˈkoʊət]

【考法 1】 *adj.* 新生的，才开始的：in an initial or **early stage**

例 inchoate feelings of affection for a man 刚刚产生的好感

近 aborning, beginning, inceptive, incipient, initial, nascent

反 adult, full-blown, full-fledged, mature, ripe 成熟的，成型的；moribund 将死的

【考法 2】 *adj.* 未完全成型的：**imperfectly formed** or developed

例 a vague, inchoate notion 模糊而不成形的想法

近 amorphous, formless, shapeless, undeveloped, unformed, unshaped

incinerate [ɪnˈsɪnəreɪt]

【考法】 *v.* 将…烧成灰烬：to cause to **burn to ashes**

例 The government is trying to stop farmers incinerating their own waste. 政府开始阻止农民们焚烧垃圾的行为。

近 burn, carbonize

反 douse, extinguish, quench, put out 扑灭

派 incineration *n.* 焚化

incipient [ɪnˈsɪpiənt]

【考法】 *adj.* 起初的，初现的：**beginning to come into being** or to become apparent

例 an incipient economic recovery 刚刚出现的经济复苏

近 aborning, beginning, inceptive, inchoate, initial, nascent

反 adult, full-blown, full-fledged, mature, ripe 成熟的，成型的；moribund 将死的

incite [ɪnˈsaɪt]

【考法】 *vt.* 煽动，激起：to **provoke** and urge on

例 incite workers to strike 煽动工人罢工

近 arouse, abet, foment, instigate, pick, provoke, raise, stir

反 dampen, deter, discourage, dishearten, dissuade 劝阻

inclement [ɪnˈklemənt]

【考法 1】 *adj.* (天气等)恶劣的：**lacking mildness**

例 inclement weather conditions 恶劣的气象条件

近 bleak, harsh, severe, stormy, tempestuous

反 bright, clear, cloudless, fair, sunny, sunshiny, unclouded 天气晴好的

【考法 2】 *adj.* 无情的，严酷的：showing no clemency; **unmerciful**

近 bitter, brutal, intemperate, rigorous

反 charitable, clement, lenient, merciful 仁慈的

派 inclemency *n.* 严酷无情

Unit 3

incogitant [ɪnˈkɑːdʒɪtənt]

【考法】 *adj.* 考虑不周的，不体谅的：thoughtless; **inconsiderate**

例 an incogitant litterbug 不体谅人的乱扔垃圾者

近 discourteous, disrespectful, ill-mannered, impertinent, inconsiderate, rude, thoughtless, ungracious

反 civil, considerate, courteous, genteel, gracious, thoughtful 体谅他人的，举止得体的

incongruent [ɪnˈkɑːŋgruənt]

【考法】 *adj.* 不全等的；不一致的：not coinciding exactly when superimposed; **not conforming** to the circumstances or requirements of a situation

例 Two triangles are incongruent. 两个三角形不全等。

近 conflicting, discordant, discrepant, dissonant, incompatible, incongruous, inconsonant

反 congruent, congruous, consistent 一致的

inconsequential [ˌɪnkɑːnsɪˈkwenʃl]

【考法 1】 *adj.* 不合逻辑的：**not** using or **following good reasoning**

例 an inconsequential line of argument 不合逻辑的论述

近 fallacious, illogical, invalid, irrational, unreasonable, unsound, weak

反 logical, rational, reasonable, sound, valid, well-founded, well-grounded 有理的，论证有力的

【考法 2】 *adj.* 不重要的：of **no significance**

例 That's an inconsequential problem compared to the other issues. 和其他问题相比，这就是一个无关痛痒的小事。

近 fiddling, frivolous, inconsiderable, insignificant, minor, minute, negligible, nugatory, petty, slight, trivial

反 consequential, eventful, important, meaningful, momentous, significant, substantial, weighty 重要的

incontrovertible [ˌɪnkɑːntrəˈvɜːrtəbl]

【考法】 *adj.* 无可争议的：**not open to question**

例 incontrovertible facts 无可非议的事实

近 certain, inarguable, incontestable, indisputable, indubitable, positive, sure, undeniable, unquestionable

反 arguable, controversial, debatable, disputable, problematic, questionable, refutable 有争议的

派 incontrovertibility *n.* 无可争议

incorrigible [ɪnˈkɔːrɪdʒəbl]

【考法 1】 *adj.* 不可救药的，积习难改的：**incapable of being corrected** or amended

例 an incorrigible criminal deserving death penalty 一个应该被判死刑的恶习难改的罪犯

近 incurable, irrecoverable, irredeemable, irremediable, irretrievable, unrecoverable, unredeemable

反 curable, reclaimable, recoverable, redeemable, remediable, retrievable, savable 可以拯救的

【考法 2】 *adj.* 无法管制的：difficult or **impossible to control** or manage

例 an incorrigible, spoiled child 被宠坏了的难管的孩子

近 headstrong, intractable, obstinate, refractory, stubborn, unmanageable, unruly, willful

反 compliant, docile, manageable, obedient, submissive, tractable 顺从的

incriminate [ɪnˈkrɪmɪneɪt]

【考法】 *vt.* 归罪于：to **accuse of a crime** or other wrongful act

例 incriminate innocent people 诬陷好人

近 charge, criminate, impeach, indict

反 absolve, acquit, exculpate, exonerate, vindicate 免罪

incubate [ˈɪŋkjubeɪt]

【考法 1】 *vt.* 孵化：to **cover and warm eggs** as the young inside develop

例 The hen incubated her eggs for two weeks. 母鸡孵蛋两周。

近 brood, hatch, sit

派 incubator *n.* 恒温箱；incubation *n.* 孵化，孵卵

【考法 2】 *vt.* 帮助，培养，促进：to cause or **aid** the development of

例 Hopefully, these youthful visits to the museum will incubate an enduring love of art. 我们希望年轻时参观博物馆能够培养人们对于艺术的持久热爱。

近 advance, cultivate, encourage, forward, further, nourish, nurse, nurture, promote

反 check, discourage, frustrate, hinder, impede, inhibit, obstruct, retard, shackle 妨碍，阻碍

inculpate [ɪnˈkʌlpeɪt]

【考法】 *vt.* 归罪于：**incriminate**

近 charge, criminate, incriminate, indict

反 absolve, acquit, exculpate, exonerate, vindicate 免罪

incursion [ɪnˈkɜːrʒn]

【考法】 *n.* 入侵：a **hostile entrance** into a territory

例 homes damaged by the incursion of floodwater 被洪水入侵破坏的房屋

近 foray, inroad, invasion, irruption, raid

反 retreat, withdrawal 撤退

indelible [ɪnˈdeləbl]

【考法 1】 *adj.* (印记等)无法擦除的：**impossible to remove**, erase, or wash away

例 indelible ink 难以擦拭的墨水

近 ineffaceable, ineradicable, inerasable, ingrained

反 eradicable, erasable, removable, washable 可抹去的

【考法 2】 *adj.* 无法忘怀的：**not easily forgotten**

例 most indelible experiences 最难以磨灭的经历

近 impressive, memorable, unforgettable

反 forgettable 容易被忘记的

Unit 4

■ INDEMNITY	■ INDICT	■ INDIFFERENT	■ INDIGENOUS	■ INDIGENT
■ INDISPENSABLE	■ INDOCTRINATE	■ INDOLENT	■ INDUCEMENT	■ INDULGENT

indemnity [ɪnˈdemnəti]

【考法】 *n.* (损害、伤害等的)保险补偿：**compensation** for damage, loss, or injury suffered

例 The widow now lives on a pension and an indemnity from her late husband's company. 这个寡妇如今依靠社保和前夫公司的保险赔偿过日。

近 compensation, indemnification, quittance, recompense, redress, remuneration, reparation, requital

indict [ɪnˈdaɪt]

【考法】 *vt.* 起诉，控告：to **accuse** of wrongdoing; charge

例 indict the mayor for fraud and embezzlement 起诉市长受贿和挪用公款

近 charge, criminate, impeach, incriminate

反 absolve, acquit, exculpate, exonerate, vindicate 免罪

indifferent [ɪnˈdɪfrənt]

【考法 1】 *adj.* 公平的：marked by **impartiality**

例 They believed their art teacher could offer an indifferent judgment on their works' merits. 他们相信艺术老师会对他们作品的价值做出公正的评价。

近 disinterested, equal, impartial, just, nonpartisan, objective, unbiased, unprejudiced

反 biased, one-sided, partial, prejudiced 有偏好的；unjust 不公平的

【考法 2】 *adj.* (质量、档次等)中规中矩的，一般的：of **average** or below average quality

例 an indifferent but drinkable cup of coffee 一杯尚可入口的咖啡

近 average, common, fair, intermediate, mediocre, medium, moderate, ordinary, passable, so-so

反 exceptional, extraordinary 极好的；inferior, poor 低档次的

【考法 3】 *adj.* 不感兴趣的，冷漠的：marked by a **lack of interest**, enthusiasm, or concern for something

例 indifferent about the result of CET-4 对四级成绩不感兴趣

近 aloof, apathetic, detached, incurious, nonchalant, numb, pococurante, remote, unconcerned, uninterested

反 attentive, concerned, interested 关切的，有兴趣的

派 indifference *n.* 漠然

indigenous [ɪnˈdɪdʒənəs]

【考法 1】 *adj.* 土产的，本地的：**originating** and living or occurring naturally in an area or environment

例 the culture of the indigenous people of that country 那个国家原住民的文化

近 aboriginal, endemic, native

反 exotic, extraneous, foreign 外来的；nonnative 非本地的

【考法2】 *adj.* 与生俱来的，先天的：being a part of the **innermost nature** of a person or thing
例 The drive to create is indigenous to humanity. 人类创造的动力是与生俱来的。
近 constitutional, essential, immanent, inborn, inbred, ingrained, innate, integral, intrinsic, natural
反 adventitious, extrinsic 外在的；acquired, studied 后天习得的

indigent [ˈɪndɪdʒənt]
【考法】 *adj.* 贫穷的：**lacking money** or material possessions
例 indigent people who require some outside assistance 需要外来援助的贫苦人民
近 beggared, destitute, impecunious, impoverished, necessitous, needy, penniless, penurious, threadbare
反 affluent, opulent, rich, wealthy 富裕的
派 indigence *n.* 贫穷

indispensable [ˌɪndɪˈspensəbl]
【考法】 *adj.* 必不可少的，不可或缺的：**impossible to do without**
例 She was becoming indispensable to him. 对他而言她逐渐变得不可替代。
近 critical; crucial, imperative, necessary, necessitous, needed, required, requisite, vital
反 dispensable 可替代的；redundant, superfluous, surplus 多余的

indoctrinate [ɪnˈdɑːktrɪneɪt]
【考法】 *vt.* 教育，灌输思想：to **instruct** especially in fundamentals or rudiments
例 indoctrinate students with the notion of egalitarianism 向学生灌输平等主义的思想
近 educate, instruct, lesson, teach, train, tutor
反 learn, study 学习

indolent [ˈɪndələnt]
【考法】 *adj.* 懒惰的：**averse to activity**, effort, or movement
例 The sweltering afternoon made us indolent. 炎热的午后使我们懒散不愿行动。
近 lazy, idle, shiftless, slothful, sluggish
反 diligent, industrious 勤奋的
派 indolence *n.* 懒惰

inducement [ɪnˈduːsmənt]
【考法1】 *n.* 动机，刺激源：a **motive** or consideration that leads one to action
例 offer an expensive watch as an inducement to ratify the proposal 赠送名贵手表以求计划得到批准
近 goad, impulse, incentive, motive, spur, stimulus
反 deterrent 抑制物
派 induce *v.* 导致，产生
【考法2】 *n.* 劝说，游说：the act of reasoning or **pleading with someone to accept** a belief or course of action
例 He gave up smoking only after a prolonged inducement by all the other family members. 在所有家庭成员坚持不懈的劝说之下，他终于愿意戒烟了。
近 conversion, convincing, persuading, suasion

indulgent [ɪnˈdʌldʒənt]
【考法】 *adj.* （对己）放纵的，（对他人）纵容的：showing, characterized by, or **given to indulgence**
例 indulgent aristocrats 生活放纵的贵族
近 decadent, forbearing, lenient, luxurious, tolerant, sybaritic
反 ascetic 禁欲的；draconian 严酷的
派 indulgence *n.* 放纵

Unit 5

■ INDURATE	■ INDUSTRIOUS	■ INEFFABLE	■ INELUCTABLE	■ INEPT
■ INERT	■ INEVITABLE	■ INEXORABLE	■ INFAMOUS	■ INFATUATE

indurate [ˈɪndjʊreɪt]
【考法1】 *adj.* 铁石心肠的，冷酷无情的：having or showing **a lack of sympathy** or tender feelings
例 an indurate heart that admits no love or mercy 一颗不认可爱或仁慈的冷酷心灵
近 affectless, callous, heartless, inhumane, merciless, obdurate, pitiless, ruthless, unsparing, cold-blooded
反 charitable, compassionate, humane, kindhearted, merciful, tender 仁慈的
【考法2】 *vt.* 使变硬：to become **physically firm** or solid
例 Great heat indurates clay. 高温使黏土变硬。
近 concrete, congeal, firm, freeze, set, solidify
反 liquefy 液化；soften 柔化

【考法3】 *vt.* 使习惯于（如艰苦或尴尬之境况）：to make able to **withstand physical hardship**, strain, or exposure

例 Such a brutal upbringing could only callous his soul and indurate his heart to the suffering of others. 这样一种残暴的培养方式只会让他的灵魂变得麻木，让他的心灵对于他人所受的折磨无动于衷。

近 fortify, inure, season, steel, strengthen, toughen

反 enfeeble, weaken, undermine 弱化，使虚弱

---

industrious [ɪnˈdʌstriəs]

【考法】 *adj.* 勤勉的：constantly, regularly, or habitually occupied, **diligent**

例 The industrious PhD spends all his summer holiday in the laboratory. 勤奋的博士整个暑假都在做实验。

近 assiduous, busy, diligent, sedulous

反 indolent, lazy, slothful 懒惰的

派 industriousness *n.* 勤奋

---

ineffable ○ [ɪnˈefəbl]

【考法】 *adj.* 难以表达的：**incapable** of being **expressed**

例 ineffable ecstasy 无法用语言表达的狂喜

近 indefinable, indescribable, inexpressible, unspeakable, unutterable

反 communicable 可传达的；expressible 可描述的

派 ineffability *n.* 不可描述性

---

ineluctable ○ [ˌɪnɪˈlʌktəbl]

【考法】 *adj.* 无法逃避的，必然的：**not to be avoided**, changed, or resisted

例 Although death is an ineluctable fate for any and every individual organism, it lays the foundation of the metabolism that perpetuates the planetary ecosystem. 尽管死亡对于任何单个的有机体而言是不可避免的宿命，但它奠定了能使整个行星生态系统永不衰竭的新陈代谢的基础。

近 certain, inescapable, inevasible, inevitable, unavoidable

反 avoidable, evadable 可避免的；uncertain, unsure（结果等）不确定的

派 ineluctability *n.* 不可避免

---

inept [ɪˈnept]

【考法1】 *adj.* 愚笨的，荒谬的：displaying a **lack of judgment**, sense, or reason

例 an inept and irresponsible remark on his paper 对他文章的荒谬而不负责任的评论

近 absurd, foolish, fatuous, preposterous, stupid, witless, unwise

反 judicious, prudent, sagacious, sapient, smart, wise 聪明的，明智的

【考法2】 *adj.* 不恰当的，不合时宜的：**not appropriate** for a particular occasion or situation

近 amiss, graceless, improper, inapposite, infelicitous, malapropos, perverse, unseemly, unsuitable

反 appropriate, becoming, felicitous, fitting, genteel, proper, seemly, suitable 恰当的

【考法3】 *adj.* 不称职的，无能力的：generally **incompetent**

例 a hopelessly inept defense attorney 严重不靠谱的辩护律师

近 incapable, inexpert, unfitted, unskillful, unqualified

反 capable, competent 有能力的；proficient, masterful 精通的，技艺精湛的

派 ineptitude *n.* 不合适

---

inert [ɪˈnɜːrt]

【考法】 *adj.*（人）懒惰缺乏活力的；（物品）惰性的：**sluggish** in action or motion; **deficient** in active properties

例 inert ingredients in drugs 药品中的惰性成分

近 dead, dormant, lethargic, idle, inactive, passive, torpid

反 active, dynamic 充满活力的；passionate 饱含激情的

派 inertia *n.* 惰性

---

inevitable [ɪnˈevɪtəbl]

【考法】 *adj.* 不可避免的，必然的：**incapable** of being **avoided** or evaded

例 The impact of the scandal on the election was inevitable. 丑闻对于选举的冲击是不可避免的。

近 certain, ineluctable, inescapable, inevasible, sure, unalterable, unavoidable

反 evitable, avoidable 可避免的；uncertain, unsure 不确定的

派 inevitability *n.* 必然性

---

inexorable [ɪnˈeksərəbl]

【考法】 *adj.* 无法劝阻的，不为所动的：**not** to be **persuaded**, moved, or stopped

例 the seemingly inexorable rise in unemployment 看起来无法阻止其高攀的失业率

近 inflexible, adamant, obdurate, relentless, rigid, unyielding

反 flexible 易受影响的；yielding 屈服的

派 inexorably *adv.* 势不可挡地

infamous [ˈɪnfəməs]

【考法】 *adj.* 臭名昭著的：having an extremely and deservedly **bad reputation**

例 an infamous city for smuggling and prostitution 因走私和卖淫而臭名昭著的城市

近 notorious, opprobrious

反 distinguished, esteemed, prestigious, reputable 声名显赫的，受尊敬的

派 infamy *n.* 声名狼藉

infatuate [ɪnˈfætʃueɪt]

【考法】 *vt.* 使迷恋：to **inspire** with **unreasoning love** or attachment

例 a naïve girl infatuated by cajolery 被甜言蜜语冲昏头脑的天真女孩

近 allure, captivate, bewitch, enchant, fascinate

反 disgust 使反感

派 infatuation *n.* 迷恋

Unit 6

■ INFERNO	■ INFILTRATE	■ INFINITE	■ INFIRM	■ INFLAME
■ INFELICITOUS	■ INFLUX	■ INFURIATE	■ INFUSE	■ INGENIOUS

inferno [ɪnˈfɜːrnoʊ]

【考法1】 *n.* 大火：an intense **fire**

例 A raging inferno posed a serious threat to the downwind villages. 肆虐的大火给下风向的村庄带来了严重的威胁。

近 conflagration, holocaust

【考法2】 *n.* 地狱：a place or a state that **resembles** or suggests **hell**

例 the inferno of war 地狱般的战场

近 hell, underworld

反 paradise, heaven, nirvana 天堂，乐土

infiltrate [ˈɪnfɪltreɪt]

【考法】 *vt.* 秘密潜入：to **enter** or take up positions in gradually or **surreptitiously**, as for purposes of espionage or takeover

例 The intelligence staff had been infiltrated by spies. 情报工作人员已经被间谍渗透了。

近 creep, insinuate, penetrate, sneak, slip

反 abscond 潜逃

派 infiltration *n.* 潜入，渗透

infinite [ˈɪnfɪnət]

【考法】 *adj.* 无尽的，无限的：having **no boundaries** or limits

例 the idea of an infinite universe 无限宇宙的概念

近 endless, boundless, limitless, immeasurable, unfathomable

反 finite 有限的；bounded, circumscribed, confined, definite, limited, restricted 有界限的，受限的

派 infinity *n.* 无限

infirm [ɪnˈfɜːrm]

【考法1】 *adj.* 虚弱的：**weak in body**, especially from old age or disease

例 her aging, infirm husband 她上了年纪、身体虚弱的丈夫

近 debilitated, effete, enervated, feeble, frail, languid, sapped, unsubstantial

反 hale, mighty, powerful, rugged, stalwart, stout, strong 强壮的，有力的

【考法2】 *adj.* 不果断的，优柔寡断的：**lacking firmness of will**, character, or purpose

例 She has little patience with the "infirm of purpose". 她对那些优柔寡断的人没什么耐心。

近 faltering, irresolute, vacillating, wavering

反 resolute 果断的

inflame [ɪnˈfleɪm]

【考法1】 *v.* 点燃，燃烧：to **set on fire**

例 A carelessly tossed cigarette inflamed the papers in the trash can. 一只被随意丢弃的香烟点燃了垃圾桶中的纸。

近 enflame, enkindle, fire, ignite, kindle, light, torch

反 douse, extinguish, quench, put out 熄灭，扑灭

【考法2】 *vt.* 使加剧：to make **more violent**

例 Retaliation served only to inflame the feud. 冤冤相报何时了。

近 aggravate, enrage, exacerbate, intensify, ire, irritate, provoke, rile, vex

反 assuage, mitigate, mollify, pacify, placate, subdue 平息

infelicitous [ˌɪnfɪˈlɪsɪtəs]

【考法1】 *adj.* 不愉快的，不幸的：not happy; **unfortunate**

例 an infelicitous moment 不幸的时刻

近 hapless, ill-fated, luckless, unfortunate, unhappy

反 lucky, happy 幸运的，令人高兴的

【考法2】 *adj.* 不适当的，不合时宜的：**not appropriate** or well-timed

例 make a very infelicitous remark 做出极不恰当的评价

近 inappropriate, indecorous, inept, malapropos, unfit, unseemly

反 apt, appropriate, becoming, proper 合适的

派 infelicity *n.* 不恰当

influx [ˈɪnflʌks]

【考法】 *n.* 涌入：a **coming in**

例 They anticipated an influx of tourists next month. 他们预期下个月会有大批游客涌入。

近 affluence, flux, income, inflow, inpouring, inrush

反 exodus 大批离去；outflow, outpouring 流出

infuriate [ɪnˈfjʊrieɪt]

【考法】 *vt.* 激怒：to **make furious**

例 be infuriated by the deliberate insults 被蓄意的中伤激怒

近 aggravate, enrage, exasperate, incense, ire, madden

反 appease, assuage, pacify, placate, propitiate 平息，安抚；delight, gratify, please 取悦，讨好

派 infuriated *adj.* 被激怒的

infuse [ɪnˈfjuːz]

【考法1】 *vt.* 灌输，使…充满：to **fill** or cause to be filled with something

例 New members infused enthusiasm into the club. 新成员为俱乐部注入了激情。

近 endue, imbue, implant, ingrain, instill, permeate, suffuse, steep

反 extract 提取

派 infusion *n.* 注入

【考法2】 *vt.* 鼓舞：**inspire**, animate

例 a sense of purpose that infuses scientific researchers 给科学研究者打鸡血一般的使命感

近 animate, exalt, motivate, stimulate

ingenious [ɪnˈdʒiːniəs]

【考法】 *adj.* 聪明的，有创造才能的：marked by originality, **resourcefulness**, and **cleverness** in conception or execution

例 Ingenious designers soon came up with a solution to the battery problem. 聪明的设计者们很快便提出了电池问题的解决方案。

近 artful, clever, imaginative, innovative, inventive, original

反 awkward 笨拙的；uncreative, unimaginative 无创造力或想象力的

Unit 7

■ INGENUITY   ■ INGENUOUS   ■ INGEST   ■ INGRAINED   ■ INGRATIATING
■ INHERENT   ■ INIMICAL   ■ INIMITABLE   ■ INIQUITY   ■ INITIATE

ingenuity [ˌɪndʒəˈnuːəti]

【考法】 *n.* 独创性，创新性：**inventive** skill or imagination

例 There is little ingenuity in his articles. 他的文章鲜有独创性。

近 creativeness, innovativeness, inventiveness, originality

反 banality, cliché 陈词滥调

派 ingenuous *adj.* 真挚的

ingenuous [ɪnˈdʒenjuəs]

【考法 1】 *adj.* 天真淳朴的：**lacking** in **cunning**, guile, or worldliness

例 Photographs captured the ingenuous smiles of young children at play. 摄影家捕捉到了演出中孩子们天真无邪的笑脸。

近 artless, innocent, guileless, naïve, simple, unaffected, unpretending, unsophisticated

反 artful, cunning, sly 狡猾的；assuming, hypocritical 虚伪做作的；sophisticated, worldly 世故的，老练的

【考法 2】 *adj.* 坦白的：openly **straightforward** or frank

例 her ingenuous thirst for knowledge 她对知识毫不掩饰的渴望

近 candid, frank, open, plain, unconcealed

反 ambiguous, equivocal, evasive 含糊其辞的

ingest [ɪnˈdʒest]

【考法】 *vt.* 摄入，咽下：to **take into** the **body** by the mouth for digestion or absorption

例 An expert claims that the average person ingests considerably more calories than is necessary or desirable. 一位专家宣称每个人平均摄取的卡路里大大超出了必要或者所需的范围。

近 eat, consume, devour, intake

反 evacuate, expel 排出；vomit 呕吐

派 ingestion *n.* 摄取

ingrained [ɪnˈɡreɪnd]

【考法】 *adj.* 本质的，根深蒂固的：forming a part of the essence or inmost being; **firmly established**

例 ingrained prejudice against foreigners 对外国人根深蒂固的偏见

近 constitutional, immanent, inborn, indigenous, inherent, innate, intrinsic

反 adventitious 外来的，偶然的；extraneous, extrinsic 非本质的，外在的

派 ingrain *vt.* 灌输，使根深蒂固

ingratiating [ɪnˈɡreɪʃieɪtɪŋ]

【考法 1】 *adj.* 讨人喜欢的：capable of **winning favor**

例 They adopted the orphan who had a most ingratiating smile. 他们收养了那名有着最惹人喜欢的笑容的孤儿

近 disarming, endearing, winsome

反 disagreeable 令人厌恶的

【考法 2】 *adj.* 逢迎的，意在奉承的：intended or adopted in order to **gain favor**

例 an repulsive ingratiating smile 令人反感的阿谀奉承的微笑

近 adulatory, deferential, fawning, flattering, toady, insinuating

派 ingratiate *vt.* 讨好

inherent [ɪnˈhɪrənt]

【考法】 *adj.* 内在的，本质的：involved in the constitution or **essential** character of something

例 a disposition inherent in human nature 人性内在的倾向

近 constitutional, elemental, essential, inborn, ingrained, innate, intrinsic

反 adventitious 外来的，偶然的；extraneous, extrinsic 外在的

派 inherently *adv.* 内在地

inimical [ɪˈnɪmɪkl]

【考法 1】 *adj.* 带有敌意的：reflecting or indicating **hostility**

例 a cold, inimical voice 冰冷而不友好的声音

近 antagonistic, hostile, opposing, unfriendly

反 amiable, amicable, friendly, hospitable 友好的；amenable 服从的

【考法 2】 *adj.* 危及某人利益的，不利的：**opposed to** one's **interests**

例 Laws were designed to enhance national security but some regard as inimical to cherished freedoms. 法律旨在维护国家安全，但有人认为它危及了人们最为珍贵的权力——自由。

近 counter, disadvantageous, negative, prejudicial, unfavorable

反 advantageous, favorable, positive, supportive, well-disposed 有利的，利好的

inimitable [ɪˈnɪmɪtəbl]

【考法】 *adj.* 无法仿效的，独特的：**not** capable of being **imitated**

例 her own inimitable style 她特立独行的作风

近 incomparable, matchless, peerless, unique, unparalleled

反 commonplace, ordinary 平凡的

派 inimitability *n.* 独特性

iniquity	[ɪˈnɪkwəti]

【考法】 *n.* 邪恶，不公正：gross **immorality** or **injustice**

例 The use of illegal narcotics is not only a destroyer of personal health but also an iniquity that undermines our society. 非法的毒品不仅仅摧残着个人健康，还是一颗危害社会的毒瘤。

近 corruption, depravity, debauchery, evil, infamy, sin, unfairness, wickedness

反 integrity, rectitude 正直；virtue 美德；disinterestedness 公正

initiate	

【考法1】 [ɪˈnɪʃieɪt] *vt.* 创始，发动促进：to **cause** or facilitate the **beginning** of

例 a chain reaction initiated by UV irradiation 紫外线激发引起的连锁反应

近 begin, start, commence, inaugurate, introduce, launch

反 terminate 终止

派 initiative *n.* 主动性，首创精神

【考法2】 [ɪˈnɪʃiət] *n.* 刚入门的新手：a **person** who is undergoing or has undergone an **initiation**

近 apprentice, beginner, novice, rookie, tyro

反 veteran 身经百战的人

Unit 8

■ INKLING	■ INNOCUOUS	■ INNOVATIVE	■ INQUISITIVE	■ INSENSIBLE
■ INSENSITIVE	■ INSENTIENT	■ INSIGHT	■ INSIPID	■ INSOLENT

⬭ inkling	[ˈɪŋklɪŋ]

【考法1】 *n.* 轻微暗示，小提示：a **slight indication** or suggestion

例 They hadn't given us an inkling of what was going to happen. 他们不给我们任何暗示将会发生什么。

近 clue, cue, hint

【考法2】 *n.* 略知：a slight knowledge or **vague notion**

例 We do not have even the faintest inkling of what the project was all about. 我们对这个项目与什么有关毫不知情。

近 glimmer

反 insight 深刻理解

innocuous	[ɪˈnɑːkjuəs]

【考法1】 *adj.* 无害的：producing **no injury**

例 The government enacted a more strict regulation on innocuous preservatives. 政府对无害防腐剂制定了更为严格的规定。

近 anodyne, benign, harmless, inoffensive, nontoxic, safe

反 damaging, detrimental, harmful, injurious, noxious, pernicious, invasive 有害的

【考法2】 *adj.* 乏味的，不会引起敌意的：**not** likely to give offense or to **arouse** strong feelings or hostility

例 He made an innocuous remark to avoid conflict. 为了避免冲突，他做了一个中庸的评价。

近 bland, inoffensive, insipid, neutral, sapless

反 provoking 刺激性的

innovative	[ˈɪnəveɪtɪv]

【考法】 *adj.* 创新性的：characterized by, tending to, or **introducing innovations**

例 an innovative macro-economic strategy 创新性的宏观经济战略

近 creative, ingenious, inventive, original

反 conservative, hidebound 保守的

派 innovation *n.* 创新

inquisitive	[ɪnˈkwɪzətɪv]

【考法】 *adj.* 过分好奇的：**inordinately** or improperly **curious** about the affairs of others

例 big sunglasses to frustrate inquisitive journalists 让狗仔队的企图无法得逞的大墨镜

近 curious, inquiring, investigative, prying

反 indifferent , unconcerned, uninterested 不感兴趣的；incurious 无好奇心的

派 inquisitiveness *n.* 好奇

insensible	[ɪnˈsensəbl]

【考法1】 *adj.* 无知觉的：having **lost consciousness**, especially temporarily

例 The security guard was knocked insensible by a sudden blow. 保安被突如其来的一击敲晕了。

近 anesthetic, insensate, senseless, unfeeling, unconscious

反 conscious 神志清醒的

【考法2】 *adj.* 漠不关心的：**not** emotionally **responsive**

例 insensible to workers' requests 对工人的要求无动于衷

近 apathetic, bloodless, callous, dull, impassive, indifferent, nonchalant, phlegmatic

反 concerned 关切的

【考法3】 *adj.* 粗俗的，没品味的：**lacking in refinement** or good taste

例 She married an insensible brute upon whom the niceties of life were completely lost. 她嫁给了一个毫无品味的凡夫俗子，从此她的生活再无任何情趣。

近 crass, crude, incult, lowbred, tasteless, uncouth, uncultivated, uncultured, unpolished, unrefined, vulgar

反 civilized, cultivated, cultured, genteel, polished, refined, smooth, tasteful 有品位的

insensitive [ɪnˈsensətɪv]

【考法1】 *adj.* 缺乏机智圆滑的，缺乏社交技巧的：**lacking tact**

例 so insensitive as to laugh at someone in pain 如此缺乏社交技巧以至于嘲笑处于悲痛中的人

近 gauche, impolite, insensible, tactless

反 considerate 为他人着想的

【考法2】 *adj.* 不敏感的，麻木的：**not responsive** or susceptible

例 insensitive to either criticism or commendation 对批评和表扬都不在乎

近 anesthetized, dead, numb, senseless, unfeeling

反 sensitive, tender 敏感的

insentient [ɪnˈsentiənt]

【考法1】 *adj.* 无感觉的，无知觉的：**lacking perception**, consciousness, or animation

例 He refused to believe that the universe as we know it evolved from the random interactions of insentient particles of matter. 他拒绝相信我们所知的宇宙是经由无生命的粒子间的相互作用演化而来的。

近 impassive, insensate, insensible, senseless, unresponsive

反 perceiving, sensible, sensitive 有知觉的

【考法2】 *adj.* 一知半解的，略懂的：**not having** or showing **a deep understanding** of something

例 an insentient therapist who failed to see what the teenager's real problem was 一个对这名青少年的真正问题所在一知半解的医生

近 impercipient, unwise

反 discerning, insightful 深邃的，有洞察力的；sagacious, sage, sapient 睿智的

insight [ˈɪnsaɪt]

【考法】 *n.* 深刻的理解：an instance of **apprehending** the true **nature** of a thing, especially through intuitive understanding

例 an insight into the global-scale environmental problems 对于全球性环境问题的深刻理解

近 discernment, perception, sagacity, sapience

反 glimmer, inkling 略懂，略知一二

派 insightful *adj.* 有洞察力的

insipid [ɪnˈsɪpɪd]

【考法1】 *adj.* (食品)清淡无味的：**lacking flavor** or zest; not tasty

例 a rather insipid soup 味道清淡的汤

近 flat, flavorless, mild, sapless, savorless, tasteless

反 piquant 辛辣的

【考法2】 *adj.* 平淡的，无聊的：**lacking** in qualities that **interest**, stimulate, or challenge

例 an insipid story of the prince and the princess 一个关于王子和公主的无聊故事

近 banal, bland, driveling, prosaic, tedious, uninteresting, vapid

反 enchanting 引人入胜的

insolent [ˈɪnsələnt]

【考法】 *adj.* 粗野的，无礼的：audaciously **rude** or disrespectful

例 an insolent child with no respect or regard for anyone 对他人不敬的无礼的小孩

近 arrogant, audacious, bold, haughty, supercilious, impertinent, impudent

反 courteous, polite 有礼貌的；respectful 恭敬的；meek, mousy, timid 胆小的

派 insolence *n.* 无礼

Unit 9

insouciant ［ɪnˈsuːsiənt］
- 【考法】 *adj.* 无忧虑的，不在乎的：**free from concern**, worry, or anxiety
- 例 an insouciant shrug 无所谓地耸耸肩
- 近 carefree, casual, indifferent, nonchalant, unconcerned
- 反 anxious, careworn 焦虑的；concerned, worried 关注的，担心的
- 派 insouciance *n.* 不在乎

instate ［ɪnˈsteɪt］
- 【考法】 *vt.* 任命：to set or **establish** in a **rank** or office
- 例 The new Secretary of the Treasury was instated on Monday. 新的财政部长于星期一被任命。
- 近 appoint, designate, inaugurate, induct, install, nominate
- 反 dismiss, oust 罢免

instigate ［ˈɪnstɪɡeɪt］
- 【考法】 *vt.* 煽动，激起：to goad or **urge forward**; to **stir up**
- 例 This incident is instigated by a small group of people with ulterior motives. 此次事件是被少数别有用心的人煽动起来的。
- 近 abet, arouse, excite, foment, goad, incite, inflame, provoke, stir
- 反 assuage, allay, mitigate, mollify, pacify, soothe 平息，缓和
- 派 instigation *n.* 煽动

instill ［ɪnˈstɪl］
- 【考法 1】 *vt.* 慢慢滴入：to cause to **enter** drop by drop
- 例 instill medication into the infected eye 将药物滴入患者受感染的眼中
- 近 inject
- 反 extract 抽取
- 【考法 2】 *vt.* 灌输：to **impart** gradually
- 例 instill a sense of responsibility to the young 向年轻人灌输一种责任感
- 近 breed, enroot, implant, inculcate, infix, infuse, ingrain, plant, sow
- 反 remove 移除
- 派 instillation *n.* 滴入；灌输

institute ［ˈɪnstɪtuːt］
- 【考法 1】 *vt.* 创立，制定：to **establish**, organize, and set in operation
- 例 institute a new department 创建一个新的部门
- 近 begin, constitute, create, found, inaugurate, launch, start, set up
- 反 abrogate, efface, rescind 废除；close, shut 关闭；phase out 淘汰
- 【考法 2】 *n.* 机构：an **organization** for the promotion of a cause
- 例 a research institute 研究机构
- 近 association, institution, society
- 派 institution *n.* 机构；习俗，制度

insubordinate ［ˌɪnsəˈbɔːrdɪnət］
- 【考法】 *adj.* 不服从权威的：**not submissive** to authority
- 例 Insubordinate soldiers are court-martialed. 抗命的士兵被送上了军事法庭。
- 近 balky, contumacious, intractable, mutinous, recalcitrant, rebellious, refractory
- 反 amenable, docile, obedient, ruly, submissive, tractable 顺从的

insular ［ˈɪnsələr］
- 【考法】 *adj.* (观念、想法等)孤立狭隘的：being, having, or reflecting a **narrow provincial viewpoint**
- 例 the insular thinking of peasant communities 农民阶级的狭隘思想
- 近 confined, local, narrow, parochial, provincial, regional, restricted
- 反 cosmopolitan, ecumenical 有国际视野的；catholic (兴趣等)广泛的；receptive 善于接受的

insulate [ˈɪnsəleɪt]

【考法】 *vt.* 使绝缘，使隔离: to place in a **detached situation**

例 greenhouse gas that insulates ground infrared radiation 能阻碍地表红外辐射的温室气体

近 block, isolate, quarantine, seclude, segregate, separate, sequester

反 connect, link, unite 连结；integrate 使成一体

派 insulation *n.* 隔绝，绝热

insurgent [ɪnˈsɜːrdʒənt]

【考法】 *n.* 叛乱分子: one who breaks with or **opposes** constituted **authority** or the established order

例 Insurgents armed with assault rifles and grenades ambushed a US convoy, resulting in heavy casualties. 持有突击步枪和手榴弹的叛乱分子偷袭了美军车队，造成重大伤亡。

近 rebel, anarchist, antagonist, malcontent, mutineer

派 insurgency *n.* 叛乱

intangible [ɪnˈtændʒəbl]

【考法】 *adj.* 无法感知的，无形的: **incapable** of being **perceived** by the senses

例 intangible value of a good reputation 良好声誉的无形价值

近 impalpable, imperceptible, imponderable, inappreciable, indiscernible, insensible, invisible

反 corporeal 肉体的，有形的；palpable, tactile, tangible, touchable 可感知的

Unit 10

■ INTEGRAL	■ INTEGRITY	■ INTELLIGIBLE	■ INTEMPERATE	■ INTENSIFY
■ INTER	■ INTERCESSOR	■ INTERDICT	■ INTERIM	■ INTERLOCK

integral [ˈɪntɪɡrəl]

【考法 1】 *adj.* 构成整体所必需的: **essential** to completeness

例 an integral part of the undergraduate curriculum 本科生课程的必修部分

近 critical, essential, indispensable, necessary, requisite, vital

反 redundant, superfluous, surplus 多余的

【考法 2】 *adj.* 完整的: **not lacking any part** or member that properly belongs to it

例 the belief that athletics are essential to an integral life 坚信运动是完整的人生所不可或缺的一部分

近 comprehensive, entire, full, grand, intact, perfect, plenary, total, whole

反 imperfect, incomplete 不完美的，不完整的；partial 部分的

integrity [ɪnˈteɡrəti]

【考法 1】 *n.* 正直: steadfast **adherence** to a strict **moral** or ethical code, devotion to telling the truth

例 After a thorough investigation into "Climategate", the panel concluded that the integrity of scientific community is still sound. 经过对"气候门事件"的彻底调查，专家组认为学术界的信誉和道德仍然是值得信赖的。

近 conscience, honesty, incorruptibility, rectitude, righteousness, scrupulousness

反 baseness 卑鄙；deceit, deceitfulness, dishonesty, lying, mendacity, untruthfulness 欺骗

【考法 2】 *n.* 完整性: the quality or condition of **being whole** or undivided

例 try to maintain the integrity of the falling empire 尽力维持日趋西山的帝国的统一

近 completeness, entireness, perfection, wholeness

intelligible [ɪnˈtelɪdʒəbl]

【考法】 *adj.* 可理解的: capable of **being understood**

例 military codenames intelligible only to those high-rank commanding officers 只有高级指挥官才能理解的军事暗号

近 accessible, apprehensible, comprehensible, fathomable, lucid, understandable

反 abstruse, recondite, inscrutable, insensible 难以理解的

派 intelligibility *n.* 可理解性

intemperate [ɪnˈtempərət]

【考法】 *adj.* 无节制的，极端的，不温和的: **not temperate** or moderate

例 The tone of the article is very intemperate. 文章的论调很极端。

近 excessive, extreme, immoderate, inordinate, overindulgent, unrestrained

反 equable 温和的；bridled, checked, constrained, controlled, curbed, governed, hampered, hindered, trammeled 受限制的，节制的

intensify [ɪnˈtensɪfaɪ]
【考法】 *vt.* 加强，激化：to **make intense** or more intensive
例 Both companies intensified their efforts to win the contract. 为了获得这份合同，两家公司都加大了投入。
近 accentuate, aggravate, amplify, deepen, enhance, magnify, redouble, strengthen
反 abate, assuage, attenuate, mitigate, moderate 减缓，降低（程度）
派 intensity *n.* 强度

inter [ɪnˈtɜːr]
【考法】 *vt.* 埋葬：to **place in** a **grave** or tomb
例 The infamous terrorist leader Bin Laden was interred at sea. 臭名昭著的恐怖分子本·拉登被葬于海中。
近 bury, entomb, inhume
反 dig, disinter, excavate, exhume, unearth 掘出

intercessor [ˌɪntərˈsesər]
【考法】 *n.* 调停者：one that **mediates**
例 attend the meeting as the intercessor 作为调停人出席会议
近 broker, buffer, conciliator, intermediate, mediator, peacemaker
反 flame-fanner 煽风点火的人
派 intercession *n.* 调停，斡旋

interdict [ˈɪntərdɪkt]
【考法1】 *vt.* 禁止：to **forbid** in a usually formal or authoritative manner
例 Though not interdicted by law, such an action is morally wrong. 尽管这种行为不被法律所禁止，但是道德上来说是不对的。
近 ban, forbid, prohibit, proscribe
反 authorize 授权；allow, permit, suffer 允许；approve, endorse, ratify, sanction 批准
派 interdiction *n.* 禁止，封锁
【考法2】 *vt.* 阻止：to **stop, seize, or interrupt** while in progress or on course
例 Federal agents are able to interdict only a small percentage of the narcotic shipments into the country. 联邦调查员们只能阻止一小部分流入国内的毒品。
近 bar, block, check, hinder, intercept, impede, obstruct
反 expedite 促进，加速

interim [ˈɪntərɪm]
【考法1】 *n.* 中间过渡时期，间隔：an interval of **time between** one **event**, process, or period and another
例 Richard Wagner's operas usually require an interim of more than 30 minutes for performers to have a break. 理查德·瓦格纳的歌剧通常需要长达30多分钟的幕间休息时间以供演员调整。
近 breach, break, gap, interruption, interval, interlude, parenthesis
反 continuation, continuity 持续
【考法2】 *adj.* 暂时的：serving in a position **for the time being**
例 an interim government to maintain social stability 维持社会稳定的临时政府
近 acting, provisional, temporary
反 eternal, permanent 永恒的

interlock [ˌɪntərˈlɑːk]
【考法】 *vi.* 连锁，连结：to become united or **joined closely**, as by hooking or dovetailing
例 The branches of the trees interlock to form a natural archway. 树枝相互缠绕在一起，形成了天然的拱门。
近 associate, connect, join, link, unite
反 sunder 拆散
派 interlocking *adj.* 连锁的

List 14

"未曾想与雄鹰争锋，来赢得他人艳羡的目光，我却凭着志在四方的信念和风雨兼程的决心，成为站在金字塔尖的蜗牛，沐浴着清风，唱响青春无悔的乐章！"

(汪洋, 2009 年 10 月, Verbal 710, Quantitative 800)

Unit 1

■ INTERMINABLE	■ INTERMITTENT	■ INTERREGNUM	■ INTERROGATE	■ INTIMATE
■ INTIMIDATE	■ INTOXICANT	■ INTRANSIGENT	■ INTREPID	■ INTRIGUE

interminable [ɪn'tɜːrmɪnəbl]

【考法】 *adj.* 无尽头的: having or seeming to have **no end**

例 A large audience fell asleep during the interminable sermon. 许多观众都在冗长的布道演说中睡着了。

近 continual, ceaseless, endless, everlasting, perpetual

反 completed 完成的

intermittent [ˌɪntər'mɪtənt]

【考法 1】 *adj.* 间歇的，断断续续的: coming and going at intervals, **not continuous**

例 intermittent rain in June 六月里断断续续的梅雨

近 episodic, erratic, occasional, periodical, recurrent, recurring

反 constant, continuous, incessant, unceasing 持续不断的

【考法 2】 *adj.* 不定期的: **lacking** in steadiness or **regularity** of occurrence

例 The husband's intermittent employment put the family in a difficult position financially. 丈夫不稳定的工作使得全家陷入了经济上的困境。

近 aperiodic, casual, catchy, discontinuous, irregular, occasional, spasmodic, sporadic, unsteady

反 habitual 习惯的，惯常的; periodic, regular, repeated 定期的，有规律的，重复的

interregnum [ˌɪntə'regnəm]

【考法】 *n.* 过渡期: **break** in continuity

例 The democratic regime proved to be a short-lived interregnum between dictatorships. 这个民主政权被证明只不过是两个独裁政权之间的短暂过渡罢了。

近 breach, break, gap, interim, interruption, interval, interlude, parenthesis

反 continuation, continuity 持续

interrogate [ɪn'terəgeɪt]

【考法】 *vt.* 质问，审问: to **question formally** and systematically

例 interrogate the prisoner of war for valuable intelligence 审问战俘以获取有价值的情报

近 ask, grill, inquire, milk, question

反 answer, reply, respond 回答，回复

派 interrogation *n.* 审讯

intimate

【考法 1】 ['ɪntɪmət] *adj.* 有紧密联系的，亲密无间的: marked by very **close association**, contact, or familiarity

例 intimate friends since childhood 孩童时期以来的密友

近 familiar, close, confidential

反 distant, remote 疏远的

【考法 2】 *adj.* 不为人知的: **not known** or meant to be known by the general populace

例 They broke up after she shared intimate information with all 500 of her closest friends. 在她把那些不为人知的消息告诉了她 500 个密友之后，他们分手了。

近 confidential, esoteric, nonpublic, secret

反 open, public 公开的

【考法 3】 ['ɪntɪmət] *n.* 密友: a **person who has a strong liking** for and trust in another

例 Usually quite aloof in public, he's actually quite relaxed with his intimates. 通常他在大众面前显得比较孤傲，但和好朋友在一起时他却是个很放松的人。

近 acquaintance, amigo, comrade, confidant, friend, insider, mate

反 stranger 陌生人; enemy, foe 敌人

【考法 4】 ['ɪntɪmeɪt] *v.* 迂回地交流，间接地沟通：to **communicate** delicately and **indirectly**
例 intimate a wish to leave 暗示想离开
近 allude, connote, hint, imply, indicate, infer, suggest
反 articulate 清晰明确地说

intimidate [ɪnˈtɪmɪdeɪt]
【考法】 *vt.* 威吓：to make timid or fearful, **frighten**
例 He refused to be intimidated by the manager. 他对经理的恐吓不为所动。
近 browbeat, bully, coerce, cow, frighten, hector, terrify
反 blandish, cajole, coax 用花言巧语讨好
派 intimidation *n.* 恐吓

intoxicant [ɪnˈtɑːksɪkənt]
【考法】 *n.* 使人陶醉的东西（尤指酒精饮料）：an agent that **intoxicates**, especially an alcoholic beverage
近 alcohol, liquor, stimulant
反 refresher 使人清醒的东西
派 intoxicating *adj.* 使人陶醉的

intransigent [ɪnˈtrænzɪdʒənt]
【考法】 *adj.* 不妥协的，固执的：characterized by **refusal to compromise** or to abandon an extreme position
例 an intransigent attitude 不妥协的态度
近 adamant, headstrong, intractable, obstinate, pertinacious, stubborn, uncompromising, unyielding
反 compliant, pliable 易受影响的；tractable, yielding 容易驾驭的
派 intransigence *n.* 顽固

intrepid [ɪnˈtrepɪd]
【考法】 *adj.* 无畏的：characterized by **resolute fearlessness**, fortitude, and endurance
例 an intrepid explorer 无畏的探险家
近 audacious, brave, bold, courageous, dauntless, fearless, gallant, valiant, valorous
反 apprehensive 恐惧的；cowardly, craven, gutless, pusillanimous, timorous 怯懦的，胆小的
派 intrepidity *n.* 无所畏惧

intrigue
【考法 1】 ['ɪntriːg] *n.* 阴谋：**a secret plan** for accomplishing evil or unlawful ends
例 The intrigue was quickly discovered, and the would-be assassins were arrested. 随着阴谋的迅速识破，未得手的刺客被逮捕了。
近 conspiracy, design, intrigue, machination, scheme
【考法 2】 [ɪnˈtriːg] *vt.* 激起…的兴趣：to **arouse** the interest, desire, or **curiosity** of
例 The children are apparently intrigued by the tale. 孩子们很明显被这个传奇故事吸引了。
近 appeal, attract, enthrall, entice, excite, fascinate, interest, occupy
反 ennui, pall 使厌倦
派 intriguing *adj.* 有趣的

Unit 2

| ■ INTRINSIC | ■ INTUITIVE | ■ INUNDATE | ■ INURE | ■ INVECTIVE |
| ■ INVEIGH | ■ INVEIGLE | ■ INVENTORY | ■ INVETERATE | ■ INVIDIOUS |

intrinsic [ɪnˈtrɪnsɪk]
【考法】 *adj.* 固有的，内在的：of or relating to the **essential** nature of a thing
例 the intrinsic worth of a gem 宝石的内在价值
近 congenial, constitutional, immanent, inborn, inherent, innate, native, natural
反 adventitious, extraneous, extrinsic 外在的

intuitive [ɪnˈtuːɪtɪv]
【考法】 *adj.* 直觉的：knowing or perceiving **by intuition**
例 The twins have an intuitive awareness of each other's feelings. 这对双胞胎天生就能感知彼此的感受。
近 instinctive
反 acquired 后天习得的
派 intuition *n.* 直觉

inundate [ˈɪnʌndeɪt]
- 【考法】 *vt.* 淹没：to **cover with** or as if with **flood**
- 例 inundated with trash e-mails 被垃圾邮件所淹没
- 近 avalanche, deluge, drown, engulf, overflow, overwhelm, submerge
- 反 drain 排空
- 派 inundation *n.* 淹没

inure [ɪˈnjʊr]
- 【考法 1】 *vt.* 使习惯接受不好的东西：to **accustom** to accept something undesirable
- 例 children inured to violence 习惯了暴力的孩子们
- 近 accustom, familiarize, habituate
- 派 inured *adj.* 习惯的
- 【考法 2】 *vt.* 使坚强：to make able to **withstand physical hardship**, strain, or exposure
- 例 The hardship of army training inured her to the rigors of desert warfare. 军营里的艰苦训练把她打造成了能适应沙漠艰苦战事的女兵。
- 近 fortify, indurate, season, steel, strengthen, toughen
- 反 enfeeble, soften, weaken, undermine 弱化，使虚弱

invective [ɪnˈvektɪv]
- 【考法】 *adj.* 侮辱性的：of, relating to, or **characterized by insult** or abuse
- 例 invective comments on female activists 对女权主义者的侮辱性评论
- 近 abusive, opprobrious, scurrile, scurrilous, truculent, vitriolic, vituperative
- 反 adulatory, flattery 阿谀奉承的；complimentary 称赞的

inveigh [ɪnˈveɪ]
- 【考法】 *vi.* 激烈抗议，表示强烈不满：to **protest** or complain bitterly or **vehemently**
- 例 inveigh against the bank industry 对银行业表示强烈不满
- 近 gripe, grouse, object, protest, remonstrate, repine
- 反 support 支持；delight, rejoice 感到高兴

inveigle [ɪnˈveɪɡl]
- 【考法】 *vt.* 诱骗：to **win over by coaxing**, flattery, or artful talk
- 例 inveigle consumers into buying the item 诱骗顾客购买商品
- 近 allure, bait, decoy, entice, entrap, seduce, tempt
- 反 demand 强求
- 派 inveigling *adj.* 诱骗性的

inventory [ˈɪnvəntɔːri]
- 【考法 1】 *n.* 存货清单：a detailed, itemized **list**, report, or record of things in one's possession, especially a periodic survey of **all goods** and materials in stock
- 例 The dealership has an unusually large inventory of pre-owned vehicles. 销售商手中有着一份巨大的二手车库存单。
- 近 budget, pool, repertoire, reservoir, stock
- 【考法 2】 *n.* (包含要点的)简介：a **short statement** of the main points
- 例 They decided to offer the public an informative inventory of everything that is known about the virus at this time. 他们决定向公众提供一份极富价值的报告，它涵盖了目前为止关于这种病毒的所有认识。
- 近 abstract, brief, epitome, outline, résumé, summarization, synopsis

inveterate [ɪnˈvetərət]
- 【考法】 *adj.* 积习的：**firmly established** by long persistence
- 例 the inveterate tendency to overlook the obvious 总是忽视显而易见事物的习惯
- 近 chronic, entrenched, ingrained, rooted, settled, hard-cored
- 反 adventitious 偶然的

invidious [ɪnˈvɪdiəs]
- 【考法 1】 *adj.* 惹人反感的：tending to **cause discontent**, animosity, or envy
- 例 the invidious task of arbitration 令人反感的仲裁任务
- 近 abhorrent, detestable, obnoxious, odious, repugnant, repellent
- 反 agreeable, gratifying, pleasant 令人高兴的
- 【考法 2】 *adj.* 羡慕嫉妒恨的：having or showing mean **resentment of another's possessions** or advantages
- 例 Inevitably, his remarkable success attracted the invidious attention of the other sales representatives. 不可避免地，他的巨大成功引来了其他销售代表羡慕嫉妒恨的眼光。
- 近 covetous, envious, jaundiced, jealous, resentful, green-eyed

Unit 3

■ INVIGORATE　　■ INVINCIBLE　　■ INVOKE　　■ IRASCIBLE　　■ IRATE
■ IRIDESCENT　　■ IRK　　■ IRONCLAD　　■ IRRADICABLE　　■ IRREDUCIBLE

invigorate ［ɪnˈvɪgəreɪt］
【考法】 *vt.* 使精神，使强壮，鼓舞激励：to **impart vigor**, strength, or vitality to
例 news that invigorates the public 给大众打鸡血的新闻
近 animate, energize, fortify, reinforce, strengthen, vitalize
反 dampen, deaden, debilitate, emaciate, sap 使衰弱；demoralize 使士气衰落
派 invigorated *adj.* 精力充沛的

invincible ［ɪnˈvɪnsəbl］
【考法】 *adj.* 不可战胜的，不可超越的：**incapable** of being **conquered**, overcome, or subdued
例 The soccer team proved to be invincible. 这支球队证明了自己是不可战胜的。
近 bulletproof, impregnable, invulnerable, unbeatable, unconquerable
反 conquerable 可被征服的；surmountable 可超越的；vulnerable 脆弱的，敏感的
派 invincibility *n.* 无敌

invoke ［ɪnˈvoʊk］
【考法 1】 *vt.* 实施：to **put into effect** or operation
例 New train timetable has been invoked. 新的火车时刻表已经生效。
近 enforce, effect, execute, implement, perform
反 suspend 暂停，搁置
【考法 2】 *vt.* 产生，造成：to **be the cause** of（a situation, action, or state of mind）
例 We should be prepared for the possibility that any solution may invoke another set of problems. 我们必须要为这样一种可能做好心理准备：任何解决方案都可能带来一系列新的问题。
近 beget, bring, catalyze, cause, create, engender, generate, induce, produce, result

irascible ［ɪˈræsəbl］
【考法】 *adj.* 易怒的：marked by hot temper and **easily provoked anger**
例 The new boss is so irascible that several employees have resigned. 由于新老板太容易发飙，许多员工已经递交了辞呈。
近 choleric, irritable, peevish, petulant
反 affable 和蔼的

irate ［aɪˈreɪt］
【考法】 *adj.* 极其愤怒的：**extremely angry**
例 an irate taxpayer 极为愤怒的纳税人
近 aggravated, apoplectic, choleric, enraged, exasperated, infuriated, ireful, mad, wrathful
反 calm, halcyon 平静的；delighted, pleased 高兴的，满意的

iridescent ［ˌɪrɪˈdesnt］
【考法】 *adj.* 五颜六色的：displaying a play of **lustrous colors** like those of the rainbow
例 an iridescent soap bubble 一个五颜六色的肥皂泡
近 nacreous, opalescent, pearlescent
反 monochromatic 单色的
派 iridescence *n.* 五彩斑斓

irk ［ɜːrk］
【考法 1】 *n.* 令人烦恼的事物：something that is a **source of irritation**
例 One of the prof's major irks is a cell phone that rings during a lecture. 课堂上突然响起的手机铃声是最让教授火大的事情之一。
近 aggravation, bother, exasperation, frustration, headache, irritant, nuisance, vexation
【考法 2】 *vt.* 使烦恼，使厌倦：to cause to be **irritating**, wearisome, or vexing to
例 She irked her friends by chewing her gum loudly during the movie. 她因为看电影时嚼口香糖弄出声响而惹怒了她的朋友们。
近 annoy, bother, fret, gall, provoke, ruffle, vex
反 appease, assuage, pacify, placate, propitiate, soothe 安抚，平息
派 irksome *adj.* 令人厌烦的

ironclad [ˈaɪərnklæd]

【考法】 *adj.* 非常坚固的，坚不可摧的：so firm or secure as to be **unbreakable**

例 pride on their ironclad fleet 对他们坚不可摧的舰队感到自豪

近 firm, invulnerable, secure, sound, tenacious, tough

反 fragile 脆弱的

irradicable [ɪˈrædɪkəbl]

【考法】 *adj.* 不能根除的：**impossible** to uproot or **destroy**

例 Smoking has become an irradicable bad habit for him. 吸烟已成了他不能根除的恶习。

近 entrenched, ineradicable, ingrained, inveterate, rooted

反 eradicable 可根除的

irreducible [ˌɪrɪˈduːsəbl]

【考法】 *adj.* （数）不可约分的：**incapable** of being **factored** into polynomials of lower degree with coefficients in some given field（as the rational numbers）or integral domain（as the integers）

例 irreducible integrals 质数

反 factorable 可约分的

Unit 4

■ IRRIGATE	■ IRRITATE	■ ISSUE	■ JABBER	■ JADED
■ JAPE	■ JARGON	■ JARRING	■ JAUNDICE	■ JAUNTY

irrigate [ˈɪrɪɡeɪt]

【考法 1】 *vt.* 灌溉：to **supply**（dry land）with **water** by means of ditches, pipes, or streams; water artificially

例 irrigate crops periodically 定期灌溉农作物

近 water

派 irrigation *n.* 灌溉

【考法 2】 *vt.* 冲洗：to **flush**（a body part）with a stream of liquid（as in removing a foreign body or medicating）

例 irrigate the wound 冲洗伤口

近 flush, rinse, wash

irritate [ˈɪrɪteɪt]

【考法】 *vt.* 刺激，惹恼：to **provoke** impatience, **anger**, or displeasure in

例 His rude interruptions really irritated her. 他粗鲁的打断激怒了她。

近 aggravate, annoy, exasperate, gall, inflame, nettle, peeve, provoke, rile, roil

反 appease, assuage, pacify, placate, propitiate, soothe 安抚，平息

派 irritant *n.* 刺激物

issue [ˈɪʃuː]

【考法 1】 *n.* （有争议的）话题，议题：a **matter that is in dispute** between two or more parties

例 focused on economic and political issues 重点关注经济和政治话题

近 nut, problem, question

【考法 2】 *v.* 发布（期刊等）：to **produce and release** for distribution in printed form

例 plans to issue a monthly newsletter 计划发布新闻月刊

近 print

【考法 3】 *v.* （使）流出：to（cause to）go, come, or **flow out**

例 strange sound issued from the abandoned house 废弃房中传来的奇怪声音

近 discharge, emit, exude, release, vent

反 withdraw 撤回

jabber [ˈdʒæbər]

【考法】 *vi.* 快而不清楚地说：to **talk rapidly, indistinctly**, or unintelligibly

例 monkeys jabbering at each other in their cages 在笼子里唧唧歪歪的猴子

近 babble, blabber, drivel, gabble, gibber, mumbo jumbo

反 speak slowly 慢慢地说

jaded [ˈdʒeɪdɪd]

【考法 1】 *adj.* 疲惫的：**depleted in strength**, energy, or freshness

例 After that long bar exam, I'm too jaded for anything but a nap. 漫长的律师资格考试结束后，我累得只想睡觉。

近 drained, exhausted, fatigued, prostrate, spent, wearied, worn-out

【考法 2】 *adj.* 厌倦的，没兴趣没热情的：having one's **patience**, interest, or pleasure **exhausted**

例 Even jaded sci-fi fans are finding this new space adventure fresh and exciting. 即使是见多识广、口味很挑的科幻小说忠粉也觉得这次的太空探险非常新鲜有趣。

近 bored, tired, wearied, fed up

反 absorbed, engaged, engrossed, interested, intrigued, rapt 有兴趣的

jape [dʒeɪp]

【考法】 *v.* 嘲弄：to say or do something jokingly or **mockingly**

例 The characters in Oscar Wilde's plays jape with a sophistication that is rarely encountered in real life. 奥斯卡·王尔德戏剧作品中的角色用一种十分世故的态度进行嘲讽，而这种态度在真实生活当中是很少见的。

近 jest, quip, wisecrack, banter, chaff, gag, jive, jolly, josh

反 revere 尊敬

jargon ['dʒɑːrgən]

【考法】 *n.* 行业术语：the **specialized or technical language** of a trade, profession, or similar group

例 medical jargon that the layman cannot understand 外行不理解的医学术语

近 argot, cant, dialect, jive, lingo, patois

jarring ['dʒɑːrɪŋ]

【考法 1】 *adj.* 刺耳的：harsh or **discordant**

例 The final chord of that song is too jarring for me. 那首歌最后的合声部分太刺耳了。

近 grating, cacophonous, strident

反 melodious 音调优美的

【考法 2】 *adj.* 震惊的：causing a **strong emotional reaction** because of unexpectedness

例 The jarring news that major financial institutions were on the verge of collapse. 有消息称主要的几个金融机构处于倒闭的边缘，真是让人震惊。

近 amazing, astonishing, astounding, blindsiding, dumbfounding, flabbergasting, jaw-dropping, jolting, shocking, startling, stunning

jaundice ['dʒɔːndɪs]

【考法】 *n.* (因嫉妒或厌世而产生的)偏见：to affect with the negativity or bitterness of jaundice; **bias**

例 the jaundice in the eyes of the two feuding neighbors 两个有积怨的邻居之间的偏见

近 animosity, animus, antagonism, antipathy, gall, hostility, rancor

反 amity 和睦，好感

jaunty ['dʒɔːnti]

【考法】 *adj.* 轻快的，活泼的：**sprightly** in manner or appearance: lively

例 a jaunty stroll 轻快的散步

近 animate, brisk, energetic, frisky, perky, racy, spirited, vivacious

反 staid, dead, inactive, inanimate, lackadaisical, languid, languishing, leaden, limp, listless, spiritless, vapid 无生气的

Unit 5

■ JEJUNE   ■ JEOPARDY   ■ JEST   ■ JETTISON   ■ JIBE
■ JINGOIST   ■ JITTERS   ■ JOCULAR   ■ JOCUND   ■ JOG

jejune [dʒɪ'dʒuːn]

【考法 1】 *adj.* 无趣乏味的：**not interesting**; dull

例 jejune lectures 无聊的讲座

近 arid, drab, dreary, leaden, monotonous, ponderous, tedious, weary

反 absorbing, engaging, engrossing, gripping, interesting, intriguing, involving, riveting, thought provoking 促人深思的，吸引人的

【考法 2】 *adj.* 幼稚的：having or showing the **annoying qualities** (as silliness) associated with **children**

例 an essay filled with jejune, simplistic opinions about international politics 充满着有关国际政治的幼稚、简单看法的文章

近 adolescent, immature, infantile, juvenile, kiddish, puerile

反 adult, grown-up, mature 成熟的

jettison ['dʒetɪsn]

【考法】 *vt.* 放弃，拒绝接受(想法、计划等)：to **get rid of** as superfluous or encumbering; omit or forgo as part of a plan or as the result of some other decision

例 The Government seems to have jettisoned the bail-out plan. 政府似乎已经放弃了这个救市计划。

近 abandon, abdicate, discard, junk, reject, scrap, shed, slough, throw away

反 rescue, salvage 救援，拯救

jeopardy [ˈdʒepərdi]

【考法】 *n.* 危险：**risk** of loss or injury; peril or **danger**

例 The city's firefighters routinely put their lives in jeopardy. 消防队员们早就把生命置之度外了。

近 distress, endangerment, imperilment, peril

反 safeness, safety, secureness, security 安全

jest [dʒest]

【考法】 *n.* 轻浮的态度，戏谑：a **frivolous** mood or manner

例 spoken in jest 戏谑地说

近 butt, derision, mockery

反 solemnity, solemn utterance 严肃

jibe [dʒaɪb]

【考法】 *vi.* 意见一致：to be in accord: **agree**

例 Your figures jibe with mine. 你的数据与我的一致。

近 accord, cohere, conform, correspond, harmonize, tally

反 conflict 冲突

jingoist [ˈdʒɪŋɡoʊɪst]

【考法】 *n.* 极端爱国激进分子（通常表现为好战的对外政策）：**extreme** chauvinism or **nationalism** marked especially by a **belligerent** foreign policy

例 jingoists who cry for war 叫嚣着鼓吹开战的激进分子

近 chauvinist, nationalist, superpatriot, war hawk

反 dove, pacifist, peacenik 反战派人士

jitters [ˈdʒɪtərz]

【考法】 *n.* 紧张，不安：a sense of **panic** or extreme **nervousness**

例 She suffered pre-wedding jitters. 她有婚前恐惧。

近 butterflies, dither, jimjams, nerves, shakes, shivers, willies

反 aplomb, calm, composure, equanimity, imperturbability, self-possession, tranquility 镇定，冷静

jocular [ˈdʒɑːkjələr]

【考法】 *adj.* 搞笑的，欢乐的：characterized by **joking, playful**

例 a jocular man who could make the most serious people laugh 搞笑的人可以使最严肃的人都开怀大笑

近 blithesome, festive, gleeful, jocund, jovial, mirthful

反 lachrymose, saturnine 悲哀的；dour, dreary, morose, serious 阴郁的

jocund [ˈdʒɑːkənd]

【考法】 *adj.* 欢快的，高兴的：**sprightly** and **lighthearted** in disposition, character, or quality

例 old friends engaged in jocund teasing 老朋友相见，互相打趣调侃

近 blithesome, jocose, jocular, jolly, jovial, mirthful, sunny

反 lachrymose, saturnine 悲哀的；dour, dreary, morose, serious 阴郁的

jog [dʒɑːɡ]

【考法1】 *n.* 慢跑：a **movement**, pace, or instance of jogging（as for **exercise**）

【考法2】 *vt.* 唤起：to **rouse** or stimulate

例 an old photo that might jog your memory 一张也许会唤起你回忆的老照片

近 arouse, excite, incite, instigate, pique, remind, stimulate, stir

反 allay, alleviate, assuage, ease, mitigate, mollify, palliate, relieve, soothe 缓和

Unit 6

■ JOLT	■ JOT	■ JOVIAL	■ JUBILANT	■ JUDICIOUS
■ JUGGERNAUT	■ KEN	■ KIDNAP	■ KINDLE	■ KINDRED

jolt [dʒoʊlt]

【考法1】 *vi.* 突然移动：to **move** or dislodge with a **sudden**, hard blow

【考法2】 *vt.* 惊吓：to cause an **unpleasant surprise** for

例 The sneak terrorist attack jolted the country out of its indolence and indifference. 偷偷摸摸的恐怖袭击将该国从懒惰和冷漠无情中惊醒。

近 appall, floor, shake up

jot	[dʒɑːt]

【考法】 *vt.* 简要记录：to **write briefly** or hurriedly

例 jot down an address 简要地记下地址

近 log, mark, put down, register, report, set down, take down, write down

jovial	[ˈdʒoʊviəl]

【考法】 *adj.* 愉快的：markedly **good-humored** especially as evidenced by **jollity** and **conviviality**

例 a jovial host 快活的主人

近 blithesome, festive, gay, gleeful, jocular, jocund, jolly, mirthful

反 lachrymose, saturnine 悲哀的；dour, dreary, morose, serious 阴郁的

jubilant	[ˈdʒuːbɪlənt]

【考法】 *adj.* 喜悦的：exultingly **joyful**

例 The nominee delivered a jubilant speech before the cheering crowd. 在欢呼的人群面前，被提名人发表了充满喜悦的演说。

近 exulting, glorying, rejoicing, triumphant

反 lachrymose, saturnine 悲哀的；dour, dreary, morose, serious 阴郁的

judicious	[dʒuˈdɪʃəs]

【考法】 *adj.* 明智的，慎重的：having or exhibiting sound **judgment**；**prudent**

例 a judicious choice 明智的抉择

近 intelligent, judgmatic, prudent, tactical, wise

反 daft, imprudent, inadvisable, inexpedient, indiscreet, impolitic, unwise 愚蠢的，轻率的

juggernaut	[ˈdʒʌɡərnɔːt]

【考法】 *n.* 无法阻挡的力量，摧毁一切的强大力量：an **overwhelming**, advancing **force** that crushes everything in its path

例 the juggernaut of industrialization 工业化无法阻挡的力量

近 steamroller

ken	[ken]

【考法1】 *n.* 视野范围：the range of **vision**

例 abstract words that are beyond the ken of children 孩子们不能理解的抽象单词

近 sight

【考法2】 *vt.* 知道、了解（人或物）：to **know** (a person or thing)

近 appreciate, apprehend, cognize, comprehend, grasp, perceive, savvy, understand

反 misapprehend, misconceive, misinterpret, misperceive, misunderstand 错误地理解

kidnap	[ˈkɪdnæp]

【考法】 *vt.* 绑架勒索：to seize and **detain** by **unlawful force** or fraud and often with a demand for ransom

例 The child was kidnapped and held for ransom. 歹徒绑架了孩子，并且向家属勒索赎金。

近 abduct

反 release, set free 释放

kindle	[ˈkɪndl]

【考法】 *vt.* 点燃：to build or fuel (a fire)；to **set fire** to；**ignite**

例 kindle interest 激发兴趣

近 enkindle, ignite, inflame, torch

反 douse, extinguish, quench, put out, snuff out 熄灭

kindred	[ˈkɪndrəd]

【考法】 *adj.* 类似的；具有相似或相近的起源、本性或性质的：having a **similar** or related **origin**, nature, or character

例 She finally found people who were kindred spirits when she joined the hiking club. 她加入登山俱乐部的时候终于发现了志向相同的人。

近 agreeable, amicable, compatible, congenial, frictionless, unanimous, united

反 disagreeable, discordant, disharmonious, disunited, incompatible, inharmonious, uncongenial 不一致的，不和谐的

Unit 7

knack [næk]
【考法】 *n.* 诀窍，聪明的做法：a **clever** trick or stratagem; a clever way of doing something
例 She's tried every knack in Cupid's book to get her guy to marry her. 她试过了所有爱情三十六计，希望那男人娶她。
近 artifice, device, gambit, ploy, scheme, sleight, stratagem
反 foolishness 愚蠢

knead [niːd]
【考法】 *vt.* 揉捏，塑造：to make or **shape** by or as if **by folding**, pressing, and stretching with the hands
例 knead dough 揉面团 ‖ knead a painful calf muscle 给疼痛的小腿肌肉按摩
近 massage, manipulate, mould, squeeze, stroke

knit [nɪt]
【考法 1】 *vt.* 编织（纱线）：to form by **interlacing yarn** or thread in a series of connected loops **with needles**
例 She knitted him a sweater for Christmas. 圣诞节她为他缝了一件毛衣。
近 braid, plait, weave
反 ravel 解开
【考法 2】 *vt.* 连接，联系：to **join closely**; unite securely
例 Sport knits the whole family close together. 体育将整个家庭紧紧地联系在一起。
近 bind, bond, combine, connect, fasten, join, link, meld, merge, tie, secure, unite
反 disassociate, disconnect, disjoin, divide, sever, split, sunder 分开

knotty ['nɑːti]
【考法】 *adj.* 多结的，复杂的，困难的：marked by or full of knots especially: so **full of difficulties** and **complications** as to be likely to defy solution
例 The candidates cautiously gave their views on an array of knotty issues. 候选人就一系列困难问题谨慎地给出了自己的看法。
近 baroque, byzantine, complicated, convoluted, intricate, involved, labyrinthine, sophisticated, tangled
反 easy, effortless, plain, simple 容易的，明显的

kudos ['kuːdɑːs]
【考法 1】 *n.* 名望，名声：**fame** and renown resulting from an act or achievement
例 Employees enjoy the kudos that the job brings as much as the financial rewards. 正如同喜欢工作带来的经济回报一样，雇员们也很享受工作所带来的名声和荣誉。
近 credit, distinction, homage, honor, laurels
反 infamy, notoriety 不好的名声
【考法 2】 *n.* 夸奖，赞扬：**acclaim or praise** for exceptional achievement
例 The attorney did pro bono work because it was the right thing to do, and not for any future kudos that it might bring. 这名律师之所以为慈善机构和穷人提供免费服务，是因为他觉得这是正确的事情，而非为了任何可能因此而产生的赞扬。
近 acclaim, accolade, applause, credit, distinction, homage, honor, laud, laurels
反 belittlement, denigration, deprecation, derogation, diminishment, disparagement 贬损

labile ['leɪbaɪl]
【考法】 *adj.* 易变的，不稳定的：continually undergoing chemical, physical, or biological change; **unstable**
例 labile mineral 不稳定的矿物质 ‖ an emotionally labile person 一个多愁善感的人
近 capricious, fluctuating, fluid, inconstant, mercurial, temperamental, unsettled, unsteady, variable, volatile
反 constant, immutable, invariable, stable, stationary, steady 稳定的

laborious [lə'bɔːriəs]
【考法 1】 *adj.* 勤奋的：hard-working; **industrious**
例 The volunteers have been commendably laborious in their cleanup of the beach. 清理海滩的志愿者们的勤奋努力值得赞扬。 ‖ He was gentle and kindly, living a laborious life in his Paris flat. 他是一个温柔、好心的人，住在巴黎的公寓里，过着勤奋的生活。
近 active, assiduous, bustling, diligent, engaged, industrious, occupied, sedulous
反 idle, inactive, indolent, inert, slothful 懒散的

【考法2】 *adj.* 费力的：marked by or requiring **long, hard work**

例 the laborious task of cleaning up the oil spill 清除泄露石油的艰苦工作

近 arduous, challenging, demanding, difficult, exacting, formidable, grueling, heavy, labored, rigorous, rough, rugged, severe, strenuous, sweaty, toilsome, tough

反 easy, effortless, facile, light, mindless, simple, undemanding 轻松的，容易的

labyrinthine [ˌlæbə'rɪnθaɪn]

【考法】 *adj.* 迷宫似的，复杂曲折的：of, relating to, resembling, or constituting a labyrinth; **extremely complex** or tortuous in **structure**

例 The labyrinthine political situation of Middle East left us totally befuddled. 中东地区复杂迷离的政治局势让我们彻底迷惑了。

近 baroque, byzantine, complicate, complicated, convoluted, intricate, involved, knotty, sophisticated, tangled

反 easy, effortless, plain, simple 容易的，明显的

lacerate ['læsəreɪt]

【考法】 *vt.* 使非常痛苦：to **cause** deep emotional **pain** to; distress

例 He was born into a family already lacerated with tensions and divisions. 他出生在一个已经被冲突和分裂折磨不堪的家庭当中。

近 afflict, distress, harrow, hurt, rend, torment, torture, wound

反 allay, alleviate, assuage, ease, mitigate, mollify, palliate, relieve, soothe 减轻(痛苦等)

lackluster ['læklʌstər]

【考法】 *adj.* 黯淡无光泽的：**lacking brightness**, luster, or vitality

例 lackluster hair 黯淡无光的头发

近 dim, dull, flat, lusterless

反 burnished, glistening, glossy, lustrous, polished, shiny, sleek 光亮的

Unit 8

■ LACONIC	■ LACHRYMOSE	■ LAMBASTE	■ LAMENT	■ LAMENTABLE
■ LAMPOON	■ LANGUID	■ LANGUISH	■ LANGUOR	■ LANK

laconic [lə'kɑːnɪk]

【考法】 *adj.* 简洁(以至于显得粗鲁或难以理解)的：using or involving the use of a **minimum of words**: **concise** to the point of seeming rude or mysterious

例 His mentor's comment tends to be laconic but very much to the point. 他导师的点评很简短，但是却总能说到点子上。

近 apothegmatic, brief, capsule, compact, compendious, curt, pithy, succinct, summary, telegraphic, terse

反 circuitous, circumlocutory, diffuse, prolix, rambling, verbose, windy, wordy 冗长的

lachrymose ['lækrɪmoʊs]

【考法】 *adj.* 催人泪下的，悲伤的：tending to cause tears, **mournful**

例 The lachrymose mourners at the funeral required a steady supply of tissues. 葬礼上多愁善感的哀悼者对纸巾有稳定的需求。

近 doleful, lamentable, lugubrious, melancholy, mournful, tearful, teary, weepy, woeful

反 cheerful, delighted, jocund, jovial 欢乐的，快乐的

lambaste [læm'beɪst]

【考法】 *vt.* 严厉斥责：to **scold sharply**; berate

例 Critics lambasted his performance. 评论家严厉斥责了他的表演。

近 assail, baste, belabor, berate, castigate, excoriate, reprimand, reproach, scathe, slam, upbraid, vituperate

反 carol, extol, glorify, hymn, laud, magnify, praise 表扬，赞美

lament [lə'ment]

【考法1】 *n.* 悼词：a **composition** expressing one's **grief** over a loss

例 her lament for her grandmother 她为她祖母写的悼词

近 dirge, elegy, requiem

【考法2】 *n.* 抱怨：an expression of dissatisfaction, pain, or **resentment**

例 the career woman's lament that there aren't any good men left 职场女性的抱怨：好男人一个没剩下

近 carp, complaint, fuss, grievance, gripe, grouch, grouse, grumble, moan, murmur

【考法 3】 *v.* 为…哀悼，表达痛苦或遗憾：to **express sorrow** or regret; mourn

例　lament an innocent death 为无辜的死者而悲痛

近　bemoan, deplore, grieve, moan, mourn, wail

反　delight, exult, joy, rejoice 感到高兴

lamentable ['læməntəbl]

【考法】 *adj.* 值得惋惜的，悲哀的：inspiring or deserving of lament or regret; **deplorable** or pitiable; mournful

例　The lamentable cries of the women for their lost sons were heard throughout the village. 女人们由于丧子之痛的哀嚎响彻整个村庄。

近　deplorable, distressful, grievous, heartbreaking, lugubrious, plaintive, plangent, sorrowful, woeful

反　cheerful, delighted, jocund, jovial 欢乐的，快乐的

lampoon [læm'puːn]

【考法】 *n.* 讽刺：a **harsh satire** usually directed against an individual

例　a lampoon of the movie business at the time 对当时电影产业的一种讽刺

近　burlesque, caricature, farce, mockery, parody, ridicule, spoof, travesty

反　eulogy, ode, paean 颂歌

languid ['læŋgwɪd]

【考法】 *adj.* 没精打采的，虚弱的：**lacking energy** or vitality; weak

例　be languid for weeks after surgery 术后的几周都无精打采的

近　debilitated, effete, enervated, feeble, frail, infirm, lackadaisical, spiritless, sapped, enfeebled

反　animated, energetic, vehement, vivacious 有精力的；mighty, powerful, stalwart, stout, strong 强壮的

languish ['læŋgwɪʃ]

【考法】 *vi.* 变得衰弱：to be or **become feeble**, weak, or enervated

例　languish during the prolonged heat wave 在持续的热浪下变得虚弱

近　decay, droop, emaciate, fade, fail, flag, sag, wither

反　burgeon, flourish, thrive, prosper 旺盛生长

languor ['læŋgər]

【考法 1】 *n.* 懒惰：physical or mental **inertness**

例　He enjoyed the languor brought on by a hot summer afternoon. 他很享受夏日午后的慵懒。

近　collapse, exhaustion, frazzle, lassitude, listlessness, stupor, torpor, prostration

反　verve, vim, animation, vitality 有活力

【考法 2】 *n.* 衰弱：**weakness** or **weariness** of body or mind

例　The tropical heat sapped our strength, leaving us in a state of unaccustomed languor. 热带的炎热气候消磨着我们的精力，让我们感到一阵不适的虚弱。

近　debilitation, enervation, enfeeblement, fragility, infirmity

反　robustness, strength, vivacity 强壮，有力

lank [læŋk]

【考法 1】 *adj.* 细长瘦弱的：**long** and **lean**

例　lank cattle 瘦牲口

近　emaciated, lean, slender, svelte, tenuous, thin

反　fat, fleshy, gross, obese 肥胖的

【考法 2】 *adj.* 不僵硬的，柔软松弛的：long, straight, and **limp**; **not stiff** in structure

例　a woman with long, lank hair 有着长而稀疏头发的女子 ‖ Right after a shower, her lank hair hung down to her shoulders. 出浴后，柔软的头发搭在她的肩上。

近　droopy, flaccid, floppy, yielding

反　inflexible, rigid, stiff, sturdy, tense 僵硬的；resilient 有弹性的

Unit 9

■ LAPSE	■ LARGESSE	■ LASH	■ LASSITUDE	■ LATENT
■ LATITUDE	■ LAUDATORY	■ LAVISH	■ LEAVEN	■ LEER

lapse [læps]

【考法 1】 *n.* 小过失：a **slight error** typically due to forgetfulness or inattention

例　a lapse in table manner 餐桌礼仪的小过错

近　blunder, fumble, gaffe, miscue, oversight, peccadillo

【考法2】 *vt.* 结束，终止：to come to an **end**
例 The contract will lapse at the end of the year. 合同将于年底到期。
近 cease, conclude, die, end, expire, finish, stop, terminate
反 continue, persist, hang on 持续

largesse [lɑːrˈdʒes]
【考法1】 *n.* 捐赠物：something given to someone **without expectation of a return**
例 The alumna's huge bequest was an unexpected largess. 校友们的巨额遗赠是一笔意料之外的财富。
近 bestowal, donation, giveaway, present
【考法2】 *n.* 慷慨：**liberality** in giving or willingness to give
例 be noted for his largesse 因慷慨而闻名
近 bountifulness, generosity, munificence, openhandedness, philanthropy
反 miserliness, parsimony, penury, stinginess 小气

lash [læʃ]
【考法1】 *n.* 击打：a **hard strike** with a part of the body or an instrument
例 She suddenly felt the lash of her drunken husband's hand on her cheek. 她突然感觉到脸颊被醉酒的丈夫扇了一耳光。
近 bang, bash, bat, beat, clap, hit, knock, punch, slam, slap, smash, stinger, stroke, swat
【考法2】 *v.* 猛击，撞击：to **strike** against **with force** or violence
例 All night long a barrage of rain lashed the windows. 倾盆大雨整夜敲击着窗户。
近 baste, hammer, lace, lambaste, punch
【考法3】 *vt.* 捆扎：to **bind** with or as if with a line
例 Secure the anchor by lashing it to the rail. 将锚绑在栏杆上使其稳固。
反 unbind 解开

lassitude [ˈlæsɪtuːd]
【考法】 *n.* 乏力，没精打采：a state or feeling of weariness, **diminished energy**, or listlessness
例 Symptoms of anaemia include general fatigue and lassitude. 贫血的通常症状包括体虚和乏力。
近 collapse, exhaustion, frazzle, languor, listlessness, stupor, torpor, prostration
反 verve, vim, animation, vitality 有活力

latent [ˈleɪtnt]
【考法】 *adj.* 潜在的，不活跃的：present or **potential** but **not evident** or active
例 a latent infection 潜伏性传染病 ‖ He has a latent talent for acting that he hasn't had a chance to express yet. 他有着表演的天赋，只不过他还没有机会来表现这一才能。
近 dormant, fallow, inert, inoperative
反 apparent, evident, manifest, obvious, plain 明显的；active 活跃的
派 latency *n.* 潜伏期

latitude [ˈlætɪtuːd]
【考法】 *n.* (行动或言论)自由：**freedom** from normal restraints, limitations, or regulations
例 Students are allowed considerable latitude in choosing courses. 学生在选课时被给予相当大的自由度。
近 authorization, license, freedom, leeway, free hand
反 limitation 限制；custody 监护，拘留

laudatory [ˈlɔːdətɔːri]
【考法】 *adj.* 表示赞扬的：of, relating to, or expressing **praise**
例 a laudatory review of the new play 对新剧目的赞扬性评论
近 adulatory, commendatory, complimentary, extolling, eulogistic, panegyric
反 derogatory, depreciatory, disparaging, pejorative 贬低的
派 laudable *adj.* 值得赞扬的

lavish [ˈlævɪʃ]
【考法1】 *adj.* 奢侈的，大量的，无节制的：characterized by or produced with **extravagance and profusion**
例 lavish buffet 奢侈的自助餐
近 copious, exuberant, gushing, lush, luxuriant, opulent, profuse, riotous
反 moderate, modest, reasonable, temperate 适度的，合理的
【考法2】 *vt.* 挥霍，浪费：to **give readily** and in large quantities; to use up **carelessly**
例 a great actor who lavished his talent in lousy movies 将才华浪费在低劣电影上的影星
近 blow, dissipate, fritter, misspend, squander, waste
反 conserve 节约

leaven ['levn]

【考法】 *vt.* 在…中加入轻松、活泼或变更的因素：to **mingle** or **permeate** with some modifying, alleviating, or vivifying element

例 He needs to leaven his speeches with more humor. 他需要在演讲中再加入点幽默元素。

近 imbue, infuse, ingrain, inoculate, inspire, permeate, steep, suffuse

反 extract 抽取

leer [lɪr]

【考法】 *vi.* 一瞥，斜眼看：to cast a **sidelong** glance

例 He gave her a leering look. 他瞥了她一眼。

近 squint

反 gape, gaze, glare, goggle, stare 盯着看

Unit 10

■ LEERY	■ LEGACY	■ LEGEND	■ LEGION	■ LENIENT
■ LETHAL	■ LETHARGIC	■ LEVELHEADED	■ LEVITY	■ LIABILITY

leery ['lɪri]

【考法】 *adj.* 怀疑的，不信任的：**suspicious** or distrustful; wary

例 be leery of strangers 对陌生人存有怀疑

近 dubious, distrustful, skeptical, suspicious, wary

反 credulous 轻信的

legacy ['legəsi]

【考法】 *n.* 遗产：something **handed down** from an **ancestor** or a predecessor or from the past

例 the legacy of the ancient philosophers 古代哲学家们的思想遗产

近 bequest, heritage, patrimony

legend ['ledʒənd]

【考法1】 *n.* 传奇，传说：a **popular myth** of recent origin

例 Some ancient civilizations had legends about spirits that inhabited trees and rocks. 一些古文明有着关于寄居于树木、岩石之中的精灵的传说。

近 fable, myth, mythos

派 legendary *adj.* 如传奇般闻名的

【考法2】 *n.* 图例：an **explanatory list** of the symbols on a **map** or chart

例 The legend in the science textbook indicated that the accompanying picture had been enlarged by 1000%. 科学课本上彩图的图例告诉我们这幅图片被放大了十倍。

近 cutline

legion ['liːdʒən]

【考法1】 *n.* 大量的人，(尤指)军团：a **large body of men** and women organized for land warfare

例 join the French Foreign Legion 加入法国外籍军团

近 army, battalion, flock, herd, horde, mob, swarm, throng

【考法2】 *adj.* 大量的：many, **numerous**

例 The problems are legion. 问题不计其数。

近 beaucoup, multifold, multitudinous, numerous

反 few, lack in number 少量的

lenient ['liːniənt]

【考法】 *adj.* 宽大仁慈的：inclined not to be harsh or strict; **merciful**, generous, or indulgent

例 the lenient sentences 仁慈的审判

近 clement, gentle, merciful, mild, sparing, tender, tolerant

反 harsh, merciless, severe, strict 残酷的，严厉的

派 lenience *n.* 仁慈

lethal ['liːθl]

【考法】 *adj.* 非常有害的，致命的：**extremely harmful**; devastating

例 This dagger is lethal. 这把匕首是致命的武器。 || launch a lethal attack 发动致命的进攻

近 baleful, deadly, deathly, fatal, mortal, murderous, pestilent, terminal, vital

反 innocuous 无害的；healthy, salubrious, wholesome 有益健康的

lethargic [ləˈθɑːrdʒɪk]

【考法】 *adj.* 没精打采的，行动迟缓的：of, relating to, or characterized by lethargy, **sluggish**

例 A big nice meal always makes me feel lethargic and sleepy. 一顿大餐吃完总是让我既慵懒又想睡。

近 dull, inert, quiescent, sluggish, torpid

反 dynamic, energetic, robust, vigorous 有精力的；active 活跃的

levelheaded [ˌlevlˈhedɪd]

【考法】 *adj.* 明智的：characteristically self-composed and **sensible**

例 a levelheaded assessment of the problem 对于问题的一个明智的评估

近 informed, justified, logical, rational, reasonable, sensible, sober, valid, well-founded

反 foolish 愚蠢的；groundless, invalid, unfounded, unjustified, unsound 没有根据的，理由不充分的

levity [ˈlevəti]

【考法】 *n.* 轻浮：excessive or unseemly **frivolity**

例 The teachers disapprove of any displays of levity during school assemblies. 老师们不允许学生在学校聚会中表现出任何轻浮的态度。

近 facetiousness, flightiness, flippancy, frivolousness, frothiness, silliness

反 earnestness, gravity, seriousness, soberness, solemnity 严肃

liability [ˌlaɪəˈbɪləti]

【考法1】 *n.* 责任：the quality or state of being **liable**

例 The company is trying to reduce its liability in this case. 在这个案件中，公司试图减少他们的责任。

近 accountability, answerability, responsibility

反 immunity 豁免权

【考法2】 *n.* 障碍，不利条件：a feature of someone or something that **creates difficulty** for achieving success

例 Their chief asset has now become a considerable liability. 他们最大的优点如今已成了不可小觑的负担。

近 burden, debit, drawback, handicap, hurdle, incommodity, manacle, saddle, trammel

反 advantage, asset, edge, plus 优点，优势

When an end is lawful and obligatory, the indispensable means to it are also lawful and obligatory.

如果一个目的是正当而必须做的，则达到这个目的的必要手段也是正当而必须采取的。

——美国政治家 林肯（Abraham Lincoln, American statesman）

List 15

"每当我们对未来充满了各种美好的期望与幻想时，就该反思一下自己现在的努力是否配得上这幻境中的将来。莫问收获，但问耕耘。"　　（刘宜君，2009 年 10 月，Verbal 730, Quantitative 800, 录取院校：斯坦福大学，计算机系）

Unit 1

■ LIBERAL	■ LIBERTINE	■ LICENTIOUS	■ LIKEN	■ LIMBER
■ LIMP	■ LIMPID	■ LINGER	■ LISSOME	■ LIST

liberal [ˈlɪbərəl]

【考法 1】 *adj.* 思想前卫的：**not bound** by traditional ways or beliefs

例 parents who take a very liberal attitude toward letting their children stay out late 思想开放，同意让他们的小孩晚归的家长们

近 nonconventional, nonorthodox, nontraditional, open-minded, progressive, radical

反 conservative, conventional, hidebound, old-fashioned, stodgy, traditional 守旧的，传统的

【考法 2】 *adj.* 慷慨的，大方的：marked by **generosity**

例 a doctor who has been very liberal in dispensing low-cost care to patients who could not otherwise afford it 一位慷慨的医生，愿意帮助无法支付低额药费的病人

近 charitable, munificent, unselfish, unsparing, unstinting

反 closefisted, miserly, niggardly, parsimonious, stingy, tightfisted 吝啬的

libertine [ˈlɪbərtiːn]

【考法】 *n.* 放荡不羁者：one who acts **without moral restraint**; a dissolute person

例 The legend of Don Juan depicts him as a playboy and libertine. 有关唐璜的传说把他描绘成一个放荡不羁的花花公子。

近 backslider, debaucher, decadent, deviate, pervert, profligate

反 ascetic 禁欲者

licentious [laɪˈsenʃəs]

【考法】 *adj.* 放荡的，性欲强的：**lacking** legal or moral **restraints**; having a strong sexua, desire

例 a moralist who decried what she regarded as the licentious and corrupt culture of the entertainment industry 一个公开谴责在她看来无比堕落和放荡的娱乐圈文化的道德家

近 concupiscent, horny, lascivious, lecherous, libidinous, lubricious, salacious, wanton

反 frigid, undersexed 性冷淡的

派 licentiousness *n.* 放荡

liken [ˈlaɪkən]

【考法】 *vt.* 显示相似，把…比作：to see, mention, or **show as similar**; compare

例 Life is often likened to a journey. 生活经常被比作一次旅行。

近 analogize, bracket, equate, equalize

反 contrast 对比，对照以产生反差

limber [ˈlɪmbər]

【考法】 *adj.* 可塑的，柔软的：capable of being shaped: **flexible**

例 She shaped the basket out of limber branches. 她用柔软的树枝编了一个筐。

近 flexible, lissome, lithesome, pliable, pliant, supple

反 inflexible, rigid, stiff, stiffened 僵硬的

limp [lɪmp]

【考法 1】 *adj.* 柔软的，松散的：**lacking firm** texture, substance, or structure

例 Her hair hung limp about her shoulders. 她的头发松散地垂在肩上。

近 droopy, flaccid, floppy, lank, yielding

反 firm, stiff, sturdy, tense 坚硬的；resilient 有弹性的

【考法2】 *adj.* 软弱的，没有精神的：**lacking strength** or firmness; weak or spiritless
例 The team's limp performance has many people calling for the head coach's resignation. 队伍不给力的表现让许多人呼吁教练下课。
近 enervated, lackadaisical, languid, languishing, languorous, spiritless
反 ambitious, enterprising 有雄心壮志的；animated, energetic, motivated 精力充沛的，有积极性的
【考法3】 *vi.* 跛行，艰难地行走：to move or proceed **haltingly or unsteadily**
例 The project limped along with half its previous funding. 项目靠着之前一半的资金艰难地进行着。
近 blunder, bumble, lumber, plod, struggle, stumble, trudge

limpid [ˈlɪmpɪd]
【考法1】 *adj.* 透明清澈的：characterized by **transparent clearness**
例 limpid streams 清澈的小溪
近 crystal, clear, lucent, pellucid, transparent
反 cloudy, murky, opaque, unclear, turbid 模糊不清的
【考法2】 *adj.* 镇定的，淡定的：**free from** emotional or mental **agitation**
例 the limpid outlook of a man who is at peace with himself as he awaits death 一个人在平静地等待死亡时所持的淡然的世界观
近 collected, composed, cool, level, peaceful, placid, possessed, sedate, serene, smooth, tranquil
反 agitated, discomposed, disturbed, flustered, perturbed 焦躁的

linger [ˈlɪŋgər]
【考法】 *vi.* 磨蹭，闲荡：to **proceed slowly**; saunter
例 Fans lingered outside the door. 粉丝们在门外徘徊。
近 crawl, creep, dally, dawdle, lag, loiter
反 hurry, run, rush 飞奔
派 lingering *adj.* 闲荡的

lissome [ˈlɪsəm]
【考法1】 *adj.* 柔软的：**easily bent**; supple
例 Rattan is such a lissome material that it can be used for all manner of furniture and baskets. 藤是一种非常柔软而有韧性的材料，可以被用于形形色色的家具和篮子之中。
近 flexible, limber, lithe, pliable, pliant, supple
反 solid 坚硬的；inflexible, rigid, stiff, stiffened 僵硬的
【考法2】 *adj.* 敏捷的，轻盈的：having the ability to **move with ease**; limber
例 a lissome ballerina 身姿轻盈的女芭蕾舞演员
近 agile, featly, feline, gracile, lithesome, nimble
反 awkward, clumsy, graceless, ungainly 笨拙的

list [lɪst]
【考法】 *v.* (使)倾斜：to set or cause to be **at an angle**
例 The sudden lift of the load on the deck listed the ship badly. 甲板上货物被突然提起，使船陡然倾斜。
近 angle, cant, heel, incline, pitch, slant, slope, tilt, tip
反 erect 竖立

Unit 2

■ LITHE　　　　　■ LOATH　　　　　■ LOATHE　　　　　■ LOFTY　　　　　■ LOLL
■ LOPSIDED　　　　■ LOQUACIOUS　　　■ LOUTISH　　　　■ LUBRICATE　　　■ LUCID

lithe [laɪð]
【考法1】 *adj.* 敏捷的，轻盈的：characterized by easy flexibility and **grace**
例 lithe dancers 轻盈优雅的舞者
近 agile, featly, feline, gracile, lightsome, nimble
反 awkward, clumsy, graceless, ungainly 笨拙的
【考法2】 *adj.* 柔软的：**easily bent** or flexed
例 lithe branches 柔软的枝条
近 flexible, limber, pliable, pliant, supple
反 solid 坚硬的；inflexible, rigid, stiff, stiffened 僵硬的

loath [loʊθ]

【考法】 *adj.* 不情愿的，讨厌的：unwilling or **reluctant**; disinclined

例 I was loath to accept the fact that he had been killed in a terrorist attack. 我极不情愿地接受了他在一场恐怖袭击中丧生的事实。

近 disinclined, indisposed, reluctant, reticent

反 eager 渴望的；disposed, inclined 有意向的

loathe [loʊð]

【考法】 *vt.* 厌恶：to **dislike** someone or something greatly; abhor

例 I loathe having to do this. 我鄙视不得不这样做。

近 abhor, abominate, despise, detest, execrate

反 adore, love 热爱

派 loathsome *adj.* 令人讨厌的

lofty [ˈlɔːfti]

【考法 1】 *adj.* 崇高的：**elevated** in character and spirit, noble

例 lofty ideals 崇高的理想

近 chivalrous, elevated, greathearted, high-minded, magnanimous, sublime

反 base, debased, ignominious, mean 可耻的

【考法 2】 *adj.* 高的：**rising** to a great height

例 lofty mountains 高耸的山峰 ‖ the ever-increasing lofty heights of the world's skyscrapers 不断攀升的摩天大楼的高度

近 altitudinous, tall, towering

反 low 低的

【考法 3】 *adj.* 自大的：having a feeling of **superiority** that shows itself in an overbearing attitude

例 She acts all lofty and superior just because she went to Stanford University. 她之所以表现得这么自大和不可一世，只因为她考进了斯坦福。

近 assumptive, bumptious, haughty, lordly, peremptory, pompous, presumptuous, supercilious, superior

反 humble, lowly, modest 谦逊的，低调的

loll [lɑːl]

【考法 1】 *vi.* 懒洋洋地行动：to act or move in a lax, **lazy**, or indolent manner

例 He lolled back in his comfortable chair. 他懒洋洋地倚在他舒适的椅子上。

近 slouch, lounge

【考法 2】 *vi.* 偷懒，打发时间：to spend time **doing nothing**

例 Some members of the decorating committee were hard at work, and others were just lolling about. 装修队的一部分人在很努力地工作，另一些则在偷懒。

近 dally, dawdle, drone, laze

lopsided [ˌlɑːpˈsaɪdɪd]

【考法 1】 *adj.* 歪的，倾斜的：**leaning** to one side

例 The portrait in the foyer was lopsided. 门厅里的画像挂歪了。

近 askew, aslant, crazy, listing, oblique, pitched, skewed, slanted, tipping, uneven

反 even, level, straight 平的

【考法 2】 *adj.* 不平衡的，不协调的：**lacking in balance**, symmetry, or proportion

例 The arrangement of the furniture was lopsided. 家具的摆放太不协调了。 ‖ a lopsided score of 4-0 四比零的压倒性比分

近 asymmetric, disproportional, irregular, off-balance, unbalanced, unequal

反 balanced 平衡的；symmetrical 对称的

loquacious [ləˈkweɪʃəs]

【考法】 *adj.* 话多的：given to fluent or **excessive talk**

例 Sometimes the loquacious talk show host barely lets her guests get a word in. 有时候多话的脱口秀主持人让她的嘉宾一句话都插不进来。

近 chatty, conservational, gabby, garrulous, talkative, voluble

反 laconic, reserved, reticent, taciturn, uncommunicative 话少的

派 loquaciousness, loquacity *n.* 话多

loutish [ˈlaʊtɪʃ]

【考法】 *adj.* 粗鲁的：having the characteristics of a lout; **awkward, stupid, and boorish**

例 a boy with a loutish air 一个举止粗鲁的男孩

近 boorish, churlish, clumsy, crude, discourteous, uncouth, uncivilized, uncultured, unrefined

反 courteous, civilized, genteel, graceful, polished, refined, urbane 有教养的

派 lout *n.* 举止粗鲁的人

lubricate [ˈluːbrɪkeɪt]

【考法】 *vt.* 使润滑：to coat（something）with a slippery substance in order to **reduce friction**

例 lubricate the gears 给齿轮打润滑油

近 grease, oil, slick, smooth, wax

派 lubricant *n.* 润滑剂

lucid [ˈluːsɪd]

【考法1】 *adj.* 有光亮的：**suffused with light**

例 Those lucid bands that spread across the arctic sky are known as aurora borealis, or the northern lights. 那些蔓延在北极天空中的光带就是北极光。

近 beaming, brilliant, dazzling, glowing, incandescent, lucent, luminous, lustrous, radiant, refulgent, splendid

反 dim, dull, lackluster 黯淡无光的

【考法2】 *adj.* 神志清醒的：having **full use of one's mind** and control over one's actions

例 She decided to make out her will while she was still lucid. 她决定趁着自己神志还清醒，列出她的遗愿。

近 balanced, clearheaded, normal, right, sane, stable

反 brainsick, crazy, insane, lunatic, mad, maniac 疯狂的

【考法3】 *adj.* 表达清晰的，简单易懂的：**easily understood**

例 The teaching assistant tried to make his instructions as lucid as possible so that everyone would understand what to do. 助教努力使自己的指令容易理解，从而让所有人都知道应该要干什么。

近 apprehensible, clear, comprehensible, intelligible, palpable, patent, pellucid, plain, understandable

反 ambiguous, enigmatic, equivocal, indistinct, obfuscated, obscure, unclear 模糊不明确的

Unit 3

| ■ LUG | ■ LUGUBRIOUS | ■ LULL | ■ LULLABY | ■ LUMBER |
| ■ LUMINARY | ■ LURCH | ■ LURK | ■ LUSH | ■ LUSTROUS |

lug [lʌg]

【考法1】 *vt.* 拖动，拉动：to **cause to follow** by applying steady force on

例 lug the lawn mower out into the backyard 把割草机拖进院子

近 drag, draw, hale, pull, tow, tug

反 drive, propel, push 推动

【考法2】 *vt.* 费力搬运：to carry **laboriously**

例 I don't understand why he's always lugging all of his books around when his locker is right over there. 我真搞不懂为什么他总是明明在有锁柜的情况下还随身扛着所有的书。

近 bear, cart, convey, ferry, haul, pack, tote, transport

lugubrious [ləˈɡuːbriəs]

【考法】 *adj.* （故作夸张的）悲哀的：**mournful**, dismal, or gloomy, especially to an exaggerated or ludicrous degree

例 his lugubrious tear-stained face 他忧郁而带着泪痕的脸庞

近 deploring, doleful, dolorous, lamentable, melancholy, morose, plaintive, rueful, saturnine, sullen, woeful

反 cheerful, delighted, jocund, jovial 快乐的

lull [lʌl]

【考法1】 *n.* 相对平静时期，间隙：a **momentary halt** in an activity

例 the lull before the storm 暴风雨前的平静

近 break, breath, interruption, recess

【考法2】 *vt.* 使镇静，使安心：to **free from distress** or disturbance

例 The absence of attacks for such an extended period had lulled the nation into a false sense of security. 长期以来没有遭受攻击让这个国家产生了一种错误的安全感。

近 allay, balm, becalm, compose, lullaby, quiet, salve, settle, soothe, still, tranquilize

反 agitate, discompose, disquiet, disturb, perturb, upset, vex 打扰，扰乱

lullaby [ˈlʌləbaɪ]

【考法1】 *n.* 催眠曲：a **song** to quiet children or **lull** them to **sleep**

例 The mother sang a lullaby to the baby every night. 这位母亲每晚都给孩子唱摇篮曲。

近 berceuse, cradlesong

【考法2】 *vt.* 使镇静，使安心：to **free from distress** or disturbance

例 Reclining peacefully on the deck, he was lullabied by the gentle motion of the ship. 他躺卧在甲板上，随着船轻轻的颠簸放松下来。

近 allay, balm, becalm, compose, lull, quiet, salve, settle, soothe, still, tranquilize

反 agitate, discompose, disquiet, disturb, perturb, upset, vex 打扰，扰乱

lumber [ˈlʌmbər]

【考法1】 *n.* 木材：**tree logs** as prepared for human use

例 A huge amount of lumber will be needed to build the house. 建这栋房子需要大量的木材。

近 timber, wood

【考法2】 *vi.* 笨拙地行动：to walk or move with heavy **clumsiness**

例 The elephant lumbered through the jungle. 大象缓缓地穿越丛林。

近 flounder, plod, stumble, trudge

反 glide, slide 轻松地滑动

【考法3】 *vt.* 使负担（从而拖累）：to place a weight or **burden** on

例 lumber the expedition with unnecessary equipment and supplies 不必要的仪器和补给品给此次远征徒增了许多负担

近 burden, encumber, freight, lade, laden, saddle, weight

反 disburden, discharge, disencumber, unlade, unload 卸下，解脱

luminary [ˈluːmɪneri]

【考法】 *n.* 杰出人物：a person who has achieved **eminence** in a specific field

例 Buddhist luminary 佛学大师 ‖ Luminaries from the worlds of sports, entertainment, and politics were at the gala. 全球体育界、娱乐圈和政界的名人都出席了此次盛会。

近 celebrity, eminence, figure, icon, notability, star, superstar

反 nobody, nonentity 小人物

lurch [lɜːrtʃ]

【考法】 *vi.* 蹒跚：to move forward while **swaying** from side to side

例 The ship lurched in the storm. 船在风暴中摇摆前行。

近 careen, dodder, falter, reel, stagger, stumble, teeter, totter, waddle

反 progress smoothly 平稳前进；march, stride, swagger 游行，大步走

lurk [lɜːrk]

【考法】 *vi.* 潜伏：to **lie in wait** in a place of concealment especially for an evil purpose

例 Dangers lurk in the path of wilderness. 在这条荒野的小路上隐伏着危险。

近 ambush, snake, steal

反 appear, come out 出来

lush [lʌʃ]

【考法1】 *adj.* 茂盛的：growing **vigorously** especially with luxuriant foliage

例 lush grass 茂盛的草

近 booming, exuberant, flourishing, lively, luxuriant, rampant, thriving, verdant, vivacious

反 blighted, faded, sere, withered 干枯的，凋谢的

【考法2】 *adj.* 多产的：**producing abundantly**

例 His lush fields were the envy of neighboring farmers. 他富饶多产的土地让邻居羡慕嫉妒恨。

近 cornucopian, fecund, fruitful, productive, prolific, rich

反 barren, dead, infertile, sterile, unproductive 贫瘠的

【考法3】 *adj.* （声音、味道）优美的，令人愉悦的：**appealing** to the senses

例 the lush sounds of the orchestra 管弦乐队奏出的悦耳声音

近 ambrosial, luscious, palatable, savory, sensuous, tasteful, tasty, voluptuous

反 flat, flavorless, insipid, stale, tasteless 乏味的

lustrous [ˈlʌstrəs]

【考法】 *adj.* 有光泽的：having a **shiny** surface or finish

例 lustrous black hair 乌黑光亮的头发

近 brilliant, burnished, gleaming, glistening, glossy, polished, refulgent, rubbed, shining, sleek, splendid

反 dim, dull, lackluster, lusterless 昏暗的

Unit 4

luxurious [lʌɡˈʒʊriəs]

【考法 1】 *adj.* 豪华的：showing obvious signs of **wealth and comfort**

例 The luxurious apartment was filled with the latest electronic gadgets and fine works of art. 豪华的公寓里满是最新式的电子产品和精美的艺术作品。

近 deluxe, lavish, luxuriant, luxury, opulent, palatial, plushy, silken, sumptuous

反 ascetic, austere, spartan 简朴的

【考法 2】 *adj.* 奢侈的：given to or marked by **excessive gratification** of one's desires

例 He squandered his family fortune in the relentless satisfaction of his luxurious tastes. 他为满足自己奢侈的品味而挥霍家族的财产。

近 decadent, indulgent, overindulgent, self-indulgent, sybaritic

反 abstemious, abstinent 克制的

派 luxury *n.* 豪华；奢侈，奢侈品

lyric [ˈlɪrɪk]

【考法 1】 *n.* (可以哼唱的)小曲：a short **musical composition** for the human voice often with instrumental accompaniment

例 The guitarist improvised and sang a gentle lyric while playing. 吉他手在弹奏的过程中即兴创作并哼唱了一首小曲。

近 ballad, ditty, jingle, vocal

【考法 2】 *adj.* 如诗歌般流畅甜美的：having a pleasantly flowing quality **suggestive of poetry or music**

例 The film's lyric photography really enhanced its romantic mood. 电影中如诗歌般的图像效果着实增强了浪漫的氛围。

近 euphonious, lyrical, mellifluous, mellow, melodious, musical, poetical

反 prosaic, prose 无聊乏味的

派 lyrics *n.* 歌词

macabre [məˈkɑːbrə]

【考法】 *adj.* 恐怖的：suggesting the **horror of death** and decay; gruesome

例 Impressively, Plants vs. Zombies presented a supposedly macabre theme in such an enjoyable way. 令人难忘的是，《植物大战僵尸》将一个本应该十分恐怖的主题用一种如此欢乐的方式呈现出来。

近 appalling, atrocious, dreadful, ghastly, gruesome, hideous, horrific, nightmarish, terrific

反 agreeable, delightful, enjoyable, pleasant 令人愉悦的

macerate [ˈmæsəreɪt]

【考法】 *vt.* 浸泡(以软化)：to make soft by **soaking or steeping** in a liquid

例 macerate the sample in ethanol 用乙醇浸软试样

近 drench, drown, impregnate, saturate, sodden, sop, souse, steep

反 wring 拧干；dehydrate, desiccate, parch, scorch, sear 烤干，烤焦

maculate [ˈmækjəleɪt]

【考法】 *vt.* 使有斑点，弄脏；玷污，损坏：to **spot**; blemish

例 Her reputation was maculated after the affair with a married man. 自从被指与一个已婚男士有染之后，她的名声受到了影响。

近 besmirch, dot, dirty, soil, spot, stain

反 clean, cleanse, purify, wash 清洗，弄干净

派 maculated *adj.* 有斑点的

maelstrom [ˈmeɪlstrɑːm]

【考法 1】 *n.* 漩涡：a powerful often **violent whirlpool** sucking in objects within a given radius

例 Their raft got caught in a maelstrom. 他们的筏被一个漩涡卷住了。

近 gulf, vortex, whirlpool

【考法 2】 *n.* 混乱、动荡的局势：a violent or **turbulent** situation

例 the maelstrom of war 战争带来的乱世

近 chaos, disorder, pandemonium, tumult, tumoil, upheaval, uproar

反 calm 风平浪静

magnificent [mæg'nɪfɪsnt]

【考法】 *adj.* 壮丽的：**strikingly** beautiful or **impressive**

例 a magnificent cathedral 宏伟壮观的大教堂

近 august, epic, glorious, grand, imperial, imposing, massive, monumental, noble, regal, splendid

反 humble, unimpressive 平凡的

派 magnificence *n.* 壮丽，壮观

maladroit [ˌmælə'drɔɪt]

【考法】 *adj.* 笨拙的：lacking or showing a **lack of nimbleness** in using one's hands

例 a maladroit movement 笨拙的动作

近 awkward, bumbling, clumsy, fumbled, gauche, graceless, heavy-handed, inept, unhandy

反 adroit, ambidexterous, deft, dexterous, handy 灵巧的

malaise [mə'leɪz]

【考法】 *n.* 不舒服：a vague feeling of **bodily discomfort**, as at the beginning of an illness

例 He complained of depression, headaches and malaise. 他抱怨说感到沮丧、头痛和身体不适。

近 debility, decrepitude, disease, feebleness, infirmity, infirmness, sickliness, unhealthiness

malcontent [ˌmælkən'tent]

【考法 1】 *n.* 不满分子：one who is in active **opposition** to an established order or government

例 The chaos was caused by a handful of malcontents. 混乱是由一小撮不满分子引起的。

近 complainer, faultfinder, grouch, rebel

【考法 2】 *adj.* 不满的：**dissatisfied** with the existing state of affairs

例 The film follows three malcontent teenagers around Paris. 电影围绕着三个不满现实的青少年在巴黎展开。

近 discontented, discontent, disgruntled, displeased, dissatisfied, ungratified

反 contented, fulfilled, gratified, pleased, satisfied 满意的

Unit 5

■ MALICIOUS	■ MALIGN	■ MALINGER	■ MALLEABLE	■ MALODOROUS
■ MANDATORY	■ MANGLE	■ MANGY	■ MANIA	■ MANIFEST

malicious [mə'lɪʃəs]

【考法】 *adj.* 恶意的：given to, marked by, or arising from malice; **deliberately harmful**

例 spread malicious gossips 散播恶意的流言蜚语

近 bad, cruel, despiteful, evil, malevolent, malign, mean, nasty, spiteful, vicious, virulent, wicked

反 benevolent, benign, benignant, charitable, kind, kindly 善良的，仁慈的

malign [mə'laɪn]

【考法 1】 *adj.* 恶意的：having or showing a desire to **cause** someone pain or **suffering** for the sheer enjoyment of it

例 Both parties to the divorce showed a malign desire to make each other's future life utterly miserable. 离婚双方都表露出了恶毒的愿望，希望对方未来的生活陷入彻底的悲剧之中。

近 bad, cruel, despiteful, evil, malevolent, malicious, mean, nasty, spiteful, vicious, virulent, wicked

反 benevolent, benign, benignant, charitable, kind, kindly 善良的，仁慈的

【考法 2】 *vt.* 诽谤：to **utter injuriously** misleading or false reports about: speak evil of

例 the belief that it is possible to win an election without maligning anyone 一种信念，那就是不需要诽谤他人而赢得选举是可能的

近 asperse, blacken, calumniate, defame, libel, smear, traduce, vilify

反 acclaim, applaud, eulogize, extol, laud, praise 赞美；defend, vindicate 辩护

malinger [mə'lɪŋgər]

【考法】 *vi.* 装病以逃避工作：to **pretend** or exaggerate incapacity or **illness**（as to avoid duty or work）

例 He claims he's ill, but I think he's just malingering. 他声称他病了，但我觉得他是装的。

近 goldbrick, shirk

反 confront, face, meet 面对

派 malingerer *n.* 装病以逃避工作的人

malleable ['mæliəbl]

【考法 1】 *adj.* 可塑的：**capable of being** extended or **shaped** by beating with a hammer or by the pressure of rollers

例 a malleable metal 有延展性的金属
近 moldable, waxy
【考法2】 *adj.* 易控制的：**capable of being** altered or **controlled** by outside forces or influences
例 The cult leader took advantage of the malleable, compliant personalities of his followers. 这个头目利用了他的信徒们容易被控制和顺从的特征。
近 ductile, elastic, fluid, modifiable, plastic, pliable, pliant, supple, variable
反 adamant, intractable, recalcitrant, refractory, ungovernable, unmanageable, unruly 难管制的

malodorous [ˌmælˈoʊdərəs]
【考法】 *adj.* 恶臭的：having an **unpleasant smell**
例 American musteline will eject amalodorous fluid when startled. 美洲鼬科动物在受到惊吓时会喷出有恶臭味的液体。
近 fetid, foul, frowsy, funky, fusty, musty, noisome, rank, reeky, smelly, stinking, stinky
反 ambrosial, aromatic, fragrant, perfumed, redolent, savory, scented, sweet 芳香的，有香味的
派 malodor *n.* 恶臭

mandatory [ˈmændətɔːri]
【考法】 *adj.* 强制的：**forcing** one's **compliance** or participation
例 GRE test is mandatory for all students, regardless of their nationality, who wish to apply for graduate schools in the United States. GRE 是每个申请美国研究生院的学生（无论国籍）所必须参加的考试。
近 compulsory, forced, imperative, incumbent, involuntary, necessary, obligatory, peremptory, required
反 elective, optional, voluntary 可自由选择的，选修的

mangle [ˈmæŋgl]
【考法1】 *vt.* 损毁，使伤残：to **injure** with deep disfiguring wounds by cutting, tearing, or crushing
例 His body was mangled beyond recognition. 他的尸体已经被损毁到无法辨认的程度了。
近 batter, deform, disfigure, distort, lacerate, mutilate, rend, wreck
反 cure, heal, rehabilitate 治愈，康复
【考法2】 *vt.* 弄砸：to **ruin** or spoil through ineptitude or ignorance
例 The orchestra had completely mangled Bach's music. 乐队彻底演砸了巴赫的音乐。
近 blow, bumble, bungle, butcher, fumble , mar, mess, ruin, foul up, screw up

mangy [ˈmeɪndʒi]
【考法】 *adj.* 卑劣的：mean; **contemptible**
例 a mangy trick 卑鄙的手段
近 base, contemptible, debased, despicable, detestable, execrable, mean, sordid, squalid
反 lofty, noble, upright, venerable, virtuous 正直的，有道德的

mania [ˈmeɪniə]
【考法】 *n.* 热衷，狂热：an excessively **intense enthusiasm**, interest, or desire; a craze
例 a mania for neatness 强烈的洁癖
近 ardor, craze, enthusiasm, fervor, obsession, passion, preoccupation, prepossession, zeal
反 apathy, indifference, nonchalance, torpor 冷漠，麻木
派 manic *adj.* 疯狂的

manifest [ˈmænɪfest]
【考法1】 *adj.* 显然的，明显易懂的：clearly apparent to the sight or **understanding**; obvious
例 He is a manifest poseur. 他显然是个装模作样的人。
近 apparent, clear, distinct, evident, lucid, obvious, palpable, patent, perspicuous, plain, transparent
反 cryptic, enigmatic, indistinct, mysterious, obfuscated, obscure, unclear 晦涩的，难懂的
【考法2】 *v.* 显现，显露：to **make evident** or certain by showing or displaying
例 His frustration is often manifested by a minor facial tic. 他的沮丧通常会从脸部的细微抽搐中表现出来。
近 bespeak, betray, demonstrate, display, evince, expose, reveal
反 conceal, hide 隐藏
派 manifesto *n.* 宣言，声明

Unit 6

■ MANIPULATE ■ MANNERED ■ MANUMIT ■ MANUSCRIPT ■ MAR
■ MARSH ■ MARTINET ■ MARVEL ■ MASH ■ MASQUERADE

manipulate ［məˈnɪpjuleɪt］
【考法 1】 *vt.* 巧妙操作：to move, arrange, operate, or control by the hands or by mechanical means, especially in a **skillful** manner
例 She manipulated the lights to get just the effect she wanted. 她巧妙操控灯光，达到了她想要的效果。
近 handle, finesse, manage
反 bungle, fumble 笨拙地做
【考法 2】 *vt.* 巧妙处理；暗中操控：to influence or manage shrewdly or **deviously**
例 He manipulated public opinion in his favor. 他巧妙地将大众观点导向了有利于他的一边。 ‖ manipulate a foreign language 熟练地掌握外语
近 machinate, maneuver
派 manipulation *n.* 操纵，控制

mannered ［ˈmænərd］
【考法】 *adj.* 不自然的，做作的：having an **artificial** or stilted character
例 a mannered speech 做作的演讲
近 affected, artificial, assumed, factitious, fake, feigned, pretended, pseudo, sham, spurious
反 natural 自然的；artless, genuine, unfeigned 真诚的

manumit ［ˌmænjuˈmɪt］
【考法】 *vt.* 解放(奴隶)：to **release from slavery** or bondage
例 Though he was an outspoken defender of liberty, this son of Virginia did not manumit his own slaves until he was on his deathbed. 尽管这位维吉尼亚之子公开地支持自由，但他直到临死前才释放自己的奴隶。
近 free, emancipate, enfranchise, liberate, loose, release, unbind, unchain, unshackle
反 detain 拘留；enchain, enfetter, enslave 奴役

manuscript ［ˈmænjuskrɪpt］
【考法】 *n.* 手稿：a book, document, or other composition **written by hand**
例 beautiful Latin manuscript on the school's diplomas 学校毕业证书上美丽的手写拉丁文
近 calligraphy, penmanship, script
反 print, type, typewriting 打字稿

mar ［mɑːr］
【考法 1】 *n.* 污点，坏点：something that **spoils the appearance** or completeness of a thing
例 mars on the furniture 家具上的污点
近 blight, blotch, defect, deformity, disfigurement, fault, flaw, imperfection, mark, pockmark, scar
【考法 2】 *vt.* 破坏，削弱：to **impair** the soundness, perfection, or integrity of; spoil
例 The once flatroad surface is now marred by numerous potholes. 曾经平整的路面如今被坑洞所破坏。 ‖ an election marred by sexual scandal 被性丑闻蒙上阴影的选举
近 blemish, compromise, cripple, damage, deface, disfigure, harm, hurt, impair, injure, spoil, vitiate
反 doctor, fix, mend, patch, renovate, repair 修补；adorn, beautify, bedeck, embellish, garnish 装饰

marsh ［mɑːrʃ］
【考法】 *n.* 沼泽，湿地：an area of soft, **wet**, low-lying land
例 The marshes along the coast support a remarkable profusion of plants and animals. 沿着海岸线一带的沼泽为大量的动植物提供了栖息所。
近 bog, fen, marshland, mire, moor, morass, quagmire, slough, swamp, wetland
派 marshy *adj.* 潮湿的

martinet ［ˌmɑːrtnˈet］
【考法】 *n.* 纪律严明之人：a **strict** disciplinarian
例 He's a retired lieutenant and a bit of a martinet. 他是一个退役的中尉，并且是一个有点纪律严明的人。
近 disciplinarian, purist, stickler
反 reprobate 放纵的人

marvel ［ˈmɑːrvl］
【考法 1】 *n.* 令人惊奇的事物：one that evokes **surprise, admiration, or wonder**
例 The robot is a marvel of modern engineering. 机器人是现代工程领域的奇迹。
近 flash, miracle, phenomenon, prodigy, splendor

【考法 2】 *v.* (因为壮观、美丽等而)表示惊讶：to **feel amazement** or bewilderment at or about
例 marvel at the tranquility of Chopin's nocturne 惊叹于肖邦夜曲中体现出来的宁静祥和
近 gape, gaze, goggle, wonder
派 marvelous *adj.* 令人惊奇的

mash [mæʃ]
【考法】 *vt.* 捣碎：to cause to become a **pulpy mass**
例 mash potatoes before adding it to the mixture 在混合之前捣碎土豆
近 crush, grind, smash, squeeze
反 agglomerate 聚集成团

masquerade [ˌmæskəˈreɪd]
【考法 1】 *n.* 面具，伪装：a **display** of emotion or behavior that is **insincere** or intended to deceive
例 Although she was deeply bored, she maintained a masquerade of polite interest as her guest droned on. 尽管她早已对客人滔滔不绝的话感到厌倦，但她还是装出了一副饶有兴致的样子以示礼貌。
近 facade, guise, mask, pretense, semblance, show, veil
【考法 2】 *vi.* 伪装，掩饰：to **disguise** oneself
例 masquerade as a policeman 化装成警察
近 act, disguise, pose, pretend
反 betray, disclose, reveal, unmask 揭露

Unit 7

| ■ MASTERY | ■ MATRICULATE | ■ MAUDLIN | ■ MAVEN | ■ MAVERICK |
| ■ MAWKISH | ■ MEAGER | ■ MEAN | ■ MEANDER | ■ MEASLY |

mastery [ˈmæstəri]
【考法】 *n.* 技艺超群，精通：possession or display of **great skill** or technique
例 She has mastery of several languages. 她熟练掌握多种语言。
近 deftness, dexterity, finesse, prowess, virtuosity
反 amateurishness 业余
派 masterful *adj.* 精通的

matriculate [məˈtrɪkjuleɪt]
【考法】 *v.* 入学；录取：to **admit or be admitted** into a group, especially a college or university
例 matriculate at Princeton 在普林斯顿入学
近 admit, enroll, inscribe, recruit, register
反 commence, graduate 毕业；delist 除名
派 matriculation *n.* 录取

maudlin [ˈmɔːdlɪn]
【考法】 *adj.* 过于感伤的：effusively or **tearfully sentimental**
例 Some naive students display an almost maudlin concern for the welfare of animals while ignoring basic social inequity. 一些幼稚的学生忽视根本的社会不公平问题，而对动物的权益表现出一种多愁善感的忧虑。
近 lachrymose, mawkish, mushy, overemotional, sentimental, tearful
反 blithe, cheerful, jocund, jovial, jubilant 高兴的；apathetic, impassive, indifferent 冷漠的

maven [ˈmeɪvn]
【考法】 *n.* 专家：one who is **experienced** or knowledgeable: expert
例 As an investment maven, he was doing well even when the market was doing poorly. 作为一名投资高手，他在市场不景气的时候也能赚钱。
近 ace, adept, connoisseur, expert, maestro, master, professional, proficient, virtuoso
反 amateur, dabbler, dilettante 业余爱好者

maverick [ˈmævərɪk]
【考法 1】 *n.* 特立独行之人：a person who **does not conform** to generally accepted standards or customs
例 Some mavericks believe that both gravity and light are electromagnetic forces. 一些特立独行的人认为，重力和光都是电磁力。
近 bohemian, deviant, heretic, iconoclast, nonconformist
反 conformer, conformist, conventionalist 遵从传统的人

【考法2】 *adj.* 标新立异的，不合常规的：**deviating** from commonly accepted beliefs or practices
例 a maverick view on marriage 关于婚姻的非传统看法
近 dissentient, dissenting, dissident, heterodox, iconoclastic, unorthodox
反 conforming, conventional, orthodox 遵从传统的

mawkish [ˈmɔːkɪʃ]
【考法】 *adj.* 过度伤感的：excessively and objectionably **sentimental**
例 a mawkish love story 令人伤感的爱情故事
近 lachrymose, maudlin, mushy, overemotional, sentimental, tearful
反 blithe, cheerful, jocund, jovial, jubilant 高兴的；apathetic, impassive, indifferent 冷漠的

meager [ˈmiːgər]
【考法】 *adj.* 贫乏的：**deficient** in quantity, fullness, or extent; scanty
例 meager cultural resources 贫乏的文化资源
近 exiguous, niggardly, poor, scanty, scarce, skimpy, slender, slim, sparing, sparse, stingy
反 abundant, ample, bountiful, copious, generous, liberal, plenteous, plentiful 大量的，富足的

mean [miːn]
【考法1】 *adj.* 卑贱的：**ignoble**; base
例 a mean trick to play on a credulous person 要在一个轻信别人的人身上的卑劣诡计
近 base, contemptible, despicable, detestable, dirty, dishonorable, execrable, ignominious, sordid
反 lofty, noble, venerable, virtuous 高尚的
【考法2】 *adj.* 吝啬的：giving or **sharing** as **little** as possible
例 a mean child who hoarded all her toys 一个把她的所有玩具都藏起来的小气孩子
近 closefisted, mingy, miserly, niggardly, parsimonious, penurious, tightfisted, ungenerous
反 generous, liberal, munificent 慷慨的；extravagant, lavish, prodigal, profligate, spendthrift 浪费的
【考法3】 *v.* 打算，怀有目的：to have in mind as a **purpose or goal**
例 I mean to win this race. 我一定要赢这场比赛。
近 aim, aspire, calculate, contemplate, design, intend, meditate, plan
【考法4】 *v.* 意味着：to serve or intend to **convey, show, or indicate**
例 The national anthem means various things to various people. 对于不同的人来说，国歌的意义不尽相同。
近 connote, denote, express, import, signify, spell
派 meaningful *adj.* 有意义的

meander [miˈændər]
【考法】 *vi.* 闲逛，漫步：to move **aimlessly and idly** without fixed direction
例 meander along the river 沿着河闲逛 ‖ vagabonds meandering through life 漂泊一生的浪子
近 amble, cruise, drift, float, ramble, roam, saunter, stroll, wander

measly [ˈmiːzli]
【考法】 *adj.* 少得可怜的，微不足道的：so **small** or unimportant as to warrant little or no attention
例 The stingy man gave the parking attendant a measly tip. 那个吝啬男给了停车保安少得可怜的小费。
近 inconsequential, inconsiderable, insignificant, minute, paltry, peanut, petty, slight, trifling, trivial
反 big, consequential, considerable, significant 大量的，重要的

Unit 8

| ■ MEASURED | ■ MEDDLE | ■ MEDIATE | ■ MEDIOCRE | ■ MEDLEY |
| ■ MEEK | ■ MEET | ■ MELLIFLUOUS | ■ MELODRAMATIC | ■ MENACE |

measured [ˈmeʒərd]
【考法】 *adj.* 深思熟虑的，审慎的：deliberated, **calculated**
例 a measured response to the terrorist attack 就恐怖袭击做出的深思熟虑的反应
近 advised, calculated, considered, knowing, reasoned, studied, thoughtful, weighed
反 casual 随意的；uncalculated, unconsidered, unstudied 没仔细考虑过的

meddle [ˈmedl]
【考法】 *vi.* 干涉，管闲事：to **intrude** into other people's affairs or business; interfere
例 Please stop meddling in my marriage. 请不要来干涉我的婚姻。
近 interfere, interlope, intermeddle, intrude, obtrude, poke, pry, snoop
反 disregard, ignore, neglect, omit, overlook 忽略，不理会
派 meddlesome *adj.* 爱管闲事的

mediate [ˈmiːdieɪt]

【考法】 *vt.* 调解，调停：to intervene between two or more disputants in order to **bring about an agreement**, a settlement, or a compromise

例 mediate a labor-management dispute 调解劳工纠纷

近 conciliate, intercede, intermediate, interpose

反 arouse, encourage, excite, foment, incite, inflame, instigate, pique, spark, stimulate, stir 煽动激起

派 mediator *n.* 调停人

mediocre [ˌmiːdiˈoʊkər]

【考法】 *adj.* 平庸的；质量中等偏下的：**moderate** to inferior in quality; ordinary

例 Without a desire for success, life is at best mediocre. 没有对成功的强烈渴望，人生最多也就是碌碌无为。

近 average, common, commonplace, fair, indifferent, medium, ordinary

反 outstanding, excellent, exceptional, extraordinary, impressive, superior 优秀的

派 mediocrity *n.* 平庸者；平庸

medley [ˈmedli]

【考法】 *adj.* 大杂烩，混合物：an unorganized collection or **mixture** of various things

例 a medley of snack foods available on the buffet table 自助餐桌上供应着各式各样的小吃

近 agglomerate, collage, hodgepodge, jumble, montage, motley, muddle, salad, shuffle, variety, welter

meek [miːk]

【考法1】 *adj.* 谦恭的：showing patience and **humility**; gentle

例 He was a meek, mild-mannered fellow. 他是个谦逊、温文尔雅的人。

近 humble, modest, unassuming, unpretentious

反 arrogant, bumptious, haughty, imperious, pompous, presumptuous, supercilious 自大的

【考法2】 *adj.* 顺从的：easily imposed on; **submissive**

例 He may be self-effacing, but he certainly isn't meek. 他可能是个很低调的人，但他绝非软骨头。

近 compliant, docile, manageable, obedient, submissive, tractable

反 adamant, headstrong, intractable, obstinate, refractory, stubborn, unruly, unyielding 倔强的，不顺从的

meet [miːt]

【考法】 *adj.* 合适的：precisely adapted to a particular situation, need, or circumstance: **very proper**

例 In this case, splitting the winnings of the contested lottery ticket seems like a meet solution. 在这种情况下，平分有争议的彩票奖金或许是个合适的解决方案。

近 applicable, appropriate, apt, becoming, befitting, felicitous, fitting, proper, right, suitable

反 improper, inapplicable, inapposite, inappropriate, inapt, infelicitous, malapropos 不合适的

mellifluous [meˈlɪfluəs]

【考法】 *adj.*（曲调）优美的：**smooth and sweet**

例 a mellifluous voice 甜美的嗓音

近 dulcet, euphonious, mellifluent, mellow, melodious

反 cacophonous, raspy 刺耳的

melodramatic [ˌmelədrəˈmætɪk]

【考法】 *adj.* 感情夸张的，伤感的：**exaggeratedly emotional** or sentimental; histrionic

例 Our office drama queen yet again made the melodramatic declaration that she was contemplating suicide. 我们办公室的"影后"又一次在危言耸听了：这回她说她准备自杀。

近 dramatic, hammy, histrionic, mannered, pretentious, stagy

反 nondramatic, nontheatrical 平淡无奇的，非戏剧性的

menace [ˈmenəs]

【考法】 *vt.* 威胁，使处于危险：to make a show of **intention to harm**; to place in danger

例 Stockpiles of nuclear weapons continue to menace the inhabitants of this planet. 大量的核武器继续威胁着这个行星上的居民。

近 compromise, hazard, imperil, jeopardize, peril, risk, threaten

反 rescue, save 救出

派 menacing *adj.* 具有威胁性的

Unit 9

mendacious　[men'deɪʃəs]

【考法】　*adj.* 撒谎的，虚假的：telling or containing **lies**

例　mendacious tales about his adventures 关于他冒险的虚假传说

近　dishonest, deceitful, fallacious, lying, spurious, untruthful

反　authentic, honest, truthful, veracious 真实的，诚实的

mentor　['mentɔːr]

【考法1】　*n.* 导师：a trusted counselor or **guide**

例　not only an lecturer but also a spirit mentor 不仅是授课者，还是精神导师

近　advisor, coach, counselor, guide, instructor, teacher

反　disciple, pupil 弟子；apprentice 学徒

【考法2】　*vt.* 教导，指导：to **give advice** and instruction regarding the course or process to be followed

例　We're looking for volunteers to mentor students in career planning. 我们正在寻找能指导学生职业规划的志愿者。

近　coach, counsel, lead, pilot, shepherd, show, tutor

反　comply, follow, observe 遵从

mercenary　['mɜːrsəneri]

【考法1】　*n.* (外国军队的)雇佣军：a professional **soldier hired** for service in a foreign army

例　hire a mercenary army to protect the VIP 雇佣了一支佣兵来保护重要人物

近　hack

【考法2】　*adj.* 唯利是图的，贪婪的：motivated solely by a desire for **monetary or material gain**

例　Virtue flies from the heart of a mercenary man. 唯利是图的人没有美德可言。

近　acquisitive, avaricious, avid, covetous, grasping, greedy, moneygrubbing, rapacious

反　benevolent, generous, liberal, philanthropic, munificent 慷慨的

mercurial　[mɜːr'kjʊriəl]

【考法】　*adj.* (情绪)善变的：characterized by rapid and unpredictable **changeableness of mood**

例　his mercurial temperament 他善变的脾气

近　capricious, changeful, fluctuating, fluid, mutable, temperamental, uncertain, variable, volatile

反　certain, constant, immutable, invariable, settled, stable, steady, unvarying 稳定的，不变的

merited　['merɪtɪd]

【考法】　*adj.* 应得的，理所当然的：being **what is called for** by accepted standards of right and wrong

例　a merited bonus 应得的奖金 ‖ The punishment, although harsh, was entirely merited. 虽然惩罚很严厉，但的确是应该的。

近　condign, deserved, due, fair, justified, right, warranted

反　undeserved, undue 不应得的；gratuitous, unjustified, unwarranted 没有根据的，无正当理由的

mesh　[meʃ]

【考法】　*v.* 诱捕：to **catch** or hold as if in a net

例　Dolphins sometimes become meshed in fishnets. 有时海豚也会被渔网缠住。

近　enmesh, ensnare, ensnarl, entoil, entrap, net, snare, tangle, trap

反　disentangle, untangle 解开，使解脱

mesmeric　[mez'merɪk]

【考法1】　*adj.* 催眠的，催眠术的：of, relating to, or induced by **mesmerism**

近　hypnotic

反　awaking 觉醒的

【考法2】　*adj.* 令人着迷的，难以抗拒的：**attracting** and holding interest as if by a spell

例　the mesmeric recital 迷人的独奏

近　attractive, alluring, captivating, charming, drawing, enchanting, riveting

反　disgusting, loathsome, repellent, repulsive 令人厌恶的；unappealing, unattractive 没有吸引力的

派　mesmerism *n.* 催眠术，难以抗拒的魅力；mesmerize *vt.* 催眠

metamorphose [ˌmetəˈmɔːrfoʊz]
【考法】 *vt.*（使）变形：to **change** into a different physical form especially by supernatural means
例 a science fiction story in which radiation metamorphoses people into giant bugs 一个描绘辐射将人变成了巨大虫子的科幻小说
近 alchemize, transfigure, transform, transmute, transpose, transubstantiate
反 remain 保持

metaphysical [ˌmetəˈfɪzɪkl]
【考法 1】 *adj.* 哲学上的，理论上的：dealing with or expressing a quality or **idea**
例 a work that deals with such metaphysical questions as the very nature of knowledge 一部探讨诸如 "知识的本质是什么" 的理论问题的著作
近 conceptual, ideal, ideational, notional, theoretical
反 concrete 具体的，实实在在的
【考法 2】 *adj.* 非尘世的：of, relating to, or being part of a reality **beyond** the observable physical **universe**
例 a metaphysical world beyond the one in which we live 在我们居住的世界之外的 "超然世界"
近 ethereal, heavenly, otherworldly, paranormal, preternatural, transcendental, unearthly, unworldly
反 mundane 世俗的；natural 自然界的

meteoric [ˌmiːtiˈɔːrɪk]
【考法】 *adj.* 流星般迅速而短暂的：similar to a meteor in speed, brilliance, or **brevity**
例 a meteoric rise to fame 一夜成名
近 ephemeral, evanescent, fleeting, momentary, rapid, transient, transitory
反 enduring, lasting, permanent, prolonged 持久的

Unit 10

| ■ METHODICAL | ■ METICULOUS | ■ METTLE | ■ MIFF | ■ MIGRATORY |
| ■ MILK | ■ MIME | ■ MIMIC | ■ MINATORY | ■ MINCE |

methodical [məˈθɑːdɪkl]
【考法】 *adj.* 井然有序的，有条理的：arranged or proceeding in regular, **systematic order**
例 a methodical summary that included lists of points to memorize 一份包含了记忆重点的有条理的总结
近 neat, orderly, organized, regular, systematic, systematized
反 disorganized, haphazard, irregular, unsystematic 杂乱的，混乱无序的

meticulous [məˈtɪkjələs]
【考法】 *adj.* 极为谨慎的：marked by **extreme or excessive care** in the consideration or treatment of details
例 He was so meticulous about everything. 他对所有事都一丝不苟。
近 careful, conscientious, exact, fussy, heedful, painstaking, punctilious, scrupulous
反 careless, feckless, heedless, thoughtless 疏忽大意的

mettle [ˈmetl]
【考法 1】 *n.* 勇气：vigor and **strength of spirit** or temperament
例 troops who showed their mettle in combat 在战场上表现出坚强勇气的部队
近 bravery, courage, dauntlessness, fortitude, guts, nerve, pluck, spirit, spunk, valor
反 cowardice, cravenness, gutlessness, pusillanimity, spinelessness 胆小，怯懦
【考法 2】 *n.* 毅力，耐力：staying quality: **stamina**
例 Those trucks had proved their mettle in army transport. 那些卡车通过在军队运输中的表现证明了它们的耐用性。
近 durability, endurance, stamina, persistence, resolution
派 mettlesome *adj.* 有毅力的

miff [mɪf]
【考法】 *vt.* 使恼怒：to cause to become offended or **annoyed**
例 be miffed by her son's disobedience 被她儿子的叛逆惹恼
近 aggravate, annoy, enrage, exasperate, incense, infuriate, ire, madden, nettle, peeve, vex
反 appease, assuage, mollify, placate, propitiate 平息，安抚；delight, gratify, please 取悦，讨好

migratory [ˈmaɪɡrətɔːri]
【考法】 *adj.* 迁移的：having a way of life that involves **moving from one region to another** typically on a seasonal basis
例 migratory birds heading south for the winter 为了越冬而往南飞的候鸟
近 migrant, mobile, nomad, nomadic, traveling
反 nonmigrant, resident, sedentary 常居一处的，不迁移的

milk [mɪlk]

【考法】 *vt.* 榨取(财富、信息等): to draw or **coerce profit** or advantage from illicitly or to an extreme degree

例 milk the workers 从工人身上榨取好处 || The interrogators milked the arrested spy, but he was dry. 审问者想尽办法套被捕间谍的话，但是无功而返。

近 drain, exploit

---

mime [maɪm]

【考法】 *v.* 模仿: to use (someone or something) as the **model** for one's speech, mannerisms, or behavior

例 mime a dog begging for food 模仿小狗乞食

近 ape, copy, copycat, emulate, mimic, simulate

---

mimic ['mɪmɪk]

【考法1】 *adj.* 仿真的，仿造的: being such **in appearance** only and made with or manufactured from usually cheaper materia

例 Police were concerned that the mimic gun, although intended only as a toy, might be confused with the real thing in certain situations. 尽管仿真枪只是玩具，但警方担忧在某些情况下它会被误认为是真枪。

近 artificial, bogus, factitious, fake, false, imitative, mock, sham, simulated, substitute, synthetic

反 genuine, natural, real 真实的

【考法2】 *vt.* 滑稽地模仿(以取笑): to **copy or exaggerate** (someone or something) in order to make fun of

例 The comedian was famous for mimicking the President's distinctive lisp. 这个喜剧演员因能滑稽地模仿那位总统特有的口齿不清而闻名。

近 burlesque, caricature, do, imitate, mock, parody, send up, spoof, travesty

【考法3】 *vt.* 模仿: to use (someone or something) as the **model** for one's speech, mannerisms, or behavior

例 She began to learn their language by mimicking the sounds they made. 她开始通过模仿发音来学习他们的语言。

近 ape, copy, copycat, emulate, simulate

派 mimicry *n.* 模仿

---

minatory ['mɪnətɔːri]

【考法】 *adj.* 带来威胁的，有凶兆的: being or showing **a sign of evil** or calamity to come

例 The novel's protagonist is haunted by a minatory black specter. 这部小说的主人公被不祥的黑色幽灵所骚扰。

近 baleful, direful, doomy, foreboding, ill-boding, inauspicious, menacing, portentous, sinister, threatening

反 unthreatening 没有威胁的; reassuring 令人安心的

---

mince [mɪns]

【考法1】 *vt.* 切碎: to cut or chop into very **small pieces**

例 I'll buy some lean meat and mince it myself. 我会买一些瘦肉然后自己切好。

近 cut, dice, grind, hash

【考法2】 *vi.* 小步走: to walk with very **short steps** or with exaggerated primness

例 The bride minced through the cathedral. 新娘踏着细小的步伐穿过教堂。

反 stride 大步走

List 16

"所谓抱负就是对现状的永不满足，有变化的生活才精彩，永远不要停下追逐梦想的脚步。"

（赵禾，2006 年 10 月，Verbal 700，Quantitative 800，
录取学校：Cornell University Ms. Financial Engineering）

Unit 1

■ MINGLE	■ MINIMIZE	■ MINT	■ MINUSCULE	■ MINUTE
■ MINUTIAE	■ MIRAGE	■ MIRE	■ MIRTH	■ MISANTHROPIC

mingle ［ˈmɪŋgl］
【考法 1】 *vi.* 参加社交活动：to take part in **social** activities
例 mingle at a cocktail party 在鸡尾酒会上与他人交往
近 associate, fraternize, socialize
【考法 2】 *vt.* 混合，结合：to **mix** so that the components become united
例 mingle the ingredients 将调料混合 ‖ mingle fact and fiction 糅杂了现实与幻想
近 mix, amalgamate, blend, commingle, immingle, intermix, merge
反 divide, separate, sunder 分开

minimize ［ˈmɪnɪmaɪz］
【考法 1】 *vt.* 将…减到最少：to **reduce to** the **smallest** possible amount, extent, size, or degree
例 All striking forces are told to minimize civilian casualties. 所有攻击部队被要求尽可能减少平民伤亡。
近 deprecate, diminish, discount, reduce
反 inflate, magnify 膨胀，扩大；maximize 最大化
派 minimum *adj.* 最小的
【考法 2】 *vt.* 刻意低估：to **underestimate** intentionally
例 minimize losses in our own company while maximize those of the rival 低估我方损失而高估对手损失
近 underestimate, underrate, undervalue
反 overestimate 高估；exaggerate 夸张，夸大
【考法 3】 *vt.* 表示鄙夷：to express **scornfully** one's **low opinion** of
例 Sore losers minimized the other team's victory. 愤愤不平的失败者对获胜方的胜利表现出鄙夷。
近 belittle, denigrate, deprecate, depreciate, derogate, diminish, disparage, trash, vilipend
反 acclaim, applaud, exalt, extol, glorify, laud, magnify, praise 欢呼，赞扬

mint ［mɪnt］
【考法 1】 *n.* 巨额：an **abundant amount**, especially of money
例 worth a mint 价值连城
近 bomb, boodle, bundle, fortune, pile, wad
反 mite, modicum 少量
【考法 2】 *adj.* 无损坏的：**unmarred** as if fresh from a mint
例 a second-handed laptop in mint condition 一台几乎全新的二手笔记本电脑
近 intact, original, perfect, pristine, unmarred, virginal
反 impaired, damaged 有损坏的；stale 陈腐的

minuscule ［ˈmɪnəskjuːl］
【考法】 *adj.* 极小的：**very small**
例 a minuscule progress 极小的进步
近 atomic, infinitesimal, microscopic, miniature, minute, tiny
反 colossal, elephantine, enormous, gargantuan, gigantic, huge, immense, mammoth, prodigious 巨大的

minute ［maɪˈnjuːt］
【考法 1】 *adj.* 仔细的，谨小慎微的：characterized by **careful scrutiny** and close examination
例 a minute description of the setting of the story 故事背景的详细介绍
近 circumstantial, elaborate, full, particular, particularized, thorough
反 brief, compendious, concise, succinct, summary, terse 摘要性的，简述的

【考法2】 *adj.* 小的，不重要的：very small or **of small importance**
例 It is not sagacious to invest excessively in minute details. 过分投入到不重要的细枝末节上是不明智的。
近 frivolous, incidental, inconsiderable, insignificant, little, minor, negligible, nugatory, slight, trifling, trivial
反 consequential, critical, crucial, momentous, significant, vital, weighty 关键的，重要的
派 minutes *n.* 会议记录

minutiae [mɪˈnuːʃiː]
【考法】 *n.* 次要的细节，小事：a minute or **minor detail**
例 plagued by minutiae 被不重要的细节困扰
近 triviality
反 gist 要点

mirage [məˈrɑːʒ]
【考法】 *n.* 海市蜃楼，幻想：something **illusory** and unattainable like a mirage
例 Reunion with her husband has become a mirage. 与她丈夫重逢已是可望而不可及的幻想。‖ A peaceful solution proved to be a mirage. 和平解决问题是不可能的了。
近 chimera, delusion, hallucination, illusion, phantom, vision
反 reality 现实

mire [ˈmaɪər]
【考法1】 *n.* 困境：a **difficult**, puzzling, or embarrassing **situation** from which there is no easy escape
例 stuck in a mire of emotional dependency 陷于感情依赖的困境中
近 dilemma, hole, impasse, jam, pickle, quagmire, rattrap, swamp
【考法2】 *vt.* 使陷入困境，拖后腿：to hamper or **hold back** as if by mire
例 be mired in the past 陷于过去的回忆不能自拔
近 bog, broil, delay, detain, entangle, entrap, retard
反 enfranchise, extricate, free, liberate, rescue 使解脱

mirth [mɜːrθ]
【考法】 *n.* 欢乐，欢笑：**gladness** or gaiety as shown by or accompanied with **laughter**
例 a man of little mirth 不苟言笑之人
近 cheer, festivity, gaiety, glee, happiness, hilarity, jocundity, joviality, lightheartedness
反 dejection, depression, desolation, despondence, doldrums, melancholy, oppression 沮丧，忧伤
派 mirthful *adj.* 高兴的

misanthropic [ˌmɪsənˈθrɑːpɪk]
【考法】 *adj.* 反人类的：having or showing a **deep distrust of human** beings and their motives
例 a solitary and misanthropic artist 一个孤立的反人类艺术家
近 antisocial, cynical, pessimistic
反 philanthropic 博爱的；uncynical 不愤世嫉俗的
派 misanthrope *n.* 反人类分子

Unit 2

misbehaving [ˌmɪsbɪˈheɪvɪŋ]
【考法】 *adj.* 调皮的，行为不端的：engaging in or marked by **childish misbehavior**
例 a new approach for disciplining a chronically misbehaving child 一个教育调皮小孩的新方法
近 annoying, devious, errant, impish, mischievous, naughty, playful, wicked
反 decorous, urbane 举止得体的

mischievous [ˈmɪstʃɪvəs]
【考法1】 *adj.* 调皮的，淘气的：playful in a **naughty** or **teasing** way
例 The mischievous child broke the vase. 那个调皮的孩子打碎了花瓶。
近 annoying, devious, errant, impish, misbehaving, naughty, playful, wicked
反 decorous, urbane 举止得体的
【考法2】 *adj.* 有害的：**causing harm** or trouble
例 mischievous rumors that defame him 恶意中伤他的谣言
近 adverse, baleful, baneful, deleterious, detrimental, evil, hurtful, injurious, nocuous, noxious, pernicious
反 beneficial 有益的；anodyne, benign, harmless, innocent, innocuous, inoffensive, safe 无害的

225

misconstrue [ˌmɪskənˈstruː]

【考法】 *vt.* 误解，曲解：to **mistake** the meaning of

例 An outsider might misconstrue the nature of the phenomenon. 局外者可能会曲解这个现象的本质。

近 garble, misapprehend, misinterpret, misperceive, misread, misrepresent, mistake

反 appreciate, apprehend, catch, comprehend, fathom, grasp, perceive, savvy, seize, understand 获知

miscreant [ˈmɪskriənt]

【考法】 *n.* 恶棍，罪犯：one who **behaves criminally** or viciously

例 robbed by a bunch of miscreants 遭到了一伙歹徒的抢劫

近 brute, culprit, devil, felon, fiend, offender, rascal, reprobate, villain

反 cavalier, chevalier（尤指对女士）彬彬有礼的绅士

misdemeanour [ˌmɪsdɪˈmiːnər]

【考法】 *n.* 轻罪：a **crime less serious** than a felony

例 charged with several misdemeanours 被指控几项轻罪

近 infraction, infringement, offense, peccadillo, violation

反 felony 重罪

miserly [ˈmaɪzərli]

【考法】 *adj.* 吝啬的：marked by grasping meanness and **penuriousness**

例 a miserly couple devoid of social conscience and responsibility 一对没有良心和社会责任感的吝啬夫妻

近 closefisted, mean, niggard, parsimonious, penurious, stingy, tightfisted

反 lavish, prodigal, spendthrift, squandering 浪费的；generous, liberal, munificent, openhanded 慷慨的

派 miser *n.* 守财奴

misfortune [ˌmɪsˈfɔːrtʃuːn]

【考法】 *n.* 不幸：**bad fortune** or ill luck

例 unable to grasp why he had been struck by such a misfortune 无法理解他为何会遇上如此不幸之事

近 adversity, calamity, cataclysm, catastrophe, disaster, ill, mischance, mishap, tragedy

反 fortune, luck, serendipity 幸事

misgiving [ˌmɪsˈɡɪvɪŋ]

【考法】 *n.* 担忧，疑虑：a feeling of **doubt** or suspicion especially concerning a future event

例 No one can dispel his misgiving. 没有人能打消他的疑虑。

近 apprehension, distrust, doubt, dread, fear, foreboding, incertitude, skepticism, suspicion

反 assurance, belief, certainty, certitude, confidence, conviction, sureness, surety, trust 信心

mishap [ˈmɪshæp]

【考法】 *n.* 不幸之事：an **unfortunate** accident

例 Mishap followed wherever he went. 不论他走到哪里，厄运总是形影相随。

近 adversity, calamity, cataclysm, catastrophe, disaster, ill, mischance, misfortune, tragedy

反 fortune, luck, serendipity 幸事

misrepresent [ˌmɪsˌreprɪˈzent]

【考法】 *vt.* 误传，篡改：to **give** an incorrect or **misleading representation** of

例 misrepresent the facts 篡改事实真相

近 belie, color, distort, falsify, garble, misinterpret, misrelate, misstate, pervert

反 clarify, explain, illuminate, illustrate 澄清，阐明

派 misrepresentation *n.* 篡改

Unit 3

| ■ MITE | ■ MITIGATE | ■ MOBILE | ■ MOCKERY | ■ MODERATE |
| ■ MODICUM | ■ MOLLIFY | ■ MOLLYCODDLE | ■ MOLT | ■ MOMENTOUS |

mite [maɪt]

【考法】 *n.* 微小的东西，很少的钱：a very **small object**, creature, or particle, a very small sum of money

例 I have only a mite left to buy lunch for the rest of the week. 我只剩下一点钱来买本周剩下几天的午饭了。

近 atom, bit, hint, iota, molecule, particle, pittance, trace

反 boodle, bundle, fortune 大笔（金钱）；colossus 巨大的事物

mitigate [ˈmɪtɪɡeɪt]
【考法】 *vt.* 减轻痛苦，使缓和：to make **less severe** or painful
例 powerful drugs that mitigate pains 强力的镇痛剂
近 allay, alleviate, assuage, ease, mollify, palliate, relieve, soothe
反 aggravate, exacerbate, intensify 加剧
派 mitigation *n.* 缓和

mobile [ˈmoʊbl]
【考法1】 *adj.* 可移动的：**capable** of **moving** or being moved
例 a mobile missile launcher 可移动导弹发射装置
近 motile, movable, portable, transportable
反 immobile, immovable 不可移动的
【考法2】 *adj.* 可变的：**changeable** in appearance, mood, or purpose
例 a highly mobile face 善变的面孔
近 adaptable, fluid, inconstant, mercurial, mutable, protean, unstable, unsteady, variable, versatile
反 fixed, steadfast, stable 稳定的，不变的
派 mobility *n.* 可移动性；mobilize *v.* 动员

mockery [ˈmɑːkəri]
【考法1】 *n.* 鄙视，嘲弄：scornfully contemptuous **ridicule**
例 Her deliberate mockery triggered a fierce fight. 她的蓄意嘲弄引起了一场激烈的打斗。
近 derision, joke, mock, ridicule, scoffing
反 respect, reverence, veneration 尊敬
【考法2】 *n.* 以嘲笑为目的的模仿：a false, **derisive**, or impudent **imitation**
例 arbitrary methods that make a mockery of justice 专断的方式是对司法公正的践踏
近 burlesque, caricature, farce, parody, sham, travesty
派 mock *v.* 愚弄，嘲弄

moderate
【考法1】 [ˈmɑːdəreɪt] *vt.* 使缓和：to **lessen** the **intensity** or extremeness of
例 Sopranos and tenors moderates their voices to fit the size of the theater. 女高音和男高音们根据剧场的大小调节他们的声音以创造合适的效果。
近 abate, diminish, dwindle, ease, lessen, lower, modulate, subside, taper, temper, wane
反 escalate, enhance, expand, heighten, intensify 扩大，升级，增强
【考法2】 [ˈmɑːdərət] *adj.* 适度的，中庸的：being **within** reasonable **limits**; not excessive or extreme
例 The new proposals regarding defense budget were met with only moderate enthusiasm. 关于国防预算的新提案只得到了平淡的回应。
近 average, conservative, fair, intermediate, mediocre, modest, reasonable, temperate
反 exorbitant, excessive 过分的；extreme, radical 极端的
派 immoderate *adj.* 不适度的

modicum [ˈmɑːdɪkəm]
【考法】 *n.* 少量：a **small portion**; a limited quantity
例 a modicum of food quota 极少量的食物配额
近 atom, iota, mite, molecule, particle
反 abundance, affluence 大量

mollify [ˈmɑːlɪfaɪ]
【考法】 *vt.* 平息，抚慰，缓和：to **calm** in temper or feeling
例 mollify the angry customer 平息消费者的怒气
近 allay, alleviate, appease, assuage, conciliate, mitigate, placate, propitiate, soothe
反 aggravate, enrage, exasperate, incense, inflame, infuriate, ire, rankle, vex 激怒；antagonize 使敌对
派 mollification *n.* 安抚

mollycoddle [ˈmɑːlikɑːdl]
【考法】 *vt.* 宠爱，溺爱：to treat with an **excessive** or absurd degree of **indulgence** and attention
例 mollycoddle his only grandson 溺爱他唯一的孙子
近 coddle, cosset, indulge, pamper, spoil
反 abuse, ill-treat 虐待

molt [moʊlt]
【考法】 *vi.* 脱（羽、皮等）：to **shed** hair, **feathers**, shell, horns, or an outer layer periodically
例 Snakes molt as they grow, shedding the old skin and growing a larger new skin. 随着年龄的增长，蛇会脱去老皮，长出大一点的新皮。
近 exfoliate, exuviate, shed
反 fledge 长羽毛

momentous [moʊˈmentəs]

【考法】 *adj.* 极重要的：of **utmost importance**; of outstanding significance or consequence

例 Battle of Stalingrad is a momentous campaign in World War. Ⅱ 斯大林格勒之战是第二次世界大战中具有重大意义的一次战役。

近 consequential, considerable, crucial, eventful, important, monumental, pivotal, significant, vital, weighty

反 inconsequential, negligible, slight, trifling, trivial 无关紧要的

Unit 4

■ MOMENTUM　　■ MONGREL　　■ MONOCHROMATIC　　■ MONOLOGUE　　■ MONOTONOUS
■ MONTAGE　　■ MORATORIUM　　■ MORBID　　■ MORDANT　　■ MORIBUND

momentum [moʊˈmentəm]

【考法】 *n.* 动力；冲力，势头：**impetus** of a physical object in motion; impetus of a nonphysical process, such as an idea or a course of events

例 Their luck began to pick up momentum. 他们的运气开始转旺。

近 boost, encouragement, goad, impetus, incentive, incitation, instigation, motivation, spur, stimulus

反 deterrent 阻碍物；obstruction, resistance 阻力

mongrel [ˈmʌŋɡrəl]

【考法】 *adj.* 杂种的，混血儿的：of **mixed origin** or character

例 homeless mongrel dogs on the streets 街上的流浪杂种狗

近 crossbred, hybrid

反 purebred 纯种的

monochromatic [ˌmɑːnəkroʊˈmætɪk]

【考法1】 *adj.* 单色的：having or consisting of **one color** or hue

例 monochromatic filter 单色滤光片

近 colorless, monochrome

反 chromatic, colorful, iridescent, motley, rainbow, variegated 五光十色的

派 monochromatism *n.* 全色盲

【考法2】 *adj.* 单调无聊的：**lacking variety**, creativity, or excitement

例 a monochromatic article eulogizing a hero 一篇无聊的赞颂英雄的文章

近 arid, dreary, drudging, dull, jejune, monotonous, pedestrian, ponderous, stale, stodgy, tiresome

反 absorbing, engaging, engrossing, gripping, interesting, intriguing, involving, riveting 吸引人的

monologue [ˈmɑːnəlɔːɡ]

【考法】 *n.* 独白：a dramatic sketch performed **by one actor**

例 deliver a tedious monologue 做了一个冗长的独白

近 soliloquy, solo, speech

反 dialogue 对话

monotonous [məˈnɑːtənəs]

【考法1】 *adj.* (声音)单调的：uttered or sounded in one **unvarying tone**

例 a monotonous apathetic voice 单调而冷漠的声音

反 vociferous 嘈杂的

【考法2】 *adj.* 清一色的，无聊的：**tediously** uniform or **unvarying**

例 a sparkle in the monotonous background 单调背景中的一个亮点

近 arid, dreary, drudging, dull, jejune, monochromatic, pedestrian, ponderous, stale, stodgy, tiresome

反 absorbing, engaging, engrossing, gripping, interesting, intriguing, involving, riveting 吸引人的

montage [ˈmɒntɑːʒ]

【考法】 *n.* 大杂烩：an unorganized **collection** or mixture of various things

例 My memories of the childhood trip are a montage of the sights of two rivers, smells of hotpots, and sounds of light railway of Chongqing. 我孩提时代旅行的记忆就是由两江风光、火锅的香味以及重庆的轻轨声杂糅而成的。

近 agglomerate, collage, hodgepodge, medley, motley, salad, variety

moratorium [ˌmɔːrəˈtɔːriəm]

【考法】 *n.* 延期，暂缓施行：a **suspension** of activity

例 a moratorium on nuclear tests 暂缓核试验

近 abeyance, delay, doldrums, dormancy, latency, quiescence, postponement, suspension

反 resumption (从中断处)继续进行

○ **morbid** [ˈmɔːrbɪd]
【考法 1】 *adj.* 疾病的，疾病所致的：affected with or induced **by disease**
例 a morbid condition 有疾病的状况
近 diseased, pathological
反 verdant 青翠的
【考法 2】 *adj.* (思想性格)变态的：characterized by preoccupation with **unwholesome thoughts** or feelings
例 read the account of the murder with a morbid interest 怀着病态的心态读谋杀报告 || exhibit a morbid fascination 展现出一种病态的迷恋
近 brainsick, crazy, deranged, lunatic, psychotic
反 hale, salubrious, wholesome 健康的
派 morbidity *n.* 病态

○ **mordant** [ˈmɔːrdnt]
【考法】 *adj.* 尖酸刻薄的：**biting** and **caustic** in thought, manner, or style
例 feel embarrassed about the mordant satire of the critics 对评论家刻薄的讽刺感到尴尬
近 acerbic, acid, acrid, barbed, caustic, corrosive, pungent, sardonic, satiric, scalding, scathing, tart
反 congenial, genial 和蔼的

moribund [ˈmɔːrɪbʌnd]
【考法 1】 *adj.* 即将结束的，垂死的：**approaching death**; about to die
例 The nation's banking industry was moribund. 这个国家的银行业危在旦夕。
近 decadent, deteriorating, dying, expiring, fading
反 beginning, nascent 初生的，刚开始的；lively, thriving, vigorous, vital 有活力的
【考法 2】 *adj.* 即将过时的：on the verge of becoming **obsolete**
例 Some social conventions have been rendered moribund in face of modernization. 不少传统习俗在现代化的影响下变得岌岌可危。
近 antiquated, archaic, dated, fossilized, moth-eaten, outdated, outworn, rusty
反 fresh, new 崭新的；promising 充满希望的

Unit 5

| ■ MOROSE | ■ MOSAIC | ■ MOSQUE | ■ MOTH-EATEN | ■ MOTILE |
| ■ MOTIVATE | ■ MOTLEY | ■ MOTTLE | ■ MOTTO | ■ MOURNFUL |

○ **morose** [məˈroʊs]
【考法】 *adj.* 忧郁的：having a **sullen** and **gloomy** disposition
例 morose job seekers who are inured to rejection 习惯了被拒的郁郁寡欢的求职者
近 bleak, chill, dark, depressed, dire, dour, gloomy, lugubrious, saturnine, solemn, sulky, sullen, surly
反 bright, cheerful, festive, jovial, jocund, sanguine, lighthearted, rejoiced 高兴的，欢快的

○ **mosaic** [moʊˈzeɪɪk]
【考法】 *n.* 综合物，马赛克般的东西：an unorganized **collection** or mixture of various things
例 a mosaic of testimony from various witnesses 从不同证人中得来的综合证词
近 agglomerate, collage, hodgepodge, jumble, montage, motley, muddle, salad, shuffle, variety, welter

○ **mosque** [mɑːsk]
【考法】 *n.* 清真寺：a building used for public **worship** by **Muslim**
例 a deadly suicide attack at the mosque 在清真寺发生的致命自杀性袭击
近 cathedral, chapel, church, temple

moth-eaten [ˈmɔːθ‚iːtn]
○ 【考法】 *adj.* 过时的：having **passed its time** of use or usefulness
例 dressed in a moth-eaten style 过时的衣着
近 antiquated, archaic, dated, fossilized, moribund, outdated, outworn, rusty
反 fresh, new 崭新的；promising 充满希望的

○ **motile** [ˈmoʊtl]
【考法】 *adj.* 能动的：exhibiting or capable of **movement**
例 Aircraft carriers are recognized as a motile combat platform. 航空母舰是一种移动作战平台。
近 mobile, movable, portable, transportable
反 immobile 不可移动的
派 motility *n.* 可运动性

motivate ['moʊtɪveɪt]

【考法】 *vt.* 刺激，激发：to **provide** with an **incentive**; move to action

例 questions that excite and motivate youth 激发青年人的问题

近 excite, galvanize, impel, innervate, provoke, rouse, stimulate

反 discourage, dishearten 使泄气

派 motivation *n.* 动机；motivated *adj.* 被激励的

motley ['mɑːtli]

【考法】 *adj.* 混杂的，富于变化的：(especially of colors) having elements of great **variety** or incongruity

例 an arrangement of motley flowers 多种不同花束的组合

近 assorted, chromatic, kaleidoscopic, heterogeneous, indiscriminate, magpie, piebald, variegated

反 homogeneous, monochromatic, monotonous, unvaried 单一的，同一性的

mottle ['mɑːtl]

【考法】 *vt.* 标记上杂色斑点：to **mark** with **spots** or blotches of different shades or colors

例 a black horse mottled with white 身上带有白色斑点的黑马

近 blotch, dapple, dot, marble, splotch, spot, stain

反 blanch 漂白

派 mottled *adj.* 斑驳的

motto ['mɑːtoʊ]

【考法】 *n.* 座右铭：a short expression of a **guiding principle**

例 "Semper fidelis" is the motto of US Marine Corps. "永远忠诚"是美国海军陆战队的格言。

近 catchword, doctrine, dogma, idiom, slogan

mournful ['mɔːrnfl]

【考法】 *adj.* 悲伤的：feeling or **expressing sorrow** or grief

例 The mournful survivors of the disaster were faced with the grim task of burying the dead. 悲伤的幸存者面临着掩埋灾难中死者尸体的可怕任务。|| Mrs. Murphy fainted at the mournful news of her son's death. Murphy 太太听到她儿子的死讯后晕了过去。

近 aching, agonized, anguished, doleful, dolorous, grievous, lamentable, lugubrious, melancholy, sad, woeful

反 cheerful, delighted, jocund, jovial, jubilant 快活的

派 mournfulness *n.* 悲伤

Unit 6

| ■ MOVEMENT | ■ MUDDY | ■ MUFFLE | ■ MULISH | ■ MUMBLE |
| ■ MUNDANE | ■ MUNIFICENT | ■ MURKY | ■ MURMUR | ■ MUTATE |

movement ['muːvmənt]

【考法】 *n.* 运动：the act or process of **moving**

例 There appears to be some movement in the bush. 树丛中似乎有动静。

近 action, motion, operation, shifting, stir

反 motionlessness, stasis 静止

muddy ['mʌdi]

【考法1】 *adj.* 不干净的：**not clean**

例 The children got muddy after playing outside. 孩子们在外面玩弄得很脏。

近 besmirched, dingy, draggled, dusty, filthy, foul, nasty, smudged, smutty, soiled, sordid, stained, sullied

反 clean, immaculate, spotless, stainless, unsoiled, unstained, unsullied 干净的

【考法2】 *adj.* 浑浊的，不清晰的：**lacking** in **clarity** or brightness

例 a muddy recording 嘈杂不清的纪录

近 cloudy, foul, murky, obscure, turbid

反 clear 清晰的

【考法3】 *vt.* 使难以理解：to **make** (something) **unclear** to the understanding

例 That point is irrelevant and will just muddy the issue we're trying to resolve. 那个观点和我们讨论的问题毫不相干，它只会妨碍我们对于问题的理解。

近 becloud, befog, blur, cloud, fog, obfuscate

反 clarify, illuminate 阐明

muffle ['mʌfl]
【考法】 *vt.* 使消声：to wrap or pad in order to **deaden the sound**
例 close the window to muffle the outside noises 关上窗户以减少外界的噪音
近 attenuate, dampen, deaden, mute, soften, stifle, suppress
反 amplify, enhance, magnify 放大，增强
派 muffler *n.* 消音器

mulish ['mjuːlɪʃ]
【考法】 *adj.* 固执的：unreasonably and inflexibly **obstinate**
例 a mulish determination to act on his own 铁了心要单打独斗
近 adamant, headstrong, immovable, intractable, obstinate, pertinacious, perverse, refractory, stubborn
反 flexible, pliable, pliant, yielding 易改变立场的，易受影响的
派 mulishly *adv.* 固执地

mumble ['mʌmbl]
【考法】 *v.* 说话含糊：to **utter** words in a low **confused** indistinct manner
例 He mumbled an apology reluctantly. 他不情愿地咕哝了句抱歉。
近 grunt, murmur, mutter, whisper
反 articulate, enunciate 清楚地表达

mundane [mʌn'deɪn]
【考法1】 *adj.* 尘世的，世俗化的：of, **relating to**, or typical of this **world**
例 As for opera, I prefer mundane to religious themes. 与宗教主题相比，我更喜欢世俗主题的歌剧。
近 carnal, earthly, materialistic, secular, sensual, worldly
反 spiritual 精神上的；ethereal 虚无缥缈的，非尘世的
【考法2】 *adj.* 平凡的：relating to, characteristic of, or concerned with **commonplaces**
例 mundane concerns of day-to-day life 关于日常生活的一般顾虑
近 common, ordinary, prosaic
反 extraordinary 非凡的

munificent [mjuː'nɪfɪsnt]
【考法】 *adj.* 慷慨的：very **liberal in giving**
例 The university received a munificent foundation grant. 那所大学收到了一笔慷慨的基金资助。
近 bountiful, charitable, generous, liberal, openhanded, unsparing
反 closefisted, mean, miserly, niggardly, parsimonious, penurious, stingy, tightfisted 小气的
派 munificence *n.* 慷慨

murky ['mɜːrki]
【考法1】 *adj.* 黯淡的，昏暗的：being **without light** or without much light
例 I didn't like walking around the murky campground without a flashlight. 我不喜欢在没有手电的情况下在营地里走动。
近 black, caliginous, darkened, dim, gloomy, stygian
反 bright, brightened, brilliant, illuminated, illumined, lucent, lucid, luminous 明亮的
【考法2】 *adj.* 模糊的，晦涩的：**lacking clarity** or distinctness
例 He felt lost in the murky bureaucratic rhetoric. 他感觉自己被官僚主义的晦涩说辞弄晕了。
近 ambiguous, arcane, cloudy, equivocal, muddy, nebulous, obscure, occult, vague
反 clear, limpid, pellucid, plain 清晰的

murmur ['mɜːrmər]
【考法1】 *n.* 小声的话语：a **low**, indistinct, continuous **sound**
例 We could hear the murmur of the audience throughout the entire performance. 我们在整个演出当中都能听到观众的窃窃私语。
近 grunt, mumble, mutter, undertone, whisper
反 roar 怒吼
【考法2】 *vi.* 低声抱怨，发牢骚：to complain in low mumbling tones; **grumble**
例 No prisoner dared murmur out loud. 没有囚犯敢大声报怨。
近 carp, fuss, gripe, grizzle, grouch, grouse, grumble, moan, repine, whine
反 crow, delight, rejoice 欢呼，高兴

mutate ['mjuːteɪt]
【考法】 *v.* (使)改变，(使)变异：to undergo or cause to **undergo mutation**
例 Some chromosomes started to mutate after exposure to X-Ray. 经 X 光照射之后部分染色体开始发生变异。
近 alter, change, fluctuate, modify, shift, transfigure, transform, vary
反 remain 保持不变；plateau, stabilize 使稳定
派 mutation *n.* 改变；变异

Unit 7

mute ［mjuːt］

【考法 1】 *adj.* 不说话的，缄默的：deliberately **refraining from speech**

例 He always remained mute no matter how much we pleaded for an answer. 不论我们怎么恳求回答，他总是保持沉默。

近 dumb, inarticulate, speechless, uncommunicative, voiceless, wordless

反 communicative, expansive, loquacious, talkative 爱说话的，话多的

【考法 2】 *vt.* 使颜色、音调等柔和：to **soften** the tone, color, shade, or hue of

例 mute a color 对颜色进行柔化

近 attenuate, soften, subdue

反 sharpen 锐化

【考法 3】 *vt.* 减弱声音：to soften or **muffle the sound** of

近 dampen, deaden, muffle, stifle

反 amplify, magnify 增强，放大

派 muted *adj.* 消声的，静音的

mutter ［ˈmʌtər］

【考法】 *vi.* 低声抱怨：to **murmur complainingly** or angrily

例 mutter about the difficult assignment 抱怨作业太难

近 carp, fuss, gripe, grizzle, grouch, grouse, grumble, moan, murmur, repine, whine

反 crow, delight, rejoice 欢呼，高兴

myopic ［maɪˈɑːpɪk］

【考法】 *adj.* 缺乏远见的，缺乏辨别能力的：a **lack of foresight** or discernment

例 a myopic view on climate change 关于气候变化缺乏远见的观点

近 shortsighted, narrow-minded

反 far-sighted, foreseeing, provident 有远见的；discerning 有辨别能力的

派 myopia *n.* 近视；鼠目寸光

myriad ［ˈmɪriəd］

【考法】 *adj.* 无限的，大量的：constituting a very large, **indefinite number**

例 the myriad stars of a summer night 夏日夜空中的无尽繁星

近 innumerable, numerous, uncountable, untold

反 few, scarce, scanty 少的，缺乏的；countable, enumerable 可数清的

nadir ［ˈneɪdɪr］

【考法】 *n.* 最低点：the **lowest point**

例 the nadir on the curve 曲线上的最低点

近 base, bottom, foot

反 acme, apex, climax, meridian, peak, pinnacle, summit, top, zenith 最高点

naïve ［naɪˈiːv］

【考法】 *adj.* 天真纯朴的：**lacking worldly experience** and understanding, simple and guileless

例 a child with a naïve charm 天真无邪的孩子

近 artless, guileless, ingenuous, innocent, natural, simple, unaffected, unsophisticated

反 sophisticated, worldly 世故的；affected, artful, assuming, dishonest, dissembling, guileful 虚伪做作的

派 naivety *n.* 天真

narcissism ［ˈnɑːrsɪsɪzəm］

【考法】 *n.* 自恋：excessive love or **admiration of oneself**

例 In his narcissism, he just assumed that everyone else wanted to hear the tiny details of his day. 在他自恋的眼中，仿佛所有人都想要听他日常生活里的细枝末节。

近 egocentricity, egotism, self-absorption

反 self-hatred 自我憎恨

派 narcissistic *adj.* 自恋的

nascent [ˈnæsnt]
【考法】 *adj.* 新生的：coming or having **recently come into existence**
例 The rise of the nascent middle class catalyzed a new economic boom. 新生中产阶级的崛起催生了一场新的经济繁荣。
近 beginning, emerging, inceptive, inchoate, incipient, initial, introductory
反 full-blown, full-fledged, mature, ripe 成熟的；moribund 将死的
派 nascence *n.* 新生的状态

natty [ˈnæti]
【考法】 *adj.* 整洁的，时髦的：trimly neat and **tidy**
例 a natty young woman 整洁漂亮的年轻女子
近 dapper, smart, spruce
反 frowsy, sloppy, slovenly 邋遢的

nauseate [ˈnɔːzieɪt]
【考法】 *v.* (使)厌恶，(使)作呕：to feel or **cause** to feel loathing or **disgust**
例 The malodor of the rotten meat made us nauseate. 腐肉的恶臭让我们恶心。
近 disgust, repel, repulse, revolt, sicken
反 delight 使愉悦
派 nausea *n.* 恶心反胃

Unit 8

■ NAUTICAL	■ NAYSAY	■ NEBULOUS	■ NEEDY	■ NEFARIOUS
■ NEGATION	■ NEGLIGENT	■ NEGOTIATE	■ NEOPHYTE	■ NERVE

nautical [ˈnɔːtɪkl]
【考法】 *adj.* 航海的：of, relating to, or characteristic of ships, shipping, sailors, or navigation **on** a body of **water**
例 nautical mile 海里
近 marine, maritime, navigational
反 aeronautic 航空的；astronautic 航天的

naysay [ˈneɪseɪ]
【考法】 *vt.* 拒绝，否认：to **oppose**, **deny**, or take a pessimistic or negative view of
近 decline, deny, deject, disallow, gainsay, oppose, refuse, reject
反 accede, agree, concur, consent 同意
派 naysayer *n.* 反对者

nebulous [ˈnebjələs]
【考法】 *adj.* 模糊的：**indistinct**, vague
例 a nebulous description of the topic 对于主题的模糊描述
近 ambiguous, arcane, equivocal, hazy, indistinct, muddy, murky, obscure, occult, vague
反 distinct 明显的；clear, definite, unambiguous, unequivocal 明确的
派 nebula *n.* 星云

needy [ˈniːdi]
【考法】 *adj.* 贫困的：being in need; **impoverished**, poor
例 As a child, she was extremely needy and had no self-confidence. 她是一个非常贫穷的小孩，因此缺乏自信。
近 destitute, impecunious, impoverished, indigent, penurious, poor, threadbare
反 affluent, opulent, wealthy 富有的

nefarious [nɪˈferiəs]
【考法】 *adj.* 极坏的，邪恶的：flagrantly **wicked** or impious
例 a nefarious scheme to assassinate the archbishop 企图刺杀大主教的邪恶阴谋
近 atrocious, degenerate, devious, evil, heinous, infamous, miscreant, vicious, villainous, wicked
反 ethical, righteous, upright, virtuous 品德高尚的；beneficial 有益的；exemplary 模范的

negation [nɪˈɡeɪʃn]
【考法】 *n.* 否定：the **opposite** or absence of something regarded as actual, positive, or affirmative
例 She issued specific negations of all of the charges against her. 她发表了明确的声明，否定了所有对她的指控。
近 contradiction, denegation, denial, gainsaying, rejection, repudiation
反 acknowledgement, affirmation, avowal 肯定，同意
派 negative *adj.* 否定的；负面的

negligent [ˈneglɪdʒənt]

【考法】 *adj.* 疏忽大意的：**failing** to give proper attention or **care**

例 negligent in taking care of the children 粗心大意地照顾孩子

近 careless, derelict, heedless, neglectful, remiss

反 attentive, careful, cautious, heedful 专心的，谨慎的

派 negligence *n.* 疏忽

negotiate [nɪˈgouʃieɪt]

【考法 1】 *v.* 商量，谈判：to arrange or settle **by** discussion and **mutual agreement**

例 negotiate the term of truce 共商停战事宜

近 arrange, bargain, concert, settle

反 break down (谈判等)失败，破产

派 negotiable *adj.* 可商量的；negotiation *n.* 商量，谈判

【考法 2】 *v.* 谋划：**plan out** usually with subtle skill or care

例 The prisoners negotiated their escape by using Morse code to tap messages to each other through the walls. 犯人们通过敲击墙壁来传达莫尔斯电码，从而密谋了他们的逃跑计划。

近 contrive, finesse, frame, machinate, maneuver, manipulate, mastermind, wangle

neophyte [ˈniːəfaɪt]

【考法】 *n.* 初学者，新手：a **beginner** or novice

例 a novice in the theater who had never even had a walk-on role 一个连龙套都没跑过的新演员

近 abecedarian, apprentice, fledgling, freshman, novice, recruit, rookie, tyro

反 veteran 老兵，身经百战的人

nerve [nɜːrv]

【考法 1】 *n.* (坚强的)意志，勇气：**power of endurance** or control; strength of mind to carry on in spite of danger

例 nerves of steel 钢铁般的意志

近 bravery, fortitude, guts, intrepidity, resolution, stamina

反 cowardice, pusillanimity 怯懦

【考法 2】 *vt.* 给予勇气，鼓励：to **give** strength or **courage** to

例 He needs to nerve himself for the big game tomorrow. 他需要为明天的大赛给自己加油鼓劲。

近 animate, brace, cheer, embolden, encourage, inspirit, steel, strengthen

反 appall 使胆寒；discourage, dishearten 使沮丧

派 nervy *adj.* 有勇气的

Unit 9

■ NETTLE	■ NEUTRALIZE	■ NEXUS	■ NIBBLE	■ NICETY
■ NIL	■ NIP	■ NITPICK	■ NOCTURNAL	■ NOISOME

nettle [ˈnetl]

【考法】 *vt.* 惹怒：to **arouse** to sharp but transitory annoyance or **anger**

例 His pompous attitude nettled several people. 他自大的性格得罪了不少人。

近 aggravate, annoy, exasperate, inflame, infuriate, irritate, peeve, pique, provoke, roil, ruffle, vex

反 appease, assuage, conciliate, mollify, placate, propitiate 安抚

neutralize [ˈnuːtrəlaɪz]

【考法 1】 *vt.* 中和：to cause (an **acid** or base) to **undergo neutralization**

例 industrial exhaust neutralized by lime 被石灰中和的工业废气

反 acidify 酸化

【考法 2】 *vt.* 破坏，使无效：to **make inoperative or ineffective** usually by means of an opposite force, influence, or effect

例 influenced by the kind of propaganda that is difficult to neutralize 被一种难以消除的宣传攻势所影响

近 annul, cancel, counteract, frustrate, negate, nullify

反 activate, vitalize 激活

派 neutralization *n.* 中和；消除

nexus ['neksəs]

【考法 1】 *n.* 连结：a means of **connection**

例 Correlativity does not sufficiently lead to causal nexus. 相关性不是因果关联的充分条件。

近 bond, connection, link, tie

【考法 2】 *n.* 核心，最重要的地带：a thing or place that is of **greatest importance** to an activity or interest

例 As the nexus for three great religions, Jerusalem has had a troubled as well as illustrious history. 作为三大宗教的圣城，耶路撒冷有着动荡而辉煌的历史。

近 base, capital, center, core, focus, kernel, heart, hub, nucleus

反 margin, periphery 边缘

nibble ['nɪbl]

【考法】 *vt.* 小口咬：to eat with **small**, quick **bites** or in small morsels

例 waves nibbling the shore 缓慢侵蚀海岸的浪

近 bite, nip, peck, sip, tipple

反 gobble 狼吞虎咽

nicety ['naɪsəti]

【考法 1】 *n.* 准确，精确：**careful** attention to **details**; delicate exactness

例 There's a nicety of detail in his meticulously painted landscapes. 在他精心绘制的景观图中，有着十分精准翔实的细节。

近 accuracy, delicacy, exactness, fineness, precision, veracity

反 coarseness, imprecision, inaccuracy, roughness 不准确，粗糙

【考法 2】 *n.* 细微之处：a **fine point** or distinction

例 the niceties of table manner 餐桌礼仪的细微之处 ‖ niceties of diplomatic protocol 外交礼节中的细节

近 detail, particular, nuance, subtlety

nil [nɪl]

【考法】 *n.* 不存在，零：**nothing**; zero

例 reduced to nil 消逝殆尽

近 nothing, nonentity, nullity, zip

反 existence 存在

nip [nɪp]

【考法 1】 *n.* 少量：a very **small amount**

例 I'll have just a nip of your sandwich. 我只吃一点点你的三明治。

近 bit, hint, little, mite, ounce, snap, trace

反 abundance, affluence, avalanche 大量

【考法 2】 *vi.* 小口吃喝：to sip (alcoholic liquor) **in small amounts**

近 nibble, sip, tipple

反 guzzle, quaff, swill 大口吃喝

nitpick ['nɪtpɪk]

【考法】 *v.* 吹毛求疵：to **criticize** by nit-picking

例 a peevish critic always ready to nitpick 一个总是吹毛求疵的古怪评论家

近 carp, cavil, fuss, niggle, quibble

派 nitpicker *n.* 吹毛求疵的人

nocturnal [nɑːk'tɜːrnl]

【考法 1】 *adj.* 夜间的：of, relating to, or occurring **in the night**

例 a nocturnal raid 夜间突袭

近 nightly, nighttime

反 daily, diurnal 白昼的

【考法 2】 *adj.* 夜间活动的：**active at night**

例 a nocturnal predator 夜间活动的捕食者

派 nocturne *n.* 夜曲

noisome ['nɔɪsəm]

【考法 1】 *adj.* 有害的，有毒的：noxious, **harmful**

例 noisome chemical fumes 有害的化学烟雾

近 deleterious, detrimental, insalubrious, noxious, unhealthy, unwholesome

反 beneficial 有益的；healthy, salubrious, wholesome 有益健康的

【考法 2】 *adj.* 恶臭的：**offensive** to the senses and especially to the sense of **smell**

例 noisome garbage 散发着恶臭的垃圾

近 fetid, foul, malodorous, smelly, stinky

反 ambrosial, aromatic, fragrant, perfumed, redolent, savory, scented, sweet 有香味的

【考法3】 *adj.* 非常令人厌恶的：highly obnoxious or **objectionable**
例 noisome habits of littering 让人反感的随地乱扔垃圾的坏习惯
近 abhorrent, appalling, disgusting, hideous, loathsome, nauseating, offensive, repugnant, repulsive
反 appealing, captivating, enchanting, fascinating 有吸引力的；agreeable, pleasant 令人愉悦的

Unit 10

■ NOMAD	■ NOMINAL	■ NONCHALANT	■ NONDESCRIPT	■ NONENTITY
■ NONPLUS	■ NONSENSE	■ NOTCH	■ NOVEL	■ NOXIOUS

nomad ['noʊmæd]
【考法】 *adj./n.* 游牧的；居无定所的人：a member of a people who have **no fixed residence** but move from place to place usually seasonally and within a well-defined territory
例 After college she became quite the nomad, backpacking through Europe with no particular destination. 大学毕业后她开始漂泊，漫无目的地游历欧洲。
近 ambulant, fugitive, gallivanting, perambulatory, peripatetic, ranging, roaming, vagabond, vagrant, wandering, wayfaring
反 settled 定居的

nominal ['nɑːmɪnl]
【考法1】 *adj.* 不重要的：so small or unimportant as to warrant little or no attention
例 His involvement was nominal. 他的参与不太重要。
近 inconsequential, inconsiderable, paltry, trifling, trivial
反 big, consequential, considerable, important, material, significant 重要的
【考法2】 *adj.* 名义上的：existing or being **something in name** or form only
例 nominal head of the party 党派的名义首领
近 formal, paper, titular

nonchalant [ˌnɑːnʃə'lɑːnt]
【考法】 *adj.* 冷漠的：having an air of easy unconcern or **indifference**
例 She was surprisingly nonchalant about winning the award. 她竟然对得奖很淡然。
近 apathetic, disinterested, insensible, insouciant, perfunctory, unconcerned
反 concerned, interested 忧虑的，有兴趣的

nondescript ['nɑːndɪskrɪpt]
【考法】 *adj.* 平凡的，不吸引人的：**lacking distinctive** or **interesting** qualities
例 Their performance was disappointingly nondescript. 他们的演出令人失望，味同嚼蜡。
近 beige, characterless, featureless, indistinctive, vanilla
反 conspicuous, remarkable, striking 明显的，惊人的

nonentity [nɑː'nentəti]
【考法1】 *n.* 不重要的人：a person or thing of **little consequence** or significance
例 She was so quiet she was almost a nonentity at the meeting. 她非常沉默，在会议上是个边缘人物。
近 cipher, half-pint, insignificancy, lightweight, nullity, snippersnapper, twerp, whippersnapper, zero, zilch
反 mogul, big shot, big wheel, bigwig, eminence, figure, magnate, personage, somebody 显要人物
【考法2】 *n.* 虚构的东西：a conception or image **created** by the imagination and having **no objective reality**
例 The arctic circle is a nonentity—you won't see it on the way to the north pole. 北极圈是虚构的概念，去北极的路上你不会见到那么一个圈。
近 chimera, conceit, daydream, delusion, fancy, figment, hallucination, illusion, phantasm, unreality, vision

nonplus [ˌnɑːn'plʌs]
【考法】 *vt.* 使迷惑，使困窘：use to be at a loss as to what to say, think, or do: **perplex**
例 I was nonplussed by his openly expressed admiration of me. 我被他公开表现的仰慕弄得很窘迫。
近 confound, confuse, discomfit, disconcert, discountenance, mortify, abash, faze, fluster

nonsense ['nɑːnsns]
【考法】 *n.* 无意义的话，废话：words or language having **no meaning** or conveying no intelligible ideas
例 Many of the words in the poem are nonsense. 这首诗歌当中很多词都是废话。
近 babble, blabber, drivel, prattle, mumbo jumbo

notch [nɑːtʃ]

【考法 1】 *n.* 刻痕：a V-shaped **cut** used for keeping a record

【考法 2】 *vt.* 通过努力获得：to **obtain**（as a goal）through effort

例 a stunning performance that notched up a second Academy Award for the actor 出色的表演为该演员拿到了第二座小金人

近 attain, bag, chalk up, clock up, gain, hit, log, make, rack up, ring up, score, win

novel [ˈnɑːvl]

【考法】 *adj.* 新奇的：strikingly **new**, unusual, or different

例 a novel scheme to collect money 一种新颖的筹钱手段

近 original, unaccustomed, unfamiliar, unheard-of, unknown, unprecedented

反 banal, timeworn, familiar, hackneyed, time-honored, tired, warmed-over 陈腐的

noxious [ˈnɑːkʃəs]

【考法 1】 *adj.* 有害的，有毒的：**harmful** to living things; **injurious to health**

例 noxious waste 有害的废弃物

近 unwholesome, baneful, deleterious, detrimental, nocuous, pernicious, wicked

反 beneficial, salubrious, anodyne, benign, harmless, hurtless, innocent, innocuous, inoffensive, safe 有益的，无害的

【考法 2】 *adj.* 产生强烈厌恶的：**causing intense displeasure**, disgust, or resentment

例 a noxious new breed of horror movie in which graphic depictions of torture are presented as entertainment 在一部新的恐怖电影中，对于酷刑生动的描述被当作娱乐，这让人很厌恶

近 abhorrent, abominable, appalling, awful, disgusting, distasteful, dreadful, foul, fulsome, gross, hideous, horrid, loathsome, nasty, nauseating, noisome, obnoxious, odious, repellent, repugnant, repulsive, revolting, scandalous

---

Education is a progressive discovery of our ignorance.

教育是一个逐步发现自己无知的过程。

——美国历史学家 杜兰特（Durant, American historian）

List 17

"敢于不断挑战极限的你将发掘拥有无限潜力的我。"

（徐碧慧，2010 年 2 月，Verbal 720，Quantitative 790，AW 4.5

录取院校：University of Oxford）

Unit 1

■ NUANCE	■ NUDGE	■ NUGATORY	■ NURTURE	■ OATH
■ OBDURATE	■ OBEDIENT	■ OBEISANCE	■ OBFUSCATE	■ OBLIGATORY

nuance ['nuːɑːns]
【考法】 *n.* 细微的差异：a **subtle distinction** or variation
例 a poem of little depth and nuance 一首没有什么深度、没有什么辨识度的诗
反 patent difference, lack of subtlety, sharp distinction, patency 明显的差别

nudge [nʌdʒ]
【考法 1】 *vt.* 用肘推以引起注意：to seek the attention of by a **push** of the **elbow**
例 accidentally nudged me as he squeezed past 他过去的时候不小心用肘碰到了我
【考法 2】 *vt.* 说服某人做某事：to try to **persuade** (someone) through earnest appeals to follow a course of action
例 The car salesman nudged me into taking a test-drive. 汽车销售员说服我进行试驾。
近 encourage, exhort, goad, press, prod, prompt

nugatory ['nuːɡətɔːri]
【考法】 *adj.* 无关紧要的：of little or no **consequence; inconsequential**
例 The book is entertaining, but its contributions to Shakespearean scholarship are nugatory. 这本书娱乐性不错，但是对于莎士比亚研究的贡献微不足道。
近 incidental, inconsequential, inconsiderable, insignificant, negligible, trifling, trivial
反 consequential, eventful, important, major, meaningful, momentous, significant, substantial, unfrivolous, weighty 重要的

nurture ['nɜːrtʃər]
【考法 1】 *vt.* 提供营养：to supply with **nourishment**
例 She nurtured her children through the winters with home-cooked soup. 她整个冬天都给孩子们喂自制的汤。
反 withhold sustenance from 停止提供营养物
【考法 2】 *vt.* 培育，培养：to **provide** (someone) **with** moral or spiritual **understanding**
例 He feels that his lifelong practice of reading the Bible daily has nurtured him in ways he cannot describe. 一生中每天都阅读圣经在潜移默化中影响了他。
近 edify, illuminate, inspire
反 impede, stunt, disregard 阻碍，漠视

oath [oʊθ]
【考法】 *n.* 誓言：a solemn, **formal** declaration or **promise** to fulfill a pledge
例 an oath to defend the nation 保卫祖国的誓言
近 pledge, troth, vow, word

obdurate ['ɑːbdərət]
【考法 1】 *adj.* 固执的：**resistant** to persuasion or softening **influences**
例 She is known for her obdurate determination. 她以坚定不移著称。
近 adamant, hard-nosed, headstrong, inflexible, intransigent, pertinacious, stubborn, unbending, uncompromising, unrelenting, unyielding, willful
反 acquiescent, agreeable, amenable, compliant, complying, flexible, pliable, pliant, relenting, yielding 温顺的
【考法 2】 *adj.* 冷酷无情的：having or showing a **lack of sympathy** or tender feelings
例 the obdurate refusal of the crotchety old man to let the neighborhood kids retrieve their ball from his backyard 那个怪老头冷酷无情地拒绝了孩子们进他后院找球的请求
近 affectless, callous, compassionless, hard-hearted, heartless, indurate, inhuman, insensate, ironhearted, merciless, remorseless, ruthless, unsparing
反 charitable, compassionate, humane, kindhearted, kindly, merciful, softhearted, sympathetic, tender, warmhearted 同情的，有爱的

obedient [ə'biːdiənt]

【考法】 *adj.* 服从的，顺从的：**submissive** to the restraint or command of **authority**

例 That girl is so obedient that she does everything the first time she is asked. 这个女孩如此顺从，叫她做事有求必应。

近 amenable, compliant, submissive, tractable

反 contumacious, imperial, balky, contrary, contumacious, defiant, disobedient, froward, incompliant, insubordinate, intractable, noncompliant, obstreperous, rebel, rebellious, recalcitrant, refractory, restive, unamenable, ungovernable, unruly, untoward, wayward, willful 顽固的，不服从的

obeisance [oʊ'biːsns]

【考法】 *n.* 敬礼，尊重：a movement of the body made in token of **respect** or **submission**

例 make obeisance to her mentors 向她的导师们致敬

派 obeisant *adj.* 恭敬的

反 impertinent, impudent, imperious 不敬的，无礼的

obfuscate ['ɑːbfʌskeɪt]

【考法】 *vt.* 使困惑，使模糊：to make so **confused** or **opaque** as to be difficult to perceive or understand

例 obfuscate the reader 让读者困惑

近 becloud, befog, blur, cloud, fog, muddy

反 demystify, elucidate, illuminate, clarify, explain clearly 澄清，阐明

派 obfuscated *adj.* 模糊的

反 lucid 清晰的

obligatory [ə'blɪɡətɔːri]

【考法1】 *adj.* 强制性的：of the nature of an obligation; **compulsory**

例 obligatory military service 强制性的服兵役

近 compulsory, imperative, involuntary, peremptory, required

反 discretionary, selective, elective, optional, voluntary 自由选择的，志愿的

【考法2】 *adj.* （见得多以至于）无聊的：used or heard so often as to be **dull**

例 the obligatory cliff-hanger endings for season finales of TV shows 电视剧总是以恶俗的惊心动魄的结局作为完季

近 banal, cliché, commonplace, hack, hackneyed, moth-eaten, musty, shopworn, stereotyped, threadbare, timeworn, trite, well-worn

反 fresh, new, novel, original, unclichéd, unhackneyed 新奇的

Unit 2

■ OBLIGING	■ OBLIQUE	■ OBLITERATE	■ OBLIVIOUS	■ OBLOQUY
■ OBSCURE	■ OBSEQUIOUS	■ OBSESS	■ OBSTINATE	■ OBSTREPEROUS

obliging [ə'blaɪdʒɪŋ]

【考法】 *adj.* 乐于助人的：willing to **do favors**

例 An obliging concierge used his pull to get us reservations at the town's hottest restaurant. 一个好心的看门人利用他的影响力帮我们在镇上最火爆的餐厅订到了座。

近 accommodative, friendly, indulgent

oblique [ə'bliːk]

【考法】 *adj.* 斜的：**inclined or twisted** to one side

例 The old woman gave the eavesdropper an oblique glance. 老妇人给了偷听者一个白眼。

近 askew, cant, inclined, leaning, listing, slanted, sloping, tilted

反 direct, even, level, straight 笔直的

obliterate [ə'blɪtəreɪt]

【考法】 *vt.* 除去：to **remove** from existence

例 The March snowstorm obliterated our hopes for an early spring. 三月的暴风雪摧毁了我们对于早春的念想。

近 efface, eradicate, expunge, expurgate, exterminate, extirpate, wipe out

oblivious [ə'blɪviəs]

【考法】 *adj.* 不知道的，不知情的：**lacking** conscious **awareness**; **not informed** about or aware of something

例 He seemed oblivious to the fact that he had hurt her. 他似乎并不知道他伤害了她。

近 incognizant, insensible, unaware, unconscious, uninformed, unwitting

反 mindful, vigilant, acquainted, cognizant, conscious, conversant, grounded, informed, knowing, mindful, witting 留意的，机警的

obloquy [ˈɑːbləkwi]

【考法 1】 *n.* 谩骂，诽谤：**abusively** detractive **language** or utterance; calumny

例 she unleashed a torrent of obloquy on her opponent. 她滔滔不绝地辱骂了对手一顿。

近 billingsgate, fulmination, invective, scurrility, vitriol, vituperation

反 adulation 极度谄媚

【考法 2】 *n.* 恶名，耻辱：the state of having **lost the esteem** of others

例 The accused murderer was condemned to live out his days in perpetual obloquy. 凶手终将在骂名中度过余生。

近 discredit, disesteem, dishonor, disrepute, ignominy, infamy, odium, opprobrium, reproach, shame

反 esteem, honor, respect 敬重，好名声

obscure [əbˈskjʊr]

【考法 1】 *adj.* 含义模糊的：**not clearly** understood or expressed; having an often intentionally **veiled** or **uncertain meaning**

例 a fantasy writer who likes to put lots of obscure references in her tales of wizards and warlocks 一个喜欢在巫师故事中添加很多含义模糊的引文的魔幻小说作家

近 ambiguous, arcane, enigmatic, equivocal, fuliginous, inscrutable, opaque

反 explicit, manifest, clear, certain, accessible, nonambiguous, obvious, plain, unambiguous, unequivocal 明晰的，没有歧义的

【考法 2】 *adj.* 平凡的，不知名的：not prominent or **famous**

例 an obscure poet 无名的诗人

近 noteless, uncelebrated, unfamous, unknown, unrecognized, unsung

反 legendary, celebrated, famed, famous, noted, notorious, prominent, renowned, well-known 有名的

派 obscurity *n.* 无名之辈

反 celebrity 名人

【考法 3】 *vt.* 使模糊：to make dark, dim, or **indistinct**

例 When it isn't obscured by smog, the view of the city from the observatory can be spectacular. 如果在晴朗的天气，从天文台看出去的城市全景非常赞。

近 blear, blur, darken, dim, overshadow, shroud

反 elucidate, brighten, illuminate, light up, lighten 阐明

obsequious [əbˈsiːkwiəs]

【考法】 *adj.* 谄媚的，奴性的：marked by or exhibiting a **fawning attentiveness**

例 She's constantly followed by obsequious assistants who will do anything. 她总是有一群谄媚的跟班，愿意为她赴汤蹈火。

反 supercilious 目中无人的

obsess [əbˈses]

【考法】 *vt.* 迷住；使困扰：to **haunt** or excessively preoccupy the mind of

例 The war obsesses her—she talks about nothing else. 那场战争总是困扰着她，她张口闭口都谈。

反 intensively disgust 极度厌恶

obstinate [ˈɑːbstɪnət]

【考法 1】 *adj.* 固执的：perversely adhering to an opinion, purpose, or course **in spite of** reason, arguments, or **persuasion**

例 obstinate resistance to change 坚决抵制改变

近 adamant, headstrong, intransigent, stubborn, uncompromising, unyielding, willful

反 acquiescent, agreeable, amenable, compliant, complying, flexible, pliable, pliant, relenting, yielding 顺从的，服从的

【考法 2】 *adj.* 难以减轻或治愈的：**not easily subdued**, remedied, or removed

例 obstinate fever 高烧不退 ‖ an obstinate headache 难以治愈的头痛

obstreperous [əbˈstrepərəs]

【考法 1】 *adj.* 难驾驭的，任性的：stubbornly resistant to control; **unruly**; given to resisting authority or another's control

例 The club's president was at his wits' end with obstreperous members who refused to cooperate. 俱乐部主席拿那些不合作的会员一点办法都没有。

近 balky, defiant, incompliant, insubordinate, intractable, rebellious, recalcitrant, refractory

反 disciplined, amenable, biddable, compliant, conformable, docile, obedient, ruly, submissive, tractable 守纪律的，顺从的

【考法 2】 *adj.* 吵闹的：engaging in or marked by **loud and insistent cries** especially of protest

例 an obstreperous crowd protesting the government's immigration policy 一堆吵闹的民众游行抗议政府的移民政策

近 blatant, clamant, clamorous, squawking, vociferant

Unit 3

obstruct [əbˈstrʌkt]

【考法 1】 *vt.* 妨碍，给…制造困难：to **impede**, retard, or interfere with; hinder; to **create difficulty** for the work or activity of
例 He was charged with obstructing justice by lying to investigators. 他被指控向检察官说谎，妨碍司法。
近 encumber, fetter, handicap, hinder, impede, inhibit, stymie, interfere with
反 facilitate, abet, aid, assist 促进，帮助

【考法 2】 *vt.* 阻挡：to **prevent passage** through by filling with something
例 an unobstructed view 无阻碍的视野
近 occlude 堵塞
反 clear, free, open up, unblock, unclog, unplug, unstop 清除(障碍)

obtuse [əbˈtuːs]

【考法】 *adj.* 愚钝的：not having or showing an ability to **absorb ideas readily**
例 Are you being deliberately obtuse? 你是故意装笨吗？
近 dumb, fatuous, mindless, oafish, opaque, senseless, unintelligent, vacuous
反 insightful, apt, brainy, bright, brilliant, clever, fast, intelligent, keen, nimble, quick, quick-witted, sharp, sharp-witted, smart 有洞察力的，智慧的

obviate [ˈɑːbvieɪt]

【考法】 *vt.* 排除，使不必要：to anticipate and prevent (as a situation) or make **unnecessary** (as an action)
例 The new treatment obviates the need for surgery. 新的疗法使手术不再是必须的。
近 avert, forestall, preclude, stave off, head off

occult [əˈkʌlt]

【考法 1】 *adj.* 难以理解的：**not easily apprehended** or understood: abstruse, **mysterious**
例 an occult reference in the text that has puzzled scholars 文章中一处晦涩的、难倒了学者们的引注
近 ambiguous, arcane, equivocal, inscrutable, opaque, impenetrable
反 bare, manifest, patent, readily fathomable 暴露的，可理解的

【考法 2】 *vt.* 使隐藏或神秘：to **keep secret** or shut off from view
例 occult their house from prying eyes by planting large trees around it 在住所周围种满大树防止别人偷窥 ‖ The actor's private life had long been occulted by a contrived public persona. 演员的私人生活一直以来被一个精心打造的公众形象所遮掩。
近 belie, blanket, cloak, conceal, cover, curtain, disguise, enshroud, mask, obscure, screen, shroud, suppress, veil, blot out, paper over
反 bare, disclose, display, divulge, expose, reveal, show, uncloak, uncover, unmask, unveil 暴露

odium [ˈoʊdiəm]

【考法】 *n.* 憎恶，讨厌：**strong dislike**, contempt, or aversion
例 Time did nothing to diminish the odium in which the traitor lived out his days. 时间也没有减少大家对这个叛徒的唾弃。
近 ignominy, infamy, obloquy, opprobrium
反 esteem, honor, respect, hankering, infatuation 尊敬，渴望，着迷

offbeat [ˌɔːfˈbiːt]

【考法】 *adj.* 不平常的：noticeably **different from** what is **generally found** or experienced
例 This writer has an enjoyably offbeat sense of humor. 这个作者有一种奇特而有趣的幽默感。
近 extraordinary, peculiar, queer, unaccustomed, uncommon, uncustomary, out-of-the-way
反 conventional, bathetic, hackneyed, common, ordinary, plain, usual 传统陈腐的，平常普通的

offhand [ˌɔːfˈhænd]

【考法】 *adj.* 即兴的，没有准备的：**without premeditation** or preparation
例 couldn't give the figures offhand 无法立即给出数字
近 ad-lib, extemporary, impromptu, improvised, unplanned, unpremeditated, unrehearsed
反 considered, planned, premeditated, prepared, rehearsed 事先谋划的

241

officious [əˈfɪʃəs]

【考法】 *adj.* 多管闲事的：**thrusting oneself** where one is not welcome or invited

例 an officious little man who was always telling everyone else how to do their jobs 一个多管闲事的人，总喜欢对他人的事情指手画脚

近 interfering, intruding, meddlesome, obtrusive, presuming, prying, snoopy

反 unobtrusive 不引人注目的

offish [ˈɔːfɪʃ]

【考法】 *adj.* 冷淡的：inclined to be distant and reserved; **aloof**

例 consistently surly and offish with the would-be suitors who came calling 对于追求者总是阴沉并且冷淡

近 aloof, detached, distant, remote, unbending, unsociable

反 sociable, cordial, friendly, social, warm 热情的

off-key [ˌɔːfˈkiː]

【考法】 *adj.* 不寻常的，不合适的：being **out of accord with** what is considered normal or appropriate

例 a high-flown, off-key speech by a newcomer 来自新手的颇有野心、不寻常的一次演讲

Unit 4

■ OMINOUS	■ OMNISCIENT	■ ONEROUS	■ OPAQUE	■ OPINE
■ OPPORTUNE	■ OPPROBRIOUS	■ ORATION	■ ORIENT	■ ORIGINAL

ominous [ˈɑːmɪnəs]

【考法】 *adj.* 凶兆的：of or being an **omen**, especially an **evil** one

例 an ominous threat of war 战争来临的凶兆

近 baleful, foreboding, inauspicious, portentous, sinister, threatening, minatory

反 auspicious, unthreatening 吉兆的，不具有威胁的

omniscient [ɑːmˈnɪsiənt]

【考法】 *adj.* 无所不知的：possessed of universal or **complete knowledge**

例 an omniscient deity 无所不知的神

反 vacuous 无知的

onerous [ˈɑːnərəs]

【考法】 *adj.* 费时间花心思的：**requiring much time, effort**, or careful attention

例 Building the scale model of the frigate was an onerous task. 建造军舰的小模型非常花时间。

近 arduous, burdensome, challenging, exacting, grueling, taxing, toilsome

反 requiring little effort, light, nondemanding, unchallenging, undemanding 轻松的，不费劲的

opaque [oʊˈpeɪk]

【考法 1】 *adj.* 不透光的：**impenetrable by light**; **neither transparent** nor **translucent**

近 blurry, dim, misty, murky, obscure, shadowy, unclear

反 diaphanous, transparent 精致透明的

【考法 2】 *adj.* 晦涩的：so **obscure** as to be unintelligible

例 opaque prose 晦涩的诗歌

近 ambiguous, arcane, enigmatic, equivocal, inscrutable, occult

反 clear, accessible, obvious, plain, unambiguous, unequivocal 清晰易懂的

opine [oʊˈpaɪn]

【考法】 *v.* 表达观点；想，认为：to **express opinions**; to sate as an opinion

例 You can opine about any subject you like. 你可以畅所欲言。

近 comment, editorialize, note, observe, reflect, weigh in

opportune [ˌɑːpərˈtuːn]

【考法】 *adj.* 合适的，适当的：suitable or **convenient** for a particular occurrence

例 an opportune moment 方便的时机

近 seasonable, well-timed

反 inconvenient, untimely, inappropriate, unseasonable 不合适的

opprobrious [əˈproʊbriəs]

【考法 1】 *adj.* 辱骂的：expressing contemptuous **reproach**; scornful or abusive

例 opprobrious language 脏话

近 scurrilous, vitriolic, vituperative, contumelious

【考法2】 *adj.* 臭名昭著的，令人鄙视的: bringing disgrace; shameful or **infamous**

例 opprobrious conduct 令人鄙视的行为

近 discreditable, disgraceful, dishonorable, ignominious, infamous, notorious, shameful, unrespectable

反 irreproachable, honorable, reputable, respectable 无可指责的，受人尊敬的

派 opprobrium *n.* 恶名

反 good repute 好名声

oration [ɔːˈreɪʃn]

【考法】 *n.* (颇有野心、自高自大的)演说: a speech delivered in a **high-flown or pompous manner**

近 address, declamation, harangue, peroration

orient [ˈɔːriənt]

【考法】 *vt.* 使确定方向，使熟悉或适应: to set or arrange in any **determinate position** especially in relation to the points of the compass; to **make familiar** with or adjusted to facts, principles, or a situation

例 orient students toward a career in medicine 指导学生从事医学的职业道路

近 accustom, familiarize, initiate, introduce, orientate

反 confuse 使迷惑

original [əˈrɪdʒənl]

【考法1】 *adj.* 创新的: independent and **creative** in thought or action: **inventive**

例 The car has a highly original design. 这车的设计很新颖。

近 ingenious, innovative, inventive

反 commonplace, banal, trite, familiar, hackneyed, time-honored, tired, warmed-over 陈腐的

【考法2】 *adj.* 最初的，最早的: coming **before** all others in time or order

例 The original plan had to be discarded when the situation changed drastically. 当环境发生剧烈变化时，最初的计划就该被放弃。

近 earliest, foremost, headmost, inaugural, initial, leadoff, maiden, pioneer, premier, virgin

反 final, last, latter, terminal, ultimate 最终的

Unit 5

■ ORTHODOX	■ OSCILLATE	■ OSSIFY	■ OSTENTATIOUS	■ OSTRACIZE
■ OUST	■ OUTGOING	■ OUTLANDISH	■ OUTMANEUVER	■ OUTSET

orthodox [ˈɔːrθədɑːks]

【考法】 *adj.* 传统的: following or agreeing with **established form**, **custom**, **or rules**

例 He believes in the benefits of both orthodox medicine and alternative medicine. 他既相信传统药物又相信替代药物的效用。

近 ceremonial, conventional, regular, routine

反 casual, freewheeling, informal, irregular, unceremonious, unconventional, unorthodox 不常见的

oscillate [ˈɑːsɪleɪt]

【考法1】 *vi.* 振动，摇晃: to **swing** backward and forward like a pendulum

反 remain static 静止

【考法2】 *vt.* 犹豫，变化: **vary** between opposing beliefs, feelings, or theories

ossify [ˈɑːsɪfaɪ]

【考法】 *v.* (使)硬化，(使)僵化: to (cause to) become **hardened** or **conventional** and **opposed to change**

例 a disease that ossifies the joints 一种会使关节僵化的疾病

反 make pliant, transcend conventions, amenable to change 使柔软，超越传统

ostentatious [ˌɑːstenˈteɪʃəs]

【考法】 *adj.* 炫耀卖弄的: marked by or fond of **conspicuous** or vainglorious and sometimes **pretentious** display

例 She wears an ostentatious diamond ring on her finger. 她手指上戴着一枚巨大的钻戒。

近 flamboyant, flaring, flashy, splashy

反 modest, artless, austere, unpretentious, conservative, quiet, understated, unflamboyant, unflashy 谦让的，朴素的，保守的

ostracize	[ˈɑːstrəsaɪz]
【考法】	*vt.* 驱逐：to **exclude** from a group
例	He was ostracized from the scientific community for many years because of his radical political beliefs. 他因激进的政治理想被驱逐出了科学界很多年。
近	banish, bounce, chase, dismiss, expel, extrude, oust, boot out, cast out, run off, drum out, kick out, throw out, turf out
反	take in, include, embrace, welcome 接纳

oust	[aʊst]
【考法 1】	*vt.* 免职：to **remove from** a position of prominence or power (as a throne)
例	be ousted from power 被赶下台
近	deprive, displace, uncrown, unthrone
反	instate, crown, enthrone, throne 任命
【考法 2】	*vt.* 驱逐：to **drive** or force **out**
例	She was ousted from her job after it was proven she'd been pilfering company supplies. 她贪污公司财物这事被证实后，她被驱逐了。
近	banish, boot out, cast out, chase, dismiss, drum out, expel, extrude, kick out, throw out, turf out, turn out

outgoing	[ˈaʊtɡoʊɪŋ]
【考法】	*adj.* 友好的，外向的：openly friendly and responsive: **extroverted**
例	a salesman whose aggressively outgoing personality could sometimes be overbearing 一个销售员如果过于热情会让人不能忍
近	companionable, extroverted, gregarious, sociable
反	antisocial, introverted, nongregarious, reclusive, unsociable, unsocial 不合群的，不善交际的

outlandish	[aʊtˈlændɪʃ]
【考法】	*adj.* 古怪的，奇异的：strikingly **out of the ordinary**; **bizarre**
例	an outlandish costume 奇装异服
近	bizarre, cranky, eccentric, erratic, offbeat, peculiar, remarkable
反	conventional, familiar, nonexotic, nonglamorous, plain-Jane, unglamorous, unromantic 常规的，平凡的

outmaneuver	[ˌaʊtməˈnuːvər]
【考法】	*vt.* 以策略取胜：to **overcome** (an opponent) by artful, clever maneuvering
例	He outmaneuvered his congressional opponent. 他以计谋战胜了国会的对手。
近	outfox, outslick, outsmart, outthink, outwit
反	yield 屈服

outset	[ˈaʊtset]
【考法】	*n.* 开端，开始：**beginning**, start
例	I wish you'd mentioned this problem at the outset. 我希望你开门见山地提这个问题。
近	alpha, commencement, genesis, inception, incipience, nascence
反	termination, close, conclusion, end, ending, omega 终止

Unit 6

■ OUTWIT	■ OVERBEARING	■ OVERLAP	■ OVERT	■ OVERTURE
■ OXYMORON	■ PACIFY	■ PADDING	■ PAEAN	■ PAINSTAKING

outwit	[ˌaʊtˈwɪt]
【考法】	*vt.* 瞒骗，以智取胜：to **surpass** in cleverness or **cunning**; outsmart
例	a plan to outwit their opponents at their own game 在擅长的领域智取对手的计划
近	outfox, outmaneuver, outslick, outsmart, outthink

overbearing	[ˌoʊvərˈberɪŋ]
【考法 1】	*adj.* 专横傲慢的：domineering in manner; **arrogant**
例	Her husband's overbearing manner made her miserable. 她的丈夫专横傲慢，让她痛不欲生。
近	authoritative, despotic, dictatorial, imperious, masterful, peremptory
反	meek, unassuming 谦逊的
【考法 2】	*adj.* 压倒一切的，(在力量或重要性上)势不可挡的；支配的，显著的：**overwhelming in power** or significance; **predominant**, coming before all others in importance
例	the overbearing problem in our nation's schools 我国中小学教育最突出的问题
近	capital, cardinal, central, chief, dominant, key, leading, master, number one, overmastering, overriding, paramount, predominant, preeminent, premier, primary, prior, sovereign, supreme

overlap [ˌouvərˈlæp]

【考法】 *v.* (与…)部分重叠：to occupy the **same area** in part

例 Baseball season overlaps football season in September. 棒球赛季和橄榄球赛季在九月有重合时间。

近 lap, overlay, overlie, overspread

overt [ouˈvɜːrt]

【考法】 *adj.* 明显的，公开的：**open** and observable; not hidden, concealed, or secret

例 overt hostility 公然的敌意

反 shadowy 模糊的

overture [ˈouvərtʃər]

【考法1】 *n.* 前言：an **introductory** section or part, as of a poem; a **prelude**

近 preamble, preliminary, prologue, warm-up, curtain-raiser

【考法2】 *n.* 序曲：an instrumental composition intended especially as an **introduction** to an extended work, such as an **opera** or oratorio

例 The parade down Main Street served as the overture for a weekend of fun and festivities. 主干道上的游行活动拉开了一周节日活动的序幕。

反 coda 结尾

oxymoron [ˌɑːksɪˈmɔːrɑːn]

【考法】 *n.* 矛盾修饰法：a **combination** of **contradictory** or incongruous words

例 The phrase "cruel kindness" is an oxymoron. "残酷的仁慈"就是矛盾修饰法的一个例子。‖ The phrase "Broadway rock musical" is an oxymoron. Broadway doesn't have the nerve to let the really hard stuff in the house. "百老汇的摇滚音乐剧"是个反讽。百老汇才不会允许吵吵闹闹的东西在里面演出。

pacify [ˈpæsɪfaɪ]

【考法】 *vt.* 使平静，安慰：to **ease the anger** or agitation of

例 pacify a crying child 安抚一个哭泣的孩子

近 appease, assuage, conciliate, mollify, placate, propitiate

反 incite, rankle, tantrum, vex, discompose, truculent 煽动，激起

padding [ˈpædɪŋ]

【考法】 *n.* 夸张，废话：the representation of something in terms that **go beyond the facts**

例 That feature writer is sometimes guilty of padding, but he keeps it from getting out of hand. 这位专栏作者有时候夸夸其谈，但是保持了适度。

近 caricature, coloring, elaboration, embellishment, embroidery, hyperbole, magnification, overstatement, stretching

反 meiosis, understatement 轻描淡写

paean [ˈpiːən]

【考法】 *n.* 欢乐颂：a **joyous song** or hymn of **praise**, tribute, thanksgiving, or triumph

例 Her retirement party featured many paeans for her long years of service to the company. 她的退休派对满是对她多年在公司辛勤工作的赞颂。

近 accolade, citation, dithyramb, eulogium, eulogy, hymn, panegyric, tribute

painstaking [ˈpeɪnzteɪkɪŋ]

【考法】 *adj.* 煞费苦心的：taking pains: expending, showing, or involving **diligent care** and effort

例 It took months of painstaking research to write the book. 这本书的写作耗费了几个月的苦心研究。

近 careful, conscientious, fussy, meticulous, scrupulous

反 slipshod, cursory, careless 漫不经心的，草率的

Unit 7

| ■ PALATABLE | ■ PALATIAL | ■ PALL | ■ PALLIATE | ■ PALLID |
| ■ PALMY | ■ PALPABLE | ■ PALTER | ■ PALTRY | ■ PAN |

palatable [ˈpælətəbl]

【考法】 *adj.* 感到愉悦满足的：giving **pleasure or contentment** to the mind or senses

例 I always associate the palatable aroma of roasting turkey with Thanksgiving. 我总是把香喷喷的烤火鸡的味道和感恩节联系起来。

近 agreeable, blessed, congenial, delectable, delightful, delightsome, dreamy, dulcet, enjoyable, felicitous, grateful, gratifying, heavenly, jolly, luscious, pleasurable, satisfying, savory

反 disagreeable, pleasureless, unpalatable, unpleasant, unwelcome 不愉悦的

	palatial	[pəˈleɪʃl]
	【考法】	*adj.* 宫殿般奢华的：of the nature of a palace, as in spaciousness or **ornateness**
	例	a palatial penthouse apartment 一套豪华的顶层公寓
	近	deluxe, lavish, luxuriant, opulent, sumptuous
	反	ascetic, austere, humble, no-frills, spartan 简朴的

	pall	[pɔːl]
	【考法】	*vi.* 失去兴趣：to lose in **interest** or **attraction**
	例	His humor began to pall on us. 他的幽默开始使我们生腻了。
	反	interest, intrigue 激发兴趣

	palliate	[ˈpælieɪt]
	【考法】	*vt.* 平息，减轻：to make **less severe** or **intense**; mitigate
	近	allay, alleviate, assuage, mitigate, mollify, relieve, soothe
	反	aggravate, exacerbate, worsen, increase intensity 加剧，恶化
	派	palliative *adj.* 缓和的，减轻的
	例	palliative drug 缓解剂

	pallid	[ˈpælɪd]
	【考法 1】	*adj.* 无生气的，缺乏活力的：**lacking** in **radiance** or **vitality**; dull
	例	The movie is a pallid version of the classic novel. 这部经典小说改编的电影很苍白无力。
	反	piquant 兴奋的
	【考法 2】	*adj.* 苍白无血色的：having an abnormally **pale** or wan complexion
	例	a pallid girl who looked as though she'd never seen the sun 一个面色苍白的姑娘，仿佛从来没有晒过太阳
	近	ashen, ashy, blanched, pasty, wan
	反	rubicund, blooming, florid, flush, full-blooded, glowing, ruddy, sanguine 红润的

	palmy	[ˈpɑːmi]
	【考法】	*adj.* 繁荣的：marked by **prosperity**
	例	the palmy days of the British drama 英国戏剧的繁荣时期
	近	flourishing, prosperous, thriving, booming, lush, roaring, halcyon
	反	failed, depressed, unprosperous, unsuccessful 不成功的，不繁荣的

	palpable	[ˈpælpəbl]
	【考法 1】	*adj.* 摸得到的：**capable** of being **touched** or felt
	例	a small but palpable lump in my neck 我脖子上有一块很小但是能摸得到的肿块
	近	touchable
	反	impalpable, intangible 无形的，触摸不到的
	【考法 2】	*adj.* 明显的，易觉察的：easily perceived; **obvious**
	例	a palpable difference 易觉察的差别
	近	apprehensible, detectable, discernible, distinguishable, sensible
	反	imperceptible, inappreciable, indistinguishable, insensible, undetectable 隐晦的，细微的

	palter	[ˈpɔːltər]
	【考法】	*vi.* 欺骗；讨价还价：to act **insincerely** or **deceitfully**; haggle, chaffer
	例	unwilling to palter over the price of the house 拒绝对房子讨价还价
	近	chaffer, deal, dicker, haggle, horse-trade, negotiate, equivocate
	反	candor 坦率

	paltry	[ˈpɔːltri]
	【考法 1】	*adj.* 无价值的；微不足道的：lacking in **importance** or worth
	例	Venture capitalists appear to be confused by such paltry amounts. 风险投资家对如此微不足道的数量感到疑惑。
	近	inconsequential, inconsiderable, insignificant, niggling, piddling, piffling, trivial
	反	significant, important, big, consequential, considerable, material 意义重大的
	【考法 2】	*adj.* 让人厌恶的，让人鄙视的：arousing or deserving of one's **loathing and disgust**
	例	a paltry, underhanded scheme to get someone fired 一个卑鄙的炒掉某人的计谋
	近	cheap, cruddy, deplorable, despicable, grubby, lame, lousy, mean, scummy, scurvy, sneaking, wretched
	反	admirable, commendable, creditable, laudable, meritorious, praiseworthy 令人尊敬的

	pan	[pæn]
	【考法】	*vt./n.* 严厉批评：a **harsh criticism**
	例	Almost all the movie critics have panned this latest sequel in a tired series. 几乎所有的影评家都批评这部最新续集，认为是狗尾续貂。
	近	blame, censure, condemn, denounce, dispraise, reprehend
	反	eulogize, extol, rave, laud, praise 称赞

Unit 8

panache [pə'næʃ]

【考法】 *n.* 炫耀: dash or **flamboyance** in style and action

例 Belanger dances with an undemonstrative panache that draws one's attention as if by seeking to deflect it; through finesse and understatement, he manages to seem at once intensely present and curiously detached. 贝朗格的舞蹈低调而华丽，似乎想通过使人走神而吸引观众的注意；他通过精湛的技艺和压抑的演绎，使他的表演让人感到忽远忽近。

反 humility, unremarkable behavior, dullness 谦逊，寻常举止，平庸乏味

pandemic [pæn'demɪk]

【考法】 *adj.* 大范围流行的: **widespread**; general

例 pandemic malaria 大规模的疟疾

反 limited 有限的

pandemonium [ˌpændə'moʊniəm]

【考法】 *n.* 喧嚣，骚动: wild uproar or **noise**

例 Christmas morning at our house is always marked by pandemonium. 我们家圣诞节的早上总是免不了一番吵吵闹闹。

近 bluster, bustle, disturbance, furor, fuss, hubbub, moil, pother, ruckus, ruction, tumult, turmoil, uproar

反 serene 安静

panegyric [ˌpænə'dʒɪrɪk]

【考法】 *n.* 赞颂之词，颂文: an **eulogistic** oration or writing

例 write a panegyric on the centennial of the Nobel laureate's birth 为诺贝尔获得者百年诞辰纪念日写一篇颂文

近 accolade, citation, commendation, dithyramb, eulogium, eulogy, hymn, paean

反 anathema, denunciation, condemnation 诅咒，谴责

panoramic [ˌpænə'ræmɪk]

【考法】 *adj.* 全景的: of an unobstructed or **complete view** of an area in every direction

近 compendious, complete, comprehensive, cyclopedic, embracive, exhaustive, thorough, in-depth

反 narrow 狭窄的

派 panorama *n.* 全景；全貌，概述

例 a panorama of American history 美国历史总览

parable ['pærəbl]

【考法】 *n.* 寓言: a story intended to **teach a basic truth** or moral about life

例 the parable in which the repentant sinner is compared to the returning prodigal son 这个寓言故事将不愿悔过的罪人和回头的浪子进行了比较

近 apologue, fable

paradigm ['pærədaɪm]

【考法】 *n.* 典范，模范: one that serves as a **pattern** or model

例 He was the paradigm of the successful man. 他是成功人士的典范。

近 archetype, example, exemplar, ideal, model, pattern, paragon

paradise ['pærədaɪs]

【考法 1】 *n.* 天堂，极乐世界: an often imaginary place or state of utter **perfection and happiness**

例 an idealist who trotted the globe looking for paradise 一个奔波于全世界以寻找一片乐土的理想主义者

近 bliss, empyrean, heaven, nirvana, utopia

反 hell, inferno 地狱

【考法 2】 *n.* 快乐，狂喜: a state of overwhelming usually **pleasurable emotion**

例 that early stage of a romance when lovers are in paradise 恋爱初期，恋人们都处于快乐兴奋的状态

近 elation, euphoria, exhilaration, intoxication, rapture, rhapsody, transport

反 dejection, depression, gloominess, melancholy 沮丧，哀伤

paradox ['pærədɑːks]

【考法】 *n.* 表面矛盾实际可能正确的话，悖论: a statement that is seemingly contradictory or **opposed to common sense** and yet is perhaps true

例 The paradox is that fishermen would catch more fish if they fished less. 有一个悖论：如果渔民减少捕鱼量的话，他们将会捕到更多的鱼。

近 dichotomy, incongruity

paragon ['pærəgɑːn]

【考法 1】 *n.* 优秀模范：a model of excellence or perfection of a kind; a peerless **example**

例 a paragon of good husband 模范好丈夫

近 archetype, example, exemplar, ideal, model, pattern, paradigm

【考法 2】 *vt.* 把…比作；显示相似：to **compare** with; parallel

例 paragon retreat with treachery 把撤退比作是背叛

近 assimilate, compare, equate, liken, match, parallel

反 contrast 对比，对照以产生反差

Unit 9

| ■ PARAMOUNT | ■ PARANOID | ■ PARAPHRASE | ■ PARCH | ■ PARENTHESIS |
| ■ PARIAH | ■ PARITY | ■ PARODY | ■ PAROXYSM | ■ PARROT |

paramount ['pærəmaʊnt]

【考法】 *adj.* 最重要的：of **chief** concern or **importance**

例 The paramount goal is to restore the colonial-era house with complete historical accuracy. 最重要的任务就是十分精确地依照历史重建殖民时期的建筑。

近 cardinal, chief, key, leading, main, predominant, preeminent, primary, principal, supreme

反 ancillary, secondary 次要的；paltry, petty, trifling, trivial 不重要的

paranoid ['pærənɔɪd]

【考法】 *adj.* 多疑的，对他人极端恐惧和怀疑：exhibiting or characterized by **extreme** and irrational **fear or distrust** of others

例 a paranoid suspicion that the phone might be bugged 疑神疑鬼地担心电话被窃听了

近 distrustful, nervous, suspicious, unbelieving, worried

反 credulous 轻信的

派 paranoia *n.* 偏执狂

paraphrase ['pærəfreɪz]

【考法】 *v.* 转述，意译，改写：to express something (as a text or statement) **in different words**

例 Could you please paraphrase your diagnosis of my health condition, using simpler language? 您能否用更通俗的话语转述一下您对我健康状况的诊断呢？

近 rephrase, restate, reword, translate

反 quote (不加以修改地)引用

parch [pɑːrtʃ]

【考法】 *v.* 炽，烤；烤干：to make extremely **dry**, especially by exposure to heat

例 parch a surface from exposure to sun 通过太阳照射烤干一个面

近 dehydrate, desiccate, dry, scorch, sear

反 douse, drench, hydrate, steep, wash, water, wet 弄湿

parenthesis [pə'renθəsɪs]

【考法】 *n.* 间断：an **interruption** of continuity; an interval

例 a parenthesis in an otherwise solid marriage 在本该是完满婚姻中的一个插曲

近 discontinuity, interim, interlude, intermission, interregnum, interruption, interstice, interval

反 continuation, continuity 持续不断；resumption 继续

pariah [pə'raɪə]

【考法】 *n.* 被排斥或鄙视的人：one that is **despised or rejected**, outcast

例 I felt like a pariah when I wore the wrong outfit to the dinner party. 当我穿着不恰当的礼服赴宴时，我感觉自己被别人狠狠地鄙视了。

近 castaway, castoff, leper, reject

反 respectable person 值得尊敬的人

parity ['pærəti]

【考法】 *n.* 相称，同等，平等：the quality or state of **being equal** or equivalent

例 achieve parity with our commercial competitors 取得与我们的商业竞争对手同等的地位

近 coequality, coordinateness, equality, equivalency, par, sameness

反 disparity, imparity, inequality 不公平；incommensurateness 不相称

parody ['pærədi]

【考法 1】 *n.* (以嘲笑原作作者的)模仿作品：a literary or musical work in which the style of an author or work is closely **imitated for** comic effect or in **ridicule**

例 The Back Dormitory Boys specialize in parody of Backstreet Boys. 后舍男生擅长恶搞后街男孩。

近 burlesque, caricature, spoof, travesty

【考法 2】 *v.* 模仿(以嘲弄)：to **copy** or exaggerate (someone or something) in order **to make fun** of
例　parody a public figure's mannerisms 模仿嘲弄一个公共人物的举止
近　imitate, mock, mimic

paroxysm [ˈpærəksɪzəm]
【考法 1】 *n.* (感情、动作的)突发：a sudden **outburst** of emotion or action
例　a paroxysm of coughing 突然一阵咳嗽
近　burst, ebullition, eruption, explosion, flare, flash, flush, gush, outburst, storm
【考法 2】 *n.* (政治、社会领域的)大动荡：a violent **disturbance** (as of the political or social order)
例　Darwin's introduction of the theory of evolution created paroxysms in both religion and science that are still being felt today. 达尔文提出的进化论给宗教界和科学界都带来了巨大的冲击，时至今日我们仍然能感觉到。
近　bouleversement, cataclysm, earthquake, hurricane, storm, tempest, tumult, upheaval, uproar

parrot [ˈpærət]
【考法】 *vt.* (机械地)模仿，复制：to repeat or **imitate**, especially **without understanding**
例　parrot others blindly 盲目地人云亦云
近　copy, ditto, duplicate, echo, quote
反　coin, create, devise, invent 创造

Unit 10

■ PARRY	■ PARSIMONIOUS	■ PARTIAL	■ PARTICULARIZE	■ PARTISAN
■ PASTICHE	■ PARTITION	■ PATENT	■ PATHOLOGICAL	■ PATINA

parry [ˈpæri]
【考法】 *vt.* 躲避(问题)：to **evade** especially by an adroit answer
例　He parried the embarrassing question with a clever reply. 他以巧妙的回答躲避了这个令人尴尬的问题。
近　avoid, dodge, elude, eschew, evade, finesse, scape, shirk, shun
反　confront, face, meet 面对；embrace 欣然接受

parsimonious [ˌpɑːrsəˈmoʊniəs]
【考法】 *n.* 过度节俭的，吝啬的：frugal to the point of **stinginess**
例　the stereotype of the dour and parsimonious Scotsman 严肃而吝啬的苏格兰人的典型代表
近　closefisted, mean, mingy, miserly, niggardly, penurious, stinting, tight, tightfisted, uncharitable, ungenerous
反　generous, liberal, munificent 慷慨的；dissolute, extravagant, prodigal, wasteful 浪费的，挥霍的

partial [ˈpɑːrʃl]
【考法 1】 *adj.* 偏袒的，偏爱的：inclined to favor one party more than the other: **biased**
例　He is partial to Maverick. 他偏爱小牛队。
近　biased, one-sided, partisan, prejudiced
反　disinterested, equitable, evenhanded, fair, impartial, neutral, objective, unbiased, unprejudiced 公平的
【考法 2】 *adj.* 部分的，不完整的：**lacking** some necessary part
例　a partial answer to the problem 一部分的解答
近　deficient, fragmental, fragmentary, half, halfway
反　complete, entire, full, intact, integral, perfect, whole 完整的
派　partially *adv.* 部分地；partiality *n.* 偏袒，偏爱

particularize [pərˈtɪkjələraɪz]
【考法】 *vt.* 详述：to go into or **give details** or particulars
例　particularize the rules you must observe 详述你需要遵守的规定
近　detail, specificate, specify
反　abbreviate, abridge, condense, shorten 删减(内容等)

partisan [ˈpɑːrtəzn]
【考法 1】 *n.* 跟随者，信徒：one who **follows** the opinions or teachings of another
例　Partisans of the charismatic leader refuse to tolerate any criticism of him at all. 跟随者们不允许任何有关于他们富有魅力的领导的负面言论。
近　acolyte, adherent, disciple, pupil, votary
反　bellwether, leader 领导者
【考法 2】 *n.* (狂热、坚定的)拥护者，支持者：one who is intensely or **excessively devoted** to a cause
例　a partisan of the revolution who was even willing to give her life for it 一个愿意为了革命献出自己生命的坚定拥护者
近　crusader, fanatic, ideologue, zealot, true believer
反　adversary, antagonist, opponent 反对者

【考法3】 *adj.* 偏袒的：inclined to favor **one side** over another

例 a shamelessly partisan news report 一篇无耻的、有倾向性的新闻报道

近 biased, one-sided, partial, prejudiced

反 disinterested, equitable, evenhanded, fair, impartial, neutral, objective, unbiased, unprejudiced 公平的

pastiche [pæˈstiːʃ]

【考法1】 *n.* (带嘲讽的)模仿：a literary, artistic, musical, or architectural work that **imitates** the style of previous work, often **with satirical intent**

例 a pastiche of Botticelli's *Birth of Venus* 波提且利画作《维纳斯的诞生》的仿品

近 burlesque, caricature, imitation, parody, spoof, travesty

反 original work 原作

【考法2】 *n.* 大杂烩：a pasticcio of incongruous parts; a **hodgepodge**

例 a pastiche of dishes from many countries 来自众多国家的饮食杂烩

近 agglomerate, collage, hodgepodge, jumble, jungle, medley, montage, motley, salad, variety, welter

partition [pɑːrˈtɪʃn]

【考法】 *n.* 分割，划分：the act or process of **dividing** something into parts

例 the partition of Czechoslovakia into the Czech Republic and Slovakia 捷克斯洛伐克被分裂成捷克共和国和斯洛伐克

近 bifurcation, breakup, cleavage, disunion, division, fractionalization, schism, scission, split, sundering

反 unification, union 联合

patent [ˈpeɪtnt]

【考法】 *adj.* 显而易见的，明显的：**readily visible** or intelligible: obvious

例 Unfortunately, the patent flaw of the proposal did not deter the city council from putting it up for a vote. 不幸的是，尽管提案中有着显而易见的缺陷，市议会依然将它拿出来进行投票。

近 apparent, blatant, conspicuous, evident, flagrant, manifest, obvious, plain

反 concealed, hidden, invisible 隐藏的，不可见的

pathological [ˌpæθəˈlɑːdʒɪkl]

【考法】 *adj.* 不正常的，病态的：being such to a degree that is extreme, excessive, or **markedly abnormal**

例 She has a pathological fear of snakes. 她对蛇有一种病态的恐惧。

近 abnormal, aberrant, anomalous, morbid

反 normal 正常的；natural 自然的

patina [pəˈtiːnə]

【考法1】 *n.* 外表：a **superficial** covering or exterior

例 a superficial patina of knowledge 表面肤浅的知识

近 façade, hull, skin, veneer

反 essential quality 本质；core, kernel 核心

【考法2】 *n.* (由内而外散发的)氛围，气场：an **appearance or aura** that is derived from association, habit, or established character

例 Although the winery is brand-new, it has been constructed and decorated to give it a patina of old-world quaintness. 尽管酿酒厂是全新建造的，但它的构造和装饰都刻意营造出一种古色古香的奇异氛围。

近 air, ambience, aroma, atmosphere, climate, flavor, halo, odor, smell, temper, vibration

List 18

"不要把背 GRE 单词当成一种负担，要把它当成记忆的游戏、扩展视角的平台。"
（宋歆怡，2008 年 10 月，Verbal 700，录取院校：Newcastle University 口译系）

Unit 1

■ PATRICIAN	■ PATRIOT	■ PATRONIZE	■ PAUCITY	■ PAUNCHY
■ PECK	■ PEDAGOGUE	■ PEDANT	■ PREDESTINE	■ PEDESTRIAN

patrician [pəˈtrɪʃn]
【考法 1】 *n.* 贵族，名门望族：a man or woman of **high birth** or social position
例 the rank of a patrician 贵族等级
近 aristocrat, noble, blue blood
反 plebeian 平民，庶民
【考法 2】 *adj.* 贵族的，地位高的：of **high birth**, rank, or station
例 come from a patrician family 出身贵族世家
近 aristocratic, genteel, gentle, grand, great, highborn, highbred, upper-class, wellborn
反 baseborn, common, humble, ignoble, low, lower-class, mean 地位低下的

patriot [ˈpeɪtriət]
【考法】 *n.* 爱国者：one who **loves** his or her **country** and supports its authority and interests
例 *The USA Patriot Act* has generated a great deal of controversy since its enactment. 自实施之日起，美国的《爱国者法案》就产生了大量的争议。‖ a fanatical patriot 狂热的爱国者
近 loyalist, nationalist, partisan
反 apostate, recreant, renegade, traitor, turncoat 叛徒；insurgent, mutineer, rebel 叛乱者
派 patriotism *n.* 爱国主义

patronize [ˈpeɪtrənaɪz]
【考法 1】 *vt.* 赞助：to **provide aid** or support for
例 a company that loyally patronizes the arts 一个一直以来坚持赞助艺术界的公司
近 advocate, back, champion, endorse, support, uphold
反 baffle, foil, frustrate, sabotage 阻挠，从中破坏
【考法 2】 *vt.* 以高人一等的态度对待：to adopt an air of condescension toward: **treat haughtily** or coolly
例 a director with an unpleasant habit of patronizing even his most gifted actors 一个有着令人讨厌的习惯的导演，他即便是对手下最有才华的演员也总是摆出傲慢的姿态
近 condescend
派 patron *n.* 赞助人

paucity [ˈpɔːsəti]
【考法】 *n.* 少量，缺乏：smallness of number; **dearth**
例 an extreme paucity of natural resources 极度缺乏自然资源
近 dearth, deficit, drought, inadequacy, insufficiency, lack, scantiness, scarcity, shortage, undersupply, want
反 abundance, adequacy, amplitude, opulence, plenitude, sufficiency, wealth 大量，丰富

paunchy [ˈpɔːntʃɪ]
【考法】 *adj.* 大腹便便的，大肚子的：having a **potbelly**
例 a paunchy middle-aged man 一个大腹便便的中年男子
近 corpulent, fat, potbellied
反 slender, slim, svelte, thin 瘦的，苗条的

peck [pek]
【考法 1】 *n.* 大量：a **considerable amount**
例 Now you're in a peck of trouble. 现在你有一堆麻烦了。
近 abundance, bunch, bundle, dozen, mass, mountain, much, multiplicity, myriad, pile, plenitude, profusion, ton, volume, wealth
反 bit, glimmer, handful, hint, little, mite, nip, ounce, peanuts, pittance, spot, sprinkle, trace 少量

【考法 2】 *v.* (不情愿地) 小口咬：to **eat** reluctantly and **in small bites**

例　Fashion models never really eat: they just peck at small meals in expensive restaurants. 时装模特们几乎不吃东西——他们只是随便咬一口昂贵餐厅里的食物。

近　bite, nibble, sip, tipple

反　devour, gobble, gorge, guzzle, quaff, swill 贪婪地吃喝，大口吃喝

pedagogue [ˈpedəgɑːg]

【考法】 *n.* 教育者，老师：a person whose occupation is to **give formal instruction** in a school

例　a boring pedagogue who is called "PPT reader" 一个被戏称为"幻灯片朗读机"的无聊老师

近　educator, instructor, preceptor, teacher

反　disciple, pupil, student 弟子，学生

pedant [ˈpednt]

【考法】 *n.* 书呆子，墨守成规之人：one who pays undue attention to book learning and **formal rules**

例　He is a perfect type of pedant. 他是个十足的书呆子。

近　doctrinaire, dogmatist

predestine [ˌpriːˈdestɪn]

【考法】 *vt.* 预先注定：to determine the fate of **in advance**

例　Our victory in the tournament was seemingly predestined. 我们在锦标赛中的胜利似乎是注定了的。

近　doom, fate, foredoom, foreordain, ordain, predestine, predetermine, preordain

派　predestination *n.* 命中注定

pedestrian [pəˈdestriən]

【考法 1】 *n.* 行人：a person **traveling on foot**

例　a lane reserved for pedestrians 行人专用道

近　footer, walker

反　rider 骑手

【考法 2】 *adj.* 平庸无奇的，令人厌倦的：**causing weariness**, restlessness, or lack of interest

例　His style is so pedestrian that the book becomes a real bore. 他的风格是如此平庸，整本书显得非常无聊。

近　arid, dreary, dull, flat, jading, jejune, monochromatic, monotonous, stale, stodgy, tedious, wearisome

反　absorbing, engaging, engrossing, gripping, interesting, intriguing, involving, riveting 吸引人的

Unit 2

■ PEEP	■ PEER	■ PEEVE	■ PEJORATIVE	■ PELLUCID
■ PEN	■ PENALTY	■ PENCHANT	■ PENITENT	■ PENSIVE

peep [piːp]

【考法 1】 *n.* 一瞥：a **brief** and sometimes furtive **look**

例　take a peep at the new neighbors 偷偷瞄了新邻居一眼

近　gander, glance, glimpse, peek

【考法 2】 *n.* 轻声：a **slight sound** or utterance

例　I haven't heard a peep out of the children for an hour. 我已经一个小时没听到孩子们的声音了。

近　mumble, murmur, mutter, twitter, whisper

反　clamor, noise, outcry, roar 喧哗，吵闹

peer [pɪr]

【考法 1】 *n.* 同等地位的人，同辈：a person who has **equal** standing with others

例　stand out among peers 在同辈当中很出众

近　coequal, compeer, coordinate, counterpart, equivalent, fellow, match, parallel

反　inferior 地位更低的人；superior 地位更高的人

派　peerless *adj.* 无与伦比的，不可比拟的

【考法 2】 *vi.* 好奇地凝视：to **look** narrowly or curiously

例　peer at the variety of marine life in the aquarium's huge tank 好奇地注视着巨大水族箱中丰富多样的海洋生物

近　blink, gape, gawk, gaze, goggle, rubberneck, stare

反　glance, glimpse 投去一瞥

peeve [piːv]
【考法】 *vt.* 打扰，惹恼：to **disturb** the peace of mind of (someone) especially by repeated disagreeable acts
例 be constantly peeved by his affected flattery 总是被他做作的谄媚所惹恼
近 aggravate, annoy, bother, exasperate, frost, gall, irk, nettle, pique, rile, ruffle, vex
反 becalm, compose, lull, lullaby, quiet, salve, settle, soothe, still, tranquilize 使镇定
派 peevish *adj.* 易怒的，脾气不好的

pejorative [pɪˈdʒɔːrətɪv]
【考法】 *adj.* 轻蔑的，贬低的：**disparaging**; belittling
例 I agree that I am ambitious, and I don't see it as a pejorative term. 我承认我"雄心勃勃"，但我并不认为这是一个贬义词。
近 belittling, contemptuous, degrading, deprecatory, depreciative, derogative, disdainful, disparaging, scornful
反 commendatory, complimentary, laudatory 赞美的

pellucid [pəˈluːsɪd]
【考法 1】 *adj.* 透明的：**admitting** the passage of **light**
例 pellucid spring water 清澈透明的泉水
近 crystal, crystalline, limpid, liquid, lucent, transparent
反 opaque 不透明的
【考法 2】 *adj.* 清晰明确的，易懂的：transparently **clear** in style or meaning
例 Her poetry has a pellucid simplicity that betrays none of the sweat that went into writing it. 她的诗歌风格十分清新简约，丝毫没有体现出她为此付出的汗水。
近 apparent, distinct, evident, lucid, manifest, obvious, palpable, patent, perspicuous, plain, straightforward
反 clouded, cryptic, enigmatic, indistinct, mysterious, obfuscated, obscure 模糊难懂的

pen [pen]
【考法 1】 *n.* 监狱：a place of **confinement** for persons held in lawful custody
例 He spent six years in a federal pen. 他在联邦监狱中度过了六年。
近 bastille, coop, jail, prison, stockade
【考法 2】 *vt.* 关押，监禁：to **close** or shut in by or as if by barriers
例 Remember to pen up the dogs when visitors come over. 客人来的时候别忘了把狗给关起来。
近 box, encage, encase, envelop, fence, hedge, immure, include, wall
反 release 释放；enfranchise, free, liberate, set free 使自由

penalty [ˈpenəlti]
【考法】 *n.* (对罪行的)处罚：a **punishment** established by law or authority for a crime or offense
例 The maximum penalty is 7 years' imprisonment. 最为严厉的惩罚是七年的有期徒刑。
近 fine, forfeit, punishment, retribution
反 honor, reward 奖励
派 penalize *vt.* 对…惩罚

penchant [ˈpentʃənt]
【考法】 *n.* 嗜好，迷恋：a **strong** and continued **inclination**
例 a penchant for Champaign 非常喜爱香槟
近 affection, bias, disposition, leaning, partiality, predilection, predisposition, proclivity, propensity, tendency
反 aversion, disfavor, disinclination, dislike, distaste, loathing, repugnance, repulsion 反感

penitent [ˈpenɪtənt]
【考法】 *adj.* 悔过的：feeling or expressing humble or **regretful** pain or sorrow for sins or offenses
例 a penitent businessman who had come to ask for forgiveness 一个来寻求宽恕的决定悔过自新的商人
近 apologetic, compunctious, regretful, remorseful, repentant, rueful, sorry
反 impenitent, remorseless, unapologetic, unrepentant 不知悔改的

pensive [ˈpensɪv]
【考法】 *adj.* 沉思的，(尤指)哀思的：given to or marked by long, quiet and often musingly sad **thinking**
例 Rainy days often put her in a pensive mood. 雨天总是让她陷入深深的思考之中。
近 broody, cogitative, meditative, melancholy, musing, reflective, ruminant, ruminative, thoughtful
反 mindless, thoughtless, unreflective 不加思考的

Unit 3

penury [ˈpenjəri]

【考法 1】 *n.* 贫穷：extreme **dearth**; barrenness or insufficiency

例 Some have pessimistically regarded the higher education in China as an invisible and irresistible path to penury. 有人悲观地把中国的高等教育看作一条通往贫穷的通道——无形但不可抗拒。

近 destitution, impecuniosity, impoverishment, indigence, neediness, poorness, poverty, want

反 affluence, opulence, richness, wealth 富裕

【考法 2】 *n.* 吝啬，节俭：extreme and often niggardly **frugality**

例 They bitterly complained about their father's penury. 他们哀怨地抱怨父亲的节俭。

近 closeness, miserliness, niggardliness, parsimony, penuriousness, stinginess, tightfistedness, tightness

反 generosity, largesse, munificence, openhandedness, philanthropy 慷慨的

派 penurious *adj.* 贫穷的；吝啬的

perambulate [pəˈræmbjuleɪt]

【考法】 *v.* 徒步穿越，走过：to **travel over** or through especially on foot for exercise or pleasure

例 We decided to lazily perambulate the entire length of the esplanade and enjoy the fresh air. 我们决定悠哉地徒步走过滨海大道，享受清新的空气。

近 amble, cross, go, navigate, pass, peregrinate, proceed, ramble, transit, travel, traverse

perceptible [pərˈseptəbl]

【考法】 *adj.* 可察觉的：capable of **being perceived** especially by the senses

例 You should be able to note a perceptible temperature change when you add the second reagents. 当你加入第二种试剂的时候，你应该能够察觉到明显的温度变化。

近 appreciable, apprehensible, detectable, discernible, distinguishable, palpable, sensible

反 impalpable, imperceptible, inappreciable, indistinguishable, insensible, undetectable 不能感知的

peremptory [pəˈremptəri]

【考法 1】 *adj.* 不容反抗的：**not allowing contradiction** or refusal; imperative

例 a peremptory order from the general 将军下达的不容反抗的命令

近 compulsory, forced, imperative, incumbent, involuntary, obligatory, required

反 elective, optional, voluntary 可选择的

【考法 2】 *adj.* 爱发号施令的：fond of **ordering people** around

例 The peremptory secretary began telling the crowd of reporters and photographers exactly where they had to stand. 爱发号施令的秘书开始部署记者和摄影师们应该站在哪里了。

近 authoritarian, despotic, dictatorial, domineering, imperious, masterful, overbearing, tyrannical, tyrannous

【考法 3】 *adj.* 傲慢的：having a **feeling of superiority** that shows itself in an overbearing attitude

例 She had such a peremptory approach to running the club that people started to avoid her. 她用一种如此傲慢自大的方式来管理俱乐部，令大家纷纷开始躲避她。

近 assumptive, bumptious, haughty, imperious, lofty, pompous, presumptuous, pretentious, supercilious

反 humble, lowly, modest 谦逊的

perfervid [pərˈfɜːrvɪd]

【考法】 *adj.* 非常热情的：marked by overwrought or **exaggerated emotion**: excessively fervent

例 perfervid love letter 热情洋溢的情书

近 ardent, demonstrative, emotional, fervid, feverish, impassioned, passionate, torrid, vehement, warm

反 cold, cool, detached, dispassionate, emotionless, impassive, unemotional 冷漠的

perfidy [ˈpɜːrfədi]

【考法】 *n.* 不忠，背信弃义：an act or an instance of **disloyalty**

例 As loyalty unites lovers, so perfidy estranges friends. 忠诚是爱情的纽带，欺诈是友谊的敌人。

近 backstabbing, disloyalty, infidelity, sellout, treachery, unfaithfulness, double cross

反 allegiance, devotion, faithfulness, fidelity, loyalty, staunchness, steadfastness 忠诚

派 perfidious *adj.* 不忠诚的

perforate [ˈpɜːrfəreɪt]

【考法】 *v.* 打孔，穿透：to **make a hole** through

例 perforate with a pin 用针穿孔

近 bore, drill, hole, pierce, punch, puncture, riddle

perfunctory [pərˈfʌŋktəri]

【考法 1】 *adj.* 例行公事的，敷衍的：characterized by routine or **superficiality** and often done merely as a duty

例 His colleague gave his usual perfunctory nod. 他的同事例行公事地向他随便点了个头。

近 automatic, cursory, mechanical, superficial

【考法 2】 *adj.* 不感兴趣的：**lacking in interest** or enthusiasm

例 She gave the list only a perfunctory glance. 她无所谓地随便瞅了名单一眼。

近 apathetic, casual, disinterested, incurious, indifferent, insouciant, nonchalant, pococurante, unconcerned

反 concerned, interested 感兴趣的

perimeter [pəˈrɪmɪtər]

【考法】 *n.* 边界，界限：the line or relatively narrow space that marks the **outer limit** of something

例 soldiers guarding the perimeter of the camp 守卫着营地边界的士兵

近 borderline, bound, boundary, circumference, confines, edge, frame, fringe, margin, periphery, skirt, verge

反 center, core, heart, kernel 核心

periodical [ˌpɪriˈɑːdɪkl]

【考法 1】 *n.* 期刊：a **publication** that appears at regular intervals

例 subscribe to three new periodicals 订阅三份新的期刊

近 book, magazine, newspaper, paper, review, serial

【考法 2】 *adj.* 周期性的，有固定间隔的：occurring or recurring at **regular intervals**

例 periodical announcements from airline personnel concerning the delay 航空公司工作人员关于延误所进行的一遍又一遍的广播

近 continual, periodic, recurrent, recurring

反 constant, continuous, incessant, unceasing 持续不断的

Unit 4

■ PERIPATETIC	■ PERIPHERAL	■ PERISH	■ PERMANENT	■ PERMEABLE
■ PERNICIOUS	■ PERORATION	■ PERPETUAL	■ PERSECUTE	■ PERSEVERE

peripatetic [ˌperipəˈtetɪk]

【考法】 *adj.* 巡游的，四处游历的：walking about or from **place to place**

例 peripatetic preachers 四处游历的传教士

近 ambulant, errant, nomadic, perambulatory, peregrine, vagabond, wandering

反 sedentary, settled 定居的

peripheral [pəˈrɪfərəl]

【考法 1】 *adj.* 外围的：related to, located in, or constituting an outer **boundary or periphery**

例 development in the peripheral areas of megacities 大城市边缘地区的发展

近 circumferential, marginal

反 central 中心的；interior 内部的

【考法 2】 *adj.* 辅助性的：available to **supply** something extra when needed

例 The IT consultant suggested that we update the drivers for all of the computer's peripheral devices. IT 咨询师建议我们更新电脑所有外围辅助设备的驱动程序。

近 accessorial, accessory, appurtenant, supplemental, supplementary

反 chief, main, principal 主要的

perish [ˈperɪʃ]

【考法】 *vi.* 死亡，消亡：to become destroyed or ruined: **cease to exist**

例 Thrive in calamity and perish in soft living. 生于忧患，死于安乐。‖ adapt or perish 适应或是消亡

近 decease, demise, die, end, expire, succumb, pass away

反 breathe, live, survive 活着，存活

permanent [ˈpɜːrmənənt]

【考法】 *adj.* 永恒的：**continuing or enduring** without fundamental or marked change; lasting **forever**

例 A temporary compromise has been accepted until a more permanent solution can be agreed upon. 在更为持久的决案被通过之前，一个暂时性的妥协方案被接受了。

近 ceaseless, dateless, deathless, endless, eternal, immortal, perpetual, undying, unending

反 ephemeral, evanescent, transient, transitory 稍瞬即逝的；provisional, temporary 暂时性的

派 permanence *n.* 永恒

permeable [ˈpɜːrmɪəbl]

【考法】 *adj.* 可渗透的：capable of being permeated or **penetrated**, especially by liquids or gases

例 a permeable fabric that allows your body heat to escape 一种能使身体热量耗散的透气纤维

近 passable, penetrable, pervious, porous

反 waterproof 防水的；impassable, impenetrable, impervious, impermeable 不能渗透的

pernicious [pərˈnɪʃəs]

【考法】 *adj.* 有害的：highly **injurious** or destructive

例 Business may be troublesome but idleness is pernicious. 工作烦人，懒散害人。

近 adverse, baleful, damaging, deleterious, detrimental, hurtful, injurious, mischievous, nocuous, noxious

反 anodyne, benign, harmless, innocent, innocuous, inoffensive, safe 温和的，无害的

peroration [ˌperəˈreɪʃn]

【考法 1】 *n.* (演讲的)结束语：the **concluding part** of a discourse and especially an oration

例 He summarized his main points in his peroration. 他在结束语中总结了自己的主要观点。

近 coda, conclusion, denouement, epilogue, finale

反 foreword, prelude, preface, prologue, overture 前言，序曲

【考法 2】 *n.* (正式的)演讲，致辞：a usually **formal discourse** delivered to an audience

例 a peroration celebrating the nation's long tradition of religious tolerance and pluralism 为庆祝该国长期以来的宗教包容力和宗教多元化所做的一个演讲

近 address, declamation, harangue, oration, speech, talk

perpetual [pərˈpetʃuəl]

【考法】 *adj.* 永恒的，不断的：**continuing forever**: everlasting

例 perpetual motion machine 永动机

近 ceaseless, dateless, deathless, endless, eternal, immortal, undying, unending

反 ephemeral, evanescent, transient, transitory 稍纵即逝的；provisional, temporary 暂时性的

派 perpetuate *vt.* 使永恒

persecute [ˈpɜːrsɪkjuːt]

【考法】 *vt.* 迫害，折磨：to **cause** persistent **suffering** to

例 people who were persecuted simply for practicing their religious faith 因为实践宗教信仰而惨遭迫害的人

近 agonize, anguish, curse, excruciate, harrow, plague, rack, torment, torture

派 persecution *n.* 迫害

persevere [ˌpɜːrsəˈvɪr]

【考法】 *vi.* 坚持不懈，不屈不挠：to **persist** in or remain constant to a purpose, idea, or task in the face of obstacles or discouragement

例 Although he was frustrated by the lack of financial resources and support, he persevered in his scientific research. 尽管因为资金不足而受阻，但他仍坚持进行科学研究。

近 carry on, endure, persist

反 renounce, succumb, surrender, yield 放弃，屈服

派 perseverance *n.* 坚持不懈

Unit 5

■ PERSIFLAGE   ■ PERSISTENCE   ■ PERSONABLE   ■ PERSPICACIOUS   ■ PERSPICUITY
■ PERTAIN   ■ PERTINACIOUS   ■ PERTINENT   ■ PERTURB   ■ PERUSE

persiflage [ˈpɜːrsɪflɑːʒ]

【考法】 *n.* 打趣：good-natured **teasing** or exchanging of clever remarks

例 Their tongue-in-cheek persiflage is sometimes mistaken for an exchange of insults by people who don't know them. 他们半开玩笑的打趣有时候被不认识他们的人误认为是在互相对骂。

近 backchat, badinage, chaff, jesting, joshing, raillery. repartee

persistence [pərˈsɪstəns]

【考法】 *n.* 坚持，持续：uninterrupted or **lasting existence**

例 The persistence of the fever for a week caused me great worry. 持续一周的发烧让我很不安。

近 ceaselessness, continuance, continuity, durability, endurance, subsistence

反 cessation, close, end, expiration, finish, stoppage, surcease, termination 停止

派 persistent *adj.* 持续不断的

personable [ˈpɜːrsənəbl]
【考法】 *adj.* 风度翩翩的，吸引人的：pleasing in personality or appearance; **attractive**
例 apparently be attracted by a personable young man 明显被一位风度翩翩的少年迷住了
近 alluring, appealing, attractive, captivating, charismatic, charming, comely, enchanting, handsome, pretty
反 grotesque, hideous, ugly 丑陋的；homely 相貌平庸的

perspicacious [ˌpɜːrspɪˈkeɪʃəs]
【考法】 *adj.* 极敏锐的，有洞察力的：having or showing **penetrating mental discernment**; clear-sighted
例 an impartial and perspicacious judge 一个明镜高悬(公正而极具洞察力)的法官
近 astute, savvy, sharp, sharp-witted, shrewd, smart
反 ignorant, oblivious, unknowing 未察觉的，无知的
派 perspicacity *n.* 敏锐，洞察力

perspicuity [ˌpɜːrspɪˈkjuːəti]
【考法】 *n.* 清晰明了：the quality of being perspicuous; **clearness and lucidity**
例 The key of modern enterprise system is the prespicuity of property right. 现代企业制度的核心是产权的明晰。
近 clarity, clearness, explicitness, lucidity, lucidness, perspicuousness
反 obscureness, obscurity, unclarity 模糊不清；ambiguity 模棱两可

pertain [pərˈteɪn]
【考法】 *vi.* 有关联：to **have a relation** or connection; relate
例 new evidence that pertains to the accident 与事故相关的新证据
近 appertain, bear, concern, refer, relate
派 pertaining *adj.* 有关系的

pertinacious [ˌpɜːrtnˈeɪʃəs]
【考法】 *adj.* 顽固的，固执地坚持的：**sticking** to an opinion, purpose, or course of action in spite of reason, arguments, or persuasion
例 The pertinacious boy won't stop crying unless his desire is satisfied. 这个固执的男孩在愿望没有满足的情况下是不会停止哭泣的。
近 adamant, headstrong, implacable, inflexible, intransigent, mulish, obdurate, perverse, stubborn, willful
反 compliant, flexible, pliable, pliant, yielding 容易受影响的，容易控制的

pertinent [ˈpɜːrtnənt]
【考法】 *adj.* 相关的，恰当的：having a clear decisive **relevance** to the matter in hand
例 He impressed the jury with his concise, pertinent answers to the attorney's questions. 他对律师提出的问题给予了简洁而恰当的回答，这给陪审团留下了深刻的印象。
近 applicable, apposite, apropos, germane, material, pointed, relative, relevant
反 extraneous, immaterial, impertinent, inapplicable, inapposite, irrelevant, pointless 无关的
派 pertinence *n.* 相关，恰当

perturb [pərˈtɜːrb]
【考法】 *vt.* 使扰乱，使烦躁不安：to **trouble the mind** of; to make uneasy
例 The naughty boy perturbed me enough to keep me awake that night. 那个捣蛋的男孩让我烦躁到当晚失眠。
近 agitate, ail, bother, discomfort, discompose, distress, unsettle, upset
反 calm, compose, quiet, settle, soothe, tranquilize 使镇定
派 perturbation *n.* 打扰，扰乱

peruse [pəˈruːz]
【考法】 *vt.* 细读：to read or **examine**, typically **with great care**
例 peruse the manuscript to check for grammatical errors 细读手稿以检查语法错误
近 examine, scrutinize
反 glance, glimpse, scan, skim 一瞥，迅速浏览

Unit 6

■ PERVADE　　　■ PESSIMISTIC　　　■ PETITION　　　■ PETRIFY　　　■ PETTY
■ PHENOMENAL　　■ PHILANTHROPIC　　■ PHILISTINE　　　■ PHLEGMATIC　　■ PIDDLING

pervade [pərˈveɪd]
【考法】 *vt.* 弥漫，充满：to be present **throughout**; permeate
例 The mixed smell of sawdust and glue pervaded the whole factory. 锯末与胶水的味道弥漫了整个工厂。
the corruption that pervades every stratum of society 充斥在社会每个阶层中的腐败
近 interpenetrate, percolate, riddle, suffuse, transfuse
派 pervasive *adj.* 弥漫的

pessimistic [ˌpesɪˈmɪstɪk]

【考法】 *adj.* 悲观的：tending to stress the negative or unfavorable or to **take the gloomiest possible view**

例 With that pessimistic attitude, it's no wonder you're depressed. 你的人生观如此悲观，难怪你会感到压抑。

近 bearish, defeatist, despairing, downbeat, hopeless

反 optimistic 乐观的

派 pessimism *n.* 悲观主义

petition [pəˈtɪʃn]

【考法 1】 *n.* 请愿，正式的申请；申请书：a solemn **supplication or request** to a superior authority; an entreaty

例 a petition for divorce 离婚申请书

近 appeal, cry, entreaty, pleading, solicitation, supplication

【考法 2】 *v.* (尤指正式地) 请求：to **make a request**, especially a formal written one

例 She is petitioning to regain custody of the child. 为了重新获得孩子的监护权，她提出了正式申请。

近 adjure, beseech, conjure, entreat, impetrate, implore, importune, plead, solicit, supplicate

派 petitioner *n.* 申请人，请愿者

petrify [ˈpetrɪfaɪ]

【考法】 *vt.* 使僵化，使失去活力：to cause to **become stiff** or stone-like; deaden

例 Pressure from family has petrified his once innovative mind. 家庭的压力使他的头脑失去了往日的创造力。

近 damp, dampen, deaden, devitalize, enervate, lobotomize, ossify

反 brace, energize, enliven, invigorate, quicken, stimulate, vitalize, vivify 使有活力

派 petrification *n.* 石化，僵化

petty [ˈpeti]

【考法】 *adj.* 细微的，不重要的：of **small importance**; trivial

例 play petty tricks 耍小聪明

近 inconsequential, inconsiderable, insignificant, measly, minute, paltry, peanut, slight, trifling, trivial

反 consequential, considerable, important, material, momentous, significant 重大的，重要的

phenomenal [fəˈnɑːmɪnl]

【考法】 *adj.* 不寻常的，非凡的：being **out of the ordinary**; extraordinary; outstanding

例 the phenomenal growth that the suburb has experienced over the last decade 过去十年间郊区所经历的令人称奇的快速发展

近 especial, exceptional, extraordinary, peculiar, preternatural, rare, singular, uncommon, unusual

反 common, normal, ordinary, typical 普通的，典型的

philanthropic [ˌfɪlənˈθrɑːpɪk]

【考法】 *adj.* 博爱的，为他人着想的：having or showing a concern for the **welfare of others**

例 the philanthropic aims of the organization 这个机构的博爱、利他的目标

近 altruistic, beneficent, benevolent, eleemosynary, good, humanitarian

反 misanthropic 反人类的；selfish 自私的

派 philanthropist *n.* 博爱的人

philistine [ˈfɪlɪstiːn]

【考法】 *n.* 市侩 (注重物质而鄙视智慧或艺术的人)：a person who is **guided by materialism** and is usually disdainful of intellectual or artistic values

例 The philistine's critics sometime limit artists' imagine. 市侩之人的批评有时会限制艺术家的想象力。

近 lowbrow, materialist

反 highbrow 文化修养高的人

phlegmatic [fleɡˈmætɪk]

【考法】 *adj.* 冷静的，无感情的，淡漠的：having or suggesting a **calm, sluggish temperament**; unemotional

例 a strangely phlegmatic response to what should have been happy news 对本该是一个让人开心的新闻的冷漠回应

近 affectless, apathetic, cold-blooded, emotionless, impassible, numb, stoic, stolid

反 demonstrative, emotional, fervent, fervid, impassioned, passionate, vehement 感情丰富的，热情的

piddling [ˈpɪdlɪŋ]

【考法】 *adj.* 微不足道的：so **trifling or trivial** as to be beneath one's consideration

例 raise a piddling objection to the plan 对计划提出一个微不足道的反对

近 inconsequential, inconsiderable, insignificant, measly, minute, paltry, peanut, slight, trifling, trivial

反 consequential, considerable, important, material, momentous, significant 重大的，重要的

Unit 7

- ■ PIEBALD   ■ PIGMENT   ■ PILFER   ■ PILLAR   ■ PILLORY
- ■ PILOT   ■ PINE   ■ PINNACLE   ■ PINPOINT   ■ PIQUANT

piebald [ˈpaɪbɔːld]

【考法 1】 *adj.* 杂色的：of **different colors**
- 例 a piebald horse 一匹杂色马
- 近 blotched, dappled, marbled, mottled, splotched, spotted
- 反 monochromatic 单色的

【考法 2】 *adj.* 混合的，杂糅而成的：consisting of many things of **different sorts**
- 例 his piebald ethnic background 他身为混血儿的背景
- 近 assorted, eclectic, heterogeneous, hybrid, magpie, mixed, motley, promiscuous, varied
- 反 homogeneous 由相同类型事物组成的

pigment [ˈpɪɡmənt]

【考法 1】 *n.* 颜料：a substance that imparts black or white or a **color** to other materials
- 例 natural red pigment 天然红色染料
- 近 colorant, dye, stain

【考法 2】 *vt.* 给…上颜色：to **color** with or as if with pigment
- 例 pigmented silk 染过色的丝绸
- 近 paint, stain, tincture, tinge, tint
- 反 blanch 漂白；decolorize 使脱色

pilfer [ˈpɪlfər]

【考法】 *vt.* 偷窃：to **steal** stealthily in small amounts
- 例 pilfer the commercial document 偷窃商业文件
- 近 appropriate, filch, hook, lift, pinch, purloin, steal, thieve

pillar [ˈpɪlər]

【考法 1】 *n.* 柱子：a firm upright **support** for a superstructure
- 例 stone pillars that supported the hall 支撑大厅的石柱
- 近 column, pier, pilaster

【考法 2】 *n.* (物质、精神等方面的)支柱：something or someone to which one looks for **support**
- 例 My father has been my pillar throughout this crisis. 整场危机之中我父亲都是我的支柱。
- 近 anchor, buttress, mainstay, reliance, standby

pillory [ˈpɪləri]

【考法】 *vt.* 当众嘲弄：to expose to **public contempt**, ridicule, or scorn
- 例 The candidate mercilessly pilloried his opponent. 候选人在大众面前无情地羞辱他的对手。‖ He resigned after being pilloried by the press. 在遭到媒体嘲弄之后他愤然辞职。
- 近 abase, debase, degrade, denounce, humiliate, ridicule
- 反 carol, eulogize, exalt, extol, laud 赞美

pilot [ˈpaɪlət]

【考法 1】 *n.* 领航员，飞行员：one employed to **steer a ship**
- 例 a jet pilot 喷气式飞机飞行员
- 近 aviator, bellwether, captain, guide, helmsman, leader, navigator

【考法 2】 *adj.* 初步的，试验性的：serving as a **tentative model** for future experiment or development
- 例 They carried out a pilot study before the larger, more expensive project was started. 在更大规模、更为昂贵的项目开始之前，他们进行了初步研究。
- 近 developmental, experimental, model, test, trial
- 反 eventual, final, ultimate 最终的

【考法 3】 *vt.* 带领通过：**lead** or conduct over a usually difficult course
- 例 The lobbyists piloted the bill through the Senate. 游说集团使法案得到参议院的批准。
- 近 conduct, direct, guide, lead, route, show, steer
- 反 follow 跟随

pine [paɪn]

【考法 1】 *vi.* 渴望，奢望：to **yearn** intensely and persistently especially for something unattainable

例 pine for a lost love 渴望那段逝去的爱情

近 ache, crave, dream, hunger, itch, long, lust, repine, thirst, yearn

反 abhor, detest, loathe 厌恶，反感

【考法 2】 *vi.* 因渴望而憔悴：to **lose vigor**, health, or flesh (as through grief)

例 Separated by their families, the lovers pined away. 这对恋人因为被家人拆散而日益憔悴。

近 decline, dwindle, fade, flag, languish, waste

pinnacle [ˈpɪnəkl]

【考法】 *n.* 顶峰：the **highest point** of development or achievement

例 a singer who has reached the pinnacle of career 已到达事业巅峰的歌手

近 acme, apex, climax, culmination, meridian, peak, summit, top, zenith

反 bottom, nadir 最低点

pinpoint [ˈpɪnpɔɪnt]

【考法 1】 *adj.* 非常精确的：located, fixed, or directed with **extreme precision**

例 The commander demanded the pinpoint location of artillery fire. 指挥官需要火炮攻击的精确位置。

近 accurate, close, delicate, exact, fine, hairline, mathematical, precise, refined, rigorous

反 coarse, cursory, rough 粗略的；imprecise, inaccurate, inexact 不准确的

【考法 2】 *vt.* 精确定位或确认：to locate, fix, determine, or **identify with precision**

例 pinpoint the target by tracking calls from his cellphone 通过跟踪手机信号精确定位目标 ‖ pinpoint the cause of failure 准确找出失败的原因

近 determine, distinguish, locate, identify, recognize, spot

反 estimate 估计

piquant [ˈpiːkənt]

【考法 1】 *adj.* 辛辣开胃的：pleasantly **pungent** or tart in **taste**

例 a piquant sauce 开胃的酱汁

近 peppery, poignant, salty, savory, spicy, zesty

反 insipid, vapid, zestless 索然无味的

【考法 2】 *adj.* 令人振奋的：appealingly **provocative**

例 a piquant glance 充满挑逗的一瞥

近 exciting, pungent, racy, stimulating

反 flat, pallid 单调的，无聊的

Unit 8

■ PIQUE	■ PIRATE	■ PITHY	■ PITILESS	■ PITTANCE
■ PLACATE	■ PLACEBO	■ PLAGIARIZE	■ PLANGENT	■ PLASTIC

pique [piːk]

【考法 1】 *vt.* 使愤怒：to **arouse anger** or resentment in

例 She was greatly piqued when they refused her invitation. 他们拒绝她的邀请让她很生气。

近 aggravate, annoy, exasperate, infuriate, irritate, peeve, provoke, rile, roil, ruffle, vex

反 delight, gratify, rejoice 使高兴

【考法 2】 *vt.* 激起，刺激：to **excite or arouse** especially by a provocation, challenge, or rebuff

例 radical remarks that pique their curiosity 引起他们兴趣的激进评论

近 arouse, encourage, excite, fire, impassion, incite, instigate, move, stimulate, stir

反 allay, alleviate, assuage, ease, mitigate, mollify, palliate, relieve, soothe 平息，缓和

pirate [ˈpaɪrət]

【考法 1】 *vt.* 盗版，盗用：to take or make use of under a guise of authority but **without actual right**

例 a pirated version of the software 盗版软件

近 arrogate, commandeer, convert, expropriate, preempt, press, seize, usurp

【考法 2】 *n.* 海盗：a **robber** on the high **seas**

例 little boys dreaming of sailing as pirates 梦想成为海盗的小男孩

近 corsair, freebooter, rover

pithy [ˈpɪθi]

【考法】 *adj.* 精练的，简洁的：precisely meaningful; forceful and **brief**

例 The professor gave a pithy introduction to this course. 教授就这门课程做了简短的介绍。

近 apothegmatic, brief, capsule, compact, compendious, concise, laconic, succinct, telegraphic, terse

反 circuitous, circumlocutory, diffuse, rambling, prolix, verbose, windy, wordy 冗长累赘的

派 pithiness *n.* 简洁，犀利

pitiless [ˈpɪtiləs]

【考法】 *adj.* 没有同情心的：**devoid of** or unmoved by **pity**

例 a pitiless humiliation 毫不留情的羞辱

近 affectless, callous, coldhearted, cruel, harsh, indurate, merciless

反 charitable, clement, compassionate, humane, merciful, sympathetic, tender 有同情心的，仁慈的

pittance [ˈpɪtns]

【考法】 *n.* 少量津贴：a **small portion**, amount, or allowance

例 The internship offers only a pittance for a salary, but it is a great opportunity to gain experience. 实习所能挣到的报酬是很少的，但是它提供了获得经验的绝佳机会。

近 bit, mite, modicum, peanuts, trace

反 cornucopia, opulence 富饶；boodle, bundle, fortune 大笔财富

placate [ˈpleɪkeɪt]

【考法】 *vt.* (通过让步以)平息抚慰：to **lessen the anger** or agitation of

例 The colonists implemented a new policy to placate local opposition. 殖民者采取了一项新政策以缓和当地的反抗情绪。

近 appease, assuage, conciliate, mollify, pacify, propitiate, tranquilize

反 anger, enrage, foment, gall, incense, inflame, infuriate, peeve, rile 激怒，使气恼

派 placation *n.* 安抚

placebo [pləˈsiːboʊ]

【考法】 *n.* 安慰性的事物：something of no intrinsic remedial value that is **used to appease or reassure** another

例 Candies are often adopted as the placebo for the dying patients. 糖果通常作为安慰剂给重症患者服用。

plagiarize [ˈpleɪdʒəraɪz]

【考法】 *v.* 剽窃，抄袭：to **steal** and pass off (the **ideas** or words of another) as one's own

例 In scientific community, plagiarizing other's paper is a felony. 在学术界，剽窃他人的论文是一项重罪。

近 steal

派 plagiarism *n.* 剽窃

plangent [ˈplændʒənt]

【考法1】 *adj.* 轰鸣的：having a **loud** reverberating **sound**

例 The camera man was stunned by the plangent roar of wild animals. 摄影师被野生动物发出的怒号吓得不知所措。

近 blaring, blasting, clamorous, deafening, earsplitting, resonant, resounding, sonorous, thunderous, vibrant

反 muffled, muted 声音被减弱的；gentle, low, soft 声音轻柔的

【考法2】 *adj.* 凄凉的，哀伤的：having an expressive and especially **plaintive** quality

例 a plangent song about a long-ago love 一首关于往日爱情的凄凉歌曲

近 doleful, dolorous, funeral, grieving, lamentable, lugubrious, plaintive, rueful, sorrowful, woeful

反 agreeable, cheerful, delightful, enjoyable, jolly, pleasing 令人愉快的

plastic [ˈplæstɪk]

【考法1】 *adj.* 可塑的：susceptible of being **modified** in form or nature

例 the plastic quality of modeling clay 模型泥的可塑性质

近 adaptable, ductile, flexible, malleable, pliable, pliant, resilient, supple

反 inflexible, rigid, stiff 僵硬的

派 plasticity *n.* 可塑性

【考法2】 *adj.* 虚假的，做作的：**lacking in natural** or spontaneous quality

例 There's usually a plastic cordiality at these corporate events. 通常在这类公司活动上都有一种虚假的热情和友好。

近 affected, assumed, bogus, factitious, fake, false, feigned, mock, phony, pretended, pseudo, spurious

反 artless, genuine, natural, spontaneous, unaffected, uncontrived, unfeigned 真诚的

Unit 9

plateau [plæˈtoʊ]

【考法 1】 *n.* 高原：a usually extensive level land area **raised** sharply **above** adjacent land on at least one side
- 例 Qinghai-Tibetan Plateau 青藏高原
- 近 highland, mesa, tableland, upland
- 反 lowland 低谷；basin 盆地

【考法 2】 *n.* 稳定时期，平台期：a relatively **stable level**, period, or state
- 例 reach a plateau of development 达到发展的稳定期
- 近 equilibrium, stage, stasis

platitude [ˈplætɪtuːd]

【考法 1】 *n.* 陈词滥调：a trite or **banal** remark or **statement**, especially one expressed as if it were original or significant
- 例 the platitude of most political oratory 政治说辞里的陈词滥调
- 近 banality, bromide, cliché, commonplace, homily, shibboleth, truism

【考法 2】 *n.* 缺乏原创性：**lack of originality**
- 近 triteness, staleness
- 反 novelty 新颖性；originality 原创性

plausible [ˈplɔːzəbl]

【考法】 *adj.* 看似有理的：**superficially** fair, **reasonable**, or valuable but often specious
- 例 a plausible argument 看起来头头是道的说理
- 近 believable, credible, likely, possible, presumable, probable
- 反 paradoxical 看似矛盾的；implausible, improbable, incredible, unbelievable, unlikely 不太可能的
- 派 plausibility *n.* 看似有理

pleat [pliːt]

【考法】 *n./vt.* 打褶：**fold**
- 近 corrugate, crease, furrow, ruffle, wrinkle
- 反 flatten, smooth 抹平

plentitude [ˈplentituːd]

【考法】 *n.* 大量：an **ample amount** or quantity; an abundance
- 例 a plentitude of lumber for the current housing market 充足的家具木材供给
- 近 abundance, affluence, cornucopia, myriad, plenty, profusion, stack, wealth
- 反 dearth, deficiency, inadequacy, insufficiency 缺乏，匮乏；mite, peanuts, pinch, pittance, trace 少量

plethora [ˈpleθərə]

【考法】 *n.* 过量，过剩：**excess**, superfluity
- 例 a plethora of advice and a paucity of assistance 给出大量建议而鲜有实质性援助
- 近 abundance, cornucopia, feast, overabundance, overflow, plentitude, profusion, surfeit, surplus
- 反 dearth, inadequacy, insufficiency, paucity, scarcity, undersupply 缺乏
- 派 plethoric *adj.* 过量的

pliable [ˈplaɪəbl]

【考法 1】 *adj.* 易弯曲的，柔软的：**supple** enough to bend freely or repeatedly without breaking
- 例 pliable optical fiber 柔软的光纤
- 近 adaptable, ductile, flexible, limber, plastic, supple
- 反 inflexible, rigid, stiff, unbending 不易弯曲的

【考法 2】 *adj.* 易受影响的，温顺的：**easily influenced**, persuaded, or swayed
- 例 He took advantage of the pliable mind of youth. 他利用了年轻人容易受他人教唆的特点。
- 近 compliant, docile, obedient, pliant, tractable, subdued
- 反 contumacious, insubordinate, intractable, obstreperous, recalcitrant, refractory, unruly 难控制的

pliant [ˈplaɪənt]

【考法 1】 *adj.* 易弯曲的：**easily bent** or flexed
- 例 a pliant young tree 易弯曲的小树

近 adaptable, ductile, flexible, limber, plastic, supple
反 inflexible, rigid, stiff 不易弯曲的；unbending 难弯曲的
【考法 2】 *adj.* 顺从的：**yielding** readily to influence or domination
例 She's proud and stubborn, you know, under that pliant exterior. 你知道，她外表温顺，内心却骄傲而固执。
近 compliant, docile, obedient, pliant, tractable, subdued
反 contumacious, insubordinate, intractable, obstreperous, recalcitrant, refractory, unruly 难控制的

plight [plaɪt]
【考法】 *n.* 困境：a situation, especially a bad or **unfortunate** one
例 He was in a plight, trying to decide whether or not to take the job. 他处在不知道是否应该接受这份工作的困境之中。
近 dilemma, jam, predicament, quandary

plod [plɑːd]
【考法】 *v.* 沉重缓慢地走：to **walk heavily** or slowly
例 The soldiers slowly plodded across the marsh. 士兵们慢慢走过沼泽地。
近 tramp, trudge
反 flit 迅速飞过；gambol 雀跃
派 plodding *adj.* 走路沉重缓慢的

Unit 10

| ■ PLUCK | ■ PLUMB | ■ PLUMMET | ■ PLUMP | ■ PLUNGE |
| ■ POLARIZE | ■ POLEMIC | ■ POLISHED | ■ POLITIC | ■ POMPOUS |

pluck [plʌk]
【考法 1】 *n.* 敢于面对困难的勇气：resourceful **courage** and daring in the face of difficulties
例 full of pluck 充满了勇气
近 backbone, courage, dauntlessness, grit, guts, resolution, spirit, spunk
反 cowardice, coward, spinelessness 胆小，怯懦
派 plucky *adj.* 勇敢的
【考法 2】 *v.* 弹奏（弦乐）：to sound (the **strings** of an instrument) by **pulling** and **releasing** them with the fingers or a plectrum
例 pluck the harp 弹奏竖琴
近 play

plumb [plʌm]
【考法 1】 *vt.* 测深度：to **measure the depth** of (as a body of water) typically with a weighted line
例 We will plumb the bay to make sure it was deep enough for the huge vessel. 为了保证水深足够容纳这艘巨轮，我们将会测量海湾的深度。
近 fathom
【考法 2】 *adj.* 垂直的：exactly **vertical**
近 perpendicular, upright, vertical
反 horizontal 水平的
【考法 3】 *adj.* 完全的，绝对的：having **no exceptions** or restrictions
派 Such a movie is plumb trash and further evidence of the deterioration of popular culture. 这样的电影就是彻头彻尾的垃圾，它进一步证明了大众文化的堕落和腐化。
近 absolute, categorical, complete, consummate, definite, pure, sheer, thorough, utter, very
反 doubtful, dubious, equivocal, questionable, uncertain 不确定的；qualified 有条件的
【考法 4】 *vt.* 仔细深入地检查；探索，探究：to **examine** closely or **deeply**
例 plumb the book's complexities 审阅这本书的复杂度 ‖ questions that plumb the depths of stupidity 探究智商下限的问题
近 explore, delve, inquire, investigate, probe

plummet [ˈplʌmɪt]
【考法】 *vi.* 突然下降：to **decline suddenly** and steeply
例 Overall GPA plummeted 0.5 points. 平均学分骤降 0.5。
近 crash, decline, descend, dip, dive, fall, plunge, sink, tumble
反 skyrocket, soar 飙升

plump [plʌmp]
【考法 1】 *adj.* 丰满的：**well-rounded** and full in form
例 In Tang Dynasty, being plump was a sign of ultimate beauty. 在唐代，身材丰满是最美丽的象征。

近 chubby, fleshy, fat, gross, obese, rotund, round
反 lean, slender, svelte, thin 纤瘦的，苗条的；angular 因消瘦而棱角分明的
【考法 2】 *v.* 鼎力支持，赞不绝口：to **give full support** or praise
例 We will plump for any candidate who supports stem cell research. 我们会鼎力支持那些拥护干细胞研究的候选人。
近 advocate, back, champion, endorse, patronize
反 baffle, foil, frustrate, sabotage 阻挠，从中破坏

plunge [plʌndʒ]
【考法 1】 *vi.* 突然下降：to **descend** or dip **suddenly**
例 Stock's value plunged. 股票价值骤然下降。
近 crash, decline, descend, dip, dive, fall, plummet, sink, tumble
反 skyrocket, soar 飙升
【考法 2】 *vt.* 插入，刺入：to cause to **penetrate** or enter quickly and forcibly into something
例 The enemy plunged the dagger into his chest. 敌人把匕首刺入他的胸膛。
近 drive, stab, stick, thrust
反 extract 拔出

polarize [ˈpoʊləraɪz]
【考法】 *vt.* 使分开对立，使两极分化：to **break** up **into opposing** factions or groupings
例 The controversy has polarized voters into pro-abortion and anti-abortion groups. 这一争议使得选民分化成支持堕胎和反对堕胎两个群体。
近 bifurcate, diverge, divide
反 coalesce, unite 合并，联合
派 polarization *n.* 两极分化

polemic [pəˈlemɪk]
【考法】 *n.* 争执：a controversial **argument**
例 The polemic between science and religion has never ceased. 科学和宗教之间的争论从未停息。
近 contention, controversy, disagreement, disputation
反 agreement 一致，协议
派 polemical *adj.* 好争论的

polished [ˈpɑːlɪʃt]
【考法 1】 *adj.* 有教养的：showing a **high degree of refinement** and the assurance that comes from wide social experience
例 He maintained a very polished tone in his correspondences. 他在通信中保持着一种极有教养的口吻。
近 cultivated, cultured, genteel, refined, urbane
反 gauche, rustic, philistine 粗俗的；uncivilized, untutored 未开化的
【考法 2】 *adj.* 擦亮的：having a **shiny** surface or finish
例 She could see her face reflected in the polished hood of the car. 她可以在引擎盖光亮的表面上看到自己的脸。
近 buffed, burnished, glistening, lustrous, rubbed, satiny, sleek
反 dim, dull, flat, lusterless 黯淡无光的
派 polish *v.* 擦亮

politic [ˈpɑːlətɪk]
【考法 1】 *adj.* 精明能干的：characterized by **shrewdness** in managing, contriving, or dealing
例 a politic secretary 能干的秘书
近 diplomatic, judicious, perspicacious, sagacious, tactful, wise
反 tactless, unsophisticated 缺乏谋略的，头脑简单的
【考法 2】 *adj.* 合时宜的，明智的：**suitable** for bringing about a desired result under the circumstances
例 It probably would not be politic to tell your boss that his latest idea is the worst thing you've ever heard. 不要现在去告诉你老板说他的想法是你听过的最糟的，这是一个不明智的做法。
近 advisable, desirable, prudent, tactical
反 imprudent, inadvisable, injudicious, unwise 不明智的，不合时宜的

pompous [ˈpɑːmpəs]
【考法 1】 *adj.* 浮夸的：excessively elevated or **ornate**
例 The candidate was given to windy and pompous rhetorical speeches. 听众们听了一场冗长而浮夸的演讲。
近 affected, bombastic, flowery, grandiloquent, magniloquent, rhetorical
反 homely 朴素的
【考法 2】 *adj.* 傲慢的：having or exhibiting **self-importance**
例 a pompous politician who insisted on boarding the plane first 一个坚持要求优先登机的傲慢政客
近 arrogant, egocentric, haughty, pontifical, presumptuous, supercilious
反 humble, modest, unpretentious 谦逊的

List 19

"多看多背多做题，不烦不倦不放弃。"

（赵墨非，Verbal 790，Quantitative 800，录取学校：UCLA 经济学 PHD）

Unit 1

■ PONDERABLE	■ PONDEROUS	■ PONTIFICATE	■ PORE	■ POROUS
■ PORTENTOUS	■ POSEUR	■ POSIT	■ POSTULATE	■ POSTURE

ponderable [ˈpɑːndərəbl]

【考法】 *adj.* 有价值的，值得考虑的：**considerable** enough to be weighed or assessed

例 Climate change has exerted a ponderable influence on world politics. 气候变化对世界政局有着不容忽视的影响。

近 appreciable, perceptible, sensible

反 inappreciable 微不足道的

ponderous [ˈpɑːndərəs]

【考法 1】 *adj.* 沉重的：of very **great weight**

例 a ponderous machine 沉重的机器

近 cumbersome, heavy, hefty, massive, onerous, weighty

反 ethereal, gossamer, light, weightless 轻飘飘的

【考法 2】 *adj.* 沉闷无聊的：oppressively or **unpleasantly dull**

例 a ponderous sermon no one really cares 没有人真正关心的沉闷无聊的布道

近 dreary, dull, flat, elephantine, monotonous, insipid, vapid

反 absorbing, engaging, engrossing, gripping, interesting, intriguing, involving, riveting 极吸引人的

pontificate [pɑːnˈtɪfɪkeɪt]

【考法】 *vi.* 傲慢地做或说：to **speak** or express opinions in a **pompous** or dogmatic way

例 pontificate to show a sense of superiority 傲慢地说以显示高人一等的优越感

反 condescend 屈尊，俯就

派 pontification *n.* 傲慢的言行；pontifical *adj.* 傲慢的

pore [pɔːr]

【考法】 *vi.* 仔细浏览，仔细研究：to **read or study attentively** (usually used with over)

例 The committee will probably pore over the results of the study for a long time before making their decision. 在正式做决定之前，委员会可能需要花很长的时间来仔细研究调查结果。

近 cogitate, consider, contemplate, deliberate, meditate, perpend, ruminate, study, weigh, chew over

反 flip, glance, leaf, riffle, skim 粗略地看，迅速浏览

porous [ˈpɔːrəs]

【考法】 *adj.* 多孔可渗透的：**admitting** the passage of gas or **liquid** through pores or interstices

例 Lava rock has a porous structure which makes the material lightweight and highly moisture-retentive. 火山岩的多孔结构使得它密度很小，同时有很高的吸湿性。

近 passable, penetrable, permeable, pervious

反 impassable, impenetrable, impermeable, impervious 无法穿透的

派 porosity *n.* 多孔性

portentous [pɔːrˈtentəs]

【考法 1】 *adj.* 预兆性的，凶兆的：being or showing a **sign of evil** or calamity to come

例 an eerie and portentous stillness 阴森神秘、充满凶兆的寂静

近 baleful, direful, doomy, foreboding, inauspicious, menacing, minatory, ominous, sinister, ill-omened

反 auspicious, propitious 吉兆的

【考法 2】 *adj.* 勾起兴趣的，令人遐想的：**eliciting amazement** or wonder

例 The way in which he could bring together opposing forces was truly portentous. 他整合两股对抗势力的方法着实令人好奇。

近 amazing, astonishing, astounding, fabulous, marvelous, miraculous, prodigious, wonderful

反 common, commonplace, ordinary 普通的

poseur [poʊˈzɜːr]

【考法】 *n.* 故作姿态、不真诚的人：an **affected** or **insincere** person

例 She is such a poseur and you will never know if she is really crying or pretending. 她就是个爱装的人，你从不知道她是真的在哭还是只是假装而已。

近 grandstander, poser

posit [ˈpɑːzɪt]

【考法】 *vt.* 假定，断定：to assume or **affirm** the existence of

例 The committee posited that he was qualified for the election. 委员会假定他是够格参加选举的。

近 assume, postulate, presuppose, premise, presume

反 falsify 证明为假

postulate [ˈpɑːstʃəleɪt]

【考法 1】 *n.* 前提条件：something taken as being true or factual and used as a **starting point** for a course of action or reasoning

例 One of the postulates that the true agnostic rejects is the assumption that it is even possible for us to know whether God exists. 我们甚至可以知道上帝是否存在——这是一个真正的不可知论者所反对的假设。

近 premise, presumption, presupposition, supposition

反 conclusion 结论

【考法 2】 *vt.* 假定为真：to **assume** or claim as **true**, existent, or necessary

例 postulate a causal relationship 假定存在因果关系

近 assume, conjecture, hypothesize, posit, presuppose, premise, presume, suppose

反 belie, disprove, falsify 证明为假

派 postulation *n.* 推测

posture [ˈpɑːstʃər]

【考法 1】 *n.* 姿势，姿态：a general **way of holding the body**

例 A good upright posture will prevent backaches. 良好的站姿可以预防背痛。

近 attitude, carriage, poise, stance, station

【考法 2】 *vi.* 故作姿态，装模作样：to assume an artificial or **pretended attitude**

例 posture to impress 故作姿态以给别人留下印象

近 attitudinize, feign, grandstand, masquerade, pose, pretend

派 posturer *n.* 故作姿态之人

Unit 2

| ■ POTABLE | ■ POTENTATE | ■ POTENTIATE | ■ POUT | ■ PRACTITIONER |
| ■ PRAIRIE | ■ PRATE | ■ PREACH | ■ PRECARIOUS | ■ PRECEDENT |

potable [ˈpoʊtəbl]

【考法 1】 *n.* 饮品，尤指有酒精饮料：a **beverage**, especially an alcoholic beverage

例 Potables are offered at bar counter for free. 饮料可以在吧台免费领取。

近 beverage, drink, juice, liquor, spirits

反 non-intoxicant, soft drink 软饮料

【考法 2】 *adj.* 适于饮用的：**suitable for drinking**

例 Price of the potable water has soared. 饮用水价格飙升。

近 drinkable, edible

反 undrinkable 不能饮用的

potentate [ˈpoʊtnteɪt]

【考法】 *n.* 有权势的人：one who **has the power** and position to rule over others

例 a son of a potentate 官二代

近 authority, autocrat, monarch, ruler, sovereign

反 figurehead（有名无权的）傀儡

potentiate [poʊ'tenʃɪeɪt]
【考法】 *vt.* 激活，加强：to make effective or active, or more effective or **more active**
例 additives to potentiate the drug 增强药效的添加剂
近 activate, energize, enhance, intensify, stir, wake, vitalize
反 deactivate 使无效；abate, attenuate, dwindle, lessen, moderate, reduce 减弱，削弱

pout [paʊt]
【考法】 *vi.* （尤指撅嘴或板着脸）表示不悦：to **show displeasure**, especially by thrusting out the lips or wearing a sullen expression
例 She pouted and didn't say a word to anyone all morning. 她整个早上都闷闷不乐，没和别人说一句话。
近 grump, mope, sulk
反 grin 露齿而笑

practitioner [præk'tɪʃənər]
【考法】 *n.* 职业人士：one who practices a **profession**
例 medical practitioner 医护人员，行医者
近 expert, guru, professional, specialist, virtuoso
反 fledgling 无经验的人；quack 冒充内行的人

prairie ['preri]
【考法】 *n.* 大草原：an extensive area of flat or rolling, predominantly **treeless grassland**
例 Canadian Prairie 加拿大大草原地区
近 grassland, meadow, plain, savanna

prate [preɪt]
【考法】 *vi.* 闲聊，空谈：to **talk** long and **idly**
例 They have been prating on the phone for hours. 他们已经煲了几个小时的电话粥了。
近 babble, chat, chatter, converse, gabble, jabber, prattle, twitter
派 prater *n.* 闲聊的人

preach [priːtʃ]
【考法】 *vi.* 传道，布道：to deliver a **sermon**
例 a minister who loves to preach 一个爱布道的牧师
近 discourse, sermonize
派 preacher *n.* 布道者

precarious [prɪ'keriəs]
【考法 1】 *adj.* 危险的，不稳定的：dangerously **lacking** in **security** or **stability**
例 a precarious livelihood 不稳定的生计
近 delicate, fragile, sensitive, touchy, unstable
反 firm, stable 稳定的；safe, secure 安全的
【考法 2】 *adj.* 可疑的，不明确的：dependent on **uncertain** premises
例 His entire argument relies on a precarious assumption. 他的整篇论证都建立在一个可疑的假设之上。
近 ambiguous, doubtful, dubious, equivocal, uncertain, unfounded
反 indubitable, unambiguous, unequivocal, unquestionable 明确的，毋庸置疑的

precedent ['presɪdənt]
【考法 1】 *n.* 先例，前例：an **earlier occurrence** of something similar
例 There has not been any precedent so far. 到目前为止还没有先例。‖ a landmark decision that set a legal precedent 在法律上首开先河的重大决议
近 example, instance, model, paradigm, pattern, standard
【考法 2】 *adj.* 先前的：**prior** in time, order, arrangement, or significance
例 Her violent behaviors may be explained by some precedent events in her troubled life. 她的暴力行径或许可以由她之前苦难生活中遭遇到的一些事件来解释。
近 antecedent, anterior, former, preceding, previous, prior
反 ensuing 继而发生的
派 unprecedented *adj.* 前所未有的

Unit 3

precipice ['presəpis]

【考法】 *n.* 悬崖峭壁：a very **steep** or overhanging place

例 a precipice too steep to climb 过于陡峭而无法攀爬的悬崖

近 bluff, cliff, crag, escarpment, palisade

反 ridge 山脊

派 precipitous *adj.* 陡峭的

precipitate [prɪ'sɪpɪteɪt]

【考法1】 *adj.* 匆忙的：acting or done with excessive or **careless speed**

例 the army's precipitate withdrawal from the field of battle 匆忙将军队从战场上撤下

近 cursory, flying, headlong, hurried, overhasty, precipitous, rash, rushed

反 deliberate 慎重考虑的；leisurely, unhurried, unrushed 从容不迫的，不慌不忙的

派 precipitation *n.* 急促；沉淀；降水

【考法2】 *vt.* 促使，导致：to **cause to happen**, especially suddenly or prematurely

例 precipitate an international crisis 产生国际危机

近 accelerate, escalate, expedite, hasten, impel, speed, trigger

反 check, encumber, enfetter, hamper, handicap, hinder, manacle, obstruct, retard, trammel 阻碍

precipitation [prɪˌsɪpɪ'teɪʃn]

【考法1】 *n.* 沉积物，尤指降水：something precipitated as a **deposit** on the earth of hail, mist, **rain**, sleet, or **snow**

例 The storm brought several inches of precipitation. 风暴带来的降水量达数英寸。

近 deposit, sediment

【考法2】 *n.* 仓促：excited and often showy or **disorderly speed**

例 I fear that I may have acted with some precipitation on this matter, so I would like to reconsider. 我害怕自己在这个事情上考虑得太仓促了，因此我想再想想。

近 haste, hastiness, hustle, precipitousness, rush

反 deliberation 深思熟虑

precipitous [prɪ'sɪpɪtəs]

【考法1】 *adj.* 非常陡峭的：very **steep**, perpendicular, or overhanging in rise or fall

例 a precipitous gorge 险峻的峡谷

近 abrupt, arduous, sheer, steep

反 flat, level 平坦的

【考法2】 *adj.* 匆忙的：acting or done with excessive or **careless speed**

例 They soon regretted their precipitous actions in international affairs. 他们很快就为他们在国际事务中的匆忙举动感到后悔。

近 cursory, flying, headlong, hurried, overhasty, precipitate, rash, rushed

反 deliberate 慎重考虑的；leisurely, unhurried, unrushed 从容不迫的，不慌不忙的

preclude [prɪ'kluːd]

【考法1】 *vt.* 预先阻止：to **make impossible**, as by action taken **in advance**

例 Age alone will not preclude him from standing as a candidate. 年龄并没有阻止他成为候选人。

近 avert, deter, forestall, obviate, prevent, stave off

【考法2】 *vt.* 排斥：to **exclude** or prevent (someone) from a given condition or activity

例 He refused to preclude the subject from discussion. 他拒绝将这个话题排出讨论范围。

近 bar, exclude, except

反 enclose 圈入

派 preclusive *adj.* 预先阻止的；除外的

precursor [priː'kɜːrsər]

【考法】 *n.* 先驱者，先导：one that **precedes** and indicates the approach of another

例 18th-century lyric poets like Robert Burns were precursors of the Romantics. 十八世纪的抒情诗人（如罗伯特·彭斯）是浪漫主义的先驱。

近 foregoer, forerunner, harbinger, herald, outrider

反 sequela, successor 后继者；descendant 后代

派 precursory *adj.* 先驱性的，开创性的

predecessor [ˈpredəsesər]

【考法】 *n.* 前任，先辈: a person who has **previously occupied** a position or office to which another has succeeded

例 a political legacy left by his predecessor 他的前任留下来的政治遗产

近 ancestor, antecedent, foregoer, forerunner, precursor

反 successor 继任者; descendant 后代

predilection [ˌpredlˈekʃn]

【考法】 *n.* 爱好，偏袒: a partiality or **disposition** in **favor** of something

例 a predilection for travel 热爱旅行

近 affection, affinity, bias, disposition, inclination, leaning, penchant, predisposition, propensity, tendency

反 aversion, loathing, nausea, repugnance, repulsion, revulsion 反感

preeminent [priˈemɪnənt]

【考法】 *adj.* 优秀的，重要的: having **paramount** rank, dignity, or importance

例 The writer's style is brilliant and his command of words, preeminent. 作者的文风和用词都十分出色。

近 distinguished, illustrious, incomparable, notable, outstanding, peerless, superb, supreme, unmatchable

反 negligible, trivial 不重要的

派 preeminence *n.* 杰出

preempt [priˈempt]

【考法1】 *vt.* 预先占有: to appropriate, **seize**, or take for oneself **before others**

例 The naughty children had preempted front-row seats that were reserved for the guests of honor. 调皮的孩子们把前排留给贵宾的座位占了。

近 appropriate, arrogate, commandeer, convert, expropriate, seize, usurp

派 preemptive *adj.* 先发制人的; 先买的

【考法2】 *vt.* 替换: to **replace** with something considered to be of greater value or priority: take precedence over

例 The special newscast preempted the usual television program. 特别新闻取代了常规电视节目。

近 displace, replace, supersede, supplant

Unit 4

■ PREEN	■ PREFACE	■ PREGNANT	■ PREMEDITATE	■ PREOCCUPATION
■ PREPONDERANT	■ PREPOSSESSING	■ PREPOSTEROUS	■ PRESAGE	■ PRESCIENCE

preen [priːn]

【考法1】 *vt.* 整理(羽毛): to **smooth** or clean (**feathers**) with the beak or bill

近 plume

反 rumple 弄皱

【考法2】 *vt.* 打扮修饰: to **dress** or groom (**oneself**) with **elaborate** care

例 She always preens herself in an elaborate suit before going to the opera. 她去听歌剧之前总要精心打扮一番，穿上最华丽的服装。

近 groom, plume, primp

【考法3】 *vt.* 自满: to **take pride** or satisfaction in (oneself)

例 He always preen himself on his ancestry. 他总是因为他的血统而洋洋得意

近 gloat, plume, pride

反 efface 隐没，使不被人注意

preface [ˈprefəs]

【考法】 *n.* 序言: a **preliminary statement** or essay introducing a book that explains its scope, intention, or background and is usually written by the author

例 An informal brunch served as a preface to the three-day conference. 一顿非正式的早午餐作为为期三天的会议的序曲。

近 exordium, foreword, introduction, overture, preamble, prelude, prologue

反 epilogue 尾声

派 prefatory *adj.* 序言的

pregnant [ˈpregnənt]

【考法1】 *adj.* 重要的，意味深长的: weighty or significant; **full of meaning**

例 the pregnant phrases of the Bible《圣经》中充满哲理的话语

近 eloquent, meaningful, momentous, profound, revelatory, significant, suggestive

反 inane 空洞的

【考法 2】 *adj.* 怀孕的：**containing** a developing embryo, fetus, or unborn **offspring** within the body

例 Being pregnant represents great news, but it comes with a lot of responsibilities. 怀孕是件大好事，但是它也带来了许多的责任。

近 enceinte, expectant, expecting, gravid

派 pregnancy *n.* 怀孕

premeditate [ˌpriːˈmedɪteɪt]

【考法】 *vi.* 预先考虑：to think, **consider**, or deliberate **beforehand**

例 carefully premeditate each step of his plan 细致谋略他计划的每一步

近 deliberate, prearrange, prepare, preplan

反 disregard, ignore, neglect, omit, overlook 忽视

派 premeditation *n.* 谋略，事先考虑

preoccupation [priˌɑːkjuˈpeɪʃn]

【考法】 *n.* 非常关心，全神贯注：**extreme** or excessive **concern** with something

例 He kept sinking back into gloomy preoccupation. 他陷入了深深的忧虑之中。

近 absorption, engagement, engrossment, immersion

反 apathy, indifference, nonchalance, unconcern 漠不关心

派 preoccupied *adj.* 全神贯注的

preponderant [prɪˈpɑːndərənt]

【考法】 *adj.* 占优势的，更重要的：having **superior** weight, force, **importance**, or influence

例 a preponderant misconception 一个影响甚广的错误概念

近 dominant, paramount, predominant, prevalent, overruling

反 secondary, subsidiary 次要的

派 preponderance *n.* 优势地位

prepossessing [ˌpriːpəˈzesɪŋ]

【考法】 *adj.* 给人好感的，有魅力的：serving to **impress favorably**

例 He was fascinated by her prepossessing appearance at first sight. 他第一眼就被她迷人的外表吸引了。

近 alluring, attractive, appealing, captivating, charming, enchanting, pleasing, riveting

反 abhorrent, appalling, disgusting, hideous, loathsome, repellent, repulsive 令人反感的

派 unprepossessing *adj.* 不吸引人的

preposterous [prɪˈpɑːstərəs]

【考法】 *adj.* 荒谬的，不符合常理的：**contrary** to nature, reason, or **common sense**

例 a preposterous conclusion of quantum mechanics 量子力学里有悖于常理的结论

近 absurd, asinine, fallacious, fatuous, lunatic, ludicrous, insane, irrational, unreasonable

反 commonsensical 常识性的；reasonable, sensible 有道理的

presage [ˈpresɪdʒ]

【考法 1】 *n.* 征兆：something believed to be a **sign or warning** of a future event

例 The sight of the first robin is always a welcome presage of spring. 第一只知更鸟的出现总是迎接春天到来的象征。

近 augury, auspice, boding, foreboding, foreshadowing, portent, prefiguring

【考法 2】 *vt.* 预示，预言：to foretell or **predict**

例 The incident may presage war. 这个事件可能是战争的征兆

近 adumbrate, augur, forecast, foretell, portend, predict, prognosticate, prophesy

prescience [ˈpresiəns]

【考法】 *n.* 预知，先见：**knowledge** of actions or events **before** they occur

例 Most believers would probably agree that complete prescience is one of God's attributes. 所有的信徒大概都会同意上帝能够预见未来。

近 foresight, forethought, providence

反 improvidence, myopia, shortsightedness 目光短浅

Unit 5

prescription [prɪˈskrɪpʃn]
【考法】 *n.* 规定，传统的规矩：something prescribed as a **rule**; especially an inherited or established way of thinking, feeling, or doing
近 convention, custom, decree, law, regulation, rule
派 prescribe *v.* 开药方；设立规定

preservative [prɪˈzɜːrvətɪv]
【考法】 *n.* 防腐剂：an additive used to **protect against decay**, discoloration, or spoilage
例 contain no chemical preservative 不含化学防腐剂
派 preserve *v.* 保存

prestige [preˈstiːʒ]
【考法】 *n.* 声望，威望：the level of **respect** at which one is regarded by others
例 The prestige of the university has been irrevocably impaired by the plagiarism scandal. 这所大学的声望已经因剽窃丑闻而受到了不可挽回的损失。
近 credit, fame, influence, reputation
反 infamy 坏名声
派 prestigious *adj.* 有名望的

presumptuous [prɪˈzʌmptʃuəs]
【考法 1】 *adj.* 放肆的，冒昧的：**overstepping** due **bounds** (as of propriety or courtesy)
例 Under such a circumstance his demand for attention was utterly presumptuous. 在那种情况下他要求被关注是极其冒昧的。
近 audacious, bold, brash, impertinent, impudent, insolent, pompous, presuming
反 courteous, decorous, genteel, gracious, urbane 举止得体的，有礼貌的
【考法 2】 *adj.* 傲慢的：having a **feeling of superiority** that shows itself in an overbearing attitude
例 The presumptuous doctor didn't even bother to explain to me the treatment that I would be receiving. 傲慢的医生连给我说明我会接受何种治疗的耐性都没有。
近 assumptive, bumptious, cavalier, haughty, imperious, lofty, overweening, peremptory, supercilious
反 humble, modest 谦卑的

pretense [ˈpriːtens]
【考法 1】 *n.* 虚假，伪装：the act of **pretending**; a false appearance or action intended to **deceive**
例 There is too much pretense in his piety. 他的虔诚大多都是伪装。
近 affectation, camouflage, deceit, disguise, imposture, mask, masquerade
反 sincerity 真诚
【考法 2】 *n.* 自大，优越感：an **exaggerated sense of one's importance** that shows itself in the making of excessive or unjustified claims
近 assumption, hauteur, imperiousness, loftiness, lordliness, pomposity, superciliousness, superiority
反 humility, modesty 谦逊

preternatural [ˌpriːtərˈnætʃrəl]
【考法】 *adj.* 超乎寻常的：**surpassing** the normal or **usual**
例 They exhibited preternatural courage in face of danger. 他们在危险面前显示出了超乎寻常的勇气。
近 aberrant, abnormal, anomalous, extraordinary, phenomenal, magical, miraculous, unearthly
反 common, ordinary, prosaic 平凡的

prevail [prɪˈveɪl]
【考法】 *vi.* 盛行，战胜：to be **greater in strength** or influence
例 a custom that still prevails 依然盛行的传统
近 conquer, dominate, overcome, reign, triumph
反 yield 屈服；lose 失败
派 prevailing *adj.* 盛行的

prevalent [ˈprevələnt]

【考法】 *adj.* 流行的，普遍的：widely or **commonly** occurring, existing, **accepted**, or practiced

例 The kinds of accidents are frequently seen in places where snowmobiles are prevalent. 这类事故在摩托雪橇盛行的地区很常见。

近 conventional, dominant, common, popular, predominant, preponderant, prevailing, rife

反 absent, rare 缺少的，稀少的；unusual 与众不同的

派 prevalence *n.* 流行，遍及

prevaricate [prɪˈværɪkeɪt]

【考法】 *vi.* 支吾其词，撒谎：to stray from or **evade the truth**

例 During the hearings the witness did his best to prevaricate. 听证会上证人在竭尽全力地支吾其词。

近 equivocate, fabricate, falsify, lie, palter

派 prevarication *n.* 支吾其词

primordial [praɪˈmɔːrdiəl]

【考法】 *adj.* 原始的，最初的：being or **happening first** in sequence of time

例 primordial forms of life 最原始的生命形态

近 ancient, early, primal, primeval, primitive

反 late, recent 最近的

Unit 6

■ PRIMP ■ PRINCIPAL ■ PRISTINE ■ PRIVATION ■ PROBE
■ PROBITY ■ PROCLIVITY ■ PROCRASTINATE ■ PROCURE ■ PROD

primp [prɪmp]

【考法】 *v.* 精心打扮：to dress, **adorn**, or arrange in a careful or **finicky** manner

例 She primps for hours before a date. 她出门约会前要花数小时打扮。

近 preen, dress up

principal [ˈprɪnsəpl]

【考法】 *adj.* 主要的，重要的：first, **highest**, or foremost in **importance**, **rank**, worth, or degree

例 The region's principal city is getting hammered by a series of terrorist attacks. 该地区的中心城市正在被一系列恐怖袭击侵扰。

近 capital, cardinal, chief, dominant, grand, main, major, paramount, predominant, preeminent, primary

反 secondary, subordinate 次要的

pristine [ˈprɪstiːn]

【考法】 *adj.* 纯净的，质朴的，未被文明腐蚀的：remaining in a **pure** state; uncorrupted by civilization; remaining **free from dirt or decay**; clean

例 a pristine forest 一片未被文明影响的森林

近 immaculate, spotless, stainless, unsoiled, unstained, unsullied

反 tainted, squalid, contaminated, besmirched, corrupted by civilization 污染的，被文明腐蚀的

privation [praɪˈveɪʃn]

【考法】 *n.* 缺乏，穷困：**lack** of what is needed for existence

例 The constant privation of sleep was starting to affect his work. 长期以来的睡眠不足开始影响他的工作。

近 deprivation, loss

反 repletion 充满

probe [proʊb]

【考法】 *v./n.* 深入调查：a **penetrating** or critical **investigation**

例 probe into his background 深入调查他的背景

近 delve, explore, inquire; delving, disquisition, exploration, inquisition

probity [ˈproʊbəti]

【考法】 *n.* 正直：faithfulness to high **moral standards**

例 A person of indisputable probity should head the disciplinary panel. 一个真正正直的人应该来领导纪律委员会。

近 honesty, integrity, rectitude, righteousness, uprightness

反 unscrupulousness, shiftiness, baseness, dishonor, lowness 肆无忌惮，欺骗

proclivity	[prəˈklɪvəti]

【考法】 *n.* 癖性，偏好：a natural propensity or **inclination**; predisposition
例 show artistic proclivities at an early age 在很小的时候就表现出了对艺术的喜好
近 aptitude, disposition, leaning, partiality, penchant, predilection, propensity
反 aversion, antipathy, disinclination 厌恶，反感

procrastinate	[proʊˈkræstɪneɪt]

【考法】 *vi.* （因为懒散）拖延：to **put off** doing something, especially out of habitual carelessness or **laziness**
例 She procrastinated and missed the submission deadline. 她一直拖拖拉拉，导致错过了截止日期。

procure	[prəˈkjʊr]

【考法】 *vi.* 获得，取得：to **get possession** of
例 procured the prisoner's release 得到了释放囚犯的许可
近 acquire, attain, garner, knock down, pull down, bring in
反 relinquish, forfeit, lose 放弃

prod	[prɑːd]

【考法】 *vt.* 促使…行动：to try to **persuade** (someone) through earnest appeals to follow a course of action
例 The strike may prod the government into action. 罢工也许会迫使政府采取行动。
近 encourage, exhort, goad, nudge, prompt, spur, egg on
反 rein 抑制

Unit 7

■ PRODIGAL	■ PRODIGIOUS	■ PROFANE	■ PROFFER	■ PROFICIENT
■ PROFLIGATE	■ PROFUNDITY	■ PROFUSION	■ PROHIBITIVE	■ PROLIFERATE

prodigal	[ˈprɑːdɪɡl]

【考法 1】 *adj.* 挥霍的：recklessly **spendthrift**
例 prodigal outlays for her clothes 买衣服时挥金如土
近 extravagant, profligate, squandering, unthrifty, wasteful
反 frugal, parsimonious, conserving, economical, economizing, penny-pinching, scrimping, skimping, thrifty 节省的，吝啬的
派 prodigality *n.* 浪费，挥霍
反 penury 贫困; husbandry 节约
【考法 2】 *n.* 败家子：someone who **spends** money **freely** or foolishly
例 The million-dollar lottery winner was such a prodigal that his windfall was exhausted after only a few years. 靠彩票中了百万的赢家是个败家子，几年之内就把这笔意外之财全部花完了。
近 fritterer, high roller, profligate, spender, spendthrift, squanderer, waster, wastrel
反 economizer, penny-pincher 吝啬的人

prodigious	[prəˈdɪdʒəs]

【考法 1】 *adj.* 巨大的：impressively **great in size**, force, or extent; **enormous**
例 a prodigious supply of canned food kept in the basement 地下室贮存着的大量罐头食品
近 colossal, elephantine, enormous, gigantic, titanic, tremendous
反 slight 微小的
派 prodigy *n.* 天才，神童
【考法 2】 *adj.* 惊人的，了不起的：causing wonder or **astonishment**
例 stage magicians performing prodigious feats for rapt audiences 舞台魔术师在全神贯注的观众们面前表演惊人的技艺
近 amazing, astonishing, astounding, awesome, fabulous, miraculous, portentous, staggering, stunning, stupendous, sublime, surprising

profane	[prəˈfeɪn]

【考法 1】 *vt.* 亵渎：to **treat** (something sacred) with **abuse**, **irreverence**, or **contempt**
例 Invading troops profaned the altar by playing poker on it. 侵略军亵渎了祭坛，竟然在上面打扑克。
近 defile, violate
派 profaned *adj.* 被亵渎的
反 unviolated, inviolable 未被亵渎的，不可亵渎的
【考法 2】 *vt.* 滥用：to put to a **bad or improper use**
例 He profaned his considerable acting talents by appearing in some wretched movies. 在一些烂俗的电影里面出现简直就是浪费他的表演才华。
近 abuse, misemploy, misuse, pervert, prostitute

proffer [ˈprɑːfər]

【考法】 *v./n.* 献出，提供：to **offer** for acceptance; tender

例 She proffered her assistance in helping the two sides reach a compromise. 她在斡旋双方达成妥协过程中尽了力。

近 extend, give, tender, trot out

反 retain, withhold 保留

proficient [prəˈfɪʃnt]

【考法】 *adj.* 熟练的，精通的：having or marked by an **advanced** degree of **competence**, as in an art, vocation, profession, or branch of learning

例 proficient in translating foreign languages 精通外语翻译

近 accomplished, complete, expert, skilled, versed, virtuoso

反 inept, incompetent, amateur, inexperienced, inexpert, jackleg, unprofessional, unseasoned, unskilled 无能的，没有经验的

profligate [ˈprɑːflɪgət]

【考法1】 *adj./n.* 挥金如土的，挥霍的：recklessly **wasteful**; wildly extravagant

例 leading a profligate life 过着骄奢淫逸的生活

近 extravagant, high-rolling, spendthrift, squandering, thriftless, unthrifty, wasteful

反 parsimonious, provident, thrift, economical, frugal, conserving 吝啬的，节俭的

【考法2】 *n.* 败家子：someone who **spends money freely** or foolishly

例 Profligate who could not really afford the grand style he maintained at Monticello, Jefferson died deeply in debt. 再也支撑不了在蒙蒂塞洛之时的大手大脚的作风，败家子杰斐逊最终深陷债务危机。

近 fritterer, high roller, spender, spendthrift, squanderer, waster, wastrel

反 economizer, penny-pincher 吝啬的人

【考法3】 *n.* 堕落的人：a person who has sunk **below the normal moral standard**

例 A drunken profligate, he was given to wretched excess in every aspect of his life. 他是一个堕落的醉鬼，在生活的方方面面都日趋堕落

近 backslider, debauchee, decadent, deviate, libertine, pervert, profligate, rake, rakehell, rip

profundity [prəˈfʌndəti]

【考法】 *n.* 深奥，深刻：something profound or **abstruse**

例 His books are a mixture of playfulness and profundity. 他的作品都是搞笑和深刻的结合体。

近 deepness, profoundness

反 superficiality 肤浅

profusion [prəˈfjuːʒn]

【考法1】 *n.* 丰富，大量：the state of being profuse; **abundance**

例 snow falling in profusion 雪量很大

近 abundance, mass, plentitude, scads, volume, wealth

反 paucity 极小量

派 profuse *adj.* 丰富的

反 scanty 缺乏的

【考法2】 *n.* 挥霍，浪费：the quality or fact of being free or **wasteful** in the expenditure of money

例 In giving gifts to his girlfriend, he was generous to the point of profusion. 在给女朋友的礼物支出一项，他慷慨到了几乎奢侈的地步。

近 extravagancy, lavishness, prodigality, wastefulness

反 economy, frugality, penny-pinching 节俭

prohibitive [prəˈhɪbətɪv]

【考法1】 *adj.* 禁止的；阻止的：tending to **prohibit** or **restrain**

【考法2】 *adj.* (价格高得)抑制购买的：so high or burdensome as to discourage **purchase** or use

例 prohibitive prices 抑制购买的高价

proliferate [prəˈlɪfəreɪt]

【考法】 *vi.* 快速繁殖；激增：to **grow or multiply by rapidly** producing new tissue, parts, cells, or **offspring**; to increase at a rapid rate

例 Rumors about the accident proliferated on the Internet. 关于事故的小道消息在网上迅速扩散。

近 balloon, boom, build up, escalate, expand, mushroom, snowball

反 decrease in amount, dwindle, contract, decrease, diminish, lessen, recede, wane 数量减少，缩小

Unit 8

■ PROLIX   ■ PROLOGUE   ■ PROLONG   ■ PROMULGATE   ■ PROOFREAD
■ PROPAGATE   ■ PROPENSITY   ■ PROPHETIC   ■ PROPITIATE   ■ PROPITIOUS

prolix [ˈproʊlɪks]
【考法】 *adj.* 啰嗦的，冗长的：tending to speak or write at **excessive length**
例 He habitually transforms brief anecdotes into prolix sagas that exhaust his listeners. 他总是将简短的小趣事变成冗长的传说故事，让听众很疲倦。
近 diffuse, garrulous, rambling, verbose, windy
反 pithy, taciturn, terse, succinct, concise, extremely brief 精炼的，寡言的

prologue [ˈproʊlɔːg]
【考法】 *n.* 序言：the **preface** or introduction to a literary work
例 The burglary, which he committed while still a teen, was but a prologue to a wasted life of crime 他青少年时犯过的入室抢劫拉开了他偷盗生涯的序幕。
近 exordium, foreword, preamble, preface, prelude, proem, prolusion
反 epilogue 结尾

prolong [prəˈlɔːŋ]
【考法】 *vt.* 延长，拖延：to **lengthen** in extent, scope, or range
例 Additives are used to prolong the shelf life of packaged food. 添加剂被用来延长包装食品的保存期限。
近 elongate, lengthen, outstretch, protract, stretch, drag (out), draw out
反 abbreviate, abridge, curtail, cut, cut back, shorten, truncate 截短

promulgate [ˈprɑːmlgeɪt]
【考法】 *vt.* 正式宣布：to **make known** openly or publicly
例 The law was promulgated in June 1988. 法律在 1988 年 6 月出台。
近 annunciate, declare, enunciate, proclaim, publicize, herald
反 keep secret 保密

proofread [ˈpruːfriːd]
【考法】 *vt.* 校对：to read (copy or proof) in order to **find errors and mark corrections**
例 She proofread the paper carefully. 她仔细把论文校对了。

propagate [ˈprɑːpəgeɪt]
【考法 1】 *v.* 繁殖：to (cause to) continue or **increase** by sexual or asexual reproduction
例 The dams along the river are interfering with the salmon's ability to propagate. 河上的大坝影响了大马哈鱼的繁殖。
近 breed, multiply, reproduce
反 fail to multiply 繁殖失败
【考法 2】 *vt.* 传播，宣传：to cause to **spread out** and affect a greater number or greater area; extend
例 the various ways in which churches can propagate the faith 不同的宣传教义的方法
近 broadcast, circulate, disseminate
反 check 阻止

propensity [prəˈpensəti]
【考法】 *n.* 倾向，癖好：an often intense natural **inclination** or preference
例 a neighbor who has an unfortunate propensity for snooping 好管闲事的邻居
近 affinity, aptitude, bent, partiality, penchant, predilection, predisposition, proclivity
反 aversion 厌恶

prophetic [prəˈfetɪk]
【考法】 *adj.* 预言的，预示的：**foretelling** events: predictive
例 Those lower-than-expected sales numbers were a prophetic indicator of the financial trouble the company would soon be in. 那些低于预期的销售数字就是公司即将陷入金融危机的先兆。
近 predictive

propitiate [prəˈpɪʃieɪt]
【考法】 *vt.* 抚慰，劝解：to conciliate (an offended power); **appease**
例 The temple was built to honor the gods in times of plenty and to propitiate them in times of trouble. 该庙宇的作用是，丰收之时感谢神明，有难之时安抚神明。
近 appease, assuage, conciliate, disarm, mollify, placate
反 enrage, incense, inflame, infuriate, ire, madden, outrage, antagonize, arouse hostility 激怒

propitious [prə'pɪʃəs]
【考法】 *adj.* 吉祥的: **favorably** disposed: pointing toward a **happy outcome**
例 propitious sign 吉祥的征兆
近 auspicious, encouraging, fair, heartening, optimistic, promising, upbeat
反 dim, discouraging, disheartening, futureless, hopeless, inauspicious, unfavorable, unpromising, unpropitious 不吉利的

Unit 9

■ PROPONENT	■ PROPRIETY	■ PROSAIC	■ PROSCRIBE	■ PROSECUTION
■ PROSELYTIZE	■ PROSPECT	■ PROSPEROUS	■ PROSTRATE	■ PROTEAN

proponent [prə'poʊnənt]
【考法】 *n.* 建议者, 支持者: one who argues in **support** of something; an advocate
例 a proponent of the use of electric-powered cars 电动能源汽车的支持者
近 advocate, apostle, champion, expounder, espouser, friend, promoter, supporter, protagonist
反 adversary, antagonist, opponent, detractor 诋毁者, 反对者

propriety [prə'praɪəti]
【考法 1】 *n.* 礼节: **conformity** to what is **socially acceptable** in conduct or speech
例 When attending a wedding, there are certain proprieties that must be followed. 参加婚礼时, 有一些礼节需要遵守。
近 decorum, form, etiquette
反 impropriety, indecency, indecorum 不合礼节
【考法 2】 *n.* 适当, 得体: the quality or state of being especially **suitable or fitting**
例 I'm not sure about the propriety of serving champagne in these glasses. 我不确定在这些杯子里倒香槟是否得体。
近 appositeness, aptness, felicity, fitness, properness, rightness, seemliness, suitability
反 improperness, impropriety, inappositeness, inappropriateness, inaptness, infelicity, unfitness, unseemliness, unsuitability, wrongness 不得体

prosaic [prə'zeɪɪk]
【考法】 *adj.* 单调的, 常见的: being of the type that is encountered in the **normal course of events**
例 prosaic advice 老掉牙的建议
近 commonplace, everyday, routine, unexceptional, unremarkable, workaday
反 abnormal, exceptional, extraordinary, odd, out-of-the-way, strange, exciting, preternatural, ingenious, imaginary 不寻常的, 有独创性的

proscribe [proʊ'skraɪb]
【考法】 *vt.* 禁止, 排斥: to prohibit; **forbid**
例 acts proscribed by law 被法律禁止的行为
近 ban, enjoin, interdict, outlaw, prohibit
反 sanction, permit, allow, let, suffer 允许

prosecution [ˌprɑːsɪ'kjuːʃn]
【考法】 *n.* 实行, 执行: the **doing** of an action
例 oversee the prosecution of the president's foreign policy 监督总统对外政策的执行情况
近 accomplishment, achievement, discharge, enactment, execution, fulfillment, implementation, performance, perpetration, pursuance
反 nonfulfillment, nonperformance 不履行, 不完成

proselytize ['prɑːsələtaɪz]
【考法】 *v.* (使) 改变信仰: to persuade to **change** to one's **religious faith**
例 The efforts of early missionaries to proselytize the Native Americans of Minnesota were largely unproductive. 早期传教士对明尼苏达土著人进行的改变信仰的努力大多无功而返。
近 convert

prospect ['prɑːspekt]
【考法 1】 *v.* 探查, 勘探: to **go into** or range over for purposes of **discovery**
例 People had arrived in the valley to prospect for gold. 人们来到山谷淘金。
近 hunt, probe, search, skirr

【考法2】 *n.* 期待，期望的事物：the act or state of **looking forward to** some occurrence

例 The prospect of a quiet, restful Sunday ended when our basement flooded. 对一个宁静休闲的周日的期待被地下室涨水打破了。

近 anticipation, contemplation, expectancy

prosperous [ˈprɑːspərəs]

【考法】 *adj.* 成功的，繁盛的：marked by **vigorous growth** and **well-being** especially economically

例 The company had a prosperous year. 公司今年业绩斐然。

近 booming, flourishing, halcyon, lush, palmy, roaring, thriving

反 depressed 萧条的；impecunious 贫穷的

prostrate [ˈprɑːstreɪt]

【考法1】 *adj./vt.* 平躺(的)/使平躺：**lying flat** or at full length

例 He was lying prostrate on the bed. 他平躺在床上。

反 erect, upright 直立的

【考法2】 *adj./v.* 衰弱的/使衰竭：to reduce to extreme **weakness** or incapacitation

例 illness that prostrated an entire family 将整个家庭拖垮的疾病

近 debilitated, effete, enervated, enfeebled, languid, sapped; debilitate, devitalize, enervate, enfeeble, etiolate, sap, tire

反 fortify, strengthen, beef up 加强

protean [ˈproʊtiən]

【考法】 *adj.* 善变的；多才多艺的：displaying great **diversity** or **variety; versatile**

例 He loved to show off his protean talent. 他喜欢炫耀自己多样的才华。

近 adaptable, universal, all-around

反 static 固定的

Unit 10

| ■ PROTOCOL | ■ PROTRACT | ■ PROTRUDE | ■ PROTUBERANT | ■ PROVIDENT |
| ■ PROVIDENTIAL | ■ PROVINCIAL | ■ PROVISIONAL | ■ PROVISORY | ■ PROVOKE |

protocol [ˈproʊtəkɔːl]

【考法】 *n.* 正确的礼仪规范：a code of **correct conduct**

例 a breach of protocol 对社交礼仪的破坏

protract [prəˈtrækt]

【考法】 *vt.* 延长，拖长：to draw out or **lengthen** in time; **prolong**

近 elongate, lengthen, prolong, stretch, drag out, draw out

反 curtail, abridge, abbreviate, shorten, cut back 缩减

protrude [proʊˈtruːd]

【考法】 *vi.* 突出：to jut out; **project**; bulge

例 a handkerchief protruding from his breast pocket 手帕从他的上衣口袋里伸出来

近 bulge, overhang, poke, project, stand out, stick out

反 concave 凹陷

protuberant [proʊˈtuːbərənt]

【考法】 *adj.* 隆起的，凸出的：**thrusting out** from a surrounding or adjacent surface often as a rounded mass

例 protuberant eyes 暴鱼眼

反 depressed 下陷的

派 protuberance *n.* 隆起

反 concavity 凹陷

provident [ˈprɑːvɪdənt]

【考法1】 *adj.* 节俭的：**frugal; economical**

例 It is possible to be provident without being miserly. 人可以做到节俭但不吝啬。

近 economical, sparing, thrifty, farsighted, provident, scrimpy

反 profligate 挥霍的

【考法2】 *adj.* 有远见的：having or showing **awareness** of and preparation **for the future**

例 Her provident measures kept us safe while we waited out the hurricane. 她之前有远见的准备措施让我们在等待飓风结束的期间安然无恙。

近 farseeing, farsighted, forehanded, foreseeing, forethoughtful, prescient, proactive, visionary

反 half-baked, half-cocked, improvident, myopic, shortsighted 目光短浅的

providential [ˌprɑːvɪˈdenʃl]
【考法】 *adj.* 天意的，幸运(的)：happening as if through **divine intervention**
例 a providential escape 幸运的逃脱
近 lucky, fluky, fortuitous
反 unfortunate, mishap, hapless, ill-fated, ill-starred, luckless, star-crossed 不幸的

provincial [prəˈvɪnʃl]
【考法】 *adj./n.* 狭隘(的)：**limited** in **perspective**; narrow and self-centered
例 an artist who has been criticized for being provincial 一个被批评非常狭隘的艺术家
近 illiberal, insular, parochial, sectarian, narrow-minded
反 ecumenical, broad-minded, catholic, cosmopolitan, liberal, open, open-minded, receptive, tolerant 世界范围的，开放的，包容的

provisional [prəˈvɪʒənl]
【考法】 *adj.* 临时的：provided or serving only for the time being; **temporary**
例 He was appointed provisional executor of the industrialist's vast estate. 在遗嘱中，他被指定为那位实业家的庞大资产的临时保管人。
近 impermanent, interim, provisionary, short-term
反 long-term, permanent 永久的

provisory [prəˈvaɪzəri]
【考法】 *adj.* 有附带条件的；临时的：depending on a proviso; **conditional**; serving in a position for the time being
例 a provisory permit to block off the street while movie scenes were being shot 一个同意在电影拍摄期间封锁道路的临时许可
近 interim, provisional, provisionary, provisory
反 unconditional, long-term, permanent 无条件的，永久的

provoke [prəˈvoʊk]
【考法 1】 *vt.* 激怒：to **incite** to **anger** or resentment
例 His teasing finally provoked her. 他的调戏最终把她激怒了。
近 arouse, excite, incite, instigate, pique, stimulate, stir, fire up
【考法 2】 *vt.* 驱使，激起：to **stir** to action or **feeling**
例 rankings that are sure to provoke an argument among film critics 必将引发影评家们争论的排名
近 abet, ferment, foment, instigate, stir up, whip up

If you put out your hands, you are a laborer; if you put out your hands and mind, you are a craftsperson; if you put out your hands, mind, heart and soul, you are an artist.

如果你用双手工作，你是一个劳力；如果你用双手和头脑工作，你是一个工匠；如果你用双手和头脑工作，并且全身心投入，你就是一个艺术家。

——美国电影 *American Heart and Soul*

List 20

"生如夏花，在追求结果绚烂的同时享受过程中的美好。"

（杨璐，2008 年 10 月，Verbal 800, Quantitative 800, AW 5.5,

录取学校：Massachusetts Inst. of Technology）

Unit 1

■ PROWESS　　■ PROWL　　■ PRUDE　　■ PRUDENT　　■ PRUDISH
■ PRUNE　　■ PRY　　■ PSEUDONYM　　■ PSYCHOLOGY　　■ PUCKER

prowess	[ˈpraʊəs]
【考法】	n. 英勇，勇敢：**superior** strength, **courage**, or daring, especially in battle
例	his prowess on the football field 他在球场上过人的勇气
近	bravery, courageousness, daring, gallantry, guts, intrepidity
反	timid, cowardice, cravenness, dastardliness, poltroonery 胆小，懦弱

prowl	[ˈpraʊl]
【考法】	v. 潜行于，巡游以猎取食物；徘徊：to **roam through** stealthily, as in **search of prey** or plunder
例	I prowled the shop looking for sales. 我在商店里转悠，寻找打折商品。

prude	[pruːd]
【考法】	n. 过分正经的人：一个过分关心自己是否得体、谦逊或正确的人：a person who is **greatly concerned** with **seemly behavior and morality** especially regarding sexual matters
例	The racy sitcom frequently satirizes exactly the sort of prude who would like to see the show taken off the air. 这部活泼生动的情景喜剧正是在讽刺那种过分正经的人，他们希望取消这种娱乐性节目。
近	bluenose, moralist, puritan
反	immoralist 不道德的人

prudent	[ˈpruːdnt]
【考法 1】	adj. 明智的：marked by **wisdom** or **judiciousness**; **wise**
例	prudent advice 明智的建议
近	advisable, desirable, judicious, politic, tactical, intelligent
反	foolish 傻的
【考法 2】	adj. 小心谨慎的，审慎的：marked by **circumspection**

prudish	[ˈpruːdɪʃ]
【考法】	adj. 过分守礼的：marked by **prudery**
例	By the prudish standards of the 19th century, any depiction of the nude was scandalous. 根据 19 世纪的保守标准，任何对裸露的刻画描述都是下流无耻的。
近	nice-nelly, prim, puritanical

prune	[pruːn]
【考法 1】	n. 梅干：a **plum dried** or capable of drying without fermentation
【考法 2】	vt. 修剪；修整：to cut off or remove dead or living parts or branches of （a plant, for example）to improve shape or growth
例	The students were asked to prune their essays. 学生们被要求修改文章。
近	shave, shear, snip, trim

pry	[praɪ]
【考法】	vi. 刺探，打听：to look or **inquire closely**, **curiously**, or impertinently
例	Don't go prying into other people's business. 别去打探别人的事。
近	interlope, intermeddle, intrude, nose, obtrude, snoop

pseudonym	[ˈsuːdənɪm]
【考法】	n. 假名，笔名：a **fictitious** name
例	Mark Twain is the pseudonym of the American writer Samuel L. Clemens. 马克·吐温是美国作家塞缪尔·L·克莱门斯的笔名。
近	alias, nom de guerre

psychology [saɪˈkɑːlədʒi]
【考法 1】 *n.* 心理学: the **science** that deals with **mental processes and behavior**
例 She studied psychology in college. 她大学专业是心理学。
【考法 2】 *n.* 心理战术: **subtle tactical action** or argument used to manipulate or **influence** another
例 He used poor psychology on his employer when trying to make the point. 他表达观点时，对老板用了拙劣的心理战术。

pucker [ˈpʌkər]
【考法】 *v.* 撅(嘴)，(使)收缩: to (cause to) become gathered, **contracted**, and wrinkled
例 pucker my lips 撅起嘴

Unit 2

■ PUCKISH　　■ PUERILE　　■ PUISSANCE　　■ PULCHRITUDE　　■ PULVERIZE
■ PUN　　■ PUNCTILIOUS　　■ PUNDIT　　■ PUNGENT　　■ PUNY

puckish [ˈpʌkɪʃ]
【考法】 *adj.* 淘气的，顽皮的: **mischievous**; **impish**
例 She had a puckish smile on her face. 她脸上挂着顽皮的笑容。
近 devilish, impish, prankish, waggish
反 sober, grave, staid 严肃的

puerile [ˈpjʊrəl]
【考法】 *adj.* 幼稚的，不成熟的: **immature**; lacking in adult experience or maturity
例 puerile remarks 幼稚的评论
近 adolescent, gréen, immature, unfledged, unformed, unripened
反 adult, experienced, grown-up, mature, ripe, sagacious 睿智的，成熟的

puissance [ˈpwɪsəns]
【考法】 *n.* 权力: **power**; might
例 The president pledged to put the full puissance of the nation into the war effort. 总统下令全国进入战争状态。
近 force, might, potency, strength, vigor, sinew
反 powerlessness, impotence, weakness 无力

pulchritude [ˈpʌlkrɪtjuːd]
【考法】 *n.* 美丽: great physical **beauty** and appeal
反 ugliness, homeliness, hideousness 丑陋，平庸

pulverize [ˈpʌlvəraɪz]
【考法】 *vt.* 将…研磨成粉；将…彻底摧毁: to pound, crush or grind to powder or dust; to bring to a **complete end** the physical soundness, existence, or usefulness of
例 Bits of pulverized rock filled the air. 被碾碎的岩石碎片充斥在空气里。
反 solidify, build, construct, erect, put up, raise, rear, set up 硬化，构建

pun [pʌn]
【考法】 *n.* 双关语: the usually **humorous** use of a word in such a way as to suggest two or more of its meanings or the meaning of another word similar in sound
例 He's a skillful pilot whose career has—no pun intended—really taken off. 她是个技术娴熟的飞行员，飞行生涯——没有别的意思——真正腾飞了。

punctilious [pʌŋkˈtɪliəs]
【考法】 *adj.* 注意细节的，一丝不苟的: strictly **attentive** to minute **details** of form in action or conduct
近 decorous, proper, starchy, stilted
反 remiss, slipshod, casual, easygoing, informal, laid-back, unceremonious 粗心的

pundit [ˈpʌndɪt]
【考法】 *n.* 权威人士，专家: a person who gives **opinions** in an **authoritative** manner usually through the mass media
例 The new laptop has gotten a thumbs-up from industry pundits. 新出的笔记本电脑受到了业界专家的一致好评。
近 savant, scholar

pungent [ˈpʌndʒənt]
【考法】 *adj.* 辛辣的，讽刺的: marked by the **use of wit** that is intended to **cause hurt feelings**
例 pungent language 辛辣讽刺的语言
近 acerbic, acid, acrid, caustic, mordant, sardonic, scalding, scathing

puny ['pjuːni]

【考法】 *adj.* 微小的，弱小的：of **inferior size**, strength, or significance; **weak**

例 I wouldn't mess with him—he makes bodybuilders look puny in comparison. 我不敢招惹他——其他健身的人和他比起来都像小孩。

近 diminutive, dwarfish, slight, subnormal

反 enormous, considerable, grand, husky, king-size, outsize, overscale, substantial, whacking, whopping 巨大的

Unit 3

■ PURITY	■ PURLIEU	■ PURLOIN	■ PURVEY	■ PUSILLANIMOUS
■ QUACK	■ QUAFF	■ QUAIL	■ QUALIFY	■ QUANDARY

purity ['pjʊrəti]

【考法】 *n.* 纯净；纯洁；纯正：the quality or state of being **clean**; the quality or state of being **morally pure**

例 struggle to live a life of purity while surrounded by wickedness 即使周围充满邪恶，也要使自己的生命纯粹、完美

近 chasteness, immaculacy, innocence, modesty

反 impurity, unchasteness, unchastity 堕落，没有节操

派 impurity *n.* 杂质；purist *n.* 纯粹主义者

purlieu ['pɜːrluː]

【考法 1】 *n.* 常去的地方：a place for spending time or for **socializing**

例 The restaurant, the preferred purlieu of the theatergoing crowd, is always packed an hour or two before showtime. 观剧的人群经常去的那间餐厅总是在演出开始前一两个小时爆满。

近 haunt, rendezvous, resort, stamping ground, stomping ground

【考法 2】 *n.* 临近的地区：an **adjoining region** or space

例 We stopped at one of the several pubs in the purlieus of the stadium. 我们在体育馆附近的一间酒吧前停下来。

近 backyard, neighborhood, vicinage, vicinity

purloin [pɜːr'lɔɪn]

【考法】 *vt.* 偷窃：to **steal**, often in a violation of trust

例 fearing that someone might attempt to purloin a copy of the script for the show's season finale 害怕该剧的完季那集剧本被盗

近 appropriate, filch, pilfer, snitch, thieve

purvey [pər'veɪ]

【考法】 *v.* (大量)供给，供应：to **supply** (food, for example); furnish

例 a little shop purveying handmade merchandise 出售手工商品的小店

pusillanimous [ˌpjuːsɪ'lænɪməs]

【考法】 *adj.* 懦弱的，胆小得令人鄙视的：lacking courage and resolution, marked by contemptible **timidity**

例 pusillanimous politicians who vote according to whichever way the political wind is blowing 胆小懦弱的政客，舆论风吹向谁就投票给谁

近 craven, dastardly, gutless, poltroon, recreant, spineless

反 brave, courageous, daring, dauntless, doughty, gallant, gutsy, intrepid, lionhearted, stalwart, stout, stout-hearted, valiant, valorous 勇敢的

quack [kwæk]

【考法】 *n.* 骗子医生，江湖郎中：a **pretender** to medical skill

例 Don't bother to see that guy, as I've heard he's a quack with no actual training. 别再找他看病了，我听说他就是个没有真才实学的江湖郎中。

近 charlatan, fake, fraud, hoaxer, mountebank, phony

反 honest practitioner 诚实从业者

quaff [kwæf]

【考法】 *vt.* 大口地喝：to **drink** (a beverage) **heartily**

例 He stopped at a bar and quaffed a few beers. 他在酒吧停下来，痛饮了几杯啤酒。

近 gulp, swig, swill

quail [kweɪl]

【考法】 *vi.* 胆怯，畏缩：to shrink back in **fear**; **cower**

例 She quailed at the thought of seeing him again. 她想到还要再见他就害怕。

近 blench, cringe, recoil, shrink, wince

反 become resolute, give bold 变得坚决、大胆

qualify [ˈkwɑːlɪfaɪ]

【考法 1】 *vt.* 限定：to **reduce** from a **general** to a particular or restricted form

派 qualified *adj.* 有限制的，不完全的

例 qualified support 有限的支持

反 unreserved, absolute, categorical 无保留的，不受限制的

【考法 2】 *vt.* 使有资格，使有能力：to **make competent**（as by training, skill, or ability）for a particular office or function

例 Raising five children has qualified her to be an advice columnist on parenting. 抚养五个孩子的经历让她成为了育儿板块的专栏作家。

近 equip, fit, prepare, ready, season, train

quandary [ˈkwɑːndəri]

【考法】 *n.* 困惑，窘境：a state of **perplexity** or **doubt**

例 I've had two job offers, and I'm in a real quandary about/over which one to accept. 我有两个工作机会，但实在是进退两难，不知道应该选哪一个。

近 catch-22, double bind

反 state of complete certainty 胸有成竹

Unit 4

| ■ QUARANTINE | ■ QUARRY | ■ QUASH | ■ QUAVER | ■ QUELL |
| ■ QUENCH | ■ QUERULOUS | ■ QUIBBLE | ■ QUIESCENT | ■ QUIXOTIC |

quarantine [ˈkwɔːrəntiːn]

【考法】 *n.* 隔离：enforced **isolation** or restriction of free movement imposed to prevent the spread of contagious disease

例 The cows will be kept in quarantine for another two weeks. 牛群还需要被隔离观察两周。

quarry [ˈkwɔːri]

【考法 1】 *n.* 采石场：an open excavation or pit from which **stone is obtained** by digging, cutting, or blasting

【考法 2】 *n.* 目标，猎物：an object of **pursuit**

例 a hunter relentlessly tracking his quarry 无情捕杀猎物的猎人

近 prey

反 predator 捕猎者

quash [kwɔːʃ]

【考法】 *vt.* 镇压，阻止：to **put a stop to**（something）by the use of force

例 quash a rebellion 镇压一次叛变

近 repress, squelch, subdue, suppress, clamp down on, crack down on

反 engender, foment 引起，煽动

quaver [ˈkweɪvər]

【考法】 *vi.* 发颤音：to speak in a **quivering voice**; utter a quivering sound

例 His voice quavered during the speech. 整个演讲过程中，他的声音都是颤抖的。

近 tremble, trill

quell [kwel]

【考法 1】 *vt.* 压制：to put down forcibly; **suppress**

例 quell riot 镇压骚乱

近 quash, repress, squash, squelch, subdue, suppress, clamp down on, crack down on

【考法 2】 *vt.* 使平静，使安静：to **pacify**; quiet

例 quell fears 减轻害怕

近 dumb, extinguish, hush, mute, settle

反 foment, instigate, rouse, incite 煽动

quench [kwentʃ]

【考法 1】 *vt.* 熄灭：to **put out**（a fire, for example）; extinguish

例 We thoroughly quenched the campfire before we headed to bed. 我们在睡前把营火完全熄灭了。

近 blanket, douse, put out, snuff out

反 fire, ignite, inflame, kindle, light 点燃

【考法2】 *vt.* 使满足：to **put a complete end to**（a physical need or desire）

例 This lemonade really quenches my thirst. 这杯柠檬汁真是解渴。

近 assuage, sate, satiate, slake

querulous [ˈkwerələs]

【考法】 *adj.* 抱怨的，爱发牢骚的：habitually **complaining**

例 a querulous voice 抱怨的声音

近 crabby, cranky, grouchy, grumpy

反 forbearing, long-suffering, patient, stoic, tolerant, uncomplaining 容忍的

quibble [ˈkwɪbl]

【考法1】 *vi.* 吹毛求疵：to find fault or **criticize** for petty reasons; **cavil**

例 She spent the entire evening quibbling about the historical inaccuracies in the television series on World War II. 她一整晚都在对那部关于二战的电视剧里的历史错误吹毛求疵。

近 carp, cavil, fuss, niggle, nitpick

【考法2】 *n.* 牵强之词：微不足道的差别或不切中要点的异议，小反对：a **minor objection** or criticism

例 My only quibble about the trip was that it rained a lot. 我对这次旅行唯一的小不满就是下雨有点多。

quiescent [kwiˈesnt]

【考法】 *adj.* 平静的，静止的：being **quiet**, still, or at rest; **inactive**

例 a group of quiescent loungers 一群平静懒散的流浪汉

近 dull, inert, lethargic, sluggish, torpid

反 rambunctious, tumultuous, active, restlessly active 骚乱的

quixotic [kwɪkˈsɑːtɪk]

【考法】 *adj.* 不切实际的，空想的：having or marked by a tendency to be guided **more by ideals than by reality**

例 She had quixotic dreams about the future. 她对未来有着幻想。

近 impractical, ideal, romantic, starry, utopian, visionary

反 clear-eyed, clear-sighted 聪明的

Unit 5

■ QUOTA	■ QUOTIDIAN	■ RABBLE	■ RABID	■ RACY
■ RAFFISH	■ RAFFLE	■ RAGE	■ RAGGED	■ RAIL

quota [ˈkwoʊtə]

【考法】 *n.* 配额，限额：a **proportional** part or share

例 The department set new sales quotas in May. 部门设定了五月的销售定额。

近 allowance, portion, proportion

反 unlimited number 不限数量

quotidian [kwoʊˈtɪdiən]

【考法】 *adj.* 每日的；平凡的：everyday; **commonplace**

例 plagued by a quotidian coughing 每天被咳嗽困扰

近 commonplace, everyday, frequent, ordinary, routine, ubiquitous

反 remarkable, striking, extraordinary, unusual, rare, infrequent, seldom 不平常的

rabble [ˈræbl]

【考法】 *n.* 混乱的人群；暴民；下层民众：a **disorganized** or disorderly **crowd of people**; the lowest class of people

例 The crown prince was reminded that even the rabble deserved his attention and compassion. 太子应该知道即使是草民，也值得他的关注和同情。

近 ragtag and bobtail, riffraff, scum, rag, trash, unwashed

rabid [ˈreɪbɪd]

【考法】 *adj.* 狂热的，不冷静的：extremely zealous or enthusiastic; **fanatical**

例 soccer fans whose rabid enthusiasm makes them go berserk when their team wins 不冷静的粉丝们在球队获胜以后变得很狂暴

近 delirious, ferocious, feverish, fierce, frantic, frenetic, violent

反 logical, detached 合常理的，客观的

racy [ˈreɪsi]

【考法】 *adj.* 活泼生动的：**vigorous**; lively

例 vivid writing and a racy plot that keeps readers turning the pages 栩栩如生的手法和生动新鲜的情节让读者手不释卷

近 animate, brisk, frisky, jaunty, perky, spirited, vivacious

反 tame, dead, inactive, inanimate, lackadaisical, languid, languorous, leaden, lifeless, limp, listless, spiritless, vapid 乏味的，死气沉沉的

raffish [ˈræfɪʃ]

【考法】 *adj.* 低俗的：marked by or suggestive of flashy vulgarity or **crudeness**

例 The dowager cringed at the thought of raffish tourists tromping all over her Persian rugs. 孀居贵妇一想到低俗的游客践踏她的波斯地毯就痛苦不已。

近 crass, lowbred, uncouth, uncultivated, uncultured, unpolished, unrefined, vulgar

反 civilized, cultivated, cultured, genteel, polished, refined, ultrarefined, well-bred 有教养的

raffle [ˈræfl]

【考法】 *n.* 垃圾，废物：**discarded** or **useless** material

例 The front lawn was littered with the raffle that the workers had left behind. 前院的草坪上满是工人们丢的垃圾。

近 chaff, deadwood, debris, dreck, dross, effluvium, litter, offal, offscouring, refuse, riffraff, rubbish, scrap, spilth

rage [reɪdʒ]

【考法】 *n./v.* 暴怒：**violent** and uncontrolled **anger**

例 Her rages rarely last more than a few minutes. 她的暴躁来得快去得也快。

近 agitation, deliriousness, delirium, distraction, furor, hysteria, rampage

ragged [ˈrægɪd]

【考法 1】 *adj.* 衣衫褴褛的：dressed in tattered or **threadbare clothes**

例 A ragged coat may cover an honest man. 不能以衣着取人。

近 raggedy, ragtag, tattered, tatterdemalion, shabby

反 kempt, neat, trim 整洁的

【考法 2】 *adj.* 凹凸不平的，不光滑的：**not** having a level or **smooth** surface

例 She cut herself on the ragged edge of the tin can's lid. 她被罐头盖的锋利边缘割伤了。

近 broken, bumpy, coarse, irregular, jagged, lumpy, pebbly, rough, roughened, rugged, scraggy

反 even, flat, level, plane 平整的；smooth 光滑的

rail [reɪl]

【考法】 *vi.* 怒骂，猛烈抨击：to **revile or scold** in harsh, insolent, or abusive language

例 We could hear the cook in the kitchen railing against his assistant and wondered if we'd ever get our food. 我们可以听到厨师在厨房怒斥他的助手，由此我们怀疑我们点的菜还能不能做好。

近 baste, berate, castigate, chastise, hammer, lambaste, rebuke, reprimand, reproach, upbraid

反 accredit, applaud, commend, eulogize, extol, laud, praise 表扬，赞扬

派 raillery *n.* 善意的打闹

Unit 6

| ■ RAKISH | ■ RAMBLE | ■ RAMBUNCTIOUS | ■ RAMSHACKLE | ■ RANCOR |
| ■ RANDOM | ■ RANKLE | ■ RANT | ■ RAPACIOUS | ■ RAPPORT |

rakish [ˈreɪkɪʃ]

【考法】 *adj.* 放荡的，行为不检点的：having or showing **lowered moral character** or standards; dissolute

例 He wore his hat at a rakish angle. 他帽子戴得吊儿郎当的。

近 debased, debauched, demoralized, depraved, dissolute, libertine, perverse, perverted, reprobate

反 good, moral, pure, righteous, virtuous 有美好品德的；uncorrupted 不放荡的

派 rake *n.* 行为不检点的人，放荡的人

ramble [ˈræmbl]

【考法 1】 *vi.* 漫步，漫游：to **move aimlessly** from place to place

例 ramble under the starlight 在星光下漫步 ‖ ramble around Beijing for a week 在北京四处漫游一周

近 amble, cruise, drift, float, meander, perambulate, roam, saunter, stroll, traipse, wander

【考法 2】 *vi.* 漫谈；长篇大论(并经常离题)地说或写：to talk at length **without** sticking to **a topic** or getting to a point
例 ramble on about dating, homework, movies, and the local football team 扯一些关于约会、作业、电影以及本地橄榄球队的闲谈
近 blather, chat, chatter, drivel, maunder, patter, prattle

rambunctious [ræmˈbʌŋkʃəs]
【考法】 *adj.* 喧闹的，骚乱的：being rough or **noisy** in a high-spirited way
例 That beach is often taken over by packs of rambunctious young people, so don't go there expecting peace and quiet. 那个海滩经常被一帮吵闹的年轻人占领，所以不要指望过去能享受到平静和安宁。
近 boisterous, clamorous, raucous, riotous, rowdy, tumultuous, turbulent
反 orderly 有秩序的；calm, noiseless, peaceful, placid, quiet, serene, silent, soundless, tranquil 安静的

ramshackle [ˈræmʃækl]
【考法】 *adj.* 摇摇欲坠的：appearing **ready to collapse**; rickety
例 a ramshackle cabin in the woods 树林中摇摇欲坠的小木屋
近 rickety, shaky, tottering
反 concrete, firm, solid, sturdy 坚固的；stable 稳定的

rancor [ˈræŋkər]
【考法】 *n.* 敌意，深仇：a bitter deep-seated **ill will**
例 A good man terminates a friendship without rancor. 君子绝交不记仇。
近 animosity, animus, antagonism, antipathy, bitterness, gall, grudge, hostility, jaundice
反 amity, harmony, goodwill, rapport, rapprochement 和睦，友好；friendship 友谊

random [ˈrændəm]
【考法】 *adj.* 随机的，随意的：**lacking** a definite plan, purpose, or **pattern**
例 We received several answers and picked one at random. 我们收到了若干答案，并随机抽取了一个。
例 aimless, arbitrary, desultory, erratic, haphazard, scattered, slapdash, stray
反 methodical, orderly, organized, regular, systematic, systematized 井然有序的，系统化的
派 randomly *adv.* 随机地；randomize *v.* 随机挑选、排列

rankle [ˈræŋkl]
【考法】 *vt.* 激怒：to **cause anger**, irritation, or deep bitterness
例 It rankles me when some schools can't even afford paper and pencils for the students. 当我获悉有些学校连纸张和铅笔都无法提供给学生时，我感到十分愤怒。
近 aggravate, enrage, exasperate, incense, inflame, infuriate, ire, madden, rile, roil
反 delight, gratify, please 使愉悦；appease, assuage, conciliate, mollify, placate, propitiate 安抚

rant [rænt]
【考法 1】 *n.* (尤指长时间的)训斥，责骂：a long **angry** speech or **scolding**
例 After complaining about the hotel's lousy service, the woman went off on another rant about the condition of her room. 在抱怨完旅店差劲的服务之后，她继续对房间的条件开骂。
近 castigation, diatribe, harangue, lambasting, philippic, reprimand, reproach, vituperation
反 encomium, eulogy, panegyric, rhapsody, tribute 赞美之词
【考法 2】 *vi.* 怒吼：to speak or write in a **noisy, angry or violent manner**
例 The old expert ranted that nobody paid any attention to his opinion. 老专家怒气冲冲地叫嚷说没人听取他的观点。
近 bluster, fulminate, huff, rave, roar, spout
反 grumble, murmur, mutter 低声抱怨

rapacious [rəˈpeɪʃəs]
【考法 1】 *adj.* 食量大的，贪食的：having a **huge appetite**
例 The manager at the buffet restaurant was apparently astonished by a team of rapacious professional basketball players. 自助餐厅的经理很明显被那一队胃口巨大的职业篮球队员们震惊了。
近 edacious, esurient, gluttonous, greedy, ravenous, voracious
【考法 2】 *adj.* 过度贪婪的：excessively grasping or **covetous**
例 Some companies are rapacious and hardly looking for the long-term value. 有些公司十分贪婪，而且不考虑长期利益。
近 acquisitive, avaricious, avid, coveting, covetous, grasping, mercenary, moneygrubbing
反 content, sated, satiated, satisfied 心满意足的
派 rapaciousness *n.* 贪婪

rapport [ræˈpɔːr]

【考法】 *n.* 和睦，友好：a **friendly relationship** marked by ready communication and mutual understanding

例 His good rapport with his students was one of the reasons why the school board named him Teacher of the Year. 他和学生的关系和睦是他被校董会提名为"年度教师"的原因之一。

近 amity, communion, concord, fellowship, harmony, rapprochement

反 animosity, antagonism, antipathy, bitterness, enmity, hostility, jaundice, rancor 敌意

Unit 7

- RAPPROCHEMENT
- RAPSCALLION
- RAPT
- RAREFY
- RASH
- RASPY
- RATIFY
- RATIOCINATION
- RATION
- RATIONAL

rapprochement [ˌræprouʃˈmɑːn]

【考法】 *n.* 和睦，友好：establishment of or state of having **cordial relations**

例 a new era of rapprochement between China and Russia 中俄两国睦邻友好关系的新纪元

近 amity, communion, concord, fellowship, harmony, rapport

反 animosity, antagonism, antipathy, bitterness, enmity, hostility, jaundice, rancor 敌意

rapscallion [ræpˈskæliən]

【考法】 *n.* 流氓，恶棍：a mean, **evil**, or unprincipled person

例 an unsafe place frequented by drunkards and rapscallions 一个酒鬼和流氓经常造访的不安全的地方

近 brute, devil, evildoer, fiend, knave, miscreant, rascal, reprobate, rogue, savage, scamp, varlet, wretch

反 saint 圣人；cavalier, chevalier（尤指对女士）彬彬有礼的绅士

rapt [ræpt]

【考法 1】 *adj.* 狂喜的，狂热的：experiencing or marked by overwhelming usually **pleasurable emotion**

例 a rock band that still attracts rapt crowds 一个仍然拥有着狂热粉丝的摇滚乐队

近 elated, elevated, enraptured, entranced, euphoric, exhilarated, intoxicated, rapturous, rhapsodic

反 crestfallen, dejected, depressed 沮丧的；doleful, gloomy, melancholy, mournful, woeful 哀伤的

【考法 2】 *adj.* 全神贯注的：**deeply absorbed**; engrossed

例 With a mixture of delight and awe, the rapt children stared at the chick in the incubator breaking out of its shell. 怀着愉快和敬畏的复杂心理，孩子们全神贯注地盯着孵化箱中的小鸡破壳而出。

近 absorbed, concentrated, deep, engrossed, enthralled, focused, immersed, intent, observant

反 absent, abstracted, distracted, inattentive 不专心的；apathetic, disinterested, unconcerned 冷漠的，不关心的

rarefy [ˈrerfaɪ]

【考法】 *vt.* 使稀薄：to **make rare**, thin, porous, or less dense: to expand without the addition of matter

例 rarefy the air 使空气变得稀薄

近 attenuate, dilute, thin

反 concentrate, condense 使稠密，浓缩

派 rarefaction *n.* 稀薄，稀疏

rash [ræʃ]

【考法】 *adj.* 草率的，仓促的：marked by or proceeding from undue haste or **lack** of deliberation or **caution**

例 That was too rash a move: for now you've lost your bishop and probably the whole chess game. 那一招棋着实是太草率了，现在你丢掉了象，很有可能会输掉整场比赛。

近 cursory, gadarene, headlong, hurried, overhasty, precipitate, precipitous, rushed

反 deliberate 慎重考虑的；leisurely, unhurried, unrushed 从容不迫的，不慌不忙的

派 rashly *adv.* 草率地，仓促地

raspy [ˈræspi]

【考法 1】 *adj.* 声音刺耳的：**harsh** and dry in sound

例 The dying man was speaking in a raspy and barely discernible voice. 将死的人在用一种沙哑刺耳且难以听清的语调说话。

近 cacophonous, coarse, croaky, harsh, grating, gravelly, gruff, husky, rasping, rusty, scratchy, throaty

反 mellifluous, sweet 声音甜美的；gentle, soft, tender 声音轻柔的

【考法 2】 *adj.* 容易生气的：**easily irritated** or annoyed

例 Overwork tends to make him raspy. 过度的工作让他变得烦躁易怒。

近 choleric, fiery, grouchy, irascible, peevish, pettish, petulant, prickly, ratty, testy

反 agreeable, amiable, good-natured, good-tempered, well-disposed 脾气/性格好的

ratify ['rætɪfaɪ]

【考法】 *vt.* (官方地)认可，批准：to give **official acceptance** of as satisfactory

例 Lincoln's home state of Illinois was the first to ratify the 13th Amendment to the U.S. Constitution, which provided for the abolition of slavery. 林肯的老家——伊利诺伊是美国第一个通过《宪法第十三修正案》的州，该决案提供了废除奴隶制的法律基础。

近 accredit, approbate, authorize, certify, endorse, finalize, formalize, pass, sanction, validate, warrant

反 decline, deny, disallow, disapprove, negative, reject, veto 否决

派 ratification *n.* 正式批准

ratiocination [ˌreɪʃiˌoʊsɪ'neɪʃn]

【考法】 *n.* 推理：the **thought processes** that have been established as leading to valid solutions to problems

例 As an expert in ratiocination, the detective Sherlock Holmes has few rivals. 作为推理专家，大侦探福尔摩斯可谓无人能及。

近 deduction, intellection, reason, reasoning, sense

ration ['ræʃn]

【考法1】 *n.* 定额供应量，配给量：an **amount allotted** or made available especially from a limited supply

例 The meat ration was down to one pound per person per week. 肉的人均供给量降至了每周一磅。

近 allotment, allowance, apportionment, portion, provision, quota, share

【考法2】 *vt.* 按比例分配：to give as a **share or portion**

例 The region has had to ration water during times of drought. 干旱时该地区不得不按比例分配水资源。

近 allocate, allot, allow, apportion, assign, distribute, lot

反 keep, retain, withhold 扣留，拒绝给予

rational ['ræʃnəl]

【考法1】 *adj.* 合乎逻辑的：consistent with or based on reason; **logical**

例 He insisted there was a rational explanation for the strange creaking noises and that there were no such things as ghosts. 他坚持认为奇怪的咯吱声一定有一个合理的解释，而不是所谓的鬼在作怪。

近 analytic, coherent, consequent, logical, reasonable, sensible, sound, valid, well-founded, well-grounded

反 illogical, incoherent, inconsequent, invalid, irrational, unreasonable, unsound, weak 不合逻辑的

【考法2】 *adj.* 理性的：**based on** sound **reasoning** or information

例 Betting all of your savings on the lottery is not a rational move. 把你所有的存款赌在彩票上可不是一个理智的决定。

近 commonsensical, firm, informed, just, justified, levelheaded, sober, solid

反 groundless, unfounded, unjustified 无理由的，无根据的

派 rationalize *vt.* 使合理化；找借口

Unit 8

■ RAVE	■ RAVEL	■ RAVISH	■ RAZE	■ REACT
■ REACTIONARY	■ REAM	■ REAP	■ REASSURE	■ REBUFF

rave [reɪv]

【考法1】 *vi.* 狂热赞扬：to make an **exaggerated display of affection** or enthusiasm

例 Critics raved about the new play. 新剧得到了评论家们的热烈赞扬。

近 drool, effuse, enthuse, fuss, rhapsodize, slobber

反 blame, censure, condemn, criticize, denounce, pan, reprehend 批评，指责

【考法2】 *vi.* (发疯般地)怒吼：to **talk** irrationally and wildly in or **as if in delirium**

例 a man standing outside the city hall, raving like a lunatic about his tax bill 站在市政大厅外、像疯子一样叫嚷着自己税单的人

近 bluster, fulminate, huff, rant, roar, spout

反 grumble, murmur, mutter 小声抱怨

ravel ['rævl]

【考法1】 *vt.* 解开，松开：to **separate** the various **strands** of

例 Since the sweater is too small, you could ravel the yarnout and make something else with it. 既然这个毛衣太小，你可以把它拆了然后织些新的东西。

近 disentangle, extricate, unbraid, unsnarl, untwine, unweave

反 braid, knit, plait, weave 编织

【考法2】 *vt.* 阐明：to **clarify by separating** the aspects of

近 clarify, clear, elucidate, untangle, unravel

反 complex, complicate, entangle, perplex, sophisticate, snarl, tangle 使复杂化

【考法3】 *vt.* 使纠缠，使复杂化：to **tangle** or complicate

例 a ravelled story 一个复杂的故事

近 complex, complicate, entangle, perplex, sophisticate, snarl, tangle

反 clarify, clear, elucidate, untangle, unravel 阐明

ravish ['rævɪʃ]

【考法】 *vt.* 使陶醉，使沉迷：to **overcome with emotion** (as wonder or delight)

例 I was completely ravished by those marvelous pictures taken by HST. 用哈勃太空望远镜拍摄的那些壮观图片让我彻底地陶醉了。

近 captivate, enchant, enrapture, enthrall, rapture, transport

反 disenchant, sober 使清醒

派 ravishing *adj.* 极美丽的

raze [reɪz]

【考法】 *vt.* 摧毁，粉碎：to **destroy completely** by or as if by knocking down or breaking to pieces

例 Excavators were began to raze old school building. 挖土机开始夷平学校的老建筑。‖ An entire city block was razed by a terrible fire. 大火摧毁了整个街区。

近 annihilate, decimate, demolish, devastate, level, nuke, pulverize, ruin, smash, vaporize, wreck, tear down

反 build, construct, erect, raise, rear, set up 建造

派 razor *n.* 剃须刀

react [riˈækt]

【考法】 *vi.* 做出反应：to act or behave **in response** (as to a stimulus or influence)

例 didn't know how to react to the cheers of the crowd 不知如何对人群的欢呼声做出回应

近 answer, reply, respond

派 reaction *n.* 反应；reactant *n.* (化学反应当中的)反应物

reactionary [riˈækʃəneri]

【考法】 *adj.* 反对变革的，极保守的：characterized by reaction, especially **opposition to progress** or liberalism; extremely conservative

例 reactionary rulers 保守的统治者

近 brassbound, conservative, die-hard, hidebound, traditionalistic, ultraconservative

反 liberal 允许变革的；progressive 进步的；radical, aggressive 激进的

ream [riːm]

【考法】 *vt.* 怒斥，训斥：to **criticize** (someone) severely or angrily especially for personal failings

例 You are so going to get reamed out when the boss learns that you wrecked the company car. 要是老板知道你把公司的车弄坏了，你肯定会挨骂的。

近 baste, berate, castigate, chastise, hammer, lambaste, rail, rebuke, reprimand, reproach, upbraid

反 accredit, applaud, commend, eulogize, extol, laud, praise 表扬，赞扬

reap [riːp]

【考法】 *v.* 收割，收获：to collect (a crop or natural resource) or to **receive** as return for effort

例 As you sow, so shall you reap. 唯有付出，才有回报。‖ She reaped large profits from her patents. 她的专利给她带来了丰厚的回报。

近 acquire, attain, capture, harvest, gain, garner, obtain, procure, secure

反 plant, seed, sow 种植，播种；forfeit, lose 丧失，没收

派 reaper *n.* 收割机

reassure [ˌriːəˈʃʊr]

【考法】 *vt.* 使安心，打消疑虑：to **restore to confidence**

例 I tried to reassure her that the dog would come back home by nightfall. 我尽力让她安心，说夜幕降临之前小狗一定会回家的。

近 assure, cheer, console, solace, soothe

反 distress, torment, torture, trouble 使忧虑，折磨

派 reassurance *n.* 消除疑虑

rebuff [rɪˈbʌf]

【考法】 *vt.* 严词拒绝：to **reject** or criticize sharply

例 She rebuffed an invitation from her colleagues. 她回绝了同事们的邀请。‖ She rebuffed him when he asked her for a date. 她拒绝了他的约会邀请。

近 decline, deny, refuse, reject, repudiate, repulse, snub, spurn

反 accept 接受；approve 赞同；welcome 欢迎

Unit 9

recalcitrant [rɪˈkælsɪtrənt]
【考法】 *adj.* 顽抗的，不顺从的：marked by stubborn **resistance** to and **defiance** of authority or guidance
【例】 a recalcitrant teenager 执拗的少年 ‖ The manager worried that the recalcitrant employee would try to undermine his authority. 经理担心那些不服管理的员工会削弱他的权威。
【近】 balky, contumacious, defiant, incompliant, insubordinate, intractable, obstreperous, rebellious, refractory, unruly
【反】 amenable, compliant, conformable, docile, governable, obedient, ruly, submissive, tractable 服从的，顺从的
【派】 recalcitrance *n.* 固执，不服从命令

recant [rɪˈkænt]
【考法】 *vt.* 撤回，放弃，改变：to **withdraw** or repudiate (**a statement** or belief) formally and publicly
【例】 The man has refused after torture to recant his heresy. 这个人在受折磨后依旧拒绝放弃他的异教信仰。
【近】 abjure, abnegate, forswear, renege, renounce, repeal, repudiate, retract, withdraw
【反】 adhere, insist, maintain, stick 坚持
【派】 recantation *n.* 改变论调

recessive [rɪˈsesɪv]
【考法1】 *adj.* （基因等）隐性的，由隐性基因控制的：of, relating to, or designating an allele that **does not produce a characteristic effect when present with a dominant allele**
【例】 a recessive disease 隐性基因控制的疾病
【反】 dominant 显性的
【考法2】 *adj.* 内向的，内敛的：**not comfortable around people**
【例】 For such a recessive genius, the most comfortable thing is working alone in his lab. 对于这样一个内向的天才而言，最舒服的事情就是一个人在实验室里干活。
【近】 backward, bashful, coy, demure, diffident, introverted, modest, retiring, self-effacing, sheepish, withdrawn
【反】 extroverted, immodest, outgoing 外向的；gregarious, sociable 好交际的
【派】 recession *n.* 后退，衰退

recidivate [riːˈsidəveit]
【考法】 *vi.* 回到原先的习惯，尤指重新犯罪：to return to a previous pattern of behavior, especially to **return to criminal habits**
【例】 The suspect has recidivated for several times. 这个嫌犯是个惯犯了。
【近】 regress, relapse, retrogress, revert
【反】 habilitate, reclaim, redeem, regenerate, rehabilitate 洗心革面，使改正
【派】 recidivism *n.* 再犯，重犯；recidivist *n.* 再次犯罪的人

reciprocate [rɪˈsɪprəkeit]
【考法1】 *vi.* 往复运动：to move **forward and backward** alternately
【例】 According to Marx's economic principle, the average price of a certain product should be reciprocating over its value. 根据马克思的经济学理论，某一商品的平均价格应该在它的价值周边波动。
【近】 fluctuate, oscillate, sway, swing, vacillate
【考法2】 *vt.* 报答，回报：to **return** in kind or degree
【例】 They reciprocated the favor by driving their neighbor to the airport. 他们开车送邻居去机场以还人情。
【近】 recompense, repay, requite, retaliate, return
【反】 owe 欠（钱、人情等）
【派】 reciprocal *adj.* 相互之间的，互惠的

reckless [ˈrekləs]
【考法】 *adj.* 不考虑后果的，大胆鲁莽的：**careless** of consequences; foolishly adventurous or bold
【例】 His reckless driving accounted for the accident. 他鲁莽的开车行为导致了这场事故。
【近】 audacious, bold, brash, brassy, brazen, careless, daredevil, rash, madcap, temerarious
【反】 careful, cautious, circumspect, guarded, heedful, prudent, wary 慎重的，小心的

recluse [ˈreklu:s]
【考法1】 *n.* 隐士：a person who **lives away** from others
【例】 He was sick of cities and crowds, so he decided to go live by himself in the woods as a recluse. 他厌倦了城市和拥挤的人群，因此他决定像隐士一样遁隐山林。
【近】 anchorite, eremite, hermit, isolate, solitary

【考法2】 *adj.* 隐居的，不爱社交的：marked by **withdrawal from society**

例 a recluse poet who left a large amount of literature legacies 一个留下了大量文学遗产的隐居诗人 ‖ My neighbor is so recluse that I only see him about once a year. 我的邻居太神秘了，一般我一年只能见他一面。

近 cloistered, hermetic, secluded, secluse, seclusive, sequestered

反 gregarious, social 好交际的

派 reclusive *adj.* 隐居的

recoil ['riːkɔɪl]

【考法】 *vi.* 退却，畏缩：to **shrink back**, as under pressure or in fear or repugnance

例 recoil from the snake 因为害怕蛇而畏缩不前 ‖ She recoiled from his touch. 她因害怕与他接触而退缩。

近 blench, cringe, flinch, quail, shrink, squinch, wince

反 confront, meet 面对

reconcile ['rekənsaɪl]

【考法】 *vt.* 使和解，协调：to restore to friendship or **harmony**

例 Historians have never been able to reconcile the two eyewitness accounts of the battle. 历史学家们一直以来都无法协调这场战役两种记载之间的矛盾。

近 accommodate, attune, conciliate, conform, coordinate, harmonize, key

反 disharmonize 使不和谐；estrange 离间

派 reconciliation *n.* 协调

recondite ['rekəndaɪt]

【考法】 *adj.* 深奥的，难解的：**difficult** or impossible for one of ordinary understanding or knowledge **to comprehend**

例 I think Quantum Mechanics and Random Process are the two most recondite courses in our curriculum this semester. 我觉得量子力学和随机过程是这学期课表中最难的两门课程。

近 abstruse, arcane, deep, enigmatic, esoteric, hermetic, occult, profound

反 facile, shallow, superficial 肤浅的；easy, simple 简单的

Unit 10

■ RECONNOITER	■ RECONSTITUTE	■ RECONVENE	■ RECTITUDE	■ RECUMBENT
■ RECUPERATE	■ REDOLENT	■ REDOUBTABLE	■ REDUNDANT	■ REEL

reconnoiter [ˌrekəˈnɔɪtə]

【考法】 *vt.* 侦察，勘查：to **make a preliminary inspection** of, especially in order to gather military information

例 The wide utilization of unmanned aerial vehicles makes it much less risky to reconnoiter a certain area. 无人飞行器的广泛运用大大减少了军事侦察的风险。

近 probe, scout, survey

派 reconnaissance *n.* 侦察

reconstitute [ˌriːˈkɑːnstətuːt]

【考法】 *vt.* 重建，（尤其是通过加水）使复原：to constitute again or anew; to **restore** to a former condition, especially **by adding water**

例 reconstitute dried coffee powder 冲咖啡 ‖ Slowly Jewish communities ravaged by Nazi Germany were reconstituted and life began anew. 被纳粹德国摧残的犹太人社区慢慢得以重建，新的生活开始了。

近 reconstruct, reorder, reorganize, reshuffle, retool

反 annihilate, decimate, demolish, devastate, level, nuke, pulverize, ruin, smash, vaporize, wreck 摧毁

派 reconstitution *n.* （加水）复原

reconvene [ˌriːkənˈviːn]

【考法】 *v.* 重新集合，重新召集：to **gather**, call together, **or summon again**, especially for a formal meeting

例 The leaders will reconvene tomorrow. 明天领导们会再次召开会议。

近 reassemble

反 adjourn, suspend 休会

rectitude ['rektɪtuːd]

【考法】 *n.* 正直：the quality or state of being straight; **moral integrity**

例 The principal encouraged the graduates to go on to live lives of rectitude. 校长鼓励毕业生们在今后的生活中做一个正直的人。

近 honesty, integrity, probity, righteousness, scrupulousness, uprightness, virtue, virtuousness

反 badness, evil, immorality, iniquity, sin, villainy, wickedness 邪恶，罪恶

recumbent [rɪˈkʌmbənt]

【考法】 *adj.* 躺着的: **lying down**, especially in a position of comfort or rest

例 lying recumbent on the floor 躺在地板上

近 decumbent, procumbent, prone, prostrate, reclining, supine

反 erect, upright 直立的

recuperate [rɪˈkuːpəreɪt]

【考法】 *v.* 恢复(健康或力量),康复: to **recover health** or strength

例 He is gradually recuperating from a serious back injury. 他正渐渐地从严重的背部损伤中恢复过来。

近 convalesce, heal, rally, recoup, recover, rehabilitate

反 deteriorate, flag, wane, weaken 衰退,变得衰弱; die, expire, perish, pass away 死亡

派 recuperative *adj.* 有助于康复的

redolent [ˈredələnt]

【考法】 *adj.* 芳香的: having or emitting **fragrance**

例 be redolent with the aroma of baking bread 充满了烤面包的香味

近 ambrosial, aromatic, fragrant, perfumed, savory, scented, sweet

反 unscented 没有香味的; fetid, foul, malodorous, noisome, rancid, reeky, stinky 恶臭的,腐臭的

派 redolence *n.* 芳香,香味

redoubtable [rɪˈdaʊtəbl]

【考法 1】 *adj.* 杰出的,值得尊敬的: **worthy of respect** or honor

例 a surprising discovery by one of the most redoubtable figures in Egyptian archaeology 埃及考古学领域最值得敬重的人物之一所做出的一个惊人发现

近 bright, distinguished, illustrious, luminous, notable, noteworthy, outstanding, preeminent, prestigious

反 average, inferior, mediocre 平庸的,中等偏下的

【考法 2】 *adj.* 可怕的: **arousing fear** or awe

例 His next opponent would be by far the most redoubtable adversary the young boxer had ever faced. 年轻的拳击手的下一个对手将会是迄今为止他见过的最可怕的敌人。

近 direful, dreadful, fearsome, formidable, frightening, ghastly, horrifying, intimidating, scary, terrifying

反 calming, comforting, consoling, lulling, pacifying, quieting, reassuring, relaxing, soothing 令人放松的

redundant [rɪˈdʌndənt]

【考法】 *adj.* 多余的,冗余的: **exceeding** what is **necessary** or normal

例 This area is already chockablock with shopping malls; another one would be redundant. 这个地区已经是商场扎堆了,再建一个完全是多此一举。

近 excess, extra, supererogatory, superfluous, supernumerary, surplus

反 deficient, inadequate, insufficient, meager, niggardly, scant, scarce, short, sparse 缺乏,稀疏

派 redundancy *n.* 过剩,过多

reel [riːl]

【考法 1】 *vi.* 感到眩晕: to be in a confused state as if **from being twirled around**

例 My head reeled with the facts and figures. 我的头脑被这些事实和数据给弄晕了。‖ His mind reeled upon hearing the news that his employer had been indicted for fraud. 当他听到雇主因为欺诈而被起诉时,他顿觉天旋地转。

近 spin, swirl, turn, whirl

反 calm 保持镇定

【考法 2】 *vi.* 蹒跚地走路: to move forward while **swaying from side to side**

例 The drunkard reeled down the alley. 醉汉蹒跚地沿着小巷走去。

近 careen, dodder, falter, lurch, stagger, stumble, teeter, totter, waddle

List 21

"GRE 考验的不是脑力，不是体力，而是心力，踏踏实实地做好每个细节，阳光真的就会出现在风雨后。"

（吕秋莹，2009 年 10 月，Verbal 750，Quantitative 800，AW 4.0

录取学校：Columbia University）

Unit 1

■ REFEREE	■ REFINE	■ REFLECT	■ REFRACTORY	■ REFULGENT
■ REFUTE	■ REGENERATE	■ REGIMEN	■ REGRESS	■ REHABILITATE

referee [ˌrefəˈriː]
【考法 1】 *n.* 仲裁者；裁判员：a person who **impartially** decides or **resolves a dispute** or controversy
例 serve as the unofficial referee in disputes over the family business 作为一个非官方协调员，解决家庭事务中的纠纷
近 adjudicator, arbiter, arbitrator, judge, umpire
【考法 2】 *vt.* （就纠纷或争议）给出意见：to **give an opinion** about（something at issue or in dispute）
例 Their father usually ends up refereeing any disputes concerning use of the big TV. 最后往往是他们的父亲决定该看什么电视频道，从而解决了相关争执。
近 adjudge, adjudicate, arbitrate, decide, determine, settle
反 consult 咨询

refine [rɪˈfaɪn]
【考法 1】 *vt.* 提纯，精炼：to **free**（as metal, sugar, or oil）**from impurities** or unwanted material
例 Oil is refined so as to remove naturally occurring impurities. 原油通过精炼可去除其中天然存在的杂质。
近 filter, garble, purify, winnow
反 adulterate, contaminate, pollute 掺杂，污染
【考法 2】 *vt.* 改善，改进：to **improve or perfect** by pruning or polishing
例 You'd better refine your backhand before the big tennis match if you want to throne. 如果你想获得冠军的话，你最好在网球大赛开赛前再提升一下反手的技术。
近 ameliorate, amend, better, enhance, enrich, help, meliorate, perfect, polish, upgrade
反 deteriorate, worsen 恶化，降低
派 refined *adj.* （物品）精雕细琢的，（人）彬彬有礼的；refinery *n.* 炼油厂

reflect [rɪˈflekt]
【考法 1】 *vt.* 反射：to prevent passage of and cause to **change direction**
例 The color of an objective is largely determined by what light it reflects. 物体的颜色很大程度上是由它能反射的光所决定的。 || Mirrors indiscriminately reflect all visible lights. 镜子不加区分地反射所有的可见光。
反 absorb 吸收
【考法 2】 *vt.* 反映，显露：to **make manifest** or apparent: show
例 Her book clearly reflects her religious beliefs. 她的书明确地反映了她的宗教信仰。 || Where you come from could be easily reflected in your accent. 你的口音可以轻易地暴露你来自哪里。
近 bespeak, betray, demonstrate, evince, manifest, reveal, show
反 conceal, cover, hide, mask, obscure, occlude, veil 隐藏
【考法 3】 *vi.* 思考：to **think seriously**
例 I reflected on my path as an undergraduate and my future as a PhD candidate. 我思考了我作为一名本科生的成长足迹以及我进修博士的未来。
近 consider, cogitate, contemplate, deliberate, meditate, muse, ponder, ruminate, think
派 reflective *adj.* 思考的，深思熟虑的

refractory [rɪˈfræktəri]
【考法】 *adj.* 倔强的，不顺从的：**resisting control** or authority
例 Refractory players will be ejected from the game. 不服从裁判命令的球员将会被驱逐出场。
近 balky, contumacious, defiant, incompliant, insubordinate, intractable, obstreperous, rebellious, unruly
反 amenable, compliant, conformable, docile, governable, obedient, ruly, submissive, tractable 服从的，顺从的

refulgent	[rɪˈfʌldʒənt]

【考法】 *adj.* 辉煌的，灿烂的：**shining radiantly**; resplendent

例 Refulgent sunlight broke through the clouds, creating huge swaths of light in the valley below us. 耀眼的阳光穿透了云层，在我们脚下的峡谷中投下了一块巨大的光斑。

近 beaming, brilliant, dazzling, incandescent, lucid, luminous, lustrous, radiant, resplendent, splendid

反 dim, dull, lackluster 黯淡无光的

派 refulgence *n.* 灿烂，光芒四射

refute	[rɪˈfjuːt]

【考法 1】 *vt.* 否认：to **declare not to be true**

例 While the spokeswoman was publicly refuting rumors of a merger, behind the scenes the CEO was working to effect that very outcome. 尽管女发言人一再公开否认合并的谣言，首席执行官却正在幕后为这一目标而努力。

近 contradict, disaffirm, disavow, disclaim, disconfirm, deny, gainsay, negate, negative, reject, repudiate

反 acknowledge, admit, avow, concede, confirm 承认

【考法 2】 *vt.* 证明为假，证伪：to **prove wrong** by argument or evidence: show to be false or erroneous

例 The triumph of Chinese athlete Liu Xiang in the 2004 Olympics effectively refuted the views that Asians are physically inferior to others. 中国运动员刘翔在 2004 年雅典奥运会上的胜利有效地驳斥了亚洲人在体格上不如其他人种的观点。

近 belie, confute, debunk, discredit, falsify, rebut, shoot down

反 confirm, prove, validate, verify 证明为真，证实

派 refutable *adj.* 可辩驳的

regenerate	[rɪˈdʒenəreɪt]

【考法 1】 *vt.* 使重获新生，使焕然一新：to **bring back to life**, practice, activity or a former condition of vigor

例 The lizard is able to regenerate its tail. 蜥蜴能够重新长出断尾。 ‖ The whole community was regenerated thanks to a government grant for repairing all the old buildings. 多亏了政府用于维修老楼的专项拨款，整个社区焕然一新。

近 recharge, refresh, rejuvenate, rekindle, renew, restore, resurrect, resuscitate, revitalize, revivify

反 degenerate, deteriorate, worsen 衰退，恶化

派 regeneration *n.* 复兴

【考法 2】 *v.* (使)洗心革面：to make **better in** behavior or **character**

例 Every time he made a mistake, he would promise to regenerate. 每次犯错后他都会保证洗心革面，下次不再犯。

近 habilitate, reclaim, redeem, rehabilitate

regimen	[ˈredʒɪmən]

【考法】 *n.* (政治上的)统治：**lawful control** over the affairs of a political unit (as a nation)

例 A new party will have regimen over the nation and, hopefully, bring some much-needed change. 一个新的政党将要上台，希望他们能带来一些迫切需要的改革。

近 administration, authority, governance, jurisdiction, regime

regress	[rɪˈgres]

【考法 1】 *vi.* 后退：to go **back**; move backward

例 To stand still is to regress. 不进则退。

近 retrogress, return, revert

反 advance, develop, evolve, progress 前进，发展

【考法 2】 *vi.* 退化，恶化：to become **worse** or of less value

例 The annual celebration has regressed to the point where it's nothing more than an excuse to get drunk. 年度的庆祝活动已经堕落成一个尽情喝醉的借口了。

近 atrophy, crumble, decay, decline, degenerate, descend, deteriorate, ebb, retrograde, rot, sink, worsen

反 ameliorate, improve, meliorate 改善

派 regressive *adj.* 后退的，退化的; regression *n.* 后退，退化

rehabilitate	[ˌriːəˈbɪlɪteɪt]

【考法 1】 *vt.* 使复原，使康复：to **restore to** a former state (as of efficiency, good management, or solvency) or a **healthy condition**

例 new policies in hopes of rehabilitating the national economy 被指望能振兴国家经济的新政策 ‖ She decided to undergo physical therapy to help rehabilitate her broken elbow. 她决定采取理疗来治疗受伤的手肘。

近 cure, fix, mend, rejuvenate, resúscitate, revitalize, revive, set up

反 debilitate, enervate, enfeeble, weaken 使虚弱; relapse 旧病复发

派 rehabilitation *n.* 康复，复原

【考法 2】 *v.* (使)洗心革面：to make **better in** behavior or **character**

例 an organization that rehabilitates criminals so they can reenter society 一个让罪犯洗心革面的机构，以便让他们能重返社会

近 habilitate, reclaim, redeem, regenerate

Unit 2

rehearsal [rɪˈhɜːrsl]

【考法】 *n.* 排练，彩排：the act of **practicing in preparation** for a public performance

例 We made a few mistakes in rehearsal, but we were pretty sure that we'd be OK on opening night. 彩排过程中我们犯了几个错误，但正式开幕式当晚我们有信心做得很好。

近 practice, trial, dry run

反 extemporization, impromptu, improvisation（无准备的）即兴表演

reign [reɪn]

【考法 1】 *n.* 统治权：the **right** or means **to command** or control others

例 A healthy nation should be governed by the reign of law and not by the will of its chief executive. 一个健康的国家应该是法制的，而非由最高领导人的意志统领。 ‖ They accused him of carrying out a reign of terror. 他们指责他搞独裁暴政。

近 arm, authority, clutch, command, control, dominion, grip, hold, mastery, sway

反 impotence, impotency, powerlessness 无权，无能

【考法 2】 *vi.* 占统治地位或盛行：to **be predominant** or prevalent

例 Chaos reigned in the classroom. 整个教室一片混乱。 ‖ Panic reigned as the fire spread. 随着大火的扩散，恐慌也迅速蔓延。

近 dominate, domineer, prevail, predominate, rule

rein [reɪn]

【考法 1】 *n.* 抑制，限制：the act or practice of **keeping** something（as an activity）**within certain boundaries**

例 The oversight committee called on the corporation to keep a much tighter rein on the activities of its contractors. 监督委员会要求这个公司对其承包商的行为采取更为严格的管控。

近 circumscription, confinement, limitation, stint

【考法 2】 *vi.* 抑制，控制：to **keep from exceeding** a desirable degree or level（as of expression）

例 A good man knows how to rein in his temper. 君子知道如何按捺住火气。

近 bridle, check, constrain, contain, curb, govern, hold, inhibit, keep, measure, manacle, regulate, restrain, rule, tame

反 liberate, loose, loosen, unleash 释放，不再加以管束

reiterate [riˈɪtəreɪt]

【考法】 *v.* 重申：to say or **state again**

例 Let me reiterate our stance. 让我来重述我们的立场。 ‖ I want to reiterate that under no circumstances are you to leave the house. 我想再次重申：无论如何你都不能离开这间房子。

近 chime, din, iterate, recapitulate, rehearse, repeat

rejoice [rɪˈdʒɔɪs]

【考法】 *vi.* 欣喜，喜悦：to **feel joy** or great delight

例 We rejoiced over our unexpected victory on the soccer field. 我们为预料之外的足球胜利而感到欢喜。

近 crow, delight, exuberate, glory, jubilate, joy, kvell, triumph

反 bemoan, bewail, deplore, grieve, lament, moan, mourn, regret, weep 感到伤感、痛苦或遗憾

派 rejoiced *adj.* 高兴的

relapse [rɪˈlæps]

【考法】 *vi.* 故态复萌，再犯：to slip or **fall back** into a former worse state

例 The patient wondered whether his illness would relapse. 病人想知道他的病会不会复发。

近 recidivate, regress, retrogress, revert

反 habilitate, reclaim, redeem, regenerate 变好，洗心革面；convalesce, rehabilitate 康复

release [rɪˈliːs]

【考法 1】 *vt.* 排放：to throw or **give off**

例 We bought an air freshener that releases a pleasing scent into the room. 我们买了一个能向房间里释放怡人香味的空气净化机。

近 cast, exhale, expel, irradiate, issue, vent

反 absorb 吸收

【考法 2】 *vt.* 释放，使获得自由：to **set free** from restraint, confinement, or servitude

例 The government was asked to release the prisoners immediately. 政府被要求立即释放囚犯。

近 discharge, disenthrall, emancipate, enfranchise, liberate, loose, loosen, manumit, unchain, unfetter

反 bind, confine, enchain, fetter, restrain 限制自由

【考法 3】 *vt.* 解雇：to **let go from office**, service, or employment

例 They released the workers who couldn't handle the new technology. 他们解雇了所有不能掌握新技术的工人。

近 bounce, cashier, dismiss, fire, remove, retire, sack, terminate

反 employ, engage, hire 雇用

relentless [rɪˈlentləs]

【考法 1】 *adj.* 残酷的，无情的：showing or promising **no abatement of severity**, intensity, strength, or pace

例 He was the most relentless teacher I have ever known. 他是我所知的最狠的老师。

近 grim, inexorable, ironfisted, merciless, mortal, ruthless, unrelenting

反 charitable, clement, merciful, lenient 仁慈的

【考法 2】 *adj.* 固执的，不肯妥协的：showing no signs of slackening or **yielding in one's purpose**

例 The team's offense was relentless in trying to score. 进攻球员毫不妥协地努力得分。

近 adamant, dogged, headstrong, mulish, obdurate, pertinacious, rigid, uncompromising, unyielding

反 acquiescent, amenable, compliant, complying, flexible, pliable, pliant, relenting, yielding 易屈服的

relevant [ˈreləvənt]

【考法】 *adj.* 有关系的，重要的：**having** a bearing on or **connection** with the matter at hand

例 Make sure your answers during the interview are short and relevant. 确保你在面试时的回答简短而恰当。
You need to bring all the relevant certificates with you. 你需要携带所有的相关证明。

近 applicable, apposite, apropos, germane, material, pertinent, pointed, relative

反 extraneous, immaterial, impertinent, inapplicable, inapposite, irrelevant, pointless 无关的

派 relevance *n.* 关联

religion [rɪˈlɪdʒən]

【考法 1】 *n.* 宗教，信仰：a body of **beliefs** and practices regarding the supernatural and the worship of one or more deities

例 The Jewish religion has followers in many parts of the globe. 犹太教在全球范围内有大量信徒。

近 credo, creed, cult, faith, persuasion

【考法 2】 *n.* （对于宗教信仰的）忠诚，虔诚：belief and trust in and **loyalty to God**

例 Without his religion, he would not have been able to survive all the difficulties he has faced over the years.
如果不是他的虔诚，他是不可能渡过这些年来遇到的所有难关的。

近 devotion, piety

反 atheism, godlessness 无神论

派 religious *adj.* 宗教的；忠诚的

Unit 3

■ RELINQUISH	■ RELISH	■ RELUCTANT	■ REMISS	■ REMODEL
■ REMONSTRANCE	■ REMORSE	■ REMUNERATE	■ REND	■ RENEGADE

relinquish [rɪˈlɪŋkwɪʃ]

【考法 1】 *vt.* 放弃（职位、权力等）：to **give up** (as a position of authority) formally

例 She relinquished his position to the company's vice president with very mixed feelings. 怀着十分复杂的情感，她放弃了公司副总裁的职位。

近 abnegate, cede, renounce, resign, surrender

反 inaugurate 就职；usurp 篡位

【考法 2】 *vt.* 移交，交出：to **give** (something) over to the **control or possession** of another usually under duress

例 The boy reluctantly relinquished the illegal fireworks to the police officer. 小男孩不情愿地把非法的烟花爆竹交给了警察。‖ The court ordered him to relinquish custody of his child. 法庭要求他交出孩子的监护权。

近 deliver, render, yield, turn in, turn over

反 keep, retain, withhold 保留，不给予

relish [ˈrelɪʃ]

【考法 1】 *n.* 喜好，偏好：an appetite for something; a strong **appreciation or liking**

例 She has great relish for early morning walks, which she takes nearly every day. 她对早晨散步有格外的喜好——几乎每天早上她都会坚持出去。

近 appetite, fancy, favor, fondness, like, love, partiality, preference, taste

反 aversion, disfavor, disgust, dislike, distaste, hatred, loathing 反感，厌恶感

【考法2】 *n.* (愿望达成时的)高兴，满足感：the feeling experienced **when** one's **wishes are met**

例 He ate the bowl of ice cream with relish. 他高兴地吃着冰激凌。

近 content, delectation, delight, enjoyment, gladness, gratification, happiness, satisfaction

反 discontent, displeasure, dissatisfaction, unhappiness 不满，不悦

【考法3】 *vt.* 享受，喜欢：to **take** keen or zestful **pleasure** in

例 He is so hungry that he will relish even plain food. 他是如此的饥饿，即使普通的食物也能让他满意。

近 adore, enjoy, like, love, rejoice, revel, savor

反 abhor, abominate, detest, dislike, hate, loathe 厌恶，讨厌

reluctant [rɪˈlʌktənt]

【考法】 *adj.* 不情愿的，反感的：feeling or **showing** aversion, hesitation, or **unwillingness**

例 I'm reluctant to let him borrow my CDs since he never gives back anything I lend him. 我很不愿意把我的 CD 借给他，因为他借了我东西从来不还。

近 averse, disinclined, indisposed, loath, unwilling

反 willing 乐意的；disposed, inclined 倾向于做某事的；eager 渴望的

派 reluctance *n.* 不愿意，不情愿

remiss [rɪˈmɪs]

【考法】 *adj.* 疏忽的，不留心的：exhibiting **carelessness** or slackness

例 I would be remiss if I didn't tell you how much I appreciated the lovely gift. 如果我不告诉你我是多么喜欢这个可爱的礼物的话，那我就太疏忽大意了。

近 careless, derelict, disregardful, heedless, lax, lazy, neglectful, neglecting, slack

反 attentive, careful, conscientious, meticulous, painstaking, scrupulous 细致的，仔细的

remodel [ˌriːˈmɑːdl]

【考法】 *vt.* 改造，改变结构：to **alter the structure** of

例 We decided to remodel the warehouse into a museum displaying the products of the company. 我们决定把仓库改造成展览我们公司产品的展馆。

近 alter, modify, recast, redo, refashion, remake, revamp, revise, rework, vary

反 fix, freeze, set, stabilize 固定

remonstrance [rɪˈmɑːnstrəns]

【考法】 *n.* 抗议，抱怨：an **expression of protest**, **complaint**, or reproof, especially a formal statement of grievances

例 She seems deaf to her son's remonstrances. 她似乎对儿子的抗议充耳不闻。‖ Aggravated by the noisy metro construction, many residents wrote letters of remonstrance to city officials. 许多被地铁建设的噪音激怒的居民向市政府投去了抗议信。

近 challenge, complaint, demur, difficulty, fuss, objection, protest, question, remonstration, stink

反 acceptance, acquiescence, agreement, approval, assent, sanction 同意，接受

remorse [rɪˈmɔːrs]

【考法】 *n.* 懊悔，悔恨：moral anguish arising from repentance for past misdeeds; **bitter regret**

例 He felt a deep remorse for having neglected his family over the years. 他为多年来忽略家人的行为表示深深的懊悔。

近 contriteness, contrition, penitence, regret, remorsefulness, repentance, rue, self-reproach, shame

反 impenitence, remorselessness 不知悔改

派 remorseful *adj.* 懊悔的，悔恨的

remunerate [rɪˈmjuːnəreɪt]

【考法】 *vt.* 支付报酬，补偿：to **pay** an equivalent to for a service, loss, or expense

例 He promptly remunerated the repair company for fixing the satellite TV. 他迅速地支付了维修公司修理卫星电视所应得的酬劳。

近 compensate, indemnify, recompense, recoup, redress, remedy, repay, requite

派 remunerative *adj.* 有报酬的

rend [rend]

【考法】 *vt.* 撕裂，猛拉：to **tear or split apart** or into pieces violently

例 Wolves rend a game to pieces. 狼群会把猎物撕成碎片。‖ pain that rends the heart 撕心裂肺般的痛

近 cleave, lacerate, ribbon, rip, rive, rupture, shred, split, tatter, tear

反 associate, coalesce, combine, conjoin, conjugate, connect, fuse, interfuse, join, link, unify 联合

renegade ['renɪgeɪd]

【考法】 *n.* 背教者，叛徒: one who **rejects** a religion, cause, **allegiance**, or group for another; a deserter

例 A band of renegades who had deserted their infantry units were making their way to Mexico. 一支背叛了他们所属的步兵编队的士兵朝着墨西哥前进。

近 apostate, betrayer, defector, deserter, recreant, traitor, turncoat

反 adherent, loyalist, partisan 忠诚者

Unit 4

■ RENOUNCE	■ RENOVATE	■ REPARTEE	■ REPATRIATE	■ REPEAL
■ REPEL	■ REPERTOIRE	■ REPINE	■ REPLETE	■ REPOSE

renounce [rɪ'naʊns]

【考法 1】 *vt.* (正式地)放弃: to **give up**, refuse, or resign usually by formal declaration

例 renounce his nationality 退出国籍

近 abnegate, cede, relinquish, resign, surrender

反 inaugurate 就职；usurp 篡位

派 renunciation *n.* 放弃

【考法 2】 *vt.* 宣布与…决裂: to **refuse to follow**, obey, or recognize any further

例 renounce the authority of the church 宣布与教会彻底决裂

近 forswear, recant, renege, repeal, repudiate, retract, withdraw

反 adhere, stick 坚持，忠于

renovate ['renəveɪt]

【考法 1】 *vt.* 修复，维修: to **restore** to a former better state (as by cleaning, repairing, or rebuilding)

例 We will have to renovate the house extensively before we can move in. 在入住之前我们必须大规模翻修一下这栋房子。

近 doctor, fix, patch, recondition, repair, revamp

反 blemish, break, damage, deface, disfigure, harm, hurt, impair, injure, mar, ruin, vandalize, wreck 破坏

【考法 2】 *vt.* 使重获新生，使焕然一新: to **bring back to life**, practice, activity or a former condition of vigor

例 The church was renovated by a new ecumenical spirit. 新的宗教领袖的到来让教堂焕发新生。

近 recharge, refresh, rejuvenate, rekindle, renew, restore, resurrect, resuscitate, revitalize, revivify

反 degenerate, deteriorate, worsen 衰退，恶化

repartee [ˌrepɑːr'tiː]

【考法 1】 *n.* 机智的回答: a quick **witty response**

例 That repartee to the reporter's question drew laughs from the bystanders. 对记者问题的机智回答引来了旁观者的笑声。

近 comeback, riposte

【考法 2】 *n.* 打趣，善意的玩笑: **good-natured teasing** or exchanging of clever remarks

例 Repartee is harder to do with text messaging. 用短信开玩笑困难多了。

近 backchat, badinage, chaff, jesting, joshing, persiflage, raillery

repatriate [ˌriː'peɪtrieɪt]

【考法】 *vt.* 遣返: to restore or **return to the country** of origin, allegiance, or citizenship

例 As soon as the war ends, the government will start to repatriate war refugees. 只要战争一结束，政府就会开始遣返战争难民。

反 banish, deport, expatriate 放逐，驱逐

repeal [rɪ'piːl]

【考法 1】 *vt.* 撤销，废除(法律等): to **rescind or annul** by authoritative act

例 The company called the furniture store to repeal the order for six new desks. 公司要求家具店撤销六张新桌子的订单。‖ In 1933, Congress passed the 21st Amendment which repealed the Prohibition Amendment of 1919, thus making the sale, distribution, and use of alcohol legal once again. 1933 年，国会通过了《第二十一修正案》，该法案废除了于 1919 年制订的《禁酒法》，从而使得酒的买卖、配送和使用再次合法化。

近 abort, abrogate, annul, cancel, disannul, invalidate, negate, null, nullify, rescind, revoke, vacate, void

反 continue, keep 继续；enact, establish, legislate 立法，制订

【考法 2】 *vt.* 宣布与…决裂: to **refuse to** follow, obey, or **recognize** any further

例 If I find that you have been lying about this, I'll instantly repeal every promise I made to you. 只要我发现在这个问题上你对我撒了谎，那我们之间的承诺就彻底破裂了。

近 forswear, recant, renege, renounce, repudiate, retract, withdraw

反 adhere, stick 坚持，忠于

repel [rɪˈpel]

【考法 1】 *vt.* 抵制：to **fight against**; resist

例 Self-discipline ensures that you can repel the things that induce you. 自律可以保证你抵制那些诱惑你的事物。‖ I repelled the temptation to stay out late and call in sick the next day. 我抵住了晚上玩通宵然后第二天谎称生病的诱惑。

近 buck, defy, fight, oppose, resist, withstand

反 capitulate, submit, succumb, surrender, yield, give in 屈服

【考法 2】 *vt.* 使厌恶：to **cause aversion** in: disgust

例 Evil odors always repel me. 臭味总是让我恶心。

近 disgust, nauseate, repulse, revolt, sicken

反 allure, attract, bewitch, captivate, charm, enchant, entice, fascinate, lure, seduce, tempt 吸引，诱惑

派 repelling *adj.* 令人厌恶的

repertoire [ˈrepərtwɑːr]

【考法】 *n.* (技术、设备或原料等的)详单：the **complete list** or supply of skills, devices, or ingredients used in a particular field, occupation, or practice

例 The chef's repertoire of specialties seems to be limited, with several of the dishes appearing over and over again in slightly varied guises. 这个厨师的所有拿手好戏看来是很有限的，因为上来的几盘菜看起来只是稍微换了一下装饰而已。

近 budget, fund, inventory, pool, reservoir, stock

repine [rɪˈpaɪn]

【考法 1】 *vi.* 抱怨，表达不满：to feel or **express discontent** or dejection

例 There is no use repining over a love that's been long lost. 抱怨早已失去的爱情是没有用的。

近 carp, complain, fuss, gripe, grouch, grouse, growl, grumble, inveigh, moan, murmur, mutter, wail, whine

反 crow, delight, rejoice 高兴

【考法 2】 *vi.* 渴望：to **long for** something

例 During the deep cold of winter, I repine for warm tropical beaches. 在寒冬，我渴望温暖的热带海滩。

近 ache, covet, crave, desiderate, hunger, itch, long, lust, pine, salivate, thirst, want, wish, yearn

反 abhor, abominate, detest, dislike, hate, loathe 厌恶，讨厌

replete [rɪˈpliːt]

【考法 1】 *adj.* 彻底吃饱了的：having one's **appetite completely satisfied**

例 Everyone is completely replete after the huge meal. 在大餐之后，每个人都吃撑了。

近 sated, satiate, satiated, stuffed, surfeited

反 empty, famished, hungry, starved, starving 挨饿的

【考法 2】 *adj.* 充满…的，富于…的：**possessing** or covered with **great numbers** or amounts of something specified

例 a scholar replete with knowledge 博学的学者

近 abounding, abundant, awash, flush, fraught, lousy, swarming, teeming, thick, thronging

反 depleted, drained, exhausted 耗竭的；deficient, incomplete, insufficient, short 缺乏的

派 repletion *n.* 装满

repose [rɪˈpoʊz]

【考法 1】 *n.* (劳作后的)休息：a **state of resting** after exertion or strain

例 The doctor ordered a period of repose for the patient suffering from insomnia. 医生要求正在饱受失眠折磨的病人好好休息一阵。

近 ease, leisure, relaxation

反 exertion, labor, toil, work 劳动，工作

【考法 2】 *n.* 平静，宁静：a state of **freedom from storm** or disturbance

例 We enjoyed the repose of a summer evening on a remote island. 我们在遥远的小岛上共享了夏日傍晚的片刻安宁。

近 calmness, hush, peace, placidity, quietness, restfulness, serenity, still, tranquility

反 commotion, pandemonium, tumult, turmoil, unrest, uproar 骚乱，动乱

【考法 3】 *vi.* 休息：to **take a rest**

例 They have to repose on couches because all beds have been occupied. 因为所有的床都有人占了，他们不得不在沙发上休息。

近 idle, loll, lounge, relax, rest

反 drudge, hustle, moil, strive, struggle, sweat, travail 努力工作

【考法 4】 *vt.* 放置，交给他人：to put（something）into the possession or **safekeeping of another**

例 The Constitution reposes the power to declare war to Congress, and to that body alone. 宪法将宣战的权力交给了国会单独保管。

近 consign, delegate, deliver, entrust, leave, pass, transfer, transmit, vest, hand over, turn over, give over

反 hold, keep, retain, withhold 保留

Unit 5

■ REPREHEND	■ REPRESS	■ REPRIEVE	■ REPROACH	■ REPROBATE
■ REPROOF	■ REPROVE	■ REPUDIATE	■ REPUGNANT	■ REPULSE

reprehend ［repri'hend］

【考法】 *vt.* 谴责，责难，批评：to **express** one's **unfavorable opinion** of the worth or quality of

例 Without exception, book reviewers reprehended the novel's trite plot. 毫无例外的，小说缺乏新意的故事情节受到了评论家们的责难。

近 berate, blame, castigate, censure, condemn, denounce, dispraise, fault, knock, lambaste, pan, upbraid

反 extol, laud, praise 表扬

派 reprehensible *adj.* 应受谴责的

repress ［ri'pres］

【考法 1】 *vt.* 镇压：to **put down by force**, usually before total control has been lost; quell

例 Military quickly repressed the rebellion in the city and restored order. 军方迅速平息了市内的暴乱，恢复了秩序。

近 crush, quash, quell, silence, squash, squelch, subdue, suppress

反 foment, incite, instigate, provoke, stir 煽动，激起

【考法 2】 *vt.* 阻止（正常的表达、活动或发展等）：to **prevent** the natural or normal **expression**, activity, or development of

例 You can't repress your feelings forever, so tell her that you love her. 你不可能永远压抑自己的感受，所以大胆地向她表白吧。

近 bridle, check, curb, muffle, smother, stifle, strangle, swallow

反 express, loose, release, take out, unleash, vent（情感等的）表达，宣泄

派 repression *n.* 阻止，镇压

reprieve ［ri'pri:v］

【考法 1】 *vt.* 对…暂缓处刑，免罪：to **postpone or cancel** the **punishment** of

例 Fourteen people, waiting to be hanged for the murder of a former prime minister, have been reprieved. 十四个因为谋杀前首相而等待绞刑的人获得了缓刑。

近 absolve, acquit, amnesty, condone, excuse, forgive, pardon, remit, respite, spare

反 penalize, punish 惩罚

【考法 2】 *vt.* 维持…运行：to **prevent**（something）**from being closed**, destroyed, etc., for a period of time

例 The library has been reprieved and will remain open for at least another year. 图书馆的状况得到了缓解，还将继续开放一年。

近 deliver, rescue, save

reproach ［ri'prəutʃ］

【考法 1】 *n.* 令人羞愧的事物，耻辱：one that **causes shame**, rebuke or blame

例 a reproach to this entire school 整个学校的耻辱

近 dishonor, opprobrium, reflection, spot, scandal, stain, stigma, taint

反 credit, honor 荣誉

【考法 2】 *vt.* 批评，责备：to **express** disapproval, **criticism**, or disappointment in（someone）

例 reproached by their mother for untidiness 因为邋遢而被他们的母亲批评

近 admonish, berate, castigate, chide, condemn, denounce, lambaste, rebuke, reprimand, reprove, upbraid

反 commend, eulogize, extol, laud, praise 表扬

派 irreproachable *adj.* 无可指责的

reprobate ［'reprəbeit］

【考法 1】 *n.* 堕落者，道德败坏的人：a morally **unprincipled person**

例 The program rehabilitates reprobates and turns them into hard-working, law-abiding citizens. 这个项目让那些堕落的人改过自新，并将他们变成勤劳守法的好公民。

近 brute, devil, fiend, miscreant, rapscallion, rascal, villain

反 saint 圣人

【考法2】 *adj.* 堕落的，放荡的：**morally corrupt**

例　He is a reprobate judge who could be bribed, and often with astonishing ease. 他是一个堕落的法官，极其容易就被贿赂了。

近　debased, debauched, degraded, depraved, dissipated, dissolute, libertine, perverse, perverted, rakish

反　good, moral, righteous, virtuous 有道德的；pure, uncorrupted 纯净的，未受污染的

【考法3】 *vt.* 谴责，痛斥：to **condemn strongly** as unworthy, unacceptable, or evil

例　He reprobated his son's unconventional lifestyle. 他怒斥他儿子不遵循传统的生活习惯。

近　blame, criticize, censure, condemn, denounce, denunciate, reprehend

反　commend, eulogize, extol, laud, praise 表扬

【考法4】 *vt.* 拒绝，不提供：to be **unwilling to grant**

例　The government will most likely reprobate the request for parole. 政府很有可能会拒绝假释的要求。

近　decline, disallow, disapprove, negative, nix, refuse, reject, repudiate, withhold

反　allow, concede, grant, let, permit, vouchsafe 允许，给予

---

reproof [rɪˈpruːf]

【考法】 *n.* 批评，反对：**criticism** for a fault, rebuke

例　The head teacher speaks in tones of gentle reproof. 校长的话语中带有轻微的批评。

近　commination, condemnation, denunciation, excoriation, rebuke, reprimand, reproach, stricture

反　commendation, eulogy, praise 赞扬；endorsement 同意

---

reprove [rɪˈpruːv]

【考法1】 *vt.* 温和地责备，警告：to **scold** or correct usually **gently** or with kindly intent

例　My piano teacher often reproves me for slouching while playing, observing that good posture helps one play better. 我的钢琴老师常常会因为懒散的坐姿而批评我，他认为良好的坐姿能让我弹得更好。

近　admonish, blame, chide, criticize, reprimand, reproach

反　lambaste 严厉地责备；commend, eulogize, extol, laud, praise 表扬

【考法2】 *vt.* 不欣赏，不喜欢：to hold an **unfavorable opinion** of

例　The older generation has always reproved the younger generation's taste in music. 老一代的人总是不喜欢新一代的音乐品味。

近　deprecate, discountenance, disesteem, disfavor, dislike, frown

反　adore, approve, endorse, enjoy, favor, like 支持，喜欢

---

repudiate [rɪˈpjuːdieɪt]

【考法1】 *vt.* 否认：to **declare not to be true**

例　She repudiated the charge that she had lied on her résumé. 她否认了她在简历中作假的指控。

近　contradict, disaffirm, disavow, disclaim, disconfirm, disown, gainsay, negate, negative, refute, reject

反　acknowledge, admit, allow, avow, concede, confirm 承认

【考法2】 *vt.* 拒绝接受：to show **unwillingness to accept**, do, engage in, or agree to

例　We didn't like the terms, so we repudiated the contract. 我们没有接受这份合同，因为我们对其中的条款表示不满。

近　balk, deselect, disapprove, negative, nix, refuse, reprobate, spurn

反　accept, agree, approve 接受，承认

派　repudiation *n.* 拒绝；否认

---

repugnant [rɪˈpʌɡnənt]

【考法1】 *adj.* 令人厌恶的：**arousing** disgust or **aversion**

例　The idea of moving again became repugnant to her. 又要搬家的想法让她感到厌恶。

近　abhorrent, abominable, awful, disgusting, distasteful, hideous, loathsome, noisome, obnoxious, repulsive

反　innocuous, inoffensive 无害的；agreeable, delightful, enjoyable, gratifying, pleasing 令人愉悦的

【考法2】 *adj.* 不和谐的，不协调的：**not** being in agreement or **harmony**

例　Technically speaking, it may not be a violation, but it is certainly repugnant to the spirit of the law. 技术上来说这还算不上违法，但是这肯定违背了法律的精神。

近　conflicting, discordant, incompatible, incongruous, inconsonant, inharmonious, mutually exclusive

反　accordant, agreeing, compatible, concordant, conformable, congruent, congruous, consistent, consonant, harmonious 和谐的

派　repugnance *n.* 厌恶；不一致

---

repulse [rɪˈpʌls]

【考法】 *vt.* 使厌恶，排斥：to rebuff or **reject with** rudeness, coldness, or **denial**

例　The scenes of violence in the film may repulse some viewers. 电影中某些暴力场景可能会使观众反感。

近　disgust, nauseate, repel, revolt, sicken

反　allure, attract, bewitch, captivate, charm, enchant, entice, fascinate, lure, seduce, tempt 吸引，诱惑

派　repulsion *n.* 排斥

Unit 6

repute [rɪˈpjuːt]

【考法】 *n.* (尤指好的)名声，名誉：a **good reputation**

例 Before his national bestseller, he was a writer of little repute. 在他的全国畅销书面市之前他是个没什么名声的作家。

近 celebrity, fame, name, renown, reputation

反 infamy, notoriety 坏名声

派 reputable *adj.* 有好名声的

requite [rɪˈkwaɪt]

【考法 1】 *vt.* 酬谢，报答：to **make repayment** or return for

例 requite her love with hatred 恩将仇报

近 indemnify, reciprocate, recompense, recoup, reimburse, remunerate, repay

【考法 2】 *vt.* 报仇：to **punish in kind** the wrongdoer responsible for

例 The future writer would later requite the abuse he suffered at the hands of his classmates by creating scathing portraits of them in his novels. 未来的作家会把在同学那里受了委屈的帐算清的——他会在小说中把他们描绘成恶人。

近 avenge, redress, retaliate, revenge

反 absolve, condone, forgive, pardon 饶恕，宽恕

requisite [ˈrekwɪzɪt]

【考法 1】 *n.* 必需品：**something necessary**, indispensable, or unavoidable

例 Calculus is a requisite for modern physics. 微积分是学习近代物理的必要知识。

近 condition, demand, necessity, need, requirement

【考法 2】 *adj.* 必不可少的，必备的：essential, **necessary**

例 Oxygen is requisite for human to survive. 氧气是维持人类生存的必要条件。

近 critical, compulsory, imperative, indispensable, mandatory, necessary, obligatory, required, vital

反 needless, unnecessary 不必要的；dispensable, optional 可替换的，可选择的

rescind [rɪˈsɪnd]

【考法】 *vt.* 废除，取消：to **make void**

例 The government refused to rescind the order of curfew. 政府拒绝撤销宵禁的决定。

近 abolish, abrogate, annul, cancel, invalidate, negate, null, nullify, recall, repeal, revoke, void

反 establish, enact 建立；continue, keep 维持，保持

reserved [rɪˈzɜːrvd]

【考法】 *adj.* 内向的，缄默的：**restrained** in words and actions

例 too reserved to offer a spontaneous criticism 过于缄默而不愿意发表真实的看法

近 closemouthed, constrained, laconic, reticent, restrained, silent, taciturn

反 communicative, expansive, talkative 健谈的；garrulous, loquacious 话多的

派 unreserved *adj.* 无保留的，外向的

residue [ˈrezɪduː]

【考法】 *n.* 剩余物：something that **remains** after a part is taken, separated, or designated

例 In the race of nature, there is no residue left for the late. 在大自然的竞争中，总是早起的鸟儿才有虫吃。

近 debris, remainder, remnant

派 residual *adj.* 剩余的

resign [rɪˈzaɪn]

【考法】 *vt.* 辞职，放弃(职位)：to **give up** one's job or **office**

例 She resigned her position at the university. 她自动放弃她在大学的职位。

近 abnegate, cede, relinquish, renounce, surrender, step down

反 assume, inaugurate 就职，承担(责任)；usurp 篡位

resilience [rɪˈzɪliəns]

【考法 1】 *n.* 弹力：the property of a material that enables it to **resume** its **original shape** or position after being bent, stretched, or compressed

近 elasticity, flexibility, malleability, pliability

反 inelasticity 无弹性

【考法2】 *n.* 恢复能力：the **ability to recover quickly** from illness, change, or misfortune

例 Her mental resilience helped her promptly walk out of the shadow of her father's death. 她的精神恢复能力让她很快地走出了父亲去世的阴影。

近 adaptability

派 resilient *adj.* 有弹性的；能迅速恢复的

resolute [ˈrezəluːt]

【考法】 *adj.* 坚定的：marked by **firm determination**

例 We are glad to have such a resolute ally. 我们很高兴能拥有这样一个坚定的盟友。

近 bound, decided, faithful, resolved, unwavering

反 faltering, hesitant, indecisive, irresolute, jittery, vacillating, wavering 犹豫的，踌躇的

派 resolution *n.* 坚定的决心

resonant [ˈrezənənt]

【考法】 *adj.* (声音)洪亮的，共鸣的：**strong** and deep **in tone**

例 A deep resonant voice rang out. 传来了洪亮的声音。

近 consonant, orotund, plangent, resounding, reverberant, sonorous, vibrant

反 faint, low, muffled, muted, smothered, soft, weak 声音模糊的，低声的

派 resonance *n.* 洪亮

Unit 7

■ RESOURCEFUL	■ RESPITE	■ RESPIRE	■ RESPLENDENT	■ RESPONSIVE
■ RESTIVE	■ RESTLESS	■ RESTRAIN	■ RESURGENCE	■ RESUSCITATE

resourceful [rɪˈsɔːrsfl]

【考法】 *adj.* 有创造力的，机智的：able to **act** effectively or **imaginatively**, especially in difficult situations

例 a resourceful man capable of dealing with difficult situations 一个能巧妙解决困局的能人

近 able, adroit, competent, talented

派 resourcefulness *n.* 足智多谋

respite [ˈrespɪt]

【考法】 *n.* 间歇，休息：an interval of **rest** or relief

例 toil without respite 埋头苦干 ‖ In the middle of each semester there came a short respite. 在每个学期的期中，会有一个短暂的休假。

近 break, lull, intermission, recess, pause, rest

反 resumption 继续进行；exertion, labor, toil, work 劳动，工作

respire [rɪˈspaɪər]

【考法】 *vi.* 呼吸：to **inhale** and **exhale air** successively

例 unable to respire due to heart attack 因心脏病发作而无法呼吸

近 breathe, inhale

反 smother, stifle, suffocate 停止呼吸，窒息

派 respiration *n.* 呼吸

resplendent [rɪˈsplendənt]

【考法】 *adj.* 华丽辉煌的：shining **brilliantly**

例 Geography teacher showed us a picture of the resplendent aurora borealis. 地理老师给我们展示了一张壮丽的北极光的照片。

近 brilliant, glorious, gorgeous, grand, magnificent, splendid, sublime, superb

反 dim, dull, lackluster 黯淡无光的

派 resplendence *n.* 辉煌

responsive [rɪˈspɑːnsɪv]

【考法】 *adj.* 反应的；敏感的：**quick to respond** or react appropriately or sympathetically

例 Children are often the most responsive members of the audience. 儿童通常是观众中最为敏感的群体。

近 prompt, sensible, sensitive, susceptible

反 dispassionate 无动于衷的；detached, indifferent 冷漠的

派 responsiveness *n.* 有反应；热诚

restive [ˈrestɪv]

【考法1】 *adj.* 急躁的，忧虑的：marked by **impatience** or **uneasiness**

例 I spent a restive night worrying about the next day's exam. 我度过了忧虑的一晚，担心明天的考试。

近 restless, nervy, uneasy, uptight

反 imperturbable 沉着的；phlegmatic 冷静的

【考法 2】 *adj.* 难以管束的：stubbornly **resisting control**
例　Tired soldiers grew restive. 疲惫的士兵变得越来越难以管理。
近　balky, contumacious, defiant, insubordinate, intractable, obstreperous, obstinate, perverse, recalcitrant, refractory
反　amenable, biddable, compliant, conformable, docile, obedient, ruly, submissive, tractable 服从的
派　restiveness *n.* 不安，躁动

restless ['restləs]
【考法】 *adj.* 不平静的：marked by or causing a **lack of quiet**, repose, or rest
例　The patient felt restless from pain. 病人因疼痛而无法平静。
近　agitating, anxious, distressful, disturbing, fraught, restive, perturbed, uneasy, unquiet, unsettled
反　halcyon, peaceful, serene, tranquil 平静的，安宁的

restrain [rɪ'streɪn]
【考法】 *vt.* 限制，控制：to **limit**, **restrict**, or keep under control
例　The old lady restrained the child from picking the flowers. 老妇人不准孩子们采摘花朵。
近　bridle, check, constrain, curb, inhibit, measure, prevent, refrain, withhold
反　discharge, release 释放
派　restrained *adj.* 受限制的

resurgence [rɪ'sɜːrdʒəns]
【考法】 *n.* 复兴：a **restoration** to use, acceptance, activity, or vigor
例　Let's witness the resurgence of classical school. 让我们见证古典乐派的复兴。
近　reanimation, rebirth, regeneration, rejuvenation, renewal, resurrection, resuscitation, revitalization
反　decay, degradation, deterioration, downfall, ebb, fall 衰落
派　resurgent *adj.* 正在复兴的

resuscitate [rɪ'sʌsɪteɪt]
【考法】 *vt.* 使复活，使苏醒：to **restore consciousness**, vigor, or life to
例　resuscitated by the kiss of the prince 因王子的吻而苏醒
近　reanimate, recharge, refresh, rejuvenate, rekindle, renew, resurrect, revitalize, revive, revivify
反　faint 昏迷
派　resuscitation *n.* 复活，复兴；resuscitated *adj.* 复活的

Unit 8

■ RETAINER　　■ RETALIATE　　■ RETARD　　■ RETINUE　　■ RETICENT
■ RETORT　　■ RETOUCH　　■ RETRACT　　■ RETRENCH　　■ RETRIBUTION

retainer [rɪ'teɪnər]
【考法】 *n.* 家仆：a person attached or owing **service** to a household
例　Knights are dressed for battle by their retainers. 骑士们在上战场之前是由他们的家仆帮助着装打扮的。
近　menial, servant
反　lord, master 主人

retaliate [rɪ'tælieɪt]
【考法】 *v.* 报复，反击：to **pay back**(as an injury)in kind
例　We swear to retaliate for our losses. 我们发誓要以牙还牙。
近　avenge, redress, requite, revenge
反　absolve, condone, forgive, pardon 饶恕，宽恕
派　retaliation *n.* 报复

retard [rɪ'tɑːrd]
【考法】 *vt.* 减速，延迟：to **cause** to move or proceed **slowly**; delay or impede
例　Language barriers retarded their negotiating progress. 语言障碍让谈判进程受阻。
近　bog, brake, decelerate, delay, detain, hamper, impede, mire, slacken
反　accelerate, catalyze, expedite, hasten, precipitate 加速，促进

retinue ['retənuː]
【考法】 *n.* 随行人员：a **group of retainers** or attendants
例　The premier inspected the factory with his retinue. 总理与随同人员一起视察了工厂。
近　associates, entourage, followers, posse, retainers
反　leader 领导者

reticent [ˈretɪsnt]

【考法 1】 *adj.* 沉默不语的：**inclined to be silent** or uncommunicative in speech
例 He was reticent about his plans. 他对他的计划三缄其口。
近 closemouthed, constrained, laconic, reserved, restrained, silent, taciturn
反 communicative, expansive, talkative 健谈的；garrulous, loquacious 话多的

【考法 2】 *adj.* 不愿意的：**slow to begin** or proceed with a course of action because of doubts or uncertainty
例 Understandably, she's reticent about becoming involved with another religious sect. 不难理解，她不愿意被牵扯进另一个宗教派别之中。
近 cagey, disinclined, dubious, indisposed, loath, reluctant
反 willing 乐意的；disposed, inclined 倾向于做某事的；eager 渴望的

retort [rɪˈtɔːrt]

【考法】 *n.* （尤指机智的）回应，回答：something spoken or written in reaction especially to a question, especially a **quick**, **witty**, or cutting **reply**
例 She responded to the heckler with a scathing but hilarious retort that instantly won over the audience. 面对故意起哄捣乱的人，她那严厉但不失幽默的回答立刻得到了观众的肯定。
近 comeback, rejoinder, repartee, reply, response, return, riposte
反 inquiry, query, question 问题，问询

retouch [ˌriːˈtʌtʃ]

【考法】 *v.* 润饰，改进：to **improve** or change（a photographic negative or print）
例 She was retouching her painting before the deadline. 在截止日期到来之前，她一直在润色她的画作。
近 ameliorate, enhance, furbish, meliorate, perfect, polish, refine, upgrade
反 deteriorate, downgrade, worsen 恶化，降低

retract [rɪˈtrækt]

【考法】 *vt.* 收回，否认：to **take back**
例 The newspaper had to retract its allegations against the mayor. 报纸不得不收回针对市长的谣言。
近 abjure, abnegate, disavow, forswear, recall, recant, renounce, repeal, repudiate, withdraw
反 tender 提出(建议，想法)；adhere, stick 坚持
派 retractable *adj.* 可收回的

retrench [rɪˈtrentʃ]

【考法】 *vi.* 削减开支：to **curtail expenses**
例 Declining business forced the company to retrench. 衰减的业务迫使公司削减开支。
近 economize, reduce, cut down
反 enlarge, expand 扩大，扩张
派 retrenchment *n.* 削减开销

retribution [ˌretrɪˈbjuːʃn]

【考法】 *n.* 报偿，报应：the dispensing or receiving of **reward or punishment** especially in the hereafter
例 The neighborhood is being torn apart by an endless cycle of gang violence and retribution. 这个社区正在被帮派间斗争和仇恨的恶性循环割裂。
近 avengement, payback, recompense, reparation, repayment, requital, retaliation, revenge, vengeance
派 retributive *n.* 报应的

Unit 9

■ RETROGRADE	■ RETROSPECTIVE	■ REVELRY	■ REVENGE	■ REVERE
■ REVISE	■ REVIVE	■ REVOKE	■ REVOLT	■ RIBALD

retrograde [ˈretrəɡreɪd]

【考法 1】 *adj.* 倒退的：**moving** or tending **backward**
例 This is a retrograde step and you will regret it. 这是后退的一步，你以后肯定会后悔的。
近 backward, receding, regressive, reversed, withdrawing
反 progressive 前进的

【考法 2】 *vi.* 退步，退化：to **decline** to a worse condition
例 The Dark Ages is the period following the fall of the Roman Empire when Western civilization seriously retrograded. "黑暗时代"指的是罗马帝国崩溃之后，西方文明严重退步的一个历史时期。
近 atrophy, crumble, decay, decline, degenerate, descend, deteriorate, ebb, regress, rot, sink, worsen
反 ameliorate, improve, meliorate 改善

retrospective [ˌretrəˈspektɪv]

【考法】 *adj.* 回顾的：**looking back** on, contemplating, or directed to the past

例 a retrospective glance at my youth 朝我少年时代投去的回顾性一瞥

近 backward

反 anticipatory, prospective 预期的，未来的

revelry [ˈrevlri]

【考法】 *n.* 狂欢，喧闹的作乐：**noisy partying** or merrymaking

例 They were exhausted after the night of revelry. 一夜狂欢后大家都筋疲力尽。

近 conviviality, festivity, gaiety, jollity, merriment, rejoicing, revel, whoopee

反 gloom, grief, melancholy, misery, mournfulness, sorrow, woe 悲哀，哀痛

revenge [rɪˈvendʒ]

【考法 1】 *n.* 报复，复仇：an act or instance of **retaliating** in order to get even

例 Both sides were determined to get revenge for losses and showed little interest in ending the feud. 双方都下定决心要为失去的东西报仇，对于结束他们之间的世仇毫无兴趣。‖ The bombing was in revenge for the assassination of their leader. 此次轰炸是对暗杀他们领袖的报复行动。

近 avengement, payback, reprisal, requital, retaliation, retribution, vengeance

反 forgiveness, pardon 饶恕，原谅

【考法 2】 *vt.* 为…复仇：to avenge（as oneself）usually by **retaliating in kind** or degree

例 He finally revenged the death of his brother. 他终于为兄弟的死报了仇。

近 avenge, redress, requite, retaliate

反 absolve, condone, forgive, pardon 原谅，宽恕

revere [rɪˈvɪr]

【考法】 *vt.*（尤指对神的）尊崇，尊敬：to offer honor or **respect** to（someone）as a divine power

例 He is revered for his valor. 他因为英勇而受到尊敬。‖ In some cultures people revere their ancestors, even leaving food offerings for them. 在一些文化中，人们非常敬重先人，甚至将一些食物留下来供他们享用。

近 adore, deify, glorify, esteem, regard, respect, venerate, worship

反 blaspheme, desecrate, profane, violate 亵渎

派 reverence *n.* 尊重；reverent *adj.* 恭敬的，虔诚的

revise [rɪˈvaɪz]

【考法】 *vt.* 更改，修正：to look over again in order to correct or **improve**

例 There are many problems involved in revising a dictionary. 修正字典会牵涉诸多问题。‖ With the snow, we'll need to revise our travel plans. 下雪了，我们不得不更改旅游计划。

近 amend, correct, emend, polish, redraft, refine, rework, upgrade

反 discard 丢弃，抛弃

派 revision *n.* 修改

revive [rɪˈvaɪv]

【考法 1】 *vi.* 恢复意识：to **return to consciousness** or life; to become flourishing again

例 His father successfully revived him with artificial respiration. 他的父亲用人工呼吸使他成功恢复意识。

近 come around

反 faint, black out 昏迷，失去知觉

【考法 2】 *vi.* 再获新生：to become **active** or flourishing **again**

例 Around midnight, I usually need to revive myself with a cup of strong coffee. 在午夜时分，我需要一杯浓咖啡来提神。‖ The success of the movie has revived her career. 这部电影的成功让她的事业焕发第二春。

近 reanimate, recharge, refresh, rejuvenate, rekindle, renew, resurrect, resuscitate, revitalize, revivify

反 degenerate, deteriorate, worsen 衰退，恶化

派 revival *n.* 复苏

revoke [rɪˈvoʊk]

【考法】 *vt.* 撤回，宣告无效：to **annul** by recalling or taking back

例 revoke a will 废除遗嘱

近 abolish, abrogate, annul, cancel, invalidate, negate, null, nullify, recall, repeal, void

反 establish, enact 建立；continue, keep 维持，保持

派 revocation *n.* 撤销，废除

revolt [rɪˈvoʊlt]

【考法 1】 *vt.* 使厌恶，使反感：to **fill with disgust** or abhorrence

例 The smell of seafood revolts him. 他对海鲜的腥味十分反感。

近 disgust, nauseate, repel, repulse, sicken

反 allure, attract, bewitch, captivate, charm, enchant, entice, fascinate, lure, seduce, tempt 吸引，诱惑

【考法2】 *vi.* 反叛 : to **renounce allegiance** or subjection（as to a government）

例 They revolted against the dictator by burning his palace. 他们通过焚烧宫殿来对抗独裁者。

近 defy, insurrect, mutiny, oppose, rebel, resist

反 obey, submit 遵从，服从

派 revolter *n.* 反叛者

ribald ['raɪbɔːld]

【考法】 *adj.*（举止、言语）下流粗俗的 : characterized by or indulging in **vulgar**, lewd humor

例 entertain the guests with ribald jokes 用荤段子来取悦客人

近 bawdy, blue, coarse, crude, dirty, filthy, gross, indecent, nasty, obscene, pornographic, profane, vulgar

反 decent, proper, seemly 恰当的，得体的

Unit 10

■ RICKETY	■ RIDER	■ RIDICULE	■ RIFE	■ RIFT
■ RILE	■ RIPEN	■ RIOT	■ RITE	■ RIVE

rickety ['rɪkəti]

【考法】 *adj.* 不稳的 : **lacking stability** or firmness

例 The rickety coalition may break at any moment. 脆弱的联盟随时都可能破裂。

近 insecure, precarious, shaky, unsound, unsteady, weak

反 firm, sound, stable, sturdy 稳定的，稳固的

rider ['raɪdər]

【考法1】 *n.* 骑马的人 : one that **rides**

近 horseman, knight

反 pedestrian, walker 行人，步行者

【考法2】 *n.*（议案的）附加条款 : a clause **appended** to a legislative bill to secure a usually distinct object

近 addendum, appendix, attachment, supplement

ridicule ['rɪdɪkjuːl]

【考法】 *vt.* 嘲笑 : to **make fun** of

例 They always ridiculed everything she said. 他们总是嘲笑她说的话。｜ The term "big bang theory" was originally coined to ridicule the belief that the universe was created by a giant explosion. "大爆炸理论"起初是为了嘲笑一种观点而创造的，这种观点认为宇宙源自一场巨大的爆炸。

近 deride, gibe, jape, jeer, lout, mock, taunt

反 commend, praise 表扬

派 ridiculous *adj.* 荒谬的

rife [raɪf]

【考法】 *adj.* 丰富的，普遍的 : possessing or covered with **great numbers** or amounts of something specified

例 a video game rife with violence and abuse 充满暴力与虐待的电子游戏

近 abounding, abundant, awash, flush, fraught, lousy, replete, swarming, teeming, thick, thronging

反 deficient, incomplete, insufficient, short 缺乏的

rift [rɪft]

【考法1】 *n.* 分裂，不和 : a **break** in **friendly** relations

例 a rift between two once allied nations 两个往昔盟国的决裂

近 crack, fissure, fracture, schism

反 reconciliation, rapprochement 调和

【考法2】 *vt.* 使开裂 : to cause to split open or **break**

例 Hills were rifted by the earthquake. 地震使得山崩地裂。

近 cleave, divide, rip, split, sunder, tear

反 associate, coalesce, combine, conjugate, join, link 接合

rile [raɪl]

【考法】 *vt.* 刺激，惹怒 : to **make agitated** and angry

例 The new work schedules riled the employees. 新的工作时间表激怒了员工。

近 aggravate, annoy, enrage, exasperate, grate, inflame, infuriate, irritate, nettle, peeve, pique, provoke, roil

反 allay, alleviate, assuage, ease, mitigate, mollify, palliate, relieve, soothe 平息，缓和

ripen ['raɪpən]

【考法】 *v.* 使成熟，变成熟：to **make** or become **ripe** or riper

例 Age ripens a good wine. 时间酿出好酒。

近 age, develop, grow, mature

反 fade, flag, shrivel, wane, wilt, wither 使枯萎

派 ripened *adj.* (酒、果实等)成熟的

riot ['raɪət]

【考法】 *n.* 喧闹，暴乱：**public violence**, tumult, or disorder

例 Special police units equipped with riot shields quickly arrived at the airport. 装备有防暴盾牌的特警们迅速抵达了飞机场。

近 clamor, commotion, disorder, ferment, tumult, turmoil, upheaval, uproar

反 serenity, tranquility 宁静；order 秩序

rite [raɪt]

【考法】 *n.* 惯例，仪式：a **prescribed form** or manner governing the words or actions for a ceremony

例 the marriage rites 婚礼仪式的章程

近 ceremony, form, observance, protocol, ritual, solemnity

派 ritual *n.* 仪式

rive [raɪv]

【考法】 *v.* 撕开：to wrench open or **tear apart** or to pieces

例 Lightning rived the tree. 闪电把树劈裂了。

近 cleave, lacerate, rend, ribbon, rip, rupture, shred, split, tatter, tear

反 associate, coalesce, combine, conjoin, conjugate, connect, fuse, interfuse, join, link, unify 联合

派 riven *adj.* 被撕开的

Jovons saw the kettle boil and cried out with the delighted voice of a child;
Marshal too had seen the kettle boil and sat down silently to build an engine.

杰文斯看见壶开了, 高兴得像孩子似地叫了起来; 马歇尔也看见壶开了, 却悄悄地坐下来造了一部蒸气机。

——英国经济学家 凯恩斯(John Maynard Keynes, British economist)

List 22

Unit 1

◼ RIVETING	◼ RIVULET	◼ ROBUST	◼ ROIL	◼ ROISTERER
◼ ROOKIE	◼ ROSTER	◼ ROSTRUM	◼ ROUSE	◼ ROYALTY

riveting ['rɪvɪtɪŋ]
【考法】 *adj.* 吸引人的，极迷人的：wholly **absorbing** or **engrossing** one's attention
例 The riveting novel has, as previously expected, become a national best-seller. 正如先前所预料的，这本引人入胜的小说成为了畅销书。
近 absorbing, arresting, engaging, engrossing, enthralling, fascinating, immersing, intriguing, involving
反 insipid, vapid 索然无味的；boring, dull, monotonous, tedious 单调的

rivulet ['rɪvjələt]
【考法】 *n.* 小河，小溪：a **small stream**
例 Dream Rivulet Diary《梦溪笔谈》
近 brook, brooklet, creek, streamlet

robust [roʊ'bʌst]
【考法】 *adj.* 精力充沛的；强壮的，健康的：**full of** health and **strength**
例 a robust older man who still bicycles 10 miles a day 一个每天骑行 10 英里的充满活力的老人
近 bouncing, dynamic, energetic, gingerly, hale, potent, strong, sound, vigorous, vital, wholesome
反 delicate, frail, weak 弱不禁风的；ailing, diseased, ill, sick, unfit, unhealthy, unsound 不健康的
派 robustness *n.* 健壮，活力四射

roil [rɔɪl]
【考法 1】 *vt.* 搅浑，使混乱：to **stir up**; disorder
例 He roiled the brook with his wood stick. 他用他的木棍将溪水搅浑。|| Financial markets have been roiled by the banking crisis. 银行业的危机搅乱了金融市场的秩序。
近 disarray, disorder, disrupt, disturb, mess, muddle, rile
反 arrange, array, order, organize, regulate 整理，使有序
【考法 2】 *vt.* 激怒：to **displease** or disturb
例 Some of his roommate's habits began to roil him. 他室友的某些习惯开始让他恼火。
近 aggravate, enrage, exasperate, incense, inflame, infuriate, irritate, provoke, rile, vex
反 delight, gratify, please 使愉快

roisterer ['rɔɪstər]
【考法】 *n.* 喝酒喧闹的人：one who **engages in merrymaking** especially in honor of a special occasion
例 the rowdy roisterers who fill the streets of New Orleans during Mardi Gras 四旬斋前最后一天遍布新奥尔良各条街道的喧闹人群
近 celebrator, merrymaker, partyer (*also* partier), partygoer, reveler
反 killjoy 扫兴的人

rookie ['rʊki]
【考法】 *n.* 新兵；新手；菜鸟：**recruit**; novice
例 The rookie replaced the injured regular at first base. 这个新手代替了受伤的一垒手。
近 apprentice, fledgling, freshman, greenhorn, neophyte, novice, recruit, tyro
反 veteran 老兵

roster ['rɔːstər]
【考法】 *n.* 值勤表，花名册：a roll or **list of personnel**
例 the roster of subscribers to the journal 杂志订阅者名册
近 catalog, checklist, list, menu, roll, schedule

rostrum [ˈrɔːstrəm]
【考法】 *n.* 讲坛，演讲坛：a **stage** for public **speaking**
例 He finally stood on the winner's rostrum. 他终于站在了胜利者的领奖台上。
近 dais, lectern, podium, stage, stand, tribune

rouse [raʊz]
【考法 1】 *vt.* 激起，煽动：to **stir up**
例 He was roused to fury. 他大为光火。
近 agitate, excite, motivate, provoke, stimulate
反 allay, alleviate, assuage, ease, mitigate, mollify, palliate, relieve, soothe 平息，缓和
【考法 2】 *vt.* 唤醒：to cause to **stop sleeping**
例 The piercing siren roused her from a deep sleep. 刺耳的警笛声将她从沉睡中唤醒。
近 arouse, awake, awaken, waken
反 lull 使睡着

royalty [ˈrɔɪəlti]
【考法 1】 *n.* 皇家身份：**regal character** or bearing
近 aristocracy, nobility
【考法 2】 *n.* 版税；专利权税：a **payment** to an author or composer for each copy of a work sold or to an inventor for each item sold under a patent
例 charge KTV owners royalty fee 向 KTV 索取版权费

Unit 2

■ RUBICUND	■ RUDIMENTARY	■ RUE	■ RUFFLE	■ RUMINATE
■ RUMPLE	■ RUN	■ RUNIC	■ RUPTURE	■ RUSE

rubicund [ˈruːbɪkənd]
【考法】 *adj.* 红润的，健康的：inclined to a **healthy rosiness**
例 A rubicund complexion indicates good health. 红色的气色意味着身体健康。
近 blooming, florid, flush, rosy, ruddy, sanguine
反 ashen, pale, pallid, wan 苍白的，虚弱的

rudimentary [ˌruːdɪˈmentri]
【考法 1】 *adj.* 初始的，未发展的：being in the **earliest** stages of **development**
例 The equipment of these past empire-builders was rudimentary. 过去这些帝国的建造者们使用的都是极其原始的工具。
近 incipient, nascent, primitive, primordial
反 developed, full-blown, mature, ripe 成熟的，发展完全的
【考法 2】 *adj.* 最根本的，基础的：consisting in **first principles**: fundamental
例 The dropout had only a rudimentary knowledge of science. 这个辍学的孩子对科学知识只有最基本的一些了解。
近 basic, elemental, essential, fundamental, rudimental, underlying
反 advanced, higher 进阶的，高级的

rue [ruː]
【考法】 *n.* 后悔，遗憾：the **feeling of regret**, remorse, or sorrow for
例 With rue my heart is laden. 我的内心充满了遗憾。
近 contriteness, contrition, penitence, regret, remorse, remorsefulness, repentance
反 impenitence, remorselessness 不知悔改
派 rueful *adj.* 后悔的

ruffle [ˈrʌfl]
【考法 1】 *n.* 皱褶，褶裥花边：a **strip** of fabric gathered or pleated on one **edge**
近 rumple, wrinkle
派 ruffled *adj.* 有褶裥边修饰的
【考法 2】 *vt.* 使粗糙：to **destroy** the **smoothness** or evenness of
例 The acid ruffled the surface of the catalyst. 酸使得催化剂的表面变得粗糙。
近 abrade, chafe, erode, roughen, rub, wear
反 glaze, smooth 使平滑

【考法 3】 *vt.* 扰乱，打扰：to **disturb** the peace of mind of（someone）especially by repeated disagreeable acts

例 The stream of minor complaints finally ruffled him into snapping, "If you don't like the way I'm doing it, do it yourself!" 一系列斤斤计较的抱怨终于让他爆发："如果你不喜欢我做事的方法，你就自己去做！"

近 annoy, bother, chafe, frost, gall, grate, itch, nettle, peeve, persecute, pique, rasp, rile, vex

反 allay, alleviate, assuage, ease, mitigate, mollify, palliate, relieve, soothe 平息，缓和

ruminate ['ruːmɪneɪt]

【考法】 *v.* 沉思：to **go over in the mind** repeatedly and often casually or slowly

例 ruminate the reason of past failures 沉思以往失败的原因

近 cogitate, contemplate, deliberate, meditate, perpend, ponder, weigh

反 ignore, neglect, overlook 忽视

派 ruminative *adj.* 沉思的

rumple ['rʌmpl]

【考法 1】 *vt.* 使皱，弄皱：to wrinkle or **form** into folds or **creases**

例 The guest rumpled the antique bedspread by sitting on it. 客人坐在古董床单上把它弄皱了。

近 crinkle, crumple, ruffle, scrunch, wrinkle

反 flatten, smooth 使表面平整；preen 整理羽毛，打扮

【考法 2】 *vt.* 打乱，使不整齐：to **undo the proper order** or arrangement of

例 The aunt would invariably rumple the little boy's hair whenever she came to visit. 不论小男孩的姨妈何时来拜访，她总是要弄乱他的头发。

近 disarray, disorder, disorganize, disrupt, disturb, mess, muddle, upset

反 arrange, array, order, organize, regulate 整理，使有序

派 rumpled *adj.* 褶皱的

run [rʌn]

【考法】 *n.*（不间断的）连续演出：an unbroken **course of performances** or showings

例 The play had a long run. 此剧一口气演了很长时间。

近 continuance, duration, persistence

runic ['ruːnɪk]

【考法】 *adj.* 神秘的：having some secret or **mysterious** meaning

例 painstaking efforts to decipher the runic inscriptions 为破解神秘的碑文付出的辛勤劳动

近 arcane, enigmatic, impenetrable, inscrutable, mysterious, mystic, occult, uncanny

反 comprehensible, fathomable 可理解的

rupture ['rʌptʃər]

【考法】 *v.* 打破；打碎，破裂：to **part** by violence

例 Jealousy ruptured our friendly relationship. 嫉妒破坏了我们之间的友谊。

近 breach, burst, disjoin, dissect, fracture, separate, split, sunder, tear

反 associate, coalesce, combine, conjoin, conjugate, connect, fuse, interfuse, join, link, unify 联合

ruse [ruːz]

【考法】 *n.* 诡计：a wily **subterfuge**

例 This is a ruse to divide them. 这是一招反间计。

近 artifice, maneuver, stratagem, trick, wile

Unit 3

| ■ RUSTIC | ■ RUSTLE | ■ SABOTAGE | ■ SACCHARINE | ■ SACRILEGE |
| ■ SADDLE | ■ SAFEGUARD | ■ SAGE | ■ SALIENT | ■ SALUBRIOUS |

rustic ['rʌstɪk]

【考法 1】 *n.* 乡下人，头脑简单的人：an **awkward or simple person** especially from a small town or the country

例 a rustic who was awed by the prices that city dwellers had to pay 一个被大城市房价所吓到的乡下人

近 bumpkin, churl, countryman, provincial, rube, yokel

反 cosmopolitan, cosmopolite, sophisticate 见多识广的人

【考法 2】 *adj.* 乡村的：of, relating to, associated with, or typical of **open areas with few buildings** or people

例 We went to a rustic area that is devoid of skyscrapers and shopping malls. 我们去了一个没有摩天大楼和购物中心的乡村原野。

近 bucolic, country, pastoral

反 urban 都市的

【考法 3】 *adj.* 粗俗的：**lacking** in social graces or **polish**
近 clumsy, discourteous, gauche, impertinent, impolite, inelegant, rude, stiff
反 graceful, polished, urbane 文雅的
派 rustically *adv.* 粗俗地

rustle [ˈrʌsl]
【考法】 *vi.* 快速地行动：to **move or act** energetically or **with speed**; to proceed or move quickly
例 The little boy rustled around enthusiastically on the first morning of the trip. 旅行的第一个早晨，小男孩充满热情地跑来跑去。
近 bolt, breeze, careen, career, hasten, hustle, jump, run, rush, scurry
反 crawl, creep 匍匐前行；poke 缓慢行动

sabotage [ˈsæbətɑːʒ]
【考法 1】 *n.* 妨害，破坏：treacherous action to defeat or **hinder a cause** or an endeavor; deliberate subversion
例 sabotage of the project by government officials 被政府官员阻止的项目
近 damage, impairment, subversion, undermining
反 assistance 支援
【考法 2】 *vt.* 从事破坏活动，阻止：to **practice sabotage** on
例 He sabotaged his opponent's campaign with rumors. 他用谣言来破坏对手的竞选活动。‖ My ex-wife deliberately sabotages my access to the children. 我的前妻故意阻止我和我的孩子们见面。
近 disrupt, foil, frustrate, obstruct, undermine
反 assist, support 支持；advance, cultivate, forward, foster, further, nurture, promote 促进

saccharine [ˈsækərɪn]
【考法 1】 *adj.* 像糖一样的，有甜味的：of, relating to, or resembling that of **sugar**
例 a powdery substance with a saccharine taste 有甜味的粉状物质
近 cloying, sugary
反 bitter 苦涩的
【考法 2】 *adj.* 做作的，矫情的：**appealing to the emotions** in an obvious and tiresome way
例 The movie was funny, but it had a saccharine ending in which everyone lives happily ever after. 电影还是很有意思的，但是结局太做作了——所有人从此都幸福地生活在了一起。
近 fruity, maudlin, mawkish, mushy, sentimental, sugarcoated
反 unsentimental 不动感情的

sacrilege [ˈsækrəlɪdʒ]
【考法】 *n.* 亵渎圣物：desecration, **profanation**, misuse, or theft of something **sacred**
例 To play Mozart's music on a kazoo is sacrilege. 用小木笛演奏莫扎特的音乐是对它的一种亵渎。
近 blasphemy, defilement, desecration, irreverence, impiety, profanation, violation
反 adoration, glorification, respect, reverence 爱慕，尊敬
派 sacrilegious *adj.* 不敬的，亵渎神明的

saddle [ˈsædl]
【考法】 *vt.* 使某人负担：to **load** or burden
例 He has saddled himself with a houseful of impecunious relatives. 一屋子的穷亲戚成了他的负担。
近 burden, encumber, freight, lade, lumber, impose, inflict, tax, weight
反 disburden, discharge, disencumber, unburden, unlade, unload 卸下

safeguard [ˈseɪfɡɑːrd]
【考法 1】 *n.* 保护措施：a technical contrivance to **prevent accident**
例 legal safeguards against fraud 防止欺诈的法律措施
近 aegis, caution, defense, fail-safe, guard, palladium, precaution, preventive, security
【考法 2】 *vt.* 保护：to **make safe**; protect
例 Sheepdogs safeguard the flock from attacks by wolves. 保护羊群免受狼群攻击的牧羊犬。
近 bulwark, cover, defend, fence, fend, guard, keep, protect, screen, secure, shield, ward
反 assail, assault, attack 攻击

sage [seɪdʒ]
【考法】 *n.* 智者：one (as a profound philosopher) distinguished for **wisdom**
例 The young prince made a pilgrimage to the sage, hoping to learn the meaning of life. 年轻的王子走上了向智者取经的道路，希望能领悟到生命的真谛。
近 expert, illuminati, master, mentor, savant, scholar
反 dolt, fool, idiot, simpleton 傻子
派 sagacious *adj.* 睿智的；sagacity *n.* 聪慧

salient [ˈseɪliənt]

【考法】 *adj.* 显著的，最突出的: standing out **conspicuously**

例 The most salient feature of the book is its papyrus cover. 该书最明显的特点就是纸莎草纸的封面。

近 conspicuous, noticeable, outstanding, prominent, remarkable, striking

反 inconspicuous, unnoticeable 不明显的

派 salience *n.* 突出; 特点

salubrious [səˈluːbriəs]

【考法】 *adj.* 有益健康的: favorable to or **promoting health** or well-being

例 Every year I go to Kunming to enjoy its cool and salubrious climate. 每年我都会去昆明享受它那凉爽宜人的气候。

近 good, healthy, restorative, salutary, tonic, wholesome

反 debilitating, deleterious, noxious, virulent 有害的，有毒的

Unit 4

■ SALUTARY	■ SALUTATION	■ SALVAGE	■ SALVE	■ SANCTIFY
■ SANCTIMONIOUS	■ SANCTION	■ SANCTUARY	■ SAND	■ SANGUINE

salutary [ˈsæljəteri]

【考法 1】 *adj.* 有益健康的: beneficial, **promoting health**

例 salutary exercise 有益健康的锻炼

近 good, healthy, restorative, salubrious, tonic, wholesome

反 debilitating, deleterious, noxious, virulent 有害的，有毒的

【考法 2】 *adj.* 有利的，利好的: **promoting** or contributing to personal or social **well-being**

例 The low interest rates should have a salutary effect on business. 低利率对于商业而言应该是有利的。 a salutary warning 善意的警告

近 advantageous, benefic, beneficent, benignant, favorable, friendly, helpful, kindly, profitable

反 bad, disadvantageous, unfavorable, unfriendly, unhelpful, unprofitable 不利的

salutation [ˌsæljuˈteɪʃn]

【考法 1】 *n.* 致敬，打招呼(表示欢迎和礼貌): a polite expression of **greeting** or goodwill

例 The veteran stepped forward, raising his hand in salutation. 老兵向前一步，举起手致敬。

近 greeting, regards, salute

反 farewell, bon voyage (离别时的)再见，一路顺风

派 salute *v.* 敬礼，致敬

【考法 2】 *n.* 赞扬: a formal expression of **praise**

例 The speaker introduced the evening's honored guest with a lavish salutation. 主持人用大量赞扬的话介绍了今晚的嘉宾。

近 accolade, citation, commendation, eulogium, eulogy, homage, hymn, paean, panegyric, tribute

salvage [ˈsælvɪdʒ]

【考法】 *vt.* (从灾难中)抢救: to **save from loss** or destruction

例 salvage the torpedoed vessel 拯救被鱼雷击中的舰艇

近 rescue, retrieve, save

反 abandon, desert, forsake 放弃，抛弃

派 salvageable *adj.* 可以挽回的

salve [sælv]

【考法】 *v.* 减轻，缓解: quiet, **assuage**

例 The company give him a raise in salary to salve his feelings. 公司决定给他加薪以安抚他的情绪。

近 allay, balm, becalm, compose, lull, lullaby, quiet, settle, soothe, still, tranquilize

反 agitate, discompose, disquiet, disturb, perturb, upset, vex 打扰，扰乱

sanctify [ˈsæŋktɪfaɪ]

【考法】 *vt.* 使神圣，将…敬为神: to **make holy**

例 The Constitution sanctified the rights of the people. 宪法认为人权是至高无上的。

近 consecrate, hallow

反 desecrate, profane 亵渎

派 sanctification *n.* 敬为神明

sanctimonious ［ˌsæŋktɪ'moʊniəs］

【考法】 *adj.* 假装虔诚的：**hypocritically pious** or devout

例 a sickening sanctimonious smile 令人厌恶的伪善的笑容

近 canting, deceiving, hypocritical

反 devout, religious, pious 虔诚的

sanction ［'sæŋkʃn］

【考法1】 *vt.* 批准，同意，认可：to **make valid** or binding usually by a formal procedure（as ratification）

例 The President sanctioned covert operations. 总统批准了秘密行动。‖ The administration will sanction almost any field trip with educational value. 基本上任何有教育意义的实地考察都可以得到批准。

近 accredit, approbate, authorize, certify, confirm, finalize, formalize, license, ratify, warrant

反 interdict, prohibit, proscribe 禁止；decline, deny, disallow, disapprove, negative, reject, veto 否决

【考法2】 *n.* 制裁：an economic or military **coercive measure** adopted usually by several nations in concert for forcing a nation violating international law to desist or yield to adjudication

例 Another trade sanction is in effect. 又一项贸易制裁生效了。

近 penalty, punishment

sanctuary ［'sæŋktʃueri］

【考法】 *n.* 避难所：a place of refuge and **protection**

例 In earlier times a criminal could use a church as a sanctuary. 在以前，犯罪分子可以将教堂当作避难所。

近 asylum, cover, harbor, haven, port, refuge, shelter

sand ［sænd］

【考法】 *vt.* 磨光：to **make smooth** by friction

例 Be sure to sand before you paint the shelf. 在上漆之前一定要先磨光。

近 buff, file, hone, rasp, rub

sanguine ［'sæŋgwɪn］

【考法1】 *adj.* 乐观的，确信的：having or showing a mind **free from doubt**

例 I'm reasonably sanguine about the adoption of the latest proposal. 我非常看好最新的那项提议获得通过。

近 assured, confident, doubtless, implicit, positive

反 doubtful, dubious, uncertain, unsure 怀疑的，不确信的

【考法2】 *adj.* 面色红润的：having a **healthy reddish** skin tone

例 A baby with a sanguine complexion is more likely to leave the hospital early than a sickly-looking one. 面色红润的新生儿比病快快的能更早出院。

近 blooming, florid, flush, glowing, rosy, rubicund

反 ashy, doughy, livid, lurid, mealy, pale, pallid, pasty, peaky, sallow, wan 面色苍白的

Unit 5

■ SANITARY	■ SAP	■ SAPIENT	■ SARCASM	■ SARTORIAL
■ SATE	■ SATIATE	■ SATIRE	■ SATIRIZE	■ SATURATE

sanitary ［'sænəteri］

【考法】 *adj.* 健康的，清洁的：of or relating to **health**

例 sanitary measures 清洁措施

近 aseptic, germfree, hygienic, sterile

反 noxious 有毒的

sap ［sæp］

【考法1】 *vt.* 削弱：to **weaken** or exhaust the **energy** or **vitality** of

例 Weeks of hard work had sapped him and left him exhausted. 连续几周辛苦工作让他筋疲力尽。

近 debilitate, devitalize, enervate, enfeeble, etiolate, prostrate

反 bolster, fortify, invigorate, beef up 增强，使有活力

【考法2】 *n.* 健康，活力：**active strength** of body or mind

例 a child full of sap and vivacity 活力满满的孩子

近 dynamism, energy, esprit, get-up-and-go, gusto, verve, vim, vitality

反 lethargy, listlessness, sluggishness, torpidity 无精打采

sapient [ˈseɪpiənt]

【考法】 *adj.* 聪明的，有洞察力的：having or showing **deep understanding** and **intelligent** application of knowledge

例 a man who is always good for valuable insights and some sapient advice 一个以见解深刻、建议明智著称的男人

近 discerning, insightful, perceptive, prudent, sagacious, sage

反 foolish, unperceptive, unwise 愚蠢的，不明智的

sarcasm [ˈsɑːrkæzəm]

【考法】 *n.* 讽刺，轻蔑：a sharp and often satirical or **ironic** utterance designed to cut or give pain

例 a voice full of sarcasm 充满轻蔑的言论

近 affront, barb, indignity, offense, slap, slight, slur

反 praise 表扬

sartorial [sɑːrˈtɔːriəl]

【考法】 *adj.* 裁缝匠的，裁缝的：of or relating to a tailor or tailored **clothes**

例 poor sartorial taste 很烂的穿衣品位

sate [seɪt]

【考法】 *vt.* 使饱足，充分满足：to glut; to **satisfy** (an appetite) **fully**

例 The information sated her curiosity. 这个消息充分满足了她的好奇心。

近 cram, glut, stuff, surfeit, satiate

反 starve 饿

satiate [ˈseɪʃieɪt]

【考法】 *vt./adj.* (使)饱足(的)，过分满足(的)：to **satisfy fully** or to excess

例 A long drink of water satiated my thirst. 一顿痛饮之后我的口渴得到了缓解。

近 replete, sate, stuff, surfeit

反 tantalize 挑逗，不去满足

satire [ˈsætaɪər]

【考法】 *n.* 讽刺诗，讽刺文学：a **literary** work holding up human vices and follies to **ridicule** or scorn

例 a satire about the music industry in which a handsome but untalented youth is turned into a rock star 一部关于一个长得帅却没才华的年轻人如何被打造成一个摇滚巨星的讽刺文学作品

近 lampoon, pasquinade

satirize [ˈsætəraɪz]

【考法】 *vt.* 讽刺：to **ridicule** or attack by means of satire

例 The movie satirizes contemporary life. 这部电影讽刺当下生活。

saturate [ˈsætʃəreɪt]

【考法】 *vt./adj.* 使饱和，浸透：to **wet thoroughly** with liquid

例 Saturate the sponge with water. 将海绵浸透。

近 bathe, douse, drench, soak, souse, bedraggle

反 wring out 拧出(水)来

Unit 6

| ■ SATURNINE | ■ SAUNTER | ■ SAVANT | ■ SAVORY | ■ SAVVY |
| ■ SCADS | ■ SCANT | ■ SCATHING | ■ SCHISM | ■ SCINTILLATE |

saturnine [ˈsætərnaɪn]

【考法1】 *adj.* 忧郁的，阴沉的：causing or marked by an atmosphere **lacking in cheer**

例 The men awaiting interrogation by the police shared a saturnine silence. 等待警察审问的人们脸色阴沉，沉默不语。

近 bleak, depressive, dismal, dreary, miserable, solemn

反 jovial, bright, cheerful, comforting, cordial, festive, heartwarming, sunshiny 欢乐的

【考法2】 *adj.* 讥讽的：having a **sardonic** aspect

例 a saturnine smile 讥讽的笑容

反 genial 友善的

saunter ['sɔːntər]

【考法】 *vi.* 闲逛，漫步：to travel **by foot** for exercise or pleasure

例 saunter slowly down the street 在街上闲逛

近 amble, ramble, range, stroll, wander, perambulate

savant [sæ'vɑːnt]

【考法】 *n.* 博学之士，学者：a person of **learning**

例 a savant in the field of medical ethics 医学伦理方面的专家

近 pundit, scholar

反 unlearned person 没有学问的人

savory ['seɪvəri]

【考法1】 *adj.* 口感好的，味道好的：**appetizing** to the **taste** or **smell**

例 Cedar is one of the most savory of all woods. 雪松是所有树木中味道最好闻的。

近 ambrosial, appetizing, dainty, palatable, scrumptious

反 noisome, fetid, foul, malodorous, putrid, rancid, reeking, smelly, stenchy, stinky 难闻的

【考法2】 *adj.* 令人愉悦的：giving **pleasure or contentment** to the mind or senses

例 Having to fire someone was not a task that the manager found at all savory. 经理发现不得不开除某人是件非常不讨好的事。

近 agreeable, blessed, congenial, delectable, delicious, delightful, dulcet, enjoyable, felicitous, grateful, gratifying, heavenly, jolly, luscious, palatable, pleasurable, satisfying, tasty, welcome

反 disagreeable, pleasureless, unpalatable, unpleasant, unwelcome 讨厌的，不受欢迎的

savvy ['sævi]

【考法1】 *n.* 老练，机智：**knowledge** gained by **actually doing** or living through something

例 political savvy 政治上的老练精明

近 chops, expertise, proficiency, know-how

反 simplicity, tactlessness, inexperience 单纯，缺乏经验

【考法2】 *v.* 明确了解：to have a **clear idea of**

例 The man growled, "Don't ever date my daughter again—you savvy?" 那男人咆哮道，"你丫以后不准再见我女儿，你丫明白？"

近 appreciate, apprehend, assimilate, behold, catch on, cognize, compass, conceive, decipher, decode, discern, grasp, perceive, recognize, register, seize, tumble to

反 miss 不理解

【考法3】 *adj.* 有见识的，精明能干的：having or showing a **practical cleverness or judgment**

例 A particularly savvy investor, he was among the first to see the potential in tech stocks. 他是一个有卓识远见的投资者，是第一批看到科技类股票升值潜力的人。

近 astute, canny, clear-eyed, clear-sighted, hard-boiled, hardheaded, heady, sharp, sharp-witted, smart

反 unknowing 无知的

scads [skædz]

【考法】 *n.* 许多，大量：a **large number** or quantity

例 scads of people showed up for the party 参加派对的人们蜂拥而至

近 abundance, plenitude, profusion, slew, spate, wealth

反 paucity 极小量

scant [skænt]

【考法】 *adj.* 不足的，缺乏的：barely or **scarcely** sufficient

例 Jobs for teenagers were scant that summer. 那年暑假适合青少年们做的工作很少。

近 exiguous, niggardly, scarce, sparse, stingy

反 considerable, copious, voluminous, profuse, myriad 大量的，相当多的

scathing ['skeɪðɪŋ]

【考法】 *adj.* 尖酸刻薄的：marked by the use of wit that is intended to **cause hurt feelings**

例 a scathing review of the book 尖刻的书评

近 acerbic, acid, acrid, pungent, scalding, snarky, tart

反 polite, calm compliment 礼貌的，平静的称赞

schism ['skɪzəm]

【考法】 *n.* 不一致：a **lack of agreement** or harmony

例 a schism between political parties 党派间的冲突

近 conflict, discordance, disharmony, dissidence, dissonance, disunion, friction, strife

反 accord, agreement, concord, harmony, peace 一致

scintillate [ˈsɪntɪleɪt]

【考法】 *vi.* 闪耀: to emit **sparks**

例 diamond ring scintillated in the sunlight 钻戒在阳光下闪闪发光

近 gleam, glimmer, glisten, glister, luster, sparkle, winkle

派 scintillating *adj.* 才华横溢的: brilliantly lively, stimulating, or witty

例 a scintillating conversation 智慧火花四溅的交谈

反 dull, foolly 迟钝的

Unit 7

■ SCION	■ SCISSION	■ SCOFF	■ SCORCH	■ SCORN
■ SCOTCH	■ SCOUR	■ SCOWL	■ SCRAPPY	■ SCRAP

scion [ˈsaɪən]

【考法】 *n.* 子孙: **descendant**, child

例 scion of a railroad empire 铁路大王的后代

反 ancestor 前辈

scission [ˈsɪʒən]

【考法】 *n.* 切断，分离，分裂: a **division** or split in a group or union: schism

例 The scission of the labor union will compromise the workers' bargaining power. 工会内部的分裂会削弱工人讨价的力量。

近 bifurcation, cleavage, dissolution, division, partition, schism, sundering

反 unification, union 统一

scoff [skɔːf]

【考法1】 *v.* 嘲笑: to treat or address with **derision**: **mock**

例 scoff at the idea 对这个提议不屑一顾

【考法2】 *v.* 狼吞虎咽: to swallow or **eat greedily**

例 He scoffed dinner before running off to the basketball game. 他风卷残云般把晚饭消灭了，就直奔向篮球场。

近 cram, devour, glut, gorge, gormandize, gulp, ingurgitate, inhale, raven

scorch [skɔːrtʃ]

【考法】 *v.* 炙烤，烘干: to **burn** on the surface; to **make dry**

例 scorching sun 火辣辣的太阳

近 dehydrate, desiccate, parch, sear, singe

反 dampen, hydrate, wash, water, wet 使潮湿

scorn [skɔːrn]

【考法】 *vt.* 轻蔑，鄙视，不屑: **reject** or dismiss as **contemptible** or unworthy

例 They were scorned as fanatics. 他们被指责为狂热分子。

近 despise, disregard, flout, contemn, disdain, slight, look down (on *or* upon)

反 adulate 谄媚；venerate, honor, respect, revere 尊敬

scotch [skɑːtʃ]

【考法】 *vt.* 停止: to **put an** abrupt **end to**

例 The prime minister scotched the rumors of her illness. 首相出面澄清了关于她生病的谣言。

近 hinder, thwart

scour [ˈskaʊər]

【考法1】 *vt.* 用力擦洗: to clean, polish, or **wash** by scrubbing **vigorously**

【考法2】 *vt.* 搜查: to look through （as a place）carefully or thoroughly in an effort **to find or discover** something

例 The police scoured the city for the criminal. 警方全城搜索罪犯。

近 comb, dig through, dredge, hunt through, rake, ransack, rifle, rummage, sort through, troll

scowl [skaʊl]

【考法】 *vi.* 皱眉（表现出不高兴）: to contract the brow in an **expression** of **displeasure**

例 scowl down at the misbehaving child 对淘气的孩子皱起眉

近 frown, pout, glare, gloom, glower, lower

反 beam, grin, smile 微笑（表示高兴）

scrappy ['skræpi]

【考法】 *adj.* 好斗的，好吵架的：having an **aggressive** and determined spirit, quarrelsome

例 She was a scrappy girl despite—or, perhaps, because of—her small size. 这个妹子好斗，但是身材娇小，不过这很可能是原因。

近 aggressive, assaultive, combative, militant, pugnacious, truculent

反 nonaggressive, nonbelligerent, pacific, peaceful, unbelligerent, uncombative, timorous 胆小的，爱好和平的

scrap [skræp]

【考法1】 *n.* 废料，废物：**discarded or useless** material

例 The rest of this stuff is just scrap, so sweep it up and throw it away. 剩下的这堆东西都是没用的，把它们打扫一下就扔了吧。

近 chaff, debris, dreck, dross, dust, effluvium, junk, litter, offal, offscouring, raffle, refuse, riffraff, rubbish, waste

【考法2】 *vt.* 抛弃：to **get rid of** as useless or unwanted

例 We've decided to scrap the first car. 我们决定丢弃第一辆车。

近 ditch, dump, jettison, junk, toss, throw away

反 retrieve 找回

【考法3】 *vt.* 终止，放弃原计划：to **put an end to** (something planned or previously agreed to)

例 We scrapped our plans to go to Paris, and set out the next day for Prague. 我们取消了去巴黎的计划，第二天启程奔赴布拉格。

近 abandon, abort, drop, recall, repeal, rescind, revoke, call off, cry off

反 continue, keep 继续，持续

Unit 8

■ SCRAWL	■ SCRIBBLE	■ SCRUPULOUS	■ SCRUTABLE	■ SCRUTINIZE
■ SCUFF	■ SCURRILOUS	■ SCURVY	■ SEAMY	■ SECLUDED

scrawl [skrɔ:l]

【考法】 *vt.* 乱涂，潦草地写：to **write** or draw awkwardly, hastily, or **carelessly**

例 He scrawled a quick note, stuck it in their mailbox, and hurried off. 他草草写了张便条，塞进他们的信箱然后匆匆跑了。

近 scratch, squiggle, scribble

反 write carefully 仔细地写

scribble ['skrɪbl]

【考法】 *v.* 潦草地书写，乱写：to cover with scribbles, doodles, or **meaningless** marks

例 Students scribbled furiously as the teacher lectured. 老师一边讲，学生们一边狂抄笔记。

近 scratch, scrawl, squiggle

scrupulous ['skru:pjələs]

【考法1】 *adj.* 正直的：guided by or in accordance with one's sense of right and wrong; **principled**

例 Less scrupulous companies find ways to evade the law. 道德程度略低的公司钻法律的空子。

近 conscionable, ethical, honest, honorable, moral, principled

反 cutthroat, dishonest, dishonorable, immoral, unconscionable, unethical, unjust, unprincipled 不道德的

【考法2】 *adj.* 一丝不苟的：taking, showing, or involving **great care and effort**

例 The task requires scrupulous attention to detail. 这项任务需要对细节一丝不苟。

近 careful, conscientious, fussy, meticulous

scrutable ['skru:təbl]

【考法】 *adj.* 可以理解的：capable of being **understood** through study and observation; **comprehensible**

例 Her machinations and motives are all too scrutable to us who know her. 她的阴谋和动机对于了解她的我们来说简直昭然若揭。

近 accessible, apprehensible, comprehensible, fathomable, legible

反 mysterious, incoherent, incomprehensible, inscrutable, insensible 神秘而不可知的

scrutinize ['skru:tənaɪz]

【考法】 *vt.* 仔细检查：to examine or **observe** with **great care**

例 I closely scrutinized my opponent's every move. 我仔细注意着对手的每一个举动。

近 examine, review, scan, survey, plumb, check (out)

反 casually glance, gloss over 随意一瞥，敷衍处理

| ♀ | scuff | [skʌf] |

【考法 1】 *v.* (使)磨损：to become scratched, chipped, or **roughened by wear**
- 例 a countertop that won't scuff 一块不易磨损的厨房台面
- 近 abrade, graze, scratch

【考法 2】 *v.* 脚步拖沓：to **move heavily** or clumsily
- 例 The miners scuffed past in heavy boots. 矿工们脚着厚重的靴子，步履蹒跚。
- 近 barge, clomp, clump, flog, flounder, lump, plod, pound, shamble, slog, slough, stamp, stomp, stumble, stump, tramp, tromp, trudge
- 反 breeze, coast, glide, slide, whisk 滑行

| ♀ | scurrilous | [ˈskɜːrələs] |

【考法】 *adj.* 说粗话的：given to the use of **vulgar**, coarse, or abusive language
- 例 scurrilous attacks on the senator 对参议院粗俗的攻击
- 近 contumelious, invective, opprobrious, truculent, vitriolic, vituperative

| ♀ | scurvy | [ˈskɜːrvi] |

【考法】 *adj.* 下流的，让人鄙视的：mean; **contemptible**
- 例 She was beset by a whole scurvy swarm of con artists. 她被一群下流的骗子艺术家蜂拥围攻。
- 近 deplorable, despicable, grubby, lousy, scummy, wretched
- 反 admirable, commendable, creditable, laudable, meritorious, praiseworthy 让人称赞的

| ♀ | seamy | [ˈsiːmi] |

【考法】 *adj.* 肮脏的，堕落的：**sordid**; **base**
- 例 the seamy side of urban life 城市生活的肮脏面
- 近 sordid, base
- 反 decent and respectable 适当而值得尊敬的

| ♀ | secluded | [sɪˈkluːdɪd] |

【考法】 *adj.* 僻静的，隐蔽的：screened or **hidden** from view
- 例 secluded monks 隐居的僧人
- 近 cloistered, covert, isolated, remote, retired, sheltered

Unit 9

■ SECRETE	■ SEDATE	■ SEDENTARY	■ SEDUCE	■ SEDULOUS
■ SEEMLY	■ SEGMENT	■ SELF-ABASEMENT	■ SELF-ABSORBED	■ SEMINAL

| ♀ | secrete | [sɪˈkriːt] |

【考法 1】 *vt.* 隐藏：to **conceal** in a hiding place: cache
- 例 The police found the weapon secreted under the driver's seat of the getaway car. 警方在逃逸车辆驾驶座下发现了隐藏的武器。
- 近 bury, cache, conceal, ensconce
- 反 divulge, display, exhibit 泄密，展示

【考法 2】 *vt.* 分泌：to **generate** and separate (a substance) from cells or bodily fluids
- 反 absorb 吸收

| ♀ | sedate | [sɪˈdeɪt] |

【考法】 *adj.* 淡定的，安静的：**free from** emotional or mental **agitation**
- 例 She remained sedate under pressure. 她在压力下仍保持镇静。
- 近 collected, composed, self-possessed, serene, tranquil, undisturbed, unperturbed, unruffled
- 反 agitated, discomposed, disturbed, flustered, perturbed, upset 不淡定的，狂乱的

| ♀ | sedentary | [ˈsednteri] |

【考法】 *adj.* 固定不动的：**not migratory**: settled
- 例 a sedentary lifestyle 很宅的生活方式
- 反 migratory, peripatetic 流动的，巡游的

| ♀ | seduce | [sɪˈduːs] |

【考法】 *vt.* 劝说(使不忠，使不服从)，诱…误入歧途：to attract or **persuade** to disobedience or disloyalty
- 例 The other firm seduced him with a better offer. 另一家公司用更高的待遇想挖他墙脚。
- 近 allure, decoy, entice, solicit, tempt, lead on
- 反 repulse, ward off 厌恶，不被吸引

sedulous [ˈsedʒələs]

【考法】 *adj.* 勤奋认真的: involving or accomplished with **careful perseverance**

例 a sedulous student 一个勤奋的学生

近 assiduous, diligent, industrious, laborious, occupied, tied-up

反 idle, inactive, unbusy, unemployed, unoccupied 懒惰的

seemly [ˈsiːmli]

【考法】 *adv.* 得体的, 遵守礼节的: **following the established traditions** of refined society and good taste

例 a young lady of seemly appearance, robust health, and keen intelligence 一个打扮得体、身体健康、头脑敏锐的姑娘

近 befitting, decent, decorous, genteel, respectable

反 uncouth, ribald, indecorous, improper, inappropriate, indecent, indelicate, unbecoming, ungenteel, unseemly 粗俗的, 不礼貌的

segment [ˈsegmənt]

【考法】 *vt./n.* 分割; 部分: to **separate** into segments

例 I think I lost one segment of this model kit. 这套模型的一个零件我找不到了。

近 member, partition, portion, section

self-abasement [ˌselfəˈbeɪsmənt]

【考法】 *n.* 自卑, 自谦: degradation or **humiliation** of oneself

反 self-asserting 自信

self-absorbed [ˌselfəbˈsɔːrbd]

【考法】 *adj.* 自恋的, 自私的: **absorbed in one's own** thoughts, activities, or interests

例 a self-absorbed man who seems utterly oblivious to the social problems of his own urban neighborhood 一个超级自私的人, 对于街坊的事情完全视而不见

近 narcissistic, self-centered, self-infatuated, self-obsessed, self-oriented, self-preoccupied

反 self-forgetting, selfless, unselfish 无私的

seminal [ˈseminl]

【考法 1】 *adj.* 有发展性的: containing or **contributing** the seeds of **later development**

反 hamper further development 阻碍进一步发展

【考法 2】 *adj.* 创新的: of, relating to, or having the power to originate; **creative**

例 a seminal novel 新颖的小说

反 derivative 派生的

Unit 10

■ SENSATION	■ SENSITIVE	■ SENTINEL	■ SEPULCHRAL	■ SEPTIC
■ SEQUELA	■ SEQUESTER	■ SERE	■ SERENDIPITY	■ SERENE

sensation [senˈseɪʃn]

【考法 1】 *n.* 感觉, 知觉: a perception associated with stimulation of a **sense** organ or with a specific body condition

例 We felt just the smallest sensation of warmth when we leaned against the radiator. 当我们靠着取暖器的时候, 我们也仅仅感到了一点点的温度。

反 anesthesia, numbness 麻木

【考法 2】 *n.* 轰动事件: a state of **intense** public **interest** and excitement

例 the rookie hitting sensation of the American League 这个菜鸟的表现轰动了整个全美大联盟

近 flash, marvel, miracle, phenomenon, portent, prodigy, splendor

反 unnoticed event 不知名的小事

sensitive [ˈsensətɪv]

【考法】 *adj.* 敏感的: **susceptible** to the attitudes, feelings, or circumstances of others

例 He's very sensitive to the sun and will burn if he's outside for any amount of time. 他的皮肤对日光非常敏感, 在外时间长了就会烧灼。

近 susceptible, vulnerable, subject (to)

反 numb 麻木的

sentinel [ˈsentɪnl]

【考法】 *n.* 哨兵，看守：a person or group that **watches over** someone or something

例 a lone sentinel kept watch over the fort 一个哨兵看守着碉堡

近 custodian, guardian, keeper, lookout, minder, sentry, warden, watchman

sepulchral [səˈpʌlkrəl]

【考法】 *adj.* 阴沉的；丧葬的：causing or marked by an atmosphere **lacking in cheer**; funereal

例 The decrepit mansion had a sepulchral tone that gave everybody a chill. 破旧的公馆有着一种坟墓的气息，让人皆为之一颤。

近 depressing, desolate, dismal, dreary, morose, sullen, tenebrous

反 merry, bright, cheery, comforting, cordial, festive, heartwarming, sunshiny 欢快的

septic [ˈseptɪk]

【考法】 *adj.* 腐败的，感染的：of, relating to, or causing **putrefaction**

反 free of infection 未被感染的

sequela [siˈkwiːlə]

【考法】 *n.* 结果：a **secondary** consequence or **result**

反 precursor 先兆

sequester [sɪˈkwestər]

【考法1】 *vt.* 使隔绝，分离：to set apart: **segregate**

例 sequester a jury 让陪审团分开讨论

近 insulate, seclude, segregate, separate, cut off

反 permit to mingle, desegregate, integrate, reintegrate 混合，综合

【考法2】 *vt.* 使隐退：to cause to withdraw into **seclusion**

例 She was sequestered in her room. 她深居简出。

sere [sɪə]

【考法】 *adj.* 干枯的，凋萎的：being **dried** and **withered**

例 a sere region that can't support agriculture 一片贫瘠不能发展农业的地区

近 arid, droughty, thirsty, waterless

反 lush, damp, dank, humid, moist, wet 葱绿的，湿润的

serendipity [ˌserənˈdɪpəti]

【考法】 *n.* 意外发现珍奇（或称心）事物的本领：the faculty of making fortunate discoveries **by accident**

例 They found each other by pure serendipity. 他俩的相识属于缘分天注定。

serene [səˈriːn]

【考法1】 *adj.* 安静的：**free from** disturbing noise or **uproar**

例 a serene vacation spot 一处宁谧的度假胜地

近 arcadian, calm, hushed, peaceful, placid, restful, still, tranquil

反 boisterous, clamorous, clattery, deafening, raucous, roistering, romping, rowdy, tumultuous, unquiet, uproarious 喧闹的

【考法2】 *adj.* 稳重的，镇静的：**unaffected** by disturbance; **calm** and unruffled

例 a serene man who was everyone's source of support 一个沉着镇静的男人，他是所有人的精神支柱

近 collected, composed, possessed, recollected, undisturbed, unperturbed, unruffled

反 agitated, discomposed, disturbed, flustered, perturbed, unhinged, unstrung, upset 暴躁的，不安的

派 serenity *n.* 平静：the quality or state of being serene

反 havoc, pandemonium, tumult, bedlam, riot, furor 混乱，骚动

List 23

Unit 1

■ SERMON	■ SERPENTINE	■ SERRATE	■ SERRIED	■ SERVILE
■ SEVERE	■ SHACKLE	■ SHADOW	■ SHALLOW	■ SHAM

sermon [ˈsɜːrmən]
【考法】 *n.* 布道，说教：**public speech** usually by a member of the clergy for the purpose of giving **moral** guidance or uplift
例 a sermon whose message was that we should love our neighbors as much as we love ourselves 主题是教导我们要像爱自己一样爱邻居的一次布道
近 homily

serpentine [ˈsɜːrpəntiːn]
【考法】 *adj.* 弯曲的：**winding** or turning one way and another
例 The country inn lies at the end of a rather serpentine road. 乡村小酒吧坐落在一条非常蜿蜒的道路的尽头。
近 curved, curvy, devious, sinuous, tortuous, twisted, winding
反 direct, straight, straightaway 直的

serrate [ˈserɪt]
【考法】 *adj.* 锯齿状的：**notched** or toothed on the edge
例 a serrate leaf 锯齿状的叶片
反 without notches, smooth 无凹口的，平滑的

serried [ˈserid]
【考法】 *adj.* 密集的：having **little space** between items or parts
例 Flowers came up every spring in their serried ranks. 大量的鲜花在春季盛开。
近 compact, dense
反 widely separated, airy, loose, open, uncrowded 稀疏的

servile [ˈsɜːrvl]
【考法】 *adj.* 低下的，卑屈的：meanly or cravenly **submissive**: **abject**
例 He had always maintained a servile attitude around people with money. 他对有钱人总是卑躬屈膝。
近 base, humble, menial, slavish

severe [sɪˈvɪr]
【考法1】 *adj.* 严厉的，要求严格的：given to **exacting standards** of discipline and self-restraint
例 a severe, uncompromising teacher 一位严厉、不妥协的老师
近 austere, harsh, ramrod, rigid, rigorous, stern
反 clement, forbearing, gentle, indulgent, lax, lenient, tolerant 温和的，随意的
【考法2】 *adj.* 难以承受的，艰难的：**difficult to endure**
例 a severe winter that was among the coldest on record 有记录的最寒冷的冬天之一
近 brutal, excruciating, grievous, onerous, oppressive, tough, trying
反 easy, light, soft 轻松的

shackle [ˈʃækl]
【考法1】 *vt.* 束缚：to deprive of freedom especially of action by means of **restrictions** or handicaps
例 unwilling to shackle the dogs to the wall of the house 不愿意把狗拴在墙边
近 chain, enchain, enfetter, fetter, gyve, handcuff, manacle, pinion, trammel
反 loose, emancipate, unbind, unfetter, unshackle 解放
【考法2】 *vt.* 限制，阻碍：to **create difficulty** for the work or activity of
例 shackled by poverty and ignorance 被贫穷和无知所阻碍
近 clog, cramp, encumber, fetter, hinder, impede, inhibit, interfere with, manacle, obstruct, short-circuit, stymie, tie up, trammel
反 aid, assist, facilitate, help 促进，帮助

shadow [ˈʃædoʊ]

【考法 1】 *vt.* 偷偷尾随：to follow especially **secretly**: **trail**

例 shadow the suspect to see what he was up to 尾随嫌犯行踪

近 chase, course, pursue, trace, track, trail

【考法 2】 *v.* 遮蔽，(使)变暗：to (cause to) become **gloomy** or dark

派 shadowy *adj.* 模糊的：faintly perceptible: indistinct

例 He had only a shadowy idea of what they wanted him to do. 他对要做的事只有一个模糊的想法。

shallow [ˈʃæloʊ]

【考法】 *adj.* 浅显的，浅薄的：having or showing a **lack of depth of understanding** or character

例 shallow generalizations 一个浅显的概览

近 facile, one-dimensional, skin-deep

反 profound 深刻的，有深度的

sham [ʃæm]

【考法 1】 *n.* 欺瞒：the quality of **deceitfulness**; empty pretense

例 condemn the rigged election as a total sham 指责这次有作弊的选举是彻头彻尾的骗局

反 debunk 揭穿真相

【考法 2】 *v.* 掩饰，假装：to **present a false appearance** of

例 sham a most unconvincing limp just to get sympathy 非常拙劣地假装自己腿脚不便，以博得同情

近 act, affect, bluff, counterfeit, cloak, dissemble, fake, simulate, pretend, profess, put on, pass for

【考法 3】 *adj.* 虚假的：not genuine; **fake**

例 street vendors selling sham designer handbags to gullible tourists 街头小贩向易上当的游客兜售山寨的设计师手包

近 bogus, forged, phony, spurious, unauthentic

反 genuine, authentic, bona fide, real, unfaked 真正的

Unit 2

■ SHIFTLESS   ■ SHIPSHAPE   ■ SHIRK   ■ SHOAL   ■ SHOPWORN
■ SHRED   ■ SHREWD   ■ SHRINK   ■ SHROUD   ■ SHRUG

shiftless [ˈʃɪftləs]

【考法】 *adj.* 胸无大志的，懒惰的：**lacking** in **ambition** or incentive: lazy

例 shiftless spongers who never thought to do anything for themselves 无志气的弃民们，从来没有想过改变自己

近 idle, indolent, slothful

反 industrious 勤奋的

shipshape [ˈʃɪpʃeɪp]

【考法】 *adj.* 井然有序的：marked by meticulous **order** and neatness

例 I like to keep my car shipshape. 我喜欢打理我的车。

近 antiseptic, kempt, orderly, prim, uncluttered, well-groomed

反 disheveled, disordered, disorderly, messy, sloven, unkempt, untidy 混乱的，不整洁的

shirk [ʃɜːrk]

【考法】 *v.* 逃避，规避：to get or **keep away from** (as a responsibility) through cleverness or trickery

例 shirk one's duty 逃避责任

近 avoid, dodge, elude, eschew, evade, shun, weasel out of

shoal [ʃoʊl]

【考法】 *adj.* 浅的：having **little depth**: shallow

例 shoal waters of the bay 海湾附近的浅水区

反 deep 深的

shopworn [ˈʃɑːpwɔːrn]

【考法】 *adj.* 陈旧的：**worn-out**, as from overuse: trite

例 the shopworn suggestion to job applicants to "just be yourself" 老掉牙的让应征者"做你自己"的提议

近 banal, cliché, commonplace, hackneyed, trite, well-worn

反 new, fresh, novel, original, unclichéd, unhackneyed 新的

shred [ʃred]

【考法】 *n.* 少量：a **small amount**; a particle

例 He struggled to retain a shred of his dignity. 他勉强挽救了一点尊严。

近 crumb, driblet, mite, scintilla, spark, speck, sprinkling, tad

shrewd [ʃruːd]

【考法 1】 *adj.* 精明的，机敏的：having or showing a practical **cleverness or judgment**

例 He's shrewd about his investments. 他是个精明的投资人。

近 crafty, cunning, devious, sly, subtle, wily, astute, savvy, sharp

反 foolish, naïve, unknowing 愚蠢的，幼稚的

【考法 2】 *adj.* 刺骨的，强烈的：causing intense **discomfort** to one's skin

例 She pulled her coat tighter against the shrewd breeze whipping down the alley. 巷子里刮着刺骨的风，她拉紧了大衣。

近 biting, bitter, keen, penetrating, piercing, raw, sharp, stinging

shrink [ʃrɪŋk]

【考法 1】 *vi.* (在数量或价值方面)降低，减小：to become **reduced** in amount or value: dwindle

例 His savings quickly shrank. 他的存款急剧减少。

近 compress, condense, constrict

反 balloon, expand, snowball, swell 增大，膨胀

【考法 2】 *v.* (使)本能性地退却(如因遇到使人惊恐的事物)，(使)退缩：to (cause to) **draw back** instinctively, as from something alarming: recoil

例 shrink back from the approaching flames 对着燃烧的火焰望而却步

近 blench, cringe, quail, recoil, squinch, wince

【考法 3】 *vi.* 表示出不情愿，犹豫：to show reluctance: **hesitate**

例 shrink from making such a sacrifice 对做出这样的牺牲犹豫不决

shroud [ʃraʊd]

【考法 1】 *n.* 隐蔽物，可起隐藏、保护或屏护作用的物体：something that **conceals**, **protects**, or **screens**

例 under a shroud of fog 在迷雾的掩护下

【考法 2】 *vt.* 将…从视线中隔离，遮蔽：to **shut off from sight**; screen

例 She shrouded the fact that the child had been adopted. 她将孩子是领养的这个事实隐藏起来。

近 belie, blanket, cloak, conceal, cover, curtain, disguise, mask, occult, screen, veil, blot out, paper over

反 bare, disclose, display, divulge, expose, reveal, show 展示，暴露

shrug [ʃrʌg]

【考法 1】 *vt.* 轻视，忽略：to **dismiss** as of little importance

例 The administration was willing to shrug off the problem. 当局有意忽略这个问题。

近 bypass, disregard, gloss, ignore, neglect, minimize, overlook, overpass, slight, slur

反 attend, heed, mind 留心，注意

【考法 2】 *v.* 脱下(衣物等)：to **rid** oneself of (a garment)

例 She shrugged off her coat and hung it up neatly. 她脱下大衣，将其整齐地挂好。

近 doff, douse, put off, take off

反 don, put on 穿上

Unit 3

■ SHUN	■ SIDESTEP	■ SIGNAL	■ SIMPLETON	■ SIMULATE
■ SIN	■ SINCERE	■ SINECURE	■ SINEW	■ SINGE

shun [ʃʌn]

【考法】 *vt.* 避开，避免：to avoid deliberately; **keep away** from

例 After his divorce he found himself being shunned by many of his former friends. 自从他离婚以来，他发现许多曾经的朋友都刻意躲着他。

近 avoid, dodge, duck, elude, eschew, evade, finesse, scape, shirk

反 accept, embrace, welcome 接受，欢迎；pursue, seek 追寻

sidestep ['saɪdstep]

【考法】 *vt.* (通过逃避而)不遵守：to **avoid having to comply with** (something) especially through cleverness

例 The eager enlistee sidestepped the regulations by lying about his age. 急切的应募者通过谎报自己的年龄躲过了规定的限制。

近 beat, bypass, dodge, shortcut, skirt

反 comply, follow, keep, obey, observe 遵守

signal ['sɪgnəl]

【考法 1】 *adj.* (在重要性、成就方面)非同寻常的: **standing above** others in rank, importance, or achievement

例 The Louisiana Purchase is cited by many historians as one of the most signal events in American history. 从法国手中购买路易斯安那被许多历史学家认为是美国历史上最重要的事件之一。‖ a signal feat 一项非同寻常的伟业

近 distinguished, illustrious, luminous, notable, noteworthy, outstanding, preeminent, prestigious, redoubtable

反 average, inferior, mediocre 一般的,低下的; insignificant, minor, unimportant 不重要的

【考法 2】 *v.* 给出信号: to **direct or notify** by a movement or gesture

例 They signaled at me to come over to their table. 他们向我打招呼要我到他们那桌去。‖ A lock on the suit-case might signal that there's something of value inside. 手提箱上的锁可能意味着里面有贵重物品。

近 beckon, flag, gesture, wave

simpleton ['sɪmpltən]

【考法】 *n.* (缺乏常识的)笨蛋: a person **lacking in common sense**; a stupid person

例 His silly antics at office parties have earned him a reputation as a simpleton. 他在办公室聚会上愚蠢古怪的行为让他被人认为是个蠢货。

近 airhead, dolt, donkey, dullard, fool, idiot, moron

反 intellectual, sage, wit 智者; genius, prodigy 天才

simulate ['sɪmjuleɪt]

【考法 1】 *vt.* 假装,模仿: to have or **take on the appearance**, form, or sound of: imitate

例 cosmetics that simulate a suntan 用来模仿晒黑效果的化妆品

近 act, affect, assume, counterfeit, dissemble, fake, imitate, pretend, profess, sham

【考法 2】 *vt.* 模拟: to **create a representation** or model of (a physical system or particular situation)

例 carry out an experiment to simulate weightlessness 进行了模拟失重状态的实验

sin [sɪn]

【考法】 *n.* 罪恶的事: an action that is or is felt to be **highly reprehensible**; morally unacceptable

例 It's a sin to waste food when people are starving. 当有人还在挨饿时浪费食物是一种罪过。

近 bad, evildoing, ill, immorality, iniquity, villainy, wrong

反 good, morality, right, virtue 美德,美好的行为

派 sinful *adj.* 罪恶的,有罪的

sincere [sɪn'sɪr]

【考法】 *adj.* 真诚的,不做作的: being **without** hypocrisy or **pretense**; true

例 She offered a sincere apology for her angry outburst. 她为她先前的盛怒表示诚挚的歉意。

近 artless, genuine, heartfelt, honest, ingenuous, innocent, natural, real, true, unaffected, unfeigned

反 affected, artful, artificial, assuming, dissembling, fake, guileful, insincere, phony, pretentious 做作的,假装的

sinecure ['saɪnɪkjʊr]

【考法】 *n.* 拿钱不干事的职务;闲差事: an office or position that **requires little or no work** and that usually provides an income

例 Brenda's job was by no means a sinecure: she actually had to work quite hard for her salary. 布伦达的工作一点也算不上闲差事: 实际上为了那点工资她必须没命地干活。

反 drudge, drudgery, moil, sweat, toil, travail 艰苦的工作,苦活

sinew ['sɪnjuː]

【考法】 *n.* 活力,力量: **vigorous strength**; muscular power

例 Money is the sinew of love as well as war. 爱情和战争都要用金钱来保证。

近 energy, firepower, force, horsepower, might, muscle, potency, power, puissance, strength, vigor

反 impotence, impotency, powerlessness, weakness 无力,虚弱

singe [sɪndʒ]

【考法】 *vt.* 轻微烧焦: to **burn superficially** or lightly

例 The iron is too hot, and you'll singe the nightdress. 熨斗太烫了,你会把睡衣烫坏的。‖ The marshmallows got a bit singed over the campfire, but we like them that way. 棉花糖因为营火而有些许烧焦,但我们还是很喜欢它的味道。

近 char, scorch, sear

反 incinerate 烧成灰烬

Unit 4

sinuous [ˈsɪnjuəs]
【考法】 *adj.* 蜿蜒的，迂回的 : marked by a long series of **irregular curves**; not direct
例 The river flowed in a sinuous path through the lush valley. 蜿蜒曲折的河流流过茂密的山谷。|| Thirty-year-old men are novel, rich in content and sinuous in plots. 三十岁的男人是小说，内容丰富，情节曲折。
近 bending, curling, curved, curving, devious, serpentine, tortuous, twisted, winding, windy
反 straight, straightaway 直的，直接的

sip [sɪp]
【考法】 *vt.* (尤指小口地)喝 : to **swallow in liquid form**, especially in small quantities
例 slowly sipping the hot soup 慢慢地喝着热汤 || She sipped her coffee while she watched the sun rise. 她一边看着日出，一边喝着咖啡。
反 gulp, guzzle, quaff, swill 大口地喝

skeleton [ˈskelɪtn]
【考法】 *n.* 骨架，框架 : something forming a **structural framework**
例 Only the charred skeleton of the house remained after the fire. 大火过后整个房子只剩下被烧焦的骨架了。We saw a skeleton of the report before it was published. 在报告发表之前，我们看到了他的整体框架。
近 architecture, configuration, edifice, fabric, framework, framing, infrastructure, shell, structure

skeptic [ˈskeptɪk]
【考法】 *n.* 怀疑者 : one who instinctively or habitually **doubts, questions**, **or disagrees** with assertions or generally accepted conclusions
例 You can either be a skeptic or not, but I believe it anyway. 至于你信不信，我反正信了。
近 disbeliever, doubter, questioner, unbeliever
反 dupe, gull, pigeon 容易上当受骗的人
派 skepticai *adj.* 持怀疑态度的；skepticism *n.* 怀疑论

skimp [skɪmp]
【考法1】 *adj.* 缺乏的，不足的 : **less plentiful** than what is normal, necessary, or desirable
例 The dieter complained about skimp meals that were served at the fat farm. 这个节食者抱怨说减肥疗养地的伙食少得可怜。
近 exiguous, meager, niggardly, poor, scant, scanty, scarce, skimpy, slender, slim, sparing, sparse, stingy
反 abundant, ample, bountiful, copious, generous, liberal, plenteous, plentiful 大量的，丰富的
【考法2】 *vi.* 节省花费，吝啬 : to **give insufficient** or barely sufficient attention or effort to or **funds** for
例 We must skimp and save if we are going to afford a vacation this summer. 要是我们这个夏天要出去旅行，那么就得开始节省出一些钱了。
近 pinch, save, scrimp, spare, stint
反 dissipate, lavish, prodigalize, squander, waste 浪费，挥霍

skirmish [ˈskɜːrmɪʃ]
【考法】 *n.* 小冲突，争论 : a **minor** or preliminary conflict or dispute
例 They had a skirmish over the rules before the debate began. 在辩论开始之前他们因为规则而吵了起来。
近 altercation, controversy, disagreement, dispute, hassle, imbroglio, quarrel, spat, squabble, tiff, wrangle
反 amity, concord, harmony, rapport, rapprochement 和睦，友好

skirt [skɜːrt]
【考法1】 *n.* 界限，边界 : the line or relatively narrow space that **marks the outer limit** of something
例 an old shack on the skirts of the town 城镇边界上的一座老房子
近 borderline, boundary, circumference, compass, confines, edge, frame, fringe, margin, perimeter, periphery, verge
反 center, core, kernel 核心
【考法2】 *vt.* 绕行，避开 : to **go around** or keep away from in order to avoid danger or discovery
例 skirt the construction zone 绕开建筑工地 || The new bill would make it harder for companies to skirt environmental regulations. 新的规定会增加公司逃脱环境监管的难度。
近 bypass, circumvent, detour, shortcut, sidestep
反 pursue, seek 追寻

slack	[slæk]

【考法 1】 *adj.* 松弛的：**not tightly fastened**, tied, or stretched

例 The rope is too slack. 绳子太松了。

近 insecure, lax, loosened, relaxed, slackened, unsecured

反 taut, tense, tight 拉紧的

【考法 2】 *adj.* 疏忽的，大意的：**failing to give proper care** and attention

例 This building contractor is known mainly for his firm's slack workmanship and slipshod construction. 这个建筑承包商因其公司不负责任的粗糙做工和马虎建造的建筑物而臭名远扬。

近 careless, derelict, disregardful, lax, lazy, neglectful, neglecting, negligent, remiss

反 attentive, careful, conscientious 专心的；alert, heedful, mindful, observant, regardful, vigilant, wary, watchful 警惕的

slake	[sleɪk]

【考法】 *vt.* 使满足：to **satisfy** (a craving); quench

例 Mountain climbing has largely slaked my desire for adventure. 登山很大程度上满足了我对探险的渴望。

近 assuage, quench, sate, satiate, satisfy

反 tantalize, tease 诱惑，挑逗；arouse, excite, pique, stimulate 激起，唤起

slant	[slænt]

【考法 1】 *n.* (看待问题、思考的) 角度，看法：a **way of looking** at or thinking about something

例 an interesting slant on the problem of underage drinking 在青少年饮酒这个问题上一个有趣的视角

近 angle, outlook, perspective, standpoint, viewpoint

【考法 2】 *adj.* 倾斜的：running in a **slanting direction**

例 The computer keyboard has a slightly slant surface so that typing is more comfortable for the wrists. 电脑键盘有一个微小的倾斜角，因此打字不会使手腕感到不适。

近 canted, graded, inclined, leaning, listing, oblique, pitched, raked, slanted, sloping, tilting

反 perpendicular, plumb, vertical 垂直的；horizontal, level 水平的

【考法 3】 *vt.* 歪曲 (事实等)：to change so much as to **create a wrong impression** or alter the meaning of

例 Reporters slanted the truth in order to push a political agenda. 为了推动政治进程，记者们歪曲了事实。

近 bend, color, distort, falsify, misinterpret, misrelate, misrepresent, misstate, pervert, twist, warp

反 clarify, clear, elucidate, illuminate, illustrate 澄清，阐明

Unit 5

■ SLATE	■ SLEW	■ SLIGHT	■ SLING	■ SLIPPERY
■ SLIPSHOD	■ SLOPPY	■ SLOTH	■ SLOUCH	■ SLOVENLY

slate	[sleɪt]

【考法】 *vt.* 列入名单，计划，安排：to **put** (someone or something) **on a list**

例 You've been slated for a three o'clock interview. 你的面试被安排在三点。

近 catalog, enroll, enter, index, inscribe, record, register, schedule

反 delete, erase 删除，除名

slew	[sluː]

【考法】 *n.* 大量，许多：a **large amount** or number

例 donate a slew of books to the university library 向大学图书馆捐赠了大量的书籍

近 abundance, bundle, dozen, multiplicity, myriad, plentitude, profusion, scad, shipload, volume, wealth

反 ace, bit, driblet, glimmer, handful, hint, mite, mouthful, nip, ounce, pittance, sprinkle, trace 少量

slight	[slaɪt]

【考法 1】 *adj.* 不重要的：**deficient in weight**, importance

例 a slight comedy that did nothing to further her career 一个对她事业发展没有任何帮助的小喜剧

近 fiddling, frivolous, inconsequential, inconsiderable, insignificant, little, minor, minute, nugatory, trifling, trivial

反 consequential, eventful, important, meaningful, momentous, significant, substantial, weighty 重要的

【考法 2】 *adj.* 轻微的：**small in degree**

例 only a slight chance of success 只有很小的成功概率 ‖ If you have even the slightest doubt, then don't do it. 只要你有一点点疑惑，那就不要去做了。

近 fragile, frail, negligible, outside, slim, small, tiny

反 distinct 显著的

【考法 3】 *vt.* 轻蔑，看不起：to **treat with disdain** or indifference

例 Those snobbish music critics slight any style of music that doesn't fit their personal taste. 那帮自命不凡的音乐评论家看不起所有不符合他们个人口味的音乐。

近 contemn, disdain, disrespect, snub, look down

反 esteem, honor, respect, revere, venerate 尊敬

【考法 4】 *vt.* 忽略，疏忽：to **fail to give proper attention** to

例 She slighted several major authors in her survey of 20th-century fiction. 她在调查 20 世纪小说时忽略了几个重要的作家。

近 bypass, disregard, ignore, neglect, overlook, overpass, shrug, slur

反 attend, heed, mind 留心，注意

sling [slɪŋ]

【考法】 *vt.* 投掷：to **send through the air** especially with a quick forward motion of the arm

例 sling stones at the checkpoint 朝着检查站扔石头

近 cast, chuck, dash, fire, fling, heave, hurl, hurtle, launch, lob, loft, pelt, pitch, toss

反 catch 接住

slippery [ˈslɪpəri]

【考法 1】 *adj.* 光滑的：causing or tending to cause something to **slide** or fall

例 The road is slippery after rain, so drive cautiously. 雨后路滑，谨慎驾驶。

近 greased, greasy, lubricated, oiled, slicked, slithery

反 coarse, rough 粗糙的

【考法 2】 *adj.* 隐秘的：given to **acting in secret** and to concealing one's intentions

例 a bar where a lot of slippery characters were known to hang out 一个有许多秘密人物出没的酒吧

近 furtive, shady, shifty, sly, sneaking, stealthy

反 aboveboard 光明正大的

【考法 3】 *adj.* 意义不明确的：**not precise** or fixed **in meaning**, elusive or tricky

例 a slippery concept that we had trouble understanding 一个我们难以理解的模糊概念

近 ambiguous, elusive, equivocal, evasive, fugitive, obscure, unintelligible, vague

反 apparent, clear, distinct, evident, manifest, obvious, palpable, patent, plain, unambiguous, unequivocal 明确的

slipshod [ˈslɪpʃɑːd]

【考法】 *adj.* 粗心的，随意的：marked by carelessness or **indifference to exactness**, **precision**, **and accuracy**

例 a slipshod piece of research 一项随意的研究 ‖ The hotel had always been run in a slipshod way. 酒店总是在以一种随意的状态运营。

近 botchy, careless, messy, slapdash, sloppy, slovenly, untidy

反 fastidious, meticulous 极仔细的；accurate, exact, precise 准确的

sloppy [ˈslɑːpi]

【考法 1】 *adj.* 邋遢的，不整洁的：**lacking neatness** in dress or person

例 a sloppy child who always seems to have spilled something on his clothes 一个外表邋遢的小孩子，他的衣服似乎总被沾上了什么东西

近 blowsy, dowdy, frowsy, slovenly, unkempt, untidy

反 dapper, dashing, sharp, smart, spruce 外表整洁的

【考法 2】 *adj.* 混乱的：**lacking in order**, neatness, and often cleanliness

例 dump the papers in a sloppy pile on the desk 把纸张随意地叠放在书桌上

近 chaotic, disarranged, disarrayed, disheveled, disorderly, jumbled, littered, rumpled, tousled, tumbled

反 bandbox, crisp, kempt, neat, orderly, organized, shipshape, snug, tidy, trim 整洁有序的

sloth [sloʊθ]

【考法】 *n.* 怠惰，懒惰：**disinclination to action** or labor: indolence

例 Sloth is the mother of poverty. 懒惰是贫穷的原因。

近 idleness, indolence, inertia, languor, laziness, lethargy, shiftlessness, sluggishness, torpor

反 assiduity, diligence, industry 勤奋

派 slothful *adj.* 懒惰的

slouch [slaʊtʃ]

【考法 1】 *n.* 懒人：a **lazy person**

例 She is no slouch when it comes to cooking. 她做起饭来可一点也不懒。

近 deadbeat, drone, idler, loafer, slug, sluggard

反 doer, hummer, hustler, rustler 活跃的人，精力充沛的人

【考法2】 *vi.* 缓慢行走：to go or **move slowly** or reluctantly

例 He slouched towards the church as if going to his own funeral. 他缓缓地向教堂走去，仿佛是要去参加自己的葬礼一般。

近 creep, drag, inch, limp, nose, ooze, plod, poke, snail

反 fly, race, speed, whiz, zip 快走

slovenly [ˈslʌvnli]

【考法】 *adj.* 邋遢的，不整洁的：**lacking neatness** in dress or person

例 For the sake of their image, the band members transformed themselves from clean-cut lads to slovenly rockers. 为了他们自身的形象，乐队成员从健康向上的青年变成了邋遢的摇滚乐手。

近 blowsy, dowdy, frowsy, sloppy, unkempt, untidy

反 dapper, dashing, neat, sharp, smart, spruce, trim 外表整洁的

Unit 6

| ■ SLUGGARD | ■ SLUGGISH | ■ SLUMBER | ■ SLUR | ■ SLY |
| ■ SMARMY | ■ SMART | ■ SMATTERING | ■ SMIRK | ■ SMOTHER |

sluggard [ˈslʌgərd]

【考法】 *n.* 懒人：an habitually **lazy person**

例 The teacher tried to wake up the sluggards who were still sleeping at that late hour. 老师尝试去叫醒那些还在睡觉的懒鬼们。

近 deadbeat, drone, idler, loafer, slouch, slug

反 doer, hummer, hustler, rustler 活跃的人，精力充沛的人

sluggish [ˈslʌgɪʃ]

【考法1】 *adj.* 缓慢的，迟缓的：markedly **slow in movement**, flow, or growth

例 The sluggish pace of the project is worrisome. 项目进展缓慢让人担忧。

近 crawling, creeping, dallying, dilatory, dragging, lagging, languid, leisurely, snaillike, tardy, unhurried

反 bolting, brisk, fast, fleet, hasty, lightning, meteoric, quick, racing, rapid, rocketing, speedy, swift 快速的

【考法2】 *adj.* 迟钝的，反应慢的：**slow to respond**（as to stimulation or treatment）

例 Reptiles are naturally sluggish at low temperatures. 在低温下爬行动物的生理机能自然会趋于迟缓。

近 dull, indolent, inert, lethargic, quiescent, sleepy, torpid

反 active, animated, bouncing, dynamic, energetic, kinetic, spirited, vigorous, vital, vivacious 有活力的

slumber [ˈslʌmbər]

【考法】 *vi.* 睡着：to be in a state of **sleep**

例 She slumbered for hours while the train rolled on. 她在火车行进过程中睡了几个小时。

近 catnap, doze, nap, rest, sleep, snooze

反 arouse, awake, waken 醒来

slur [slɜːr]

【考法1】 *n.* 耻辱：a **mark of guilt** or disgrace

例 Your drunken behavior at the wedding has cast a slur on this family. 你在婚礼上醉酒后的行为给整个家族都带来了耻辱。

近 blot, brand, onus, smirch, smudge, spot, stigma, taint

反 award, credit, glory, honor 荣誉，荣耀

【考法2】 *vt.* 含糊地发音：to pronounce **indistinctly**

例 If you slur your words, the visa officer will have a hard time following you. 如果你说话含糊不清，签证官就很难听懂你的话。

近 mumble, murmur, mutter

反 articulate, enunciate 清楚地表达

【考法3】 *vt.* 疏忽，忽略：to slide or slip over **without due** mention, **consideration**, or emphasis

例 This documentary slurs over certain important facts as it offers a very biased case for a conspiracy theory. 这部纪录片忽略了许多重要的客观事实，而只给出了带有偏见的阴谋论解释。

近 bypass, disregard, forget, ignore, overlook, overpass, slight

反 attend, heed, mind 留心，注意

sly [slaɪ]

【考法 1】 *adj.* 狡猾的: **clever or cunning**, especially in the practice of deceit

例 The movie pairs a sly, dissembling ex-con with an upstanding, straight-arrow cop. 电影把一个狡猾、善于骗人的出狱犯和正直、坦率的警察搭配在了一起。

近 beguiling, cagey, crafty, cunning, designing, devious, foxy, guileful, scheming, shrewd, subtle, tricky, wily

反 artless, guileless, ingenuous, innocent, undesigning 天真纯朴的，无伪装的

【考法 2】 *adj.* 隐秘的，偷偷的: given to **acting in secret** and to concealing one's intentions

例 The maid took a sly look at the letter on the table. 女仆偷偷地看了一眼桌上的信。

近 furtive, shady, shifty, slippery, sneaking, stealthy

反 aboveboard 光明正大的

smarmy [ˈsmɑːrmi]

【考法】 *adj.* 虚情假意的，过分恭维的: **hypocritically**, complacently, or effusively **earnest**

例 He is slightly smarmy and eager to impress. 他有点虚伪，急于给人留下印象。

近 fulsome, oily, slick, soapy, unctuous

反 artless, earnest, genuine, heartfelt, sincere, unaffected 真诚的，真挚的

smart [smɑːrt]

【考法 1】 *adj.* 反应敏捷的，聪颖的: characterized by **sharp quick thought**

例 a smart child who could do well in school 一个能在学校取得良好成绩的聪明孩子

近 alert, brainy, bright, brilliant, clever, exceptional, fast, intelligent, keen, nimble, quick, sharp

反 airheaded, brainless, doltish, dumb, fatuous, mindless, obtuse, senseless, simple, stupid, vacuous, witless 愚钝的

【考法 2】 *adj.* 整洁的: being **strikingly neat** and trim in style or appearance

例 Dressed in their smart new uniforms, the cadets proudly paraded around the grounds of the military school. 穿着整洁的制服，军校的学员们骄傲地在训练场上游行。

近 dapper, natty, neat, sharp, snappy, spruce, trim

反 disheveled, frowsy, sloppy, slovenly, unkempt 不整洁的

【考法 3】 *vi.* 感到疼痛，感到痛苦: to **suffer acutely**, as from mental distress, wounded feelings, or remorse

例 The injection only smarted for a moment. 打针只会痛一小会儿。 || He is still smarting over criticism of his clumsy performance. 那些对他笨拙表演的批评仍然让他感到痛苦。

近 ache, hurt, pain, suffer

反 allay, alleviate, assuage, ease, mitigate, mollify, palliate, relieve, soothe 缓和

smattering [ˈsmætərɪŋ]

【考法 1】 *n.* 浅薄的知识: **superficial** piecemeal **knowledge**

例 a smattering of Greek grammar 略懂希腊语法

反 erudition 博学；insight 深刻的见解

【考法 2】 *n.* 少量: a **small** scattered number or **amount**

例 Only a smattering of spectators presented. 只有少数几个观看者出席了。

近 ace, bit, driblet, glimmer, handful, hint, mite, mouthful, nip, ounce, pittance, sprinkle, trace

反 abundance, bundle, dozen, multiplicity, myriad, plentitude, profusion, scad, shipload, slew, volume, wealth 大量

smirk [smɜːrk]

【考法】 *vi.* (自鸣得意地)笑: to smile in an affected, often **offensively self-satisfied** manner

例 She tried not to smirk when they announced the winner. 当他们宣布她获得了胜利时，她尽可能地保持不露出笑容。

近 grin, simper

反 cry, weep 哭泣；groan, moan, sigh 叹息

smother [ˈsmʌðər]

【考法 1】 *vt.* 使窒息: to be or cause to be **killed by lack of** breathable **air**

例 Children should never be left in cars alone because they could become trapped and smothered. 小孩子不应该被单独留在车中，因为他们很容易被困并且窒息死亡。

近 asphyxiate, choke, stifle, strangle, suffocate

【考法 2】 *vt.* 抑制(表达、说出)，压制: to **refrain** from openly showing or uttering

例 He quickly smothered his inappropriate laughter at the funeral ceremony. 他很快就控制住了自己在葬礼上不适当的笑声。 || Management smothered the true facts of the case. 管理层隐瞒了案件的真相。

近 bridle, check, choke, control, curb, muffle, quash, quell, repress, squelch, suppress

反 unleash, vent (感情)爆发，宣泄；express 表达

Unit 7

smug ［smʌg］
【考法 1】 *adj.* 自大的，自鸣得意的：having too high an **opinion of oneself**
例 The winner was so smug that he lost the support of the crowd. 胜利者过于自大，失去了群众的支持。
近 complacent, egoistic, overweening, pompous, proud, self-satisfied, vain
反 egoless, humble, modest 谦逊的
【考法 2】 *adj.* 整洁的，有序的：being clean and in **good order**
例 The suburb's smug lawns and tree-lined streets bespeak a comfortable affluence. 郊区整齐有序的草坪和种满树木的街道体现出那里生活的舒适和丰富。
近 dapper, kempt, orderly, shipshape, spruce, tidy, trim, uncluttered, well-groomed
反 disheveled, disordered, messy, slovenly, unkempt, untidy 邋遢的，混乱的

smuggling ［ˈsmʌglɪŋ］
【考法】 *n.* 走私，私运：secret **importation or exportation contrary to the law** and especially without paying duties imposed by law
例 He was arrested for smuggling drugs into the country. 他因为向境内走私毒品而被逮捕。
近 bootlegging, contraband

snare ［sner］
【考法 1】 *n.* 无法逃脱的困境：something that **catches and holds**
例 Someday you'll find that your lies are a snare from which you can't escape. 总有一天你会发现，你所说过的谎话都会变成你无法逃脱的困境。 ‖ caught in the snare of drug addiction 处于吸毒上瘾的困境之中
近 entanglement, mesh, morass, net, noose, quagmire, quicksand, toil, trap
【考法 2】 *vt.* 捕捉：to **capture by** or as if by use of a snare
例 They snared a rabbit earlier in the day. 今天的早些时候他们捕获了一只兔子。 ‖ The car salesman successfully snared three potential customers. 汽车销售员成功地让三个潜在客户上钩了。
近 catch, enmesh, ensnare, ensnarl, entrap, tangle
反 disentangle 解开；free, liberate 释放

snarl ［snɑːrl］
【考法 1】 *v.* 纠缠，纠结：to **twist** together into a usually confused mass
例 You'll be awfully sorry if you snarl your fishing line. 要是你把渔网给缠在一起，你肯定会非常后悔的。 ‖ The new regulation has succeeded in nothing but snarling up rush-hour traffic throughout the city. 新的政策将全城高峰时期的交通变得更为复杂难解。
近 entangle, ensnarl, interlace, intertwine, intertwist, interweave, knot, ravel, tangle
反 disentangle, extricate, unravel, unsnarl, untwine, untwist 解开
【考法 2】 *vi.* 咆哮，怒吼：to give vent **to anger** in surly language
例 She snarled at me after I kept badgering her with questions. 在我不断用问题骚扰她之后，她终于忍不住爆发了。
近 bark, fulminate, rant, roar, scream, shout, storm, vent
反 calm 冷静下来

sneer ［snɪr］
【考法】 *vt.* (轻蔑地)嘲笑：to speak in a **scornful**, contemptuous, or derisive manner
例 They would invariably sneer every time they passed the hapless nerds. 每次经过那个不幸的书呆子身边时，他们总是会报以不变的嘲笑。
近 deride, gibe, laugh, jeer, jibe, mock, ridicule
反 esteem, honor, respect, revere, venerate 尊敬

snobbish ［ˈsnɑːbɪʃ］
【考法】 *adj.* 谄上傲下的，自大的：being or characteristic of a person who has an **offensive air of superiority** and tends to ignore or disdain anyone regarded as inferior
例 I expected her to be snobbish but she was warm and friendly. 我本以为她会是个自大的人，结果她非常热心和友好。
近 aristocratic, bumptious, elitist, haughty, imperious, persnickety, pompous, presumptuous, supercilious
反 egoless, humble, modest 谦逊的，不自大的

snub	[snʌb]
【考法】	*vt.* 轻视，不理睬：to treat with **contempt or neglect**
例	The snob in town always snubbed anyone she thought was beneath her. 镇上那个自命不凡的人总是对那些她认为不如她的人不屑一顾。
近	contemn, disdain, disrespect, slight, look down
反	esteem, honor, respect, revere, venerate 尊敬

soak	[souk]
【考法】	*vt.* 使…湿透：to **make thoroughly wet** or saturated by or as if by placing in liquid
例	That downpour soaked my hair, and now I look like a sight. 那场大雨把我的头发淋湿了，所以我现在看起来格外滑稽。‖ We ran for home as soon as the rain started, but our clothes still ended up soaked. 我们一发觉下雨就开始往家里跑，但我们的衣服还是湿透了。
近	douse, drench, drown, impregnate, macerate, saturate, sodden, sop, souse, steep
反	dehydrate, dry, desiccate 脱水；parch, sear, scorch 烤干，烧焦；wring 拧干

sober	[ˈsoubər]
【考法1】	*adj.* 严肃的：marked by **seriousness**, gravity, or solemnity of conduct or character
例	She made a sober reply to what was only a teasing comment. 她很严肃地回复了那个恶搞的评论。‖ Illness is a sober reminder of our mortality. 疾病是死亡给我们发出的严肃警告。
近	earnest, grave, humorless, sedate, severe, sober, solemn, staid, weighty
反	facetious, flip, flippant, humorous, jesting, jocular, joking, playful 轻佻的，幽默有趣的
【考法2】	*adj.* 节制的：given to or marked by **restraint** in the satisfaction of one's appetites
例	The millionaire decided to live a sober life after bankruptcy. 那个百万富翁破产以后决定过有节制的生活。
近	abstentious, abstinent, continent, self-denying, temperate
反	hedonistic, licentious, self-indulgent, sensual, sybaritic, voluptuary 纵欲的，享乐主义的
【考法3】	*adj.* 有理有据的：based on **sound reasoning** or information
例	a sober assessment of the situation 关于局势有理有据的分析
近	firm, informed, justified, levelheaded, logical, rational, reasonable, sensible, solid, valid, well-founded
反	groundless, illogical, invalid, unfounded, uninformed, unjustified, unreasonable, unsound 没有道理的

sodden	[ˈsɑːdn]
【考法1】	*adj.* 湿透的：containing, covered with, or thoroughly **penetrated by water**
例	We stripped off our sodden clothes and wrung them dry. 我们脱下湿透了的衣服并将它们拧干。
近	awash, bathed, doused, drenched, logged, saturated, soaked, watered, waterlogged
反	arid, dry 干燥的
【考法2】	*vt.* 使…湿透：to **wet thoroughly** with liquid
例	Soldiers' boots were soddened by endless hours in muddy trenches. 长时间身处泥泞的战壕使得士兵的靴子湿透了。
近	douse, drench, drown, impregnate, macerate, saturate, soak, sop, souse, steep
反	dehydrate, dry, desiccate 脱水；parch, sear, scorch 烤干，烧焦；wring 拧干

Unit 8

■ SOLACE	■ SOLDER	■ SOLEMNITY	■ SOLICITOUS	■ SOLID
■ SOLILOQUY	■ SOLITUDE	■ SOLVENT	■ SOMATIC	■ SOMBER

solace	[ˈsɑːləs]
【考法1】	*n.* 安慰：**comfort in sorrow**, misfortune, or distress
例	The kind words brought a little solace to the grieving widow. 这些同情的话语给痛苦的寡妇带来了些许安慰。
近	consolation, relief
【考法2】	*vt.* 安慰，安抚：to comfort, cheer, or **console**, as in trouble or sorrow
例	I did my best to solace those bereaved children. 我尽力去安抚那些失去双亲的孩子们。
近	cheer, comfort, console, soothe
反	agonize, distress, harrow, torment, torture, trouble 使痛苦，折磨

solder	[ˈsɑːdər]
【考法】	*v.* 连接，联合：to join or **unite**
例	Wires are soldered onto the circuit board. 电线被焊接在电路板上。‖ The agreement soldered the factions into an alliance. 两个派系因这份协议而结成同盟。
近	associate, coalesce, combine, conjoin, conjugate, connect, couple, fuse, interfuse, join, link, marry, unify
反	disassociate, disconnect, disjoin, divide, sever, split, sunder 分开

solemnity [səˈlemnəti]

【考法】 *n.* 庄严，严肃：the quality or condition of being **solemn**

例 Solemnity is a trick of the body to hide the fault of the mind. 一本正经的态度是肉体为了掩饰精神上的缺陷而耍的花招。‖ The coronation ceremony requires absolute solemnity. 加冕典礼需要绝对的庄严肃穆。

近 earnest, graveness, gravity, intentness, seriousness, sobriety, solemnness, staidness

反 facetiousness, flightiness, flippancy, frivolity, frivolousness, levity, lightheartedness, play 轻佻，欢快

solicitous [səˈlɪsɪtəs]

【考法 1】 *adj.* 为他人操心的，体谅他人的：given to or made with heedful anticipation of the needs and **happiness of others**

例 The solicitous husband had already cleaned the house and cooked dinner by the time his wife returned home from work. 这个十分体谅妻子的好丈夫在他妻子回家之前就把家里清理干净，还把晚餐都做好了。

近 attentive, considerate, kind

反 heedless, inconsiderate, thoughtless, unthinking 不关心的

派 solicitude *n.* 关切，挂念

【考法 2】 *adj.* 迫切的，渴望的：showing **urgent desire** or interest

例 The family is solicitous to put this whole unfortunate affair behind them and to move on with their lives. 这个家庭迫切希望能忘记那些不幸的事情，开始崭新的生活。

近 agog, anxious, ardent, avid, desirous, eager, enthusiastic, greedy, hungry, keen, thirsty, voracious, wild

反 apathetic, indifferent, uneager, unenthusiastic 无所谓的

solid [ˈsɑːlɪd]

【考法 1】 *adj.* 固态的，坚固的：having a consistency that does **not easily yield to pressure**

例 The ice cream is too solid to scoop right now. 冰淇淋现在太硬了，根本舀不动。

近 compact, hard, rigid, stiff, unyielding

反 flabby, soft, spongy, squashy, squishy 柔软的，容易挤压的

【考法 2】 *adj.* 有理有据的：based on **sound reasoning** or information

例 the only solid conclusion that the jury could have reached 陪审团唯一可能做出的合理结论

近 firm, informed, justified, levelheaded, logical, rational, reasonable, sensible, sober, valid, well-founded

反 groundless, illogical, invalid, unfounded, uninformed, unjustified, unreasonable, unsound 没有道理的

【考法 3】 *adj.* 坚定的，不迟疑的：**not showing weakness** or uncertainty

例 Some people see a solid handshake as a sign of strong character. 有人认为握手毫不迟疑的人有着很强势的性格。

近 forceful, hearty, iron, lusty, robust, stout, strong, sturdy, vigorous

反 uncertain, weak 迟疑的，软弱的

派 solidify *vt.* 使固化

soliloquy [səˈlɪləkwi]

【考法】 *n.* (尤指自言自语的)独白：a dramatic or literary form of discourse in which a character talks to himself or herself or reveals his or her thoughts **without addressing a listener**

例 A soliloquy always reveals the character's thoughts and feelings. 一段独白经常反映出人物的思想和感情。

近 monologue

反 chorus, ensemble 合唱

solitude [ˈsɑːlətuːd]

【考法】 *n.* 孤独，避世：the quality or state of **being alone** or remote from society

例 He sought the kind of solitude where his thoughts would be his only companions. 他在寻找一种孤独感，只有他的思想陪伴着他。‖ She wished to work on her novel in solitude. 她想一个人安静地完成小说。

近 aloneness, insulation, privacy, seclusion, segregation, separateness, sequestration, solitariness

反 camaraderie, companionship, company, comradeship, fellowship, society 陪伴

solvent [ˈsɑːlvənt]

【考法 1】 *adj.* 有偿付能力的：**able to pay** all legal **debts**

例 They're going to have to prove that the company is now solvent. 接下来他们必须要证明公司的偿贷能力。

反 bankrupt 破产的

【考法 2】 *n.* 溶剂：a substance in which **another substance is dissolved**, forming a solution

例 Some organic solvents, such as benzene, pyridine, furan, are poisonous to human's reproductive system. 一些有机溶剂(比如苯、吡啶、呋喃)对人体的生殖系统有毒性。

反 solute 溶质

somatic [səˈmætɪk]

【考法】 *adj.* 肉体的：**of the body**, especially as distinguished from a body part, the mind, or the environment

例 a somatic disorder that was once thought to be "all in the patient's head" 曾被认为"全是病人头脑中的问题"的生理机能紊乱

近 animal, bodily, carnal, corporal, corporeal, fleshly, material, physical

反 mental, spiritual 精神上的；nonmaterial, nonphysical 非肉体的

somber [ˈsɑːmbər]

【考法 1】 *adj.* 昏暗的，无光的：so **shaded** as to be dark and gloomy

例 The prison's somber interrogation room has the desired effect of striking fear and despair into the prisoner. 牢房中阴暗的问讯间有着能让囚犯感到恐惧和绝望的效果。

近 black, caliginous, dark, dim, gloomy, lightless, murky, obscure, pitch-dark, rayless, stygian

反 bright, brilliant, illuminated, lit, lightsome, lucent, lucid, luminous 光亮的

【考法 2】 *adj.* 悲伤的，不愉快的：causing or marked by an atmosphere **lacking in cheer**

例 Her death put us in a somber mood. 她的死让我们陷入了悲伤沮丧的情绪之中。

近 depressing, dire, dismal, funereal, lugubrious, melancholy, miserable, morbid, morose, saturnine, sullen

反 cheerful, delighted, festive, gay, jocund, jovial 快乐的

Unit 9

■ SOMNOLENCE	■ SONNET	■ SOOTHE	■ SOP	■ SOPHISM
■ SOPHISTICATED	■ SOPORIFIC	■ SORDID	■ SOUND	■ SPARSE

somnolence [ˈsɑːmnələns]

【考法】 *n.* 瞌睡，嗜睡：the quality or state of desiring or **needing sleep**

例 Somnolence is likely to be the most typical reaction to this novel. 读这部小说最典型的感受就是想睡觉。

近 doziness, drowsiness

反 insomnia, sleeplessness, wakefulness 失眠

sonnet [ˈsɑːnɪt]

【考法】 *n.* 十四行诗：a **14-line verse form** usually having one of several conventional rhyme schemes

例 a sonnet that celebrates love 一首歌颂爱情的十四行诗

反 doggerel 幽默不正式的诗，打油诗

soothe [suːð]

【考法 1】 *vt.* 带来慰藉，安慰：to **bring comfort**, solace, or reassurance to

例 There seemed to be no words sufficient to soothe the widow. 任何话语好像都不足以安慰这个寡妇。

近 cheer, comfort, console, solace

反 agonize, distress, harrow, torment, torture, trouble 使痛苦，折磨

【考法 2】 *vt.* 使镇静，使安心：to **free from distress** or disturbance

例 He took her in his arms and soothed her. 他把她抱在怀中以让她镇静下来。

近 becalm, compose, lull, lullaby, quiet, quieten, salve, settle, still, tranquilize

反 agitate, discompose, disquiet, disturb, perturb, upset, vex 打扰，使不安

【考法 3】 *vt.* 弱化，缓解：to make more bearable or **less severe**

例 Hot tea with honey will soothe a sore throat. 加了蜂蜜的热茶可以缓解喉咙的酸痛。

近 abate, allay, alleviate, assuage, ease, mitigate, mollify, palliate, relieve, soften

反 aggravate, exacerbate, intensify 恶化

sop [sɑːp]

【考法 1】 *n.* 安慰物：something yielded to **placate or soothe**

例 provide with the salary raise as a sop 提高工资作为安慰

近 balm, emollient, placebo, salve, unguent

反 irritant, stimulant 刺激物

【考法 2】 *n.* 贿赂，回扣：something given or promised in order to **improperly influence a person's conduct** or decision

例 As a sop to the teachers' union for supporting his reelection campaign, the mayor promised to push for the abolition of the residency requirement. 市长答应推动废除获得绿卡的限制条件，以此作为换取选举中教师联盟支持的条件。

近 backhander, boodle, cumshaw, fix

【考法3】 *vt.* 浸湿，湿透：to **wet thoroughly**

例 My book fell in the swimming pool and was thoroughly sopped before I could fish it out. 我的书掉进了游泳池，在我把它捞出来之前已经彻底湿透了。

近 douse, drench, drown, impregnate, macerate, saturate, soak, sodden, souse, steep

反 dehydrate, dry, desiccate 脱水；parch, sear, scorch 烤干，烧焦；wring 拧干

sophism ［ˈsɑːfɪzəm］

【考法】 *n.* 假推理，诡辩：**deceptive** or fallacious **argumentation**

例 Political selection is more dependent on sophism and less on economic literacy. 政治选举更多的是依靠诡辩，而非简练的文笔。

近 sophistry

sophisticated ［səˈfɪstɪkeɪtɪd］

【考法1】 *adj.* 精明的，老于世故的：having acquired **worldly knowledge or refinement**; lacking natural simplicity or naiveté

例 On the train I met a surprisingly sophisticated and widely traveled child. 在火车上我见到了一个老练得让人惊讶的、见多识广的孩子。

近 cosmopolitan, debonair, knowing, smart, suave, urbane, worldly

反 guileless, ingenuous, innocent, naïve 天真的

【考法2】 *adj.* 复杂的：very **complex** or complicated

例 a very sophisticated machine that is a marvel of modern design 一个十分复杂的机器，是现代设计的最高成就

近 baroque, byzantine, complicated, convoluted, elaborate, intricate, involved, knotty, labyrinthine, tangled

反 plain, simple 简单的

派 sophistication *n.* 精明；复杂

soporific ［ˌsɑːpəˈrɪfɪk］

【考法1】 *n.* 催眠的药剂，安眠药：a drug or other substance that **induces sleep**

例 Alcohol is a poor soporific because it disturbs sleep patterns, and so can worsen sleep disorders. 酒精是一种欠佳的安眠药，因为它会干扰睡眠的固定模式，从而恶化睡眠紊乱的情况。

近 hypnotic

反 stimulant 兴奋剂

【考法2】 *adj.* 催眠的：causing or tending to **cause sleep**

例 This medication is soporific, so do not drive after taking it. 种药物是催眠的，服用之后切忌开车。‖ the soporific heat of summer 夏日里催人欲睡的炎热

近 narcotic, opiate, slumberous, somniferous, somnolent

反 arousing, waking, invigorating, stimulating 刺激性的

【考法3】 *adj.* 慵懒的，困倦的：of, relating to, or marked by **sleepiness or lethargy**

例 A big lunch always makes me soporific in the afternoon. 中午一顿大餐总是让我下午感到困倦。

近 dozy, drowsy, sleepy

反 awake, conscious, wakeful 清醒的；alert 警醒的；sleepless, insomniac 无法入睡的

sordid ［ˈsɔːrdɪd］

【考法1】 *adj.* 肮脏的，不干净的：**not clean**

例 I will not let my children grow up in such a sordid environment. 我绝不会让我的孩子在这样一个肮脏的环境之中成长。

近 besmirched, dirty, dusty, filthy, foul, grubby, muddy, nasty, smudged, soiled, stained, sullied, unclean

反 clean, immaculate, spotless, stainless, unsoiled, unstained, unsullied 干净的

【考法2】 *adj.* 卑鄙的：marked by **baseness** or grossness

近 Behind his generous donation were sordid motives. 在他慷慨捐资的背后有着卑鄙的动机。

近 base, contemptible, despicable, detestable, dishonorable, execrable, ignominious, mean, vile, wretched

反 honorable, lofty, noble, straight, upright, venerable, virtuous 高尚的，值得尊敬的

sound ［saʊnd］

【考法1】 *adj.* 牢固的，不可动摇的：marked by the ability to **withstand stress without structural damage** or distortion

例 The bridge is structurally sound. 这座大桥在结构上是稳固的。

近 bombproof, fast, firm, stalwart, strong, sturdy

反 ramshackle 摇摇欲坠的；rickety, unstable, unsteady 不稳定的

【考法2】 *adj.* 健康的，强壮的：**free from injury** or disease; exhibiting normal health

例 The horse is getting old, but still perfectly sound. 虽然在变老，但这匹马依然相当健康。

近 bouncing, fit, hale, healthy, hearty, robust, well, well-conditioned, wholesome

反 ailing, diseased, ill, sick 生病的；decrepit, enfeebled, feeble, infirm 虚弱的

【考法3】 *adj.* (逻辑上)严谨的: based on **valid reasoning**

例 Sound reasoning alone should tell you that the result is invalid. 从纯粹严谨的逻辑演绎出发，这个结论是不正确的。

近 analytic, coherent, consequent, rational, reasonable, sensible, valid, well-founded, well-grounded

反 illegitimate, illogical, incoherent, inconsequent, invalid, irrational, unreasonable, unsound, weak (逻辑上)站不住脚的

派 soundness *n.* (逻辑上的)无瑕疵

sparse [spɑːrs]

【考法】 *adj.* 稀疏的，稀少的: **less plentiful** than what is normal, necessary, or desirable

例 Many slopes are rock fields with sparse vegetation. 许多山坡都是不长植物的石坡。

近 exiguous, meager, niggardly, poor, scant, scanty, scarce, skimpy, slender, slim, sparing, stingy

反 abundant, ample, bountiful, copious, generous, liberal, plenteous, plentiful 大量的，丰富的

Unit 10

- SPARTAN
- SPAT
- SPATE
- SPECIFIC
- SPECIOUS
- SPECK
- SPECTATOR
- SPECTRUM
- SPECULATE
- SPENDTHRIFT

spartan [ˈspɑːrtn]

【考法】 *adj.* 简朴的，节约的: marked by **simplicity**, frugality, or avoidance of luxury and comfort

例 Accommodations on the windjammer are spartan but clean and comfortable nevertheless. 帆船上的装饰十分朴素，但是干净、舒适。

近 austere, plain, simple, stark

反 deluxe, luxurious, plush 奢华的

spat [spæt]

【考法】 *n.* (小的)争吵: a brief petty **quarrel** or angry outburst

例 Like any other couple, they have their spats. 像其他夫妻一样，他们也会有争执。|| They were typical sisters, spatting one minute, playing together the next. 她们是典型的姐妹: 上一分钟还在吵架，下一分钟就又玩在一起了。

近 altercation, controversy, disagreement, dispute, imbroglio, quarrel, squabble, tiff, wrangle

反 amity, concord, harmony, rapport, rapprochement 和睦，友好

spate [speɪt]

【考法1】 *n.* 突发的洪水: **sudden flood**

近 bath, deluge, flood, inundation, overflow, torrent

反 drought 干旱

【考法2】 *n.* 大量: a **large number** or amount

例 a spate of books about GRE 很多关于 GRE 的书

近 abundance, bundle, dozen, multiplicity, myriad, plentitude, profusion, scad, shipload, slew, volume, wealth

反 ace, bit, driblet, glimmer, handful, hint, mite, mouthful, nip, ounce, pittance, sprinkle, trace 少量

specific [spəˈsɪfɪk]

【考法1】 *adj.* 特有的，独特的: of a particular or **exact sort**

例 We need a specific type of pen to sign the diplomas. 我们需要一种特制的笔来签署学位证书。

近 concrete, distinct, especial, peculiar, precise, special, unique

反 general, generic, universal 普遍的

【考法2】 *adj.* 明确的: so **clearly expressed** as to leave no doubt about the meaning

例 specific instructions regarding the interrogation of prisoners 有关如何审问犯人的明确指示

近 clear, definite, definitive, explicit, express, unambiguous, unequivocal, univocal

反 ambiguous, equivocal, implicit, indefinite, inexplicit, unspecific, vague 模糊的

specious [ˈspiːʃəs]

【考法】 *adj.* 似是而非的，欺骗性的: having a **false look of truth** or genuineness

例 a specious argument that really does not stand up under close examination 经不起仔细推敲的论证

近 beguiling, deceitful, deceiving, deluding, delusive, delusory, fallacious, false, misleading

反 aboveboard, forthright, straightforward 明确的

335

speck [spek]
【考法】 *n.* 小点，少量：a very **small amount**: bit
例 She writes without even a speck of humor. 她字里行间一点幽默感也没有。
近 ace, bit, driblet, glimmer, handful, hint, mite, mouthful, nip, ounce, pittance, sprinkle, trace
反 abundance, bundle, dozen, multiplicity, myriad, plentitude, profusion, scad, shipload, slew, volume, wealth 大量

spectator ['spekteɪtər]
【考法】 *n.* 观众，目击者，旁观者：one who looks on or **watches**
例 join the organization as a temporary spectator 作为短期观察员加入该组织 ‖ The accident attracted a large crowd of spectators. 事故引来了大量的围观群众。
近 bystander, observer, onlooker, viewer, watcher
反 actor, performer, player 表演者

spectrum ['spektrəm]
【考法】 *n.* 光谱；范围，系列：a broad **sequence or range** of related qualities, ideas, or activities
例 the whole spectrum of 20th-century thought 20 世纪所有不同的思潮 ‖ A political spectrum is a way of modeling different political positions by placing them upon one or more geometric axes symbolizing independent political dimensions. 所谓的政治光谱是一种将不同的政治立场可视化的模型，它通过一条或者多条几何坐标轴来定位不同的政治态度。
近 diapason, gamut, scale, spread, stretch

speculate ['spekjuleɪt]
【考法 1】 *v.* 推测，揣测：to **take to be true** on the basis of insufficient evidence
例 I speculate that someone has been using this cabin as a trysting place. 我猜测有情侣把这个小屋当做他们幽会的地方。
近 assume, conjecture, daresay, imagine, presume, speculate, suppose, surmise, suspect
反 prove, substantiate, validate 证明
【考法 2】 *vi.* 投机倒卖：to buy or sell in expectation of profiting **from market fluctuations**
例 speculate on the oil market 在石油市场上投机倒卖

spendthrift ['spendθrɪft]
【考法 1】 *n.* 挥霍者，败家子：a person who **spends improvidently** or wastefully
例 The spendthrift managed to blow all of his inheritance in a single year. 这个败家子只用了一年就把自己继承的遗产挥霍一空。
近 fritterer, profligate, spender, squanderer, waster, wastrel
反 economizer, penny-pincher 节约的人；hoarder, miser, niggard 吝啬鬼
【考法 2】 *adj.* 挥霍的，不节俭的：given to **spending money freely** or foolishly
例 Spendthrift consumers amassed a mountain of debt on their credit cards. 那些爱挥霍财富的消费者们在他们的信用卡上累积了一大笔债务。
近 extravagant, improvident, squandering, thriftless, unthrifty, wasteful
反 conserving, economical, frugal, penny-pinching, provident, scrimping, skimping, thrifty 节俭的

The supreme happiness of life is the conviction that we are loved.
生活中最大的幸福是坚信有人爱我们。

——法国小说家 雨果（Victor Hugo, French novelist）

List 24

Unit 1

■ SPENT	■ SPINDLY	■ SPINY	■ SPLEEN	■ SPLICE
■ SPONTANEOUS	■ SPOOF	■ SPORADIC	■ SPRAWL	■ SPRIGHTLY

spent ［spent］
【考法】 *adj.* 精疲力竭的：**drained of energy** or effectiveness
例 After all that exertion, we were completely spent. 在完成所有的锻炼之后我们已是筋疲力尽。
近 beaten, bleary, done, drained, enervate, exhausted, fatigued, jaded, prostrate, tired, wearied, worn-out
反 active, energetic, invigorated, peppy, strengthened, strong, tireless, vitalized, wearyless 充满活力的

spindly ［'spɪndli］
【考法】 *adj.* 细长纤弱的：**frail or flimsy** in appearance or structure
例 I prefer having rather spindly legs. 我更希望有一双细腿。
近 gangling, gangly, lanky, spindling
反 squat 矮胖的

spiny ［'spaɪni］
【考法 1】 *adj.* 多刺的：bearing **spines**, prickles, or thorns
例 low spiny bushes of sage 低矮多刺的长满鼠尾草的灌木丛
近 brambly, prickly, thorny
反 even, flat, plane, smooth 平滑的
【考法 2】 *adj.* 棘手的，麻烦的：**requiring exceptional skill** or caution in performance or handling
例 This promises to be a spiny problem to negotiate. 这有可能成为谈判过程中棘手的问题。
近 catchy, delicate, difficult, knotty, problematic, sensitive, sticky, ticklish, thorny, tough, troublesome
反 easy, effortless, manageable, painless, simple, straightforward, uncomplicated, undemanding 简单的

spleen ［spliːn］
【考法】 *n.* 怒气，怨恨：feelings of **anger or ill will** often suppressed
例 She vented her spleen on her boyfriend and felt much better for having done so. 在她把怒气一股脑地倾泻到她男朋友身上之后，她感觉好多了。
近 angriness, choler, furor, fury, indignation, ire, madness, outrage, rage, wrath
反 delight, pleasure 高兴，愉悦

splice ［splaɪs］
【考法】 *vt.* 接合，叠接：to **unite** (as two ropes) by interweaving the strands, or to join (as two pieces of film) at the ends
例 He taught me to edit and splice film. 他教我如何剪辑和叠接胶卷。
近 associate, coalesce, combine, conjoin, conjugate, connect, couple, fuse, interfuse, join, link, marry, unify
反 disassociate, disconnect, disjoin, divide, sever, split, sunder 分开

spontaneous ［spɑːn'teɪniəs］
【考法】 *adj.* 自发的，不经思索的：acting or activated **without apparent thought** or deliberation
例 Hugging a crying child is simply a spontaneous reaction. 拥抱一个哭泣的小孩是很自然而然的反应。
近 automatic, impulsive, instinctive, involuntary, mechanical, natural
反 calculated, deliberate, intentional, planned, predetermined, premeditated, studied 有计划的，故意的

spoof ［spuːf］
【考法 1】 *n.* 轻松幽默的模仿，小恶搞：a work that imitates and **exaggerates** another work **for comic effect**
例 Many viewers thought that the spoof of a television newscast was the real thing. 许多观众认为这则新闻报道被恶搞之后的作品才是真实的东西。
近 burlesque, caricature, mimicking, parody, travesty

【考法2】 *v.* 诱骗，诱使相信：to cause to **believe what is untrue**

例 The public was spoofed by a supposedly plausible report of a UFO encounter. 一个听起来真实的 UFO 遭遇报告欺骗了大众。

近 beguile, cozen, delude, dupe, fool, hoax, misguide, misinform, mislead, trick

反 disabuse, disenchant, disillusion, undeceive 使醒悟

sporadic [spəˈrædɪk]

【考法】 *adj.* 偶尔的，零星发生的：**not often occurring** or repeated

例 On the whole, situation has significantly improved with only sporadic disturbances. 总体而言，局势得到了明显的改善，现在只有偶尔发生的骚乱。

近 few, infrequent, occasional, odd, rare, scarce, seldom, uncommon

反 frequent, habitual, repeated 时常发生的

sprawl [sprɔːl]

【考法】 *v.* 杂乱无序地发展；蔓生，蔓延：to grow, develop, or spread **irregularly** and without apparent design or plan

例 The city sprawls down the whole coast. 城市顺着整条海岸线蔓延。

近 ramble, scramble, straddle

派 sprawling *adj.* 蔓延的，不规则伸展的

sprightly [ˈspraɪtli]

【考法】 *adj.* 活泼的，充满活力的：**full of** spirit and **vitality**

例 He was deeply impressed by the sprightly Gypsy dance. 活力四射的吉普赛舞蹈给他留下了深刻印象。

近 active, airy, animated, brisk, energetic, frisky, gay, jaunty, kinetic, mettlesome, racy, spirited, vital, vivacious

反 dead, inactive, inanimate, lackadaisical, languid, languishing, leaden, lifeless, listless, spiritless, vapid 没精神的

Unit 2

■ SPUR	■ SPURIOUS	■ SPURN	■ SQUABBLE	■ SQUALID
■ SQUALL	■ SQUANDER	■ SQUAT	■ SQUINT	■ SQUELCH

spur [spɜːr]

【考法1】 *n.* 刺激物：something that **arouses action** or activity

例 The threat of losing its only sports franchise was the spur the city council needed to finally do something about the rising crime rate. 有可能失去唯一的体育赛事举办权，这成为了促使市政府决定就攀升的犯罪率采取相关措施的因素。

近 boost, catalyst, impetus, incentive, incitement, instigation, momentum, motivation, provocation, stimulus

反 deterrent, disincentive 阻碍物

【考法2】 *n.* 支撑物：a structure that **holds up** or serves as a foundation for something else

例 a weak wall that might need a spur 一面或许需要支撑的墙

近 brace, buttress, mount, prop, reinforcement, shore, underpinning

【考法3】 *vt.* 刺激，激励：to **incite** or stimulate

例 Appreciation spurred his ambition. 赞扬激起了他的雄心壮志。

近 arouse, excite, exhort, goad, instigate, prod, stir, urge

反 bridle, check, constrain, curb, deter, fetter, hamper, inhibit, manacle, shackle 制止，阻碍，束缚

spurious [ˈspjʊriəs]

【考法】 *adj.* 假的，伪造的：**lacking authenticity** or validity in essence or origin; not genuine

例 In statistics, a spurious relationship is a mathematical relationship in which two events or variables have no direct causal connection, but it may be wrongly inferred that they do, due to either coincidence or the presence of a certain third, unseen factor. 在统计学中，"伪相关关系"是两个不存在因果关联的事件或变量，因为巧合或是不可见的第三方因素，而被误判为存在因果联系。

近 apocryphal, bogus, counterfeit, fake, forged, phony, sham

反 authentic, bona fide, genuine, real 真实的

派 spuriously *adv.* 伪造地，虚假地

spurn [spɜːrn]

【考法】 *vt.* 摈弃，拒绝：to **reject with disdain** or contempt

例 They spurned his recommendation. 他们拒绝了他的推荐。 ‖ Fiercely independent, the elderly couple spurned all offers of financial help. 这对老夫妻极其独立，回绝了所有经济援助。

近 decline, disapprove, negative, refuse, reject, reprobate, repudiate

反 accede, accept, agree, approve, assent, consent, embrace 同意，接受

派 spurned *adj.* 被摒弃的，被拒绝的

squabble	[ˈskwɑːbl]
【考法】	*n.* 口角，小争吵：a noisy **quarrel**, usually about a trivial matter
例	a brief squabble over what to do next 关于接下来该做什么发生了争吵
近	altercation, argument, controversy, disagreement, dispute, imbroglio, quarrel, spat, skirmish, wrangle
反	harmony 和谐

squalid	[ˈskwɑːlɪd]
【考法1】	*adj.* 污秽的，肮脏的：**dirty** and wretched
例	The migrants have been living in squalid conditions. 移民们一直生存在肮脏的条件下。
近	black, dirty, filthy, foul, impure, nasty, slipshod, slovenly, unclean
反	clean, immaculate, spotless, unsoiled, unsullied 干净的
【考法2】	*adj.* 道德败坏的：morally **repulsive**
例	the squalid atmosphere of intrigue and betrayal 充满了阴谋与背叛的不正之风
近	base, despicable, ignoble, scurvy, sordid, vile, wretched
反	moral, noble 品格高尚的

squall	[skwɔːl]
【考法1】	*n.*（通常伴随着雨或雪的）风暴，暴风雪，暴风雨：a brief, sudden, **violent windstorm**, often accompanied by rain or snow
例	A snow squall is expected tonight. 今晚预计有暴风雪。
近	blizzard, hailstorm, snowstorm, tempest
【考法2】	*v.* 尖叫：to **scream** or cry loudly and harshly
例	The baby squalled in pain. 婴儿因为疼痛而大叫。
近	cry, howl, screech, shout, shriek, shrill, squeal, thunder, yelp, yell
反	murmur, mutter, whisper 低声细语

squander	[ˈskwɑːndər]
【考法1】	*vt.* 使分散：to cause（members of a group）to move widely **apart**
例	A single blast of the shotgun squandered the herd of deer. 猎枪的一声枪响让鹿群四处逃窜。
近	disband, dispel, disperse
反	assemble, cluster, collect, concentrate, congregate, gather, ingather 使聚集，使集中
【考法2】	*vt.* 浪费：to **spend wastefully** or extravagantly
例	He squandered his inheritance on women and gambling. 他把他继承的遗产浪费在女人和赌博上。
近	blow, dissipate, fritter, lavish, misspend, waste
反	conserve, husband 节约，节俭
派	squandering *adj.* 浪费的

squat	[skwɑːt]
【考法】	*adj.* 又矮又胖的：being compact and **broad in build** and often **short in stature**
例	a squat but adroit craftsman 一个又胖又矮，但是手艺灵巧的工匠
近	chunky, dumpy, heavyset, squatty, stocky, stout, stubby, stumpy, thickset
反	gangling, lanky 瘦高的

squint	[skwɪnt]
【考法】	*vi.* 斜视，睥睨：to look or **glance sideways**
例	The driver squinted as the sun hit his windshield. 阳光使得驾驶员不得不把眼睛偏向一边。
近	leer
反	gaze, goggle 直视

squelch	[skweltʃ]
【考法1】	*vt.* 压制，镇压（运动）：to put a **stop** to（something）**by** the use of **force**
例	The authority tried to squelch the workers' protest. 政府试图镇压工人的抗议游行。
近	crush, muffle, quell, repress, squash, subdue, suppress, crack down
反	abet, aid, assist, back, help, support, prop up 支持，帮助
派	squelcher *n.* 镇压者
【考法2】	*vt.* 击溃，使无言以对：to **put down or silence**, as with a crushing retort
例	His irritated glare squelched any other potential objectors. 他怒目而视，使得其他反对者都不敢说话。
近	dumb, extinguish, mute, quiet, settle, still, shut up
反	foment, incite, instigate, provoke, stir 激发，激起

Unit 3

stabilize [ˈsteɪbəlaɪz]

【考法】 *v.* 使稳定；变得稳定：to **make or become stable**, steadfast, or firm

例 a policy that intended to stabilize the situation in Iraq 一项旨在维护伊拉克局势稳定的政策 ‖ The country's population has stabilized at 3.2 million. 这个国家的人口维持在三百二十万。

近 ballast, poise, steady

反 destabilize 使不稳定；overthrow, overturn, subvert 推翻，颠覆

派 stability *n.* 稳定性

stalwart [ˈstɔːlwərt]

【考法 1】 *adj.* 无所畏惧的：feeling or displaying **no fear** by temperament

例 The stalwart soldiers in the army of Alexander the Great, who willingly followed him to the ends of the known world. 亚历山大大大帝军队中无所畏惧的士兵们愿意跟随亚历山大奔赴世界的尽头。

近 bold, courageous, dauntless, fearless, gallant, intrepid, manful, stout, stouthearted, valiant, valorous

反 cowardly, craven, fearful, gutless, nerveless, pusillanimous, spineless, spiritless, timorous 怯懦的

【考法 2】 *adj.* (体魄等)强健的：marked by outstanding **strength** and **vigor** of body, mind, or spirit

例 a lithe yet stalwart athlete 身体轻柔但结实的运动员

近 brawny, firm, muscular, rugged, sinewy, sound, stout, strong, sturdy

反 delicate, feeble, frail, weak, wimpy 脆弱的

【考法 3】 *adj.* 坚定的：**firm** and **resolute**

例 a stalwart supporter of the UN 联合国的坚定支持者

近 adament, obstinate, unbending, willful

stamina [ˈstæmɪnə]

【考法】 *n.* 耐力：physical or **moral strength** to resist or withstand illness, fatigue, or hardship

例 A marathon challenges a runner's stamina. 马拉松挑战参赛者的耐力。

近 endurance, tolerance

反 frailty 脆弱

stammer [ˈstæmər]

【考法】 *vi.* 口吃，结巴：to **speak with** involuntary **pauses** or repetitions

例 The frightened child started to stammer. 受到惊吓的小孩开始结巴地说话。

近 falter, stutter

反 articulate 清楚地说

startle [ˈstɑːrtl]

【考法】 *vt.* 使吓一跳，使大吃一惊：to **frighten or surprise** suddenly and usually not seriously

例 They were startled at the prohibitive price. 他们被高得离谱的价格吓到了。

近 amaze, astonish, astound, dumbfound, rock, scare, shock, stun, stupefy

反 reassure 消除(恐惧或疑虑)

派 startling *adj.* 惊人的

static [ˈstætɪk]

【考法 1】 *adj.* 静态的；停滞的：characterized by a **lack of movement**, animation, or progression

例 Both your pictures are of static subjects. 你的两张照片都是静物。‖ a static economy 停滞不前的经济

近 inactive, fixed, immobile, immotile, immovable, inert, stable, stagnant, stationary, still

反 active, dynamic, lively, vibrant 充满活力的；mobile, movable 可移动的

【考法 2】 *adj.* 无改变的：showing **little change**

例 a static population 没有变化的人口

近 inflexible, invariable, rigid, stiff, steadfast

反 capricious, changeful, fluid, mercurial, temperamental, versatile, volatile 容易变化的

派 stasis *n.* 静止不变

stature [ˈstætʃər]

【考法 1】 *n.* 高度，身高：natural **height** (as of a person) in an upright position

例 a man of surprisingly great stature 拥有惊人身高的人

近 altitude, elevation, inch

【考法2】 *n.* 才干，水平: **quality** or **status** gained by growth, development, or achievement
例 This club has grown in stature over the last 20 years. 过去二十年间里这家俱乐部的水平得到了提升。
近 merit, quality, value, virtue, worth

steadfast [ˈstedfæst]
【考法】 *adj.* 坚定的，忠诚的: **firm in belief**, determination, or adherence
例 Her comrades remained steadfast despite brutal tortures. 尽管经受了残酷的折磨，她的同志们都依然坚定忠诚。
近 constant, dedicated, devoted, devout, loyal, pious, staunch, steady, true-blue
反 disloyal, perfidious, recreant, traitorous, treacherous, unfaithful 不忠的

stealth [stelθ]
【考法1】 *n.* 秘密行动: the act or action of **proceeding furtively**, secretly, or imperceptibly
例 Both sides advanced by stealth. 双方都隐秘地行军。
【考法2】 *adj.* 秘密的: intended **not to attract attention**
例 The SWAT team carried out a stealth raid on the house, which was believed to be harboring a terrorist cell. 特警们对这间被认为是恐怖分子老巢的房屋进行了秘密的突袭。
近 backstairs, clandestine, covert, furtive, private, sneak, stealthy, surreptitious, undercover, underground
反 open, overt, public 公开的，光明正大的
派 stealthy *adj.* 秘密的，隐秘的

steep [stiːp]
【考法1】 *vt.* 浸泡: to **make** thoroughly **wet**
例 Steep the tea for five minutes. 浸泡茶叶五分钟。
近 drench, drown, impregnate, macerate, saturate, sodden, sop, souse
反 desiccate, dry, parch, sear 烘烤，烤干；wring 拧干
【考法2】 *adj.* 陡峭的: having an incline **approaching** the **perpendicular**
例 a very steep rock face that is nearly impossible to climb 一面非常陡峭、不可能攀爬的岩石
近 abrupt, precipitate, sheer
反 gradual 逐渐变化的；flat 平坦的
【考法3】 *adj.* 过分的，过高的: going **beyond** a normal or acceptable **limit** in degree or amount
例 We would like to hire him, but his salary demands are just too steep. 我们很想雇用他，可是他对于薪水的要求实在是太高了。
近 exorbitant, extravagant, extreme, immoderate, inordinate, insane, lavish, overdue, overweening, plethoric, stiff
反 moderate, modest, reasonable, temperate 适度的

Unit 4

■ STENCH	■ STENTORIAN	■ STERILE	■ STICKLER	■ STIFF
■ STIFLE	■ STIGMA	■ STINT	■ STINGY	■ STIPPLE

stench [stentʃ]
【考法】 *n.* 臭气，恶臭: a strong, **foul odor**
例 We finally discovered the dead rat that was causing the stench in the living room. 我们终于发现是死老鼠带来了卧室里的恶臭。
近 fetor, funk, malodor, reek, stink
反 aroma, fragrance, perfume, scent 香气

stentorian [stenˈtɔːriən]
【考法】 *adj.* 声音洪亮的: extremely **loud**
例 an tenor with a stentorian voice 拥有洪亮声音的男高音 ‖ The professor's stentorian voice was enough to keep even the drowsiest student awake. 教授洪亮的声音足以使最困的学生保持清醒。
近 blaring, blasting, clamorous, deafening, earsplitting, plangent, resounding, roaring, sonorous, thunderous
反 gentle, low, soft 声音轻柔的

sterile [ˈsterəl]
【考法1】 *adj.* 贫瘠的: **not productive** or effective
例 a sterile land which used to be a forest 曾经是森林的一块贫瘠土地
近 barren, effete, fruitless, impotent, infertile
反 verdant（因长满植物而）青翠的；fat, fertile, fruitful 肥沃的

341

adj. 无菌的: **free from** live **bacteria** or other microorganisms
例 The hospitals in the war-torn city often lack necessary drugs and sterile surgical supplies. 在这个被战争所蹂躏的城市中，医院里通常缺乏必需的药物和无菌手术用品。
近 aseptic, germfree, hygienic
反 insanitary, unhygienic 不卫生的；contaminated, polluted 受污染的
派 sterilize *v.* 消毒，杀菌

stickler [ˈstɪklər]
【考法】 *n.* 坚持细节的人，一丝不苟的人: one who **insists on exactness** or completeness in the observance of something
例 a stickler for perfection 完美主义者 ‖ a stickler for neatness 有洁癖的人
近 disciplinarian, pedant, purist, martinet

stiff [stɪf]
【考法1】 *adj.* 僵硬的，无法弯曲的: **lacking** in **suppleness** or flexibility
例 a stiff cardboard packing box 不易弯折的硬纸板盒 ‖ When I got out of bed this morning my back was stiff as a board. 今早起床时我的背和木板一样僵硬。
近 immalleable, impliable, inflexible, petrified, rigid, unbending, unyielding
反 flexible, floppy, pliable, pliant, supple, yielding 柔软的
【考法2】 *adj.* (在社交场合)缺乏优雅的，不自在的: **lacking social grace** and assurance
例 She always felt stiff and ill-at-ease whenever she was introduced to her father's friends. 每当她被介绍给父亲的朋友时，她总会感到浑身不自在和不舒服。
近 clumsy, gauche, graceless, inelegant, rustic, stilted, uncomfortable, uneasy, wooden
反 graceful, suave, urbane 风度翩翩的
【考法3】 *adj.* 过分的，过高的: going **beyond** a normal or acceptable **limit** in degree or amount
例 Don't you think that's a pretty stiff fine for such a minor infraction? 你难道不觉得对于这么小的一个错误，罚款实在太高了么?
近 exorbitant, extravagant, extreme, immoderate, inordinate, insane, lavish, overdue, overweening, plethoric, steep
反 moderate, modest, reasonable, temperate 适度的
【考法4】 *adj.* 艰苦的，费力的: **requiring** considerable physical or mental **effort**
例 We'll have a stiff climb to actually reach the summit. 我们还有一段艰苦的征途才能登顶。
近 arduous. challenging, difficult, formidable, grueling, laborious, strenuous, sweaty, testing, toilsome, tough
反 easy, effortless, facile, light, mindless, simple, soft, undemanding 容易的

stifle [ˈstaɪfl]
【考法】 *vt.* 抑制(声音、呼吸等)；阻止，扼杀: to cut off (as the voice or breath); to keep in or **hold back**
例 stifle free expression 限制言论自由
近 choke, muffle, mute, repress, smother, strangle, suffocate, suppress
反 foment, incite, instigate, provoke, stir 激发，激起
派 stifling *adj.* 抑制的

stigma [ˈstɪgmə]
【考法】 *n.* 耻辱，污名: a **mark of shame** or discredit
例 the stigma of cowardice 懦弱的污名 ‖ There's a social stigma attached to receiving welfare. 接受福利有一种社会耻辱感。
近 blemish, brand, onus, slur, smirch, smudge, spot, stain, taint
反 award, credit, honor 荣誉；fame, glory, renown, repute 好名声

stint [stɪnt]
【考法】 *vi.* 吝惜，节省: to **be** sparing or **frugal**
例 They never stint with their praise. 他们从不吝啬他们的赞美之词。
近 scrimp, skimp
反 blow, dissipate, fritter, lavish, misspend, squander, waste 浪费

stingy [ˈstɪndʒi]
【考法1】 *adj.* 小气的，吝啬的: being **unwilling** or showing unwillingness **to share** with others
例 too stingy to tip the waiter 小气到不肯给小费
近 closefisted, mean, mingy, miserly, niggardly, parsimonious, penurious, sparing, stinting, tightfisted
反 bountiful, charitable, freehanded, generous, liberal, munificent, openhanded 慷慨的
派 stinginess *n.* 小气
【考法2】 *adj.* 极少量的: **less plentiful** than what is normal, necessary, or desirable
例 Many people may consider this a rather stingy amount of food. 很多人都会认为这是分量很少的食物。
近 exiguous, poor, scant, scanty, scarce, skimpy, sparse
反 abundant, ample, bounteous, copious, plenteous, plentiful 大量的

	stipple	['stɪpl]

【考法】 *v.* (雕刻时)点刻；用点标记：to **mark with small spots** especially unevenly

例 They crossed a field stippled with purple lavender. 他们穿越了一片有紫色薰衣草点缀的田野。

近 blotch, dapple, dot, freckle, mottle, speckle, splotch, sprinkle, spot

Unit 5

■ STIPULATE	■ STITCH	■ STOCK	■ STOCKADE	■ STODGY
■ STOKE	■ STOIC	■ STOLID	■ STOMACH	■ STONEWALL

stipulate	['stɪpjuleɪt]

【考法】 *v.* 规定，特定要求：to **specify** or arrange in an **agreement**

例 Total disarmament was stipulated in the peace treaty. 和平条约中要求彻底解除武装。

近 claim, designate, detail, particularize, qualify

反 relinquish, surrender, yield, waive 放弃（权利等）

派 stipulation *n.* 规范，要求

stitch	[stɪtʃ]

【考法】 *n.* 突然剧痛：a **sharp unpleasant sensation** usually felt in some specific part of the body

例 He had to drop out of the race when the stitch in his side became too painful. 因为他突然感到剧痛，所以不得不放弃比赛。

近 ache, pang, prick, shoot, smart, sting, throe, tingle, twinge

反 comfort, ease, easiness 舒适的感觉

stock	[stɑːk]

【考法 1】 *n.* 库存，储备：the **inventory** of goods of a merchant or manufacturer

例 This type of product is currently out of stock. 这种商品已经脱销。

近 inventory, pool, repertoire, reserve, reservoir

【考法 2】 *adj.* 普通的，常备的：**commonly used** or brought forward

例 the stock answers to sensitive questions 对于敏感问题的常备回答

近 common, conventional, general, ordinary, prosaic, routine, standard, universal

反 unique 独特的

stockade	[stɑːˈkeɪd]

【考法 1】 *n.* 栅栏，围栏：an **enclosure** or pen made with posts and stakes

例 a heavy stockade that protected the troops 保护驻扎部队的厚厚的栅栏

近 barricade, barrier, blockade, fence, wall

【考法 2】 *n.* 监狱：a place of **confinement** for persons held in lawful custody

例 All POWs were kept in a remote stockade. 所有的战俘都被关在一个遥远的监狱里。

近 bastille, coop, jail, pen, prison

stodgy	['stɑːdʒi]

【考法 1】 *adj.* 平庸的，乏味的：**dull**, unimaginative, and commonplace

例 The sitcom was offbeat and interesting in its first season, but has since become predictable and stodgy. 这部情景喜剧的第一季是离奇而有趣的，但是后几季就变得老套和乏味。

近 arid, dreary, dull, flat, jading, jejune, monochromatic, monotonous, pedestrian, stale, tedious, wearisome

反 absorbing, engaging, engrossing, gripping, interesting, intriguing, involving, riveting 吸引人的

派 stodginess *n.* 乏味，无趣

【考法 2】 *adj.* 非常守旧的：extremely **old-fashioned**

例 Without notice she received a letter from his stodgy father. 毫无征兆地，她收到了一封来自她保守父亲的信。

近 conservative, hidebound, intolerant

反 avant-guard 先锋派的；radical 激进的

stoke	[stoʊk]

【考法 1】 *vt.* 添加燃料：**supply** with **fuel**

例 She was stoking the furnace. 她正给火炉添木头。

近 fuel, rekindle

【考法 2】 *vt.* 增大，促进：to **make greater** in size, amount, or number

例 stoke workers' commitment to the company by raising their salaries 通过加薪来提升员工对公司的忠诚度

近 aggrandize, amplify, augment, boost, enlarge, escalate, expand, extend, multiply, raise

反 abate, decrease, diminish, downsize, dwindle, lessen, lower, minify, reduce, subtract 减少

stoic	['stoʊɪk]
【考法】	*adj.* 隐忍的，冷静的: seemingly indifferent to or **unaffected by pleasure or pain**
例	stoic resignation in the face of hunger 默默忍受着饥饿
近	aloof, apathetic, detached, forbearing, indifferent, impassive, phlegmatic, stolid, tolerant, unemotional
反	demonstrative, emotional, fervent, fervid, impassioned, passionate, vehement 充满热情的

stolid	['stɑːlɪd]
【考法】	*adj.* 无动于衷的，感情麻木的: having or revealing **little emotion** or sensibility
例	Her face showed nothing but stolid indifference. 她的脸上只露出了麻木和冷漠。
近	apathetic, catatonic, deadpan, emotionless, impassive, indifferent, numb, phlegmatic, stoic
反	demonstrative, emotional, fervent, fervid, impassioned, passionate, vehement 充满热情的
派	stolidity *n.* 麻木，无动于衷

stomach	['stʌmək]
【考法】	*vt.* 容忍: to **bear** without overt reaction or resentment
例	I can't stomach his bragging. 我受不了他自吹自擂了。
近	abide, brook, countenance, endure, handle, stand, tolerate
反	decline, refuse, reject, repudiate, spurn 拒绝

stonewall	[ˌstoʊn'wɔːl]
【考法】	*v.* 拒绝(合作)，阻挠: to be **uncooperative**, **obstructive**, or evasive
例	lobbying efforts to stonewall passage of the legislation 意在阻止法律通过的游说行动
近	blockade, filibuster, hinder, impede, obstruct
反	collaborate, cooperate 合作

Unit 6

■ STOUTHEARTED	■ STRATAGEM	■ STRAIT	■ STRAND	■ STRATIFY
■ STRAY	■ STRENGTH	■ STRIATE	■ STRICTURE	■ STRIDE

stouthearted	[ˌstaʊt'hɑːrtɪd]
【考法】	*adj.* 勇敢的: having a **stout** heart or **spirit**
例	a stouthearted army officer who risked his life to save his men 为了拯救部下宁愿牺牲自己的勇敢军官
近	bold, brave, courageous, dauntless, fearless, gallant, intrepid, stalwart, stout, valiant, valorous
反	cowardly, craven, fearful, gutless, nerveless, pusillanimous, spineless, spiritless, timorous 怯懦的

stratagem	['strætədʒəm]
【考法】	*n.* 谋略，策略: an artifice or trick in war for **deceiving** and outwitting the enemy
例	a stratagem to secure customer loyalty 用来稳固客户忠诚度的计谋
近	artifice, device, gambit, gimmick, intrigue, maneuver, ruse, scheme, trick, wile

strait	[streɪt]
【考法 1】	*n.* 海峡: a narrow **channel joining** two larger bodies of **water**
例	Thousands of vessels pass through the straits annually. 每年数以千计的货轮要通过这个海峡。
近	channel, narrow, neck
反	isthmus 地峡
【考法 2】	*n.* 痛苦: a state of great **suffering** of body or mind
例	She was in dire straits over the loss of her mother's cherished necklace. 她因为丢失了母亲最珍贵的项链而陷入了极端的痛苦之中。
近	affliction, agony, anguish, excruciation, misery, pain, torment, torture, travail, tribulation, woe

strand	[strænd]
【考法 1】	*n.* 绳、线之一股: a **single filament**, such as a fiber or thread, of a woven or braided material
例	a strand of DNA DNA 中的一条链
近	thread
【考法 2】	*vt.* 遗弃，使置于困境: to **leave in a** strange or an **unfavorable place** especially without funds or means to depart
例	The convoy was stranded in the desert. 车队被困在了沙漠之中。
近	abandon, desert, forsake, maroon, quit
反	evacuate, reclaim, rescue 救出

stratify ['strætıfaı]

【考法】 *vt.* 将…分成各种等级：to **divide into classes**, castes, or social strata

例 Income distribution often stratifies a society. 收入分配往往将社会分层。

近 assort, categorize, classify, differentiate, distinguish, separate

反 homogenize 使均匀；commingle, mingle 混合

派 stratification *n.* 分层化

stray [streı]

【考法 1】 *adj.* 漫无目的的：**lacking** a definite plan, **purpose**, or pattern

例 No stray sighting of UFO's has been rigorously analyzed by scientists. 在无规律出现的 UFO 事件之中，尚未有被科学家严谨分析的案例。

近 aimless, arbitrary, desultory, erratic, haphazard, scattered, slapdash

反 methodical, orderly, organized, regular 有条理的，有组织的；systematic, systematized 系统性的

【考法 2】 *vi.* 离群，迷途，偏离：to **move away** from a group, **deviate** from the correct course, or go beyond established limits

例 stray from the main road 偏离了主干道

近 deviate, digress, err, wander

strength [streŋθ]

【考法 1】 *n.* 力量：the **ability to exert effort** for the accomplishment of a task

例 We are facing an army of great strength. 我们面对的是一支强大的军队。

近 energy, force, might, potency, power, puissance, sinew, vigor

反 impotence, impotency, powerlessness, weakness 无力

【考法 2】 *n.* （抵抗攻击、压力的）强度：the **ability to withstand force** or stress without being distorted, dislodged, or damaged

例 This cheap shelve unit doesn't have the strength to hold all those books. 这个廉价的书架不足以支撑所有的书本。

近 firmness, soundness, sturdiness

反 insecurity, instability, precariousness, shakiness, unstableness, unsteadiness 不稳固

派 strengthen *vt.* 增强

striate ['straııt]

【考法】 *vt.* 加条纹：to **mark with striations** or striae

例 The inner surface of the bark is smooth, of a pale, yellowish brown and very finely striated. 树皮的内部十分光滑，显着偏暗偏黄的棕色，并且有着十分精细的条纹。

近 furrow, streak, stripe

派 striated *adj.* 有条纹的

stricture ['strıktʃər]

【考法】 *n.* 责难，批评：an adverse **criticism**

例 The reviewer made several strictures upon the author's style. 评论家就作者的文风发出了不少责难。

近 censure, condemnation, denunciation, excoriation, obloquy, rebuke, reprimand, reproach, reproof

反 commendation, eulogy 表扬，赞扬

stride [straıd]

【考法】 *vi.* 迈大步走：to move with or as if with **long steps**

例 The man strode to the door and slammed it. 男人大步走向门口，狠狠地把门摔上。

近 march, pace, parade

反 mince 碎步走

Unit 7

| ■ STRIDENT | ■ STRIKE | ■ STRINGENT | ■ STRIP | ■ STRUT |
| ■ STUDIO | ■ STULTIFY | ■ STUPOR | ■ STUNT | ■ STURDY |

strident ['straıdnt]

【考法】 *adj.* 刺耳的：characterized by **harsh**, insistent, and discordant **sound**

例 plagued by the strident noise 被刺耳的噪声所折磨

近 grating, harsh, hoarse, jarring, rasping, raucous, squawky

反 mellifluous （声音）甜美的；harmonious 和谐的

派 stridence *n.* 喧闹，刺耳

strike [straɪk]

【考法 1】 *n.* 攻击：the act or action of setting upon with **force or violence**

例 The first strike was directed at a munitions warehouse. 第一轮攻击的目标是军火仓库。

近 aggression, assault, charge, offense, onset, onslaught, raid, rush

【考法 2】 *vt.* 铸造（奖牌）：to **form by stamping**, printing, or punching

近 build, fabricate, forge, form, make, mold, shape

【考法 3】 *vt.* 击打：to aim and usually **deliver a blow**, stroke, or thrust（as with the hand, a weapon, or a tool）

例 The drunkard angrily stuck the security guard. 酒鬼愤怒地殴打保安。

近 bat, beat, hammer, hit, knock, nail, punch, swat

【考法 4】 *vt.* 袭击，攻击：to take sudden, **violent action** against

例 A rattlesnake strikes its prey with lightning speed. 响尾蛇以惊人的速度攻击了它的猎物。

近 assail, beset, storm, set on

【考法 5】 *vt.* 撞击：to come into usually **forceful contact** with something

例 One bullet-train struck the other one which had been forced to stop on a viaduct due to lightning strike, resulting in huge casualties. 一辆动车撞向了另一因雷击而停在高架桥上的动车，造成了巨大的人员伤亡。

近 bang, bash, bump, collide, crash, impact, impinge, ram, slam, smash, swipe, thud

派 striking *adj.* 引人注目的

stringent [ˈstrɪndʒənt]

【考法 1】 *adj.* 紧绷的：**tight**, constricted

近 inflexible, rigid, taut

反 lax, loose, slack 松弛的

【考法 2】 *adj.* 严格的：**marked by rigor**, strictness, or severity especially with regard to rule or standard

例 Its drug-testing procedures are the most stringent in the world. 它的药检程序是世界上最严格的。

近 draconian, exacting, ironhanded, rigorous, severe, strict, uncompromising

反 lenient 宽大的，仁慈的

strip [strɪp]

【考法】 *vt.* 脱衣，剥去：to **remove clothing**, covering, or surface matter from

例 Guards stripped and started to search the prisoners. 守卫剥光了犯人，开始搜身。

近 denude, disrobe, doff, unclothe, undress

反 dress, gown, robe 穿衣；bedeck 穿衣打扮

strut [strʌt]

【考法 1】 *vi.* 趾高气扬地走：to **walk** with a **pompous** and affected air

例 A pompous general strutted off the parade ground. 盛气凌人的将军从阅兵场上趾高气扬地走过。

近 parade, prance, stalk, swagger

【考法 2】 *n.* 支柱，压杆：a structural element used to brace or **strengthen a framework** by resisting longitudinal compression

近 brace, buttress, column, girder, support, underpinning

studio [ˈstuːdioʊ]

【考法】 *n.* 工作室，画室，摄影室：the **working place of a painter**, sculptor, or photographer

例 move to a larger studio 搬进更大的工作室

近 workshop

stultify [ˈstʌltɪfaɪ]

【考法】 *vt.* 使无效，抑制：to deprive of vitality and **render futile** especially by enfeebling or repressive influences

例 The accident stultified his previous efforts. 这场意外使他过去的努力都白费了。

近 constipate, stagnate, stifle, trammel

反 encourage, foster, nourish 鼓励，培养

派 stultifying *adj.* 抑制的

stupor [ˈstuːpər]

【考法】 *n.* 迟钝，麻痹，无知觉：a condition of greatly dulled or completely **suspended sense** or sensibility

例 The heartbreaking man lapsed into an alcoholic stupor. 那个伤心的男人陷入了无知觉的酒醉状态。

近 coma, dullness, languor, lethargy, lassitude, listlessness, torpidity, torpor

反 alertness, vigilance 警惕，警戒；vigor, vim, vitality, vivacity 活力，精力

stunt [stʌnt]

【考法】 *vt.* 阻碍(成长): to **hinder** the normal **growth**, development, or progress of

例 The inhospitable climate had stunted all vegetation. 不佳的气候条件抑制了所有植物的生长。

近 check, curb, dwarf, suppress

反 advance, boost, foster, nourish, nurture, promote 培养，促进

sturdy [ˈstɜːrdi]

【考法】 *adj.* 强健的，结实的: marked by or reflecting physical **strength** or vigor; substantially made or built

例 sturdy young athletes 年轻有力的运动员 ‖ Remember to wear sturdy boots because we will be going over sharp rocks and uneven terrain. 别忘了穿一双靠谱的靴子，因为我们要在锋利的岩石和崎岖的地面上行走。

近 durable, firm, robust, rugged, stalwart, stout, strong, sound, tough, vigorous

反 delicate, feeble, frail, weak, wimpy 脆弱的；rickety, unsound, unstable, unsteady 不稳固的

派 sturdiness *n.* 强健

Unit 8

▣ STYGIAN	▣ STYMIE	▣ SUBDUE	▣ SUBJECT	▣ SUBJUGATE
▣ SUBLIME	▣ SUBLIMINAL	▣ SUBMERGE	▣ SUBMISSIVE	▣ SUBORDINATE

stygian [ˈstɪdʒiən]

【考法】 *adj.* 极阴暗的: **extremely dark**, gloomy, or forbidding

例 the stygian blackness of the cave 山洞里令人恐惧的黑暗

近 black, caliginous, dark, dim, gloomy, pitch-black

反 bright, brilliant, illuminated, illumined, light, lightsome, lucent, lucid, luminous 明亮的

stymie [ˈstaɪmi]

【考法】 *vt.* 阻碍: to **present an obstacle** to

例 stymied by red tape 被冗长的政策条款所阻碍

近 encumber, fetter, handcuff, handicap, hinder, impede, inhibit, manacle, obstruct, shackle, trammel

反 aid, assist, facilitate, help 帮助，促进

派 stymieing *adj.* 阻碍的

subdue [səbˈduː]

【考法】 *vt.* 使顺从；征服: to **conquer** and bring into subjection; to bring under one's control by force of arms

例 They subdued the native tribes after years of fighting. 他们经过多年征战终于征服了当地的部落。

近 conquer, defeat, squelch, subjugate, vanquish

反 capitulate, surrender 投降；lose 失败

派 subdued *adj.* 臣服的；柔和的

subject [ˈsʌbdʒekt]

【考法 1】 *n.* 臣民，受支配的人: one that is placed **under authority** or control

例 Because of the tense situation in that country, British subjects were advised to return home as soon as possible. 因为该国紧张的局势，英国公民被建议尽快返回英国国内。

近 citizen, national

反 alien 外来人；potentate 统治者

【考法 2】 *adj.* 取决于(其他因素)的: contingent on or **under the influence** of some later action

例 The price of seafood is subject to weather conditions. 海鲜的价格受天气影响。

近 affected, conditional, contingent, dependent, reliant, subordinate

反 independent, unconditional 独立的，无条件的

subjugate [ˈsʌbdʒugeɪt]

【考法 1】 *vt.* 征服，镇压: to **bring under control** and governance as a subject

例 I would rather die than be subjugated. 我宁死也不愿臣服。

近 conquer, dominate, overpower, pacify, quash, squelch, subdue, vanquish

反 capitulate, surrender 投降；lose 失败

派 subjugation *n.* 征服

【考法 2】 *vt.* 剥夺…的自由: to **make subservient**

近 enfetter, enslave, enthrall

反 discharge, emancipate, enfranchise, liberate, manumit, release, unfetter 解放，释放

sublime [sə'blaɪm]

【考法 1】 *adj.* 崇高的，庄严的：of **high** spiritual, **moral**, or intellectual worth

例 the sublime virtue of having given all one's worldly goods to the poor 将所有财产都捐给穷人的崇高美德

近 chivalrous, elevated, gallant, greathearted, lofty, magnanimous, noble

反 base, debased, degenerate, degraded, ignoble, low 可鄙的

【考法 2】 *adj.* （因为杰出、尊贵、美丽等而）令人惊叹的：tending to **inspire awe** usually because of elevated quality（as of beauty, nobility, or grandeur）or transcendent excellence

例 the sublime beauty of the canyon 峡谷令人惊叹的美丽

近 amazing, astonishing, astounding, awesome, fabulous, miraculous, portentous, prodigious, staggering, stunning, stupendous, wonderful

反 common, ordinary 平常的，普通的

派 sublimity *n.* 庄严，壮观

subliminal [ˌsʌb'lɪmɪnl]

【考法】 *adj.* 下意识的，潜在意识的：**below** the threshold of conscious **perception**

例 subliminal advertising in movies 电影中的潜意识广告

近 concealed, hidden, subconscious

反 apparent, clear, evident, manifest, obvious, patent 明显的

submerge [səb'mɜːrdʒ]

【考法】 *vt.* 使淹没：to put **under water**

例 The river bursted its banks, submerging an entire village. 河水冲上了堤岸，淹没了整个村庄。

近 dip, douse, drench, drown, immerse, inundate, sop, submerse

反 emerge 显现

派 submerged *adj.* 被淹没的

submissive [səb'mɪsɪv]

【考法】 *adj.* 服从的，顺从的，恭顺的：**submitting** to others

例 submissive employees 顺服的员工 ‖ It's not in her nature to be submissive. 服从不是她的本性。

近 amenable, biddable, compliant, conformable, docile, obeisant, obsequious, servile, subservient, tractable

反 contumacious, defiant, intractable, obstreperous, rebellious, recalcitrant, refractory, unruly 不顺从的

派 submission *n.* 服从，顺从

subordinate

【考法 1】 [sə'bɔːrdɪnət] *adj.* 下级的；次要的：belonging to a **lower** or inferior class or **rank**

例 His contention is that environment plays a subordinate role to heredity in determining what we become. 他的观点就是：在决定我们成长的因素——环境和遗传之中，前者处于更次要的地位。

近 inferior, junior, lower, minor, secondary, subject, tributary

反 greater, higher, major, primary, prime, senior, superior 更优等的，更高等的

【考法 2】 [sə'bɔːrdɪneɪt] *vt.* 征服：to bring **under one's control** by force of arms

例 It is one of the lessons of history that more powerful civilizations often subordinate weaker ones. 强大的文明往往征服弱势的文明，这是历史的教训之一。

近 conquer, dominate, overpower, pacify, subdue, subject, subjugate, vanquish

反 capitulate, surrender 投降；lose 失败

Unit 9

subservient [səb'sɜːrviənt]

【考法】 *adj.* 奉承的，屈从的：**obsequiously** submissive

近 amenable, biddable, compliant, conformable, docile, obeisant, obsequious, servile, submissive, tractable

反 contumacious, defiant, intractable, obstreperous, rebellious, recalcitrant, refractory, unruly 不顺从的

派 subservience *n.* 服从

subside [səb'saɪd]

【考法】 *vi.* 下陷，下沉，减弱：to **tend downward**

例 Local officials say the flood waters have subsided. 当地官员表示洪水已经退去。 ‖ As the noise of the siren subsided, I was able to fall back to sleep. 随着警笛声的减弱，我可以再次睡着了。 ‖ The pain will subside in a couple of hours. 几个小时之内疼痛感就会退去。

近 abate, decline, decrease, diminish, drop, dwindle, ebb, fall, lessen, moderate, recede, wane

反 balloon, burgeon, escalate, expand, grow, increase, intensify, rise, snowball, soar, wax 上升，增大

派 subsidence *n.* 下沉

subsidiary [səbˈsɪdieri]

【考法 1】 *adj.* 次要的：of **secondary importance**

例 The river has several subsidiary streams. 这条河拥有数条支流。

近 minor, secondary, subordinate, tributary

反 capital, cardinal, central, chief, key, leading, main, paramount, predominant, primary, principal, supreme 主要的，重要的

【考法 2】 *adj.* 起辅助作用的：furnishing **aid** or **support**

例 Attached are subsidiary materials. 附件中是辅助资料。

近 accessory, auxiliary, contributory, supplemental, supporting, upholding

subsidy [ˈsʌbsədi]

【考法】 *n.* 补助金，津贴：**monetary** assistance granted by a government to a person or group in **support** of an enterprise regarded as being in the public interest

例 a subsidy to manufacturers during the war 战争期间对制造商的补贴金

近 allotment, allowance, appropriation, grant, subvention

派 subsidize *vt.* 提供补助

substantial [səbˈstænʃl]

【考法 1】 *adj.* 物质的：of, relating to, or **having substance**

例 a world of dreams, even less substantial than a rainbow 一个梦想中的世界，甚至比彩虹还虚无缥缈

近 corporeal, concrete, gross, material, objective, physical, tangible

反 tenuous, vaporous 空洞的，空幻的；diaphanous, ethereal, immaterial 非物质的

【考法 2】 *adj.* 有重大意义的：**considerable in importance**, value, degree, amount, or extent

例 made a substantial progress 取得了实质性的进展

近 consequential, considerable, earthshaking, important, meaningful, momentous, significant, weighty

反 inconsequential, inconsiderable, insignificant, little, minor, negligible, slight, trifling, trivial 微不足道的

substantiate [səbˈstænʃieɪt]

【考法 1】 *vt.* 证实：to **support with proof** or evidence

例 There is little scientific evidence to substantiate the claims. 现在还缺乏足够的科学证据来证实这种言论。

近 attest, authenticate, confirm, corroborate, justify, validate, verify

反 controvert, disprove, rebut, refute 反驳

派 substantiated *adj.* 经证实的

【考法 2】 *vt.* 使实体化：to **give material** form to

例 The artist's intense feelings are substantiated by his paintings' bold colors and broad brush strokes. 画家强烈的情感通过他画作中鲜艳的色彩和很宽的笔画体现出来。

近 embody, epitomize, externalize, incarnate, incorporate, manifest, materialize, personalize

反 disembody 使脱离形体

substantive [səbˈstæntɪv]

【考法】 *adj.* 本质的，关键的：of or **relating to the essence** or substance

例 The substantive information is their political stance. 关键信息是他们的政治立场。

近 constitutional, elemental, essential, fundamental, substantial, vital

反 inconsequential, inconsiderable, insignificant, insubstantial, negligible, nominal 不重要的

subterfuge [ˈsʌbtərfjuːdʒ]

【考法】 *n.* 诡计：**deception** by artifice or stratagem in order **to conceal**, escape, or evade

例 The spy obtained the documents by subterfuge. 间谍通过狡猾的计谋获得了文件。

近 artifice, cheat, chicanery, deception, fraud, trickery, wile

subtle [ˈsʌtl]

【考法 1】 *adj.* 微妙的，难以感知的：(so slight as to be) **difficult** to understand or **perceive**

例 subtle differences in meaning between the words 单词词义之间的细微差别

近 delicate, elusive, evasive, faint, fine, impalpable, intangible, nice, slight

反 blatant, conspicuous, obvious, patent, plain 明显的；open, public 公开的

派 subtlety *n.* 微妙；微妙的想法

【考法 2】 *adj.* 巧妙的，间接或带有欺骗性的：**clever** at attaining one's ends by indirect and often **deceptive means**

例 used subtle methods of persuasion 采用了十分巧妙的劝说方式

近 beguiling, crafty, cunning, cute, designing, devious, foxy, guileful, scheming, shrewd, sly, tricky, wily

反 artless, guileless, ingenuous, innocent, undesigning 天真纯朴的，无伪装的

	subvert	[səb'vɜːrt]

【考法】 *vt.* 颠覆：to **overturn** or overthrow from the foundation

例 an alleged plot to subvert the state 一个旨在推翻政权的谣传中的阴谋

近 overthrow, overturn, topple

反 reinforce 加强

派 subversion *n.* 颠覆

Unit 10

■ SUCCINCT	■ SUCCOR	■ SUFFOCATE	■ SUFFUSE	■ SULK
■ SULLEN	■ SUMMARY	■ SUMMIT	■ SUMMON	■ SUMPTUOUS

succinct [sək'sɪŋkt]

【考法】 *adj.* 简明的，简洁的：characterized by **clear**, **precise** expression in few words

例 His speech is always succinct and perspicacious. 他的发言总是简洁而一针见血。

近 apothegmatic, brief, compact, compendious, concise, laconic, pithy, summary, telegraphic, terse

反 circuitous, circumlocutory, diffuse, long, prolix, rambling, verbose, windy, wordy 冗长的

派 succinctness *n.* 简洁，扼要

succor ['sʌkər]

【考法】 *vt.* 救援，援助：to go to the **aid** of

例 We see it as our duty to succor anyone in need. 我们视帮助他人为自己的职责。

近 aid, assist, help, relieve, support

suffocate ['sʌfəkeɪt]

【考法】 *vt.* 使窒息：to **deprive of oxygen**

例 The law requires the owner of a discarded refrigerator to remove its door so that a child won't get trapped inside and suffocate. 法律要求废弃冰箱的所有者移除箱门，从而防止儿童被困其中而窒息致死。

近 asphyxiate, choke, smother, stifle, strangle

派 suffocating *adj.* 令人窒息的，压抑的

suffuse [sə'fjuːz]

【考法】 *vt.* (色彩等)弥漫，染遍，充满：to **spread through** or over, as with liquid, color, or light

例 a room suffused with warm sunlight 一个充满温暖阳光的房间

近 flush, fill, imbue, infuse, interpenetrate, percolate, pervade, transfuse

派 suffusing *adj.* 弥漫的

sulk [sʌlk]

【考法】 *vi.* 生气，愠怒：to be sullenly aloof or withdrawn, as in silent **resentment** or protest

例 He would sulk for hours whenever he didn't get what he wanted. 每当他的愿望没被满足时，他都会生几个小时的闷气。

近 frown, grump, mope, pout

反 crow, delight, exuberate, jubilate, rejoice, triumph 感到高兴，雀跃

派 sulky *adj.* 生气的，不悦的

sullen ['sʌlən]

【考法】 *adj.* 闷闷不乐的：causing or marked by an atmosphere **lacking in cheer**

例 She remained sullen amid festivities alone. 她独自一人在喜庆的气氛中闷闷不乐。‖ sullen skies that matched our mood on the day of the funeral 葬礼当天与我们很搭调的沉闷天气

近 bleak, cheerless, dark, depressing, dire, gloomy, glum, gray, lugubrious, morose, saturnine, sulky, surly

反 bright, cheerful, cheering, cordial, festive, gay, lighthearted 欢快的，高兴的

summary ['sʌməri]

【考法 1】 *n.* 摘要：an **abstract**, abridgment, or compendium especially of a preceding discourse

例 Many book reports choose to begin with a summary of the book. 许多书评以该书的摘要开始。

近 abstract, brief, epitome, outline, recapitulation, synopsis, summarization

反 elaboration 详细解释

【考法 2】 *adj.* 就地的，立即的：done or executed **on the spot** and without formality

例 a summary trial and speedy execution 就地判决和快速处决

反 prolonged, protracted 拖延的

[ˈsʌmɪt]

【考法】 *n.* 顶点：the **highest point**

例 the summit of his ambition 他雄心壮志的顶点

近 acme, apex, climax, crescendo, crest, crown, culmination, meridian, peak, pinnacle, top, zenith

反 bottom, nadir 最低点

summon [ˈsʌmən]

【考法1】 *vt.* 召集，召唤：to **call together**

例 The general summoned all his troops before the operation. 行动之前，将军把所有的部队召集到了一起。

近 assemble, convene, convoke, muster, rally

反 dismiss 解散

【考法2】 *vt.* 传唤（出庭、出席）：to **command** by service of a summons, especially **to appear in court**

例 He was summoned to answer charges. 他被传唤出庭应对起诉。

近 call, hail

sumptuous [ˈsʌmptʃuəs]

【考法】 *adj.* 豪华的，奢侈的：**extremely** costly, rich, **luxurious**, or magnificent

例 The hotel claims to offer sumptuous furnishings and exquisitely prepared cuisine. 酒店宣称有奢华的装潢和精心准备的食物。

近 deluxe, lavish, lush, luxurious, opulent, palatial, resplendent, splendid, superb

反 ascetic, austere, humble, spartan 简朴的

And gladly would learn, and gladly teach.

勤于学习的人才能乐于施教。

——英国诗人 乔叟（Chaucer, British poet）

List 25

"面对辞藻堆砌的高峰，我们不应因身处词汇匮乏的谷底而绝望，征服都是从脚下开始的。"

（姚佳雄，Verbal 700，Quantitative 800，AW4.5，

录取院校：Johns Hopkins University）

Unit 1

■ SUNDER	■ SUPERCILIOUS	■ SUPERFICIAL	■ SUPERFLUOUS	■ SUPERIMPOSE
■ SUPINE	■ SUPPLE	■ SUPPLANT	■ SUPPLEMENT	■ SUPPLICATE

sunder [ˈsʌndər]
【考法】 *vt.* 分裂，分离：to **break apart** or in two
例 a city sundered by racial conflict 一个因种族冲突而分裂的城市
近 disassociate, disconnect, disjoin, disunite, divide, part, rend, rive, separate, sever, unyoke
反 bond, connect, join, link, unify, unite, yoke 连接，结合
派 asunder *adv.* 分开地，分裂地

supercilious [ˌsuːpərˈsɪliəs]
【考法】 *adj.* 高傲的，傲慢的：feeling or showing **haughty** disdain
例 The aristocrat reacted to their breach of etiquette with a supercilious smile. 贵族对他们破坏礼节的行为报以傲慢的一笑。
近 arrogant, assumptive, bumptious, haughty, imperious, pompous, presumptuous, overbearing, superior
反 humble, moderate, modest 谦逊的

superficial [ˌsuːpərˈfɪʃl]
【考法】 *adj.* 表面的，肤浅的：**lacking** in **depth**, solidity, and comprehensiveness
例 The official's superficial report on the situation provoked wide blame on the Internet. 官员对于情况的敷衍陈述激起了网络上的广泛谴责。
近 cursory, facile, perfunctory, shallow, sketchy, skin-deep
反 profound 深刻的；comprehensive, exhaustive 全面的
派 superficiality *n.* 表面现象

superfluous [suːˈpɜːrfluəs]
【考法】 *adj.* 多余的，过剩的：**exceeding** what is **sufficient** or necessary
例 a complicated algorithm that could filter all superfluous information 一个能滤除所有多余信息的复杂算法
近 excessive, extra, redundant, surplus
反 deficient, inadequate, insufficient, scanty, scarce, short, skimpy, sparse 不足的
派 superfluity *n.* 多余，过剩

superimpose [ˌsuːpərɪmˈpoʊz]
【考法】 *vt.* 添(声)加(色)(使形象、某因素或性质更加清楚)：to **add** as a **distinct** feature, element, or quality
例 She superimposed her own interpretation when she retold the story. 她重复故事的时候，加入了自己的解释。

supine [ˈsuːpaɪn]
【考法】 *adj.* 懒散的，倦怠的，消极的，漠不关心的：showing **lethargy**, passivity, or blameworthy **indifference**
例 a supine legislature that is afraid to take action 害怕采取行动的不作为的立法机关
近 inert, passive, dormant, torpid
反 vigilant 警惕的

supple [ˈsʌpl]
【考法】 *adj.* 易弯曲的，柔软的：readily **bent**; **pliant**
例 supple limbs 柔软的四肢 ‖ a supple mind 灵活的头脑
近 bendy, flexible, limber, lissome, lithe, pliable, pliant, lithesome
反 inflexible, stiff, rigid 坚硬的
派 suppleness *n.* 柔软

supplant [səˈplænt]

【考法】 *vt.* 排挤，篡夺…的位置: to **usurp the place of**, especially through intrigue or underhanded tactics

例 Old traditions were fading away and being supplanted by modern ways. 老传统逐渐式微，被现代方式所取代。

近 displace, displant, substitute, supersede, cut out

supplement [ˈsʌplɪmənt]

【考法】 *n./v.* 增补，补充: something that serves to **complete** or make up **for a deficiency** in something else

例 recommends taking a vitamin C supplement to prevent colds 建议补充维生素 C 来预防感冒

近 addendum, addition, expansion, increment, proliferation, step-up

supplicate [ˈsʌplɪkeɪt]

【考法】 *v.* 恳求，乞求: to **make a request** to（someone）in an **earnest or urgent** manner

例 God is not just someone to be supplicated in times of trouble. 我们不应该只在困难时候才向主祷告。

近 beseech, conjure, entreat, impetrate, implore, solicit, plead to, appeal to

反 demand 强求

Unit 2

| ■ SUPPOSITION | ■ SUPPRESS | ■ SURCHARGE | ■ SURFEIT | ■ SURRENDER |
| ■ SURREPTITIOUS | ■ SUSCEPTIBILITY | ■ SUSPEND | ■ SUTURE | ■ SVELTE |

supposition [ˌsʌpəˈzɪʃn]

【考法】 *n.* 猜想，推测: an opinion or judgment based on **little or no evidence**

例 It's pure supposition on your part that there's something illegal going on next door. 你说隔壁在进行非法勾当纯属猜测。

近 hypothesis, proposition, surmise, premise, presumption

反 certainty 确定

suppress [səˈpres]

【考法 1】 *vt.* 抑制（表情）: to **inhibit the expression** of（an impulse, for example）; check

例 suppress a smile 忍住笑容

近 repress, smother, stifle, choke back, hold back

反 stimulate 激励

【考法 2】 *vt.* 用暴力终止，镇压: to **put a stop to**（something）by the use of **force**

例 Nothing could suppress the rising tide of protest. 任何事物都无法控制越来越激烈的游行示威活动。

近 clamp down on, crack down on, put down, quash, repress, silence, slap down, snuff out, squash, squelch, subdue

surcharge [ˈsɜːrtʃɑːrdʒ]

【考法】 *v./n.* 过高收费: to **charge**（someone）too **much** for goods or services

例 The airline has added a $30 fuel surcharge on all international flights. 该航空公司对所有国际航线上涨了 30 美元的燃油税。

近 gouge, soak, sting

surfeit [ˈsɜːrfɪt]

【考法】 *v./n.*（使）过量，（使）饮食过度: to feed or **supply** to **excess**

例 He surfeited himself with chocolate. 他巧克力吃多了。

近 overabundance, overage, overflow, plethora, redundancy, superfluity, surplus

反 deficiency, deprivation, insufficient supply, famish, starve 短缺，匮乏

surrender [səˈrendər]

【考法 1】 *vt.* 交出，放弃，投降: to **give**（something）**over to** the control or possession of another usually under duress

例 surrender a contractual right 放弃契约上规定的一项权利

近 abnegate, cede, relinquish, renounce, resign

反 appropriate 挪用，占为己有

【考法 2】 *vt.* 使沉溺于: to **give（oneself）over** to something especially unrestrainedly

例 He surrendered himself to grief. 他沉湎于悲伤之中。

近 deliver, give up, indulge, yield

surreptitious [ˌsɜːrəpˈtɪʃəs]

【考法】 *adj.* 偷偷摸摸的，保密的: undertaken or done so as to **escape being observed** or known by others

例 He took a surreptitious glance at her knees. 他偷偷瞟了一下她的膝盖。

近 backstairs, clandestine, covert, furtive, privy, underground, underhanded, behind-the-scenes

反 barefaced, aboveboard, open, overt, public 光明正大的

susceptibility [səˌseptəˈbɪləti]

【考法】 *n.* 易受感染的性质或状态: the quality or state of having **little resistance** to some outside agent

例 A weak immune system causes increased susceptibility to disease. 弱的免疫系统会增大患病的概率。

近 defenselessness, vulnerability, weakness

反 immunity, invulnerability 免疫

suspend [səˈspend]

【考法 1】 *vi.* 暂停，中止: to **bring to a formal close** for a period of time

例 suspend the trial 暂停审判

近 prorogue, recess

反 invoke 实行

【考法 2】 *vt.* 悬挂: **hang**

例 suspend a banner proclaiming the town's "Heritage Days" from the archway 在拱门上方悬挂一条庆祝该镇"遗产日"的条幅

反 erect, let fall 使直立，落下

suture [ˈsuːtʃər]

【考法】 *n./v.* 缝合: the process of **joining** two surfaces or edges together along a line by or as if by sewing

例 The doctor cleaned, sutured, and bandaged the wound. 医生将伤口清洗、缝合、包扎。

反 incision, avulse 切开，撕脱

svelte [svelt]

【考法】 *adj.* (女人)体态苗条的，优雅的: slender or graceful in figure or outline; **slim**

例 The svelte dancer seemed to float across the stage. 苗条的舞者看起来就像轻盈地漂浮在舞台上。

近 bony, lean, skinny, slender, slim

反 plump, corpulent, paunchy and awkward 丰满的，大腹便便而笨拙的

Unit 3

■ SWAGGER	■ SWEAR	■ SWELTERING	■ SWERVE	■ SWILL
■ SWINDLE	■ SYBARITE	■ SYCOPHANT	■ SYLLABUS	■ SYLLOGISM

swagger [ˈswæɡər]

【考法 1】 *vi.* 大摇大摆地走，趾高气昂地走: to conduct oneself in an **arrogant** or superciliously **pompous** manner

例 The young man confidently swaggered across the room. 年轻人高傲地在房间里走来走去。

近 prance, sashay, stalk

【考法 2】 *vi.* 自夸，吹嘘: to **boast**, brag

例 I would swagger if I'd won first place in the bowling tournament. 如果我赢得保龄球锦标赛的冠军，我肯定会自夸。

近 brag, vapor, vaunt, gasconade

swear [swer]

【考法 1】 *vi.* 咒骂: to use profane or obscene language: **curse**

例 No one is allowed to swear in this house. 这个房间里禁止说脏话。

近 blaspheme, curse, cuss

反 accolade 赞美

【考法 2】 *v.* 宣誓: to promise or pledge with a solemn **oath**; vow

例 He swore his oath of allegiance to the queen. 他宣誓效忠女王。

近 attest, depose, covenant, pledge, vow

sweltering [ˈsweltərɪŋ]

【考法】 *adj.* 酷热的: oppressively **hot**

例 The air conditioning was broken, and it was sweltering in the room. 空调坏了，房间里酷热难耐。

近 boiling, scorching, searing, sultry, torrid, fiery

反 algid, arctic, bone-chilling, freezing, frigid, frozen, glacial, ice-cold, iced, icy 严寒的

swerve	[swɜ:rv]
【考法】	*vi.* 突然改变方向: to **turn aside abruptly** from a straight line or course
例	The car swerved sharply to avoid the squirrel in the road. 为了避开路上的松鼠，汽车猛地转向。
近	detour, deviate, diverge, sheer, swing, veer
反	maintain direction, straighten 保持方向，直行

swill	[swɪl]
【考法】	*vt.* 痛饮，大口地吃: to **drink greedily**, to **eat greedily** or to excess
例	Considering the way she swills carbonated drinks, she ought to own stock in Pepsi company. 鉴于她对碳酸饮料消费的贡献，百事公司应该给她分点股份。
近	gulp, quaff, swig
反	sip 啜饮

swindle	[ˈswɪndl]
【考法】	*vt.* 欺骗，骗取: to **cheat** or defraud of money or property
例	Hundreds of people were swindled out of their savings. 几百人都被骗去了存款。
近	bilk, con, hustle, fiddle, gyp, bunco, flimflam

sybarite	[ˈsɪbəraɪt]
【考法】	*n.* 沉溺于奢侈逸乐者，酒色之徒: a person **devoted** to pleasure and **luxury**; a voluptuary
例	The prince was remembered as a self-indulgent sybarite. 王子酒色之徒的名声远扬。
近	debauchee, decadent, hedonist, sensualist
反	spartan, ascetic 禁欲者

sycophant	[ˈsɪkəfænt]
【考法】	*n.* 马屁精: a servile self-seeking **flatterer**
例	When her career was riding high, the self-deluded actress often mistook sycophants for true friends. 当这位演员的事业如日中天之时，她常常把一些马屁精误以为真朋友。
近	fawner, flunky, lickspittle, toady, apple-polisher, bootlicker, brownnoser

syllabus	[ˈsɪləbəs]
【考法】	*n.* 提纲，摘要；课文、演讲或研究课题的概要或提纲: an outline or a **summary** of the main points of a text, lecture, or course of study
例	Have you got next year's syllabus? 你拿到明年的教学大纲了吗？

syllogism	[ˈsɪlədʒɪzəm]
【考法】	*n.* 由一般到个别的推理，演绎: **reasoning** from the general to the specific; **deduction**
例	The syllogism was at the core of traditional deductive reasoning, where facts are determined by combining existing statements, in contrast to inductive reasoning where facts are determined by repeated observations. 从一般到个别的推理是传统演绎推理的核心，事实结论由综合现存知识所确定，而归纳推理中的事实结论则由重复观测来确定。
派	syllogize *v.* 用三段论论证

Unit 4

■ SYMBIOSIS	■ SYMMETRY	■ SYNCHRONOUS	■ SYNERGIC	■ SYNONYMOUS
■ SYNOPSIS	■ SYNTHESIS	■ TACIT	■ TACITURN	■ TACKLE

symbiosis	[ˌsɪmbaɪˈoʊsɪs]
【考法】	*n.* 共生关系: the **living together** in more or less intimate association or close union of two dissimilar
例	The bird lives in symbiosis with the hippopotamus. 这种鸟和河马是共生关系。
反	unrelated growth 无关联的生长

symmetry	[ˈsɪmətri]
【考法】	*n.* 对称: **balanced proportions**
例	The building has perfect symmetry. 这栋房子是完美的对称构造。
近	balance, coherence, consonance, proportion
反	disproportion, asymmetry, discordance, disproportion, disunity, imbalance, incoherence, violence 不均衡，混乱

synchronous [ˈsɪŋkrənəs]

【考法】 *adj.* 同时期的，同步的: having **identical period** and **phase**

例 The synchronous arrival of a baby sister and loss of a beloved grandmother strongly affected the girl. 妹妹的出生和奶奶的去世同时发生，给这个女孩造成了巨大的影响。

近 coetaneous, coeval, coexistent, concurrent, contemporaneous, simultaneous

反 occurring at different times, noncontemporaneous, out-of-phase 发生在不同时代的

synergic [sɪˈnɜːrdʒɪk]

【考法】 *adj.* 合作的: working together: **cooperating**

例 synergic muscles 协同肌肉

反 antagonistic 敌对的

synonymous [sɪˈnɑːnɪməs]

【考法】 *adj.* 同义的: having the **same** or a **similar meaning**

例 Paris has always been synonymous with elegance, luxury and style. 巴黎在人们心中就是优雅、奢侈和时尚的同义词。

synopsis [sɪˈnɑːpsɪs]

【考法】 *n.* 摘要，概要: a brief **outline** or general view; an **abstract** or a **summary**

例 Just give me a synopsis of the movie. 把电影的大致情节给我说说就行。

近 abstract, brief, digest, recapitulation, roundup, summarization, epitome

synthesis [ˈsɪnθəsɪs]

【考法】 *n.* 合成，综合: the **combination** of parts or elements so as to form a whole

例 a philosophy that is a kind of synthesis of several schools of Western and Eastern thought 哲学是东西方很多思想流派的综合

近 admixture, alloy, amalgamation, compound, conflation, fusion, meld

反 analysis, taking apart 分解

tacit [ˈtæsɪt]

【考法】 *adj.* 暗示的: **implied** or indicated（as by an act or by silence）but **not actually expressed**

例 tacit consent 默许

近 implied, unexpressed, unspoken, unvoiced, wordless

反 explicit, express, expressed, spoken, stated, voiced 明确表达的，直率的

taciturn [ˈtæsɪtɜːrn]

【考法】 *adj.* 沉默寡言的，话少的: temperamentally **disinclined to talk**

例 A taciturn man never initiates a conversation. 一个寡言的人从不主动和人说话。

近 laconic, reserved, reticent, tight-lipped, uncommunicative

反 garrulous, loquacious, glib, expansive, prolix, voluble 多话的

tackle [ˈtækl]

【考法】 *vt.* 着手处理: to **start work** on energetically

例 Once I clean the kitchen, I think I'll tackle the bathroom. 等我把厨房打扫干净了，就去收拾浴室。

近 dive into, wade in

Unit 5

■ TACT	■ TACTILE	■ TACTLESS	■ TALISMAN	■ TAINT
■ TAMPER	■ TANGENT	■ TANGIBLE	■ TANGY	■ TANTALIZE

tact [tækt]

【考法】 *n.* 机敏，精明，不冒犯: a **keen sense** of what to do or say in order to **maintain good relations** with others or avoid offense

例 She talked to her neighbor with supreme tact. 她和邻居说话十分圆滑。

近 diplomacy

反 clumsiness, insensitivity, tactlessness 笨拙

tactile [ˈtæktl]

【考法】 *adj.* 有触觉的，能触知的: perceptible by **touch**: **tangible**

例 The thick brushstrokes give the painting a tactile quality. 粘稠的笔触给了这幅画一种厚实的感觉。

tactless ['tæktləs]

【考法】 *adj.* 不机智的，笨拙的：bluntly **inconsiderate** or **indiscreet**

例 tactless comments 不明智的评论

近 graceless, ill-advised, imprudent, indelicate, injudicious, undiplomatic

反 advisable, discreet, judicious, prudent, tactful, wise 小心谨慎的，明智的

talisman ['tælɪzmən]

【考法】 *n.* 护身符：something worn or kept to **bring good luck** or **keep away evil**

例 A pendant of white nephrite jade is often worn by Indians as a talisman to ward off heart disease. 印度人通常戴一串软玉挂件作为护身符，防止心脏病发作。

近 amulet, fetish, mascot, mojo, periapt, phylactery

taint [teɪnt]

【考法】 *vt.* 使(品质)污损：to affect slightly with something **morally bad** or undesirable

例 A tendency toward conceitedness taints that athlete's status as a role model. 该运动员自负的倾向玷污了其行为模范的地位。

近 blemish, darken, mar, spoil, tarnish, vitiate

派 tainted *adj.* 污损的

反 pristine, unspoiled, wholesome, unadulterated 纯洁的，健全的

tamper ['tæmpər]

【考法1】 *v.* 恶意窜改，损害：to handle thoughtlessly, ignorantly, or **mischievously**

例 tamper with tradition 坏了规矩

近 diddle with, fiddle with, fool with, mess with

【考法2】 *vi.* 玩弄：to tinker with **rashly or foolishly**

例 Don't tamper with my feelings. 不要玩弄我的感情。

tangent ['tændʒənt]

【考法】 *n./adj.* 离题(的)，不相关(的)：diverging from an original purpose of course: **irrelevant**

例 tangent remarks 不相关的评论

近 excursive, digressive

反 essential 重要的

tangible ['tændʒəbl]

【考法1】 *adj.* 可感知的：**capable** of being **perceived**

近 palpable, touchable

反 impalpable, intangible, unable to perceive 无法感知的

【考法2】 *adj.* 确凿的，真实的：possible to be treated as fact; **real or concrete**

例 tangible evidence 确凿的证据

tangy ['tæŋi]

【考法】 *adj.* 刺激的：having a **powerfully stimulating** odor or flavor

例 a tangy sauce with a strong aftertaste 味道刺激的酱料，回味无穷

近 pungent, strong

反 bland, mild, smooth 不刺激的

tantalize ['tæntəlaɪz]

【考法】 *vt.* 激起，挑逗，引诱：to **excite** (another) by exposing something desirable while keeping it out of reach

例 He was tantalized by the possibility of earning a lot of money quickly. 有人用迅速致富引诱他。

反 comfort, console, solace, alleviate, assuage, relieve, satiate 安慰，缓和

Unit 6

■ TANTAMOUNT　　■ TANTRUM　　■ TAPER　　■ TARDY　　■ TARNISH
■ TASTY　　■ TATTY　　■ TAUNT　　■ TAUT　　■ TAWDRY

tantamount ['tæntəmaʊnt]

【考法】 *adj.* 等价的，与…相等的：**equivalent** in value, significance, or effect

例 a relationship tantamount to marriage 到了谈婚论嫁地步的关系

反 incommensurate 不相称的

tantrum [ˈtæntrəm]

【考法】 *n.* 勃然大怒，发脾气：a fit of **bad temper**

例 have a tantrum 大发脾气

近 blowup, explosion, fit

反 pacification 平静

taper [ˈteɪpər]

【考法 1】 *v.* (使)逐渐变细：to **become** gradually **narrower** or **thinner** toward one end

例 taper to a point 逐渐变细成为一点

近 abate, decline, diminish, dwindle, shrink, wane, drain away

【考法 2】 *v.* 逐渐减少，减弱：to **diminish** or lessen **gradually**

例 The storm finally tapered off. 风暴逐渐平静下来。

近 subside, die down, phase down, fall away, let up

tardy [ˈtɑːrdi]

【考法 1】 *adj.* 缓慢的，迟缓的：moving **slowly**: sluggish

例 He was tardy to work. 他做事拖拖拉拉。

近 crawling, creeping, dallying, dawdling, dilatory, dragging, lagging, languid, sluggish

反 bolting, brisk, fleet, flying, meteoric, rocketing, scooting, scudding, scurrying, swift, whirling 迅速的

【考法 2】 *adj.* 延后的，迟的：**delayed** beyond the expected or proper time

例 a tardy arrival 迟到

近 behind, belated, delinquent, overdue

反 early, inopportune, precocious, premature, unseasonable, untimely 提早的

tarnish [ˈtɑːrnɪʃ]

【考法】 *vt.* 玷污：to affect slightly with something **morally bad** or undesirable

例 An arrest for shoplifting tarnished her reputation. 因在商店行窃被捕玷污了她的名誉。

近 blemish, mar, stain, vitiate

tasty [ˈteɪsti]

【考法】 *adj.* 美味的；令人愉悦的：giving **pleasure or contentment** to the mind or senses

例 the tasty prospect of getting his revenge 他报仇成功的诱人前景

近 agreeable, delectable, delightful, satisfying, savory

反 uninteresting, disagreeable, unpalatable, unpleasant, unwelcome 无趣的，令人失望的

tatty [ˈtæti]

【考法】 *adj.* 破旧的，褴褛的：somewhat worn, **shabby**, or dilapidated

例 a tatty shirt 破旧的衬衣

近 dilapidated, scruffy, seedy, sleazy, tatterdemalion, threadbare

反 smart 整洁漂亮的

taunt [tɔːnt]

【考法】 *vt.* 嘲弄性质疑，挑衅：to reproach or **challenge** in a mocking or insulting manner: **jeer at**

例 The boys continually taunted each other. 男孩子们不断互相挑衅。

近 bait, hassle, haze, heckle, needle, ride

taut [tɔːt]

【考法 1】 *adj.* 紧绷的：**not loose** or flabby

例 taut muscles 紧实的肌肉

反 lax, loose, slack 松弛的

【考法 2】 *adj.* 整洁的：kept in **proper order** or condition, kept in **trim shape**; neat and tidy

例 a taut ship 保养得不错的船

近 kempt, orderly, shipshape, trim

tawdry [ˈtɔːdri]

【考法】 *adj.* 俗丽的，花哨而庸俗的：cheap and **gaudy** in appearance or quality; ignoble

例 a tawdry attempt to smear his opponent 企图污蔑对手的下三滥的手段

近 meretricious, gaudy, flashy, garish

反 exquisite 高雅的

Unit 7

taxing ['tæksɪŋ]

【考法】 *adj.* 繁重的，费力的：**requiring much time**, **effort**, or careful attention

例 The journey proved to be very taxing. 旅途很艰辛。

近 arduous, burdensome, exacting, grueling, laborious, onerous, toilsome

反 light, easy 轻快的

tedious ['tiːdiəs]

【考法】 *adj.* 冗长乏味的：**tiresome** because of length or **dullness**: **boring**

例 a tedious public ceremony 冗长无聊的公开仪式

近 drab, dreary, jading, monotonous, stale, stodgy, stuffy, weary, drudging

反 entertaining, absorbing, stimulating, engaging, engrossing, gripping, interesting, intriguing, involving, riveting 令人愉快的，吸引人的

teeter ['tiːtər]

【考法 1】 *vi.* 蹒跚，不稳定地行走：to move **unsteadily**: wobble

例 She teetered down the street in her high heels. 她穿着高跟鞋，摇摇晃晃地沿街走着。

近 careen, dodder, lurch, reel

反 stabilize 使…稳固

【考法 2】 *vi.* 犹豫不决：to show **uncertainty** about the right course of action

例 He was teetering on the brink of making a decision about college. 他正在为选择哪所大学而犹豫不决。

近 balance, dither, falter, hang back, scruple, shilly-shally, stagger, vacillate, waver, wobble

反 dive in, plunge in 积极做

teetotalism [ˌtiː'toʊtlɪzəm]

【考法】 *n.* 禁酒：the principle or practice of complete **abstinence** from **alcoholic** drinks

反 intemperance 饮酒过度

telling ['telɪŋ]

【考法】 *adj.* 有效的，显著的：**effective**, expressive

例 the most telling evidence 最有力的证据

近 compelling, conclusive, convincing, forceful, persuasive, satisfying

反 inconclusive, indecisive, ineffective, uncompelling, unconvincing, unpersuasive 无效的

temerity [tə'merəti]

【考法】 *n.* 鲁莽，冒失：**foolhardy** disregard of danger; **recklessness**

例 She was punished for her temerity. 她因冒失吃到了苦头。

近 audacity, brashness, presumption, presumptuousness

反 circumspection, cautious approach, pusillanimity 谨慎

temporize ['tempəraɪz]

【考法】 *vi.* 行动躲躲闪闪以争取时间、躲避争论等：to **act evasively** in order to gain time, avoid argument, or postpone a decision

例 "Colonial officials . . . ordered to enforce unpopular enactments, tended to temporize, to find excuses for evasion"(J. H. Parry) "被命令来执行不受欢迎法案的殖民地官员们倾向于敷衍了事，寻找逃避的理由"(J.H. 帕里）

temperate ['tempərət]

【考法 1】 *adj.* (言行举止)有分寸的：**avoiding extremes** in behavior or expression

例 He is rather temperate in his appraisal of the movie, calling it good but not great. 他对这部电影的赞赏很适度，说其"还好"而不是"很棒"。

反 immoderate, extreme, frivolous 极端的

【考法 2】 *adj.* 有节制的：given to or marked by **restraint** in the satisfaction of one's appetites

例 a soft-spoken, serious-minded person of temperate habits 一个说话温和、认真严肃的人，其兴趣爱好都很适度

近 abstentious, abstinent, continent, self-abnegating, self-denying, sober

反 self-indulgent 放纵的

tempestuous [tem'pestʃuəs]

【考法】 *adj.* 突然的，剧烈的：marked by **sudden or violent** disturbance

例 In terms of social change, the 1960s are generally considered the most tempestuous decade in recent American history. 就社会变革来说，20世纪60年代是近现代美国历史上最动荡的十年。

近 cataclysmal, tumultuous, turbulent

反 serene 平静的

tenable ['tenəbl]

【考法】 *adj.* 有据可依的，无懈可击的：**capable** of being held or **defended**；**reasonable**

例 a tenable theory 一个站得住脚的理论 ‖ a tenable outpost 一个守得住的前哨

近 defendable, justifiable, maintainable, supportable, sustainable

反 unjustified, unsound, specious, indefensible, fallacious 不合理的

Unit 8

■ TENACIOUS   ■ TENDENTIOUS   ■ TENDER   ■ TENUOUS   ■ TEPID
■ TERMINOLOGY   ■ TERMINUS   ■ TERROR   ■ TERSE   ■ TESTIMONY

tenacious [tə'neɪʃəs]

【考法1】 *adj.* 顽固的，不屈不挠的：**persistent** in maintaining something valued or habitual

例 a tenacious advocate of civil rights 公民权利的坚定捍卫者

近 dogged, insistent, persevering, pertinacious

反 negotiable, vacillated 可商量的，踌躇的

【考法2】 *adj.* 粘着的：tending to **adhere to** objects upon contact

例 You'll have enough time getting those tenacious gum off of your wool sweater. 你有足够的时候去把羊毛毛衣上面那块粘着的泡泡糖弄下来。

近 adherent, adhesive, clingy, glutinous, tacky, viscid

反 nonadhesive 不具有粘性的

tendentious [ten'denʃəs]

【考法】 *adj.* 有偏见的：marked by a tendency in favor of a particular point of view: **biased**

例 He made some extremely tendentious remarks. 他的一些评论颇具偏向性。

近 partial, distorting, subjective, biased

反 unbiased, unprejudiced 公平的

tender ['tendər]

【考法1】 *vt.* 正式提出：to **offer** formally

例 tender a letter of resignation 正式提交辞职信

近 extend, proffer, trot out

反 withdraw 撤回

【考法2】 *adj.* 考虑周到的，关心同情的：having or marked by **sympathy** and **consideration** for others

例 an especially tender teacher who loves having kids with special educational needs in her class 特别无微不至的老师，爱着那些需要特别教育的孩子们

近 beneficent, benevolent, benignant, compassionate, softhearted

反 atrocious, barbarous, bestial, brutal, callous, cruel, fiendish, inhuman, insensate, sadistic, savage, truculent, uncompassionate, vicious 尖酸刻薄的

tenuous ['tenjuəs]

【考法】 *adj.* 没有实际内容的，空洞的：having **little substance**; flimsy

例 a tenuous argument 站不住脚的论点

反 substantial 实质的

tepid ['tepɪd]

【考法】 *adj.* 不太热心的：showing **little or no interest** or enthusiasm

例 a tepid response 冷漠的回应 ‖ the tepid conservatism of the fifties 五十年代那种温和的保守主义

近 lukewarm, halfhearted, uneager, unenthusiastic

反 ardent, ebullient, feverish, keen, passionate, wholehearted 热心的

terminology [ˌtɜːrmə'nɑːlədʒi]

【考法】 *n.* 专业术语：the **special terms or expressions** of a particular group or field

例 the terminology favored by sportscasters 体育节目转播员喜欢用的那些术语 ‖ medical terminology that can be hard for the patient to understand 那些病人们难以理解的医学术语

近 argot, cant, dialect, jargon, jive, lingo, patois, patter, slang

terminus	[ˈtɜːrmɪnəs]	

terminus [ˈtɜːrmɪnəs]

【考法】 *n.* 终点，终点站：the final point; the **end**

例 Stockholm is the terminus for the southbound train. 斯德哥尔摩是向南去的列车的终点站。

反 outset, sustain 开始，持续

terror [ˈterər]

【考法】 *n.* 极度恐惧：a state of **intense fear**

例 Many civilians fled in terror. 很多黎民百姓极度恐慌，逃难去了。

近 anxiety, dread, fearfulness, fright, horror, panic, trepidation

terse [tɜːrs]

【考法】 *adj.* 简洁的，简明的：**brief** and to the point; effectively concise

例 He dismissed me with a terse "no". 他用一个简单的"不"把我打发了。

近 compact, compendious, laconic, pithy, succinct

反 circuitous, circumlocutory, diffuse, long-winded, prolix, rambling, verbose, windy, wordy 冗长啰嗦的

testimony [ˈtestɪmoʊni]

【考法】 *n.* 证词，声明：firsthand **authentication** of a fact

例 The jury heard 10 days of testimony. 陪审团进行了 10 天的听证。

近 attestation, confirmation, documentation, substantiation, testament, validation

反 disproof 反驳

Unit 9

■ TESTY	■ TETHER	■ THEATRICAL	■ THERAPEUTIC	■ THORNY
■ THREADBARE	■ THRONG	■ THWART	■ TICKLISH	■ TIFF

testy [ˈtesti]

【考法】 *adj.* 易怒的，暴躁的：**easily annoyed**: **irritable**

例 That coworker would be easier to get along with if she weren't so testy all the time. 如果那个同事不是一直那么易怒的话，她还是挺好相处的。

近 choleric, irascible, peevish, perverse, pettish, petulant

反 affable, good humor, unable to irritate, imperturbable, patient 和蔼可亲的，冷静的，有耐心的

tether [ˈteðər]

【考法 1】 *vt.* (用绳、铁链)拴系，束缚：to **fasten** or **restrain** by or as if by a tether

例 They tethered the horses in the shade. 他们把马拴在棚子里。

反 detach, tear loose 分开，撕裂

【考法 2】 *n.* 能力或忍耐力的极限：the **limit** of one's strength or resources

例 drought-stricken farmers at the end of their tether 受干旱打击的农民已经忍无可忍

theatrical [θiˈætrɪkl]

【考法】 *adj.* 做作的，夸张的，矫揉造作的：marked by **exaggerated** self-display and **unnatural** behavior

例 assume a theatrical pose 摆出夸张的姿势

近 dramatic, histrionic, melodramatic, stagy

反 natural, understated, reserved, restraint 自然的，保留的

therapeutic [ˌθerəˈpjuːtɪk]

【考法】 *adj.* 治疗的，有疗效的：of or relating to the **treatment** of **disease** or disorders by remedial agents or methods

例 Gentle exercise can be therapeutic for hospital patients. 适量的运动对病人恢复有好处。

近 curative, healing, officinal, remedial, restorative

thorny [ˈθɔːrni]

【考法 1】 *adj.* 多刺的：**full of thorns**

例 Stay out of the thorny brambles unless you want a ton of scratches. 离那些长满刺的荆棘丛远一点，除非你想满身都是窟窿。

反 smooth 平滑的

【考法 2】 *adj.* 棘手的：full of **difficulties** or controversial points: ticklish

例 a thorny problem 棘手的问题

近 catchy, delicate, knotty, prickly, ticklish

threadbare	[ˈθredber]

【考法 1】 *adj.* 陈腐的: overused to the point of being worn out; **hackneyed**

例 a novel filled with nothing but threadbare clichés 一部满是陈词滥调的小说

近 banal, cliché, commonplace, hackney, shopworn, trite

【考法 2】 *adj.* 贫穷的: **lacking** money or material **possessions**

例 She never knew that she had so many threadbare relatives until she won the lottery. 赢了彩票之后才知道她有这么多穷亲戚。

近 beggared, destitute, down-and-out, famished, impecunious, impoverished, indigent, necessitous, needful, pauperized, penniless, penurious, poverty-stricken, skint

反 affluent, deep-pocketed, flush, opulent, silk-stocking, wealthy, well-heeled, well-off, well-to-do 富裕的

【考法 3】 *adj.* 破烂的: **worn or torn** into or as if into rags

例 I love that threadbare shirt, but after 10 years of wear, it is time to throw it away. 我很喜欢那件旧旧的衬衣，但是已经穿了 10 年了，是该扔了。

近 frayed, raggedy, ratty, seedy, shabby, tattered, worn-out

throng	[θrɔːŋ]

【考法】 *v./n.* 大量聚集: to **crowd** together **in great numbers**

例 commuters thronging the MTR platform 持月票的乘客拥向地铁站

近 flock, mob, swarm

thwart	[θwɔːrt]

【考法】 *vt.* 阻挠: to **oppose** successfully

例 She did all she could to thwart his plans. 她竭尽所能阻挠他的计划。

近 baffle, balk, checkmate, discomfit

反 advance, cultivate, encourage, forward, foster, further, nurture, promote, support, aid, bolster, abet, foment, facilitate 促进，支持

ticklish	[ˈtɪklɪʃ]

【考法 1】 *adj.* 易怒的: **easily offended** or upset; touchy

例 He is always ticklish whenever people refer to his baldness. 大家一提起他的秃头，他就暴怒。

近 huffy, tetchy, thin-skinned

反 imperturbable 镇静的

【考法 2】 *adj.* 棘手的，对技巧要求高的: requiring **exceptional skill or caution** in performance or handling

例 Trying to tell him that his zipper is down without embarrassing him will be a ticklish task. 如何体面得体地提醒他拉链没关好是一个技巧活儿。

近 catchy, delicate, difficult, dodgy, knotty, prickly, problematic, sensitive, spiny, sticky, thorny, touchy, tough, tricksy

tiff	[tɪf]

【考法】 *n./v.* 小争吵: a **petty quarrel**

例 The couple got into a little tiff about what color sheets to buy for their bed. 夫妇俩对于买什么颜色的床单争吵起来。

近 altercate, bicker, brabble, hassle, quarrel, quibble, row, scrap, spat, squabble

Unit 10

■ TIGHTFISTED	■ TIMEWORN	■ TIMID	■ TIMOROUS	■ TINGE
■ TINKER	■ TINT	■ TIRADE	■ TOADY	■ TONIC

tightfisted	[ˈtaɪtˌfɪstɪd]

【考法】 *adj.* 吝啬的: close-fisted; **stingy**

例 The company is pretty tightfisted when it comes to bonuses. 这个公司分红的时候很吝啬。

近 mean, miserly, parsimonious, penurious, sparing, stinting

反 bounteous, bountiful, charitable, freehanded, generous, liberal, munificent, openhanded, unsparing, unstinting 慷慨大方的

timeworn	[ˈtaɪmˌwɔːrn]

【考法】 *adj.* 陈腐的: **hackneyed**, stale

例 timeworn jokes 老掉牙的笑话

近 banal, cliché, commonplace, hackneyed, stereotyped, threadbare, trite

反 fresh, new, novel, original, unclichéd, unhackneyed 新奇的

timid	[ˈtɪmɪd]
【考法】	*adj.*胆小的，不自信的：**lacking** in **courage** or **self-confidence**
例	He gave her a timid smile. 他给了她一个羞赧的微笑。
近	fainthearted, fearsome, scary, timorous, tremulous
反	stalwart, adventurous, audacious, bold, daring, dashing, gutsy, venturous 坚定勇敢的

timorous	[ˈtɪmərəs]
【考法】	*adj.*胆小的：of a timid disposition: **fearful**
例	be as timorous as a rabbit 像兔子一样胆小
近	timid, undaring, quailing, recoiling, scary, skittish
反	stalwart, intrepid, adventurous, audacious, bold, daring, dashing, gutsy, venturous 大胆的

tinge	[tɪndʒ]
【考法】	*vt.*给…着上少量的色彩：to **color** with a slight shade or stain: **tint**
例	Just slightly tinge the frosting with yellow food coloring to give it a lemony look. 略微在霜糖表面加一点黄色色素，有一点柠檬的感觉就可以了。
近	dye, pigment, stain, tincture, tint, suffuse
反	decolorize 使脱色

tinker	[ˈtɪŋkər]
【考法】	*v.*乱修，乱调整：to handle **thoughtlessly**, ignorantly, or mischievously
例	tinker with the engine 胡乱调整发动机
近	diddle with, fiddle with, fool with, mess with, toy with, twiddle with
反	adjust, repair 调整，修理

tint	[tɪnt]
【考法】	*v.*涂浅色，微染：apply a usually **slight** or pale **coloration to**
例	tint with only one color 只用一种颜色染色
近	dye, pigment, stain, tincture, tinge, suffuse
反	decolorize 使脱色

tirade	[ˈtaɪreɪd]
【考法】	*n.*长篇抨击性演讲：a long **angry** or violent speech, usually of a **censorious or denunciatory** nature; a diatribe
例	a tirade of angry protest 一个表达愤怒的抗议的长篇抨击性演讲
近	harangue, diatribe, jeremiad, philippic, rant
反	eulogy, encomium, panegyric, tribute 颂词

toady	[ˈtoʊdi]
【考法】	*n./v.*马屁精；拍马屁：one who **flatters** in the hope of **gaining favors**
例	He criticized that I was a toady. 他批评说我是一个马屁精。
近	sycophant, groveler, flatterer

tonic	[ˈtɑːnɪk]
【考法】	*adj.*滋补的，有益健康的：producing or **stimulating** physical, mental, or emotional **vigor**; **beneficial** to the health of body or mind
例	tonic medicine 补药
近	medicinal, restorative, salubrious, salutary, salutiferous, sanative, wholesome
反	insalubrious, noxious, unhealthful, unhealthy, unwholesome 不健康的

List 26

"若干年前，有人跟我说，没有GRE的人生是不完整的。现在我跟别人说，没有GRE的人生确实不是完整的。"

（李丹，录取院校：Princeton University, Civil and Environmental Engineering）

Unit 1

■ TOPSY-TURVY ■ TORPID ■ TORPOR ■ TORRENTIAL ■ TORRID
■ TORTUOUS ■ TOUT ■ TOY ■ TRACTABLE ■ TRANQUILITY

topsy-turvy [ˌtɑːpsiˈtɜːrvi]
【考法】 *adj.*混乱的：**lacking in order**, neatness, and often cleanliness
例 He left his room topsy-turvy. 他把他的房间弄得很乱。
近 disordered, chaotic, messy, anarchic, jumbled
反 kempt, neat, orderly, organized, shipshape, tidy, trim, uncluttered, well-ordered 有序的

torpid [ˈtɔːrpɪd]
【考法1】 *adj.*麻木的，没有知觉的：lacking in **sensation** or feeling
例 My tongue and throat remained torpid for a time following the endoscopy. 胃镜检查之后，我的舌头和喉咙一直是麻木的。
近 asleep, benumbed, dead, insensitive, numbed, unfeeling
反 feeling, sensible, sensitive 有同情心的，敏感的
【考法2】 *adj.*迟钝的，行动迟缓的：**slow** to move or act
例 a torpid sloth that refused to budge off its tree branch 趴在树枝上一动不动的树獭
近 dull, inert, lethargic, quiescent, sleepy, sluggish, torpid
反 active 活跃的

torpor [ˈtɔːrpər]
【考法1】 *n.*缺乏兴趣：**lack of interest** or concern
例 After a lifetime of setbacks, defeats, and failures, he could only greet the latest bad news with a resigned fatalism and dull torpor. 一生都充满了挫折、失败，他只能用宿命论和麻木不仁来迎接又一次的坏消息。
近 apathy, casualness, complacence, disinterestedness, disregard, incuriosity, insouciance, nonchalance
反 concern, interest, regard 有兴趣
【考法2】 *n.*（肉体或精神上的）迟钝，懒散：physical or mental **inertness**
例 Following Thanksgiving dinner, we spent the rest of the day lounging about in a contented torpor. 吃完感恩节晚餐后，我们慵懒地靠在沙发上度过剩下的时间。
近 languor, lassitude, listlessness, stupor
反 vigor, vim, vitality, vivacity 活力

torrential [təˈrenʃl]
【考法】 *adj.*急流的：caused by or resulting from action of **rapidstreams**
例 a torrential rain 倾盆大雨
反 trickling 涓涓细流的

torrid [ˈtɔːrɪd]
【考法1】 *adj.*酷热的：**intensely hot**
例 the dry, torrid summers in southern Arizona 南亚利桑那州干燥、炎热的夏天
近 hot, scalding, scorching, sweltering
反 arctic, bone-chilling, freezing, frigid, frozen, glacial, icy 寒冷的
【考法2】 *adj.*热情的，情感深厚的：having or expressing **great depth of feeling**
例 torrid love affair 炙热的爱
近 ardent, burning, fervid, flaming, glowing, impassioned, incandescent, intense, passionate, vehement
反 dispassionate, emotionless, impassive, unemotional 冷漠的

tortuous	[ˈtɔːrtʃuəs]
【考法】	*adj.* 转弯抹角的：marked by devious or **indirect** tactics; crooked, tricky
例	a tortuous path 一条蜿蜒的道路
近	bending, curling, curvy, devious, serpentine, sinuous, twisted, windy
反	direct, straightforward 直接的

tout	[taʊt]
【考法】	*vt.* 极力赞扬：to promote or **praise** energetically; publicize
例	tout victory in the war 鼓吹战果
近	acclaim, laud, praise, ballyhoo
反	asperse, censure, denounce, berate, rate, revile, vituperate 指责

toy	[tɔɪ]
【考法】	*vi.* 草率或不认真地对待：to **handle thoughtlessly**, ignorantly, or mischievously
例	That microscope is a delicate instrument, not something to be toyed with. 那台显微镜是精密仪器，不是随随便便的一个玩具。
近	diddle with, fiddle with, fool with, mess with, monkey with, tinker with, twiddle with

tractable	[ˈtræktəbl]
【考法】	*adj.* 易驾驭的，温顺的：readily **giving in** to the command or authority of another
例	a tractable horse 一匹温顺的马
近	obedient, amenable, docile, flexible, manageable, compliant, submissive, tame
反	balky, contumacious, defiant, disobedient, incompliant, insubordinate, obstreperous, rebellious, recalcitrant, refractory, restive, unamenable, ungovernable, unruly, untoward, wayward, willful 任性的，难以驯服的

tranquility	[træŋˈkwɪləti]
【考法】	*n.* 宁静，淡定：a state of **freedom from storm** or disturbance
例	enjoyed the tranquillity of the snow-covered field at dusk 享受傍晚时分被雪覆盖的田野的静谧
近	calm, quiet, silence, serenity
反	bustle, commotion, hubbub, pandemonium, tumult, turmoil, unquietness, unrest, uproar 喧闹，骚乱

Unit 2

■ TRANSCEND	■ TRANSFIGURE	■ TRANSGRESS	■ TRANSIENT	■ TRANSITORY
■ TRANSLUCENT	■ TRANSPARENT	■ TRAVAIL	■ TRAVERSE	■ TRAVESTY

transcend	[trænˈsend]
【考法】	*vt.* 超越，超过极限：to rise above or go **beyond the limits** of
例	a person who believes that any true understanding of God transcends human intelligence 认为对上帝的真正理解是超越人类智商极限的人
近	break, outreach, outrun, overpass, overreach, overrun, overshoot, overstep, surpass

transfigure	[trænsˈfɪɡjər]
【考法】	*vt.* 使改变外观：to **alter** the outward **appearance** of; **transform**
例	transfigure the AutoCAD drawings with elegant symbols 用优美的符号使 AutoCAD 图变得美观
近	alchemize, metamorphose, transform, transmute, transpose, transubstantiate, make over

transgress	[trænzˈɡres]
【考法】	*vt.* 违背；犯错：to **fail to keep**; to **commit an offense**
例	Don't even think about transgressing the drug laws of that Asian country, for punishments are severe and there's nothing that our government can do to intervene. 别指望违背那个亚洲国家的药品相关法，因为惩罚非常严厉，我们政府完全无法干涉。
近	breach, break, contravene, fracture, infringe, offend, traduce
反	follow, mind, obey, observe, comply with, conform to 遵守

transient	[ˈtrænʃnt]
【考法】	*adj.* 短暂的，瞬时的：passing with time; **transitory**
例	transient pleasure 短暂的快乐
近	transitory, ephemeral, evanescent, fleeting, temporary

反	ceaseless, dateless, deathless, endless, enduring, eternal, everlasting, immortal, lasting, long-lived, permanent, perpetual, timeless, undying, unending 永恒持久的

transitory ［ˈtrænsətɔːri］

【考法】 *adj.*短暂的：existing or **lasting only a short time**; short-lived or temporary

例 Most of life's joys are transitory. 尘世间的欢乐都是过眼烟云，转瞬即逝。

近 transient, ephemeral, evanescent, fleeting, temporary

反 ceaseless, dateless, deathless, endless, enduring, eternal, everlasting, immortal, lasting, long-lived, permanent, perpetual, timeless, undying, unending 永恒持久的

translucent ［trænsˈluːsnt］

【考法】 *adj.*透明的：**permitting** the **passage** of **light**; clear, **transparent**

例 translucent dewdrop 透明的露珠

近 transparent, limpid, pellucid, lucent, lucid, transpicuous

反 opaque 不透明的

transparent ［trænsˈpærənt］

【考法 1】 *adj.*透明的：**capable of transmitting light**

近 translucent, limpid, pellucid, lucent, lucid, transpicuous

反 cloudy, opaque 不透明的

【考法 2】 *adj.*没有歧义的，清晰易懂的：**not subject to misinterpretation** or more than one interpretation

例 His meaning in leaving the conversation is transparent: he doesn't want to talk about his combat experiences. 他结束这个话题的意图很明显：不想谈论当年参战的经历。

近 obvious, clear, apparent, patent, understandable, apprehensible, comprehensible, fathomable

反 ambiguous, clouded, cryptic, enigmatic, equivocal, indistinct, mysterious, obfuscated, obscure, unapparent, unclarified, unclear, unclouded 难以理解的

travail ［ˈtræveɪl］

【考法】 *n./v.*辛苦劳动：work, especially when **arduous** or involving painful effort

例 writer's literary travail 作家辛勤的文学创作 ‖ Labor Day is the day on which we recognize those men and women who daily travail with little appreciation or compensation. 劳动节是我们向那些平日辛勤劳作但是很少受到大家关注并得到应有补偿的工人致敬的日子。

近 drudgery, fatigue, grind

traverse ［trəˈvɜːrs］

【考法】 *vt.*横穿：to travel or **pass across**, over, or through

例 The spider traversed the wall from end to end. 蜘蛛侠攀岩走壁。

近 course, cover, cross, cut across, navigate, pass over, perambulate, peregrinate, proceed along, transit, travel

travesty ［ˈtrævəsti］

【考法】 *n./v.* 拙劣的、嘲弄性模仿：an **exaggerated** or grotesque **imitation**, such as a parody of a literary work

例 a travesty of his classmate's manner 滑稽的模仿其他同学的举止

近 caricature, burlesque, parody, spoof, mock

反 paragon 完美的模范

Unit 3

■ TREACHEROUS	■ TRENCHANT	■ TREPIDATION	■ TRESPASS	■ TRIBUTE
■ TRICKLE	■ TRITE	■ TRIVIAL	■ TRUANT	■ TRUCE

treacherous ［ˈtretʃərəs］

【考法】 *adj.*背叛的：marked by **betrayal** of fidelity, confidence, or trust

例 a treacherous ally 不忠的盟友

近 faithless, disloyal, perfidious, recreant, traitorous, unfaithful, unloyal, betraying

反 constant, dedicated, devoted, staunch, down-the-line, faithful, fast, loyal, steadfast, steady, true 忠诚的

trenchant ［ˈtrentʃənt］

【考法 1】 *adj.*锐利的：keen, **sharp**

例 Even the most trenchant sword could not sever the bonds of loyalty between them. 即使最锋利的刀剑也不能切断他们之间的忠诚。

近 keen, sharp

反 blunt, blunted, dull, obtuse 钝的

【考法2】 *adj.* (言辞) 一针见血的: vigorously effective and **articulate**

例 trenchant criticisms 一针见血的批评

近 incisive

反 vague 含糊的

trepidation [ˌtrepɪˈdeɪʃn]

【考法】 *n.* 恐惧，战栗: the emotion experienced in the presence or threat of danger; **apprehension**

例 trepidation about starting a new career 对开创一项新事业感到恐惧

近 fear, fright, horror, apprehension

反 boldness, bravery, dauntlessness, intrepidity 大胆

trespass [ˈtrespəs]

【考法】 *vi.* 非法侵入；违反，冒犯: to **enter unlawfully** upon the land of another; to commit an **offense**

例 I consider him to be trespassing against all of us when he trespasses against any one of us. 当他冒犯我们当中一个人的时候，他就冒犯了我们全部。

近 transgress, invade, intrude

反 withdraw, retreat 撤退

tribute [ˈtrɪbjuːt]

【考法】 *n.* 称颂，颂词: a gift, payment, **declaration**, or other acknowledgment of **gratitude**, respect, or admiration

例 pay a high tribute to 赞颂

近 accolade, eulogy, encomium, panegyric, tribute 颂词

反 denunciation, condemnation, criticism, censure, reproof, reprobation 批评，指责

trickle [ˈtrɪkl]

【考法】 *vi.* 一滴一滴地流，缓缓地流: to issue or **fall in drops**

例 Tears trickled down her cheeks. 眼泪从她的脸上一滴一滴地流下。

反 pour, roll, stream, gush 喷涌

trite [traɪt]

【考法】 *adj.* 陈腐的，陈词滥调的: **hackneyed** or boring from much use, not fresh or original

例 "You win some, you lose some" is a trite expression. "有得必有失"是老生常谈了。

近 bathetic, cliché, hackneyed, threadbare, timeworn, banal

反 fresh, new, novel, original, unclichéd, unhackneyed 新鲜的

trivial [ˈtrɪviəl]

【考法】 *adj.* 琐碎的，无足轻重的: of **little** worth or **importance**

例 Why spend so much time on trivial decisions, like whether the cola should be regular or diet? 为什么花这么多时间在这种琐碎的决定上，比如可乐要喝一般的还是健怡的?

近 inconsiderable, insignificant, minor, petty, inconsequential, paltry, trifling

反 consequential, material, momentous, weighty, indispensable, substantive, grandiose, massive 重要的

truant [ˈtruːənt]

【考法】 *adj./n./vi.* 逃避责任(的)；逃避责任者: **shirking responsibility**; one who **shirks duty**

例 play truant 逃学

近 shirk, malinger, goldbrick, avoid, escape, evade, parry, sidestep, circumvent, fence, hedge, avert, elude, shun, skirt, dodge, bilk, eschew

反 dutiful 尽职尽责的

truce [truːs]

【考法】 *n.* 休战，休战协定: a **suspension** of **fighting** especially of considerable duration by agreement of opposing forces

例 truce agreement 休战协议

近 armistice, cease-fire, peace

Unit 4

truculent ['trʌkjələnt]

【考法 1】 *adj.* 尖酸刻薄的：marked by **harsh insulting** language
例 a theater critic who was notorious for his titanically truculent reviews 一个以超大量尖酸刻薄言论著称的话剧评论家
近 contumelious, invective, opprobrious, scurrilous, vitriolic, vituperative

【考法 2】 *adj.* 好战的，好斗的：feeling or displaying **eagerness to fight**
例 in an aggressively truculent manner 以好斗的、进攻性的方式
近 belligerent, bellicose, combative, militant, aggressive, feisty
反 nonaggressive, nonbelligerent, pacific, peaceable, peaceful, uncombative, uncontentious 好和平的

trudge [trʌdʒ]

【考法】 *vi.* 吃力而笨拙地走：to move **heavily or clumsily**
例 trudge over hill 翻山越岭
近 plod, lug, slog, flounder
反 breeze, glide, slide, waltz, whisk, flit 快速通过

trumpet ['trʌmpɪt]

【考法】 *v.* 大声说出或宣告：to **make known** openly or publicly
例 The losing party lost no time in trumpeting allegations of election fraud. 落败的政党马不停蹄地开始公开宣称选举存在作假。
近 advertise, annunciate, blare, broadcast, declare, proclaim, promulgate, release, give out

truncate ['trʌŋkeɪt]

【考法】 *vt.* 截短；缩短（时间、篇幅等）：to **shorten** by or as if by cutting off
例 a truncated version of the 11 o'clock newscast following the awards show, which ran over its time slot 颁奖典礼之后缩短版的 11 点新闻节目，已经超出了预定时长
近 abbreviate, abridge, curtail, retrench
反 elongate, extend, lengthen, prolong, protract 延长

truss [trʌs]

【考法】 *v.* 系紧，扎紧：to gather **into a tight mass** by means of a line or cord
例 After stuffing the turkey, the chef quickly trussed it so the forcemeat wouldn't fall out during roasting. 把填料塞进火鸡后，大厨迅速把它扎紧防止在烘烤过程中肉馅掉出来。
近 band, bind
反 unbind, untie 解开

tumult ['tuːmʌlt]

【考法】 *n.* 骚动，暴动：a **disorderly** commotion or **disturbance**, a riot
例 His mind was in a tumult. 他心烦意乱。
近 disorder, disturbance, commotion, convulsion, ferment, turmoil, pandemonium, uproar
反 quietude, quiescence, serenity, tranquility 安静

turbid ['tɜːrbɪd]

【考法】 *adj.* 混浊的：**deficient in clarity** or purity
例 a turbid stream 一条混浊的河
近 muddy, murky, obscure
反 clear, limpid, lucid, pellucid, crystalline 清澈的

turbulent ['tɜːrbjələnt]

【考法 1】 *adj.* 动荡的：marked by sudden or violent **disturbance**
例 a turbulent period in history 历史上的动荡时期
近 cataclysmal, stormy, tempestuous, tumultuous

【考法 2】 *adj.* 湍急的，汹涌的：marked by **turmoil** or disturbance especially of natural elements
例 The turbulent rapids of the river were certainly daunting to those of us who were new to river rafting. 湍急的流水必定让我们这些初玩漂流的人吓得不轻。
近 rough, rugged, stormy, tempestuous

turgid ['tɜːrdʒɪd]

【考法】 *adj.* 浮夸的，过分装饰的: excessively **embellished** in style or language

例 turgid prose 浮华的散文

近 flatulent, bombastic, pompous

反 simple, austere, unadorned, undecorated, unembellished 简朴的

turmoil ['tɜːrmɔɪl]

【考法】 *n.* 骚动，混乱: a state or condition of extreme confusion, **agitation**, or **commotion**

例 My mind is in a turmoil. 我心里很乱。

近 commotion, agitation, tumult, turbulence, disorder, ferment, clamor

反 calm, ease, peace, peacefulness, quiet, tranquility, silence, serenity 安静

Unit 5

■ TURNCOAT	■ TURPITUDE	■ TWIG	■ TYPO	■ TYRO
■ UBIQUITOUS	■ UNASSAILABLE	■ UNCANNY	■ UNCOUTH	■ UNCTUOUS

turncoat ['tɜːrnkoʊt]

【考法】 *n.* 叛徒: one who **switches** to an opposing side or party; specifically: **traitor**

例 He was labeled as a turncoat. 他是一个叛徒。

近 renegade, traitor, apostate, recreant, betrayer, quisling

反 loyalist, partisan, adherent, supporter 支持者，追随者

turpitude ['tɜːrpətuːd]

【考法】 *n.* 卑鄙: inherent **baseness**: depravity

例 moral turpitude 道德上的卑鄙

近 abjection, corruptness, debasement, debauchery, decadency, degeneration, degradation, demoralization, depravity, dissipatedness, dissoluteness, libertinism, perversion, rakishness

反 probity 正直

twig [twɪg]

【考法】 *v.* 了解: to **have a clear idea** of

例 It took me a while to twig the true nature of the relationship between the two women. 我花了很长时间才搞清楚这俩女人之间的关系。

近 appreciate, apprehend, cognize, compass, conceive, decipher, decode, dig, discern, perceive, recognize, savvy, seize, sense, tumble to, catch on to, make out

typo ['taɪpoʊ]

【考法】 *n.* 打字错误: an **error** in typed or typeset material

例 make one typo on the memo 在样张上打错一个字

近 misprint, bug

tyro ['taɪroʊ]

【考法】 *n.* 新手，业余爱好者: a **beginner** in learning: **novice**

例 a tyro in the art of piano 钢琴界的新手

近 novice, apprentice, neophyte, rookie, amateur, dabbler, dilettante, fledgling, recruit

反 old hand, old-timer, vet, expert, professional, veteran 专家

ubiquitous [juːˈbɪkwɪtəs]

【考法】 *adj.* 无所不在的，普通的: being **everywhere** at the same time; **often observed** or encountered

例 The conflict between opposites is ubiquitous. 对立的冲突无所不在。

近 omnipresent, universal, general, common

反 extraordinary, infrequent, rare, seldom, uncommon, unfamiliar, unusual, unique, particular 独特的，不常见的

unassailable [ˌʌnəˈseɪləbl]

【考法】 *adj.* 无可争辩的，无法否认的，不可亵渎的: **not to be violated**, criticized, or tampered with

例 an unassailable article 无可争辩的文章

近 undeniable, inviolable, sacrosanct, irrefutable, indisputable, unexceptionable, unimpeachable

反 controversial 有争议的

	uncanny	[ʌnˈkæni]

uncanny [ʌnˈkæni]

【考法】 *adj.* 离奇的，奇异的: being so **extraordinary or abnormal** as to suggest powers which violate the laws of nature

例 The silence was uncanny. 静得出奇。

近 magical, miraculous, phenomenal, preternatural, superhuman, supernormal, transcendent, transcendental, unearthly

反 ordinary, commonplace, normal 平凡的

uncouth [ʌnˈkuːθ]

【考法】 *adj.* 粗俗的，没有品位的: **lacking in refinement** or good taste

例 The movie's uncouth humor seemed to be purposely offensive. 电影里一些恶俗的幽默貌似是故意的。

近 crass, rude, discourteous, disgracious, ungraceful, crude, ill-bred, ill-mannered, uncivil, unrefined

反 genteel, cultivated, cultured, polished, urbane, seemly 得体的，有教养的

unctuous [ˈʌŋktʃuəs]

【考法1】 *adj.* 油嘴滑舌的，谄媚的: overly or insincerely **flattering**

例 an unctuous appraisal of the musical talent shown by the boss's daughter 拍老板马屁，说他女儿在音乐方面有着非常卓越的天赋

近 adulatory, gushing, hagiographic, oily, oleaginous, soapy

【考法2】 *adj.* 夸张的，做作的: characterized by **affected, exaggerated**, or insincere earnestness

例 an unctuous effort to appear religious to the voters 过分做作想在选民面前表现得虔诚

近 artificial, backhanded, counterfeit, fake, feigned, hypocritical, phony, pretended

反 artless, candid, genuine, heartfelt, honest, sincere, undesigning, unfeigned 真实的

Unit 6

■ UNDERDOG	■ UNDERGIRD	■ UNDERMINE	■ UNDERSCORE	■ UNDERSTATE
■ UNDERSTUDY	■ UNEXCEPTIONABLE	■ UNFLAPPABLE	■ UNGAINLY	■ UNIMPEACHABLE

underdog [ˈʌndərdɔːg]

【考法】 *n.* 受害者，输家: a **loser/victim** or predicted loser in a struggle or contest

例 She always supports for the underdog. 她经常支持受害者。

近 loser, victim

反 bully 欺凌弱小者

undergird [ˌʌndərˈgɜːrd]

【考法】 *vt.* 加强，巩固…的底部: to support or **strengthen** from beneath

例 Facts and statistics undergird his commentary. 事实和数据支持了他的评论。

近 strengthen, support, fortify, reinforce, bear, bolster, brace, buttress, carry, stay, sustain, underpin, uphold, prop up, shore up

反 undermine, weaken, debilitate, enfeeble, enervate 削弱

undermine [ˌʌndərˈmaɪn]

【考法】 *vt.* 削弱，破坏: to **weaken**, **injure**, or **impair**, often by degrees or imperceptibly

例 undermine a fortress 挖地道破坏堡垒

近 weaken, debilitate, enfeeble, enervate

反 strengthen, support, fortify, reinforce 加强

underscore [ˌʌndərˈskɔːr]

【考法】 *vt.* 强调: **to emphasize**; stress

例 underscore the value of education 强调教育的重要性

近 accentuate, italicize, stress, underline, bring out

反 deemphasize, downplay 轻描淡写

understate [ˌʌndərˈsteɪt]

【考法】 *vt.* 保守陈述: to state or present with **restraint** especially for effect

例 understate a problem 低调处理问题

近 downplay

反 vaunt, exaggerate, overstate 夸大

派 understated *adj.* 不夸张的；朴素的：avoiding obvious emphasis or embellishment
近 conservative, low-key, muted, repressed, restrained, sober, subdued, unflashy, unpretentious
反 flamboyant, flaring, flashy, garish, gaudy, glitzy, ostentatious, splashy 夸张的；华丽的

understudy [ˈʌndərstʌdi]
【考法】 *n.* 替补演员：one who is prepared to act another's part or **take** over **another's duties**
例 be an understudy to sb 作为某人的替补
近 deputy

unexceptionable [ˌʌnɪkˈsepʃənəbl]
【考法】 *adj.* 无懈可击的：not open to objection or criticism，**beyond reproach**
近 unassailable, undeniable, irrefutable, indisputable, unimpeachable
反 assailable, controversial 有争议的

unflappable [ˌʌnˈflæpəbl]
【考法】 *adj.* 镇定的，从容不迫的：**not easily upset** or excited
例 a unflappable general 一个镇定的将军
近 collected, composed, disimpassioned, imperturbable
反 perturbable, shakable, disturbed, nervous 紧张的

ungainly [ʌnˈɡeɪnli]
【考法】 *adj.* 笨拙的，不雅的：having or showing an **inability** to move **in a graceful manner**
例 ungainly movements 笨拙的动作
近 clumsy, awkward, blundering, maladroit
反 coordinated, graceful, adroit, dexterous, lissome 协调的，灵巧的

unimpeachable [ˌʌnɪmˈpiːtʃəbl]
【考法】 *adj.* 无可置疑的：beyond doubt; **unquestionable**
例 an unimpeachable evidence 无可置疑的证据
近 unassailable, undeniable, irrefutable, indisputable, unexceptionable
反 assailable, controversial, open to question 可争辩的

Unit 7

■ UNKEMPT	■ UNLETTERED	■ UNPRETENTIOUS	■ UNPRODUCTIVE	■ UNREQUITED
■ UNRULY	■ UNTENABLE	■ UNTOLD	■ UNTOWARD	■ UNWITTING

unkempt [ˌʌnˈkempt]
【考法】 *adj.* 凌乱的，无序的：**lacking in order**, neatness, and often cleanliness
例 unkempt hotel rooms 凌乱的酒店房间
近 slovenly, slipshod, sloppy, unneat, untidy, topsy-turvy, jumbled
反 bandbox, neat, orderly, organized, shipshape, tidy, trim, uncluttered, well-ordered 有序的，井井有条的

unlettered [ˌʌnˈletərd]
【考法】 *adj.* 未受教育的，文盲的：not adept at reading and writing; **deficient in the knowledge** that can be acquired from books; **illiterate**
例 unlettered sector of society 未受教育的地区
近 ignorant, illiterate, uneducated, untutored
反 educated, knowledgeable, erudite, literate, schooled, well-informed, well-read 博学的，受过教育的

unpretentious [ˌʌnprɪˈtenʃəs]
【考法 1】 *adj.* 低调的，谦逊的：lacking pretension or affectation; **modest**
例 an unpretentious virtuoso 一位谦虚的大师
近 demure, down-to-earth, lowly, meek, unassuming, humble, modest, unostentatious
反 arrogant, bumptious, conceited, egotistic, fastuous, haughty, imperious, lordly, overweening, peremptory, pompous, presuming, presumptuous, self-asserting, supercilious, superior, toplofty, uppish, flamboyant, ostentatious 傲慢的，自负的
【考法 2】 *adj.* 坦诚的，自然的：**free from** any intent to **deceive** or impress others
例 a simple and unpretentious account about growing up in the rural South 一段简单坦率的关于在南部乡村成长经历的叙述

近 artless, genuine, honest, ingenuous, innocent, naive, simple, sincere, true, unpretending

反 affected, artful, artificial, assuming, dissembling, dissimulating, fake, guileful, insincere, phony 做作的，虚伪的

unproductive [ˌʌnprəˈdʌktɪv]

【考法】 *adj.*徒然的，无效的：**not productive**; idle

例 Her attempts to write a novel have been unproductive. 她一直想写本小说的努力只是徒然。

近 abortive, barren, fruitless, otiose, profitless, unavailing, unprofitable, unsuccessful, useless, vain

反 deadly, effective, effectual, efficacious, efficient, potent, productive, profitable, successful, virtuous, telling 有效的

unrequited [ˌʌnrɪˈkwaɪtɪd]

【考法】 *adj.*无报答的，无报酬的：**not reciprocated** or returned in kind

例 unrequited love 无报答的爱

近 unreciprocated

反 remunerative, gainful, lucrative, profitable 有报酬的

unruly [ʌnˈruːli]

【考法】 *adj.*难驾驭的，不守规矩的：**difficult** or impossible **to discipline**, control, or rule

例 an unruly child 一个不听话的孩子

近 indocile, indomitable, intractable, recalcitrant, uncontrollable, undisciplined, ungovernable, unmanageable, insubordinate

反 amenable, biddable, compliant, conformable, docile, obedient, submissive, tractable, subdued, mild, manageable, disciplined 顺从的，守纪律的

untenable [ʌnˈtenəbl]

【考法】 *adj.*防守不住的，站不住脚的：not able to be **defended**

例 an untenable position 一个站不住脚的立场

近 assailable, controversial, open to question 可质疑的

反 unassailable, undeniable, irrefutable, indisputable, unexceptionable, unimpeachable 无可指责的，无懈可击的

untold [ʌnˈtoʊld]

【考法】 *adj.*数不清的，无数的：too great or **numerous** to count

例 untold wealth 不知其数的财富

近 incalculable, innumerable, countless, innumerous, uncountable, uncounted

反 countable, enumerable, numberable, quantifiable, calculable 可以计算的

untoward [ʌnˈtɔːrd]

【考法1】 *adj.*倒霉的，不吉利的：**not favorable**, **unpropitious**

例 an untoward incident 不幸的事故

近 unpropitious, unlucky, misfortunate, unfortunate

反 auspicious, propitious, favorable, fortunate 吉利的，幸运的

【考法2】 *adj.*难以驯服的，难以驾驭的：given to **resisting control or discipline** by others

例 a program for untoward teenagers that is designed to give them the kind of discipline that their parents were unable or unwilling to administer 一个以任性、桀骜不驯青少年为对象的项目，旨在弥补家长管教不周之处

近 froward, headstrong, intractable, recalcitrant, refractory, unruly, wayward, willful

反 controllable, governable, manageable, tractable 易管教的，顺从的

unwitting [ʌnˈwɪtɪŋ]

【考法1】 *adj.*不知道的，未觉察的：not knowing, **unaware**

例 Please forgive my unwitting interruption of your conversation. 请原谅我无意间打断了你们的谈话。

近 unaware, ignorant

反 acquainted, aware, cognizant, conscious, conversant, grounded, informed, knowing, mindful 有意识的

【考法2】 *adj.*偶然的，并非有意的：happening **by chance**; **not intended**

例 an unwitting mistake made in copying the material 在打印过程中一个无心的过失

近 casual, chance, fluky, fortuitous, inadvertent, incidental, unintentional

反 calculated, deliberate, intended, intentional, planned, premeditated, prepense 故意的，蓄意的

Unit 8

unwonted [ʌnˈwoʊntɪd]

【考法】 *adj.* 不习惯的，不寻常的：**not habitual** or **ordinary**; **unusual**

例 He's honored for the unwonted courage he showed in battle. 他因在战争中表现出的过人的勇气而受到嘉奖。

近 uncommon, unordinary, unusual

反 wonted, usual, routine, habitual, accustomed, customary 平常的

upbraid [ʌpˈbreɪd]

【考法】 *vt.* (严厉地)谴责，责骂：to **reproach severely**

例 upbraid sb with his ingratitude 责备某人忘恩负义

近 baste, scold, revile, berate, vituperate

反 laud, extol, glorify, hymn, magnify, panegyrize, flatter, fawn, cringe, adulate 赞扬

uphold [ʌpˈhoʊld]

【考法】 *vt.* 支持，赞成：to give **support** to

例 He determined to uphold her views in the face of all challenges. 他下定决心支持她的观点，尽管全世界都反对她。

近 support, bolster, advocate, champion, endorse, espouse

urbane [ɜːrˈbeɪn]

【考法】 *adj.* 彬彬有礼的，文雅的：notably **polite** or finished in manner

例 a gentlemanly and urbane host of elegant dinner parties 优雅晚宴的主人颇有绅士风度，彬彬有礼

近 debonair, civilized, genteel, cultivated, cultured, polished, refined, well-bred, courteous, gracious

反 boorish, churlish, classless, clownish, loutish, uncouth 粗鲁的

usurp [juːˈzɜːrp]

【考法】 *vt.* 篡夺，篡位：to **seize** and hold (the **power** or rights of another, for example) by force and **without legal authority**

例 usurp the throne 篡夺王位

近 arrogate, commandeer, convert, expropriate, pirate, preempt, press, seize, take over

反 abdicate 退位；crown 授予职位

utter [ˈʌtər]

【考法 1】 *vt.* 出(声)，说(话)：to **articulate** (words); pronounce or speak

例 She tried not to utter a sound as the doctor gave her a flu shot. 她克制自己不在医生打针的时候喊出来。

近 articulate, bring out, enunciate, verbalize, vocalize

【考法 2】 *adj.* 完全的，绝对的：complete; absolute; **entire**

例 be at an utter loss what to do 完全不知道怎样才好

近 entire, total, stark, sheer, unqualified

反 partial 部分的

vaccinate [ˈvæksɪneɪt]

【考法】 *v.* 预防接种疫苗：to inoculate with a vaccine in order to **produce immunity** to an infectious disease, such as diphtheria or typhus

例 vaccinate sb for smallpox 为某人接种牛痘疫苗以防天花

近 immunize

vacillate [ˈvæsəleɪt]

【考法 1】 *vi.* 犹豫不决：to waver in mind, will, or feeling; **hesitate** in choice of opinions or courses

例 Parents vacillate between saying no and yes, but actually neither response seems satisfactory to their children. 父母总是犹豫不定，不知道是该同意还是该反对，但是事实上哪种答案对他们的孩子都不理想。

近 hesitate, dither, waver, teeter, falter

反 resolute, decide, dive in, plunge in 决定

【考法 2】 *vi.* 摇动，摇摆：to sway from one side to the other; **oscillate**

近 oscillate, fluctuate

反 equipoise 平衡；静止

vacuous [ˈvækjuəs]

【考法】 *adj.* 茫然的，愚蠢的：marked by **lack of** ideas or **intelligence**

例 a movie that was derided for its vacuous dialogue 一部因为对白十分愚蠢而被嘲讽的电影

近 airhead, brainless, dull, dumb, fatuous, foolish, inane, moronic, obtuse, simple, stupid, witless

反 apt, bright, brilliant, clever, intelligent, keen, sharp, smart 聪明的

派 vacuity *n.* 愚蠢；空虚，空白

vagary [ˈveɪɡəri]

【考法】 *n.* 不可预测的思想或行为：an **erratic**, **unpredictable**, or extravagant manifestation, action, or notion

例 Recently he had been prone to strange vagaries. 最近他逐渐变得行为古怪起来。

近 caprice, fancy, freak, humor, vagrancy, whimsy

Unit 9

■ VAGUE	■ VALEDICTION	■ VALIANT	■ VALID	■ VANQUISH
■ VAPID	■ VAPORIZE	■ VARIANCE	■ VARIEGATED	■ VARNISH

vague [veɪɡ]

【考法 1】 *adj.* 表达不清的：**not clearly expressed**

例 The diplomat gave as vague a reply as he could at the press conference. 外交官在记者招待会上尽其所能来含糊其辞。

近 ambiguous, enigmatic, equivocal, indefinite, inexplicit, unclear

反 clear, definite, express, explicit, specific 清楚明确的

【考法 2】 *adj.* 轮廓不清晰的：**lacking definite shape**, form, or character

例 the vague outline of a building through the dense fog 浓雾中建筑物模糊的轮廓

近 dim, faint, foggy, hazy, indistinct, indistinguishable, misty, murky, nebulous, obscure, opaque

反 pellucid 清澈透明的

valediction [ˌvælɪˈdɪkʃn]

【考法 1】 *n.* 告别：an act of **bidding farewell**

近 farewell, goodbye

反 greeting 欢迎；debut 初次登台，首次亮相

【考法 2】 *n.* 告别词：an **address** or statement of **farewell** or leave-taking

例 a valediction given by the college president upon his retirement 大学校长退休时的告别演说

派 valedictory *adj.* 告别的

valiant [ˈvæliənt]

【考法】 *adj.* 勇敢的，英勇的：possessing or acting with **bravery** or boldness

例 a valiant and moral knight 一个勇敢和有道德感的骑士 ‖ Despite their valiant efforts, they lost the game. 尽管他们英勇奋战，但还是输掉了比赛。

近 audacious, bold, brave, courageous, dauntless, fearless, gallant, intrepid, stalwart, stout, valorous

反 cowardly, craven, gutless, nerveless, pusillanimous, spineless, timorous 胆怯的

派 valiance *n.* 英勇

valid [ˈvælɪd]

【考法】 *adj.* 逻辑上正确的：logically **correct**

例 Only further experiments will show whether your theory is valid. 只有进一步的实验才能验证你的理论是否正确。‖ Your argument isn't valid because you're taking what should be the conclusion and using it as a premise. 你的论述逻辑上是错误的，因为你把本该是结论的东西当成了前提条件。

近 analytic, coherent, consequent, rational, reasonable, sensible, sound, well-founded, well-grounded

反 groundless, illegitimate, illogical, incoherent, inconsequent, invalid, irrational, unreasonable, unsound（逻辑上）站不住脚的

派 validity *n.* 合乎逻辑

vanquish [ˈvæŋkwɪʃ]

【考法】 *vt.* 打败，征服：to **defeat** in a conflict or contest

例 He vanquished his inner fear. 他战胜了内心的恐惧。

近 conquer, dominate, overpower, pacify, subdue, subject, subjugate, subordinate

反 capitulate, surrender, yield 投降，屈服

vapid	[ˈvæpɪd]
【考法】	*adj.* 无趣的，乏味的：**lacking** liveliness, animation, or **interest**
例	a song with vapid lyrics 一首歌词乏味的歌曲
近	driveling, dull, flat, inane, insipid, jejune, sapless, tasteless
反	absorbing, arresting, engaging, engrossing, enthralling, fascinating, immersing, intriguing, riveting 吸引人的

vaporize	[ˈveɪpəraɪz]
【考法1】	*vt.* 使（液体）蒸发：to **convert**（as **by** the application of **heat** or by spraying）into vapor
近	gasify
反	condense（气体）液化
【考法2】	*vt.* 彻底消灭：to **destroy** by or as if by converting into vapor
例	The entire fleet was vaporized. 整个舰队都被消灭了。
近	annihilate, decimate, demolish, devastate, extinguish, nuke, pulverize, raze, ruin, smash, wreck
反	build, construct, erect, establish, raise, rear 建造
派	vaporous *adj.* 模糊的，空洞的

variance	[ˈveriəns]
【考法】	*n.* 不一致，不和谐：a **lack** of agreement or **harmony**
例	Persistent variance within the band eventually caused it to break up. 乐团中持续不断的分歧最终导致了它的解散。
近	conflict, disaccord, discordance, disharmony, dissent, division, friction, schism, variation, war
反	accord, agreement, concord, concordance, harmony, peace 和谐，一致
派	variant *adj.* 有差异的，不同的

variegated	[ˈveriɡeɪtɪd]
【考法】	*adj.* 杂色的，斑驳的：having discrete markings of **different colors**
例	variegated costumes of the dancers in the nightclub 夜总会舞者身上色彩斑驳的服装
近	chromatic, kaleidoscopic, iridescent, motley, rainbow
反	monochromatic 单色的；colorless 无色的
派	variegation *n.* 杂色

varnish	[ˈvɑːrnɪʃ]
【考法1】	*vt.* 上清漆，使有光泽：to give a **smooth** and **glossy** finish to
例	Don't sit on that chair- I've just varnished it. 不要坐在那张椅子上——我刚刚上过漆。
近	adorn, bedeck, bedizen, decorate, embellish, garnish, ornament
【考法2】	*vt.* 粉饰（令人不悦的东西）：to cover or **conceal**（as something **unpleasant**）with something that gives an attractive appearance
例	She tried to varnish her mistakes. 她试图掩盖她的失误。
近	blanch, extenuate, gloss, palliate, sugarcoat, veneer
反	bare, disclose, discover, divulge, expose, reveal, uncloak, uncover, unmask, unveil 揭露

Unit 10

■ VAULT	■ VAUNT	■ VEER	■ VEHEMENT	■ VENAL
■ VENDOR	■ VENEER	■ VENERATE	■ VENIAL	■ VENOM

vault	[vɔːlt]
【考法1】	*vi.* 跳起，跳跃：to **propel oneself upward** or forward into the air
例	The horse vaulted over the obstacle with ease. 骏马轻松地跃过障碍物。
近	bound, hop, jump, leap, spring
【考法2】	*vi.* 一跃而至：to accomplish something as if by **leaping suddenly** or vigorously
例	She vaulted into a position of wealth. 她一夜暴富。

vaunt	[vɔːnt]
【考法】	*vi.* 吹嘘：to speak **boastfully**
例	He always vaunted his country's military might. 他总是吹嘘他的国家的军事实力。
近	boast, brag, brandish, swagger
反	belittle, deprecate, diminish, minimize, underrate, undervalue 轻视，瞧不起
派	vaunting *adj.* 吹嘘的

veer [vɪr]

【考法】 *v.* (使)转向，(使)改变航线：to **change direction** or course

例 He veered the car abruptly to the right to avoid a collision. 他向右猛打方向盘以避免撞击。

近 avert, deviate, deflect, divert, redirect, swerve, swing, wheel

反 straighten (使)直行

vehement ['viːəmənt]

【考法】 *adj.* (情感)强烈的，热情的：having or expressing **great depth of feeling**

例 a vehement defender of the rights of minorities 一个感情强烈的少数民族维权者

近 ardent, demonstrative, emotional, fervid, impassioned, intense, passionate, perfervid, torrid

反 cold, cool, dispassionate, emotionless, impassive, unemotional 冷淡的

派 vehemence *n.* 强烈

venal ['viːnl]

【考法】 *adj.* 贪污受贿的：**open to corrupt** influence and especially bribery

例 a judge who is known for being venal and easily bought 一名以贪污受贿、容易被收买闻名的法官

近 bribable, corruptible, dirty, purchasable

反 incorruptible 不受贿赂的；scrupulous 正直的

vendor ['vendər]

【考法】 *n.* 小贩，商贩：one that **sells** or vends

例 We're thinking of making a deal with that other software vendor. 我们在考虑和那个软件供应商做交易。

近 broker, dealer, merchandiser, retailer, seller, trader

反 buyer, consumer, purchaser 消费者

veneer [və'nɪr]

【考法 1】 *n.* 薄木板，用以贴在家具外面的饰面板：a **thin surface layer**, as of finely grained **wood**, glued to a base of inferior material

近 cover, façade, mask

反 center, core, kernel 核心

【考法 2】 *vt.* 粉饰(不好的东西)：to cover over with a veneer; especially to **conceal** (as a **defect** of character) under a superficial and deceptive attractiveness

近 blanch, extenuate, gloss, palliate, sugarcoat, varnish

反 bare, disclose, discover, divulge, expose, reveal, uncloak, uncover, unmask, unveil 揭露

venerate ['venəreɪt]

【考法】 *vt.* 尊敬：to **regard with** reverential **respect** or with admiring deference

例 She is venerated by the public as a saint. 她被当作圣人，受万众景仰。

近 adore, deify, esteem, regard, respect, revere

反 despise, disdain, disregard, flout, scorn 轻视，蔑视

派 veneration *n.* 尊敬

venial ['viːniəl]

【考法】 *adj.* 可宽恕的：**easily excused** or forgiven

例 Taking the restaurant's menu as a souvenir seems like a venial offense. 把餐厅的菜单当成纪念品带走似乎是一个可以宽恕的罪行。

近 condonable, excusable, forgivable, pardonable, remissible, remittable

反 heinous, indefensible, inexcusable, mortal, unforgivable, unpardonable 罪大恶极的，不可饶恕的

venom ['venəm]

【考法 1】 *n.* 毒液：**poisonous matter** normally secreted by some animals as snakes, scorpions, or bees

例 an antidote to snake venom 蛇毒的解药

近 toxic, toxin

反 antidote 解药

【考法 2】 *n.* 恶意，恶毒的用心：the **desire to cause pain** for the satisfaction of doing harm

例 She spoke of him with venom in her voice. 她对他的评论怀揣着恶意。

近 despite, malevolence, maliciousness, malignance, malignity, meanness, nastiness, spite, viciousness

反 comity, friendship, goodwill 友善

List 27

Unit 1

■ VERACIOUS	■ VERBATIM	■ VERBOSE	■ VERDANT	■ VERIFY
■ VERISIMILAR	■ VERITABLE	■ VERNACULAR	■ VERSATILE	■ VERSE

veracious ［vəˈreɪʃəs］
【考法 1】 *adj.* 诚实的，说实话的：being in the habit of **telling the truth**
例 a veracious witness 诚实的证人 ‖ He has a reputation for being veracious, so people generally take his word for things. 他诚实的名声让其他人通常都相信他说的话。
近 honest, truthful
反 dishonest, lying, mendacious, prevaricating, untruthful 说谎的，不诚实的
派 veracity *n.* 诚实
【考法 2】 *adj.* 精确的，准确的：**precise**, accurate
例 a novel that presents a fairly veracious and unvarnished picture of the lives of affluent suburbanites 一部准确而不加修饰地描述郊区富人生活的小说
近 accurate, exact, precise, proper, right, true
反 false, improper, inaccurate, incorrect, inexact, untrue, wrong 不准确的

verbatim ［vɜːrˈbeɪtɪm］
【考法】 *adv.* 逐字地，一字不差地：in the **exact words**
例 You can't just copy the encyclopedia article verbatim for your report - that's plagiarism. 你不能一字不差地抄百科全书上的内容——这是剽窃。
近 ad verbum, directly, exactly, word for word
反 inaccurately, inexactly 不准确地
派 verbalism *n.* 言辞，措词

verbose ［vɜːrˈboʊs］
【考法】 *adj.* 冗长的，啰嗦的：containing **more** words **than necessary**
例 a verbose orator 啰嗦的演讲者 ‖ She has a verbose writing style. 她的文风很啰嗦。
近 circuitous, circumlocutory, diffuse, garrulous, long-winded, prolix, rambling, verbose, windy
反 brief, compact, concise, pithy, succinct, terse 简洁的
派 verbosity *n.* 冗长，啰嗦

verdant ［ˈvɜːrdnt］
【考法】 *adj.* （因长满植物而）翠绿的，郁郁葱葱的：**green with vegetation**; covered with green growth
例 verdant fields 翠绿的田野
近 green, grown, leafy, luxuriant, overgrown
反 barren, impoverished, infertile, leafless, sterile 贫瘠的

verify ［ˈverɪfaɪ］
【考法】 *vt.* 校验，证实：to **determine** or test the truth or **accuracy** of, as by comparison, investigation, or reference
例 We need to verify your passport. 我们需要校验阁下的护照。
近 attest, authenticate, certify, corroborate, substantiate, support, validate, vindicate
反 disprove, rebut, refute 反驳，驳斥
派 verified *adj.* 经证实的；verification *n.* 证实

verisimilar ［ˌverɪsɪˈmɪlər］
【考法】 *adj.* 似乎真实的：**appearing to be true** or real
例 a verisimilar tale 一个似乎为真的传奇
近 likely, plausible, probable
反 implausible, incredible, unbelievable 难以置信的

veritable	[ˈverɪtəbl]

【考法】 *adj.* 真正的，确实的：being in fact the thing named and **not false**, unreal, or imaginary
例　a veritable manuscript 一份原稿
近　authentic, credible, genuine, real, true, unquestionable, bona fide
反　bogus, counterfeit, fake, false, mock, phony, pseudo, sham, spurious 伪造的，虚假的

vernacular	[vərˈnækjələr]

【考法1】 *n.* 方言：a **nonstandard language** or dialect of a place, region, or country
例　phrases that occur in the common vernacular 常见方言中的词组
近　argot, cant, dialect, jargon, lingo, slang
【考法2】 *adj.* 非正式的，口头的：used in or **suitable for speech** and not formal writing
例　write essays in a very easy-to-read, vernacular style 用一种易懂的口头化风格写作
近　conversational, informal, nonliterary, vulgar
反　bookish, formal, learned, literary 书面的，正式的

versatile	[ˈvɜːrsətl]

【考法1】 *adj.* 多才多艺的，全能的：able to do many **different** kinds of **things**
例　We have found a versatile baseball player who can play any position. 我们发现了一个能打任何位置的全能型球员。
近　adaptable, all-around, ambidextrous, protean, universal
反　limited 受限制的，有限的
【考法2】 *adj.* 易改变的：changing or **fluctuating readily**
例　a versatile disposition 多变的性格
近　capricious, changeable, fluid, inconstant, mercurial, skittish, temperamental, variable, volatile
反　certain, changeless, constant, immutable, invariable, settled, stable, stationary, steady, unchangeable, unvarying 固定的，不变的

verse	[vɜːrs]

【考法1】 *vt.* 使精通，使熟悉：to **familiarize** by close association, study, or experience
例　well versed in the theater 精通剧院 ‖ While in prison, he versed himself in the rights of the incarcerated. 当他身处监狱时，他通过自学熟悉了囚犯所享有的权利。
近　acquaint, familiarize, inform
反　misinform, mislead 误导
【考法2】 *n.* 诗歌：a composition using **rhythm** and often rhyme to create a **lyrical effect**
例　compose a short verse for his father's birthday 为他父亲的生日创作了一首小诗
近　ballad, lyric, poetry, song
反　prose 散文

Unit 2

■ VERTIGO	■ VERVE	■ VESSEL	■ VESTIGE	■ VESTIGIAL
■ VETERAN	■ VETO	■ VEX	■ VIABLE	■ VICARIOUS

vertigo	[ˈvɜːrtɪɡoʊ]

【考法】 *n.* 眩晕：a **dizzy** confused state of mind
例　He had a dreadful attack of vertigo at the top of the tower. 他站在塔顶，感到一阵令人窒息的眩晕。
近　dizziness, giddiness
反　sobriety 清醒

verve	[vɜːrv]

【考法】 *n.* 活力，热情：**vitality**, liveliness
例　The instrumentalists played with skill and verve. 器乐表演者们有着高超的技巧与饱满的热情。
近　animation, dynamism, energy, exuberance, liveliness, robustness, vibrancy, vigorousness, vim, vitality
反　lethargy, listlessness, sluggishness, torpidity 精神不振

vessel	[ˈvesl]

【考法1】 *n.* 管：a **tube** or canal (as an artery) in which a **body fluid** is contained and conveyed or circulated
例　blood vessel 血管
近　artery, vein

【考法 2】 *n.* 船，舰艇：a **watercraft** bigger than a rowboat
例 the largest military vessel afloat 最大的军用舰艇
近 boat, cruiser, destroyer, ferry, ship, watercraft

vestige [ˈvestɪdʒ]
【考法】 *n.* 微小的遗迹，小痕迹：the **smallest** quantity or **trace**
例 A few strange words carved on a stone were the only vestige of the lost civilization. 石碑上刻着的几个奇怪的字符是这个失落文明的唯一遗迹。|| the fossilized vestige of a dinosaur that traversed that muddy landscape millions of years ago 数百万年横跨那块泥泞土壤的恐龙的化石碎片
近 echo, ghost, relic, remain, remnant, residual, shadow, trace
派 vestigial *adj.* 残留的；退化的

vestigial [veˈstɪdʒiəl]
【考法】 *adj.* 退化的，发育不全的：(of certain organs or parts of organisms) having attained a **simple structure** and reduced size and function during the evolution of the species
例 snake that has vestigial limbs 拥有退化四肢的蛇
近 incomplete, rudimentary, undeveloped
反 adult, full-blown, full-fledged, matured, ripe, ripened 成熟的，发育完全的

veteran [ˈvetərən]
【考法 1】 *n.* 老兵；有丰富经验的人：an old soldier; one having **knowledge** or ability gained **through long experience**
例 As a veteran of overseas travel, she offered us solid advice about planning our trip. 作为一名资深的海外旅行家，她给我们提供了许多关于旅行规划的中肯建议。
近 doyen, expert, master, maven, warhorse
反 beginner, colt, fledgling, freshman, greenhorn, neophyte, novice, recruit, rookie, tenderfoot, tyro 新手
【考法 2】 *adj.* 经验丰富的，资深的：having or showing exceptional **knowledge**, **experience**, or skill in a field of endeavor
例 She is a veteran teacher who can mentor new teachers. 她是一位资深教师，可以教新教师。
近 accomplished, adept, consummate, experienced, masterful, professed, skilled, versed, virtuoso
反 amateur, inexperienced, inexpert, unprofessional, unseasoned, unskilled, unskillful 业余的，经验不足的

veto [ˈviːtoʊ]
【考法】 *n./vt.* 否决，禁止：to **forbid** or **prohibit** authoritatively
例 The President vetoed the bill. 总统否决了提案。|| We wanted to do a cross-country trip, but our parents vetoed it. 我们想来一次跨国旅行，但是父母不肯批准。
近 blackball, decline, disallow, disapprove, kill, negative, refuse, reject
反 accredit, approbate, authorize, clear, confirm, finalize, formalize, ratify, sanction, warrant 批准

vex [veks]
【考法】 *vt.* 使烦恼，使恼怒：to **bring** trouble, distress, or **agitation** to
例 She was vexed by her son's failure to clean his room. 她因为儿子不清理房间而恼怒。
近 aggravate, annoy, bother, exasperate, gall, grate, irk, nettle, peeve, rile
反 appease, assuage, conciliate, mollify, placate, propitiate 平息
派 vexation *n.* 烦恼

viable [ˈvaɪəbl]
【考法】 *adj.* 可行的：capable of **being done** or carried out
例 a viable solution to the problem 解决问题的一个可行方案
近 achievable, attainable, doable, feasible, practicable, realizable, workable
反 hopeless, impossible, impracticable, infeasible, unattainable, unviable, unworkable 不可行的
派 viability *n.* 可行性

vicarious [vaɪˈkeriəs]
【考法】 *adj.* 代理的，取代的：performed or suffered by one person as a **substitute for another** or to the benefit or advantage of another
例 use Internet as a vicarious form of social life 把互联网当作一种虚拟的社交生活
近 indirect, substitute, surrogate
反 firsthand 直接的

Unit 3

vicious ['vɪʃəs]

【考法 1】 *adj.* 凶恶的，恶毒的：having or showing the **desire to inflict** severe pain and suffering on others
- 例 vicious slander 恶意诽谤
- 近 atrocious, barbaric, barbarous, brutal, butcherly, fiendish, heartless, inhumane, sadistic, savage, truculent
- 反 benign, benignant, compassionate, humane, kind, kindhearted, merciful, sympathetic 仁慈的
- 派 viciousness *n.* 邪恶

【考法 2】 *adj.* 猛烈的：marked by **violence or ferocity**
- 例 a vicious storm ripped through the region 在境内肆虐的强烈风暴
- 近 dreadful, excruciating, explosive, fearsome, ferocious, fierce, intensive, profound, vehement, violent
- 反 light, moderate, soft 轻柔的

vicissitude [vɪ'sɪsɪtuːd]

【考法】 *n.* 自然变化，变迁兴衰：**natural change** or mutation visible in nature or in human affairs
- 例 vicissitude of daily life 日常生活的跌宕起伏
- 近 fluctuation, mutation, shift, variation
- 反 uniformity 一致性，无差异
- 派 vicissitudinous *adj.* 有变化的

victimize ['vɪktɪmaɪz]

【考法】 *vt.* 使受骗：to **subject to deception** or fraud
- 例 victimized by a confidence man with a slick story 被一个骗子用圆滑的故事欺骗
- 近 cheat, cozen, deceive, defraud, dupe, fool, hoax, swindle
- 反 disabuse, disenchant, disillusion, undeceive 使醒悟

vigilant ['vɪdʒɪlənt]

【考法】 *adj.* 警醒的，警惕的：**alertly watchful** especially to avoid danger
- 例 Police warned the public to be vigilant and report anything suspicious. 警方要求公众保持警惕，并上报任何有嫌疑的人或事。|| When traveling through the city, tourists should be extra vigilant. 在这个城市旅行的游客应该保持格外的警惕。
- 近 alert, attentive, awake, cautious, observant, sharp, watchful
- 反 careless, heedless, inattentive, unmindful, unthinking, unwary 不谨慎的
- 派 vigilance *n.* 警惕

vignette [vɪn'jet]

【考法】 *n.* 简介，短文：a **vivid representation** in words of someone or something
- 例 The general's memoirs are filled with revealing vignettes of some of the war's most compelling personalities. 将军的回忆录里充满了短小的文章，它们揭露了战争中最引人注意的人物。
- 近 definition, delineation, depiction, picture, portrait, portraiture, portrayal, rendering, sketch

vigorous ['vɪɡərəs]

【考法 1】 *adj.* 精力旺盛的：having **active strength** of body or mind
- 例 He remains vigorous despite being over 80 years old. 尽管他已年过 80，但仍活力不减。
- 近 brisk, dynamic, energetic, lively, robust, spirited, vital
- 反 dull, lethargic, listless, sluggish, torpid 没有精神的

【考法 2】 *adj.* 强健的：able to **withstand hardship**, strain, or exposure
- 例 vigorous and sturdy little sheep bred to live in mountainous regions 在山区喂养的强壮的小羊
- 近 hard, hardened, inured, rugged, stout, strong, sturdy, tough, toughened
- 反 delicate, soft, tender, weak 脆弱的
- 派 vigor *n.* 精力

vilify ['vɪlɪfaɪ]

【考法】 *vt.* 诽谤，辱骂：to **utter slanderous** and abusive **statements** against
- 例 be vilified by the press because of her radical views 因为她激进的观点而被媒体抨击
- 近 asperse, blacken, calumniate, defame, libel, malign, smear, traduce
- 反 acclaim, applaud, commend, praise 表扬
- 派 vilification *n.* 辱骂

vim [vɪm]

【考法】 *n.* 活力，精力 :robust **energy** and enthusiasm

例 A little rest should give me back some of my vim. 稍事休息我应该就能回复些许精力。

近 animation, bounce, dynamism, energy, liveliness, robustness, verve, vibrancy, vigorousness, vitality

反 lethargy, listlessness, sluggishness, torpidity 精神不振

vindicate [ˈvɪndɪkeɪt]

【考法 1】 *vt.* 为…平反，为…辩护，使无罪 :to **free from** allegation or **blame**

例 The evidence would completely vindicate him. 这个证据将彻底证明他的清白。

近 absolve, acquit, exculpate, exonerate

反 incriminate 使有罪

【考法 2】 *vt.* 证明，证实 :to **give evidence** or testimony to the truth or factualness of

例 Recent discoveries have generally vindicated the physicist's theories. 近期的发现整体上证明了物理学家的理论。

近 attest, authenticate, certify, corroborate, substantiate, support, validate, verify

反 disprove, rebut, refute 反驳，驳斥

vindictive [vɪnˈdɪktɪv]

【考法】 *adj.* 复仇的，有寻仇倾向的 :disposed to **seek revenge**

例 vindictive hatred for his brother 对他兄弟的仇恨

近 avenging, resentful, retaliatory, revengeful, vengeful

反 forgiving, merciful, relenting 仁慈的

Unit 4

■ VIRTUOSO	■ VIRTUOUS	■ VIRULENT	■ VISCID	■ VISCOUS
■ VISIONARY	■ VITALITY	■ VITIATE	■ VITRIOLIC	■ VITUPERATE

virtuoso [ˌvɜːrtʃuˈoʊsoʊ]

【考法 1】 *n.* 艺术鉴赏家，专家 :a person with **masterly skill** or technique in the arts

例 a violin virtuoso 资深小提琴艺术家

近 adept, connoisseur, maestro, master, maven, proficient, wizard

反 amateur, inexpert 业余爱好者，非专业玩家

【考法 2】 *adj.* 经验丰富的，技艺精湛的 : having or showing **exceptional knowledge**, experience, or skill in a field of endeavor

例 The American virtuoso cellist Lynn Harrell joins the orchestra as soloist in Shostakovich's technically challenging *Cello Concerto No 2*. 来自美国的技艺精湛的大提琴家林恩·哈勒尔作为独奏者加入了乐队，共同演绎肖斯塔科维奇充满挑战的《第二大提琴协奏曲》。

近 accomplished, adept, consummate, experienced, masterful, professed, skilled, versed, veteran

反 amateur, inexperienced, inexpert, unprofessional, unseasoned, unskilled, unskillful 业余的，经验不足的

派 virtuosity *n.* 精湛技艺

virtuous [ˈvɜːrtʃuəs]

【考法】 *adj.* 品德高尚的，正直的 : having or **showing** virtue, especially **moral excellence**

例 Virtuous behavior is its own reward. 美德本身就是一种回报。 ‖ She felt that she had made a virtuous decision by donating the money to charity. 她觉得把钱捐赠给慈善基金是一个高尚的决定。

近 decent, ethical, honest, honorable, moral, noble, righteous, straight, upright

反 bad, evil, immoral, indecent, sinful, unethical, unrighteous, wicked, wrong 邪恶的

virulent [ˈvɪrələnt]

【考法 1】 *adj.* 有毒的 : extremely **poisonous** or venomous

例 virulent bacteria 有毒的细菌

近 poisonous, toxic, venomous

反 innocuous 无害的；healthy, salubrious, wholesome 有益健康的

【考法 2】 *adj.* 凶残的 : marked by a rapid, severe, and **destructive course**

例 a virulent look on her face 面露凶色

近 cruel, malevolent, malicious, malignant, spiteful, vicious

反 benevolent, benign, benignant, loving 仁慈的

派 virulence *n.* 毒性；恶毒

viscid [ˈvɪsɪd]

【考法】 *adj.* 有粘性的：having a **glutinous** consistency

例 viscid tree resin 粘性的树脂

近 adherent, adhesive, clingy, gluey, glutinous, tenacious, viscous

反 slick 光滑的

viscous [ˈvɪskəs]

【考法】 *adj.* 粘稠的，粘的：**viscid**; sticky

例 viscous syrup that takes forever to pour from a narrow-neck bottle 不知要花多久才能从窄口瓶中倒出来的粘稠糖浆

近 glutinous, syrup, viscid

反 fluid, watery 流体的，易流动的

visionary [ˈvɪʒəneri]

【考法 1】 *adj.* 空想的，不切实际的：having or marked by a tendency to be **guided** more **by ideals** than by reality

例 a visionary plan for a manned flight to Mars 一个构想中的载人火星计划

近 idealistic, imaginary, impractical, quixotic, romantic, utopian

反 pragmatic 实事求是的，务实的

【考法 2】 *adj.* 幻觉的：not real and existing only **in the imagination**

例 claimed to have had visionary experiences of hell 宣称有过到达地狱的幻觉

近 chimerical, dreamy, fabulous, fantastic, illusory, phantom, unreal

反 actual, existent, existing, real 真实存在的

【考法 3】 *adj.* 有远见的：having or marked by **foresight** and imagination

例 a visionary and legendary leader 一个有远见的传奇领袖

近 farseeing, farsighted, forehanded, foreseeing, forethoughtful, prescient, proactive, provident

反 improvident, myopic, shortsighted 目光短浅的

vitality [vaɪˈtæləti]

【考法】 *n.* 活力，生命力：physical or mental **vigor** especially when highly developed

例 Her vitality seemed to spread to everyone around her. 她的活力似乎能影响身边的每一个人。

近 animation, bounce, dynamism, energy, liveliness, robustness, verve, vibrancy, vigorousness, vim

反 lethargy, listlessness, sluggishness, torpidity 精神不振

派 vitalize *vt.* 激发，使有活力

vitiate [ˈvɪʃieɪt]

【考法 1】 *v.* 削弱，损害：to **reduce the value** or impair the quality of

例 Too many grammatical errors can vitiate the soundness of your writing, so double-check is recommended before submission. 太多的语法错误会削弱你论证的力度，所以建议交稿前检查几遍。

近 blemish, cripple, deface, degrade, deteriorate, flaw, harm, impair, mar, undermine

反 doctor, fix, mend, patch, rebuild, recondition, reconstruct, renovate, repair, revamp 修复，再生

【考法 2】 *v.* (在道德、审美上)降低，堕落：to **debase in moral** or aesthetic status

例 Penchant for coarse language vitiates what is otherwise a refined literary style. 使用粗俗语言的倾向使得本该是一个高雅的文体变得不堪入目。

近 abase, cheapen, corrupt, debauch, demean, demoralize, deprave, pervert, profane, prostitute, subvert

反 elevate, ennoble, uplift 使高尚

派 vitiated *adj.* 受损害的；堕落的

vitriolic [ˌvɪtriˈɑːlɪk]

【考法】 *adj.* (言辞)刻薄的：bitterly **scathing**

例 vitriolic criticism 刻薄的批评

近 acerbic, acid, acrid, bitter, biting, caustic, corrosive, harsh, mordant, scalding, scathing, sharp, tart

反 balmy, benign, bland, delicate, light, mellow, mild, nonabrasive, soft, soothing, tender 柔和的

派 vitriol *n.* 刻薄的话语

vituperate [vaɪˈtuːpəreɪt]

【考法】 *vt.* 谩骂，责骂：to **abuse or censure** severely or abusively

例 He was vituperated for betraying his friends. 他因为背叛朋友而被责骂。

近 abuse, assail, belabor, berate, castigate, excoriate, lambaste, reprimand, scold, rail, revile, upbraid

反 admire, commend, laud, praise 赞赏

派 vituperative *adj.* 辱骂的

Unit 5

vivacious ［vɪˈveɪʃəs］
【考法】 *adj.* 活泼的，快活的：**lively** in temper, conduct, or spirit
例 a vivacious girl who became a successful sales rep 一个成为成功销售代表的活泼女孩
近 active, animated, bouncing, brisk, energetic, frisky, kinetic, mettlesome, spirited, sprightly, vital, zippy
反 dead, inactive, inanimate, languid, languorous, leaden, lifeless, listless, spiritless, vapid 无活力的
派 vivacity *n.* 活力，活泼

vociferous ［voʊˈsɪfərəs］
【考法】 *adj.* 喧哗的，大叫大嚷的：making, given to, or marked by noisy and **vehement outcry**
例 Vociferous opponents of the bill protested angrily outside the Congress. 议案的反对者在国会外愤怒地进行声势浩大的抗议活动。
近 blatant, boisterous, clamant, clamorous, obstreperous, strident, yowling
反 reticent, taciturn 沉默的；serene, tranquil 宁静的

volatile ［ˈvɑːlətl］
【考法】 *adj.* 多变的：characterized by or subject to **rapid** or unexpected **change**
例 a boss of volatile moods 一个性情多变的老板 ‖ The stock market can be very volatile. 股市瞬息万变。
近 capricious, changeable, fluid, inconstant, mercurial, skittish, temperamental, variable, versatile
反 certain, changeless, constant, immutable, invariable, settled, stable, stationary, steady, unchangeable, unvarying 固定的，不变的
派 volatility *n.* 易变性，易挥发性

volition ［vəˈlɪʃn］
【考法】 *n.* 意志，自愿选择的行为：the act or power of **making one's own choices** or decisions
例 beyond his volition or control 超出了他的意志和控制范围
近 choice, decision, discretion, will
反 coercion, compulsion, constraint, duress, force, pressure 强迫，迫使

voluble ［ˈvɑːljəbl］
【考法】 *adj.* 健谈的，话多的：characterized by **ready** or rapid **speech**
例 The voluble gadfly ruined the party. 聚会被那个话又多又让人讨厌的人破坏了。
近 chatty, eloquent, garrulous, glib, loquacious, talkative, vocative
反 reticent, taciturn 沉默的；laconic, reserved, succinct 惜字如金的
派 volubility *n.* 口若悬河

voluminous ［vəˈluːmɪnəs］
【考法】 *adj.* 卷数多的，大量的，庞大的：having **great** volume, fullness, size, or **number**
例 try to keep a track of voluminous academic database 尝试追踪数目庞大的学术数据库
近 colossal, considerable, elephantine, enormous, gargantuan, gigantic, mammoth, numerous, oversize
反 scanty, scarce 缺乏的；dwarf, little, small, undersized 数量少的

voluptuous ［vəˈlʌptʃuəs］
【考法】 *adj.* 奢侈逸乐的，沉溺酒色的：given to or spent in **enjoyments** of **luxury**, pleasure, or sensual gratifications
例 They spent a long and voluptuous holiday in Venice. 他们在威尼斯度过了一个漫长而奢华的假期。
近 carnal, epicurean, luscious, lush, luxurious, indulgent, sensual, sensuous
反 ascetic, spartan, self-denying 克己的，自制的
派 voluptuary *n.* 酒色之徒

voracious ［vəˈreɪʃəs］
【考法 1】 *adj.* 有很大食量的，贪吃的：having a **huge appetite**
例 He has a voracious appetite. 他的食量惊人。
近 edacious, esurient, gluttonous, swinish
反 abstemious, abstentious 有节制的

【考法2】 *adj.* 贪婪的，如饥似渴的：having or marked by an **insatiable** appetite for an activity or pursuit
例 a voracious reader who locked himself up in the study 一个把自己锁在书房里如饥似渴读书的人
近 acquisitive, avid, covetous, grasping, greedy, hungry, rapacious, ravenous, thirsty
反 apathetic, indifferent, uneager, unenthusiastic 无所谓的
派 voracity *n.* 食欲，贪婪

votary ['voʊtəri]
【考法】 *n.* 崇拜者，信徒：a person who is **fervently devoted**, as to a leader or ideal; a faithful follower
例 votaries of the religious leader 宗教领袖的追随者们
近 acolyte, adherent, devotee, disciple, fan, fanatic, partisan, pupil, zealot
反 bellwether, leader 领导；apostate, defector, renegade, traitor, turncoat 叛徒

vouch [vaʊtʃ]
【考法】 *v.* 担保，声称为真：to declare (something) to be true or genuine; to **give a guarantee**
例 willing to vouch for her integrity 愿意担保她的人格
近 attest, avouch, guarantee, testify, warrant

Unit 6

■ VULGAR	■ VULNERABLE	■ WADDLE	■ WAFFLE	■ WAFT
■ WAG	■ WAN	■ WANDERLUST	■ WANE	■ WANT

vulgar ['vʌlgər]
【考法1】 *adj.* 粗俗的，无教养的：morally **crude**, undeveloped, or unregenerate
例 He is a vulgar man but his music is quite divine. 虽然他是一个粗俗的人，但他的音乐却十分神奇。
近 bawdy, coarse, crass, crude, dirty, filthy, gross, lowbred, indecent, nasty, obscene, ribald, rude, uncouth
反 civilized, cultivated, cultured, genteel, polished, refined, urbane, well-bred 有教养的
【考法2】 *adj.* 口头的，非正式的：used in or **suitable for speech** and not formal writing
例 Latin was once the language of scholars, and English the vulgar language used by common people. 很久以前拉丁语才是学术界的官方语言，而英语是普通百姓所使用的。
近 conversational, informal, nonliterary, unliterary, vernacular
反 bookish, formal, learned, literary 书面的，正式的

vulnerable ['vʌlnərəbl]
【考法】 *adj.* 易受攻击的，脆弱的：**open to attack** or damage
例 The troops were deployed in a vulnerable position. 部队被部署在了一个容易遭受攻击的位置。 || The fort was undefended and vulnerable. 堡垒没有设防，十分脆弱。
近 assailable, endangered, exposed, subject, susceptible
反 guarded, protected, shielded 有保护的；invincible, invulnerable 无敌的
派 vulnerability *n.* 弱点，易受伤害

waddle ['wɑːdl]
【考法】 *vi.* 摇摇摆摆地走：to walk with short steps that **tilt the body from side to side**
例 The duck waddled back into the water. 鸭子一摇一摆地回到了水中。
近 careen, dodder, reel, teeter, totter
派 waddling *adj.* 摇摇摆摆的

waffle ['wɑːfl]
【考法】 *vi.* 胡扯：to **talk** or write **foolishly**
例 This lecturer will waffle on for hours. 这个老师会胡说八道地扯几个小时。
近 babble, blather, drivel, gabble, prattle
反 articulate 清楚地说

waft [wɑːft]
【考法】 *v.* 飘荡，漂浮：to **float** easily and gently, as on the air
例 Heavenly aromas wafted from the kitchen. 令人欣悦的香气从厨房飘出。 || A feather wafted past us and settled on the grass. 一片羽毛飘过我们身边，落在草地上。
近 buoy, drift, glide, hang, hover, raft
反 flounder, sink 沉没；submerge 下沉

wag	[wæg]

【考法 1】 *n.* 幽默诙谐的人：a **humorous** or droll person

例 Some wag wrote a droll satire on the scandal. 一些有才的人就丑闻写了一篇搞怪的讽刺文章。

近 comedian, comic, droll, humorist, joker, wit

【考法 2】 *v.* 摆动：to **move to and fro or up and down** especially with quick jerky motions

例 The dog wagged its tail. 狗摆动着它的尾巴。

近 swish, switch, waggle

wan	[wæn]

【考法】 *adj.* 苍白的，病态的：suggestive of **poor health**

例 She looks a little wan after all that tiring work. 在完成那些繁重的工作之后她看起来有些虚弱。

近 ashen, ashy, blanched, livid, lurid, sickly, pale, pallid

反 blooming, florid, flush, full-blooded, glowing, red, rosy, rubicund, ruddy, sanguine 红润的，健康的

wanderlust	['wɑːndərlʌst]

【考法】 *n.* 旅行癖：a very strong or irresistible **impulse to travel**

例 His wanderlust would not allow him to stay long in one spot. 他对旅行的渴望让他不可能在一处久待。

wane	[weɪn]

【考法】 *vi.* 减少，衰退，降低：to **decrease** in size, extent, or degree

例 In the evening the storm finally waned. 傍晚时分风暴终于减弱了。‖ The moon waxes and then wanes. 月有阴晴圆缺。

近 abate, decline, diminish, dwindle, ease, ebb, fall, lessen, lower, moderate, recede, shrink, subside, taper

反 accumulate, balloon, burgeon, enlarge, escalate, expand, grow, increase, intensify, mushroom, rise, snowball, soar, wax 增加，扩大，上升

派 waning *adj.* 衰退的，减少的

want	[wɑːnt]

【考法 1】 *n.* 短缺：the condition or quality of **lacking** something usual or necessary

例 There's a notable want of teachers in rural areas. 农村地区存在着严重的师资短缺问题。

近 absence, dearth, deficiency, drought, famine, inadequacy, insufficiency, lack, paucity, scarcity, shortage

反 abundance, adequacy, amplitude, opulence, plenitude, plenty, sufficiency, wealth 丰富，大量

【考法 2】 *vt.* 渴望：to have a strong **desire** for

例 I want a new car so badly! 我太想要一辆新车了！‖ She wanted more time to finish the test. 她希望能有更多的时间来完成考试。

近 ache, covet, crave, hunger, itch, long, lust, pine, repine, thirst, wish, yearn

反 abhor, abominate, despise, detest, execrate, hate, loathe 厌恶，反感

Unit 7

■ WARMONGER	■ WARP	■ WARRANT	■ WARY	■ WASTREL
■ WATERSHED	■ WAX	■ WAYLAY	■ WELTER	■ WHEEDLE

warmonger	['wɔːrmʌŋɡər]

【考法】 *n.* 好战者：one who **urges** or attempts to stir up **war**

例 Fortunately, the warmongers met with overwhelming opposition. 幸运的是，好战者们碰到了巨大的阻力。

近 belligerent, hawk, jingoist, war hawk

反 dove, pacifist 和平主义者

warp	[wɔːrp]

【考法 1】 *vt.* 使偏向：to **turn** from a correct or proper course

近 avert, deflect, divert, veer

反 straighten 使变直，使回归正轨

【考法 2】 *vt.* 扭曲，变形：to **twist**（something）out of a natural or normal shape or condition

例 The heat caused the wood to warp. 高温使得木头变形了。

近 deform, misshape, screw, torture

派 warped *adj.* 弯曲的，变形的

【考法 3】 *vt.* 曲解：to change so much as to create a wrong impression or **alter the meaning** of

例 The faulty English translation really warps the meaning of the original Chinese text. 错误的英语翻译曲解了中文的原意。

近 distort, falsify, misinterpret, misrepresent, twist

反 clarify, clear, explain, illuminate, illustrate 澄清

warrant [ˈwɔːrənt]

【考法 1】 *vt.* 向⋯保证质量：to **assume responsibility for the satisfactory quality** or performance of

例 The computer company unconditionally warrants all of its products for one full year. 这个电脑公司对所有的产品提供为期一年的质量保证。

近 assure, avouch, guarantee, vouch

【考法 2】 *vt.* 批准，认可：to **give official acceptance** of as satisfactory

例 The law warrants these measures. 法律允许这些措施。

近 approbate, authorize, clear, confirm, finalize, formalize, ratify, sanction

反 decline, deny, disallow, disapprove, negative, reject, veto 禁止，否决

派 warranted *adj.* 担保的；warranty *n.* 保证，承诺

wary [ˈweri]

【考法】 *adj.* 小心的，机警的，谨慎的：marked by keen **caution**, cunning, and watchfulness

例 keep a wary eye out for signs of the enemy 对敌人的形迹保持警惕

近 alert, cautious, chary, circumspect, conservative, guarded, heedful, vigilant, watchful

反 careless, heedless, incautious, unguarded, unmindful, unwary 不谨慎的

派 wariness *n.* 谨慎，小心

wastrel [ˈweɪstrəl]

【考法】 *n.* 肆意挥霍的人，败家子：one who **expends** resources foolishly and **self-indulgently**

例 He ended up being a wastrel and a drunkard. 他最后成了一个花天酒地的败家子，还是一个酒鬼。

近 fritterer, profligate, spender, spendthrift, squanderer, waster

反 economizer, penny-pincher 节约的人；hoarder, miser, niggard 吝啬鬼

watershed [ˈwɔːtərʃed]

【考法】 *n.* 重要关头，分水岭：a crucial dividing point: **turning point**

例 a watershed moment in her life 她命运的分水岭

近 climax, corner, event, landmark, milestone

wax [wæks]

【考法 1】 *vi.* 月亮渐满：to **increase in phase** or intensity, used chiefly **of the moon**, other satellites, and inferior planets

反 wane 月亮渐亏

【考法 2】 *vt.* 用蜡涂、处理或上光：to **coat** (something) with a slippery substance in order to reduce friction

例 wax the floor 给地板打蜡

近 grease, oil, slick

反 coarsen, rough, roughen 使粗糙

【考法 3】 *vi.* 增大，增强：to **increase** in size, numbers, strength, prosperity, or intensity

例 The commitment of the young volunteers to the cause seems to wax. 青年志愿者们对于这项事业的投入似乎在增多。

近 accelerate, accumulate, appreciate, balloon, boom, burgeon, enlarge, escalate, expand, proliferate, rise

反 contract, decrease, diminish, dwindle, lessen, recede 减少，减弱

派 waxing *adj.* 增加的

waylay [weɪˈleɪ]

【考法】 *vt.* 埋伏，伏击：to lie in wait for or **attack** from ambush

例 Unsuspecting tourists are often waylaid by gangs. 不警惕的旅客们常常被犯罪团伙偷袭。‖ We were way-laid by a group of protestors with rocks. 我们被一群示威者用石头偷袭了。

近 ambush, assault, lurk

welter [ˈweltər]

【考法】 *n.* 混乱，动乱：a state of wild **disorder**

例 There was a welter of pushing and shoving. 到处是推搡和拥挤的混乱局面。‖ The troop withdrawal would plunge the country into a welter of anarchy and endless civil war. 撤军会使得这个国家陷入无政府的动乱状态和无尽的内战中。

近 disturbance, furor, hurricane, pandemonium, turmoil, uproar, whirl

反 calm, peace, tranquility 平静，宁静；order 秩序

wheedle [ˈwiːdl]

【考法】 *v.* (用花言巧语)诱惑，哄骗：to persuade or attempt to **persuade by flattery** or guile

例 wheedle him into working for them 哄骗他为他们工作 ‖ She pleaded and wheedled, but I wouldn't be swayed. 她软磨硬泡地求我，但我仍不动摇。

近 adulate, blandish, cajole, coax

反 coerce, compel, demand, force, oblige, require 迫使，强求

Unit 8

whet [wet]
- 【考法】 *vt.* 磨快：to **sharpen** by rubbing on or with something（as a stone）
- 例 whett the dagger with the grindstone 用磨石把匕首磨锋利
- 近 edge, grind, hone, stone, strop
- 反 blunt, dull 使变钝

whiff [wɪf]
- 【考法 1】 *n.* 微风：a quick puff or **slight gust** especially of air, odor, gas, smoke, or spray
- 例 A whiff of fresh air reinvigorated him. 一股清新的空气让他恢复了活力。
- 近 breath, puff
- 反 blast 强烈的气流
- 【考法 2】 *n.* 细微的信号，轻微痕迹：an almost **imperceptible sign** of something
- 例 Even a whiff of appreciation for everything I've done for her would have been nice. 她哪怕是对我为她的付出流露出一丁点的感激之情也好啊。‖ Humanity is unregenerable and hates the language of conformity, since conformity has a whiff of the inhuman about it.（Anthony Burgess）人性是不能改造也无法统一的，因为一致性本身带有一点点不人道的意味。（安东尼·伯吉斯）
- 近 flicker, glimmer, suggestion, touch, trace

whimsical ['wɪmzɪkl]
- 【考法】 *adj.* 反复无常的：prone to **sudden illogical changes** of mind, ideas, or actions
- 例 It's hard to make plans with such a whimsical friend. 和这样一个反复无常的朋友制定计划是很困难的。
- 近 capricious, fickle, freakish, mercurial, volatile
- 反 resolute, unwavering 坚决的
- 派 whimsicality *n.* 反复无常

wholesome ['hoʊlsəm]
- 【考法】 *adj.* 有益身心健康的：**promoting** mental, moral, or social **health**
- 例 try to eat a more wholesome diet 尽可能有更健康的饮食习惯
- 近 healthy, restorative, salubrious, recuperative, tonic
- 反 insalubrious, noxious, unhealthy, unwholesome 不健康的，有害的
- 派 wholesomeness *n.* 健康

wicked ['wɪkɪd]
- 【考法】 *adj.* 邪恶的：**morally** very **bad**
- 例 a wicked urge to steal just for the sake of stealing 纯粹为了偷盗而偷盗的邪恶冲动
- 近 dark, evil, immoral, iniquitous, nefarious, sinful, vicious, villainous
- 反 decent, ethical, good, honest, honorable, moral, righteous, sublime, upright, virtuous 高尚的
- 派 wickedness *n.* 邪恶

wince [wɪns]
- 【考法】 *vi.* 畏缩：to **shrink back** involuntarily as **from pain**
- 例 wince at the horrible corpses 在令人恐惧的尸体面前畏缩
- 近 blench, cringe, quail, quiver, recoil, shrink, tremble
- 反 confront, face, meet 直面；challenge 挑战

windbag ['wɪndbæg]
- 【考法】 *n.* 健谈的人：an exhaustively **talkative** person
- 例 With a windbag like that, who needs a wind farm to meet our energy needs? 有了他这样一个多话的"吹风机"，谁还要风力发电厂来满足电力需求呢？
- 近 babbler, conversationalist, gabbler, gasbag, prattler

windy ['wɪndi]
- 【考法】 *adj.* 冗长的：characterized by wearisome **verbosity**
- 例 a windy saleswoman who told us a lot more than we wanted to know about vacuum cleaners 一个啰嗦的女销售员，一个劲地说着我们不想知道的关于吸尘器的细节
- 近 circuitous, circumlocutory, diffuse, garrulous, prolix, rambling, verbose
- 反 compact, concise, crisp, pithy, succinct, terse 简洁的

winsome ['wɪnsəm]

【考法】 *adj.* 迷人的，漂亮的：generally **pleasing and engaging** often because of a childlike charm and inno-cence

例 fascinated by her winsome smile 为她动人一笑所倾倒

近 adorable, charming, disarming, enchanting, endearing, sweet, winning

反 abhorrent, abominable, detestable, hateful, loathsome, odious 令人厌恶的

派 winsomeness *n.* 迷人

wit [wɪt]

【考法 1】 *n.* 机智，智慧：the natural **ability to** perceive and **understand**

例 lack the wit to judge 缺乏判断的智慧

近 astuteness, brilliance, foxiness, intelligence, keenness, perspicacity, sagacity, sharpness, shrewdness

反 brainlessness, dullness, fatuity, lunacy, silliness 愚蠢

【考法 2】 *n.* 智者，有智慧的人：a person of exceptional **intelligence**

例 a man who fancied himself as a great wit 一个把自己想象成智慧的化身的男子

近 illuminati, pundit, sage, savant, scholar

反 dolt, fool, idiot, simpleton 傻子

派 witty *adj.* 有智慧的

Unit 9

■ WITHDRAW　　■ WITHER　　■ WITHHOLD　　■ WIZEN　　■ WOBBLE
■ WORLDLY　　■ WORSHIP　　■ WRANGLE　　■ WRETCHED　　■ WRY

withdraw [wɪð'drɔː]

【考法】 *v.* 撤退：to **take back** or away

例 The army was forced to withdraw from the frontline. 部队被迫从前线撤回。

近 recede, retreat, fall back

反 advance 前进；place, position, put 放置，安置

派 withdrawal *n.* 撤退；withdrawn *adj.* 性格内向的，离群的

wither ['wɪðər]

【考法】 *vi.* 枯萎，凋谢：to **become** dry and **sapless**

例 Amaranth is a legendary flower that never withers. 传说中的 Amaranth 是一种永不凋谢的花。

近 dry, fade, shrivel, wane, wilt, wizen

反 revive 复活；bloom, flourish, prosper, thrive 繁茂

派 withering *adj.* 凋谢的，凋亡的

withhold [wɪð'hould]

【考法】 *vt.* 抑制；扣压，不给予：to hold back from action; to **refrain from** granting, **giving**, or allowing

例 withhold sensitive information 限制敏感信息的传播

近 decline, disallow, disapprove, detain, refuse, reject, reprobate, restrain, retain

反 allow, concede, grant, permit 授予

wizen ['waɪzn]

【考法 1】 *v.* (使)凋谢，(使)枯萎：to **become** dry, shrunken, and **wrinkled** often as a result of aging or of failing vitality

近 dry, mummify, shrivel, wither

反 revive 复活；bloom, flourish, prosper, thrive 繁茂

【考法 2】 *adj.* 凋谢的，枯萎的：shriveled or **dried up**

近 faded, withered

反 blooming 盛开的

wobble ['wɑːbl]

【考法 1】 *vi.* 摇晃，颤抖：to **move or proceed** with an irregular rocking or staggering motion or **unsteadily** and clumsily from side to side

例 The drunk stood up, wobbled for a moment, and fell forward. 醉汉站了起来，晃动了一阵，然后向前倒了下去。

近 rock, totter

反 stabilize 使稳定

【考法 2】 *vi.* 犹豫不决：to **show uncertainty** about the right course of action

例 We cannot tolerate the government wobbling at this critical time. 我们不能容忍政府在这种关键时刻犹豫不决。

近 falter, stagger, teeter, vacillate, waver

worldly ['wɜːrldli]

【考法 1】 *adj.* 世间的，世俗的：of this world **rather than spiritual** or religion affairs

例 preoccupied with worldly concerns 纠缠于世俗的忧虑 || It is time you woke up and focused your thoughts on more worldly matters. 现在你应该停止做梦，然后把自己的精力集中在更现实的问题上了。

近 carnal, corporeal, material, mundane

反 mental, spiritual 精神的；heavenly 天国的

【考法 2】 *adj.* 老练的：**experienced** in human affairs

例 My little sister was worldly and sophisticated, quite unlike me. 与我截然不同的是，我的妹妹在为人处世方面非常老练。

近 cosmopolitan, sophisticated

反 ingenuous, innocent, naïve, unsophisticated 天真的

worship ['wɜːrʃɪp]

【考法 1】 *n.* 崇拜，敬仰：extravagant **respect** to an object of esteem

例 the belief in swords and the worship of force 刀剑信仰与武力崇拜

近 adulation, adoration, deification, idolatry, reverence, veneration

反 dislike, dismissal, disregard, hatred, loathing, scorn 反感，厌恶

【考法 2】 *v.* 崇拜，膜拜：to **offer honor or respect** to (someone) as a divine power

例 The ancient Greeks worshipped many different gods. 古希腊人崇拜不同的神明。

近 adore, deify, glorify, revere, venerate

反 blaspheme, desecrate, profane, violate 亵渎

wrangle ['ræŋɡl]

【考法 1】 *n.* 纷争，争端：an often noisy or angry expression of **differing opinions**

例 There was a bit of a wrangle over how much money to give the high school for its sports programs. 这个高中应该获得多少体育项目的拨款引起了一阵纷争。

近 altercation, controversy, disagreement, dispute, fight, imbroglio, quarrel, squabble

反 harmony 和谐

【考法 2】 *vi.* 争吵：to **quarrel** noisily or angrily

例 Local residents wrangled for hours about property taxes. 当地居民就房产税的问题争吵不休。

近 altercate, argue, bicker, controvert, hassle, quibble, spat, tiff

派 wrangler *n.* 争吵的人

wretched ['retʃɪd]

【考法 1】 *adj.* 极差的：very **poor in quality** or ability

例 the wretched conditions of the refugee camp 难民营极恶劣的条件

近 bad, coarse, inferior, low-grade, mediocre, miserable, poor, rubbishy, terrible, trashy

反 excellent, fine, first-class, first-rate, good, high-grade, superior 优质的

【考法 2】 *adj.* 沮丧的：deeply afflicted, **dejected**, or distressed in body or mind

例 She was wretched for weeks after breaking up with her boyfriend. 她与男友分手后郁闷了几个星期。

近 blue, crestfallen, dejected, doleful, dolorous, gloomy, melancholy, mournful, rueful, sorrowful, woeful

反 blissful, buoyant, cheerful, delighted, glad, happy, joyful, jubilant 欢乐的

派 wretchedness *n.* 沮丧

wry [raɪ]

【考法 1】 *adj.* 扭曲的：abnormally **twisted** or **bent** to one side

例 a wry smile 扭曲的笑容

近 bending, crooked, curving, devious

反 common, normal, usual 正常的

【考法 2】 *adj.* 坚持错误的：**stubborn** in adherence **to wrong** opinion or principles

近 headstrong, obstinate, pertinacious, perverse, stubborn, wrongheaded

反 amenable, compliant, complying, flexible, pliable, pliant, relenting, yielding 容易改变立场的

Unit 10

xenophobe [ˈzenəfəʊb]

【考法】 *n.* 仇视（或畏惧）外国人（或外国事物）者：one unduly **fearful of what is foreign** and especially of people of foreign origin

例 But from what I know, no way could this thoroughly US-educated woman（from the age of 12）be a xeno-phobe. 但根据我的了解，这个从 12 岁起就接受彻底的美国教育的女人不可能是抵触外国事物的人。

反 xenomania 崇洋媚外的人

派 xenophobia *n.* 仇外情绪

yoke [jəʊk]

【考法】 *v.* 连接：to **become joined** or linked

例 yoke several ideas together to propose a novel theory 将几个想法结合起来提出一个全新的理论

近 chain, conjugate, hook, interconnect, join, link, unite

反 disconnect, disjoin, dissever, disunite, separate, sunder, unchain, unlink, unyoke 分开

yokel [ˈjəʊkl]

【考法】 *n.* 乡下人，天真纯朴的人：a naive or gullible **inhabitant of a rural area** or small town

例 a lame comedy about the misadventures of yokels in the big city 讲述乡下人在大都市中不幸遭遇的蹩脚喜剧

近 bucolic, bumpkin, churl, provincial, rustic

反 cosmopolitan 云游四海的人

zeal [ziːl]

【考法】 *n.* 热心，热诚：**enthusiastic devotion** to a cause, ideal, or goal and tireless diligence in its furtherance

例 preaches with fanatical zeal 带着狂热进行传教

近 ardor, devotion, enthusiasm, fervidness, fervor, passion

反 apathy, indifference, nonchalance, torpor, unconcern 麻木，冷漠

派 zealous *adj.* 狂热的

zealot [ˈzelət]

【考法】 *n.* 狂热者，极端主义者：someone whose views and actions are very **extreme**, especially in **following a** particular **political or religious belief**

例 In matters of taste, the art patron and collector Peggy Guggenheim was a zealot: she was for the strangest, the most surprising, the most satisfying, the best, the unique. 就品位而言，艺术赞助人和收藏家 Peggy Guggenheim 是一个狂热者：她总是倾向于最新奇、最让人满意和最独特的佳品。

近 enthusiast, extremist, fanatic, fiend, freak, partisan, maniac, nut

反 moderate 温和派

派 zeal *n.* 狂热

zenith [ˈzenɪθ]

【考法】 *n.* 最高点，巅峰：**culminating** point

例 at the zenith of his power 他到达了权力巅峰

近 acme, apex, apogee, climax, crescendo, crest, peak, pinnacle, summit, top

反 bottom, nadir 最低点

zesty [ˈzesti]

【考法】 *adj.* 刺激的，开胃的：appealingly **piquant** or lively

例 a zesty sauce 味道刺激的酱汁

近 peppery, piquant, pungent, salty, savory, spicy, zingy

反 bland, insipid, vapid, zestless 乏味的

List 28*

Unit 1

■ ABREAST	■ ABSENT	■ ACCLAIM	■ ACCOMPLISH	■ ACCORD
■ ACKNOWLEDGE	■ ACQUIRE	■ ACQUISITIVE	■ ADJUDICATE	■ ADVERSITY

abreast [ə'brest]
【考法 1】 *adv.* 并排地：beside one another with bodies **in line**
例 a group of youths riding four abreast 四个一排骑着车的一群年轻人
近 alongside, side by side
反 aimlessly, desultorily, erratically, haphazardly, irregularly, randomly, willy-nilly 混乱地
【考法 2】 *adj.* 熟知的：up to a particular standard or level especially of **knowledge of recent developments**
例 She tried to keep abreast of the latest fashion trends. 她总是尽可能地跟上时尚的潮流。
近 acquainted, conversant, informed, knowledgeable, versed, well-informed
反 ignorant, unacquainted, unfamiliar, uninformed, unknowledgeable 无知的，不熟悉的

absent ['æbsənt]
【考法 1】 *adj.* 未出现的，缺乏的：**not present**, attending or existing
例 The city's usual stir of activity was conspicuously absent due to the report of an escaped lion from the zoo. 一则动物园狮子逃跑的消息让这座城市缺少了往日的繁华热闹。
近 away, lacking, missing, nonexistent, wanting
反 existent, present 存在的，出现的
【考法 2】 *adj.* 不专心的，走神的：**lost in thought**
例 He seemed absent because he nodded but didn't say anything. 他只点了点头但没说话，看起来像是走神了。
近 abstracted, distracted
反 alert, vigilant, watchful, wary 警惕的；attentive, heedful, mindful, preoccupied 专注的

acclaim [ə'kleɪm]
【考法 1】 *n.* 称赞：**public acknowledgment or admiration** for an achievement
例 Many people were involved in the search, but the person who actually found the missing girl got all the acclaim. 许许多多的人都参与了搜救行动，但是只有真正找到那个迷失的小女孩的人才受到了称赞。
近 accolade, applause, credit, distinction, homage, honor, kudos, laud, laurels
【考法 2】 *vt.* 赞扬，赞颂：to declare enthusiastic **approval** of
例 He was acclaimed as the country's greatest modern painter. 他被盛赞为国内最优秀的现代画家。
近 accredit, applaud, cheer, commend, endorse, exalt, hail, praise, salute, tout
反 castigate, excoriate, lambaste, pan, slam 猛烈抨击

accomplish [ə'kɑːmplɪʃ]
【考法】 *vt.* 完成，实现：to carry through (as a process) to **completion**
例 I don't think we can accomplish our goal unless we cooperate. 我认为只有合作才能实现我们的目标。
近 achieve, commit, execute, fulfill, make, perpetrate, prosecute, carry out
反 fail 失败
派 accomplishment *n.* 成就；accomplished *adj.* 有造诣的

accord [ə'kɔːrd]
【考法 1】 *n.* 一致：a state of **consistency**
例 This map doesn't seem to be in accord with the current layout of the streets. 这幅地图似乎与当前的街道情况不尽一致。
近 accordance, agreement, conformity, congruence, congruity, consensus, consonance, harmony, tune
反 conflict, disagreement, incongruence, incongruity, incongruousness 不一致

【考法 2】 *vi.* 相符合，相一致: to be consistent or **in harmony**

例 a theory that accords with the known facts 与已知事实相一致的理论 ‖ He claims that the newspaper's quote does not accord with what he actually said. 他声称报纸引用的与他真正所说的话并不相符。

近 agree, chord, cohere, coincide, conform, correspond, fit, harmonize, jibe, sort, square, tally

反 differ, disagree 不相同，不一致

派 accordance *n.* 一致，和谐

【考法 3】 *vt.* 授予，给予: to **grant or give** especially as appropriate, due, or earned

例 Women were finally accorded the right to vote in 1920. 女性最终在 1920 年获得了投票权。

近 accord, award, grant, vest, vouchsafe

反 withhold 保留，不给予; recant, retract, withdraw 撤回，收回

acknowledge [əkˈnɑːlɪdʒ]

【考法】 *vt.* 承认: to **admit** the existence, reality, or truth of

例 He refused to acknowledge the fact that her daughter has gone. 他拒绝承认女儿已经死去的事实。

近 admit, agree, allow, concede, confess, grant, own

反 deny 否认

派 acknowledgement *n.* 承认

acquire [əˈkwaɪər]

【考法】 *vt.* 获取，获得: to **get as one's own**

例 bacteria that acquire tolerance to antibiotics 产生了抗药性的细菌 ‖ I have never acquired a taste for wine. 我从来就不具备对葡萄酒的品味能力。

近 attain, capture, draw, gain, garner, get, make, obtain, procure, realize, reap, secure, win, bring in

反 forfeit, lose 丧失

派 acquired *adj.* 后天的

acquisitive [əˈkwɪzətɪv]

【考法】 *adj.* 贪婪的: strongly **desirous** of acquiring and possessing

例 Acquisitive developers are trying to tear down the ancient temple and build a shopping mall instead. 贪婪的开发商打算铲平这座古老的神庙，取而代之建造一座购物中心。

近 avaricious, avid, coveting, covetous, grabby, grasping, mercenary, moneygrubbing, rapacious

反 benevolent, generous, liberal, philanthropic, munificent 慷慨的

adjudicate [əˈdʒuːdɪkeɪt]

【考法】 *v.* 裁决，判定: to hear and **settle**（a case, dispute or conflict）

例 When my wife and I asked the salesclerk to adjudicate our disagreement, she agreed with me that the white shoes looked better. 我和我妻子要求售货员来裁决我们之间的争论，她同意我的观点，认为白色的鞋子看起来更漂亮。

近 adjudge, arbitrate, decide, determine, judge, referee, settle, umpire

adversity [ədˈvɜːrsəti]

【考法】 *n.* 厄运，逆境: a state, condition, or instance of serious or continued **difficulty** or adverse fortune

例 The fire is the test of gold, adversity of strong man.（Martha Graham）烈火试真金，逆境炼勇士。——玛莎·葛兰姆 ‖ They finally overcame all the adversities of the Great Depression and rebuilt their fortunes. 他们终于度过了大萧条的困境，开始重新创造他们的财富。

近 ill, hardship, misadventure, mischance, mishap, tragedy

反 fortune, fluke, luck, serendipity 好运气

Unit 2

■ AFFECTATION	■ AFFIRM	■ AFFIX	■ AFFLICTION	■ AGAPE
■ AGILITY	■ AGONIZE	■ AGREEABLE	■ ALIENATE	■ ALLOY

affectation [ˌæfekˈteɪʃn]

【考法】 *n.* 虚伪，做作: the act of taking on or displaying an attitude or mode of behavior **not natural** to oneself or **not genuinely felt**

例 His little affectations irritated her. 他做作的小动作激怒了她。

近 façade, guise, mannerism, pose, pretense, show

反 artlessness, genuineness, innocence, naivety 天真，淳朴

affirm [əˈfɜːrm]

【考法】 *vt.* 声称…为真，肯定…属实：to assert (as a judgment or decree) as **valid or confirmed**

例 He was unwilling to affirm without further study that the painting is an original Rembrandt. 在缺乏进一步研究的情况下，他不愿意声称这幅画作是出自伦勃朗的正品。

近 allege, assert, aver, avouch, avow, contend, declare, insist, maintain, profess, protest, purport, warrant

反 deny, gainsay, disclaim, recant 否定，反对

派 affirmation *n.* 肯定，确认

affix [əˈfɪks]

【考法】 *vt.* 粘合：to **attach physically**

例 affix a stamp to a letter 把邮票贴在信封上

近 attach, bend, fix

反 detach, undo, unfasten, unhook 松开，分开

affliction [əˈflɪkʃn]

【考法】 *n.* 痛苦，悲伤，折磨：a state of **great suffering** of body or mind

例 She listened with deep affliction as her daughter told her about the latest trouble she was in. 听着女儿诉说自己目前艰难的处境，她感到深深的心痛。

近 agony, anguish, dolor, excruciation, grief, hurt, misery, pain, rack, torment, torture, travail, tribulation, woe

反 bliss, cheer, delight, ecstasy, elation, euphoria, exhilaration, exuberance, exultation, felicity, joy, jubilation, pleasure, rapture 喜悦，高兴

agape [əˈɡeɪp]

【考法】 *adj.* 急切盼望的：having or showing signs of **eagerly awaiting** something

例 At the sound of the sleigh bells the children were all agape, waiting for Santa to appear. 听到雪橇铃声，孩子们开始急切地等待圣诞老人的到来。

近 agog, anticipant, anticipatory

反 apathetic, indifferent, unconcerned, uninterested 不感兴趣的，不为所动的

agility [əˈdʒɪləti]

【考法】 *n.* (身手)敏捷：**quickness**, **ease and grace** in physical activity

例 His agility on the parallel bars has won him several medals. 他在双杠上的矫捷身姿助他赢得了数枚奖牌。

近 deftness, dexterity, nimbleness, sleight, spryness

反 awkwardness, clumsiness, gaucheness, gawkiness, gracelessness, ungainliness (行动)笨拙

agonize [ˈæɡənaɪz]

【考法 1】 *vt.* 折磨，使痛苦：to cause to suffer **agony**

例 She got into more trouble, further agonizing her poor mother. 她惹上了更多的麻烦，进一步加剧了她可怜的母亲所遭受的痛苦。

近 bedevil, beset, besiege, curse, excruciate, harrow, persecute, plague, rack, torment, torture

反 comfort, console, solace, soothe 安抚，安慰

派 agony *n.* 痛苦；agonizing *adj.* 痛苦的

【考法 2】 *vi.* 感到痛苦：to **suffer agony**, torture, or anguish

例 She agonized for days over the moral issues involved. 一连几天她都为卷入的道德纠纷而感到痛苦。

近 anguish, bleed, hurt, mourn, sorrow, suffer

反 cheer, crow, delight, exult, joy, rejoice 感到高兴

agreeable [əˈɡriːəbl]

【考法 1】 *adj.* 令人愉悦的：**pleasing to the mind or senses** especially as according well with one's tastes or needs

例 Would you mind putting on some agreeable music for dinner? 你介意晚饭时放一些令人愉快的音乐吗？
the agreeable melancholy resulting from a sense of the transitoriness of natural beauty 因为感慨自然之美稍纵即逝而产生的令人愉悦的忧伤

近 congenial, delectable, delicious, delightful, dulcet, enjoyable, felicitous, gratifying, heavenly, palatable, pleasing, satisfying, savory

反 abhorrent, abominable, disagreeable, disgusting, loathsome, nauseating, repellent, repugnant, repulsive, revolting 令人厌恶的

【考法 2】 *adj.* 随和的：having an **easygoing and pleasing manner** especially in social situations

例 I have an agreeable art teacher who lets me do pretty much whatever I want. 我的艺术老师性格随和，允许我去做我想做的事情。

近 affable, genial, good-natured, good-tempered, gracious, mellow, nice, pleasant, sweet, well-disposed

反 choleric, dyspeptic, fussy, grouchy, irascible, irritable, peevish, touchy 脾气不好的，易怒的

【考法 3】 *adj.* 相一致的：being **in harmony**

例 These new security measures are not agreeable with our core concepts of personal freedom. 这些新的安保措施和我们所信仰的个人自由的核心理念彼此抵触。

近 amicable, compatible, congenial, consistent, consonant, frictionless, kindred, unanimous, united

反 disagreeable, discordant, disunited, incompatible, inharmonious 不一致的

alienate [ˈeɪliəneɪt]

【考法 1】 *vt.* 使…疏远：to make **unfriendly**, **hostile**, or **indifferent** especially where attachment formerly existed

例 His heartless treatment of their mother during the divorce proceeding has completely alienated the two children. 他在离婚过程中对妻子表现出来的残酷，已经彻底地让两个孩子与他疏远起来。

近 alien, disaffect, disgruntle, sour

反 reconcile 使…重归于好

【考法 2】 *vt.* 转让，让渡：to **convey or transfer**（as property or a right）usually by a specific act rather than the due course of law

例 A landowner has a right to alienate his right of ownership - in other words, he can sell the land if he wants to. 地主拥有转让所有权的权力——也就是说如果愿意，他可以出售他的土地。

近 assign, cede, convey, deed, make over

反 expropriate 接纳他人财产

派 unalienable *adj.* 不可予夺的，不可转让的

alloy

【考法 1】 [ˈælɔɪ] *n.* 合金；混合物：a distinct entity formed by the **combining of two or more different things**

例 Brass is an alloy, consisting of copper and zinc. 黄铜是一种由铜和锌组成的合金。 ‖ Television news has always been an alloy of journalism and show business. 电视新闻一直以来都是新闻界和演艺圈的混合体。

近 admixture, amalgam, cocktail, composite, compound, fusion, intermixture, mix, mixture, synthesis

反 element（构成整体的）单个元素

【考法 2】 [əˈlɔɪ] *vt.* 掺杂，降低…的纯度：to **debase by the addition** of an inferior element

例 idealism that was alloyed with political skill 因为掺入了政治技巧而被削弱的理想主义

近 adulterate, contaminate, dilute, extend, lace, pollute, sophisticate, thin

反 purify 纯化

派 unalloyed *adj.* 纯粹的，未掺杂的

Unit 3

■ AMBIVALENT	■ ANACHRONISTIC	■ ANALOGOUS	■ ANNEX	■ ANNOTATE
■ ANTEDATE	■ ANTIPATHY	■ ANTIQUATED	■ ANTITHETICAL	■ APPARITION

ambivalent [æmˈbɪvələnt]

【考法】 *adj.*（尤指感情、态度）矛盾的：having a mixture of **opposing feelings**

例 He maintained an ambivalent attitude to religion throughout his life. 他一生都对宗教抱有矛盾的心理。

近 conflicting, contradictory, mixed

反 certain, decided, definite, positive, resolute, sure, unquestioning 明确的，毫无疑问的

派 ambivalence *n.* 矛盾心理

anachronistic [əˌnækrəˈnɪstɪk]

【考法】 *adj.* 时代错误的：**chronologically misplaced**

例 Despite the occasional anachronistic word or concept, he has a good feel for the period. 尽管有时会犯一些语言和概念上的时代性错误，但他对于那个时代的整体把握还是不错的。

近 anachronic, anachronous

反 accurate 准确的

analogous [əˈnæləgəs]

【考法】 *adj.* 相似的，可比较的：having qualities in **common**

例 Bad-mouthing your sister is analogous to slapping her in the face - it's just as bad. 说你姐姐的坏话和当面扇她耳光是类似的——它们都是不好的行为。

近 akin, cognate, comparable, connate, corresponding, matching, parallel, resembling, similar, suchlike

反 different, disparate, dissimilar, diverse, unlike 不同的，不相似的

annex [əˈneks]

【考法 1】 *vt.* 添加，合并：to **join**（something）to a mass, quantity, or number so as to bring about an overall increase

例 plan to annex the supply room so as to make the classroom bigger 计划将工具房并入教室，从而扩充其容量

近 adjoin, affix, append, attach, subjoin, tack

反 abate, deduct, remove, subtract 削减

【考法2】 *vt.* 吞并，夺取（土地等）：to **incorporate**（a country or other territory）within the domain of a state

例 Rome annexed the Nabatean kingdom in 106 AD. 公元前 106 年罗马帝国吞并了古城那巴顿。

近 acquire, appropriate, arrogate, expropriate, seize, take over

反 lose 失去

annotate [ˈænəteɪt]

【考法】 *vt.* 给…作注解：to furnish（a literary work）with critical **commentary or explanatory notes**

例 The advent of e-books enables user to freely annotate what they are reading without worrying about being fined by libraries. 电子书的出现使得用户可以在不用担心被图书馆处以罚金的情况下自由地在读物上作注。

近 commentate, footnote, gloss

派 annotation *n.* 注解，注释

antedate [ˌæntiˈdeɪt]

【考法】 *vt.* 比…早，早于：to be of an **earlier date** than

例 The church antedates the village itself. 这座教堂甚至在村庄之前就存在了。‖ Dinosaurs antedate cavemen by millions of years. 恐龙比穴居人要早几百万年出现。

近 antecede, forego, predate, preexist

反 follow, postdate, succeed 晚于

antipathy [ænˈtɪpəθi]

【考法1】 *n.* 厌恶，反感：settled **aversion** or **dislike**

例 I feel no antipathy towards any of my opponents in the tournament. 我对锦标赛中碰到的任何对手都不存在反感。

近 animosity, animus, antagonism, bitterness, enmity, gall, grudge, hostility, jaundice, rancor

反 amity 友好，和睦；liking, partiality, predilection, prepossession 偏爱，喜爱

【考法2】 *n.* 令人反感的事物：an **object of aversion**

例 Cruelty to animals is one of my most deeply felt antipathies. 虐待动物是让我反感的行为之一。

近 abhorrence, abomination, anathema, aversion, detestation, execration

反 beloved, darling, dear, love 令人喜爱的人或事物

antiquated [ˈæntɪkweɪtɪd]

【考法】 *adj.* 古老的，过时的：outmoded or discredited by reason of age: being **out of style** or fashion

例 We saw an antiquated hand-cranked rope-making machine at the textiles museum. 我们在纺织博物馆里看到了一台手摇式古董制绳机。‖ antiquated methods of farming 过时的耕种技术

近 antique, archaic, dated, fossilized, moribund, moth-eaten, obsolete, outdated, outmoded, outworn, prehistoric, rusty

反 contemporary, current, modern, recent 当前的，现代的

antithetical [ˌæntɪˈθetɪkl]

【考法】 *adj.* 完全对立的，相反的：being in **direct and unequivocal opposition**

例 Spiritual ideals seem antithetical to the materialism embraced by modern society. 精神上的理想境界往往同当代社会所推崇的唯物主义相抵触。

近 antipodal, antipodean, contradictory, contrary, diametric, opposite, polar

反 equivalent, identical, same 完全一致的，相等的

派 antithesis *n.* 对立，相反

apparition [ˌæpəˈrɪʃn]

【考法】 *n.* 鬼魂，幽灵：a **ghostly figure**

例 An eccentric claimed to have photographed an apparition in her very own house. 一个行为怪异的人声称在她的住所里拍到了一张幽灵的照片。

近 ghost, phantasm, phantom, shade, shadow, specter, spirit, spook, sprite, vision, visitant, wraith

反 entity, substance 实体

Unit 4

| ■ APPLICABLE | ■ APPREHENSIVE | ■ ARABLE | ■ ARBITRARY | ■ ARCANE |
| ■ ARGUMENT | ■ ARID | ■ ARRAY | ■ ASSAIL | ■ ASYMMETRY |

applicable [ˈæplɪkəbl]

【考法1】 *adj.* 可用的，可行的：capable of being **put to use** or account

例 Is that Act applicable in this case where suspect is a foreigner? 那条法规适用于这个案件么，案件中的嫌犯不是本国公民？

近 actionable, applicative, applied, functional, practicable, serviceable, useful, workable

反 impractical, inapplicable, unusable, unworkable, useless 不可用的，不可行的

【考法2】 *adj.* 相关的，有关的：**having to do with** the matter at hand

例 He rarely makes comment that is applicable to our discussion. 他的评论很少和我们讨论的题目搭边。

近 apposite, apropos, germane, material, pointed, relative, relevant

反 extraneous, immaterial, impertinent, inapposite, irrelevant, pointless 无关的

【考法3】 *adj.* 合适的，恰当的：**meeting the requirements** of a purpose or situation

例 He has been busy in selecting the most applicable word for his PhD thesis. 他一直忙于为自己的博士论文选择最为恰当的词汇。

近 appropriate, apt, becoming, befitting, felicitous, fitting, meet, pretty, proper, right, suitable

反 improper, inappropriate, inapt, incongruous, malapropos, misbecoming, unbecoming, unfitting, unmeet, unseemly, unsuitable, wrong 不恰当的

apprehensive [ˌæprɪˈhensɪv]

【考法1】 *adj.* 知晓的，理解的：having specified facts or feelings actively **impressed on the mind**

例 I am fully apprehensive of the opinions, I assure you. 我向你保证这些观点我都理解了。

近 alive, aware, cognizant, mindful, sensible, sentient, ware, witting

反 ignorant, insensible, oblivious, unaware, unconscious, unmindful, unwitting 不知晓的，无知觉的

【考法2】 *adj.* 恐惧的，害怕的：**anxious** or **fearful** about the future

例 People apparently haven't recovered from the devastating terrorist attack and are still terribly apprehensive about the future. 人们显然没有从那场严重的恐怖袭击中恢复过来，对于未来仍然充满了恐惧。

近 afraid, aghast, fearful, frightened, horrified, hysterical, scared, shocked, terrified

反 dauntless, fearless, intrepid, unafraid 无所畏惧的；confident 充满自信的

派 apprehension *n.* 理解；忧虑，恐惧

arable [ˈærəbl]

【考法】 *adj.* 适合耕种的：fit for or used for the **growing of crops**

例 explore the west for arable land 向西探索适合耕种的土地

近 cultivable, tillable

反 barren, sterile, infertile, unfruitful, unproductive 贫瘠的

arbitrary [ˈɑːrbətreri]

【考法1】 *adj.* 专横的，独断专行的：having or showing a tendency to **force one's will on others** without any regard to fairness or necessity

例 an arbitrary piano teacher who makes all her students do the same exercises over and over again 一个让学生反复练习相同曲子的专横的老师

近 dictatorial, imperious, peremptory, willful

【考法2】 *adj.* 独裁的，拥有无限权力的：exercising power or authority **without interference by others**

例 a nation with no tradition of democracy, only a long history of arbitrary rulers 一个从来没有民主传统，只有长期的独裁统治的国家

近 autocratic, czarist, despotic, monocratic, tyrannic, tyrannous

反 limited（权力）受限的；democratic 民主的；republican 共和国的

【考法3】 *adj.* 缺乏计划的，随意的：**lacking a definite plan**, purpose, or pattern

例 The order of the names of the 10 semifinalists is entirely arbitrary. 半决赛上十名上场选手的顺序完全是随机的。

近 aimless, desultory, erratic, haphazard, scattered, slapdash, stray, willy-nilly

反 methodical, orderly, organized, regular, systematic, systematized 有序的，有组织的

arcane [ɑːrˈkeɪn]

【考法1】 *adj.*（语言）晦涩的，隐晦的：having an often intentionally **veiled** or **uncertain** meaning

例 The rebate form uses arcane language, the only purpose of which seems to be to disqualify buyers from actually getting a rebate. 折扣单上的条文晦涩难懂，这样做的唯一目的也许就是让消费者不能真正地享受到折扣。

近 ambiguous, dark, elliptical, equivocal, murky, mysterious, mystic, nebulous, occult, opaque

反 accessible, clear, obvious, plain, unambiguous, unequivocal 清晰明了的，明确的

【考法2】 *adj.* 深奥的，难以理解的：**difficult** for one of ordinary knowledge or intelligence **to understand**

例 Grammatical rules seem extremely arcane to generations of students who were never taught grammar in the first place. 对那些从未学习过语法的几代学生来说，语法规则犹如天书。

近 abstruse, cryptic, deep, enigmatic, esoteric, hermetic, impenetrable, inscrutable, recondite, uncanny

反 easy, facile, shallow, simple, superficial 浅显易懂的

argument [ˈɑːrɡjumənt]

【考法1】 *n.* 争吵，争论：an often noisy or angry **expression of differing opinions**

例 The couple's arguments were often loud enough to be heard all over the neighborhood. 这对夫妻吵架的声音往往大到能被所有邻居听见。

近 altercation, controversy, disagreement, dispute, hassle, imbroglio, quarrel, squabble, tiff, wrangle

【考法2】 *n.* (逻辑上的)论证 : a coherent series of statements leading **from a premise to a conclusion**

例 In his argument the author committed several logical fallacies which undermined its soundness. 在该作者的论述中出现了若干逻辑谬误，从而降低了它的论证力度。

近 account, accounting, argumentation, case, explanation, rationale, reasoning

【考法3】 *n.* 观点，论点 : an **idea** or **opinion** that is put forth in a discussion or debate

例 It is and will always be my argument that we have too many problems here on earth to concern ourselves with manned trips to Mars. 我现在和以后的观点都将会是：在我们解决地球上的问题之前，不应该花太多的心思考虑载人火星计划的事情。

近 assertion, point, position, stand, thesis

---

arid [ˈærɪd]

【考法1】 *adj.* 干燥的 : marked by **little or no precipitation** or humidity

例 arid wastelands unfit for human habitation 不适合人类居住的干燥荒原

近 droughty, dry, sere, thirsty, waterless

反 damp, dank, humid, moist, wet 湿润的，潮湿的

【考法2】 *adj.* 无趣的，无聊的 : causing weariness, restlessness, or **lack of interest**

例 a technically perfect but arid musical performance 技术纯熟但音乐毫无感染力的表演

近 dreary, dull, flat, humdrum, jading, jejune, monochromatic, monotonous, pedestrian, stale, stodgy, tedious, wearisome

反 absorbing, engaging, engrossing, gripping, interesting, intriguing, involving, riveting 有趣的，吸引人的

---

array [əˈreɪ]

【考法1】 *n.* 排列，阵列 : a regular and imposing grouping or **arrangement**

例 a marching band's carefully choreographed array 前进中的乐队所摆出的经过精心编排的队列阵形

近 arrangement, disposal, disposition, distribution, ordering, sequence, setup

反 disorder, disorganization 混乱，无序

【考法2】 *vt.* 排列，摆放 : to **arrange or display** in or as if in an array

例 data arrayed in descending order 按照降序排列的数据 ‖ He arrayed his baseball cards in order of their rarity and consequent monetary value. 他把他的棒球卡按照稀有程度以及随之附有的价值排列。

近 arrange, classify, codify, dispose, marshal, organize, range, systematize, draw up, lay out

反 derange, disarrange, disarray, disorder, mess, rumple, upset 弄乱，打乱

【考法3】 *vt.* 装饰，装修 : to **dress or decorate** especially in splendid or impressive attire

例 He had already arrayed himself in his best clothes. 他已经穿上了他最好的服装。 ‖ a door arrayed for the holidays with a beautiful evergreen wreath 在节日里被美丽的常青花环妆点的大门

近 adorn, beautify, bedeck, bedizen, blazon, embellish, emblaze, emboss, enrich, garnish, ornament, trim

反 blemish, deface, disfigure, mar, scar, spoil 破坏，损毁

---

assail [əˈseɪl]

【考法1】 *vt.* 抨击，严厉批评 : to **criticize harshly** and usually publicly

例 The union organizers assailed the chemical company for failing to provide a safe working environment. 工会主席严厉批评这家化工企业不能为员工提供安全的生产环境。

近 abuse, bash, belabor, blast, castigate, excoriate, lambaste, savage, scathe, slam, trash, vituperate

反 acclaim, commend, compliment, hail, laud, praise 表扬，称赞

【考法2】 *vt.* 攻击，猛攻 : to take sudden, **violent action against**

例 He was assailed by a young man with a knife. 他被一个持刀的年轻人袭击。

近 assault, attack, beset, charge, raid, rush, storm, strike, set on

反 defend, guard, protect, shield 防御，守卫

派 assailable *adj.* 易受攻击的

---

asymmetry [ˌeɪˈsɪmətri]

【考法】 *n.* 不对称，不平衡 : **lack of balance** or symmetry

例 functional asymmetry of cerebral hemispheres 大脑两半球功能的不对称性

近 disproportion, imbalance

反 symmetry 对称；balance, proportion 平衡

派 asymmetric *adj.* 不对称的

Unit 5

---

atrophy [ˈætrəfi]

【考法】 *vi.* 萎缩，衰退 : to **waste away**; wither or deteriorate

例 The years following the closing of the last textile mill, the town atrophied. 随着最后一家纺织厂的倒闭，整个城镇开始衰退。

近 crumble, decay, decline, degenerate, descend, devolve, ebb, regress, retrograde, rot, sink, worsen
反 ameliorate, improve, meliorate 改善，提升

attest [əˈtest]

【考法】 *vt.* 证实，为…作证：to **give evidence** or testimony to the truth or factualness of

例 Her fine work attests her ability. 她的优秀作品能够证明她的能力。‖ I can attest that she was at the party. 我可以证明她当时在聚会上。

近 argue, authenticate, certify, corroborate, substantiate, support, testify, validate, verify, vindicate
反 contradict, disprove, gainsay, rebut, refute 反驳，否定

attune [əˈtuːn]

【考法】 *vt.* 使协调，使和谐：to bring **into harmony**

例 After years spent in academia, he found it difficult to attune himself to the corporate culture. 在学术圈摸爬滚打多年之后，他发现自己很难融入企业文化之中。

近 accommodate, conciliate, conform, coordinate, key, reconcile
反 disharmonize 使不和谐；disarray, disorder, disorganize, disrupt 弄乱，打乱
派 attunement *n.* 调音；协调

august [ɔːˈgʌst]

【考法1】 *adj.* 威严的，庄重的：having or showing a **formal and serious or reserved manner**

例 Unsurprisingly, the head of the bank is an august white-haired gentleman. 不出所料，银行的总裁是一名白发苍苍的、令人顿生敬意的绅士。

近 distinguished, imposing, portly, solemn, staid, stately
反 flighty, frivolous, giddy, goofy, silly, undignified 轻浮的，不庄重的

【考法2】 *adj.* 盛大的，令人印象深刻的：**large and impressive** in size, grandeur, extent, or conception

例 an august golden anniversary celebration for the company 该公司盛大的周年庆祝会

近 baronial, epic, grandiose, imperial, magnificent, majestic, massive, monumental, noble, regal, splendid
反 common, humble, mediocre, ordinary, unimposing, unimpressive 普通的，一般的

auspicious [ɔːˈspɪʃəs]

【考法】 *adj.* 好兆头的：pointing **toward a happy outcome**

例 They began the season with an auspicious win against their strongest football rival. 他们在赛季之初就战胜了最强的对手，为整个赛季赢得了好兆头。

近 bright, encouraging, golden, heartening, hopeful, promising, propitious
反 baleful, dark, direful, doomy, foreboding, gloomy, menacing, minatory, ominous, portentous, sinister, threatening 不祥的，凶兆的

austere [ɔːˈstɪr]

【考法1】 *adj.* 朴素的，朴实无华的：markedly **simple** or unadorned

例 For the private office of the CEO of the large corporation, the room is unexpectedly austere. 出人意料的是，这家大公司总裁的私人办公室居然十分朴素。

近 plain, spartan, stark, unadorned
反 deluxe, lavish, luxurious, plush, sumptuous 奢华的；elaborate, fancy 花哨的
派 austerity *n.* 节俭，朴素

【考法2】 *adj.* 严肃的，令人生畏的：**stern and cold** in appearance or manner

例 an austere fortress at the top of some formidable cliffs 建立在悬崖峭壁之上的一座令人畏惧的堡垒 ‖ In his memory his deceased grandfather is an austere, distant, cold person. 在他的记忆之中，已过世的祖父是一个严肃、冷漠而难以接近的人。

近 dour, fierce, flinty, forbidding, formidable, gruff, intimidating, lowering, rough, rugged, severe, steely
反 benign, benignant, gentle, mild, tender 和蔼的，温柔的

automatic [ˌɔːtəˈmætɪk]

【考法1】 *adj.* (机器等)自动的：acting or operating in a manner essentially **independent of external influence or control**

例 Will your next car be a manual or an automatic? 你下辆车是手动挡还是自动挡？ ‖ Modern subways are equipped with automatic screen doors. 现代地铁都装备了自动屏蔽门。

近 automated, robotic, self-acting, self-operating, self-regulating
反 manual 手动的

【考法 2】 *adj.* 自发的，情不自禁的：acting or done **spontaneously or unconsciously**
例 Carl's automatic use of the brakes narrowly averted a collision. 卡尔不经意间踩了刹车勉强避免了一场车祸。
近 impulsive, instinctive, involuntary, mechanic, mechanical, natural, spontaneous
反 calculated, deliberate, intentional, planned, predetermined, premeditated, studied 有计划的，蓄意的
派 automatically *adv.* 自动地

avowal [əˈvaʊəl]
【考法】 *n.* 承认，公开宣布：a solemn and often public **declaration** of the truth or existence of something
例 With jingoism rampant, the peace candidate felt compelled to make an avowal of his patriotism. 在沙文主义肆虐的情况下，这位爱好和平的候选人被迫公开承认自己是个爱国主义者。
近 affirmation, assertion, asseveration, avouchment, claim, declaration, insistence, profession
反 disavowal 否认，否定

backfire [ˌbækˈfaɪər]
【考法】 *vi.* 产生相反的结果，事与愿违：to have the **reverse** of the desired or expected effect
例 My plan to throw her a surprise party backfired when she ended up sobbing that everyone had forgotten her birthday. 我本想为她的生日开一个聚会作为惊喜，但没想到事与愿违，她啜泣着说所有人都忘记了她的生日。
近 boomerang
反 succeed 成功

backslide [ˈbækslaɪd]
【考法】 *vi.* （情况等）倒退，变坏：to **revert to a worse condition**
例 Keep these things in mind to help prevent you from backsliding. 牢记这些东西，它们能防止你旧病复发。
近 degenerate, lapse, recidivate, relapse, retrograde, retrogress
反 advance, progress 进步，前进

Unit 6

■ BAFFLE	■ BAFFLING	■ BASH	■ BASK	■ BEHOLDEN
■ BEHOOVE	■ BEIGE	■ BELLIGERENCE	■ BELLIGERENT	■ BESET

baffle [ˈbæfl]
【考法 1】 *vt.* 挫败，阻挠：to **frustrate or check** (a person) as by confusing or perplexing
例 baffled by the language barrier 因语言障碍而受阻
近 balk, beat, check, discomfit, foil, frustrate, thwart
反 advance, cultivate, encourage, forward, foster, further, nurture, promote 促进，鼓舞
【考法 2】 *vt.* 使疑惑：to throw into a state of **mental uncertainty**
例 I was baffled by many of the scientific terms used in the article. 这篇文章中的各种学术词汇让我很困惑。
近 befog, befuddle, bewilder, confound, discombobulate, disorient, maze, mystify, perplex, puzzle, vex
反 clarify, elucidate 澄清，阐明
派 baffling *adj.* 令人困惑的

baffling [ˈbæflɪŋ]
【考法】 *adj.* 令人疑惑的，难以理解的：making great mental demands; **hard to comprehend** or solve
例 I was constantly ill, with a baffling array of symptoms. 我常常生病，伴随着一系列令人困惑的症状。
近 befuddling, bewildering, confounding, confusing, enigmatic, puzzling, perplexing
反 apparent, distinct, evident, lucid, manifest, obvious, patent, pellucid, perspicuous, plain, transparent 明确的，明显的

bash [bæʃ]
【考法 1】 *n.* 猛击：a **forceful blow**
例 He has not been the same ever since he received that bash on his head. 自从他脑袋被别人打了之后，他就变得大不一样。
近 bang, bat, beat, crack, hit, knock, lash, poke, pound, punch, slam, slap, smash, spank, stroke, swat
【考法 2】 *vt.* 攻击，用力击打：to **strike violently** and often repeatedly
例 The angry child kept bashing her toy with a hammer until it broke. 愤怒的小孩用锤子不断地敲击她的玩具，直到它彻底被破坏。
近 baste, batter, buffet, hammer, lace, maul, nail, smash, strike

【考法3】 *vt.* 抨击，严厉批评: to **criticize harshly** and usually publicly

例 In all of talk radio no other host seems to enjoy bashing liberals as much as he does. 在所有电台节目中再没有像他一样热衷于抨击自由主义者的主持人了。

近 abuse, assail, belabor, blast, castigate, excoriate, lambaste, savage, scathe, slam, trash, vituperate

反 acclaim, commend, compliment, hail, laud, praise 表扬，称赞

bask [bæsk]

【考法】 *vi.* 休息，悠然自得: to **lie or relax** in a pleasant warmth or atmosphere

例 We blissfully basked at the seashore over the long holiday. 我们在海滩上躺着晒太阳，享受着漫长的假期。

近 loll, lounge, relax, repose

反 drudge, grind, hustle, labor, moil, plod, slave, sweat, toil, travail, work (辛苦地)干活，工作

beholden [bɪˈhoʊldən]

【考法】 *adj.* 欠他人人情的: **owing** something, such as **gratitude**, to another

例 Not wanting to be beholden to anyone, he insisted on paying his own way. 因为不想欠别人的人情，所以他坚持出自己的那一份钱。

近 indebted, obligated, obliged

behoove [bɪˈhuːv]

【考法】 *vt.* 对…有利: to be **necessary**, **proper** or **advantageous** for

例 It behooves you at least to try. 你至少也应该尝试一下。

近 befit, beseem, fit, serve, suite

beige [beɪʒ]

【考法】 *adj.* 缺乏特征的: **lacking distinction**

例 Some food critics have dismissed that chef's version of French cuisine as beige and boring. 一些美食评论家认为那名厨师所做的法国菜平凡无奇，令人厌倦。

近 characterless, faceless, featureless, indistinctive, neutral, noncommittal, vanilla

反 diagnostic, discriminating, distinct, distinctive, distinguishing, identifying, peculiar, typical 有特征的

belligerence [bəˈlɪdʒərəns]

【考法】 *n.* 好斗，好战: an **aggressive or truculent** attitude, atmosphere, or disposition

例 Among the Native American tribes of the colonial period, the Iroquois were known for their belligerence. 在殖民时期的美洲土著部落中，易洛魁人因为他们的好战而著名。

近 aggressiveness, assaultiveness, bellicosity, combativeness, contentiousness, disputatiousness, feistiness, militance, pugnacity, quarrelsomeness, scrappiness, truculence

反 pacifism 爱好和平

belligerent [bəˈlɪdʒərənt]

【考法】 *adj.* 好斗的，好战的: inclined to or exhibiting **assertiveness**, **hostility**, or **combativeness**

例 The coach became quite belligerent and spit at an umpire after being thrown out of the game. 教练变得好斗起来，以至于在被罚出场外之后转身向裁判吐口水。

近 aggressive, agonistic, assaultive, bellicose, combative, contentious, disputatious, feisty, gladiatorial, militant, pugnacious, quarrelsome, truculent, warlike

反 dove, pacific, peaceful 爱好和平的

派 belligerence *n.* 好战，好斗

beset [bɪˈset]

【考法1】 *vt.* 使苦恼，骚扰: to **cause persistent suffering** to

例 He has been beset by a lack of self-confidence virtually his entire life. 事实上他的一生都被缺乏自信所困扰。

近 agonize, anguish, bedevil, besiege, curse, excruciate, harrow, persecute, plague, rack, torment, torture

反 comfort, console, solace, soothe 安抚，安慰

【考法2】 *vt.* 攻击，袭击: to **set upon**

例 The settlers were beset by savages. 这些移民遭到了野蛮人的袭击。 || The unsuspecting tourists were suddenly beset by robbers. 丝毫没有准备的游客遭到了歹徒的突然袭击。

近 assail, assault, attack, charge, raid, rush, storm, strike, set on

反 defend, guard, protect, shield 防御，守卫

Unit 7

■ BEWITCHING ■ BLACKMAIL ■ BLUFF ■ BOGUS ■ BORE
■ BRANDISH ■ BRIM ■ BUMBLE ■ BUSTLE ■ CACHET

bewitching [bɪˈwɪtʃɪŋ]

【考法】 *adj.* 迷人的，令人着迷的: having an often mysterious or magical power to **attract**

例 a bewitching woman who has never lacked for suitors 一个从不缺乏追求者的迷人女子

近 alluring, appealing, attractive, captivating, charismatic, enchanting, engaging, entrancing, glamorous, luring, magnetic, seductive

反 repellent, repelling, repugnant, repulsive, revolting 令人反感的

blackmail [ˈblækmeɪl]

【考法】 *n./vt.* 敲诈，勒索：**extortion of money** or something else of value from a person by the threat of exposing a criminal act or discreditable information

例 It looks like these pornographic pictures were being used for blackmail. 看起来有人用这些不雅照进行敲诈勒索。

近 extortion

bluff [blʌf]

【考法 1】 *adj.* 直率的，(说话)直截了当的：being or characterized by **direct**, **brief**, and **potentially rude** speech or manner

例 Frankly speaking, he is a bluff but good-hearted teacher. 老实说，这个老师说话很直接，但是心地善良。

近 abrupt, brusque, crusty, curt, downright, forthright, snippy, straightforward, unceremonious

反 circuitous, mealy-mouthed (说话)拐弯抹角的

【考法 2】 *vt.* 欺骗：to cause to believe what is untrue; **deceive**

例 I successfully bluffed the interviewer into believing that I could really speak French and thus would be the perfect person to serve in the newspaper's Paris bureau. 我成功地欺骗了面试官，让他相信我会法语，从而成为报社在巴黎办事处的不二人选。

近 bamboozle, beguile, cozen, deceive, delude, dupe, fool, hoax, misguide, misinform, mislead, trick

反 disabuse, disenchant, disillusion 使清醒

bogus [ˈbouɡəs]

【考法 1】 *adj.* 伪造的，假冒的：**being such in appearance only** and made or manufactured with the intention of committing fraud

例 The evidence turned out to be completely bogus and the suspect may be innocent. 由于证据被发现是彻底伪造的，嫌犯很有可能是无辜的。

近 counterfeit, fake, false, forged, inauthentic, phony, queer, sham, snide, spurious, unauthentic

反 authentic, genuine, real, unfaked, bona fide 真实的

【考法 2】 *adj.* 虚伪的，做作的：**lacking** in natural or **spontaneous quality**

例 There was often a lot of bogus conviviality at the company's parties. 公司的聚会上往往有着虚伪的欢乐。

近 affected, assumed, contrived, factitious, feigned, plastic, pretended, pseudo, simulated, unnatural

反 artless, natural, spontaneous, unaffected, uncontrived, unfeigned, unforced 真诚的，不虚伪的

bore [bɔːr]

【考法 1】 *n.* 令人厌烦的人或事物：one that **causes boredom**

例 For once, the graduation speaker wasn't a real bore. 就这一次，毕业演讲者不是那么令人厌倦。

近 drip, droner, snoozer, yawner

【考法 2】 *vt.* 使厌倦，使厌烦：to **make weary** by being dull, repetitive, or tedious

例 The professor's lifeless and unimaginative teaching style bored the students to death. 教授毫无生气和想象力的教学方式让学生厌倦至极。

近 jade, pall, tire, weary

反 absorb, engage, engross, enthrall, fascinate, grip, interest, intrigue 使充满兴趣，使全神贯注

派 boring *adj.* 令人厌烦的；boredom *n.* 厌烦，乏味

brandish [ˈbrændɪʃ]

【考法】 *vt.* (带有威胁性地)挥舞：to **shake** or wave (as a weapon) **menacingly**

例 I could see that the suspect was brandishing a knife and was in no way inclined to surrender. 我可以看到嫌犯在挥舞着一把刀，完全没有要投降的倾向。

近 shake, swing, wave

反 drop 放下(武器等)

brim [brɪm]

【考法 1】 *n.* 边缘，边界：an upper or **outer margin**

例 The brim of the teacup was banded with gold. 茶杯的边缘被镀上了金。

近 borderline, bound, boundary, circumference, confines, edge, frame, fringe, margin, perimeter, periphery, skirt, verge

反 center, core, heart, kernel 核心

【考法2】 *vi.* 充满: to be or become **full often to overflowing**

例 a secondhand bookstore that was brimming with bargains 一个到处都是减价品的二手书店 ‖ eyes brimming with tears 饱含热泪的双眼

近 bristle, bulge, burst, bustle, buzz, crawl, hum, overflow, pullulate, swarm, teem

反 lack, need, want 缺少，缺乏

【考法3】 *vt.* 加满，倒满: to put into (something) **as much as can be** held or contained

例 He brimmed the glass with milk, and now I'm afraid that I will spill it. 他向杯子里倒了太多牛奶，我现在担心会不会洒出来。

近 charge, cram, heap, jam, load, pack, stuff

反 clear, empty, evacuate, vacate, void 清空

bumble ['bʌmbl]

【考法1】 *vi.* 含糊不清地说，杂乱无章地说: to speak **rapidly**, **inarticulately**, and usually unintelligibly

例 Overcome with stage fright, I could only bumble through the speech. 由于怯场，我结结巴巴地说完了演讲稿。

近 babble, drivel, drool, gabble, gibber, jabber, prattle, sputter

反 articulate, enunciate, pronounce 清楚地说

【考法2】 *vi.* 笨拙地行动: to move, act, or proceed **clumsily**

例 I sort of bumbled through the dance number, hoping that it would soon end. 我笨拙地跟着曲子舞蹈，心里指望着它快点结束。

近 blunder, flounder, limp, lumber, plod, struggle, stumble, trudge

反 coast, drift, glide, sail, slide (轻松地)行动，滑动

bustle ['bʌsl]

【考法1】 *n.* 忙乱，喧闹: **noisy**, **energetic**, and often obtrusive activity

例 the hustle and bustle of the big city 熙熙攘攘的大都市 ‖ I couldn't concentrate in all the bustle of the student lounge. 学生休息室里过于嘈杂，我无法专心。

近 bluster, coil, disturbance, furor, hurricane, pandemonium, stir, storm, tumult, turmoil, uproar, welter, whirl

反 calm, hush, peace, quiet, rest, stillness, tranquillity 宁静，祥和; order 秩序

【考法2】 *vi.* (快速地)行走，奔忙: to **move briskly** and often ostentatiously

例 The hostess bustled about, taking care of last-minute preparations for the party. 女主人四处走着，为聚会做最后的准备。

近 blast, bolt, careen, career, dash, fly, hustle, rush, rustle, speed, whirl

反 crawl, creep, lag, poke 缓慢行进

cachet [kæ'ʃeɪ]

【考法】 *n.* 威望，声望: a **mark or quality**, as of distinction, individuality, or authenticity

例 Federal courts have a certain cachet which state courts lack. 联邦法院拥有州立法院所不具备的威信。

近 credit, distinction, esteem, homage, kudos, prestige

反 infamy, notoriety 不好的名声

Unit 8

■ CALAMITY	■ CALCULATED	■ CALIBRATE	■ CANNY	■ CANONIZE
■ CAPTIOUS	■ CAREEN	■ CAREFREE	■ CASCADE	■ CELLULAR

calamity [kə'læməti]

【考法】 *n.* 大灾难: a **disastrous event** marked by great loss and lasting distress and suffering

例 This latest breakdown of the car is inconvenient, but not a calamity. 最近的汽车抛锚确实带来了不便，但还不是一场灾难。 ‖ an economic calamity 金融风暴

近 apocalypse, cataclysm, catastrophe, debacle, disaster, tragedy

反 benediction, boon, felicity, godsend, manna, windfall 天赐好运，幸事

calculated ['kælkjuleɪtɪd]

【考法】 *adj.* 经过计算(成败得失)的，经过深思熟虑的: engaged in, undertaken, or displayed after **reckoning or estimating** the statistical probability of success or failure

例 He took a calculated risk and got in on the ground floor of the new enterprise. 他深思熟虑一番之后决定冒这个险，踏出了迈向新计划的第一步。

近 advised, considered, deliberate, knowing, measured, reasoned, studied, thoughtful, weighed

反 automatic, casual, instinctive, spontaneous, unstudied 随意的，不假思索的

calibrate	[ˈkælɪbreɪt]

【考法】 *vt.* 校准，调校：to **check**, **adjust**, **or determine** by comparison with a standard （the graduations of a quantitative measuring instrument）

例 We need to calibrate the sextants navigation. 我们要为航行校准六分仪。

近 adjust, align, gauge, graduate, measure

派 calibration *n.* 校准

canny	[ˈkæni]

【考法】 *adj.* 精明的，聪明的：**careful and shrewd**, especially where one's own interests are concerned

例 He is a canny card player who is good at psyching out his opponents. 他是一个善于琢磨对手心思的精明的扑克玩家。

近 astute, clever, hardheaded, heady, knowing, savvy, sharp, shrewd, smart

反 ignorant, unknowing 无知的；foolish, idiotic, imbecile, moronic, silly, thoughtless, witless 愚笨的

canonize	[ˈkænənaɪz]

【考法 1】 *vt.* 过分宠爱，过分崇拜：to love or **admire too much**

例 a singing star so canonized by his fans that they refuse to believe anything bad about him 一个受到粉丝疯狂追捧的歌星，粉丝们不会相信任何关于他的负面新闻

近 adore, adulate, canonize, dote, worship

反 abhor, abominate, belittle, despise, detest, disdain, dislike, disparage, hate, loathe 厌恶，鄙视

【考法 2】 *vt.* 使崇高，使神圣：to assign a **high status or value** to

例 Some movie buffs canonized David Fincher as today's most preeminent director. 一些影迷把戴维·芬彻视作当今世界上最为出色的导演。

近 aggrandize, deify, dignify, elevate, ennoble, enshrine, ensky, enthrone, glorify, magnify

反 abase, degrade, demean, humble, humiliate 贬低，瞧不起

captious	[ˈkæpʃəs]

【考法】 *adj.* 吹毛求疵的，爱挑毛病的：marked by an often ill-natured inclination to **stress faults and raise objections**

例 a captious and cranky eater who has never met a vegetable he didn't hate 一个古怪又挑剔的食客，从来就没有他不讨厌的蔬菜

近 carping, caviling, critical, faultfinding, hypercritical, judgmental, overcritical

反 appreciative 表示欣赏的

careen	[kəˈriːn]

【考法 1】 *vi.* 蹒跚而行，不稳地行走：to **lurch or swerve** while in motion

例 He careened unsteadily to the couch after hitting his head. 在撞到头以后，他摇摇摆摆地走向沙发。

近 dodder, lurch, reel, sway, teeter, totter, waddle, wobble

【考法 2】 *vi.* 狂奔，快速运动：to **rush** headlong or carelessly

例 Sounding its siren, an ambulance careened through the intersection. 救护车响着警笛飞驰过十字路口。

近 blast, bolt, bustle, career, dash, fly, hustle, rush, rustle, speed, whirl

反 crawl, creep, lag, poke 缓慢行进

carefree	[ˈkerfriː]

【考法】 *adj.* 无忧无虑的：free from care as having **no worries or troubles**

例 passengers on a luxury cruise ship enjoying a carefree vacation 在豪华游轮上享受着无忧旅途的乘客
carefree college students on spring break 春假期间无忧无虑的大学生

近 blithe, debonair, gay, insouciant, lighthearted, lightsome, slaphappy, unconcerned

反 careworn 焦虑的

cascade	[kæˈskeɪd]

【考法】 *n.* (尤指小的)瀑布：a steep usually **small** fall of water

例 The river forms a series of cascades as it drops a total of 200 feet in elevation. 这条河前后海拔差达 200 英尺，故而形成了一系列的小瀑布。

近 fall, waterfall

反 cataract 大瀑布

cellular	[ˈseljələr]

【考法】 *adj.* 多孔的：containing cavities; having a **porous** texture

例 the cellular construction of a beehive 蜂巢的多孔结构

近 porous

Unit 9

ceremonious [ˌserəˈmoʊniəs]

【考法】 *adj.* 讲究礼节的，庄重的：marked by or showing **careful attention to set forms** and details

例 A century ago everyday life was much more ceremonious than in our anything-goes era. 一个世纪之前的生活和我们现在这个随便怎么都无所谓的年代相比，多出了许多要讲究的礼节。

近 correct, decorous, formal, nice, proper, punctilious, starchy, stiff, stilted

反 casual, easygoing, informal, unceremonious 随意的，不正式的

certitude [ˈsɜːrtɪtuːd]

【考法】 *n.* 确信无疑：the state of being or feeling **certain**

例 I believes with certitude that he is the best candidate for the job. 我确信他是这项工作的最佳人选。

近 assurance, assuredness, certainty, confidence, conviction, doubtlessness, positiveness, sureness, surety

反 doubt, dubiety, incertitude, uncertainty 不确定

channel [ˈtʃænl]

【考法 1】 *n.* 水渠：an open man-made **passageway for water**

例 Water was drained from the swamp through a specially constructed channel. 这块沼泽通过一条特别修建的水渠源源不断地向外输水。

近 aqueduct, canal, conduit, course, flume, racecourse, raceway, watercourse, waterway

【考法 2】 *n.* 海峡：a narrow body of water **between two land masses**

例 the world record for swimming the channel between Alaska and Chukotskiy 游泳横渡阿拉斯加和楚科奇之间的海峡(即白令海峡)的世界纪录

近 narrows, neck, sound, strait

【考法 3】 *vt.* 将…导向，投入：to cause to **move to a central point** or along a restricted pathway

例 a youth who channeled all of his energy into sports 一个将所有精力都投入体育之中的少年

近 canalize, channelize, conduct, direct, funnel, pipe, siphon

chaperone [ˈʃæpəroʊn]

【考法】 *vt.* 同行，护送：to **go along with** in order to provide assistance, protection, or companionship

例 Three parents will chaperone the students on the school trip. 本次班级旅行将有三名家长同行。

近 accompany, attend, companion, company, convoy, escort, squire

反 abandon, desert, ditch, dump, forsake 抛弃，不顾

charisma [kəˈrɪzmə]

【考法】 *n.* 魅力，吸引力：a special magnetic **charm** or appeal

例 a movie star with unique charisma 有着独特魅力的电影明星 ‖ The candidate was lacking in charisma. 这位候选人就是缺乏了这点个人魅力。

近 allure, appeal, attractiveness, captivation, enchantment, fascination, glamor, seductiveness, witchery

反 repulsion, repulsiveness 反感，厌恶

派 charismatic *adj.* 有魅力的，吸引人的

cherished [ˈtʃerɪʃt]

【考法】 *adj.* 受喜爱的，珍爱的：**granted special treatment** or attention

例 a cherished heirloom that has been in the family for generations 在这个家族里流传了几代的备受珍爱的传家宝 ‖ He described the picture with his wife as his most cherished possession. 他把这张与妻子的合影看作自己最为珍爱的财富。

近 beloved, dear, favored, favorite, fond, loved, pet, precious, special, sweet

反 abhorred, abominated, despised, detested, disdained, disliked, execrated, hated, loathed 被厌恶的

chivalrous [ˈʃɪvlrəs]

【考法】 *adj.* 有骑士风度的，(尤指对女性)彬彬有礼的：marked by **gracious courtesy and high-minded consideration**(especially to women)

例 The elderly gentleman still engages in chivalrous behavior, such as opening doors for people. 这位年迈的绅士仍然坚持着有风度的行为，比如帮别人开门。

近 big, elevated, gallant, great, greathearted, high, high-minded, lofty, lordly, magnanimous, natural, sublime

反 base, debased, degenerate, degraded, ignoble, ignominious, low 品行低劣的，可鄙的

派 chivalry *n.* 骑士风度

chorale [kəˈrɑːl]

【考法 1】 *n.* 赞美诗：a **hymn or psalm** sung to a traditional or composed melody **in church**

例 practice a chorale to perform in church 练习吟唱要在教堂表演的赞美诗

近 anthem, canticle, carol, hymn, paean, psalm, spiritual

【考法 2】 *n.* 合唱班，合唱团：an organized **group of singers**

例 a chorale that is regarded as being among the best in the state 一个被认为是国内一流的合唱班

近 choir, chorus, consort, ensemble

clamor [ˈklæmər]

【考法】 *n.* 喧闹，喧哗，噪声：**loud**, confused, and usually **inharmonious** sound

例 A clamor arose from the crowd as the prisoner was brought forward. 当犯人被带上前时，人群中发出一阵骚动。‖ the clamor of a dozen people practicing the trumpet at once 一群人同时练习小号时发出的噪音

近 blare, bluster, cacophony, clangor, discordance, howl, racket, rattle, roar, tumult, uproar, vociferation

反 quiet, silence, still, stillness 寂静；calm, lull, serenity, tranquility 宁静，祥和

派 clamorous *adj.* 喧闹的

clan [klæn]

【考法】 *n.* (有共同爱好的)团体，帮派：a group **united by a common interest** or common characteristics

例 That clan of football fans has parties every weekend on which the New England Patriots play. 只要是新英格兰爱国者队有比赛的周末，那帮球迷就会举行聚会。

近 body, bunch, circle, clique, community, coterie, coven, crowd, fold, network, pack, ring, set

反 clannish *adj.* 派系的；团结的

Unit 10

■ CLEAVE	■ CLING	■ COARSE	■ COHESIVE	■ COLLABORATE
■ COMMISERATE	■ COMPATIBLE	■ COMPELLING	■ COMPLACENT	■ COMPLEMENTARY

cleave [kliːv]

【考法 1】 *vi.* 紧贴，坚持：to **adhere** firmly and closely or loyally and unwaveringly

例 You should resolutely cleave to the facts in your report. 你应该在报道中坚持客观的原则。

近 adhere, cling, hew, stick

反 defect 叛变

【考法 2】 *vt.* 分隔，割裂，劈开：to **divide** by or as if by a cutting blow

例 His spade cleaved the firm sand with a harsh crunch. 他的锹凿开了坚实的砂土，发出尖锐刺耳的嘎扎声。

近 cut, decouple, disconnect, disjoin, dissever, dissociate, divide, part, ramify, sever, slice, split, sunder

反 join, link, unify, unite 连接，接合

cling [klɪŋ]

【考法 1】 *n.* 粘结，粘合：a **physical sticking** to as if by glue

例 For certain types of materials that plastic wrap has very little cling. 对于某些材料，那种塑料覆膜的粘性不好。

近 adherence, bonding, cohesion

【考法 2】 *vi.* 紧贴；支持：to **adhere** as if glued firmly

例 a dozen magnets clinging to the refrigerator 贴靠在冰箱门上的一打磁石 ‖ The couple continued to cling to the old ideas of child rearing long after they had gone out of fashion. 这对夫妇仍然坚持关于抚养孩子的老观念，尽管它们已经过时。

近 adhere, cleave, hew, stick

反 defect 叛变

coarse [kɔːrs]

【考法 1】 *adj.* 粗糙的，表面不平整的：**not** having a level or **smooth** surface

例 the coarse surface of the sandpaper 砂纸的粗糙表面

近 broken, bumpy, irregular, jagged, lumpy, pebbly, ragged, rough, roughened, rugged, scraggy

反 even, flat, level, plane 表面平整的；smooth 表面光滑的

【考法 2】 *adj.* (声音)刺耳的，粗声粗气的：harsh, raucous, or **rough in tone**

例 a coarse laugh from the living room 客厅里传来的一阵刺耳笑声

近 croaking, croaky, grating, gravel, gruff, husky, rasping, raspy, rusty, scratchy, throaty

反 gentle, gliding, golden, liquid, mellifluent, mellifluous, mellow, soothing, sweet, tender (声音)柔美的

【考法 3】 *adj.* 粗俗的：**lacking** in delicacy or **refinement**

例 They don't know how to behave, and are coarse and insulting. 他们不知道正常的行为礼节，因此显得粗俗而无理。

近 crass, crude, gross, incult, lowbred, raffish, rude, uncouth, uncultivated, unpolished, unrefined, vulgar

反 civilized, cultivated, cultured, genteel, polished, refined, smooth, tasteful 有教养的，举止得体的

【考法4】 *adj.* （质量）低劣的: of low, common, or **inferior quality**

例 coarse imitations of quality merchandise 高级商品的粗劣仿制品

近 execrable, inferior, lousy, mediocre, miserable, rotten, rubbishy, shoddy, sleazy, terrible, trashy, wretched

反 excellent, fine, superior （品质）优良的

cohesive [koʊˈhiːsɪv]

【考法】 *adj.* 有粘性的；有凝聚力的: exhibiting or producing **cohesion or coherence**

例 a cohesive social unit 有凝聚力的社会个体 ‖ cohesive soils 有粘性的土壤

近 adherent, adhesive, clingy, gluey, glutinous, gummy, tacky, tenacious, viscid

反 non-adhesive, non-viscous 无粘性的

派 cohesion *n.* 粘结；凝聚力

collaborate [kəˈlæbəreɪt]

【考法】 *vi.* 合作: to **work jointly** with others or together especially in an intellectual endeavor

例 The two men collaborated on a blockbuster in 1986 which gained both of them fame. 两人在 1986 年合作出演了一部十分卖座的电影，由此名噪一时。

近 band, concert, cooperate, concur, conjoin, conspire, join, league, unite

反 stonewall 拒绝合作

派 collaboration *n.* 合作，协作

commiserate [kəˈmɪzəreɪt]

【考法】 *vi.* 表示怜悯，同情: to feel or express **sympathy**

例 He commiserated over their failure. 他对他们的失败表示同情。 ‖ We commiserated with him but there was little we could do to make the situation better. 我们很同情他的遭遇，但是也只能表示无能为力。

近 ache, bleed, compassionate, condole, sympathize, yearn

compatible [kəmˈpætəbl]

【考法】 *adj.* 一致的，能共存的: capable of existing together **in harmony**

例 I don't think that they could be compatible as roommates. 我不觉得他们做了室友之后能和谐相处。 a theory that is compatible with what we already know about early man 一个与对远古人类的已有知识不存在矛盾的理论

近 accordant, coherent, concordant, conformable, congruent, congruous, consonant, harmonious

反 conflicting, incompatible, incongruous, inconsistent, inharmonious 有冲突的，矛盾的

compelling [kəmˈpelɪŋ]

【考法1】 *adj.* 极具说服力的: having the power to **persuade**

例 make a compelling argument against military intervention 就反对军事干预提出了很有说服力的论证 ‖ If you can't present any compelling evidence to prove your innocence, you will be found guilty. 如果你找不出任何能证明你清白的有力证据，你就会被定罪。

近 conclusive, convincing, decisive, effective, forceful, persuasive, satisfying, strong, telling

反 feeble, weak 说服力不足的

【考法2】 *adj.* 迫切的，紧迫的: needing **immediate attention**

例 There is no compelling need to raise taxes at this time. 现在没有迫切提升税率的必要。

近 burning, clamant, critical, crying, dire, emergent, exigent, imperative, imperious, importunate, instant, necessitous, pressing, urgent

反 minor, negligible, trivial, unimportant 不重要的，琐碎的

complacent [kəmˈpleɪsnt]

【考法1】 *adj.* 自满的，自鸣得意的: feeling or showing an often **excessive or unjustified satisfaction** and pleasure in one's status, possessions, or attainments

例 a complacent junior accountant who was certain of her indispensability to the company 一个确信自己对于公司而言无可替代而自满的年轻会计

近 assured, consequential, egoistic, overweening, pompous, prideful, proud, smug, vain, vainglorious

反 egoless, humble, modest, uncomplacent 谦逊的，谦卑的

派 complacency *n.* 自满

【考法2】 *adj.* 无所谓的，不关心的: having or showing a **lack of interest or concern**

例 We can't afford to be complacent about rural illiteracy rates. 我们不能对农村的文盲率坐视不理。

近 apathetic, casual, disinterested, insouciant, nonchalant, perfunctory, pococurante, unconcerned

反 attentive, concerned, heedful, interested, mindful 关注的，感兴趣的

complementary [ˌkɑːmplɪˈmentri]

【考法】 *adj.* 互补的: mutually **supplying each other's** lack

例 The complementary contributions of the cooking and cleanup committees were essential to the success of the barbecue. 负责食物和卫生的两个小组之间的相互配合是野炊成功的关键。

近 correlative, interdependent, reciprocal, supplemental, supplementary

反 contradictory, incompatible 矛盾的

List 29*

"人最大的悲剧是眼睁睁地让梦想一点点蜕变成空想。与其纠结每个小节的意义，不如放手一搏，不求无憾，但求无悔。"

（翟冰，录取院校：Texas A&M University，生物学系）

Unit 1

■ COMPLICATE　　■ COMPREHEND　　■ CONCRETE　　■ CONDEMN　　■ CONDITIONAL
■ CONFLAGRATION　　■ CONFLATE　　■ CONFORM　　■ CONJURE　　■ CONSENT

complicate [ˈkɑːmplɪkeɪt]
【考法】 *vt.* 使复杂化：to make **complex or difficult**
例 Don't complicate matters by getting the parents involved. 不要把父母牵扯进来，这会让问题更复杂。
近 complex, embarrass, entangle, ravel, perplex, sophisticate, tangle
反 simplify, streamline 简化
派 complicated *adj.* 复杂的，麻烦的

comprehend [ˌkɑːmprɪˈhend]
【考法 1】 *vt.* 理解，了解：to **grasp** the nature, significance, or meaning of
例 the age at which children can comprehend the difference between right and wrong 一个小孩可以开始分辨是非的年龄 || With internet, television, cellphone and even radio down, we are unable to comprehend what has happened. 互联网、电视、手机乃至无线电都不起作用了，我们无法获知发生了什么。
近 appreciate, apprehend, assimilate, behold, catch, cognize, conceive, discern, grasp, perceive, recognize, savvy, see, seize, sense, understand
反 misapprehend, misconceive, misinterpret, misperceive, misunderstand 误解
【考法 2】 *vt.* 包括，包含：to **contain or hold within** a total scope, significance, or amount
例 Our notion of morality should comprehend much more than proper sexual behavior. 我们的道德观范围不应该仅仅止步于恰当的性行为。
近 carry, contain, embrace, encompass, entail, involve, number, subsume, take in
反 exclude, leave, omit, preclude 排除，忽略
派 comprehensive *adj.* 全面的，综合的；comprehension *n.* 理解；comprehensible *adj.* 可理解的

concrete [ˈkɑːŋkriːt]
【考法 1】 *adj.* 实体的，实在的：relating to or composed of **matter**
例 concrete objects like rocks and trees 像石头、树这一类的实物
近 physical, substantial, substantive
反 airy, diaphanous, gossamery, immaterial, tenuous, thin, vaporous 虚无缥缈的，非实体的
【考法 2】 *adj.* 事实性的，明确的：existing **in fact** and not merely as a possibility
例 Concrete evidence, and not just a theory, must be presented at a trial. 在法庭上需要出示确凿的证据，而非臆测。
近 effective, existent, factual, genuine, real, true, very, de facto
反 conjectural, hypothetical, ideal, platonic, suppositional, theoretical 猜测的，理论上的

condemn [kənˈdem]
【考法】 *vt.* 谴责（…为不道德的、邪恶的）：to **declare to be reprehensible**, **wrong**, **or evil** usually after weighing evidence and without reservation
例 a policy widely condemned as racist 一个被广泛谴责为种族歧视的政策 || It is a sign of human progress that slavery, which was once common, is now universally condemned. 曾经很平常的奴隶制如今却沦落到人人谴责的境地，这不能不说是人类文明的进步。
近 anathematize, censure, damn, decry, denounce, execrate, reprimand, reprehend, reproach, reprobate
反 commend, endorse, extol, laud, praise 赞扬，赞颂

conditional [kənˈdɪʃənl]
【考法】 *adj.* 有条件的，受制约的：subject to, implying, or **dependent** upon a condition
例 a conditional offer 有条件限制的录取 || Their support is conditional on their approval of his proposals. 他们认可他的提案是有条件的。
近 contingent, dependent, subject, tentative
反 absolute, categorical, unconditional 不受制约的；independent 独立的

conflagration [ˌkɑːnfləˈɡreɪʃn]

【考法 1】 *n.* 大火：a **large destructive fire**

例 All the stock was destroyed in a warehouse conflagration. 仓库里所有的货物都被一场大火烧毁了。

近 holocaust, inferno

【考法 2】 *n.* 武装冲突，战争：a state of **armed violent struggle** between states, nations, or groups

例 What began as a skirmish over disputed territory erupted into a conflagration that swept the continent. 这场席卷整个大陆的战争是由之前关于有纠纷的领土的小冲突引发的。

近 conflict, war, warfare

反 peace 和平；truce 休战

conflate [kənˈfleɪt]

【考法】 *vt.* 混合：to **turn into a single mass** or entity that is more or less the same throughout

例 The movie conflates documentary footage and dramatized reenacts so seamlessly and ingeniously that viewers may not know what is real and what is not. 电影将纪实档案和娱乐性的夸张如此巧妙无缝地糅合起来，以至于观众不知道哪一部分是真实的，哪一部分是虚构的。

近 amalgamate, combine, composite, fuse, homogenize, immingle, incorporate, integrate, interfuse, meld, merge, mingle, mix

反 disunite, divide, part, separate, sunder 使分离

派 conflation *n.* 合并

conform [kənˈfɔːrm]

【考法 1】 *vt.* 使协调：to **bring into harmony** or accord

例 We have to conform this new rule with existing policy regarding student-run organizations on campus. 我们必须要让这些新规定与现行的校园学生社团的政策相协调。

近 accommodate, attune, conciliate, coordinate, key, reconcile

反 disharmonize 使不和谐

【考法 2】 *vt.* 调整（以适应）：to **change** (something) so as **to make it suitable** for a new use or situation

例 I can be funny or serious, for I always conform my behavior to the situation. 我会根据情况调整举止，因此我有时候会很活泼，有时候会很严肃。

近 acclimate, acclimatize, accommodate, adjust, condition, doctor, edit, fashion, fit, put, shape, suit, tailor

【考法 3】 *vi.* 遵照，遵从：to be **obedient** or **compliant**

例 an independent-minded person who refuses to conform to another's wishes 一个思想独立、拒绝遵照他人的意愿行动的人

近 adhere, comply, follow, goose-step, mind, observe

反 defy, disobey, rebel 不服从，反抗

派 conformist *n.* 墨守成规的人；conformism *n.* 守旧

conjure [ˈkʌndʒər]

【考法 1】 *vt.* 请求，恳求：to charge or **entreat earnestly** or solemnly

例 I conjure you to hear my plea for mercy. 请您发发慈悲吧。‖ He conjured them with his dying breath to look after his children. 临终前他恳求他们照顾他的孩子。

近 appeal, beseech, besiege, entreat, impetrate, implore, importune, petition, plead, pray, solicit, supplicate

【考法 2】 *vt.* 在脑海中浮现，想起：to **form a mental picture** of

例 With certain flowers I instantly conjure up memories of our Caribbean honeymoon. 这些鲜花让我立即回想起我们加勒比海的蜜月之旅。

近 conceive, dream, envisage, envision, fancy, fantasize, feature, ideate, image, picture, vision, visualize

consent [kənˈsent]

【考法 1】 *n.* 同意，赞同：the **approval** by someone in authority for the doing of something

例 We had to get our neighbor's consent in order to trim the tree from his side. 想要从邻居家那边修剪树木，我们得先得到他的同意。

近 allowance, approval, authorization, clearance, concurrence, granting, license, sanction, warrant

反 interdiction, prohibition, proscription 禁止

【考法 2】 *vi.* 同意：to give assent or **approval**

例 consent to being tested in her neurobiology experiment 同意在她神经生物学的实验中作测试对象 ‖ refuse to consent to the marriage 拒绝这桩婚事

近 acquiesce, agree, approve, assent, subscribe

反 dissent 反对；deny, veto 否决

Unit 2

consign [kən'saɪn]

【考法】 *vt.* 转交，转移(给他人)：to give, transfer, or deliver into the hands or **control of another**

例 The record shows that the deliveryman had consigned our package to a next-door neighbor. 记录显示邮递员把我们的包裹转投给隔壁邻居了。 ‖ a writer consigned to oblivion 湮没无闻的作家

近 commend, commit, confide, delegate, deliver, entrust, hand, recommend, repose, transfer, transmit, vest

反 hold, keep, retain 保留

consternation [ˌkɑːnstərˈneɪʃn]

【考法】 *n.* 惊愕，恐慌，恐惧：a state of **paralyzing dismay**

例 The two girls stared at each other in consternation without any idea about what to do. 两个小女孩惊恐地望着对方，显得不知所措。

近 alarm, apprehension, dread, fear, fright, horror, terror, trepidation

反 bravery, courage, dauntlessness, fearlessness, fortitude, intrepidity, stoutness, valor 勇气，无畏

constrict [kən'strɪkt]

【考法】 *vt.* 压缩，压紧：to make smaller or narrower by or as if by **binding or squeezing**

例 lives constricted by poverty 因为贫穷而拮据的生活 ‖ Severe migraine can be treated with a drug which constricts the blood vessels. 某些能使血管收缩的药物可用来治疗严重的偏头痛。

近 capsule, collapse, compact, condense, constringe, contract, narrow, squeeze, telescope

反 decompress, expand, open, outspread, outstretch 扩张，使伸展

contemplate [ˈkɑːntəmpleɪt]

【考法】 *v.* 沉思，仔细思索：to view or **consider** with continued attention

例 contemplate the vastness of the universe 沉思着宇宙的广袤无垠 ‖ She contemplated the problem for several hours before reaching a decision. 关于这个问题，她苦苦思索了几个小时后才做出决定。

近 cogitate, consider, deliberate, meditate, mull, perpend, pore, revolve, ruminate, study, weigh, wrestle

反 disregard, ignore, overlook, slight 忽视

派 contemplation *n.* 沉思，思索

contempt [kən'tempt]

【考法】 *n.* 蔑视，鄙视：open dislike for someone or something considered **unworthy of one's concern or respect**

例 my undying contempt for people who abuse animals 我对于虐待动物者的无尽鄙视 ‖ Her contempt for illiterate was obvious. 你可以很明显地看出她对文盲的鄙夷。

近 contemptuousness, despisement, despite, despitefulness, disdain, misprision, scorn

反 admiration, esteem, estimation, regard, respect, reverence, veneration 尊敬，敬仰

派 contemptible *adj.* 可鄙的；contemptuous *adj.* 蔑视的

contend [kən'tend]

【考法 1】 *vi.* 竞争，争夺：to **strive or vie in contest** or rivalry or against difficulties

例 two traditional rivals contending for the championship 两个争夺冠军头衔的老对手

近 battle, fight, race, rival, vie

反 capitulate, quit, succumb, surrender, give in 投降

【考法 2】 *vt.* 声明，声称：to **state as a fact** usually forcefully

例 He contended that his opponent was wrong about practically everything. 他宣称对手几乎在所有问题上都犯了错误。 ‖ He contended that his considerable experience made him the best candidate. 他声称因为他见多识广，所以是最佳人选。

近 affirm, allege, assert, aver, avouch, avow, declare, insist, maintain, profess, protest, purport, warrant

反 deny, gainsay 否认

contradict [ˌkɑːntrəˈdɪkt]

【考法】 *vt.* 否认，反驳；与…相矛盾：to assert the **contrary** of; to imply the opposite or a denial of

例 contradict a rumor 反驳谣言 ‖ Your actions contradict your words. 你的行为和你说的话相互矛盾。

近 deny, disaffirm, disavow, disclaim, disconfirm, disown, gainsay, negate, negative, refute, reject, repudiate

反 acknowledge, admit, avow, concede, confirm 承认

派 contradictory *adj.* 矛盾的，相反的

contrived [kənˈtraɪvd]

【考法】 *adj.* 不自然的，刻意的：**lacking** in natural or **spontaneous quality**

例 We are bored with the contrived applause of a TV studio audience that has been told when to clap. 摄影棚中的观众会被告知什么时候鼓掌，这种经过刻意安排的掌声让我们倍感厌倦。

近 affected, assumed, bogus, factitious, feigned, plastic, pretended, pseudo, simulated, unnatural

反 artless, natural, spontaneous, unaffected, uncontrived, unfeigned, unforced 真诚的，不虚伪的

convene [kənˈviːn]

【考法1】 *vt.* 召开，召集：to bring together in assembly by or as if by command

例 convene the members of the council for an emergency session 召集委员会的成员进入紧急议程

近 assemble, call, muster, summon

反 disband, dispel, disperse, dissipate, dissolve, squander 驱散，驱逐

【考法2】 *vi.* 聚集，集合：to come together in a body

例 The students convened in the auditorium to hear the principal's address. 学生们在大礼堂集合，聆听校长的致辞。

近 cluster, collect, concenter, concentrate, conglomerate, congregate, converge, gather, meet, rendezvous

派 convention *n.* 集会，大会

correlate [ˈkɔːrəleɪt]

【考法】 *vt.* 使…相关联：to establish a **mutual or reciprocal relation** between

例 a demanding father who always correlated success with hard work 一个总将成功和辛勤工作挂钩的严格父亲 ‖ In this work, we correlate the simulation in the lab and the observation in the field to examine the validity of our theory. 本文中，我们将实验室的模拟结果和实际观测数据联系起来以验证理论的真实性。

近 connect, identify, link, relate

反 separate 分离

派 correlation *n.* 关联，关系

Unit 3

■ COUNTERPART   ■ COUNTERPRODUCTIVE ■ COURTEOUS   ■ COY   ■ CREDIBLE
■ CREDIT   ■ CROW   ■ DAMN   ■ DAMPEN   ■ DASHING

counterpart [ˈkaʊntərpɑːrt]

【考法】 *n.* (地位、功能) 对等的人或物：one having the **same function or characteristics** as another

例 She worked with her counterpart in the other office to get the job done. 她与另一个办公室的同职人员一起完成这项工作。 ‖ U.S. presidents and his British counterpart 美国总统和英国首相

近 coequal, compeer, coordinate, equivalent, fellow, like, match, parallel, peer, rival

counterproductive [ˌkaʊntərprəˈdʌktɪv]

【考法】 *adj.* 反效果的，阻碍预期目标的：**not producing** or tending to hinder the attainment of a **desired goal**

例 Violence as a means to achieve an end is counterproductive. (W. E. Brock) 用暴力来达到目标往往是事与愿违的。——W. E. 布洛克 ‖ His uncontrollable anger is very counterproductive to his attempt at saving his marriage. 他无法自控的愤怒只会对他拯救婚姻的意愿起反作用。

近 feckless, hamstrung, ineffective, ineffectual, inefficacious, inefficient, inexpedient

反 effective, effectual, efficacious, efficient, expedient, operant 行之有效的

courteous [ˈkɜːrtiəs]

【考法】 *adj.* 礼貌的，谦恭有礼的：marked by **polished manners**, gallantry, or ceremonial usage of a court

例 Their customer service department always gives courteous responses, even to rude people. 哪怕是对粗鲁的消费者，他们的客服部门总是用一种非常有礼貌的态度回复。

近 civil, civilized, couth, genteel, gracious, mannerly, suave, urbane, well-bred

反 discourteous, ill-bred, ill-mannered, impertinent, impolite, impudent, insolent, rude 粗鲁的，不礼貌的

派 courtesy *n.* 礼貌，谦恭

coy [kɔɪ]

【考法1】 *adj.* 故作羞涩的：affectedly and usually **flirtatiously shy or modest**

例 Not wanting him to know that she was interested in him, she acted very coy at the dance. 她在舞会上故意装得很娇羞的样子，不想让他知道她喜欢他。

近 coquettish, demure, kittenish

【考法2】 *adj.* 不愿与人交往的，内向的：**tending to avoid people** and social situations

例 She was modest without being coy. 她很低调，但又不至于内向。

近 backward, bashful, diffident, introverted, modest, recessive, retiring, sheepish, shy, withdrawn

反 extroverted, immodest, outgoing 外向的

credible [ˈkredəbl]

【考法】 *adj.* 可信的，值得信赖的：**worthy of being accepted** as true or reasonable

例 It's not perfect, but is at least a credible explanation. 尽管还不算完美，但这好歹也算是可信的解释了。‖ a credible account of an accident 事故的可靠报道

近 believable, creditable, likely, plausible, presumptive, probable

反 implausible, improbable, incredible, unbelievable, unlikely 不可信的，难以置信的

派 credibility *n.* 可靠性，公信力

credit [ˈkredɪt]

【考法1】 *n.* 信任，信赖：**mental conviction of the truth** of some statement or the reality of some being or phenomenon

例 I give full credit to this report on the prevalence of cheating among college students today. 我非常相信这则有关大学中作弊成风的报道。

近 belief, credence, faith, trust

反 disbelief, doubt, dubiety, incertitude 不信任，不确定

【考法2】 *n.* 表扬，赞扬：public **acknowledgment or admiration** for an achievement

例 She deserves all the credit, since she did all the work. 是她完成了所有的工作，因此荣誉都应该属于她。

近 acclaim, accolade, applause, commendation, distinction, endorsement, homage, honor, kudos, laud

反 denunciation, excoriation, rebuke, reprimand, reproach, reproof, stricture 谴责，责难

crow [kroʊ]

【考法1】 *vi.* 感到高兴：to feel or express **joy or triumph**

例 Being the home of the new Super Bowl champs was the first thing that city residents had to crow about in a very long time. 当地的队伍获得超级碗美式足球冠军赛是长期以来让这个城市居民感到高兴的第一件事情。

近 delight, exuberate, glory, jubilate, joy, rejoice, triumph

反 bemoan, bewail, grieve, lament, weep 感到悲伤，叹息

【考法2】 *vi.* 自鸣得意：to praise or express **pride in one's own possessions**, qualities, or accomplishments often to excess

例 He is already crowing over his victory. 他已经在那里为自己的胜利而自鸣得意了。

近 blow, brag, swagger, vapor, vaunt

damn [dæm]

【考法1】 *vt.* (在道德上)谴责：to declare to be **morally wrong or evil**

例 a cleric who damned gambling and strong drink 一位严厉谴责赌博和酗酒的牧师

近 anathematize, censure, decry, denounce, execrate, reprehend, reprobate

反 bless, eulogize, exalt, extol, glorify, laud, praise 赞颂

【考法2】 *adv.* 非常地，极其地：to a **great degree**

例 Let's have a damn good party. 让我们尽情享乐狂欢吧。

近 deadly, desperately, exceedingly, extremely, greatly, heavily, highly, incredibly, really, seriously, very

反 little, negligibly, nominally, slightly, somewhat 一点点，稍微

dampen [ˈdæmpən]

【考法1】 *vt.* (特指稍稍地)弄湿：to make or become slightly or moderately **wet**

例 dampen a paper towel with water and use it to clean up the mess 把纸巾弄湿用来清洁

近 bedew, damp, douse, drench, impregnate, saturate, soak, souse, steep

反 dehydrate, desiccate, dry, parch, scorch, sear 使脱水，烤干

【考法2】 *vt.* 抑制，压抑(感情、精力等)，泼冷水：to check or **diminish the feeling, activity or vigor** of

例 Nothing could dampen their enthusiasm. 没有什么能扼杀他们的激情。‖ The oppressive heat dampened our spirits. 让人难以忍受的酷暑让我们精神不振。

近 benumb, blunt, castrate, deaden, devitalize, enervate, geld, lobotomize, petrify

反 brace, energize, enliven, invigorate, quicken, stimulate, vitalize, vivify 使充满活力

dashing [ˈdæʃɪŋ]

【考法】 *adj.* 爱好冒险的，大胆的：inclined or willing to **take risks**

例 the dashing heroes in stories about the American West 美国西部故事中那些勇敢无畏的英雄

近 adventurous, audacious, daring, emboldened, enterprising, gutsy, nerved, nervy, venturous

反 cowardly, craven, pusillanimous, timid, timorous 胆小的

Unit 4

dated ['deɪtɪd]

【考法】 *adj.* 过时的：having **passed its time of use** or usefulness; out-of-date

例 His jokes are awfully dated, referring to things that happened years ago. 他的笑话全是些关于几年前的事情的过时货。

近 antiquated, archaic, fossilized, medieval, moribund, moth-eaten, obsolete, outdated, outmoded, outworn, prehistoric, rusty

反 contemporary, current, modern, recent 当前的，现代的

deadlock ['dedlɑːk]

【考法1】 *n.* 僵局：**a state of inaction or neutralization** resulting from the opposition of equally powerful uncompromising persons or factions

例 The deadlock was broken with a key compromise. 一个关键性的妥协打破了僵局。

近 gridlock, halt, impasse, logjam, stalemate, standoff, standstill

【考法2】 *vt.* 使陷入僵局，使停顿：to bring or come **to a deadlock**

反 expedite 加速进程

debonair [ˌdebə'ner]

【考法1】 *adj.* 无忧无虑的，不在乎的：having or showing **freedom from worries or troubles**

例 His debonair dismissal of my inquiry concerning his financial situation led me to believe that nothing was wrong. 对于我提出的有关他个人财务状况的问题，他表现得毫不担忧，这使我相信(他的财务)确实没有出问题。

近 blithe, carefree, gay, insouciant, lighthearted, lightsome, slaphappy, unconcerned

反 careworn 焦虑的

【考法2】 *adj.* 风度翩翩的：having or showing very **polished and worldly manners**

例 The debonair gentleman charmed all of the ladies in the room. 风度翩翩的绅士吸引了房间里的所有女士。

近 civilized, graceful, polished, refined, smooth, sophisticated, suave, svelte, urbane

反 boorish, churlish, loutish, uncouth 粗鲁的，粗野的；clumsy, gauche, graceless 笨拙的

decadent ['dekədənt]

【考法1】 *adj.* 堕落的，腐败的：having or showing **lowered moral character** or standards

例 Opponents of gambling casinos claim that gambling is a decadent form of entertainment. 赌场的反对者们宣称赌博是一种堕落腐化的娱乐形式。

近 debased, debauched, degenerate, depraved, dissolute, perverse, perverted, reprobate, warped

反 pure, uncorrupted 纯净的，未腐化的

【考法2】 *n.* 放纵的人：a person whose life is **devoted to luxury and sensual pleasures**

例 a decadent who squandered her once considerable family fortune 一个挥霍了大量家族财富的人

近 debauchee, hedonist, libertine, sensualist, sybarite, profligate

反 ascetic 苦行者，禁欲者

【考法3】 *n.* 道德上堕落的人：a person in a condition or process of mental or **moral decay**

例 avant-garde artists who were scorned by the bourgeoisie as talentless decadents 被中产阶级鄙视为没有才华的堕落者的前卫艺术家

近 deviate

反 saint 圣人

· decry [dɪ'kraɪ]

【考法】 *vt.* 强烈反对，否定：to express **strong disapproval** of

例 Scientists were quick to decry the claims of the psychic. 通灵者的说法很快就遭到了科学家的反对。decry the excessive emphasis on sex 谴责对于性的过分重视

近 belittle, denigrate, denounce, deprecate, depreciate, derogate, disapprove, dismiss, disparage, minimize

反 acclaim, applaud, exalt, extol, glorify, laud, magnify, praise 表扬，称颂

deflect [dɪ'flekt]

【考法】 *vt.* 使偏斜，使转向：to **turn aside** especially **from a straight course** or fixed direction

例 The goalie deflected the ball with his hands. 守门员用双手将球击出。‖ They are trying to deflect the public attention from the troubled economy. 他们试图将公众的注意力从经济的困境中转移开。

近 divert, redirect, swing, veer, wheel, whip

派 deflection *n.* 偏转，偏离

defray [dɪˈfreɪ]

【考法】 *vt.* 支付: to **undertake the payment** of

例 The government has committed billions toward defraying the costs of the war. 政府为战争付出了数十亿元的代价。‖ I don't have sufficient fund to defray the expense. 我身上的现金不够买单。

近 disburse, expend, pay

反 acquire, earn, gain, garner, procure, realize, secure, win 获得，获取；charge 收取

deign [deɪn]

【考法】 *vi.* （不情愿地）屈尊，俯就: to **condescend reluctantly** and with a strong sense of the affront to one's superiority that is involved

例 I would never deign to answer that absurd accusation. 我根本不屑于去解释那样一个荒谬的指责。

近 condescend, stoop

delegate [ˈdelɪɡət]

【考法 1】 *n.* 代理人，代表: a person authorized to act as **representative for another**

例 The real estate developer sent a delegate to the town meeting to represent his interests. 房地产开发商派了一名能代表自己利益的代理前往镇上开会。‖ the U.N. delegates from African countries 非洲国家的驻联合国代表

近 agent, assignee, commissary, deputy, emissary, envoy, legate, minister, proxy, representative

派 delegation *n.* 代表团

【考法 2】 *vt.* 移交（权力、任务等）: to put（something）into the **possession or safekeeping of another**

例 The manager is reluctant to delegate authority to subordinates while abroad. 经理不愿意在国外期间将自己的权力转交给下级。

近 commit, confide, consign, deliver, entrust, repose, transfer, transmit, vest, give over, hand over, turn over

反 hold, keep, retain 保持，持有

delineate [dɪˈlɪnieɪt]

【考法 1】 *vt.* 勾勒，用线条描绘: to indicate or represent **by drawn or painted lines**

例 lights delineating the narrow streets 勾勒狭窄街道线条的路灯

近 define, silhouette, sketch, trace

【考法 2】 *vt.* 描写，描绘: to **describe**, **portray**, or set forth with accuracy or in detail

例 delineate the steps to be taken by the government 具体描述了政府所应该采取的措施 ‖ The film does a remarkable job of delineating the emotions that immigrants feel upon their arrival in a strange country. 这部电影成功地描绘了移民者踏上陌生国土时的心情。

近 depict, display, draw, image, limn, paint, picture, portray, render

反 color, distort, falsify, garble, misrepresent, misstate, pervert, twist, warp 曲解，篡改本意

派 delineation *n.* 描绘

Unit 5

■ DEMOTE	■ DEPENDABLE	■ DEPLORABLE	■ DESPERATE	■ DICHOTOMY
■ DICTATE	■ DIKE	■ DISCREET	■ DISENCHANT	■ DISHEARTEN

demote [ˌdiːˈmoʊt]

【考法】 *vt.* 降职，降级: to reduce to **a lower grade** or rank

例 The court-martial's decision was to demote the officer responsible for the failed mission. 军事法庭决定对为此次任务失败负责的军官进行降职处理。

近 break, bust, degrade, disrate, downgrade, reduce

反 advance, elevate, promote, raise 提升，晋升

派 demotion *n.* 降职

dependable [dɪˈpendəbl]

【考法】 *adj.* 可靠的，值得信赖的: capable of being **depended on**

例 a dependable source of income 可靠的收入来源 ‖ He was a good friend and a dependable companion. 他是一个好朋友，一个值得信赖的好伙伴。

近 calculable, reliable, responsible, safe, secure, solid, trustable, trustworthy

反 undependable, unreliable, unsafe, untrustworthy 不值得信赖的

deplorable [dɪˈplɔːrəbl]

【考法 1】 *adj.* 可鄙的，可耻的: worthy of severe **condemnation or reproach**

例 We will not tolerate such deplorable behavior in a house of worship. 我们绝不能容许这样一种可鄙的行为出现在礼拜堂中。

近 despicable, dirty, grubby, lousy, mean, nasty, paltry, scurvy, wretched

反 admirable, commendable, creditable, laudable, meritorious, praiseworthy 值得表扬的

【考法2】 *adj.* 悲惨的，可悲的：of a kind to **cause great distress**

例 Many of them work under deplorable conditions. 许多人的工作环境十分悲惨。

近 distressful, distressing, grievous, heartbreaking, heartrending, lamentable, tragic, unfortunate, woeful

desperate [ˈdespərət]

【考法】 *adj.* 绝望的：feeling or showing **no hope**

例 a desperate spirit crying for relief 一个渴望宽慰的绝望的灵魂

近 despondent, despairing, forlorn, hopeless

反 hopeful, optimistic 充满希望的，乐观的

dichotomy [daɪˈkɑːtəmi]

【考法】 *n.* 一分为二，分割：a **division into two** especially mutually exclusive or contradictory groups or entities

例 a dichotomy between the academic world and the industrial world 学术界和工业界的割裂

近 bifurcation, breakup, cleavage, division, fractionalization, partition, schism, scission, split, sundering

反 unification, union 统一

dictate [ˈdɪkteɪt]

【考法1】 *n.* 指令，命令：a **command** by one in authority

例 follow the dictates of my conscience 遵从我的良心准则 ‖ The army must abide by the dictates of the new government. 军队必须服从新政府的命令。

近 behest, charge, commandment, decree, direction, directive, edict, imperative, injunction, instruction, order

【考法2】 *vt.* (仗着地位、权力) 下令：to **request** the doing of by virtue of one's authority

例 The general dictated that the terms of surrender be negotiated by his senior staff. 将军下令投降书中的若干条款由手下的高级将领进行讨论。

近 call, decree, direct, impose, mandate, ordain, order, prescribe

反 cancel, countermand, rescind 撤销命令

派 dictator *n.* 独裁者

dike [daɪk]

【考法1】 *n.* 堤坝，水坝：a bank usually of earth constructed to **control or confine water**

例 An elaborate system of dikes was built to protect the lowlands from the relentless onslaught of the sea. 建立了一套精密复杂的堤坝系统，使低地不再受到海水的无情侵袭。

近 dam, embankment, levee

【考法2】 *n.* 水沟，水渠：a **long narrow channel** dug in the earth

例 Water flowed along the dike to the small pond. 水沿着沟渠流入小池塘。

近 ditch, gutter, trench

discreet [dɪˈskriːt]

【考法1】 *adj.* (言行) 谨慎的：having or showing **good judgment and restraint** especially in conduct or speech

例 He was very discreet, only saying what was necessary. 他是个十分谨慎的人，从来不说多余的话。

近 intelligent, judicious, prudent

反 imprudent, indiscreet, injudicious 不谨慎的

【考法2】 *adj.* 不易察觉的：**not readily seen or noticed**

例 With a discreet gesture, she signaled to her husband that she was ready to leave the party. 她用一个不起眼的手势向丈夫暗示准备离开聚会。‖ follow at a discreet distance 远远地跟踪

近 inconspicuous, invisible, unnoticeable, unobtrusive

反 apparent, conspicuous, distinct, evident, manifest, noticeable, obvious, patent, visible 明显的

disenchant [ˌdɪsɪnˈtʃænt]

【考法】 *vt.* 使清醒：to **free from illusion**

例 If you thought that you could pass this course without doing any work, let me be the first to disenchant you. 如果你觉得你不做任何功课也能及格，那就让我做第一个让你清醒的人。

近 disabuse, undeceive

反 beguile, cozen, delude, dupe, fool, gull, hoax, hoodwink, misguide, misinform, mislead 诱骗

dishearten [dɪsˈhɑːrtn]

【考法】 *vt.* 使沮丧，使失去信心：to cause to **lose spirit or morale**

例 We were greatly disheartened by the news that our grandmother was seriously ill. 听到祖母病重的消息，我们都很沮丧。

近 chill, daunt, demoralize, discourage, dismay, dispirit, frustrate, unnerve

反 embolden, encourage, hearten, nerve, steel 使大胆，鼓励

Unit 6

■ DISJUNCTIVE　　■ DISPROVE　　■ DISTINCTIVE　　■ DOCTRINAIRE　　■ DOMINEER
■ DRAB　　■ DRAMATIC　　■ DREAD　　■ DUPLICATE　　■ DYNAMIC

disjunctive ［dɪs'dʒʌŋktɪv］
【考法】 *adj.*分离的：marked by **breaks or disunity**
例 a disjunctive narrative sequence 散乱的叙述顺序
反 conjunctive, connective 连接的
派 disjunction *n.* 分离

disprove ［,dɪs'pruːv］
【考法】 *vt.*反驳，证明为假：to **prove to be false** or wrong
例 Magellan's circumnavigation of the globe disproved any lingering notions that the earth is flat. 麦哲伦的环球旅行彻底反驳了任何残存的"地球是平的"的观念。
近 belie, confound, confute, debunk, disconfirm, discredit, falsify, rebut, refute, shoot down
反 confirm, establish, prove, validate, verify 证实，证明为真

distinctive ［dɪ'stɪŋktɪv］
【考法 1】 *adj.*完全不同的：being **not of the same kind**
例 She seems to alternate between two distinctive hairstyles. 她的发型似乎在两种截然不同的样式中变换。
近 disparate, dissimilar, distant, distinct, distinguishable, diverse, unalike, unlike
反 identical, indistinguishable, same 相同的；alike, analogous, kindred, like, parallel, similar 相似的
派 distinction *n.* 区别，差别
【考法 2】 *adj.*特征性的，典型的：**serving to identify** as belonging to an individual or group
例 Jerusalem has a distinctive Middle East flavor. 耶路撒冷有着典型的中东风情。
近 characteristic, classic, diagnostic, discriminating, distinguishing, identifying, peculiar, symptomatic, typical
反 atypical, uncharacteristic, untypical 非典型的

doctrinaire ［,dɑːktrə'ner］
【考法】 *adj.*教条主义的，照本宣科的：given to or marked by the forceful expression of **strongly held opinions**
例 A doctrinaire conservative, the columnist takes special delight in baiting liberals. 这个专栏作家是个谨遵教条的顽固保守主义者，他很享受挑衅那些自由主义者的感觉。
近 dogmatic
反 latitudinarian（宗教方面）能容纳不同意见的

domineer ［,dɑːmə'nɪr］
【考法】 *vt.*专制统治：to exercise arbitrary or **overbearing control**
例 Her husband and mother-in-law domineer her. 她生活在她丈夫和婆婆的高压统治下。
近 tyrannize
派 domineering *adj.* 专横的，盛气凌人的

drab ［dræb］
【考法】 *adj.*单调的，无聊的：characterized by **dullness and monotony**
例 The new city hall turned out to be another drab pile of masonry for the town. 新的市政大厅结果又是城镇里一座单调无趣的砖瓦堆积物。
近 arid, dreary, drudging, humdrum, jading, jejune, monochromatic, monotonous, pedestrian, ponderous, stale, stodgy, tedious, tiresome, wearisome
反 absorbing, engaging, engrossing, gripping, interesting, intriguing, involving, riveting 令人感兴趣的

dramatic ［drə'mætɪk］
【考法】 *adj.*显著的，惹人注意的：**striking** in appearance or effect
例 a dramatic drop in the temperature overnight 夜晚气温的显著下降
近 arresting, bold, brilliant, catchy, conspicuous, flamboyant, prominent, remarkable, splashy, striking
反 discreet, inconspicuous, invisible, subtle, unnoticeable, unobtrusive 不易引起注意的
派 dramatically *adv.* 显著地

dread ［dred］
【考法】 *n.*恐惧：great **fear** especially in the face of impending evil
例 We were filled with dread when we saw the rapids we would be rafting down. 当我们看到竹筏驶向激流时，我们的内心被恐惧所占据。
近 alarm, apprehension, consternation, fear, fright, horror, terror, trepidation
反 bravery, courage, dauntlessness, fearlessness, fortitude, intrepidity, stoutness, valor 勇气，无畏
派 dreadful *adj.* 令人恐惧的

duplicate

【考法 1】 [ˈduːplɪkət] *n.* 复制品：either of two things **exactly alike** and usually produced at the same time or by the same process

例 a duplicate of a house key 房间钥匙的复制品 ‖ Your computer is almost a duplicate of mine. 你的电脑和我的几乎一模一样。

近 copy, dupe, duplication, facsimile, imitation, mock, reduplication, replica, replication, reproduction

反 archetype, original, prototype 原型

【考法 2】 [ˈduːplɪkeɪt] *vt.* 复制：to **make a copy** of

例 A cell duplicates itself when it divides. 当一个细胞分裂时，它会完全按着自己的样子复制。‖ Art students are trying to duplicate paintings in the museum's collection as part of their training. 艺术生们正在努力临摹博物馆中的作品，作为他们训练的一部分。

近 clone, copycat, imitate, reduplicate, render, replicate, reproduce

反 originate 原创

派 duplicable *adj.* 可模仿的

【考法 3】 *vt.* 重复，反复：to **do over or again** often needlessly

例 We were unable to duplicate the experiment with the same result in our own lab, so we're suspicious. 我们不能在自己的实验室中重复之前的实验并得到相同的结果，因此我们很怀疑。

近 redo, reiterate, renew, repeat

dynamic [daɪˈnæmɪk]

【考法】 *adj.* 有力量的，有活力的：marked by usually continuous and **productive activity** or change; energetic

例 He has become a dynamic new challenger for the title of champion. 他成为了有望冲击冠军、有活力的新选手。‖ a dynamic speech expressing her goals and values 宣扬她的目标和理念的慷慨激昂的演讲

近 brisk, energetic, flush, forceful, gingery, kinetic, lusty, peppy, robust, sprightly, vital, vivacious

反 dull, lethargic, listless, sluggish, torpid 无精打采的

Unit 7

■ ECLECTIC	■ EFFICACIOUS	■ ELUDE	■ ENAMORED	■ ENDEAVOR
■ ENTHRALL	■ EQUILIBRIUM	■ ERRONEOUS	■ ESCORT	■ ETHOS

eclectic [ɪˈklektɪk]

【考法】 *adj.* 混合的，多元化的：composed of elements drawn **from various sources**

例 The museum's eclectic collection has everything from a giraffe skeleton to medieval musical instruments. 博物馆里的展品丰富多样，从长颈鹿的骨架到中世纪的乐器都有。

近 assorted, diverse, heterogeneous, indiscriminate, magpie, mixed, motley, piebald, ragtag, varied

反 homogeneous, uniform 同一性的

efficacious [ˌefɪˈkeɪʃəs]

【考法】 *adj.* 有效的：having the power to **produce a desired effect**

例 Taking break with a cup of coffee while studying is one of the most efficacious ways of rejuvenating the mind that I have ever discovered. 在紧张的学习中休息一会，喝杯咖啡，是我发现的最能提神的方法之一。

近 effective, effectual, efficient, fruitful, operative, potent, productive

反 bootless, fruitless, ineffective, ineffectual, inefficient, inoperative, unproductive, useless 无效的

elude [iˈluːd]

【考法 1】 *vt.* 躲闪，躲避：to **avoid adroitly**

例 manage to elude capture 成功躲过追捕 ‖ The millionaire had been eluding his fair share of taxes for years before getting caught. 在被逮捕之前，这名百万富翁逃税已经有若干年了。

近 avoid, dodge, duck, eschew, evade, finesse, scape, shirk, shun, sidestep, weasel

反 confront 直面，面对

【考法 2】 *vt.* 使无法理解，使困惑：to **escape the perception**, understanding, or grasp of

例 a metaphor that eluded them 一个让他们无法理解的比喻

近 baffle, befog, befuddle, bewilder, confound, discombobulate, disorient, maze, mystify, perplex, puzzle, vex

反 clarify, elucidate, explicate, expound, illuminate, illustrate 解释，阐明

派 elusive *adj.* 隐秘的；难懂的

enamored [ɪˈnæmərd]

【考法】 *adj.* 迷恋的，热爱的：filled with an **intense or excessive love** for

例 Many teenage girls became enamored of the movie idol for her boyish good looks. 很多年轻的女孩子因为该影星男性化的帅气面庞而对她深深迷恋。

近 besotted, bewitched, captivated, crazy, dotty, enraptured, fascinated, infatuated, mad, nuts, obsessed

反 apathetic, detached, indifferent, insouciant, nonchalant 无所谓的，冷漠的

endeavor [ɪnˈdevər]

【考法 1】 *n.* 努力，奋斗：a **conscientious or concerted effort** toward an end

例 We hope that this latest endeavor will yield much information about the atmosphere of the planet. 我们希望这最后一次的努力能够获取关于该行星大气层的大量信息。

近 attempt, essay, striving, struggle, trial, undertaking

【考法 2】 *vt.* 努力做，拼搏：to **devote serious and sustained effort**

例 endeavor to improve the quality of life in the inner city 努力改善市内的生活质量 ‖ They endeavored to create a government that truly serves its people. 他们在努力地创立一个一心为人民服务的政府。

近 assay, drudge, hustle, moil, plod, slave, strain, strive, sweat, seek, toil, travail, tug

反 drop, quit 放弃

enthrall [ɪnˈθrɔːl]

【考法】 *vt.* (像用魔咒般)吸引：to **hold the attention** of as if by a spell

例 Enthralled by the flickering aurora in the sky, we lost all track of time. 我们被夜空里变化莫测的极光深深地吸引，以至于忘却了时间。

近 absorb, arrest, bedazzle, enchant, engross, fascinate, grip, hypnotize, immerse, mesmerize, spellbind

反 bore, jade, pall, tire, weary 使厌恶，使厌倦

派 enthralling *adj.* 吸引人的

equilibrium [ˌiːkwɪˈlɪbriəm]

【考法 1】 *n.* 均势，平衡：a condition in which **opposing forces are equal** to one another

例 We must find an equilibrium between commercial development and conservation of our natural treasures. 我们必须在发展经济和保护自然资源之间找到一个平衡点。

近 counterpoise, equilibration, equipoise, poise, stasis

反 disequilibration, disequilibrium, imbalance, nonequilibrium, unbalance 不平衡

【考法 2】 *n.* (感情上的)平静：**evenness of emotions** or temper

例 That stunning insult left me speechless, and several minutes passed before I recovered my equilibrium. 那个令人震惊的侮辱弄得我哑口无言，我花了好几分钟才使心情得以平静。

近 aplomb, calmness, composure, countenance, imperturbability, placidity, repose, sangfroid, serenity, tranquillity

反 agitation, discomposure, perturbation 不安，焦躁

erroneous [ɪˈrouniəs]

【考法】 *adj.* 错误的，不正确的：**containing** or characterized by **error**

例 The news article about the new drug was filled with much erroneous information. 有关新药的新闻报道里充斥着大量的错误信息。

近 inaccurate, incorrect, inexact, invalid, mistaken, unsound, untrue, untruthful, wrong

反 accurate, correct, errorless, exact, precise, right, sound, true, valid, veracious 正确的，准确的

escort

【考法 1】 [ˈeskɔːrt] *n.* 护卫队，护送者：a person or group of persons **accompanying another** to give protection or as a courtesy

例 The mayor served as the First Lady's escort for her tour of the city. 市长陪同第一夫人参观了城市。

近 attendant, companion, guard, guide

【考法 2】 [ɪˈskɔːrt] *vt.* 同行，护送：to **go along with** in order to provide assistance, protection, or companionship

例 A senior student from the college escorted my parents and me on our tour of the campus. 来自学院的一个师兄陪同我和我父母参观了校园。‖ a VIP escorted by an army of bodyguards and journalists 被一群保镖和记者包围的重要人物

近 accompany, attend, chaperone, companion, company, convoy, squire

反 abandon, desert, ditch, dump, forsake 抛弃，不顾

ethos [ˈiːθɑːs]

【考法】 *n.* 道德准则：the **code of good conduct** for an individual or group

例 Rigorous self-discipline was central to the ethos of the ancient Spartans. 严格的自律是古代斯巴达人所尊崇的核心道德准则。

近 ethics, morality, morals, norms, principles, standards

Unit 8

■ EXORCISE   ■ EXPLICATE   ■ EXTERMINATE   ■ EXTRAPOLATE   ■ FABULOUS
■ FAD   ■ FALLIBLE   ■ FANCIFUL   ■ FAVORITISM   ■ FEATURELESS

exorcise [ˈeksɔːrsaɪz]

【考法】 *vt.* 除去：to **get rid of** (something troublesome, menacing, or oppressive)

例 Please exorcise that offensive word from your vocabulary. 请把那个粗鲁的词从你的字典里删掉。

近 cashier, cast, ditch, dump, fling, jettison, lose, pitch, reject, scrap, shed, slough, throw, toss, unload
反 adopt, employ, use, utilize 采用，使用
派 exorcism *n.* 除魔，驱鬼

explicate [ˈeksplɪkeɪt]
【考法】 *vt.* 解释，说明：to give a **detailed explanation** of
例 The physicist did his best to explicate the wave theory of light for the audience of laymen. 物理学家尽其所能向一群非专业的听众解释了光的波动性理论。
近 clarify, clear, construe, demonstrate, demystify, elucidate, explain, expound, illuminate, illustrate, interpret, simplify, unriddle
反 obscure 使晦涩
派 explication *n.* 解释

exterminate [ɪkˈstɜːrmɪneɪt]
【考法】 *vt.* 根除，消灭：to get rid of completely usually by **killing off**
例 We hope that the fumigant exterminates the whole colony of cockroaches, for any survivors may be resistant to any poison. 我们希望所有的蟑螂都能被这种杀虫熏剂根除，因为任何幸存者都可能产生抗药性。
近 annihilate, decimate, efface, eradicate, expunge, extirpate, liquidate, obliterate, raze, sweep, wipe out
反 conserve, preserve, protect 保护；rescue, save 拯救
派 extermination *n.* 消灭

extrapolate [ɪkˈstræpəleɪt]
【考法】 *vt.* (通过逻辑)推断：to form an **opinion** or reach a conclusion **through reasoning** and information
例 We can extrapolate from past economic recessions the probable course of the current one. 通过以往经济衰退我们可以推断出本次危机的可能发展趋势。
近 conclude, decide, deduce, derive, gather, judge, reason, understand
反 conjecture, guess, speculate, surmise (无根据地)猜测，揣测
派 extrapolation *n.* 推论

fabulous [ˈfæbjələs]
【考法1】 *adj.* 传说中的：based on, described in, or being a **fable**
例 The city of Phoenix is named after a fabulous bird that every 500 years destroys itself with fire, only to rise again from its own ashes. 凤凰城的名字来源于传说中的一种鸟，它每隔 500 年会在火焰中自我毁灭，然后再从灰烬中重生。
近 fabled, legendary
【考法2】 *adj.* 幻想中的，不真实的：not real and existing only **in the imagination**
例 a story of a fabulous land where the people know nothing of war and live together in perfect harmony 一个有关世外桃源的故事，当地的居民不知道战争为何物，和谐融洽地生活在一起
近 chimerical, dreamy, illusory, phantom, unreal, visionary
反 actual, existent, existing, real 真实存在的
【考法3】 *adj.* 令人惊讶的，令人称奇的：**causing wonder** or astonishment
例 the fabulous endurance of a marathon runner 马拉松参赛者令人惊讶的耐力
近 amazing, astonishing, astounding, miraculous, portentous, prodigious, staggering, stunning, stupendous, sublime, wonderful
反 common, ordinary 平常的，普通的
【考法4】 *adj.* 极好的：**extremely pleasing** or successful
例 We had a fabulous time on our vacation. 我们的假期赞极了。
近 awesome, divine, fantastic, heavenly, marvelous, noble, prime, splendid, superb, superior, terrific
反 atrocious, awful, execrable, lousy, pathetic, poor, rotten, terrible, wretched 极差劲的

fad [fæd]
【考法】 *n.* (短暂的)流行，时尚：a practice or interest that is very **popular for a short time**
例 Once the fad for that kind of music had passed, nobody would have been caught dead listening to it. 一旦那种流派的音乐流行风刮过之后，就没有人会来听它出丑了。
近 buzz, craze, enthusiasm, fashion, trend, vogue
反 classic 经典；standard 标准

fallible [ˈfæləbl]
【考法】 *adj.* 可能出错的：tending or likely to be **erroneous** or capable of making an error
例 They are only human and all too fallible. 他们都是人类，因此难免犯错。|| a hasty, fallible generalization 有可能出错的仓促结论
近 errant
反 fail-safe, foolproof, infallible, unfailing 万无一失的，不可能出错的
派 fallibility *n.* 易错

fanciful [ˈfænsɪfl]

【考法 1】 *adj.* 幻想中的，不真实的: not real and existing only **in the imagination**

例 a fanciful tale of a monster in the woods 一个有关栖息在丛林中的怪兽的传说故事

近 chimerical, fabulous, fantastic, fictional, fictitious, ideal, invented, mythical, notional, phantom, visionary

反 actual, existent, existing, real 真实存在的

【考法 2】 *adj.* 不切实际的，荒谬的: conceived or made **without regard for reason** or reality

例 She harbors the fanciful notion that she has a talent for singing. 她怀着一个不切实际的空想: 她有着歌唱家的天赋。

近 absurd, bizarre, crazy, foolish, insane, nonsensical, preposterous, unreal, wild

反 realistic, reasonable 现实的，有理的

favoritism [ˈfeɪvərɪtɪzəm]

【考法】 *n.* 偏爱，偏袒: the showing of **special favor**

例 Favoritism blinded the administrator to the benefits of the proposed system for distributing work. 偏袒使得经理无法意识到这一待讨论的分配系统所带来的收益。

近 favor, one-sidedness, partiality, prejudice, tendentiousness

反 impartiality, neutrality, objectivity, open-mindedness, unbiasedness 公平，公正

featureless [ˈfiːtʃərləs]

【考法】 *adj.* 缺乏特征的: **lacking distinguishing characteristics** or features

例 the featureless landscape of the steppe 大草原上缺乏特色的地貌

近 beige, characterless, faceless, indistinctive, neutral, noncommittal, vanilla

反 diagnostic, discriminating, distinct, distinctive, distinguishing, identifying, peculiar, typical 特征的

Unit 9

■ FEISTY	■ FELONY	■ FEROCIOUS	■ FERVENT	■ FIGMENT
■ FITFUL	■ FLEETING	■ FORAGE	■ FOREBODE	■ FOREGROUND

feisty [ˈfaɪsti]

【考法】 *adj.* 好斗的，好争论的: having or showing a lively **aggressiveness**

例 At 66, she was as feisty as ever. 尽管已经 66 岁高龄，她还是一样好斗。

近 aggressive, agonistic, assaultive, bellicose, belligerent, combative, contentious, disputatious, gladiatorial, militant, quarrelsome, truculent

反 pacific, peaceful, peace-loving 热爱和平的

felony [ˈfeləni]

【考法】 *n.* 重罪: one of several **grave crimes**, such as murder, rape, or burglary, punishable by a more stringent sentence than that given for a misdemeanor

例 a felony punishable by life imprisonment 可被判处无期徒刑的重罪

近 crime

反 misdemeanor, peccadillo 轻罪

ferocious [fəˈroʊʃəs]

【考法 1】 *adj.* 极端的，剧烈的: marked by **unrelenting intensity**

例 Ferocious heat wave kept people indoor. 剧烈的热浪使人不能出门。

近 dreadful, excruciating, explosive, fearsome, fierce, intensive, profound, vehement, violent

反 light, moderate, soft 轻柔的

【考法 2】 *adj.* 激烈的，爆发性的: marked by **bursts of destructive force** or intense activity

例 Ferocious forest fires threatened to destroy hundreds of homes in the scrubland. 肆虐的森林大火威胁着灌木丛林地中数百户居民的住所。

近 cyclonic, explosive, furious, paroxysmal, rabid, stormy, tempestuous, tumultuous, turbulent, volcanic

反 nonviolent, peaceable, peaceful 平静的，平和的

【考法 3】 *adj.* 凶猛的，残暴的: violently **unfriendly or aggressive** in disposition

例 captured and slaughtered by the ferocious tribesmen 被残暴的部落居民所抓获并惨遭屠杀

近 feral, grim, savage, vicious

反 gentle, mild, unaggressive 温和的，不具攻击性的

派 ferocity *n.* 凶猛，残暴

fervent	[ˈfɜːrvənt]
【考法】	*adj.* 充满感情的，热情洋溢的：exhibiting or marked by **great intensity of feeling**
例	a fervent speech that called for tolerance and compassion for those who are physically challenged 一个充满热情的演说，它呼吁人们对残疾人持有一颗包容和同情的心
近	ardent, demonstrative, fervid, flaming, glowing, impassioned, incandescent, passionate, perfervid, torrid, vehement, zealous
反	cold, cool, dispassionate, emotionless, impassive, unemotional 冷漠的

figment	[ˈfɪgmənt]
【考法】	*n.* 虚构的事物，幻觉：something **made up** or contrived
例	Unable to find any tracks in the snow the next morning, I was forced to conclude that the shadowy figure had been a figment of my imagination. 第二天一早，我没有在雪地上发现任何足迹，由此我不得不相信昨晚幽灵一样的物体只是我的空想。‖ Thus far, the invisible human being has been nothing more than a figment of fantasy writers. 到目前为止，隐形人还仅仅是玄幻小说作家笔下的构想。
近	chimera, conceit, daydream, delusion, dream, fancy, fantasy, hallucination, illusion, phantasm, vision
反	fact, materiality, reality 客观存在的事物

fitful	[ˈfɪtfl]
【考法】	*adj.* 无规律的，缺乏周期的：having an **erratic or intermittent** character
例	He drifted off into a fitful sleep. 他慢慢地陷入了时睡时醒的状态。
近	aperiodic, casual, discontinuous, episodic, erratic, intermittent, irregular, occasional, sporadic, unsteady
反	constant, continuous, incessant 持续不断的；periodic, regular, repeated 定期的

fleeting	[ˈfliːtɪŋ]
【考法】	*adj.* 稍纵即逝的，短暂的：lasting only **for a short time**; passing swiftly
例	They have been waiting for more than 4 hours but caught only a fleeting glimpse of the movie star. 他们苦等了四个多小时，却最终只匆匆地瞟到了电影明星一眼。
近	brief, ephemeral, evanescent, flash, fugitive, impermanent, passing, temporary, transient, transitory
反	ceaseless, deathless, eternal, everlasting, immortal, lasting, permanent, perpetual, timeless 永恒的

forage	[ˈfɔːrɪdʒ]
【考法】	*vi.* 寻找：to make a **search**
例	go foraging for change for the parking meter 寻找付停车费的零钱
近	chase, hunt, pursue, quest, rummage, search
反	ignore, neglect 忽视，忽略；conceal, hide 隐藏
派	forager *n.* 为动物寻找饲料的人

forebode	[fɔːrˈboʊd]
【考法】	*v.* 预示，预兆：to **show signs** of coming ill or misfortune
例	That police car parked outside the house doesn't forebode well. 门外停着的那辆警车可不是什么好兆头。
近	augur, predict, promise
派	foreboding *n.* 预感，预兆

foreground	[ˈfɔːrgraʊnd]
【考法】	*vt.* 强调，重视：to **indicate the importance** of by centering attention on
例	He repeatedly foregrounded his experience in international affairs in the course of his campaign for the presidency. 在竞选总统的过程中，他一再强调自己在处理国际事务方面的经验。‖ The lionization of Vladimir Nabokov as one of North America's literary giants has thrown the spotlight on his peripheral activities and has thus served to foreground his efforts as an amateur entomologist. 弗拉基米尔·纳博科夫被追捧为北美的文学巨匠之一，这使得他的其他生活方面也受到关注，例如他想成为业余昆虫学家的努力被不断提及。
近	accent, accentuate, emphasize, feature, highlight, illuminate, press, punctuate, stress
反	de-emphasize, understate, play down 轻描淡写

Unit 10

■ FORFEIT	■ FORSAKE	■ FROSTY	■ GAWKY	■ GERMINATE
■ GLACIAL	■ GLIDE	■ GLOWER	■ GRAFT	■ GRIT

forfeit	[ˈfɔːrfət]
【考法】	*n.* 罚金：a sum of money to be paid as a **punishment**
例	The forfeit for each baseball player involved in the brawl was $5,000. 参加打架的篮球运动员都受到了五千美元的罚款处理。
近	damages, fine, forfeiture, mulct, penalty
反	bonus, premium, prize 奖金

forsake [fərˈseɪk]

【考法】 *vt.* 彻底放弃，抛弃：to **renounce** or turn away from entirely

例 Forsaking most of our possessions, we evacuated just before the hurricane struck. 我们抛下了绝大多数的财产，终于在海啸来袭之前撤离了。 || Her boyfriend has forsaken her. 她的男朋友将她抛弃了。

近 abandon, desert, maroon, quit, renounce, strand

反 reclaim 重新获得；hold, keep, retain, withhold 保留

派 forsaken *adj.* 被抛弃的

frosty [ˈfrɔːsti]

【考法1】 *adj.* 寒冷的：having a **low** or subnormal **temperature**

例 a frosty autumn that was a sign of the brutal winter that followed 一个极为寒冷的秋天，它预示着随之而来的、可能更加冷酷的冬季

近 algid, arctic, bitter, chilling, coldish, cool, freezing, frigid, gelid, glacial, icy, nippy, numbing, polar, snappy

反 ardent, blazing, burning, fervent, fervid, molten, roasting, scalding, scorching, searing, sultry, sweltering, torrid 炎热的

【考法2】 *adj.* 无强烈感情的，冷淡的：lacking in friendliness or warmth of feeling

例 She gave the telemarketer on the phone a frosty "No, thank you" and hung up. 她向电话那头的推销员冷冷地说了一句"不，谢谢"之后就挂掉了电话。

近 antiseptic, apathetic, brittle, chilly, cold-blooded, frozen, indifferent, unfriendly, unsympathetic, wintry

反 cordial, friendly, genial, hearty, sympathetic, warm, warm-blooded, warmhearted 友善的，热心的

gawky [ˈɡɔːki]

【考法】 *adj.* (举止) 笨拙的：having or showing an **inability to move in a graceful manner**

例 The pathetic gawky woman was once a lithe ballerina but got severely injured in a car accident. 这个可怜的步态笨拙的妇女本来是一名轻巧优雅的芭蕾舞女演员，但是在一次车祸中受了重伤。

近 awkward, clumsy, gawkish, graceless, uncoordinated, ungainly

反 agile, graceful, lithe, nimble 灵巧的，敏捷的；elegant 优雅的

派 gawkiness *n.* 笨拙

germinate [ˈdʒɜːrmɪneɪt]

【考法1】 *vi.* 发芽：to **begin to grow**

例 Some seed varieties germinate very quickly. 有一些种子的变异体能够迅速发芽。

近 burgeon, shoot, sprout

反 fade, flag, wilt, wither 枯萎

派 germination *n.* 萌芽

【考法2】 *vi.* 出现：to **come into being**

例 A truly marvelous proof of this theorem germinated in his mind. 这个定理的一种绝妙证明方法浮现在他的脑海之中。

近 develop, evolve, grow

反 disappear, vanish 消逝，消失

glacial [ˈɡleɪʃiəl]

【考法1】 *adj.* 极冷的：**extremely cold**

例 The air from the sea felt glacial. 海上的空气冷极了。

近 algid, arctic, bitter, chilling, coldish, cool, freezing, frigid, frosty, gelid, icy, nippy, numbing, polar, snappy

反 ardent, blazing, burning, fervent, fervid, molten, roasting, scalding, scorching, searing, sultry, sweltering, torrid 炎热的

【考法2】 *adj.* 冷漠的，无感情的：**devoid of warmth** and cordiality

例 The Duchess gave him a glacial look and moved on. 公爵夫人冷冷地看了他一眼，然后就继续上路了。

近 antiseptic, apathetic, brittle, chilly, cold-blooded, frozen, indifferent, unfriendly, unsympathetic, wintry

反 cordial, friendly, genial, hearty, sympathetic, warm, warm-blooded, warmhearted 友善的，热心的

glide [ɡlaɪd]

【考法】 *v.* 轻松地行动，轻松地通过：to move or proceed **smoothly**, **continuously**, and **effortlessly**

例 swans gliding over the lake 在湖面悠然划水的天鹅 || looking for a college course that he could just glide through 正在寻找一门他很容易就能通过的课程

近 bowl, breeze, brush, coast, cruise, drift, roll, sail, skim, slide, slip, stream, sweep, whisk

反 flounder, struggle 挣扎

glower [ˈɡlaʊər]

【考法】 *vi.* 怒目而视：to look or **stare with** sullen annoyance or **anger**

例 Baseball fans glowered at their TVs as they watched their favorite team lose. 看着他们支持的球队输球，棒球迷们恶狠狠地盯着电视屏幕。 || He just glowered without speaking. 他一言不发地怒视着我。

近 glare, gloom, lower, scowl

反 beam, grin, smile 笑

graft [ɡræft]

【考法】 *vt.* 移植，移接：to **implant** (living tissue) **surgically** or as if surgically

例 The top layer of skin has to be grafted onto the burns. 顶层的皮肤需要被移植到烧伤的伤口上。‖ graft old traditions onto the new ones 把老传统移植到新的习俗中

近 implant, transplant

grit [ɡrɪt]

【考法】 *n.* （面对困难时所表现出来的）毅力：the strength of mind that enables a person to **endure pain or hardship**

例 She was an athlete with true grit, continuing her training despite bad weather and an injury. 她是一个有着惊人毅力的真正的运动员，即便是在受了伤外加天气恶劣的情况下仍然坚持训练。

近 backbone, constancy, fiber, grittiness, guts, intestinal fortitude, pluck, spunk

反 cowardliness, cravenness, gutlessness, pusillanimity, spinelessness 懦弱

We often hear of people breaking down from overwork, but in nine cases out of ten they are really suffering from worry or anxiety.

我们常常听人说，人们因工作过度而垮下来，但是实际上十有八九是因为饱受担忧或焦虑的折磨。

—— 英国银行家 卢伯克. J. (John Lubbock, British banker)

List 30*

Unit 1

■ GROGGY	■ GRUDGE	■ GRUMBLE	■ HALFHEARTED	■ HECKLE
■ HIERARCHICAL	■ HOBBLE	■ HUMDRUM	■ HUMILIATE	■ HYPOTHETICAL

groggy [ˈɡrɑːɡi]
【考法 1】 *adj.* 虚弱的，（走路）不稳的：**weak and unsteady** on the feet or in action
例 She was feeling a bit groggy when I saw her. 当我看到她的时候她显得有些走路不稳。
近 rickety, rocky, shaky, unbalanced, unsound, unstable, unsteady, wobbly
反 balanced, stable, steady, sound 平衡的，稳定的
【考法 2】 *adj.* 无法思考的，头脑不清的：**not able to think or move** normally because of being tired, sick, etc.
例 I'm still a little groggy from my nap. 我还没完全从睡梦中清醒过来。‖ The medicine sometimes makes patients groggy. 这种药偶尔会让病人感到头脑不清醒。
近 dazed, dopey, muddleheaded, muzzy, punch-drunk, punchy, stupefied, zonked, zonked-out
反 clearheaded, unconfused 头脑清楚的

grudge [ɡrʌdʒ]
【考法】 *n.* 怨恨，仇恨：a feeling of deep-seated resentment or **ill will**
例 There has been a grudge between the two families for years. 两家之间积怨已深。‖ He has had a deep grudge against her ever since she snubbed him at the dance. 自从她在舞会上对他不理不睬之后，他就对她怀有深深的怨念。
近 animosity, animus, antagonism, antipathy, bitterness, gall, hostility, jaundice, malice, rancor, resentment
反 amity 和睦，友好
派 grudging *adj.* 勉强的，不情愿的

grumble [ˈɡrʌmbl]
【考法】 *vi.* （尤指低声地）抱怨，埋怨：to **complain** in a surly manner; mutter discontentedly
例 The governed will always find something to grumble about. （Crane Brinton）被统治者总能找到发牢骚的理由。——克莱恩·布林顿
近 carp, croak, fuss, gripe, grouch, grouse, grump, moan, murmur, mutter, repine
反 crow, delight, rejoice 感到高兴

halfhearted [ˌhɑːf ˈhɑːrtɪd]
【考法】 *adj.* 不感兴趣的，不热情的：**lacking heart**, spirit, or interest
例 a halfhearted attempt to clean the house before the arrival of the in-laws 在亲家到来前草草地收拾房间了事
近 lukewarm, tepid, uneager, unenthusiastic
反 eager, enthusiastic, keen, passionate, warm 充满热情的；hearty, wholehearted 全心投入的

heckle [ˈhekl]
【考法】 *vt.* 起哄，使难堪：to **harass** and try to disconcert with questions, challenges, or gibes
例 a controversial singer who was constantly heckled by the fans 一个时常被粉丝起哄的有争议的歌手
Several protesters were heckling the speaker at the rally. 不少示威者在集会上起哄让发言者难堪。
近 badger, bait, hassle, haze, hector, needle, ride, taunt

hierarchical [ˌhaɪə ˈrɑːrkɪkl]
【考法】 *adj.* 分等级的，等级制的：**classified** according to various criteria into successive levels or layers
例 the traditional hierarchical system of military organization 军队中传统的等级制度
近 graded, graduated, ranked
派 hierarchy *n.* 等级制度

hobble [ˈhɑːbl]
【考法 1】 *vi.* 跛行，蹒跚而行：to walk or move along **haltingly or with difficulty**
例 She picked up her cane and hobbled across the room. 她拿起了手杖，一拐一拐地穿过房间。
近 falter, halt, limp, stagger, totter
反 stride 大步走

423

【考法 2】 *vt.* 阻碍，妨碍：to **hamper the action** or progress of

例　We were hobbled by the snowstorm from getting out to do some Christmas shopping. 暴风雪阻碍了我们圣诞购物的计划。

近　encumber, fetter, handicap, hamper, hinder, impede, inhibit, manacle, obstruct, shackle, stymie, trammel

反　aid, assist, facilitate 帮助

humdrum ['hʌmdrʌm]

【考法 1】 *n.* 千篇一律，单调：a tedious **lack of variety**

例　She has been loathing the humdrum of daily life in a small town for a long time. 一直以来她对小城镇里一成不变的生活都感到厌倦。

近　monotone, monotonousness, sameness

反　diversity, variety 多样性

【考法 2】 *adj.* 无聊的，乏味的：**lacking** variety or **excitement**

例　trapped in a humdrum but well-paid job 陷于无聊但是收入可观的工作之中

近　arid, drab, dreary, drudging, jading, jejune, monochromatic, monotonous, pedestrian, ponderous, stale, stodgy, tedious, tiresome, wearisome

反　absorbing, engaging, engrossing, gripping, interesting, intriguing, involving, riveting, thrilling 令人感兴趣的

humiliate [hjuːˈmɪlieɪt]

【考法】 *vt.* 羞辱，使丧失尊严：to reduce **to a lower position** in one's own eyes or others' eyes

例　No student feels humiliated for not having the "right" clothes because everyone is wearing a school uniform. 因为所有学生都统一穿着学校的校服，所以没有人会因为"不正确"的衣着而感觉尊严扫地。‖ He humiliated me in front of my parents and I swear to retaliate. 他在我的父母面前让我难堪，我发誓要报复他。

近　abase, chasten, cheapen, debase, degrade, demean, discredit, disgrace, dishonor, shame, sink, smirch

反　aggrandize, canonize, deify, elevate, exalt 使崇高

派　humiliation *n.* 羞辱，蒙羞

hypothetical [ˌhaɪpəˈθetɪkl]

【考法 1】 *n.* 假设，前提条件：something taken as being true or factual and used as a **starting point** for a course of action or reasoning

例　He believes that predictions of the extinction of certain species as the result of global warming are based upon too many hypotheticals. 他认为所谓全球变暖会导致某些物种灭绝的说法基于过多的假设。

近　assumption, given, postulate, premise, presumption, presupposition, supposition

反　conclusion, consequence, deduction, induction, inference 结论

【考法 2】 *adj.* 假定的：existing only as an **assumption** or **speculation**

例　We talked about what we would do in various hypothetical emergencies. 我们讨论了在各种假定的紧急情况下的对策。

近　conjectural, speculative, supposed, suppositional

反　actual, factual, real 事实的

Unit 2

■ IDIOSYNCRASY　　■ IDLE　　■ ILL-BRED　　■ ILLUSTRIOUS　　■ IMPERISHABLE
■ IMPLICIT　　■ IMPOSTER　　■ IMPUNITY　　■ INCENTIVE　　■ INCUMBENT

idiosyncrasy [ˌɪdiəˈsɪŋkrəsi]

【考法】 *n.* 独特而奇怪的习惯：an **odd or peculiar habit**

例　His only idiosyncrasy is his inveterate wearing of sneakers, even with business suits. 他唯一的怪癖就是无时无刻都穿着运动鞋——哪怕身上是西装革履。

近　crotchet, eccentricity, individualism, mannerism, oddity, peculiarity, quirk, singularity, trick, twist

反　conformity, sameness 合乎(礼节等)，千篇一律

idle ['aɪdl]

【考法 1】 *adj.* 闲置的，未使用的：**not turned to** normal or appropriate **use**

例　The car was idle for two weeks while they went on vacation. 因为他们出去旅行了，他们的车闲置了两周。

近　dead, dormant, fallow, free, inert, inoperative, latent, unused, vacant

反　active, alive, employed, functioning, operative, running, working 使用中的

【考法 2】 *adj.* 懒散的：shiftless, **lazy**

例　an idle employee who always seems to be either on break or at lunch 一个懒散的员工似乎不是在休息就是在吃饭

近　indolent, lazy, shiftless, slothful

反　diligent, industrious 勤奋的

派　idlly *adv.* 懒散地

【考法3】 *v.* 懒散度日，无所事事：to pass（time）**without working** or while avoiding work

例 idle the afternoon away 打发下午的时光

近 dally, dillydally, drone, laze, loaf, loll, lounge

反 drudge, grind, hustle, labor, moil, plod, slave, sweat, toil, travail, work（辛苦地）干活，工作

ill-bred ['ɪl'bred]

【考法】 *adj.* 没有教养的，没有礼貌的：badly brought up or showing bad upbringing：**impolite**

例 Only an ill-bred, conceited person would demand that everyone cater to his whims. 只有一个没有教养、狂妄自大的人才会要求所有人都去迎合他的想法。

近 discourteous, disrespectful, impertinent, impolite, inconsiderate, rude, uncivil, ungracious, unmannerly

反 civil, considerate, courteous, genteel, gracious, mannerly, polite, urbane, well-bred 有礼貌的，得体的

illustrious [ɪ'lʌstrɪəs]

【考法】 *adj.* 著名的，杰出的：well known and very **distinguished**

例 the most illustrious scientists of the century 本世纪最为杰出的科学家

近 distinguished, luminous, noble, notable, noteworthy, outstanding, preeminent, prestigious, redoubtable, signal

反 average, inferior, mediocre 平凡的，较差的

imperishable [ɪm'perɪʃəbl]

【考法1】 *adj.* 不能被摧毁的：**impossible to destroy**; not subject to decay

例 Energy is imperishable. 能量本身是不能被毁灭的。

近 inextinguishable

反 destructible, extinguishable, perishable 可被毁灭的

【考法2】 *adj.* 不朽的，永恒的：enduring or **occurring forever**

例 My memories are within me, imperishable. 我的回忆已经和我融为一体，永恒不变。

近 ageless, continuing, eternal, everlasting, immortal, lasting, perennial, perpetual, timeless, undying

反 emphemeral, evanescent, fleeting, transient, transitory 稍纵即逝的

implicit [ɪm'plɪsɪt]

【考法1】 *adj.* 不言而喻的，心照不宣的：capable of being **understood** from something else **though unexpressed**

例 The implicit agreement among members of the outing club is that everyone pays his or her own way on all trips. 野外俱乐部成员之间一条心照不宣的约定就是：沿途所有开销都 AA。

近 implied, unexpressed, unspoken, unvoiced, wordless

反 explicit, expressed, spoken, stated, voiced 明确声明的

【考法2】 *adj.* 无疑问的，无保留的：being **without doubt** or reserve

例 Members of the expedition must have implicit trust in their leaders. 远征队员必须百分之百信任他们的领队。

近 assured, clear, confident, doubtless, positive, sanguine, sure

反 doubtful, dubious, uncertain, unsure 不确定的，存有疑惑的

imposter [ɪm'pɑstər]

【考法】 *n.* 冒名顶替者，骗子：one that **assumes false identity** or title for the purpose of deception

例 The man who claimed to be my townsman turned out to be an impostor. 那个自称是我老乡的人结果是个骗子。

近 charlatan, fake, fraud, hoaxer, humbug, mountebank, phony, pretender, quack, quacksalver, ringer, sham

impunity [ɪm'pjuːnəti]

【考法】 *n.* 免责，免受处罚：exemption or **freedom from punishment**, harm, or loss

例 She mistakenly believed that she could insult people with impunity. 她错误地认为她可以肆无忌惮地羞辱他人，不受处罚。

近 exemption, immunity

反 liability 责任

incentive [ɪn'sentɪv]

【考法】 *n.* 刺激，诱因：something that **incites** or has a tendency to incite to determination or action

例 The handsome reward for the missing wallet was an incentive for me to start looking. 找到丢失钱包的可观报酬激励我展开搜寻。‖ A little bonus will give employees an incentive to work harder. 一点点奖金就可以刺激雇员更加努力地工作。

近 boost, goad, impetus, incitement, instigation, momentum, motivation, motive, provocation, spur, stimulant, stimulus, yeast

反 deterrent, disincentive 抑制剂，阻碍物

incumbent [ɪnˈkʌmbənt]

【考法】 *adj.* 义不容辞的，必须的：imposed as an **obligation** or **duty**

例 It is incumbent upon individuals to sacrifice for their country when it is in danger. 当国家受难时，个人应该义不容辞地为国做出牺牲。‖ It is incumbent upon the press to act not in its own best interests, but in society's best interests. 对于媒体来说，为社会的利益(而非自身利益)服务是其应尽的义务。

近 compulsory, forced, imperative, involuntary, necessary, obligatory, peremptory, required

反 elective, optional, voluntary 可选择的

Unit 3

■ INDECOROUS   ■ INFRACTION   ■ JUSTIFY   ■ LAG   ■ LANCE
■ LAX   ■ LICENSE   ■ LIONIZE   ■ LUDICROUS   ■ LUMINOUS

indecorous [ɪnˈdekərəs]

【考法】 *adj.* 不合乎礼节的，不得体的：**conflicting with accepted standards** of good conduct or good taste

例 How can you make such an indecorous joke for a solemn moment in the marriage ceremony? 你怎么能在庄严肃穆的结婚典礼上开那样一个不得体的玩笑呢？

近 amiss, graceless, improper, inapposite, infelicitous, malapropos, perverse, unbecoming, unfit, unseemly, unsuitable, wrong

反 appropriate, becoming, befitting, decorous, felicitous, fit, genteel, meet, proper, seemly, suitable 得体的，合乎礼节的

infraction [ɪnˈfrækʃn]

【考法】 *n.* 违背，违犯：a **failure to uphold the requirements** of law, duty, or obligation

例 Speeding is only a minor infraction, but vehicular homicide is a serious felony. 超速只是小的违章，但是用机动车故意杀人就是重罪了。

近 breach, contravention, infringement, transgression, trespass, violation

反 observance 遵守

justify [ˈdʒʌstɪfaɪ]

【考法】 *vt.* 证明…的合理性，为…辩解：to **prove** or show **to be just**, **right**, or reasonable

例 fail to justify the need for a new expressway at this time 没能证明当前修建新的高速公路的合理性 ‖ The storm warning justified his leaving early. 他的早退因为风暴预警而显得理所当然。

近 excuse, rationalize, warrant

派 justification *n.* (正当的)理由

lag [læg]

【考法 1】 *adj.* 最终的，最后的：**following all others** of the same kind in order or time

例 We're now in the lag end of the project. 现在我们到了项目的尾声阶段。

近 bottommost, closing, concluding, final, hindmost, last, latest, rearmost, terminal, terminating, ultimate

反 beginning, earliest, first, foremost, inaugural, initial, maiden, opening, original, pioneer, primary 最初的

【考法 2】 *vi.* 缓慢行走：to proceed or develop with comparative **slowness**

例 The tired puppy was lagging behind the rest of the pack. 疲倦的小狗在队伍的后面缓缓地走着。

近 crawl, creep, dally, dawdle, dillydally, linger, loiter, poke, tarry

反 blast, bolt, bustle, careen, career, dash, fly, hustle, rush, rustle, speed, whirl 疾行，快速行走

派 lagging *n.* 延迟

【考法 3】 *vi.* 萎靡，失去活力：to **lose bodily strength** or vigor

例 During the fourth quarter the whole team seemed to lag. 到了第四节整支队伍似乎都已经精疲力竭了。

近 decay, droop, emaciate, fade, fail, languish, sink, waste, wilt, wither, mope

反 convalesce, rally, rebound, recover, recuperate 康复，复原

lance [læns]

【考法 1】 *n.* 长矛，标枪：a weapon with a **long straight handle and sharp head or blade**

例 The lance struck squarely on the knight's shield, knocking him from his horse. 标枪正中骑士的盾牌，将他掀于马下。

近 javelin, pike, shaft, spear

派 lancer *n.* (19 世纪法国的)枪骑兵

【考法 2】 *vt.* 刺穿，刺破：to **penetrate** or hold (something) with a pointed object

例 Doctors used to lance infected sores, so that they could drain clean. 以前医生会刺破受感染的疮，从而使脓液流出。

近 gore, harpoon, jab, pierce, puncture, spike, stab, stick

lax [læks]

【考法 1】 *adj.* 松弛的，不紧的，不严格的：**not tense**, **firm**, or **rigid**

例 exercises to improve lax muscles 改善松弛的肌肉的锻炼 ‖ The guidelines for the essay contest were fairly lax, permitting a wide variety of topics. 本次作文大赛的要求相对比较宽松，允许写多种类型的主题。

近 flabby, flaccid, insecure, loose, loosened, relaxed, slackened, unsecured

反 taut, tense, tight 紧固的，牢固的；hard, harsh, rigid, rigorous, severe, stern, strict 严格的

【考法 2】 *adj.* 懒惰的，漫不经心的：**failing to give proper care** and attention

例 The university has been lax about enforcing these rules. 学校对于这些规定的施行显得漫不经心。

近 careless, derelict, disregardful, heedless, lazy, neglectful, neglecting, negligent, remiss, slack

反 attentive, careful, cautious, conscientious, heedful, mindful, vigilant, wary 注意的，留心的

license [ˈlaɪsns]

【考法 1】 *n.* 许可，认可：the **approval** by someone in authority for the doing of something

例 The company is seeking license to operate several more power plants in the state. 公司正在寻求在国内多建造几个电厂的许可。‖ A restaurant owner has to get a license to serve food and drink. 餐厅营业者必须获得食物和饮品的销售许可。

近 allowance, authorization, clearance, concurrence, consent, empowerment, granting, sanction, warrant

反 interdiction, prohibition, proscription 禁止

【考法 2】 *n.* 自由：the right to act or **move freely**

例 Military commanders on the ground must be granted considerable license, as wars cannot be micromanaged by people back in Washington. 战地指挥官应该被赋予相当大的自由，因为一场战争只靠华盛顿的人是不可能打赢的，他们无法进行具体指挥。

近 freedom, latitude, liberty

反 confinement, custody, imprisonment 拘留，囚禁

【考法 3】 *n.* 放荡：**disregard for standards** of personal conduct

例 a night of drinking and license at the nightclub 在夜店里放纵饮酒取乐的一夜

近 debauchery, hedonism, libertinage, libertinism, licentiousness, profligacy, voluptuousness

反 abstinence, asceticism, sobriety, temperance 节制，克制

【考法 4】 *vt.* 准许，授权使用：to **permit or authorize** especially by formal license

例 A state statute licenses county sheriffs to choose their own deputies. 州法律允许郡上的司法长官选择自己的副手。‖ licensed to use deadly force 获准使用致命火力

近 accredit, certify, commission, empower, enable, invest, qualify, vest, warrant

反 disqualify 取消资格；forbid, interdict, prohibit, proscribe, veto 禁止

lionize [ˈlaɪənaɪz]

【考法】 *vt.* 追捧，把…捧为名人：to look on or treat (a person) as a **celebrity**

例 She was lionized everywhere after her novel won the Pulitzer Prize. 在她的小说获得普利策奖之后，她无论走到哪都受到追捧。

近 aggrandize, canonize, deify, dignify, elevate, ennoble, enshrine, ensky, enthrone, glorify, magnify

反 abase, degrade, demean, humble, humiliate 贬低，瞧不起

ludicrous [ˈluːdɪkrəs]

【考法】 *adj.* 荒唐的，可笑的：meriting **derisive laughter** or scorn as absurdly inept, false, or foolish

例 He made a ludicrous and easily detected attempt to forge his father's signature on a note to school. 他试图在要上交学校的纸条上伪造父亲的签名，这实在是既可笑又容易被发现的花招。

近 absurd, comical, derisive, derisory, farcical, laughable, ridiculous, pathetic, preposterous, risible, silly

反 logical, rational, reasonable, sensible 有道理的

luminous [ˈluːmɪnəs]

【考法 1】 *adj.* 发光的，有光泽的：**emitting or reflecting** usually steady, suffused, or glowing **light**

例 The luminous moon bathed the snow-covered fields with a pearly glow. 在明亮的月光下，雪地仿佛被罩上了一层珍珠般的光晕。

近 beaming, bright, candescent, dazzling, effulgent, glowing, incandescent, lambent, lucent, lucid, lustrous, radiant, refulgent, shiny, splendid

反 dim, dull, lackluster 黯淡无光的

派 luminosity *n.* 发光；亮度

【考法 2】 *adj.* 杰出的，重要的：**standing above** others in rank, importance, or achievement

例 some of the most luminous writers in the nation's history 该国历史上最杰出的一批作家

近 astral, brilliant, distinguished, illustrious, notable, noteworthy, preeminent, prestigious, redoubtable, signal

反 average, inferior, mediocre 一般的，中庸的

Unit 4

lurid [ˈlʊrɪd]

【考法 1】 *adj.* 恐怖的，令人反感的：**causing** horror or **revulsion**

例 We quickly drove past the lurid scene of the crash. 我们迅速驶过了可怕的车祸现场。

近 appalling, atrocious, dreadful, frightful, ghastly, gruesome, hideous, horrid, horrific, macabre, monstrous, nightmarish

反 agreeable, appealing, delicious, delightful, enjoyable, enticing, inviting, pleasant, satisfying 令人愉悦的

【考法 2】 *adj.* 面色苍白的，病态的：wan and ghastly **pale in appearance**

例 The doctor was alarmed by the patient's lurid complexion. 病人惨白的面色给医生敲响了警钟。

近 ashen, ashy, blanched, cadaverous, doughy, livid, mealy, paled, pallid, pasty, peaked, wan

反 blooming, florid, flush, full-blooded, glowing, rosy, rubicund, ruddy, sanguine 红润的，健康的

machination [ˌmæʃɪˈneɪʃn]

【考法】 *n.* 诡计：a **scheming or crafty action** or artful design intended to accomplish some usually evil end

例 The incredibly complicated machination to assassinate the president inevitably failed. 刺杀总统的诡计极其复杂，最终不可避免地失败了。

近 conspiracy, design, intrigue, plot, scheme

madcap [ˈmædkæp]

【考法 1】 *n.* 热爱冒险的人：a person who **seeks out very dangerous or foolhardy adventures** with no apparent fear

例 an incorrigible madcap who loves drag racing and white-water rafting 一个热爱飙车和激流竹筏的无药可救的冒险狂

近 daredevil, madman

【考法 2】 *adj.* 大胆的，鲁莽的：behaving or acting impulsively or rashly; **foolishly adventurous or bold**

例 They switched from one madcap scheme to another. 他们从一个鲁莽的方案换到了另一个。

近 audacious, bold, brash, daredevil, overbold, overconfident, reckless, temerarious

反 careful, cautious, circumspect, guarded, heedful, prudent, wary 谨慎的，小心的

magnitude [ˈmæɡnɪtuːd]

【考法 1】 *n.* 重要，重大：**greatness in significance** or influence

例 The magnitude of the issue is severely underestimated. 这个事件的重要性被严重低估了。

近 account, consequence, importance, moment, momentousness, significance, weight, weightiness

反 insignificance, littleness, puniness, slightness, smallness, triviality 不重要

【考法 2】 *n.* 巨大：**greatness in size** or extent

例 The mountain's sheer magnitude usually leaves tourists speechless. 巨大的山脉往往让旅游者哑口无言。

近 enormousness, giantism, gigantism, hugeness, immenseness, massiveness, prodigiousness, vastness

反 diminutiveness, minuteness, tininess 微小

malevolent [məˈlevələnt]

【考法】 *adj.* 恶意的，恶毒的：having, showing, or arising from intense often **vicious ill will**, **spite**, or **hatred**

例 The novel grossly oversimplified the conflict as a struggle between relentlessly malevolent villains on one side and faultless saints on the other. 小说把这场冲突彻底简化成凶残恶毒的坏人和完美无瑕的圣人间的斗争。

近 cruel, despiteful, evil, malicious, malign, malignant, mean, nasty, spiteful, vicious, virulent

反 benevolent, benign, benignant 善意的，和善的

派 malevolence *n.* 恶意，恶毒

malignant [məˈlɪɡnənt]

【考法】 *adj.* 恶毒的，邪恶的：having or showing a **desire to cause someone pain** or suffering for the sheer enjoyment of it; disposed to do evil

例 She has a malignant wish to poison everyone who was smarter, richer, or better-looking than she was. 她有一个恶毒的愿望，那就是毒死所有比她聪明、有钱或者是比她更漂亮的人。

近 atrocious, brutal, cruel, despiteful, malevolent, malicious, malign, mean, nasty, spiteful, vicious, virulent

反 benevolent, benign, benignant 慈善的，和蔼的；merciful 仁慈的

maneuver [məˈnuːvər]

【考法】 *vt.* 巧妙地操纵: to **guide with adroitness and design** or to bring about or secure as a result of skillful management

例 They maneuvered him into signing the contract. 他们巧妙地诱使他签下合同。|| The host maneuvered the conversation so as to avoid the touchy subject of her divorce. 主人巧妙地控制着对话的内容，以避免触及有关她离婚的敏感话题。

近 contrive, finagle, finesse, frame, machinate, manipulate, mastermind, negotiate, wangle

反 botch, bungle, fumble, mishandle, muff, scamp, mess up 弄砸

marginal [ˈmɑːrdʒɪnl]

【考法 1】 *adj.* 边缘的: located at or **near a border**

例 Marginal locations in the open-air market are a bit cheaper. 露天市场边缘的地段通常都要便宜些。

近 frontier

反 interior 内部的

【考法 2】 *adj.* 不重要的: **not of central importance**

例 regard violence as a marginal rather than a central problem 并不把暴力问题当作重要的核心问题来看

近 inconsequential, inconsiderable, insignificant, minor, minute, negligible, nugatory, slight, trifling, trivial

反 consequential, eventful, important, meaningful, momentous, significant, substantial, weighty 重要的

meditate [ˈmedɪteɪt]

【考法】 *vt.* 思索，沉思: to **focus** one's thoughts on

例 meditate a visit to her professor 思索着去拜访她的导师 || I have been meditating a career change for months. 我这几个月一直在考虑换一个工作。

近 cogitate, consider, contemplate, deliberate, mull, perpend, ponder, ruminate, study, weigh, wrestle

反 disregard, ignore, overlook, slight 忽视

派 meditation *n.* 沉思

menial [ˈmiːniəl]

【考法 1】 *n.* 仆人，奴仆: a **servant**, especially a domestic servant

例 Immigrants to that country faced fierce prejudice and could expect to find work only as menials. 前往那个国家的移民遭到了严重的歧视，他们也许只能找到仆人一类的工作。

近 domestic, retainer, steward

反 lord, master, mistress 主人

【考法 2】 *adj.* 卑贱的，低下的: showing, expressing, or offered in a **spirit of humility or unseemly submissiveness**

例 low-paid menial jobs such as cleaning the street 一些低收入的卑贱工作，比如扫大街

近 base, humble, lowly, servile, slavish, subservient

反 arrogant, haughty, imperious, lordly, supercilious, superior 自大的，狂妄的

Unit 5

| ■ MERETRICIOUS | ■ MILIEU | ■ MILITARY | ■ MISAPPREHENSION | ■ MONARCH |
| ■ MONOPOLIZE | ■ NIRVANA | ■ NOSTALGIA | ■ NOTORIETY | ■ NOURISH |

meretricious [ˌmerəˈtrɪʃəs]

【考法】 *adj.* 艳俗的，俗气的: attracting attention in a **vulgar manner**

例 The paradise they found was no more than a meretricious wasteland of casinos and bars. 他们发现的所谓"天堂"只不过是一块有着赌场和酒吧的俗气不堪的荒漠罢了。

近 flamboyant, flaring, flashy, garish, gaudy, glaring, loud, ostentatious, tawdry

反 conservative, quiet, understated, unflamboyant 低调的，不张扬的

milieu [miːˈljɜː]

【考法】 *n.* 环境，氛围: the **physical or social setting** in which something occurs or develops

例 Young, innovative artists thrive in the freewheeling milieu that a big city offers. 在大都市所提供的自由氛围中，年轻而富有创造力的艺术家们在事业上蓬勃发展。|| a historical milieu conducive to democracy 有助于民主制度的历史背景

近 ambient, atmosphere, climate, context, environment, environs, medium, setting, surroundings, terrain

military [ˈmɪləteri]

【考法】 *adj.* 军事的，军用的: of or relating to **soldiers**, **arms**, **or war**

例 NATO struggles with how to proceed military operation against Libya. 北约就如何延续针对利比亚的军事行动出现了内部分歧。|| an encyclopedia of modern military aircraft 现代军用飞行器百科全书

近 martial, service

反 civilian 民用的

misapprehension [ˌmɪsæprɪˈhenʃn]

【考法】 *n.* 错误的理解、判断：a **failure to understand** correctly; a **wrong judgement**

例 tried to eliminate all misapprehensions about the planned riverfront development 尽可能消除所有关于河流沿岸发展计划的误解 ‖ a common misapprehension about how our language functions 有关我们的语言如何运作的常见误judgment

近 incomprehension, misconstruction, misconstruing, misimpression, misinterpretation, misknowledge, misreading, misunderstanding, miscalculation, misjudging, misjudgment, misstep, slip, slipup

monarch [ˈmɑːnərk]

【考法 1】 *n.* 君主，帝王：one who **rules** over a people with a sole, supreme, and usually hereditary authority

例 The ruling monarch of Britain at that time was Queen Elizabeth I. 伊丽莎白一世是当时英国的君主。

近 autocrat, lord, potentate, ruler, sovereign

【考法 2】 *n.* 巨头，大亨：a **person of rank**, **power**, **or influence** in a particular field

例 the reigning monarchs of the recording industry 唱片业的巨头们

近 baron, captain, king, lion, lord, magnate, mogul, prince, tycoon

反 nobody, nothing, zero 不起眼的人物

派 monarchy *n.* 君主制

monopolize [məˈnɑːpəlaɪz]

【考法】 *vt.* 垄断，主宰：to have **complete control** over

例 They are virtually monopolizing the market. 他们实际上已经垄断了整个市场。‖ To their surprise it was the vice president who monopolized the conversation. 令他们惊讶的是，主导整个谈话的居然是副总裁。

近 control, dominate, govern, reign, rule, sew up

派 monopoly *n.* 垄断，垄断权

nirvana [nɪrˈvɑːnə]

【考法 1】 *n.* 彻底放松的状态：a state of being **disregardful or unconscious** of one's surroundings, concerns, or obligations

例 The spa experience was a week of pure nirvana. 去做了一周的温泉水疗，这种经历真是彻底的放松。

近 forgetfulness, obliviousness

反 alertness, awareness, cognizance, consciousness 警觉，知觉

【考法 2】 *n.* 天堂，极乐世界：an often imaginary place or state of **utter perfection and happiness**

例 They believe in a continuous cycle of births and deaths until the soul is perfected and achieves nirvana. 他们相信生命会不断轮回，直到灵魂变得完美并升入天堂。

近 empyrean, fantasyland, heaven, lotusland, utopia

反 hell, inferno 地狱

nostalgia [nəˈstældʒə]

【考法 1】 *n.* 思乡之情：the state of being **homesick**

例 Overwhelmed by nostalgia, she started to cry. 被思乡之情淹没的她开始啜泣。

近 homesickness

【考法 2】 *n.* 怀旧，怀念：a wistful or excessively **sentimental yearning for return** to or of some past period or irrecoverable condition

例 He felt a wave of nostalgia for the life he had left behind him. 他开始怀念往昔的时光。

近 reminiscence

反 oblivion 遗忘

派 nostalgic *adj.* 怀旧的

notoriety [ˌnoʊtəˈraɪəti]

【考法 1】 *n.*（尤指因为丑闻而出名的）名人：a person who is **widely known** and usually much talked about, especially for **something bad**; a notorious person

例 a television show featuring notorieties from 20 years of scandals 以二十年来因各色丑闻而出名的名人为卖点的电视节目

近 figure, icon, luminary, megastar, name, notable, personage, standout, star, superstar

反 nobody, noncelebrity 不知名的人

【考法 2】 *n.* 坏名声：the quality or condition of being notorious; **ill fame**

例 She gained notoriety when nude photographs of her appeared in a magazine. 她的裸照出现在杂志上让她"声名远播"。‖ His comment about the President has given him a notoriety that he enjoys very much. 他对于总统的评论让他获得了很让他满意的"名声"。

近 infamy, obloquy, odium, opprobrium

反 anonymity, oblivion, obscurity 不知名，默默无闻；celebrity, fame, renown, repute 好名声

nourish [ˈnɜːrɪʃ]

【考法 1】 *vt.* 养育，抚养：to **provide with food** or other substances necessary for life and growth

例 He willingly nourished a child that was not his own. 他主动抚养了一名不是他亲生的孩子。

近 breed, foster, nurse, nurture, raise, rear

【考法 2】 *vt.* 培养，促进：to **help the growth** or development of

例 a friendship nourished by trust 在信任的基础之上开出的友谊之花

近 advance, cultivate, encourage, forward, further, incubate, promote

反 discourage, frustrate, hinder, inhibit 阻碍，妨碍

Unit 6

■ NOVICE	■ NULLIFICATION	■ NUMB	■ OAF	■ OBSERVANT
■ OBSOLETE	■ ONSET	■ ORDEAL	■ OSTENSIBLE	■ OUTGROWTH

novice [ˈnɑːvɪs]

【考法】 *n.* 新手，初学者：a person **new** to a field or activity

例 a novice chess player 象棋初学者

近 apprentice, colt, fledgling, freshman, greenhorn, neophyte, newcomer, recruit, rook, tenderfoot, tyro, virgin

反 doyen, maven, veteran 有经验的人

nullification [ˌnʌlɪfɪˈkeɪʃn]

【考法】 *n.* (尤指法律条文等正式的) 废除，废弃：the **doing away** with something by formal action

例 the nullification of a treaty 废除条约

近 abolishment, abrogation, annulment, cancellation, invalidation, negation, repeal, rescindment, voiding

反 enactment, legislation 立法；establishment, founding, institution 建立

numb [nʌm]

【考法 1】 *adj.* 失去感觉的：**devoid of sensation** especially as a result of cold or anesthesia

例 I have been sitting in the same position for too long and now my feet are numb. 我一个姿势坐得太久，以至于双腿都发麻了。

近 asleep, benumbed, dead, insensitive, numbed, torpid, unfeeling

反 feeling, sensible, sensitive 有感觉的

【考法 2】 *adj.* 麻木的，无感情的：**devoid of emotion**

例 Apparently in shock, he answered the police officer's questions with a numb expression on his face. 他显然是受到了惊吓，在回答警官的问题时一脸茫然。 ‖ Years of physical and emotional abuse had rendered the woman numb and withdrawn. 长年累月的肉体和精神上的折磨已让她麻木而寡言。

近 affectless, apathetic, catatonic, deadpan, emotionless, impassible, passionless, phlegmatic, stoic, stolid

反 demonstrative, emotional, fervent, fervid, impassioned, passionate, vehement 充满感情的

oaf [oʊf]

【考法】 *n.* 愚蠢的人：a **stupid person**

例 Anyone who took him for an oaf and tried to cheat him would be in for a nasty surprise. 任何把他当成傻子然后想借机欺骗他的人就等着大吃一惊吧。

近 airhead, dolt, dope, dullard, dumbhead, fool, idiot, imbecile, moron, simpleton

反 brain, intellectual, sage, wit 智者；genius, prodigy 天才

observant [əbˈzɜːrvənt]

【考法 1】 *adj.* 警惕的，警觉的：**paying close attention** usually for the purpose of anticipating approaching danger or opportunity

例 Good reporters are keenly observant of everything around them. 优秀的记者应该对身边所有的事情都保持高度的警惕。 ‖ If you were more observant, you would perceive that something is troubling her deeply. 如果你能再警觉一些的话，你就会发现她正被某些东西困扰。

近 alert, attentive, awake, cautious, sharp, vigilant, watchful

反 careless, heedless, inattentive, unmindful, unthinking, unwary 不谨慎的

【考法 2】 *adj.* 严格遵守(规章、制度或原则)的：diligent in **observing** a law, custom, duty, or principle

例 observant of the speed limit 严格遵守速度限制 ‖ pious and religiously observant families 虔诚而严守教规的家庭

近 law-abiding

派 observance *n.* 遵守(规定)

obsolete [ˌɑːbsəˈliːt]

【考法】 *adj.* 过时的，被淘汰的：no longer in use or **no longer useful**

例 I was told my old printer was obsolete and I couldn't get replacement parts. 我被告知我的打印机已经被淘汰了，因此无法更换配件。‖ an obsolete word 一个已经废弃不用的单词

近 antiquated, archaic, dated, fossilized, medieval, moribund, moth-eaten, outdated, outmoded, outworn, prehistoric, rusty

反 contemporary, current, modern, recent 当前的，现代的

onset [ˈɑːnset]

【考法1】 *n.* 攻击，进攻：**attack**, **assault**

例 withstand the onset of the army 抵挡住了敌人军队的进攻

近 aggression, assault, charge, offense, onslaught, raid, rush, strike

反 defense 防御

【考法2】 *n.* 起始，开始：the point at which something **begins**

例 If you take enough vitamin C at the onset of a cold, you'll probably recover faster. 如果你感冒刚一开始就服用足量的维生素 C，你可能会康复得更快。

近 alpha, baseline, commencement, dawn, genesis, inception, kickoff, launch, nascence, outset, threshold

反 close, conclusion, end, ending, omega, termination 结束

ordeal [ɔːrˈdiːl]

【考法】 *n.* 严峻的考验：a **severe trial** or experience

例 The hikers were finally rescued after a three-day ordeal in the wilderness. 在野外度过了三天的严峻考验之后，登山者们终于获救了。

近 calvary, crucible, fire, gauntlet

反 delight, enjoyment, pleasure 令人愉快的事物

ostensible [ɑːˈstensəbl]

【考法】 *adj.* 表面上的，佯装的：**appearing to be true** on the basis of evidence that may or may not be confirmed

例 It must be the ostensible reason for their visit while their actual motives may be malignant. 这肯定只是他们上门拜访的表面原因，他们背后的动机说不定恶劣至极。

近 apparent, assumed, evident, ostensive, presumed, putative, reputed, seeming, supposed, prima facie

反 actual, real 真实的

派 ostensibly *adv.* 表面上

outgrowth [ˈaʊtɡroʊθ]

【考法】 *n.* 结果，后果：a condition or occurrence **traceable to a cause**

例 Crime is often an outgrowth of poverty. 犯罪往往可以归因于贫穷。‖ A predictable outgrowth of the suburb's ever growing population will be the need for more schools. 郊区人口攀升所导致的一个可以预见的后果就是需要更多的学校。

近 aftereffect, aftermath, consequence, fate, fruit, outcome, precipitate, product, result, sequel, sequence

反 antecedent, cause, occasion, reason 原因；origin, root, source 源头

Unit 7

■ OUTMODED	■ OVERRIDE	■ OVERSHADOW	■ OVERWHELM	■ OVERWROUGHT
■ PALAVER	■ PALPITATION	■ PANACEA	■ PECULIARITY	■ PEDAGOGICAL

outmoded [ˌaʊtˈmoʊdɪd]

【考法】 *adj.* 过时的，废弃的：**no longer** acceptable, current, or **usable**

例 outmoded computers that can be recycled 可回收的废旧电脑

近 antiquated, archaic, demoded, fossilized, moribund, moth-eaten, obsolete, outworn, prehistoric, rusty

反 contemporary, current, modern 现代的，当代的

override [ˌoʊvərˈraɪd]

【考法】 *vt.* 不顾：to **set aside**

例 The Congress overrode the President's veto and passed the law. 国会不顾总统的否决，强行通过了那项法令。‖ He overrode all opposition to his plans. 他对所有的反对意见不予理睬。

近 disregard, ignore, neglect, overlook, overpass, pass over

反 comply, observe 遵守

overshadow [ˌouvərˈʃædou]

【考法 1】 *vt.* 使变黯淡: to **make dark**, **dim**, or indistinct

例 Large trees overshadow the yard and darken the house for much of the day. 大树遮挡了射入院子里的阳光, 使得屋子里一天之中的大多数时候都很昏暗。‖ Her mother's illness overshadowed her childhood. 她母亲的疾病让她的童年缺乏亮色。

近 becloud, befog, blacken, blear, blur, darken, dim, fog, haze, mist, obscure, overcast, overcloud, shroud

反 brighten, illuminate, illumine, lighten 照明, 照亮

【考法 2】 *vt.* (在重要性上)超越, 超过: to **exceed in importance**

例 The forward's outstanding performance should not overshadow the achievements of the rest of the team. 其他队员的贡献不应该因前锋的精彩表现而被忽略。

近 eclipse, outrank, outshine, outstrip, overbalance, overweigh

反 fall behind 落后

overwhelm [ˌouvərˈwelm]

【考法 1】 *vt.* 淹没: to **cover** with or as if with a flood

例 That spring the massive runoff from melting snows overwhelmed the valley. 那个春天, 整个山谷被融雪形成的洪流吞没了。

近 deluge, drown, engulf, inundate, overflow, submerge, submerse, swamp

反 drain 抽干

【考法 2】 *vt.* (感情上、精神上)使无所适从, 使难以承受: to **subject to** incapacitating emotional or **mental stress**

例 Just the thought of how much work there is to do overwhelms me. 仅仅是想想还有多少工作没完成就几乎让我喘不过气了。

近 devastate, oppress, overcome, overmaster, overpower, prostrate, whelm

反 relieve 使舒缓

派 overwhelming *adj.* 势不可挡的, 无法抗拒的

overwrought [ˌouvərˈrɔːt]

【考法 1】 *adj.* 十分激动的, 非常不安的: being in a state of increased activity or **agitation**

例 She became overwrought when she heard that her child was missing. 当她得知自己孩子失踪的消息后变得极其激动和不安。

近 agitated, excited, frenzied, heated, hectic, hyperactive, overactive

反 calm, collected, composed, placid, serene, tranquil 冷静的, 沉着的

【考法 2】 *adj.* (装饰、文风等)过分华丽的: elaborately and often **excessively decorated**

例 The author's prose is overwrought with purple passages and florid metaphors. 这个作者的散文里充满了词藻华丽的段落和比喻, 显得有些过分。

近 baroque, bedizened, flamboyant, florid, fussy, gingerbreaded, ornate, overdecorated

反 austere, plain, severe, stark, unadorned 朴素的

palaver [pəˈlævər]

【考法 1】 *n.* 对话, 交流: an **exchange of views** for the purpose of exploring a subject or deciding an issue

例 seemingly endless palaver between the negotiating parties 谈判双方之间看似没有尽头的对话

近 argument, colloquy, conference, consult, council, counsel, debate, dialogue, parley

【考法 2】 *vi.* 闲聊: to talk **profusely or idly**

例 Mothers were palavering and drinking coffee while watching their children play. 母亲们一边看着她们的孩子玩耍, 一边喝着咖啡闲谈。

近 babble, chatter, converse, gabble, jabber, prate, prattle, rattle, twitter

palpitation [ˌpælpɪˈteɪʃn]

【考法】 *n.* (有节奏的)舒张收缩: a rhythmic **expanding and contracting**

例 a palpitation of the blood vessels 血管有节奏的舒张收缩

近 beat, beating, pulse, throb

panacea [ˌpænəˈsiːə]

【考法】 *n.* 万能药, 万灵药: a **remedy for all ills** or difficulties

例 a woman who seems to believe that chicken soup is a panacea for nearly everything 一个相信鸡汤是万能灵药的妇女 ‖ Bicycles are not a panacea for the traffic problem. 自行车并不是解决交通问题的万能药。

近 catholicon, cure-all, elixir, nostrum

peculiarity [pɪˌkjuːliˈærəti]

【考法】 *n.* 特征, 特点: a **distinguishing characteristic**

例 It is a peculiarity of the house that there is no front door. 没有大门是这座房子的一个特色。

近 attribute, character, criterion, diagnostic, differentia, feature, fingerprint, hallmark, mark, note, particularity, quality, specific, trait

pedagogical [ˌpedə'gɑːdʒɪkl]

【考法】 *adj.* 教学的；教师的：of, relating to, or befitting a **teacher or education**
例 I have no brow of such a pedagogical tone. 我一点也不喜欢这种说教的口吻。
近 preceptorial
反 pupillary 学生的

Unit 8

■ PEEL	■ PERCEPTIVE	■ PERILOUS	■ PERQUISITE	■ PETULANT
■ PIONEER	■ PIOUS	■ PITFALL	■ PIVOTAL	■ PLACID

peel [piːl]

【考法 1】 *vt.* 剥去…的皮：to **strip off** an outer layer of
例 She can peel apples with lightning speed. 她能以飞快的速度削苹果。
近 bark, flay, hull, husk, shell, shuck, skin, strip
【考法 2】 *vi.* 脱去（衣服等）：to **take off** one's **clothes**
例 peel off the wet clothes 脱去湿衣服
近 doff, douse, put off, shrug off, take off
反 don, put on 穿上

perceptive [pər'septɪv]

【考法 1】 *adj.* 敏锐的：able to **sense slight** impressions or **differences**
例 Due to their ability to rotate their ears, cats are very perceptive when it comes to pinpointing the source of a sound. 由于猫能够转动它们的耳朵，所以它们能十分敏锐地确定声源的位置。
近 delicate, fine, keen, quick, sensitive, sharp
反 dead, imperceptible, insensible, insensitive, numb 反应慢的，麻木的
【考法 2】 *adj.* 洞察力强的：having or showing **deep understanding** and intelligent application of knowledge
例 A perceptive teacher was able to discover what was really troubling the youth. 一个洞察力强的老师应该能察觉真正困扰青年的是什么。
近 discerning, insightful, prudent, sagacious, sage, sapient
反 brainless, dumb, foolish, idiotic, imbecile, moronic, silly, simple, slow, stupid, thoughtless, unintelligent, unwise, witless 愚钝的

perilous ['perələs]

【考法】 *adj.* 危险的：involving **potential loss or injury**
例 perilous journey through hostile territory 穿过敌方领土的危险行程
近 dangerous, grave, grievous, hazardous, jeopardizing, menacing, risky, serious, threatening, venturesome
反 harmless, innocent, innocuous, safe, unthreatening 安全的，无害的

perquisite [ˌpɜːrkwɪzɪt]

【考法】 *n.* 额外的好处：something **given in addition** to what is ordinarily expected or owed
例 Give the movers a perquisite if they do a good job. 如果搬家工人做得好就给他们一些小费。 ‖ The use of a company car is one perquisite of the job. 能使用公司的汽车是这份工作的附加好处之一。
近 cumshaw, dividend, donative, extra, gratuity, gravy, lagniappe, perk, tip

petulant ['petʃələnt]

【考法】 *adj.* 易怒的，爱发脾气的：**easily irritated** or annoyed
例 He is a petulant and fussy man who is always blaming everyone else for his problems. 他是一个对细节非常在意而又容易生气的人，还总是把自己的问题怪罪到别人的头上。
近 choleric, grouchy, grumpy, irascible, irritable, peevish, perverse, pettish, prickly, raspy, ratty, stuffy, testy
反 forbearing, obliging, patient, stoic, tolerant 容忍的，忍让的
派 petulance *n.* 易怒，坏脾气

pioneer [ˌpaɪə'nɪr]

【考法 1】 *n.* 扩荒者，先驱者：one of the **first to settle** in a territory
例 the hardships that the pioneers endured while taming the wilderness 在驯服自然的过程中扩荒者所受到的种种磨难 ‖ a pioneer in aviation 航空业的先驱
近 colonist, colonizer, homesteader, settler
反 follower 跟随者

【考法2】 *adj.* 最初的，最早的：**coming before** all others in time or order

例 the nation's pioneer institutions for the education of African-Americans 该国为了非裔美国人的教育而设立的第一批教育机构

近 earliest, foremost, headmost, inaugural, initial, leadoff, maiden, original, premier, virgin

反 final, last, latest, terminal, terminating, ultimate 最后的，终结的

【考法3】 *vt.* 开创，创造：to **open up**（an area）or prepare（a way）

例 He single-handedly pioneered the university's institute for medical research. 他单枪匹马创建了这所大学的医学研究所。|| rockets that pioneered outer space 开创了外太空纪元的火箭

近 begin, constitute, establish, inaugurate, initiate, innovate, institute, introduce, launch, plant, set up

反 close, end, shut, terminate, phase out 终止，淘汰

派 pioneering *adj.* 先驱性的，先导性的

pious [ˈpaɪəs]

【考法1】 *adj.*（信仰上）虔诚的：marked by or showing reverence for deity and **devotion to divine worship**

例 a pious woman who decided to become a nun 一个决心成为修女的虔诚女子

近 devout, godly, religious, sainted, saintly

反 antireligious, faithless, godless, impious, irreligious, ungodly, unholy 不虔诚的，无宗教信仰的

【考法2】 *adj.* 忠诚的：**firm in one's allegiance** to someone or something

例 a pious supporter of his school's athletic teams, during winning and losing seasons alike 学校体育队的忠诚支持者，不论他们是输还是赢

近 constant, dedicated, devoted, loyal, staunch, steadfast, steady, true

反 disloyal, fickle, inconstant, perfidious, recreant, traitorous, treacherous, unfaithful 不忠诚的，善变的

pitfall [ˈpɪtfɔːl]

【考法1】 *n.* 陷阱：a pit flimsily covered or camouflaged and used to **capture and hold animals** or men

例 caught in a pitfall 掉下了陷阱 || Renting a house can be full of pitfalls for the unwary. 对于那些不谨慎的人来说租房也是危机四伏的。

近 catch, gimmick, gotcha, hitch, joker, snag, snare, trap

【考法2】 *n.*（不易察觉的）危害：a **hidden** or not easily recognized **danger** or difficulty

例 One of the pitfalls of ignorance is that people will also assume you are stupid. 无知的一个危害就是，人们总会假设你一无所知。

近 hazard, imminence, menace, peril, risk, threat, trouble

pivotal [ˈpɪvətl]

【考法】 *adj.* 最关键的，最为重要的：of the **greatest possible importance**

例 The report was missing a pivotal piece of information. 报告遗漏了最为重要的信息。

近 critical, crucial, decisive, key, vital

反 inconsequential, inconsiderable, insignificant, marginal, minor, minute, negligible, nugatory, slight, trifling, trivial 不重要的

placid [ˈplæsɪd]

【考法1】 *adj.* 宁静的，风平浪静的：**free from storms** or physical disturbance

例 a vacation in the placid lake community 在宁静的湖区度过的假日

近 calm, halcyon, hushed, peaceful, quiet, serene, still, stilly, tranquil, untroubled

反 boisterous, clamorous, noisy, raucous, roistering, rowdy, tumultuous, uproarious 喧闹的

【考法2】 *adj.* 冷静的，淡定的：**free from** emotional or mental **agitation**

例 I know an exceptionally placid mother who was rarely upset by her six children. 我认识一个异常淡定的母亲，她几乎从未因为自己的六个孩子而烦恼过。

近 collected, composed, coolheaded, level, limpid, possessed, recollected, sedate, undisturbed, unperturbed

反 agitated, discomposed, disturbed, flustered, perturbed, upset 不安的，焦虑的

派 placidity *n.* 宁静，安宁

Unit 9

■ PLAYFUL	■ PLEBEIAN	■ PLENITUDE	■ PLODDER	■ PLUSH
■ POACH	■ POINTER	■ PRAGMATIC	■ PREMEDITATE	■ PREREQUISITE

playful [ˈpleɪfl]

【考法】 *adj.* 爱开玩笑的，好打闹的：given to good-natured **joking or teasing**

例 The little girl was lighthearted and playful. 小女孩无忧无虑的，喜欢和别人打闹。

近 antic, coltish, elfish, fay, frisky, frolicsome, larky, rollicking, sportive

反 earnest, grave, serious, sober, solemn, somber 严肃的

plebeian [plə'biːən]

【考法】 *adj.* 平民的，社会下层的: belonging to the class of people of **low social or economic rank**

例 a man who rose to greatness but never forgot his plebeian past 一个仕途通达、但从未忘却自己平民出身的人

近 baseborn, common, humble, inferior, lowborn, lumpen, mean, prole, proletarian, unwashed, vulgar

反 aristocratic, genteel, gentle, highborn, highbred, lofty, noble, patrician, wellborn 上流社会的

plenitude ['plenɪtuːd]

【考法1】 *n.* 丰富，充沛: an amount or supply **more than sufficient** to meet one's needs

例 a region blessed with a plenitude of natural resources 充满着上帝赐予的丰富资源的地区

近 abundance, cornucopia, feast, plentitude, plethora, wealth

反 deficiency, inadequacy, insufficiency, undersupply 匮乏，不足

【考法2】 *n.* 大量: a **considerable amount**

例 She has gathered a plenitude of information on the topic. 有关这个话题她收集了大量的资料。

近 bunch, bundle, dozen, multiplicity, myriad, plateful, plenty, profusion, ream, scads, spate, stack, volume

反 ace, bit, glimmer, handful, hint, mite, nip, ounce, pittance, speck, spot, trace 少量

plodder ['plɑːdər]

【考法】 *n.* 行走缓慢的人: someone who **moves slowly** or more slowly than others

例 The guide halted the tour group so that the plodders who had fallen behind could catch up. 导游让队伍停下来，以便那些落在后头的行动缓慢的人可以跟上。

近 crawler, dallier, dawdler, dragger, laggard, lagger, lingerer, loiterer, snail, straggler

反 speedster 速度快的人

plush [plʌʃ]

【考法1】 *adj.* (味道等)浓郁的: having an **abundance** of some characteristic **quality** (as flavor)

例 a plush, ripe wine 味道浓郁醇美的红酒

近 concentrated, full, heady, lusty, muscular, potent, rich, robust, strong

反 delicate, light, mild, thin, weak (味道等)淡的

【考法2】 *adj.* 奢华的，豪华的: notably **luxurious**

例 a plush castle filled with priceless art and antiques 一座充满了无价艺术品和古董的奢华城堡

近 deluxe, lavish, luxuriant, luxurious, opulent, palatial, silken, sumptuous

反 ascetic, austere, humble, spartan 朴素的，平凡的

poach [poʊtʃ]

【考法】 *vt.* 水煮: to **cook in a liquid** heated to the point that it gives off steam

例 He poached an egg for breakfast. 他煮了一个荷包蛋做早饭。

近 coddle, parboil, simmer, stew

pointer ['pɔɪntər]

【考法1】 *n.* (仪表上的)指针: a **scale indicator** on a watch, balance, or other measuring instrument

例 The pointer on my bathroom scale must be stuck - I know I lost weight. 浴室磅秤里的指针肯定坏了——我知道我体重应该有下降的。

近 hand, index, indicator, needle

【考法2】 *n.* 忠告，建议: a useful **suggestion or hint** usually from an expert

例 Here are a few pointers to help you make a choice. 这里有一些能帮助你作抉择的建议。

近 advice, hint, lead, recommendation, tip

pragmatic [præg'mætɪk]

【考法】 *adj.* 实用主义的，务实的: a **practical approach** to problems and affairs

例 Pragmatic men of power have had no time or inclination to deal with social morality.(K. B. Clark) 务实的当权者不会有时间或者意向去处理社会道德的问题。——K. B. 克拉克 ‖ a pragmatic man, not given to grand, visionary schemes 一个不迷恋花哨空想的计划，而更注重实际的人

近 down-to-earth, earthy, hardheaded, matter-of-fact, practical

反 fanciful, idealistic, impractical, unrealistic, utopian, visionary 幻想的，不务实的

派 pragmatism *n.* 实用主义，务实主义

premeditate [priː'medɪteɪt]

【考法】 *vt.* 预谋: to **think about** and revolve in the mind **beforehand**

例 He's carefully premeditating each step of his plan of campaign. 他正在仔细地计划竞选计划中的每一个步骤。

近 forethink, precogitate, predetermine

反 disregard, ignore, overlook, slight 忽略

派 premeditated *adj.* 有预谋的

prerequisite [ˌpriːˈrekwəzɪt]

【考法】 *n.* 先决条件，前提：something that is **necessary to an end** or to the carrying out of a function

例 Competence is prerequisite to promotion. 能力是提升的必要条件。‖ I don't think a large dwelling place is a prerequisite for a happy life. 我并不认为大的住所就能带来幸福的生活。

近 condition, essential, must, necessity, precondition, requirement, requisite, sine qua non

Unit 10

■ PREROGATIVE	■ PROCLAIM	■ PROJECT	■ PROPRIETARY	■ PROTOTYPE
■ RAMPANT	■ RAVENOUS	■ REDEEM	■ REFRESHING	■ REMNANT

prerogative [prɪˈrɑːgətɪv]

【考法】 *n.* 特权，权力：an exclusive or special **right**, **power**, or **privilege**

例 It is your prerogative to refuse to attend religious services. 你有权力不参加宗教活动。

近 appanage, birthright, entitlement, privilege, right

proclaim [prəˈkleɪm]

【考法】 *vt.* 宣告，使…公之于众：to **declare publicly**, typically insistently, proudly, or defiantly and in either speech or writing

例 I was wearing a button that proclaimed my choice for President. 我身上挂着一个纽扣，它能够彰显我支持谁当总统。‖ He launched a coup and proclaimed himself President. 他发动了一场政变，然后宣称自己已成为总统。

近 advertise, announce, blare, blazon, broadcast, declare, enunciate, herald, promulgate, publicize, publish, release, trumpet

反 conceal, hide 隐藏；silence, suppress 压制（观点的发表）

project

【考法 1】 [ˈprɑːdʒekt] *n.* 方案，计划：a **specific plan** or design

例 an ambitious project to develop the city's underground transport 一项开发城市地下交通系统的雄心勃勃的计划

近 arrangement, blueprint, design, plan, program, scheme, strategy, system, road map

【考法 2】 [prəˈdʒekt] *vi.* 凸出：to **extend outward** beyond a usual point

例 Some boulders projected dangerously out above the trail. 一些巨石非常危险地在道路上凸了出来。

近 balloon, beetle, billow, bunch, jut, overhang, poke, pouch, pout, protrude, swell

【考法 3】 *vt.* 预测，预计：to calculate, estimate, or predict (something in the future), **based on present data or trends**

例 project next year's expenses 预测明年的开销

近 augur, estimate, extrapolate, forecast, predict, predetermine, presage

派 projected *adj.* 计划的；projection *n.* 凸起物；投影

proprietary [prəˈpraɪəteri]

【考法 1】 *n.* 所有权：**ownership**

近 dominion, ownership, possession, property, proprietorship

【考法 2】 *adj.* 私营的：**privately owned** and managed and run as a profit-making organization

例 a proprietary hospital 私人医院

近 private

反 public 政府提供的；state-owned 国有的

prototype [ˈproʊtətaɪp]

【考法】 *n.* 原型：an **original model** on which something is patterned

例 The manufacturer exhaustively tested the prototype of the vehicle before approving production. 生产商在将该车型投入生产之前对样机进行了详细的测试。

近 archetype

反 copy, imitation, replica, reproduction 复制品

rampant [ˈræmpənt]

【考法 1】 *adj.* （植物）生长茂盛的：**growing thickly** and vigorously

例 a rampant growth of weeds in the neglected yard 废弃的院子里杂草疯长

近 lush, luxuriant, prosperous, weedy

反 sparse 稀疏的

【考法2】 *adj.* 猖獗的，不受限制的：<u>occurring without restraint</u> and frequently, widely, or menacingly
例 Mayor promised to put a stop to the rampant crime that plagued the city. 市长承诺要采取措施，终止那些扰乱城市治安的猖獗的犯罪活动。 ‖ rampant corruption in city government 市政府中猖獗的腐败
近 abandoned, intemperate, runaway, unbounded, unbridled, unchecked, uncontrolled, unhampered, unhindered, unrestrained
反 bridled, checked, constrained, controlled, curbed, governed, hampered, hindered, restrained, temperate 受制约的

ravenous [ˈrævənəs]
【考法】 *adj.* 食量大的，贪食的；贪婪的：having a **huge appetite**; greedy for gratification
例 He had moderated his ravenous appetite. 他控制了自己的食欲。 ‖ ravenous for power 渴望权力
近 edacious, esurient, gluttonous, greedy, rapacious, voracious
反 content, sated, satiated, satisfied 心满意足的

redeem [rɪˈdiːm]
【考法1】 *vt.* 实践，履行（诺言等）：to do what is **required** by the terms of
例 The coach redeemed his promise to take the players out for ice cream if they improved their fielding over the season. 教练履行了他的诺言：如果球员们能够在赛季中提升防守能力的话，他就请他们吃冰淇淋。
近 answer, complete, comply, fill, fulfill, keep, meet, satisfy
反 breach, break, transgress, violate 违反，违背
【考法2】 *vt.* 改过自新：to **make better** in behavior or character
例 The unfaithful husband made a determined effort to redeem himself in the eyes of his wife and children. 不忠的丈夫下定决心要在妻子和孩子的监督下改过自新。
近 habilitate, reclaim, regenerate, rehabilitate
派 redeemable *adj.* 可赎回的，可挽救的

refreshing [rɪˈfreʃɪŋ]
【考法】 *adj.* 令人身心振奋的，提神的：having a **renewing effect** on the state of the body or mind
例 A glass of cold water is very refreshing on such a hot day. 大热天里的一杯冰水真是让人心旷神怡。 ‖ It is refreshing to hear some good news about him. 能听到他的好消息真是让人振奋。
近 bracing, cordial, invigorating, rejuvenating, restorative, reviving, stimulating, stimulative, vitalizing
反 deadening, debilitating, draining, enervating, enfeebling, exhausting, sapping, wearying 令人虚弱的

remnant [ˈremnənt]
【考法】 *n.* 残余，剩余物：something **left over**
例 a remnant of his past glory 他辉煌过去的一丝残余 ‖ The shop is selling remnants of cloth at half price. 商店在半价抛售剩余的衣物。
近 debris, remainder, remains, residue, vestige

The man who has made up his mind to win will never say "impossible".
凡是决心取得胜利的人是从来不说"不可能的"。
——法国皇帝 拿破仑（Bonaparte Napoleon, French emperor）

438

List 31 *

Unit 1

■ RENEGE	■ REPLENISH	■ REPLICATE	■ RESIDUAL	■ RESTITUTION
■ RESURRECT	■ RETENTIVE	■ RETRIEVE	■ REVERBERATE	■ RHETORICAL

renege [rɪˈniːg]
【考法】 *vt.* 放弃，摒弃: to solemnly or **formally reject** or go back on（as something formerly adhered to）
例 She refused to renege the principles by which she had always lived her life, even if it resulted in losing her business. 尽管有可能使她失去她的事业，但她仍然拒绝放弃生命中所坚持的那些原则。
近 abnegate, forswear, recant, renounce, repeal, repudiate, retract, withdraw
反 adhere 坚持
派 renegade *n.* 叛徒

replenish [rɪˈplenɪʃ]
【考法】 *vt.* 补充: to **fill** or make complete **again**; add a new stock or supply to
例 He went to replenish her glass. 他去为她续杯了。
近 refill, reload
反 consume, drain, empty, exhaust 清空，耗尽

replicate [ˈreplɪkeɪt]
【考法1】 *vt.* 复制，复刻: to **make an exact likeness** of
例 We replicated the famous painting in our art class. 我们在艺术课上临摹一幅名画。
近 clone, copy, copycat, duplicate, imitate, reduplicate, render, reproduce
反 originate 原创
【考法2】 *vt.* 重复，反复: to make or **do again**
例 I cannot replicate your results when I do the experiment myself. 我自己的实验里无法重复你的结果。
近 redo, reiterate, renew, repeat
派 replicable *adj.* 可复制的，能复现的

residual [rɪˈzɪdʒuəl]
【考法】 *adj.* 剩余的，残存的: of, relating to, or characteristic of a **residue**
例 residual radiation from nuclear tests 核试验所遗留下来的残余辐射
近 leftover, remaining, vestigial
反 comprehensive, entire, full, integral, total, whole 全部的，完整的

restitution [ˌrestɪˈtuːʃn]
【考法】 *n.* 补偿，赔偿: a making good of or giving an equivalent **for some injury**
例 The victims are demanding full restitution. 受害者要求全额补偿。
近 damages, indemnity, quittance, recompense, recoupment, redress, remuneration, reparation, reprisal, requital

resurrect [ˌrezəˈrekt]
【考法】 *vt.* 使重生，使复苏: to **bring back to life**, practice, or activity
例 People believed that his body would be resurrected. 人们相信他的身体将会复活。‖ Attempts are being made by both parties to resurrect the stalled arms negotiations. 双方正在努力重启受阻的武器谈判。
近 reanimate, recharge, regenerate, rejuvenate, rekindle, renew, resuscitate, revitalize, revive, revivify
反 kill 杀死
派 resurrection *n.* 重生，复苏

retentive [rɪˈtentɪv]
【考法】 *adj.* 记性好的: having the ability or capacity to **retain knowledge or information** with ease
例 Her retentive memory helped her sail through the history test. 她的好记性帮助她顺利通过了历史考试。
反 absentminded, forgetful, oblivious 健忘的
派 retentiveness *n.* 好记性

retrieve [rɪˈtriːv]
【考法】 *vt.* 寻回，找回: to **get back again**

例 I need to retrieve the book from my friend so I could return it to the library. 我需要先把书从朋友那里拿回来才能还给图书馆。

近 reacquire, recapture, reclaim, re-collect, recoup, recover, regain, repossess, retake

反 lose, mislay, misplace 丢失

reverberate [rɪˈvɜːrbəreɪt]
【考法】 *vi.* 回荡，回响: to **continue or be repeated** in a series of reflected **sound waves**

例 The sound of thunder reverberated from one end of the mountain to the other. 打雷的声音在山间不断回荡。

近 echo, reecho, resonate, resound

派 reverberation *n.* 回响，回音

rhetorical [rɪˈtɔːrɪkl]
【考法1】 *adj.* 语言上的，文字上的: of or relating to **words or language**

例 The next war that those two nations fight won't be rhetorical - it will be with bombs and bullets. 两国之间的下一场战争可不会是斗嘴皮子——他们会来真格的。

近 lexical, linguistic, vocabular, wordy

【考法2】 *adj.* 言辞华丽（却往往无内涵）的: full of fine words and **fancy** expressions **but** mostly **meaningless** words and phrases

例 You can skip over the rhetorical passages and still get the gist of the essay. 你可以跳过那些词藻华丽的段落，直接获取文本的主旨。‖ The new governor delivered a long rhetorical speech about our state's bright future but laid out no specific programs for ensuring it. 新的执政官发表了词藻华丽的长篇演说，畅谈国家的美好未来，但却没有提出实现这一目标的具体措施。

近 bombastic, flatulent, florid, fustian, gaseous, gassy, grandiloquent, oratorical, orotund, purple, windy

反 prosaic 平凡无奇的; plain, simple 简单的

Unit 2

■ RIGMAROLE	■ RUTHLESS	■ SACROSANCT	■ SCOURGE	■ SCREEN
■ SCRIMP	■ SCRUPLE	■ SECEDE	■ SECTARIANISM	■ SECULAR

rigmarole [ˈrɪɡməroʊl]
【考法】 *n.* 混乱而无意义的话: language marked by abstractions, jargon, euphemisms, and circumlocutions; **confused or meaningless talk**

例 The security guard gave me some kind of rigmarole about passes and authorizations. 保安不知所云地跟我说了一些关于通关和授权的话。

近 abracadabra, babble, drivel, gabble, gibber, jabber, nonsense, prattle

ruthless [ˈruːθləs]
【考法】 *adj.* 没有怜悯心的，残忍的: having **no pity**

例 an office supervisor with a ruthless disregard for others' feelings 一个从不顾及他人感情的无情领导

近 cruel, heartless, inhumane, ironfisted, iron-hearted, pitiless, merciless, mortal, relentless, remorseless

反 charitable, compassionate, humane, kindhearted, merciful, sympathetic, tender 有同情心的，善良的

sacrosanct [ˈsækroʊsæŋkt]
【考法】 *adj.* 极为神圣的，不可侵犯的: **most sacred** or holy

例 The teacher's book of grades is sacrosanct, and someone could be expelled for changing anything in it. 老师记录成绩的小册子是极为神圣的，任何篡改它的人都可能受到被退学的惩罚。

近 hallowed, holy, inviolable, sacred, unassailable, untouchable

反 blasphemous, irreverent, profane, sacrilegious 亵渎的

scourge [skɜːrdʒ]
【考法】 *n.* 祸害: a **source of harm** or misfortune

例 The sheer ubiquity of food seems to be the scourge of humanity, as evidenced by the obesity epidemic. 无所不在的食品似乎要成为人类的祸害了，这一点可以从肥胖病的泛滥得以佐证。

近 affliction, bane, curse, nemesis

反 benefit, blessing, boon, felicity, godsend, manna, windfall 恩赐，福音

screen [skriːn]
【考法1】 *n.* 掩护物，屏障: something that **shelters**, **protects**, **or hides**

例 The target will be difficult to reach as it is behind a screen of anti-aircraft batteries. 目标在防空炮火的掩护之下难以靠近。‖ Please keep away from the screen door. 请不要倚靠屏蔽门。

近 aegis, ammunition, armor, cover, guard, protection, safeguard, security, shield, wall, ward

【考法2】 *vt.* 保护，使…免受攻击：to **drive** danger or **attack away** from

例 Gunships were called in to help screen the troops from further attacks. 武装直升机被呼叫对步兵进行支援，使之免受进一步的攻击。

近 defend, fence, fend, forfend, protect, secure

反 assail, assault, attack 攻击

【考法3】 *vt.* 掩护，遮蔽：to keep secret or **shut off from view**

例 Bushes screened the swimming pool from passersby on the street. 灌木丛将游泳池和街上的行人隔绝开来。

近 belie, cloak, conceal, curtain, disguise, enshroud, mask, obscure, occult, shroud, veil

反 disclose, expose, reveal, uncloak, uncover, unmask, unveil 揭露

---

scrimp [skrɪmp]

【考法】 *vi.* 节俭：to **avoid** unnecessary **waste** or expense

例 They had to scrimp and save for years in order to be able to afford a house. 他们不得不节俭度日才能攒够钱买房。

近 conserve, economize, husband, pinch, save, skimp, spare

反 dissipate, lavish, squander, waste 浪费

---

scruple [ˈskruːpl]

【考法】 *n.* (良心上的)不安：an **uneasy feeling about the rightness** of what one is doing or going to do

例 The survey showed that many students had few scruples about cheating on papers or exams. 调查显示，很多学生对于在论文中或考试时作弊没有丝毫的愧疚。

近 compunction, misgiving

反 assurance, certainty, certitude, confidence, conviction, sureness 确信

---

secede [sɪˈsiːd]

【考法】 *vi.* 脱离，退出(组织、团体、联盟等)：to **withdraw from an organization** (as a religious communion or political party or federation)

例 They threatened to secede from the coalition. 他们以退出联盟相要挟。

近 demit, disaffiliate, quit, withdraw

反 enlist, enroll, join, sign up 加入

---

sectarianism [sekˈteriənɪzəm]

【考法】 *n.* 宗派主义，顽固：stubborn or intolerant **adherence to** one's opinions or **prejudices**

例 An ideological sectarianism prevented the political party from ever being anything more than a fringe group. 意识形态上的顽固和保守使得这个政党只能成为一个边缘团体。

近 dogmatism, illiberalism, intolerance, narrow-mindedness, partisanship, small-mindedness

反 broad-mindedness, liberalism, open-mindedness, tolerance 开明

---

secular [ˈsekjələr]

【考法】 *adj.* 世俗的，尘世的：of or relating to the **worldly or temporal**

例 That's an issue for the secular authorities, not the church. 这个问题和宗教无关，是一件世俗事务。

近 carnal, earthborn, earthbound, fleshly, material, mundane, sublunary, temporal, terrene, terrestrial, worldly

反 heavenly, unearthly, unworldly 非尘世间的; spiritual 精神上的; religious 宗教的; clerical 牧师的

Unit 3

■ SEQUEL	■ SHIFT	■ SHIFTY	■ SIMILE	■ SKITTISH
■ SPARING	■ SPLINTER	■ SPLUTTER	■ SQUEAMISH	■ STASIS

---

sequel [ˈsiːkwəl]

【考法】 *n.* 结果：a **result** or consequence

例 Higher prices are a logical sequel to higher costs for manufacturers. 从逻辑上来说，更高的价格是生产商付出更高的生产成本的结果。

近 aftermath, conclusion, consequence, fate, fruit, outcome, product, result, sequence

反 antecedent, causation, cause, occasion, reason 起因，原因

---

shift [ʃɪft]

【考法1】 *vt.* 改变…的位置：to **change** the place or **position** of

例 She shifted the vase closer to the wall so that it wouldn't get knocked over. 她把花瓶靠墙挪动了一点，以防止它被碰倒。

近 budge, dislocate, displace, disturb, relocate, remove, reposition, transfer, transpose

反 anchor, fix, freeze, secure, set 使固定

【考法 2】 *vi.* 改变，变化：to **pass from** one form, state, or level to another

例 She watched the aurora in fascination as its colors shifted from green to blue. 她着迷地看着极光的色彩从绿变成蓝。

近 fluctuate, mutate, snap, vary

反 plateau, stabilize 达到稳定点，不变

【考法 3】 *vt.* 交换：to give up (something) and take something else **in return**

例 My father and I shifted seats just before takeoff so that I could sit by the window. 起飞前我和我父亲交换了座位，这样我就可以靠窗坐了。

近 commute, exchange, substitute, swap, switch, trade

shifty ['ʃɪfti]

【考法】 *adj.* (显得)狡诈的，(显得)欺诈的：having, displaying, or suggestive of **deceitful character**

例 shifty practices such as turning back the odometers on used cars 一些欺骗性的花招，比如把旧车的里程表调零 ‖ He had a shifty face so I won't trust him. 他看起来贼目鼠眼的，我不会相信他。

近 crooked, deceitful, deceptive, duplicitous, fraudulent, guileful, rogue, shady, sharp, underhanded

反 aboveboard, honest, straight 正派的，光明正大的

simile ['sɪməli]

【考法】 *n.* 明喻：a figure of speech **comparing two unlike things** that is often introduced by like or as

例 Even though both similes and metaphors are forms of comparison, similes indirectly compare the two ideas and allow them to remain distinct in spite of their similarities, whereas metaphors compare two things directly. For instance, a simile that compares a person with a bullet would go as follows: "Chris was a record-setting runner as fast as a speeding bullet." A metaphor might read something like, "When Chris ran, he was a speeding bullet racing along the track." 尽管明喻和暗喻都是比喻的手法，明喻会间接地对两个对象进行比较，同时允许差异的存在，而暗喻则直接对两者进行比较。比如说，用明喻来把一个人比作子弹会这样说："克里斯是一个不断打破记录的选手，他跑得就和高速子弹一样快。"而暗喻可能会说："当克里斯奔跑的时候，他就是一颗在赛场上高速飞行的子弹。"

反 metaphor 暗喻

skittish ['skɪtɪʃ]

【考法 1】 *adj.* 容易受到惊吓的，胆小的：**easily frightened**

例 The kitty is skittish around people she doesn't know. 小猫看到不认识的人就会显得特别胆小害怕。

近 fainthearted, fearful, fearsome, mousy, scary, timid, timorous, tremulous

反 adventuresome, adventurous, audacious, bold, daring, dashing, gutsy, venturesome, venturous 大胆的

【考法 2】 *adj.* 容易激动的：**easily excited** by nature

例 The skittish colt leapt up when we approached. 一看到我们靠近，小马驹就激动地猛跳起来。

近 flighty, fluttery, hyper, hyperactive, hyperkinetic, jittery, jumpy, nervous, skittery, spasmodic, spooky

反 imperturbable, nerveless, unexcitable, unflappable, unshakable 不为所动的，沉着的

【考法 3】 *adj.* 善变的，多变的：**likely to change** frequently, suddenly, or unexpectedly

例 The skittish housing market had both buyers and sellers on edge. 变幻莫测的房市让买家和卖家都坐立不安。

近 capricious, changeful, flickery, fluctuating, fluid, inconstant, mercurial, mutable, temperamental, uncertain, unstable, unsteady, volatile

反 changeless, constant, immutable, invariable, settled, stable, stationary, steady, unvarying 不变的

sparing ['sperɪŋ]

【考法 1】 *adj.* 节俭的，节约的：marked by or practicing **careful restraint** (as in the use of resources)

例 The sparing couple are trying to save up enough for a house. 节俭的夫妻希望能够攒钱买套房。

近 economical, economizing, provident, scrimping, thrifty

反 prodigal, profligate, spendthrift, squandering, wasteful 浪费的

【考法 2】 *adj.* 不足的，缺乏的：**less plentiful** than what is normal, necessary, or desirable

例 Unfortunately, the explanation of the health insurance plan was somewhat sparing on details. 不幸的是，健康保险计划上的说明似乎不够详细。‖ The map is sparing of information. 这张地图的信息量太少了。

近 exiguous, niggardly, poor, scant, scanty, scarce, skimp, skimpy, slender, slim, spare, sparse, stingy

反 abundant, ample, bountiful, copious, generous, liberal, plenteous, plentiful 足量的

splinter ['splɪntər]

【考法 1】 *n.* 尖细条，刺：a **sharp**, **slender piece**, as of wood, bone, glass, or metal, split or broken off from a main body

例 She got a splinter from the unfinished wall. 她的手被还没有装修的墙扎了一根刺。

近 chip, flake, sliver, spall, splint

反 chunk, slab 厚板

【考法2】 *vt.* 将…切成细条: to split or **break into sharp, slender pieces**

例 splinter the carrots into little sticks 把胡萝卜切成丝

近 slice

---

splutter [ˈsplʌtər]

【考法】 *vi.* 急切而不清楚地说: to speak **hastily and incoherently**, as when confused or angry

例 They begin to splutter and move restlessly about if they feel time is slipping away without some return. 当他们感到时间在悄悄流逝却一无所得时，他们便开始激动地说话，不安地走动。

近 babble, drivel, gabble, gibber, jabber, sputter, stammer, stutter

反 articulate, enunciate, pronounce 清楚地说

---

squeamish [ˈskwiːmɪʃ]

【考法】 *adj.* 恶心的，晕船的: affected with **nausea**

例 The rolling of the ship made the young sailor squeamish. 摇晃的船只让年轻的水手感到恶心。

近 ill, nauseated, qualmish, queasy, queer, queerish, sick, sickish

反 healthy, well 状态良好的

---

stasis [ˈsteɪsɪs]

【考法】 *n.* 平衡，停滞: a condition of **balance** among various forces

例 For the time being, the populations of the national park's predators and prey remain in stasis. 目前国家公园中捕食者和猎物的数量保持着一定的平衡。‖ Language is a primary element of culture, and stasis in the arts is tantamount to death. (Charles Marsh) 语言是文化当中的主要元素，艺术的停滞和平衡就等同于死亡。——查尔斯·马什

近 counterpoise, equilibration, equilibrium, equipoise, poise

反 disequilibration, disequilibrium, imbalance, nonequilibrium, unbalance 不平衡

Unit 4

■ STAUNCH	■ STEREOTYPE	■ STIGMATIZE	■ SUBSTITUTE	■ SUCCUMB
■ SUPERSEDE	■ SURLY	■ SURMISE	■ SURMOUNT	■ SURPASS

---

staunch [stɔːntʃ]

【考法】 *adj.* 忠诚的，坚定的: **steadfast in loyalty** or principle

例 a staunch believer in the democratic system 民主制度的坚定拥护者 ‖ No matter what happens I will be your staunchest supporters. 不论发生什么，我都会是你最忠诚的支持者。

近 constant, dedicated, devoted, devout, faithful, fast, loyal, pious, steadfast, steady, true, true-blue

反 disloyal, inconstant, perfidious, recreant, traitorous, treacherous 不忠诚的; fickle 善变的

---

stereotype [ˈsteriətaɪp]

【考法】 *n.* 成见，老套的理念: a **conventional**, **formulaic**, **and oversimplified** conception, **opinion**, or image

例 The noble savage was a stereotype that appealed to 18th-century intellectuals, who viewed European civilization as decadent and corrupt. "高贵的野蛮人"这一概念是为了迎合十八世纪的文人而提出的，他们将欧洲文明视作堕落和腐化的文明。

近 concept, conception, generality, notion

---

stigmatize [ˈstɪɡmətaɪz]

【考法】 *vt.* 使蒙上污名: to characterize or brand as **disgraceful or ignominious**

例 Urban construction workers are often stigmatized by the rest of society as lazy and dirty. 城市里的建筑工人往往被社会里的其他人污蔑为是懒惰而肮脏的。

近 abase, debase, degrade, demean, discredit, disgrace, dishonor, foul, humiliate, shame, sink, smirch

反 aggrandize, canonize, deify, elevate, exalt 提升(名誉、声望等)

---

substitute [ˈsʌbstɪtuːt]

【考法1】 *n.* 取代者，替代品: a person or thing that **takes the place** or function **of another**

例 If you like, you can use nuts as a substitute for coconut in that recipe. 如果您不反对，我们可以将菜单里的椰子换成坚果。

近 backup, cover, fill-in, relief, replacement, reserve, stand-in, surrogate

【考法2】 *vt.* 取代，替代: to take **the place of**

例 substitute moral power for physical force 用道德的力量取代暴力 ‖ BFR molecules have some atoms substituted by bromide atoms, which makes it fire-resistant. 在溴化阻燃剂的分子中，一部分原子被溴原子取代，从而使它不易燃烧。

近 displace, relieve, replace, supersede, supplant, cut out

派 substitution *n.* 取代

succumb [sə'kʌm]

【考法 1】 *vi.* 屈服: to **yield to superior strength** or force or overpowering appeal or desire

例 She refused to succumb to her fears and defiantly walked through the dark cemetery. 她拒绝向自己的恐惧屈服，而是倔强地走过了幽暗的墓地。

近 bow, capitulate, concede, submit, surrender, give in

反 resist 抵抗

【考法 2】 *vi.* 死亡: to be brought to an end (as **death**) by the effect of destructive or disruptive forces

例 The patient lay so still and pale that everyone thought he had succumbed, and then he opened his eyes. 面色惨白的病人静静地躺在床上，正当所有人都以为他已经过世时，他突然睁开了眼睛。‖ The doctor worked tirelessly until finally he, too, succumbed to the plague. 医生不知劳累地工作，直至最后，他也死于瘟疫。

近 decease, demise, expire, perish, pass away

反 endure, stand 忍受住; breathe, live, survive 存活

supersede [ˌsuːpər'siːd]

【考法】 *vt.* 取代，替代: to **displace** in favor of another

例 That edition of the dictionary that you have has been superseded by a more recent one. 你买的那版字典已经被最近新出的版本取代了。

近 displace, relieve, replace, substitute, supplant, cut out

surly ['sɜːrli]

【考法】 *adj.* 脾气不好的: irritably sullen and **churlish in mood** or manner

例 The surly receptionist told us we would have to wait outside in the rain. 态度粗暴的接待员说我们必须在外面等——哪怕是在下雨。

近 acid, bearish, bilious, cantankerous, disagreeable, dyspeptic, ill-humored, ill-natured, ornery, splenetic

反 amiable, good-humored, good-natured, good-tempered 性格好的

surmise

【考法 1】 ['sɜːrmaɪz] *n.* (根据不足的)推测，揣测: a thought or idea **based on scanty evidence**

例 My surmise is that the couple's "good news" is the announcement that they are going to have a baby. 我猜那对夫妻说的"好消息"就是他们要有小孩了。

近 guess, hypothesis, shot, supposition, theory

反 fact 事实

【考法 2】 [sər'maɪz] *vt.* 推测: to form a notion of **from scanty evidence**

例 From his tone I surmised that he was unhappy. 从他的语气中我猜测他并不高兴。

近 assume, conjecture, daresay, imagine, infer, presume, speculate, suppose, suspect

反 demonstrate, prove, substantiate, validate 证明

surmount [sər'maʊnt]

【考法】 *vt.* 战胜，获得胜利: to **achieve a victory** over

例 an Olympic swimmer who surmounted endless obstacles to achieve her goals 一个克服重重困难最终实现目标的奥运游泳运动员

近 conquer, defeat, overbear, overcome, overmatch, prevail, subdue, triumph, win

反 lose 失败

surpass [sər'pæs]

【考法 1】 *vt.* 超越，强于: to **become better**, greater, or stronger than

例 She always tried to surpass her older brother at anything he did, which results in his diffidence. 她在任何一个方面都要比她哥哥优秀，由此导致了他自信心的缺乏。

近 beat, better, eclipse, exceed, excel, outclass, outmatch, outshine, outstrip, overtop, transcend

反 fall behind 落后

【考法 2】 *vt.* 突破(界限、记录等): to go **beyond the limit** of

例 The sales of the band's newest CD have surpassed the combined sales of its last two albums. 乐队新专辑的发售量甚至超过了前两张销售量的总和。

近 break, outreach, outrun, overpass, overreach, overrun, overstep

Unit 5

■ SURROGATE　　■ SURVEILLANCE　　■ TAME　　　　　　■ TANGLE　　　　■ TEEMING
■ TEMPORAL　　　■ TENTATIVE　　　■ THICK-SKINNED　■ THRILL　　　　■ TIMELY

surrogate ['sɜːrəgət]

【考法】 *n.* 替代品: one that **takes the place** of another

例 For some people, Google Earth is never a justified surrogate for actual travel. 对于一部分人而言，谷歌地球不是实地旅行的合理替代品。

近 backup, cover, fill-in, relief, replacement, reserve, stand-in, substitute

surveillance [sɜːrˈveɪləns]
【考法】 *n.* 监视，监控：**close observation** of a person or group, especially one under suspicion
例 government surveillance of suspected terrorists 政府对于恐怖分子嫌疑人的监控
近 oversight, supervision, watch

tame [teɪm]
【考法1】 *adj.* 被驯化的：**reduced from a state of native wildness** especially so as to be tractable and useful to humans
例 Every evening, a wild Canada goose is at the food trough with our tame geese. 每天傍晚的食槽边总会出现一只野生加拿大鹅和我们饲养的家鹅一起进食。
近 domestic, domesticated, tamed
反 feral, savage, undomesticated, untamed, wild 野生的
【考法2】 *adj.* 无聊的，乏味的：**lacking spirit**, zest, interest, or the capacity to excite
例 That action movie was so tame I fell asleep about 20 minutes into it. 那部动作片实在是太无聊了，我刚开场二十分钟就睡着了。
近 arid, drab, dreary, drudging, humdrum, insipid, jading, jejune, monochromatic, monotonous, pedestrian, ponderous, stale, stodgy, tedious, tiresome, wearisome
反 absorbing, engaging, engrossing, gripping, interesting, intriguing, involving, riveting 令人感兴趣的
【考法3】 *vt.* 控制，抑制：to **keep from exceeding** a desirable degree or level (as of expression)
例 Try to tame your language when you are in front of the kids. 在孩子面前注意一下你的措辞。
近 bridle, check, constrain, contain, curb, govern, hold, inhibit, keep, measure, regulate, rein, restrain, rule
反 unleash 宣泄 (感情等)

tangle [ˈtæŋgl]
【考法1】 *n.* 困惑，不解：a state of **perplexity** or complete bewilderment
例 My mind has been in a tangle ever since I learned some information about an old, deceased acquaintance. 自从我获知一位已故的老熟人的一些消息之后我就陷入了困惑之中。
近 bafflement, befuddlement, bemusement, bewilderment, confusedness, distraction, muddle, mystification, perplexity, puzzlement, whirl
反 assurance, certainty, certitude, confidence, conviction, sureness 确信
【考法2】 *vt.* 纠缠，使…纠结：to seize and hold in or as if **in a snare**
例 He was at last tangled in the web of lies that he had told to everyone. 他最终被自己所编织的谎言缠住了。
近 enmesh, ensnare, ensnarl, entrap, mesh, net, snare, trap
反 disentangle 解开

teeming [ˈtiːmɪŋ]
【考法】 *adj.* 大量的：possessing or covered with **great numbers** or amounts of something specified
例 oceans teeming with life 孕育着无穷生命的海洋
近 abundant, ample, awash, cornucopian, flush, fraught, lousy, replete, swarming, thick, thronging
反 bare, barren, blank, devoid, empty, stark, vacant, void 贫瘠的，空无一物的

temporal [ˈtempərəl]
【考法】 *adj.* 世俗的，尘世的：of or relating to **earthly life**
例 The master told his disciples not to worry about temporal concerns, but instead focus on spiritual matters. 大师要弟子们不要为尘世间的纷争而苦恼，而是将精神集中于灵魂上的思考。
近 carnal, earthborn, earthbound, fleshly, material, mundane, secular, sublunary, terrene, terrestrial, worldly
反 heavenly, unearthly, unworldly 非尘世间的；spiritual 精神上的；religious 宗教的

tentative [ˈtentətɪv]
【考法】 *adj.* 暂时性的，尝试的：**not fully** worked out or **developed**
例 Our plans are only tentative at this point and will depend on whether you can come. 我们的计划只是暂时性的，具体还要看你能否前来。
近 ad interim, impermanent, interim, provisional, provisionary, provisory, short-term, temporary, trial
反 final 最终的；ceaseless, endless, eternal, immortal, permanent, perpetual, undying 永久性的

thick-skinned [ˌθɪkˈskɪnd]
【考法】 *adj.* 冷漠无情的，不顾及他人感受的：largely **unaffected** by the needs and feelings of other people
例 She was so thick-skinned that she was clueless about the fact that the joke had hurt her friend's feelings. 她很少顾及他人的感受，以至于根本没有意识到那个玩笑伤害了她朋友的感情。
近 affectless, callous, cold-blooded, heartless, indurate, inhumane, insensitive, merciless, obdurate, ruthless
反 charitable, compassionate, humane, kindhearted, merciful, sympathetic, tender, warmhearted 慈善的

thrill [θrɪl]

【考法 1】 *n.* 强烈的兴奋感，快感：a **pleasurably intense stimulation** of the feelings

例 Everyone gets a real thrill out of the Independence Day fireworks. 每个人都因独立日的焰火表演而感到无比的兴奋。

近 bang, boot, exhilaration, frisson, jollies, kick, rush, titillation, wallop

【考法 2】 *vt.* 使兴奋，使激动：to cause to experience a sudden sharp feeling of **excitement**

例 I was thrilled to hear that you got the promotion that you'd been so desperately wanting. 听到你终于获得了梦寐已久的升职，我感到非常激动。

近 arouse, charge, electrify, excite, exhilarate, galvanize, intoxicate, provoke, stimulate, titillate, pump up

反 bore, jade, pall, tire, weary 使厌倦

派 thrilling *adj.* 刺激的；thriller *n.* 恐怖电影

timely [ˈtaɪmli]

【考法 1】 *adj.* 及时的，无拖延的：done, carried out, or given **without delay**

例 When I order a pizza, I expect it to be delivered in a timely manner. 当我在外面点了披萨饼，我就希望它能按时送到。

近 immediate, punctual, speedy

反 belated, late, tardy 迟到的，延迟的

【考法 2】 *adj.* 恰到好处的，合乎适宜的：**appropriate** or adapted to the times or the occasion

例 Timely invitation to lunch came just as I was starting to feel hungry. 正当我开始感到饥饿的时候，就有人适时地邀请我吃午饭了。

近 opportune, seasonable, well-timed

反 inopportune, unseasonable, untimely 不合时宜的

Unit 6

■ TOPSY-TURVY	■ TRIFLE	■ TRIFLING	■ TYCOON	■ TYRANT
■ UMBRAGE	■ UNANIMOUS	■ UNAVAILING	■ UNREMITTING	■ VERSED

topsy-turvy [ˌtɑːpsi ˈtɜːrvi]

【考法】 *adj.* 混乱的，不整洁的：**lacking in order**, **neatness**, and often cleanliness; totally disordered

例 The office is still topsy-turvy even though we moved in months ago. 尽管我们几个月前就搬了进来，办公室还是混乱不堪。‖ turn our ordered life topsy-turvy 把我们原本有序的生活彻底打乱

近 chaotic, confused, disarranged, disarrayed, disheveled, disorderly, jumbled, messed, rumpled, sloppy, unkempt, untidy

反 bandbox, crisp, kempt, neat, orderly, organized, shipshape, tidy, trim, well-ordered 整洁的，有序的

trifle [ˈtraɪfl]

【考法 1】 *n.* 不重要的事：something of **little importance or value**

例 Let us not speak of trifles when our nation may be going to war. 战事在即，我们还是先放下这些琐事吧。

近 bagatelle, frippery, triviality

派 trifling *adj.* 不重要的

【考法 2】 *vi.* 不正经地对待，玩弄：to behave amorously **without serious intent**

例 Do not trifle with me unless you mean to ask me to marry you. 如果你不是真心想和我结婚，就请不要来玩弄我的感情。

近 coquet, dally, flirt, frivol, toy

trifling [ˈtraɪflɪŋ]

【考法】 *adj.* 细微的，不重要的：**lacking in significance** or solid worth

例 Deciding what you want to do for a living is no trifling matter. 决定维持生计的行当可不是一件小事。‖ trifling differences between the theatrical and DVD versions of the movie 这部电影影院版和 DVD 版的细微区别

近 frivolous, inconsequential, inconsiderable, insignificant, minor, minute, negligible, nugatory, slight, trivial

反 consequential, eventful, important, meaningful, momentous, significant, substantial, weighty 重要的

tycoon [taɪˈkuːn]

【考法】 *n.* 大亨，巨头：a **person of rank**, **power**, or **influence** in a particular field

例 an oil tycoon who's widely considered the most powerful man in the county 被认为是郡上最有势力的一个石油大亨 ‖ The automobile tycoon is on the verge of bankruptcy. 汽车巨头濒临破产的边缘。

近 baron, captain, king, lion, lord, magnate, mogul, monarch, prince

反 nobody, nothing, zero 不起眼的人物

tyrant	[ˈtaɪrənt]
【考法】	*n.* 暴君: a ruler who exercises absolute power **oppressively or brutally**
例	The people universally feared the tyrant, who was notorious for his frequent use of torture. 人们都非常恐惧这个暴君，因为他有着经常折磨人的臭名。
近	dictator, oppressor, pharaoh, strongman
派	tyranny *n.* 暴政，苛政

umbrage	[ˈʌmbrɪdʒ]
【考法】	*n.* 不悦，生气: the **feeling of being offended or resentful** after a slight or indignity
例	He would take umbrage at the slightest suggestion of disrespect. 哪怕是一点点的不敬也会让他不悦。
近	dudgeon, huff, miff, offense, peeve, resentment
反	contentment, delight, gratification, happiness, pleasure 满意，高兴

unanimous	[juˈnænɪməs]
【考法】	*adj.* 一致同意的: having the agreement and **consent of all**
例	a unanimous vote to upgrade the school's computer facilities 一致同意对学校的计算机设备进行升级
近	consentaneous, uncontested
派	unanimity *n.* 一致同意

unavailing	[ˌʌnəˈveɪlɪŋ]
【考法】	*adj.* 徒劳的，无果的: **producing no results**
例	an unavailing effort to avert a war 试图避免战争的徒劳尝试
近	abortive, barren, bootless, fruitless, ineffectual, unproductive, unprofitable, unsuccessful, useless, vain
反	effective, effectual, efficacious, fruitful, potent, productive 有效的; successful 成功的

unremitting	[ˌʌnrɪˈmɪtɪŋ]
【考法】	*adj.* 连续不断的: going on and on **without any interruptions**
例	Unremitting rain lasted for six days. 连续下了六天的雨。
近	ceaseless, continual, continuing, incessant, nonstop, perpetual, unbroken, uninterrupted
反	discontinuous, intermittent 不连续的，有间断的

versed	[vɜːrst]
【考法 1】	*adj.* 熟知的: **having information** especially as a result of study or experience
例	versed in the latest developments in aeronautics 熟知航空业的最新发展情况
近	abreast, acquainted, conversant, informed, knowledgeable, well-informed
反	ignorant, unacquainted, unfamiliar, uninformed, unknowledgeable 无知的
【考法 2】	*adj.* 精通的: having or showing **exceptional knowledge**, experience, or skill in a field of endeavor
例	well versed in the techniques of laser surgery 精通激光手术方面的技术
近	accomplished, adept, complete, consummate, experienced, expert, master, practiced, professed, skilled, veteran, virtuoso
反	amateur, inexperienced, inexpert, jackleg, unprofessional, unseasoned, unskilled 业余的，不精通的

Unit 7

■ VILE	■ VOCATION	■ VOUCHSAFE	■ VOYEUR	■ WANTING
■ WAYWARD	■ WEATHER	■ WILLFUL	■ WILLY-NILLY	■ WILT

vile	[vaɪl]
【考法 1】	*adj.* 丑陋的: **unpleasant to look at**
例	a truly vile combination of colors 着实丑陋的混搭色调
近	grotesque, hideous, homely, monstrous
反	aesthetic, attractive, beautiful, comely, cute, fair, gorgeous, handsome, ravishing, seemly 漂亮迷人的
【考法 2】	*adj.* (道德上)可鄙的，卑鄙的: **morally despicable** or abhorrent
例	Nothing is so vile as intellectual dishonesty. 没什么比智力上的欺骗更为可鄙的了。
近	base, contemptible, despicable, detestable, dishonorable, execrable, ignominious, mean, nasty, paltry, sordid, wretched
反	honorable, lofty, noble, straight, upright, venerable, virtuous 有道德的，高尚的

vocation	[voʊˈkeɪʃn]
【考法】	*n.* 职业: the work in which a person is regularly **employed**
例	She finally made soccer her vocation instead of just a hobby. 她终于将足球从爱好升级为谋生的职业。
近	calling, employment, occupation, profession, trade, work
反	hobby 爱好
派	vocational *adj.* 职业的，为职业做准备的

vouchsafe [ˌvautʃˈseɪf]

【考法】 *vt.* 允诺，给予：to **grant** or furnish often **in a gracious or condescending manner**

例 refuse to vouchsafe an explanation 拒绝给出任何解释

近 accord, award, grant, vest

反 withhold 保留，不给予；recant, retract, withdraw 撤回，收回

voyeur [vɔɪˈɜːr]

【考法】 *n.* 窥淫狂：one obtaining sexual gratification from **observing unsuspecting individuals** who are partly undressed, naked, or engaged in sexual acts

例 They accidentally found out that their ostensibly benign neighbor is actually a voyeur. 他们偶然间发现那个表面和善的邻居居然是一个偷窥狂。

近 peeper

派 voyeurism *n.* 偷窥癖

wanting [ˈwɑːntɪŋ]

【考法 1】 *adj.* 未出现的，缺少的：**not present** or in evidence

例 Grass is almost entirely wanting in that arid wasteland. 那片荒漠几乎没有长一丝青草。

近 absent, lacking, missing, nonexistent

反 existent, present 存在的，出现的

【考法 2】 *adj.* 未达到要求的：**not being up to standards** or expectations

例 He examined her work and found it wanting. 他检查了她的工作，发现不合要求。‖ We tried her cooking and found it to be very wanting. 我们试了试她的厨艺，结果发现很不尽人意。

近 deficient, dissatisfactory, ill, inferior, lousy, paltry, poor, unacceptable, unsatisfactory, wretched

反 acceptable, adequate, passable, tolerable 可接受的；satisfactory 令人满意的

wayward [ˈweɪwərd]

【考法】 *adj.* 刚愎自用的，不服管束的：**following one's own** capricious, wanton, or depraved **inclinations**

例 He had always been the most wayward of their three children. 他总是三个小孩里最不听话的一个。wayward children with a history of behavioral problems 过去行为上有些问题的调皮小孩

近 balky, contrary, contumacious, defiant, intractable, obstreperous, rebellious, recalcitrant, refractory, unruly

反 amenable, biddable, compliant, conformable, docile, obedient, ruly, submissive, tractable 顺从的

weather [ˈweðər]

【考法】 *vt.* 安全度过（危机等），经受住：to **come through** (something) safely

例 We have weathered worse crises, and so we'll survive this one. 更为严重的危机我们都闯过了，这个也不会有问题的。‖ They weathered a terrible storm while at sea. 他们在海上平安渡过了一场巨大的风暴。

近 survive

反 decease, die, expire, perish, succumb, pass away 死亡，消亡

willful [ˈwɪlfl]

【考法 1】 *adj.* 固执的，倔强的：obstinately and often perversely **self-willed**

例 Finally the parents sought professional counseling for the willful child. 最终家长不得不为倔强的小孩寻求专业咨询。

近 adamant, headstrong, immovable, implacable, inconvincible, inflexible, intransigent, mulish, obdurate, pertinacious, perverse, stubborn, unyielding, wrongheaded

反 acquiescent, agreeable, amenable, compliant, flexible, pliable, pliant, relenting, yielding 易受影响的

【考法 2】 *adj.* 故意的：done **deliberately**

例 a willful attempt to cheat her siblings out of their rightful inheritance 想将继承权从她的兄弟姐妹手里骗过来的企图

近 conscious, deliberate, intended, intentional, knowing, purposeful, voluntary, willed, witting

反 accidental, chance, haphazard, inadvertent, incidental, random 不经意的，偶然的

willy-nilly [ˌwɪli ˈnɪli]

【考法 1】 *adv.* 不论是否愿意地：whether **desired or not**

例 After her boss fell sick, she willy-nilly found herself directing the project. 在她老板生病后，她发现自己不论愿不愿意，都得接手这项工程。

近 helplessly, inescapably, inevitably, perforce, unavoidably

【考法 2】 *adj.* 无秩序的，随意的：**without order** or plan

例 willy-nilly taxing laws 杂乱无序的税收法

近 aimless, arbitrary, desultory, erratic, haphazard, scattered, slapdash, stray

反 methodical, orderly, organized, regular, systematic 有序的，有组织的

wilt [wɪlt]

【考法 1】 *vi.* (花、植物等)萎蔫: to become **limp or flaccid**

例 The plants wilted after I forgot to water them for three whole days. 在我整整三天忘记浇水之后，植物们全都萎蔫了。

近 flag, hang, loll, sag, swag

【考法 2】 *vi.* 精神萎靡，憔悴: to feel or exhibit the effects of **fatigue or exhaustion**

例 She had wilted a bit after walking around the hot and humid city. 在炎热潮湿的城市中行走使得她略显憔悴。
His brain wilted from hitherto unprecedented weariness. 在前所未有的疲劳面前，他开始变得脑力衰弱。

近 decay, droop, emaciate, fade, fail, lag, languish, sink, waste, wither

反 convalesce, rally, rebound, recover, recuperate 康复，复原

Unit 8

■ WILY　　　■ WIRETAP　　　■ WISTFUL　　　■ WREST　　　■ WRONGHEADED

wily ['waɪli]

【考法】 *adj.* 狡诈的，狡猾的: clever at attaining one's ends by indirect and often **deceptive means**

例 He is an experienced and wily old statesman. 他是一个经验丰富而狡诈的老政治家。 ‖ His wily plan only rebounded on himself. 聪明反被聪明误。

近 beguiling, cagey, crafty, cunning, devious, foxy, guileful, scheming, shrewd, slick, sly, subtle, tricky

反 artless, guileless, ingenuous, innocent, undesigning 天真的，单纯的

wiretap ['waɪərtæp]

【考法】 *n./vt.* 偷听，窃听: to tap a telephone or telegraph wire in order to **get information**

例 This line is not clean as CIA might have wiretapped it. 这条线路不安全，因为中情局可能已经在监听了。

近 eavesdrop, overhear, tap

wistful ['wɪstfl]

【考法】 *adj.* (带着忧伤而)渴望的，怀念的: full of **yearning or desire** tinged **with melancholy**

例 There was a wistful look in his eyes when he spoke of his childhood. 当他谈起他的童年时，眼眶中不禁流露出一种带有忧伤的怀念之情。

近 longing, nostalgic, reminiscent, yearning

反 apathetic, indifferent, insouciant, nonchalant, perfunctory, unconcerned 无所谓的，不感兴趣的

wrest [rest]

【考法 1】 *vt.* 拧，扭动: to pull, force, or move by violent **wringing or twisting movements**

例 wrest the lid off this pickle jar 把泡菜罐的盖子拧下来

近 twist, wrench, wring

【考法 2】 *vt.* 辛苦地获得: to **gain with difficulty** by or as if by force, violence, or determined labor

例 farmers who were used to wresting a living from the barren land 一度依靠贫瘠的土地辛苦度日的农民

近 scrape, scrounge, squeeze

wrongheaded [ˌrɔːŋ'hedɪd]

【考法】 *adj.* 固执己见的，坚持(错误观点)的: **stubborn in adherence** to wrong opinion or principles

例 In spite of other's objections, he is always wrongheaded in his opinions. 他总是不管他人的反对而固执地坚持自己哪怕是错误的观点。

近 adamant, headstrong, immovable, implacable, inconvincible, inflexible, intransigent, mulish, obdurate, pertinacious, perverse, stubborn, unyielding, willful

反 acquiescent, agreeable, amenable, compliant, flexible, pliable, pliant, relenting, yielding 易受影响的